WLM
100

A Textbook of Human Psychology

A Textbook of
Human Psychology

Edited by

H. J. Eysenck
Professor of Psychology, University of London and

G. D. Wilson
*Associate Professor of Psychiatry, University of
Southern California School of Medicine*

MTP

Published by
MTP Press Ltd
St Leonard's House
Lancaster
England

ISBN 0 85200 131-2 (cloth)
     0 85200 137-1 (paper)

Printed in Great Britain by R. & R. Clark Ltd, Edinburgh

CONTENTS

Introduction

THE CONTRIBUTORS. *All contributors are present or former lecturers at the Institute of Psychiatry, University of London.*

INTRODUCTION

There are so many good textbooks in the field of human psychology that anyone producing a new one must have a good excuse, ready to explain his temerity. Our reason for bringing together the various authors who have contributed the chapters of this book is a very simple one. Most textbooks are written just for future professional psychologists, i.e. for students who are going to adopt psychology as their life's work, and whose main area of concentration is psychology. These students are, of course, a very important group, yet psychology is becoming more and more important to professionals in other fields as well —psychiatrists and doctors generally, sociologists, educationalists, social workers, penologists, and many, many more. Indeed, hardly any profession which deals with people has reached a standard of perfection where training in scientific knowledge of people would not be useful; these many non-professional psychologists are not very well catered for in the standard type of textbook which takes up much time and space with discussions of issues which may be important and interesting to the psychologist, but which are irrelevant to the many non-specialists who wish to gain insight into the main findings of psychology which might be relevant to their own work.

We have tried to keep this particularly in mind when designing this book. We hope, therefore, that it will fulfil a useful double role: firstly, as a practical *introductory* textbook for full-time psychology students and, secondly, as a *comprehensive* textbook for students and professionals in other fields who need a proper understanding of psychology.

This book is largely based on the psychology course that is taught to psychiatrists in training here at the Institute of Psychiatry in London. It tends to give emphasis to the more applied and 'human' areas of psychology—personality, social, developmental and abnormal psychology in particular—but there is also a large section on basic psychological processes because we believe that a firm foundation in the general principles of behaviour is essential to effective applications in the abnormal, or any other, field. It is, therefore, a general psychology textbook. It differs from other such texts not so much in content as in approach. We have concentrated on presenting as much factual material as possible within the space available, minimising the amount of history and philosophy that abounds in many psychology texts. In this sense the book is more comparable to modern textbooks of 'harder' sciences such as physics and physiology. Theories are considered important, but only theories that are scientific in the sense that they continuously interact with empirically derived facts. Theories which seldom make contact with facts (e.g. Jung's theory of archetypes) are generally ignored.

There is one other point about which we would like to be explicit. Textbooks often state different theories regarding a particular phenomenon, or set of phenomena, without giving any opinion as to which of these theories might be judged superior to the others. In a textbook directed just at future scientists, this is not unreasonable; but in a book such as this it seemed more acceptable to make judgements and to deal largely with a particular theory, if we felt that this theory was superior to its rivals in its explanatory powers and in its support in experimental research. Similarly, textbooks often deal with discredited researches, simply because textbooks have always dealt with these studies in the past; it seemed pointless to us to discuss the research first, and then point out why it was not worth discussing. We have preferred to omit the study in question altogether. In some cases, discredited methods which at one time were widely used, and a knowledge of which might be useful in reading older texts, have been very briefly discussed and the main reasons given for not going into details; projective techniques are an example of this genre. Theories which have been widely held, but which have not found ready support in experiment, have not been dealt with, even critically, as already pointed out; the only exceptions are psychoanalysis and Laing's existentialism. These theories have achieved such widespread popularity that we felt it necessary to show in some detail why they are not highly regarded by psychologists.

It is sometimes said that introductory textbooks offer a more systematic treatment if they are authored rather than edited. We believe that the science of psychology has reached such proportions that no one man can claim all-round expertise, and it is especially when a broad area has to be condensed into a chapter of twenty pages or less that it is necessary to have a specialist to do the job. Only a specialist has sufficient perspective within an area to be able to abstract the most important material, and only a specialist is sufficiently familiar with the current literature to be able to sift out genuine discoveries and developments from temporary fads and fashions. The chapters in this book have been mainly prepared by the members of our own Department who are currently teaching those topics; they will be recognised as distinguished researchers who have made substantial contributions to the literature in their respective fields. Where possible, the chapters are based on lecture notes that have evolved progressively over several years, being continually improved and refined as a result of the teaching experience and feedback from the students. This, we believe, is one of the primary advantages that this text may have over its predecessors.

We have tried to write at a level which would be intelligible to the layman as well as the professional, and without too many references, the very profligacy of which he might find confusing. This has not always been easy and occasionally we have failed. Our failures are, however, more often due to difficulties inherent in the subject matter of a given chapter than to malevolence of the author; it is easier to write at an elementary level about Interviewing than about Memory, for instance. We have tried to combine scholarly exactness with simplicity and clarity; such compromises are inherently difficult and no doubt we have not succeeded in every instance. Yet the effort seemed worth making. We have tried to organise the field in such a way that the reader would go away with an overall pattern, some hint of a general organisation of mental activity, in his mind; we have aimed at presenting a model of man and have applied this model to various practical problems, such as criminality, mental disorder, etc. This, of course, is the most difficult task of all and we are not optimistic that reviewers will concede that we have had even a moderate success. Nevertheless, we feel that psychology should strive for something of the kind; the usual collection of unrelated chapter headings does not inspire students with confidence in the existence of a unitary subject called 'psychology'. We hope that students will get the feeling of this model toward which psychology is groping, and will feel inspired to try to apply it in practice; as we shall argue, such applications as have been made of it in various spheres have by no means been completely unsuccessful.

We have kept the book as short as possible so that it might also be useful to students as a practical aid to retention for examination purposes (the limitations of lecture notes in this connection are well known and, in any case, the process of taking notes tends to interfere with appreciation of the lecture). This leaves the lecturer free to elaborate on the material in the text and discuss interesting recent developments in the field. Most of the material contained in this book is dealt with in much greater detail in reference books such as *The Handbook of Abnormal Psychology* (Eysenck, 1973) and it may often help the student to consult this work in addition. Obviously some sacrifices have to be made for the sake of brevity, but we have tried as far as possible to keep the book interesting and informative as well as understandable and manageable.

Hans J. Eysenck and Glenn D. Wilson

Institute of Psychiatry,
University of London,
January, 1976

BASIC PROCESSES

Chapter 1

PSYCHOLOGY AS A BIO-SOCIAL SCIENCE

H. J. Eysenck

Psychology is so all-pervasive and so important that it enters into our every thought and action; by definition almost, the facts and theories of psychology are central to our mental and physical activities. Psychology, clearly, is about *us* if it is about anything: our behaviour, our minds, our emotions, our intelligence, our crimes and mental disorders, our problems. This means that ever since human beings came to the fore in the evolutionary struggle, they have concerned themselves with psychological questions. Some of these questions are philosophical in nature—Who are we? Why are we here? How did we come to be the way we are? Why do we differ so profoundly from each other? Other questions have a more practical turn—How can we make other people do what we want them to do? Who is best suited for this or that position? Will she be a good wife for me? Is he trustworthy? Psychology is still split into a pure and an applied section, although this differentiation tends to get more and more blurred. In any case, psychology has a long past; but it has a very short history. The history of psychology as a science is just about 100 years long; it was only in 1879 that Wilhelm Wundt founded the first formal psychological laboratory in Leipzig. Its growth has been very rapid since those early days, but it is still very young in comparison with long-established sciences like physics, or chemistry. Both past and history have been reviewed in great detail, and with many fascinating details about the many famous people who contributed to them, by Boring (1950); the *History of Experimental Psychology* presents an excellent account of how psychology grew to its present stature.

PSYCHOLOGY AND BEHAVIOURISM

Just as an elephant is easier to recognise than to describe, so is psychology; psychologists tend to know what they are about, but they do not always agree on a definition of their speciality. Literally, psychology is the science of the mind or soul, but psychologists at the time of the first world war rebelled against such an unenlightening name; we are merely defining one unknown in terms of another. They also rebelled against the method of controlled introspection which was then the most widely used method of experimental psychology; nothing of any value seemed to have grown out of all the countless hours spent looking into one's own mind, or getting some colleagues or senior students to look into theirs.

Furthermore, what one found there seemed to be determined by what one expected to find—or what one's teacher expected to find; Würzburg psychologists found different content in their minds to Göttingen psychologists, in much the same way that patients treated by Freudian analysts dream in Freudian symbols, while patients treated by Jungian analysts dream in Jungian symbols. This rebellion, led by the founder of the Behaviourist school, J. B. Watson, suggested that psychology is concerned with behaviour, not with minds; it is only behaviour (including in this term all the events taking place inside the body, such as muscular contractions, nerve signals, hormonal secretions and the like, as well as outwardly visible movements, speech, etc.) that can be observed objectively and can thus serve as the basis for a properly scientific discipline. Psychology as the science of behaviour is now almost universally agreed by psychologists to be the best label we can pin to our subject matter; mind and soul are recognised as relics from the Cartesian dualism which split matter and mind asunder in such a way that no-one could put them together again, a dualism which is fairly universally recognised nowadays to have served its purpose, and to be of little use in dealing with the observable world of living things.

The tenets of behaviourism are often misunderstood, and it may be worthwhile to point out that there are different varieties of behaviourism. Two in particular must be sharply differentiated, if only because it is the first of these that is usually held up to ridicule by critics, while it is the second which is actually embraced by psychologists working in the experimental tradition. In the first place, then, we have *philosophical behaviourism*; this makes statements about the real existence of matter and the non-existence of mind, consciousness, etc.—statements which are reminiscent of naive realism (a rather old-fashioned philosophical doctrine, not taken seriously by professional philosophers), and which are just embarrassing to most psychologists who do not have much interest in philosophy anyway. In the second place, we have *methodological behaviourism*; this makes statements about the kinds of evidence that we need in psychology, and the kinds of proof required in order to substantiate scientific hypotheses. Methodologically, we are all behaviourists; we recognise that behaviour is our subject matter, this being the only objective 'given' that we can study, and that is in the public domain. Peter Medawar once jokingly said that the essence of behaviourism lay in the distinction between saying: 'The dog was sad' and 'The dog howled'—there is much truth in this remark. We can observe that the dog is howling; to deduce that the dog is sad constitutes an anthropomorphic jump into uncertainty that takes us straight out of science.

Note that methodological behaviourism does not say (as does philosophical behaviourism) that we have no consciousness; such nonsensical declarations scientists leave with advantage to philosophers. Behaviourists would tend to agree on some such statement as this: Verbal communication is behaviour, and is therefore a proper source of information for psychologists. Whether it can be admitted as a true indicator of some inner state depends on whether or not corroborative evidence is available. The fact that I say 'I have a headache' cannot be accepted necessarily as evidence that I have a headache; I may simply be trying to get out of some engagement by pleading illness. But it cannot be rejected as meaningless either; I often tell the truth. One would look for corroborative, behavioural evidence of the 'headache' if one really had serious doubts; thus one might apply physiological measures of muscular stress to the frontalis muscles which are usually involved in genuine headaches. But be that as it may, it is possible to agree on certain procedures which incorporate verbal behaviour with other types of behaviour and make it subject to psychological analysis.

VERBAL BEHAVIOUR

Verbal behaviour is often self-validating. If you wish to know whether I am colour blind, you can present me with certain colours, of equal brightness, and ask me to name them; that I can do so is *ipso facto* evidence of my not being colour blind; it is not necessary to speculate about the state of my consciousness. A purist might prefer to condition certain behaviours to the colours, and see whether the conditioned responses occur in me; thus he might teach me to salivate on seeing red by always giving me something to eat after showing me a patch of red colour. But this would be regarded as absurd even by the most conscientious behaviourists; speech is universally admitted as a reasonable aspect of human behaviour.

The kind of interplay that serves to establish verbal behaviour as meaningful in psychological research may be illustrated by an example. This example deals with verbal conditioning, a technique in which the subject is presented with cards saying something like:

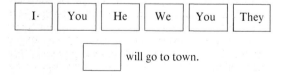

will go to town.

Each card has a different sentence on it, and the subject has to read the sentence, making use of whichever personal pronoun he wishes. The experiment continues for some 20 trials or so, to see with what frequency the subject uses each pronoun. Then begins the conditioning trial; whenever the subject uses a preselected pronoun (e.g. 'They'), the experimenter nods, or says 'good', or makes some appropriate noise. Gradually the subject begins to use this pronoun more and more, and the increase in use of the conditioned pronoun is the score on the test. People differ greatly with respect to the degree of conditioning evidenced, and it was predicted, for reasons which will become apparent in a later chapter, that introverted people would respond better to the conditioning paradigm. Many studies have been published, some of which found introverts better, others extroverts, and others found no difference.

These results can be reconciled if we go on to say that often the subject guesses what is going on; he acquires 'awareness' of the contingencies involved in the experiment. Now the prediction only applies to unaware subjects; extroverts may condition poorly, but when aware of what is going on may be more likely than introverts to wish to please the experimenter, and hence play the game for him. If this were so, we would expect that with subjects lacking in 'awareness', introverts would condition better; in subjects with 'awareness', extroverts might give a better performance. When subjects were verbally interrogated about what they thought had been happening in the experiment, they could be grouped into 'aware' and 'unaware', and indeed personality correlated with performance in contradictory ways in the two groups, as expected. Now the verbal statements of 'awareness' might be considered analogous to introspection, but in this case we have weighty external evidence to reassure us that the verbal statement is in fact true; it gives evidence of knowledge, and fits in with a larger theoretical system which predicts what should happen. As far as the argument

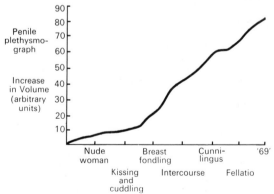

Figure 1.1 Increase in size of penis as a function of content of imagery

goes, therefore, we may accept verbal statements in this situation, and for this purpose. Not to do so would deprive us of important information which could not be gained in any other way. Refusal of relevant and important evidence would be a sign of rigidity and bias.

Even such apparently nebulous terms as 'imagery' can be tied down securely to observable facts. Let us suppose that I tell you to imagine certain situations, say of a sexual nature. You tell me what you see in your imagination. Can a behaviourist accept this as evidence? Figure 1.1 shows the results of an experiment in which the subject was instructed to imagine, each for 20 seconds, the seven items listed on the abscissa. On the ordinate are given figures taken from a penis plethysmograph, which is an instrument which measures with considerable accuracy the size of his penis. It will be seen that the more erotic the image, the greater the enlargement of the penis. We may accept the reality of the internal process because it is tied down securely to observable and measurable events preceding (instructions) and following (penis plethysmograph) the unobservable event.

THE DEFINITION OF PSYCHOLOGY

We have so far concentrated on methods of investigation and on the usefulness of the behaviouristic doctrine; we are still far away from being able to define psychology. To say that it deals with human behaviour is fine and accurate as far as it goes; however, there are other sciences or disciplines which also claim to deal with human behaviour—sociology, physiology, anthropology, economics, genetics and many others might be mentioned here. How can we demarcate the realm of psychology, and indicate in which way it is differentiated from these other disciplines? The first answer might be that it cannot be done at all; academic subjects are in large part artefacts of the curriculum—divisions which are made for the convenience of administrators, and of students who cannot be expected to learn more than a given, limited amount of material in their three or four years at university. There is no absolute line of demarcation between psychology and physiology, or psychology and sociology, such that we might say: 'This investigation is clearly physiology, not psychology', or: 'That study falls within the purview of psychology, not sociology.' But having said this, there is a way in which we can differentiate these various subjects, in principle, at least; there will still be overlap, but the main outlines of the various subjects may become clearer.

Consider Figure 1.2. It delineates two large groups of subjects. On the left, we have a sample of the biological sciences—genetics, physiology, neurology, anatomy, biochemistry, pharmacology, etc. On the right, we have a sample of the social disciplines—history, sociology, anthropology, economics, sociometry, etc. Like a circus rider skilfully straddling two horses (or like a man sitting down between two chairs!) psychology clearly partakes of both groups of sciences. This may be an obvious statement to make, but it has tremendous consequences: psychology is both a biological and a social science. The ramifications of this statement will be discussed in what follows; here let us merely note that clearly physiology is a biological science, sociology a social one; these and the other disciplines mentioned do not meet, except where they are related through some psychological content or theory. This is the importance of psychology and this is the reason for its existence: psychology alone makes the attempt to tie together these different and heterogeneous groups of subjects and mediate between them. Is this a sensible thing to do, and why should anyone try to carry out such a difficult and perhaps impossible task?

Physiology deals with segmental processes; it is concerned with minutiae of reflex activity, carefully studying one reflex at a time, or with specific organ systems of one kind or another. Such segmental studies are of the utmost importance, but they do not tell us what happens when these segments are activated *in vivo* as part of a larger whole—man. Take a particular example. During the first world war, there was much interest in night blindness; obviously a sentry who cannot see in the dark would be a danger to himself and his whole company, and it was clearly important to know the likely number of night-blind soldiers. Physiologists had studied the conditions giving rise to night-blindness, and gave a reassuring answer—given that enough carrots were available, only a very small number of people were likely to be affected. In actual combat, it soon became clear that the answer given was out by several thousand per cent; there were quite large numbers of night blind soldiers in all the armies involved in the

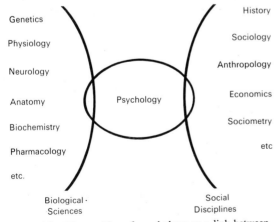

Genetics

Physiology

Neurology

Anatomy

Biochemistry

Pharmacology

etc.

Psychology

History

Sociology

Anthropology

Economics

Sociometry

etc

Biological·Sciences

Social Disciplines

Figure 1.2   The position of psychology as a link between the biological and social sciences

gigantic struggle. The reason soon became obvious. The fine adjustments involved in focussing and seeing in the dark could easily be thrown out of gear by fear; neurotic soldiers suffered from night blindness in a functional sense. There was nothing physiologically wrong with their physical equipment, but the upsurge of autonomic excitement which was produced by situations of real or imaginary danger made it impossible for them to make use of their equipment. The physiologist could say, quite truthfully, that he had been asked quite a different question, and that his answer had been correct. This was no consolation to those who had originally asked the question; they were concerned with the interaction of physiological systems, i.e. with a psychological problem. This is not to say that psychology is better (or worse) than physiology; it is simply different. It looks upon the physiological equipment of man from the point of view of use in actual life, and this use in actual life usually implies certain social connotations. The physiologist quite rightly declines to leave his laboratory and take into account variables he has not been trained to deal with; the psychologist has no choice but to study these variables and try to integrate them with whatever he may learn from the physiologist.

The sociologist, on the other hand, is concerned entirely with social variables; such institutions as marriage, government and criminality are his concern. But of course these institutions are run by individuals, by persons, and it takes a psychologist to undertake the study of persons in institutions. Similarly for economics; economics lays down general laws according to which behaviour should function, but the psychologist knows only too well that people don't usually do what they are supposed to do—such as buy in the cheapest market, and sell in the dearest. Psychological experiments have shown that when identical goods are sold at different prices, many people pay two or three times the lowest price, even though the choice is right in front of their noses. Economics may be able to formulate laws covering rational behaviour, but psychologists have found time and time again that human behaviour is only intermittently rational. Hence on the social side too, psychology is needed to mediate the general and abstract laws of sociology, economics, and the other 'dismal sciences' which throng the right side of our diagram.

Psychologists thus have the duty to look at man as a whole, and to take into account both his biological nature and the social context within which he alone can exist. This is not an easy task, and it is hardly to be wondered at that many psychologists have concentrated on isolated aspects of the job. There are physiological psychologists who are often difficult to distinguish from physiologists; there are social psychologists equally difficult to distinguish from sociologists. Even among behaviourists interested in

quite general experimental work that would place them somewhere at the centre of our diagram, there are often to be found odd notions such as that of the 'empty organism'—a doctrine according to which physiology is too backward to tell us anything of interest about psychological processes, or even that physiology is never likely to be able to make an important contribution to psychology. In line with such thinking, psychologists must 'go it alone' and elaborate functional relations between stimuli and responses; these, it is declared, are the fundamental bits and pieces out of which a proper science will eventually be built.

THE STIMULUS–RESPONSE SYSTEM

For many years this view, enshrined in the symbolism of the 'S–R bond', was to be found in every introductory textbook, and it must be said that the notion underlying it had an intuitive appeal to many students. If you can discover which stimuli produce which responses, or if you can investigate the laws according to which new S–R bonds are fashioned, by learning or conditioning, then you can manipulate responses by suitably manipulating stimuli. This stress on manipulation has always been strongly associated with behaviourism; note J. B. Watson's well-known saying: 'Psychology as the behaviourist views it is a purely objective experimental branch of natural science. Its theoretical goal is the prediction and control of behaviour.' Can we indeed obtain 'control' over behaviour by simply manipulating stimuli? As we shall see, this whole notion is so grossly oversimplified that scientific investigation and experimentation has suffered greatly by the restrictions imposed by it.

Behaviourists often argued that their model was in line with the models adopted by workers in the 'hard' sciences. A physicist may study the expansion of metals as a function of heat, or an astronomer the Doppler effect (red-shift) as a function of the distance of stellar objects. True, some form of functionalism is implied in the typical equation written by scientists, $a = (f)b$. However, there is something missing in this whole argument. Different metals expand differently with heat, and in order to get any meaningful answer we have to specify the precise nature of the metal (or alloy) we are using. Similarly, different organisms respond differently to different stimuli, and unless we take this into account we will be quite unable to make any meaningful predictions—let alone exert any kind of control! Accordingly, we may have to expand our formula to read: S–O–R; the stimulus strikes the organism, interacts with the innate and acquired properties of the organism, and the organism then emits a response. Why did this obvious point take so long to penetrate, and why is it still honoured more in the breach than in the observance?

The answer must be speculative, but undoubtedly

there is a good historical reason. Biological workers interested in psychology tended to have a strongly genetic approach to the subject; often human behaviour was assumed to be generated by 'instincts' which dictated precisely what type of response should be made to different types of stimuli. Opponents of this doctrine had little difficulty in showing that it was not of much use in psychology; accounting for sociable behaviour in terms of an 'instinct' of sociability was clearly a circular process which did not 'explain' anything. The doctrine of instincts fell into disrepute, and a whole-hogging environmentalism took over which allied itself with the doctrine of the 'empty organism', to produce modern behaviourism which still often echoes Watson's proud boast that if you gave him control of the environment, then he could make young children into anything he chose, from genius to beggarman. Alas, things are not as simple as that; the organism arrives on the scene fully fitted out with genes and chromosomes which determine its capacities and emotional reactivity, its abilities and personality, to a very marked degree—as we shall see in later chapters. A simple-minded disbelief in genetics has always characterised manipulative societies, such as the U.S.A. and the U.S.S.R.; genetics seems to set limits to the power of the state to transform itself and its citizens into some Utopian ideal, and a *tabula rasa* hypothesis seems much more acceptable. The impressive empirical work of ethologists, studying different animal species in great detail in their every-day lives, has revived the doctrine of instincts, although in a much more sophisticated form, and altogether the pendulum is swinging back towards a position less eccentrically emphasising only the one side of the heredity–environment interaction equation. (Some behaviourists, rather reluctantly, have recognised the importance of the organism by postulating that S–R relations are influenced to some extent by the 'history of reinforcement' of the organism, i.e. by the rewards and punishments it received in the past; this purely environmental view of O has to be supplemented by recognition of the genetic determinants of behaviour.)

A more complete chain of events might look like Figure 1.3, which takes into account the most important aspects of human behaviour. We begin with the stimulus, recognising that there is an important difference between physical stimuli (S_P) and social stimuli (S_S), and that there may also be internal stimuli (S_I) which emanate from the person's viscera. These stimuli strike the organism, which is in a state of readiness to react to them in certain ways, determined partly by genetic (G), partly by environmental (E) antecedents. The organism then emits responses, which may be mediated by the autonomic nervous system, i.e. are emotional in nature (R_A), which may be cognitive, i.e. thoughts or ideas (R_C), or which may be motor movements (R_M). These

responses finally lead to an effector state ($E\pm$) which may be either pleasant (indicated by the + sign) or unpleasant (indicated by the − sign). The pleasantness or otherwise of this state constitutes the positive. or negative reinforcement produced by the whole chain of events; this in turn modifies the organism (through

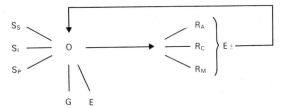

Figure 1.3   A model of behaviour

learning and conditioning) in such a way that in future it will seek or avoid the stimuli which herald the final effector state. We have come a long way from the simple S–R formula, and many psychologists still yearn for the relative simplicity of that formula; however, the evidence for its inadequacy is too strong to allow us to return to it.

Different groups of psychologists concern themselves with different parts of the larger formula given in Figure 1.3. For instance O is the field studied by behavioural geneticists; S_P–O is studied by workers in the traditional field of perception. S_S–O constitutes the relatively new field of social perception; where traditional workers would use lights and sounds carrying no meaning as their stimuli, workers in this new field would be concerned with facts such as that poor youngsters overestimate the size of high-value coins, or that college students take longer to recognise words which refer to unpleasant or pornographic items ('perceptual defence'). S_P–R_A would be a field of study in which Pavlovian conditioning would be characteristic; S_P–R_M would be concerned with operant conditioning, as we shall see later on in the book. $E\pm$ would be concerned with motivation. It will be obvious then that while in every behavioural act the whole chain is involved, it may be necessary for experimental purposes to study one particular aspect or connection within the chain, and to try to 'hold constant' the remainder—however difficult that may be.

THE INTERACTION OF SOCIAL AND BIOLOGICAL FACTORS

The fact that human beings are at one and the same time biological organisms and the products of a social environment means that we are inevitably concerned, at all times, with the paradigm of *interaction*. Biological and social factors and influences are constantly interacting with each other, and no attempt to understand psychology can possibly succeed which does not bear this in mind. There are in psychology sociotropes and biotropes, people who stress one or the other side alone, and at best give lip service to the other; such men are dangerous. The danger involved in such one-sided enthusiasm is simply that we try to impose on nature our prejudices, rather than allow nature to teach us what the facts are; scientists have to have their share of humility and take their cue from nature.

The danger is particularly apparent when. the psychological problems in question have social and political aspects. In the early days of the century, for instance, many psychologists held a strongly genetic position which ascribed all (or nearly all) differences in intelligence, to take but one example, to heredity, including the large differences in I.Q. observed between white and black Americans; from this allegedly scientific basis strongly racist conclusions were then drawn. The science of genetics gave no support to these assumptions, and of course the racist conclusions would in any case have had no scientific support, being purely political in nature. Later on, largely as a reaction, many psychologists held a similarly extreme view emphasising environment and stating as a fact that all races had innately identical intelligence, with the observed differences being due to environmental deprivations of various kinds. These beliefs were based on no firmer evidence than those rejected; the wish, in both cases, was the father of the child.

Both heredity and environment clearly play their part in observable, phenotypic behaviour; such an interactionist doctrine suggests the importance, not of emphasising one or the other, but of discovering with some precision the relative contributions of the two factors in any particular situation. This requires complex and difficult experimental investigations, and the construction of genetic models which are testable against the facts unearthed. Much is now known about the relative part played by heredity and environment in the causation of I.Q. differences, at least as far as people living in the U.S.A., the U.K., and the European continent are concerned; when it comes to racial differences no results are available which carry similar conviction.

One particular area of dispute between sociotropes and biotropes has been the relevance of animal work. Ever since Pavlov used the conditioning paradigm derived from his work with cats and rats, psychologists have argued about the relevance of the results to human learning and conditioning. The arguments against 'rat psychology' are quite strong. It is said that species differences are much too large to enable us to argue from one species to another, least of all from such lowly animals as rats to animals having the power of speech, like man. There may be superficial similarities between rats running mazes and children learning some simple motor habits, but these do not extend to specifically human learning, which involves speech, thought and other human attributes not found in rats. Similarly, the motivating conditions of the two species are quite different—rats are usually motivated in the laboratory by hunger and thirst, more rarely by sex, and most frequently by electric shock, while motivations for humans, at least those living in affluent Western countries, tend on the whole to be more subtle and less obvious. It may make sense to talk about 'drive reduction' theories of motivation in hungry, thirsty, or otherwise deprived rats; it may be difficult to see how relevant this is to human beings living in stable societies. If we are interested in the abilities, motivations, etc. which made Shakespeare write his sonnets, or which made Newton evolve his theory of gravitation, we are unlikely to get too much help from rats running mazes, or avoiding shock in a shuttle box, or even pressing levers in a Skinner box. For these and many other obvious reasons, rat psychology is in bad repute with many people, and students often dismiss it contemptuously as useless. This is probably a one-sided point of view.

Biologically, rats share with us certain very impressive similarities. They possess, like us, a central nervous system, issuing in a cortex; they have an autonomic system which mediates emotional expression; they have sense organs very similar to ours. They respond to physical stimuli much as we do; they respond to drugs in ways not too dissimilar to ourselves. They can learn, and they become conditioned, in ways which are qualitatively and quantitatively similar, in considerable detail, to our ways. To stress the differences, to the exclusion of the similarities, is one-sided, just as it would be one-sided to look at the similarities alone and conclude that rats were perfect replicas of humans. The issue simply cannot be resolved by *a priori* statements, or in terms of common sense assessment; it boils down to a precise evaluation of those areas where rats can be used with some degree of confidence as analogues of human beings, and those where the differences are too great to make this useful. Consider a few examples to illustrate the possible usefulness of animal analogues in this context.

THE RELEVANCE OF ANIMAL EXPERIMENTS

There is a well-known behaviour pattern among rats called the 'Columbus effect'. A male rat will tire of being with the same female rat for any length of time, and his number of mountings and intromissions will decline. Furnish him with a new partner and his vigour will return. This parallels a well-documented pattern in human behaviour; number of copulations in marriage declines steeply during the first year, and then declines more gradually; this gradual decline is probably due to increasing age, but the precipitate decline during the first year is very similar to the

Columbus effect. Now it is of course perfectly true to argue that men are not rats; human behaviour is not governed exclusively (as is rat behaviour) by biological mechanisms. The institution of marriage, the persistence of love, the mutual usefulness of members of a pair bond are social influences which may counteract the biological determination of the Columbus effect. It would be as unrealistic (and hence as unscientific) to disregard the social forces entering the equation, as it would be to disregard the biological ones. Work with rats may clarify the precise nature of the latter; to that degree it is useful. Work with rats will tell us little about the former; to that extent it can be misleading.

As another example, take Pavlov's work on conditioning with dogs (Pavlov, 1927). He carefully and precisely worked out the main laws according to which conditioning takes place, and these laws have been shown to apply in very much the same manner to human beings. It is much easier to work with dogs, and our knowledge has increased enormously due to Pavlov's extensive studies. Now obviously it is also necessary to demonstrate that what is true of dogs is also true of humans; consequently a great deal of experimental work has also been done with humans. This work was inspired by Pavlov's findings, and directed in every particular by the theories and laws he had based on his discoveries. Pavlovian conditioning plays a vital part in human behaviour; it lies at the basis of neurotic behaviour, to take but one example. But of course, here also, the animal work only gives us the biological side of things; even in Pavlovian conditioning there is a social side to consider, and this cannot be discovered from animal work alone. Thus it would be one-sided and unscientific to reject Pavlov's findings because they were based on animal work, or to accept them uncritically as applying without change to human beings. We can learn from animals, but we cannot learn all there is to be known from animals.

As a third example, consider the important work of J. Masserman (1943) with cats. He would teach cats to get food from a box; next he would electrify the box so that the cats would get a shock when touching it. This is a situation of approach–avoidance conflict; the hungry cats have a strong drive (hunger) which propels them towards the box, but they also have an aversive drive (pain avoidance) which pushes them in the opposite direction, away from the box. This approach–avoidance situation has been studied in great detail by N. Miller (see Gray, 1971), whose work will be discussed in some detail later in this book; it is very conducive to the genesis of neurotic behaviour (Eysenck, 1974). This was observable in Masserman's cats; it has also been found true in human behaviour. Again, it is of course true that human and cat behaviour are not identical; the conflicts generated by approach–avoidance situations

are different in the two cases, being less closely bound to biological stimuli (food, shock) in humans. Nevertheless, the similarities are considerable; they enable us to achieve a much better understanding of neurosis. As has been well said:

> 'Masserman the cat man,
>> Makes cats neurotic;
> Are cats and humans,
>> Really asymptotic?

Can we really take over general laws largely based on animal work, and apply them to human problems? Consider a particular problem, that of children who bang their heads. This is a terribly dangerous practice; children have been known to kill themselves, or to detach their retinae by the banging and become blind. What can be done about it? Physicians used to advise strapping the children to a chair; this certainly prevents them from banging their heads, but it is hardly a procedure which can be used for any length of time, and is really a counsel of despair. Psychoanalysts advised love and affection; whenever the child started to bang his head, mothers were told to go and hug and kiss the child. This is a humane method, but unfortunately a counter-productive one; the children banged their heads more and more! Readers might like to stop here and think how they would deal with this problem, using common sense as a guide; in the next paragraph we will then go on to discuss suggestions emanating from animal work.

Towards the turn of the century, E. L. Thorndike announced the Law of Effect; this states, essentially, that animals (including people) will tend to repeat those activities and actions which in the past have led to pleasant, acceptable consequences, and to shun those activities and actions which in the past have led to unpleasant, noxious consequences. B. F. Skinner, another American psychologist, took up this notion half a century later and based his *law of reinforcement* on extensive work with rats and pigeons; positive reinforcement (a technical name for reward) led to repetition, negative reinforcement to abandonment of the particular activities preceding either. This general sort of approach (which is similar to the philosophical doctrine of hedonism, but goes beyond it in many ways, and is much more specific in its recommendations) leads to a quite clear-cut approach to our head-bangers. Whenever the child starts to bang his head, the mother is instructed to pick him up and take him to a small room; there he is locked in for 10 minutes, all alone. The mother shows no emotion, and neither does she scold the child when he is let out again after his period of 'detention' is up. This 'time out' procedure provides negative reinforcement for the action preceding it (i.e. the head banging), just as hugging and kissing the child, in accordance with the psychoanalytic recommendation, provides positive reinforcement. No wonder the psychoanalytic method makes things worse; the child is actually being rewarded for misbehaving! The behaviouristic method works extremely well, and quickly; most children are cured within a matter of weeks. The cure is permanent, and does not lead to 'symptom substitution', as many psychiatrists feared; in other words, no alternative symptoms appear when the head banging is stopped. With a small group of children something stronger than 'time out' is needed; a slight electric shock, administered when- ever the head banging starts, followed by 'time out', may be required.

This example of 'behaviour therapy' (which will be discussed in much more detail in a later chapter) may deserve some more detailed study. In the first place, it shows that general laws derived from animal work can be applied with considerable success to human behaviour. At the same time, these laws can be used to explain why other types of treatment (such as psychoanalytic treatment) fail to work. Clearly, rats and humans are not so distant on the evolutionary scale that certain uniformities cannot be discovered and used to cross the species boundaries. The method of treatment so discovered may seem obvious once the suggestion has been made, but for many years common sense, medical ingenuity, and psychoanalytic insight all failed miserably in their efforts to find a solution to this particular problem. In the same way, it seems obvious to us that the earth circles round the sun, and that apples and planets obey the law of gravitation; these self-evident truths were far from self-evident 500 years ago, and required great scien- tific acumen and insight to establish. The laws of positive and negative reinforcement may also seem obvious when stated so broadly; they are of course much more precise and detailed than anything we have stated so far, and go well beyond common sense, or philosophical hedonism.

PROBLEMS OF APPLIED PSYCHOLOGY

The example shows that behaviouristic methods, derived from animal studies, can work; there are many other examples which will be found in later pages of this book. It used to be quite popular to deny that such methods could ever work; this objection has not survived the many obvious successes of behaviour therapy. Now it is more popular to say that these methods are simply ways of inducing conformity in people, and that manipulation of other persons, as is implied in all behaviouristic methods, is inherently wrong and inhumane. This type of objection is more difficult to answer because there is an element of truth in it. Nevertheless, we believe it to be mistaken. Let us note first of all that from birth to the grave man attempts to manipulate others, and is in turn manipu- lated by them. The baby is 'manipulated' to suck at the mother's breast, and later on to take solid food and come off the mother's breast. The child is

'manipulated' to learn reading and writing, and all the other things which he needs in order to live happily in society. The adolescent is 'manipulated' to take a job, earn a living, and maintain a family. The girl is 'manipulated' into bed by her boyfriend. The voter is 'manipulated' to give his vote to politicians whose concern for his welfare is more verbal than real, and more apparent before than after the election. We are all 'manipulated' by advertisements to buy this rather than that. Opponents of racial discrimination search for methods to 'manipulate' racists successfully. Sometimes manipulation is disguised as appeal to reason, but this is not usually a very convincing mask. Wisdom begins with the realisation that all social living implies manipulation of one person by another; manipulation is the essence of social living—only the hermit is free from it.

Equally important as the fact of manipulation is the motive for manipulation. It is idle to say that all manipulation is bad; without it we would still be animals living in a state of nature—our lives being nasty, brutish, and short. It is easy to say: 'Do your thing'; the question is of course whether 'your thing' is completely innate (which seems extremely unlikely), or whether it is due to various social influences— which imply 'manipulation'. Some kinds of manipu- lation are obviously of help to the person concerned; the baby would starve if his mother did not orient his mouth correctly to the breast, and the head banger might kill himself if we did not advise the mother correctly. It is not reasonable to say: 'Well, let him kill himself if that is what he wants'. The child is not able to foresee the consequences of his actions and certainly does not wish to kill himself. Or consider the patient who comes to the behaviour therapist with acute phobic fears and generalised anxieties. He is driven to distraction by his troubles and may be near suicide; if methods of 'manipulation' exist which can cure him and restore him to mental health, and if he is only too desirous of being 'manipulated' in this fashion, would it not be inhumane to withhold treatment? Again, the grown man often thanks those who in his youth 'manipulated' him in such a way that he learned to read, thus opening up to him a vast new world of delight and happiness; had he been left alone, without any pressure at all, he might still be illiterate. Children, as they grow up, often reproach their laissez-faire parents, saying: 'Why didn't you make me do that?' when some deficit becomes apparent in their education or upbringing, which could easily have been dealt with earlier on.

On the other hand, manipulation can obviously also be bad, in the sense that it is used for the interest of the manipulator, rather than of the person manipu- lated. It seems hardly necessary to give examples; advertising which makes use of natural fears of death, disease, social isolation and other negative feelings for the purpose of selling useless and possibly dangerous drugs, creams, etc., is too well-known to all of us. More interesting are those cases where a good case could be made either way. Consider homosexuality. Many homosexuals come to the therapist asking for treatment; they do not wish to live out their lives in their present state. Assuming that aversion therapy (which will be discussed later on) is able to make them heterosexual, is this a case of 'bad' manipulation? The question seems to hinge on whether or not the patient really and truly wishes to be changed, or whether he is merely reacting to social prompting—by family, a court order, or some other agency. In the former case there seems to be no reason to consider the case in a different category from the patient suffering from anxiety; there may be difficulties in being sure of one's facts, but in principle we would not seem to have the right to withhold treatment from a patient who is suffering and wishes to be cured. In the latter case, we may take one of two positions. We may declare that social pressure is immoral, and that the therapist should refuse to undertake the treatment. Or we may take the view that the therapist as therapist can do nothing to alter social pressures, but must leave the decision to the patient; if the patient decides that under the circumstances he would prefer to opt for treatment, then it is not up to the therapist to refuse to implement this decision. If the patient is clearly unwilling, but society is insistent, then the therapist of course has an ethical duty to the patient, rather than to society; under no circumstances would he be justified in 'manipulating' the patient against his will.

In all this, behaviourists do not encounter difficulties which are in any way different from those encountered by psychiatrists, psychoanalysts, social workers, and many other people concerned with social treatment of any kind. The principles of action suggested above are no different from those which might be accepted by other workers in this field; behaviouristic methods do not differ in principle from those of other groups. Nor can we pretend that there is always a 'true' answer to the problems thrown up by society; there is often room for genuine disagreement among well-meaning persons desperately trying to do the right thing. The behaviourist psychologist, any more than the psychoanalyst, or the psychiatrist, is not a moral philosopher by training; he is just as likely to make mistakes as the next person. Notwithstanding this obvious human fallibility, it should not be assumed that he is any less well-meaning, or any less conscious of his ethical duties, than other workers in this field.

REHABILITATION OF CRIMINALS AS AN ETHICAL ISSUE

A more complicated issue arises when we come to criminals. Here behaviour therapists have suggested new methods of treatment which hold out a promise of rehabilitation better than any of the existing methods—token economies, conditioning methods, modelling, and many others. (Needless to say, none of these resemble in any way, shape or form the methods used in such films as 'A Clockwork Orange'. Not only are these inhuman to such an extent that they would never be used by any clinical psychologist, but also they are extremely unlikely to work. Discussion of modern methods of treatment is often made impossibly difficult because most people derive their views from films such as this rather than from reading the official documents.) Now it is sometimes suggested that crime is the product of the social system, and that rehabilitation of criminals simply serves to support the system and make criminals 'conform' to the rules of that system. Accordingly, it is suggested that such methods of rehabilitation are not acceptable. It is undoubtedly true that to some extent the definition of crime is a social matter; homosexuality is a crime in some countries, but not in others. Adultery is a crime in some American states, but not in England. However, murder and theft are crimes practically everywhere, including both capitalist and communist countries; no society can exist without explicit rules of conduct, the breaking of which is punished in some way or other. Furthermore, the purpose of such punishment is in part the rehabilitation of the culprit; deterrence and retaliation are the other two purposes, but they are probably less important in the long run. No known tribe, country, or civilisation has ever been able to do without punishment of antisocial conduct; it would seem reasonable to prefer humane methods (such as those advocated by behaviour therapists) to inhumane ones (such as are all too frequently found in many countries).

Furthermore, overemphasis on the social side of antisocial behaviour does not take into account the biological. It is well-documented that criminality has a strong hereditary component; identical twins are far more often concordant for criminality than are fraternal twins, a fact which strongly implicates genetic factors. Furthermore, when babies are taken from criminal and non-criminal parents and adopted by criminal and non-criminal foster parents, it is found that the adolescent and grown-up foster children take after their biological parents, not their foster parents—in spite of the fact that it is the latter who have provided them with their environment for practically their whole lives. In other words, antisocial behaviour is partly an innate characteristic of people, a characteristic which would emerge in any society. Here as always it is necessary to bear in mind that man is both a social and a biological animal; no answer to our problems is likely to be found useful and practicable which does not take into account one or the other of these two complementary factors.

Last but not least, objections to behavioural treatment of criminality do not take into account the wishes of the criminals themselves. Contrary to *a priori* thinking, criminals very often do not see themselves as opponents of the 'system' which society has imposed on them; quite the contrary is true. They often see themselves as strong defenders of the system, and may be more conservative than other, comparable groups of the population (Siddiqi *et al.*, 1973). Their reactions to homosexuals, baby bashers and sex criminals are often such that these offenders have to be protected against the wrath of the 'normal' criminals. Furthermore, criminals (particularly young criminals) very often express a strong desire for rehabilitation, and volunteer readily to take part in experiments carried out in prisons, borstals, and other institutions. The ethics of submitting unwilling prisoners to behavioural treatment are doubtful, to say the least; in any case, the methods are unlikely to work with any but true volunteers. But to refuse these volunteers a chance to become happy and contented citizens on political and other grounds which are not shared by the prisoners in question themselves seems equally unethical; to do so would impose on other people one's own ideals and views. Much more could be said about these ethical problems which beset all our efforts to use modern methods of psychology for the betterment of mankind; clearly these problems are very real, and equally clearly it is very difficult to know what the true answers might be—even given that there are any true answers. We are perhaps not likely to go too far wrong if we adopt as our motivation the benefit of the individual sufferer; compassion may mislead us sometimes, but it is unlikely to lead us too far in the direction of dangerous inhumanity.

In short, behaviourist psychology is in exactly the same position as all science, as far as application is concerned; whether it is well or ill applied, to the benefit or the detriment of mankind, depends on mankind itself, not on the scientists in question. When Rutherford split the atom, he was convinced that this discovery would never be of any practical use. Since then, we have seen this discovery applied to the making of atom bombs, casting their menacing shadows over mankind as a whole; we have also seen it applied to the creation of energy urgently needed by mankind to replace the rapidly ebbing reserves of natural fuels. Without Rutherford's discovery we might be marginally safer from destruction by war; we would also be certain to run out of electricity and other forms of energy by the turn of the century, or even earlier. This would condemn hundreds of millions of people to death, and the rest of mankind to a much more hazardous and less comfortable life than they enjoy at the moment. It is as wrong to look only at the dark side of scientific inventiveness as it is to look only at the bright side; we have to learn to look fearlessly at both sides, and then come to realistic conclusions about the balance in terms of the quality of human life.

SHOULD PSYCHOLOGY BE SCIENTIFIC?

In this introductory chapter, we have spoken of behaviouristic psychology as if it were the only kind of psychology in existence. In so far as we are talking about psychology as a scientific discipline, this is clearly true. Methodological behaviourism, unlike philosophical behaviourism, really means little else but a commitment to the application of scientific method to psychological problems; it does not lay down precise rules and laws as to just how this should be done. It thus lacks content; to say that one disagrees with behaviourism is almost meaningless, unless of course what is meant is philosophical behaviourism which we have already agreed is irrelevant to the development of psychology as a science. The only conceivable meaning that dislike of methodological behaviourism may have is a dislike of the application of science to human problems; such a dislike is certainly quite widespread, and has given rise to a kind of literary, philosophical psychology which is professed by existentialists, writers, and philosophers who have usually not received any training in academic psychology. At first sight, some of the criticisms made by these people sound sensible and attractive; when one looks closer, however, they are found to be based on erroneous notions of what science means, and what it aims at.

Thus critics will say that behaviouristic models of human conduct are grossly oversimplified, that they leave out essential features of human conduct, and that they reduce man, the glory of creation, to a mechanical ape. Another criticism which is often voiced is that psychologists do not deal with precisely those aspects of behaviour, like love, or creativity, or altruism, which are specifically human, and which are of much more interest to readers than those topics featured in most textbooks—visual acuity, rote learning, or the formation of conditioned reflexes. To some degree these criticisms are of course true; most people would prefer to see a Shakespeare play, read a Wordsworth sonnet, or listen to a discussion on the nature of love by a group of writers, actors and much-married film stars, rather than study the mathematical formulae in Thurstone's book on factor analysis, read through thousands of scientific papers dealing with the extinction of conditioned reflexes, or carry out endless experiments on the physiological concomitants of emotional arousal. But to state such an obvious truth is to say nothing about the aims of scientific psychology; it simply means that most people prefer being amused to working hard. Scientific knowledge is additive; literary insight is not. We may argue that Shakespeare had more insight into human nature than does the average psychologist; it would be difficult to dissent. But similarly top tennis players, or golf stars, or international footballers, probably have more insight into the behaviour of globular, inflated rubber spheres when struck by hard objects than does the average physicist. This knowledge, however, is private; it cannot be transferred to other people. If we wish to land a rocket filled with people on the moon, we still turn to physicists, rather than to sportsmen. Would Shakespeare's insight have led us to find a proper therapy for head bangers? Poetic insight is fun, and it may even have cathartic effects on certain individuals; nevertheless it does not help us solve practical problems in the psychological field. Whether psychology does all that much better is a moot point; we will be better able to discuss this at the end of this book. But psychology is constantly growing more and more able to deal with its problems; the knowledge it possesses is additive. Writers cannot claim the same for their craft; there is a notable absence of Shakespeares in the modern theatre!

Psychology oversimplifies, does not deal with important problems which concern the man in the street, and puts forward a model of human behaviour which is not too complimentary. It does these things, not because of some wayward strain in the psychologists who do all these things, but simply because it is a science. Inevitably all science oversimplifies, most of all when it is still young and relatively ignorant. Astronomy for centuries treated the earth as if it were a perfect sphere; this is grossly inaccurate and 'oversimplified'. The earth is flattened over the poles, and pear-shaped in addition; these facts were not of any great importance for the purposes of astronomers intent on understanding our planetary system. They are now important when we are trying to send rockets to the moon, and consequently they are now being taken into account. It is the task of science to bring order into the chaos of blooming, buzzing confusion which constitutes experience; it does so by isolating invariant bits of experience, and studying these in depth. It has been incredibly successful in doing so, but of course there is a price to pay. If we throw a man and a pig from the tower of Pisa, they will arrive at the same time on the flat ground below the tower; this can be used to demonstrate Galileo's law of falling bodies, although it seems to equate pigs and humans. For the purpose of the scientist in studying the laws of falling bodies, this distinction is irrelevant; no insult is intended either to pigs or humans. Science is based on abstraction, and abstraction comes only with difficulty to most people. Nevertheless, if we want to study psychology scientifically, we must use abstraction in the same way, and to the same extent, as do other sciences. Without simplification we could not even start; the acid test of whether we have done our job properly is not whether the result appeals to the layman, but whether we arrive at a model which can be used to predict and explain the facts with which we are concerned. Thus our criterion is a technical one, and success can only be measured in technical terms; features of our model which offend the outsider may be essential in accounting for the facts. A scientific model is not meant to be a portrait!

Whether psychology deals with problems which are important to the man in the street or not cannot be decided by the man in the street; it is not necessarily apparent to the layman whether fundamental research is or is not relevant to one of his problems. Skinner's work on pigeons learning to peck at a coloured disc may seem quite irrelevant to anything of practical importance, but it has led to valuable practical methods of treating psychotic patients, criminals, and other groups. Rutherford's work on the atom, as already mentioned, seemed quite irrelevant to any practical problems, yet it produced some of the most 'relevant' solutions to problems of war and peace that have ever been produced. It is simply impossible for the outsider (and often even for the insider) to say what the practical relevance of a scientific investigation may be in the future; what is certain is that direct attacks on practical problems have in the past had a poor rate of success. Fundamental problems have to be solved before any direct attack may be possible, and only the expert can assess the value of such fundamental work. And even the expert can often be wrong in his assessment!

The model of human conduct put up by modern psychology is not complimentary for the same reason that Copernicus's heliocentric model of the planetary system was judged to be uncomplimentary to mankind, by displacing the earth from the centre of the Universe, or Darwin's doctrine of evolution an insult to human values, by failing to make man unique in creation. We are not only social beings, but biological beings as well; this biological background we share with rats, jackals and pigeons. Thirst, hunger and sex are fundamental drives for human beings, just as they are for other animals; fear, rage and lust are powerful emotions which govern our conduct as surely as they govern the conduct of cats, racoons and dogs. No model would begin to do the job which did not embody these facts prominently and explicitly. The model must of course, also contain other features—some features are clearly difficult to replicate in animal work, and the study of human beings in all their complexity is required in order to make the model more lifelike. This is a tremendous task, and if psychology has not made as much headway as one might have wished, the reason is partly its youth, and partly the fact that society has not supported psychology to an extent which would enable it to forge ahead as fast as it might otherwise have done. But adequate or not, the present model is the best we have. In the same way, Newton's model was the best available 300 years ago; by modern standards it was defective in many, many different ways. Yet it did good service until dethroned by a better one. Scientists learn to put up with simple models, in the hope that investigation and criticism of the model will lead to new facts and theories which will in due course improve the model out of all recognition, or change it altogether. By a process of conjectures and refutations (Popper, 1963) science pulls itself up by its bootstraps, constantly improving its models, and the fit of these models to the facts. It is not sufficient for the critic to say that he doesn't like what he sees;

this is not constructive criticism. The task of the critic in science is to propose a better theory, buttress it with new facts, and apply it in new and original ways. Psychology must be a science if it is to transcend popular wisdom, and the insight of the playwright and novelist; it has made a good beginning, even though some critics would like to write at the end of the report: 'Could do better'. As long as psychologists remember the dual nature of man as a biological animal and a social organism, psychology no doubt will do better in the near future.

References

Boring, E. G. (1950). *A History of Experimental Psychology* (New York: Appleton, Century, Crofts)

Eysenck, H. J. (1974). *The Natural History of Neurosis*. In: *Stress and Anxiety*, **Vol. 1**, D. Spielberger and I. G. Sarason (editors) (London: Wiley)

Gray, J. A. (1971). *The Psychology of Fear and Stress* (London: Weidenfeld, Nicolson)

Masserman, J. M. (1943). *Behavior and Neurosis* (Chicago: Univ. of Chicago Press)

Pavlov, I. P. (1927). *Conditioned Reflexes* (Oxford: University Press)

Popper, K. R. (1963). *Conjectures and Refutations* (London: Routledge Kegan Paul)

Siddiqui, J. A., Haara, A. and Schnabel, W. (1973). Conservative policemen, even more conservative prisoners: A factor–analytical investigation using Wilson and Patterson's Conservatism Scale. *Psychol. Beitr.*, **15**, 106–118

Chapter 2

PERCEPTION

C. D. Frith

INTRODUCTION

Perception is the transformation of the physical world into 'mental images'. In this brief account of the scientific study of perception I shall be less concerned with the brain mechanisms underlying these mental images and more concerned with the nature of the images themselves and how they differ from the physical world that they represent; for if the transformation is to be useful the mental image must be 'different' from the physical world. If the brain contained a perfect representation of the world then the problem of how to interpret and use this picture would still remain. Thus the map is a better analogy of the mental image than the photograph. The map retains only a very limited amount of information about the country it represents. It makes use of conventional signs, contour lines and imaginary grids. The uselessness of the 'perfect' map is illustrated by the following anecdote from a collection by Borges and Casares (1971).

'In that Empire, the Art of Cartography achieved such Perfection that the Map of one single Province occupied the whole of a City, and the Map of the Empire, the whole of a Province. In time, those Disproportionate Maps failed to satisfy and the Schools of Cartography sketched a Map of the Empire which was the size of the Empire and coincided at every point with it. Less Addicted to the Study of Cartography, the Following Generations comprehended that this dilated Map was Useless and, not without Impiety, delivered it to the Inclemencies of the Sun and of the Winters. In the Western Deserts there remain piecemeal Ruins of the Map, inhabited by Animals and Beggars. In the entire rest of the Country there is no vestige left of the Geographical Disciplines.'

Suárez Miranda, *Viajes de Varones Prudentes*, libro cuarto, cap. XIV (Lérida, 1658)

To economise on effort and so as not to overload a limited memory capacity, the organism seeks to ignore as much of the environment as possible. Much can simply be discarded because it is of no relevance to the survival of the organism. Of more interest are those perceptual processes which ignore aspects of the environment because they are *redundant*. One aspect of the environment is redundant if some other aspect provides the same information. Thus people with beards tend to be men and other sexual characteristics can be ignored. It used also to be the case that people with long hair tended to be women. When this recently ceased to be so considerable confusion resulted for a time. To make use of redundancy the organism has to detect relationships between different aspects of the environment. It must discover principles of organisation in the environment or even impose organisation upon the environment. By emphasising these aspects of perception I relate it closely to higher order functions such as abstract thinking, pattern detection, concept formation and even language.

The processes that I propose are involved in perception, are precisely the same as those used by a scientist or a statistician in dealing with the large masses of data he collects. He too discards irrelevant data and tries to represent populations by a few measures such as the mean and the standard deviation. He too seeks for relationships between the variables he measures.

Perceptual processes then are concerned with reducing the very large amount of information available in the environment into a small amount used by the organism. This can be seen as a necessary strategy to overcome the organism's very limited memory capacity. Such a relation between memory capacity and abstract thinking (the organising process in perception) has been described by Borges (1964) and Luria (1969). In both the cases described (one fictional and one fact) a phenomenal memory resulted in a severe impairment of the capacity for abstract thought, for if every member of a set can be remembered there is no need to discover a rule for generating the set.

THE RAW SENSES

Sense receptors respond to various forms of energy. The elements in the retina respond to light waves, those in the ear to mechanical vibrations and so on. At this stage a vast amount of possible information is ignored. We can see neither infrared nor ultraviolet light and most of us cannot hear the cries of bats. Information carried by these forms of energy is apparently irrelevant to our survival. A striking illustration of the selectivity of the senses is provided by the touch receptors. In this modality the face and hands (in humans) are represented in the brain in enormous detail and in the rest of the body hardly at all (Figure 2.1). In other animals, different parts of the

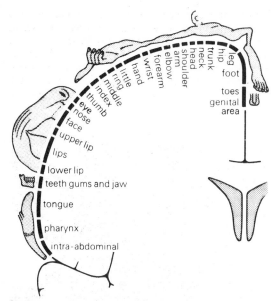

Figure 2.1 Diagram of section cut through a human brain showing the representation of body parts as measured by evoked potentials recorded from each point of the cortex upon stimulation of the skin at the parts of the body shown. (Redrawn from W. Penfield and T. Rasmussen, *The Cerebral Cortex of Man*. New York: Macmillan, 1952)

body are heavily represented as is appropriate to their particular life style.

Psychophysics

One of the earliest ways in which psychologists tried to investigate the mental representation of the physical environment was by studying the sensations associated with particular physical levels of a stimulus. We can ask the question, 'how much does the energy level of a stimulus (the brightness of a light or the loudness of a sound) have to be increased in order to produce a just noticeable change in sensation?' The answer to this question seems to be of almost universal application. The relation between physical energy and sensation is usually a logarithmic one. This is known as the Weber–Fechner law. If the light intensity is low a small change in intensity is easily noticed. If the light is very bright then the change has to be large before it is noticed. The same principle applies, among other things, to wages and salaries. A farm worker earning £20 a week will certainly notice an increase of £2 a week, whereas a company director would certainly not notice such an increase even if he were successfully avoiding tax. As a result wage and salary increases are nearly always in terms of percentages, which is equivalent to using a logarithmic scale.

The transformation performed on stimulus energy by the nervous system has the effect of concentrating its processing capabilities on low energy stimuli at the expense of high energy stimuli.

Thresholds

In talking about the relation between stimulus energy and sensation I have avoided discussing how sensation is measured. On the whole people are very bad at describing sensations, but they are very good at detecting changes in sensation. Thus in the experiments relating stimulus energy to sensation the experimenter would increase stimulus energy until the observer said that his sensation had changed. The minimum change in stimulus energy needed to produce a change in sensation is called the *difference threshold*. A similar parameter of sensation that has been measured even more frequently is the *absolute threshold*. This is the minimum intensity for a light or a sound or whatever to be detectable. Many sensations can have absolute thresholds in this sense. Thus we can measure the fastest rate at which a light can flicker and still be distinguishable from a steady light. We can measure the shortest distance apart for two points to be felt as two rather than one.

Most of these thresholds are sensitive to gross changes in the state of the organism such as might be brought about by drugs or brain damage (Milner and Teuber, 1968).

There is however a methodological problem in measuring thresholds in this way. An observer is often uncertain whether he saw the dim flash of light or not. What will he say in this situation? If he is a radar operator detecting enemy ICBMs he may not wish to set off World War III accidentally, and therefore, when in doubt, he will say he saw nothing. If on the other hand he is detecting birds in the path of a civilian airliner he would rather give a false alarm than perhaps cause the death of many passengers. In these examples it is clear that the observers would have very different thresholds. The second observer would report much dimmer lights than the first. These differences are not due to differences in sensation, but result from a difference in the willingness to give the two responses 'yes' or 'no'. This is called a *response bias*. It is clearly sometimes important to distinguish changes in sensation from changes in response bias (Tanner & Swets, 1954).

Clark (1969) studied the effects of a placebo, which his subjects believed to be analgesic, on the pain threshold. He found that the placebo increased the pain threshold. However a more detailed analysis showed that sensitivity to pain had not changed, merely the subjects' willingness to report pain. With a real analgesic, on the other hand, the change in threshold was associated with a change in sensitivity to pain.

Contour extraction

Phenomena such as thresholds are automatic, i.e. largely determined by the nature of the peripheral sense organs. These processes seem to have little to do with abstract thinking and the other higher order abilities mentioned in the introduction. The mechanism to be described next is also automatic and peripheral. Nevertheless it performs a sophisticated transformation upon incoming information which has much in common with the higher order processes.

The world about us, contrary to the view of the impressionist painters, does not consist of a multitude of dots of different colours and brightnesses. What we see tends to occur in large blocks. Objects such as houses, trees and animals tend to have outlines that separate them from their backgrounds. This separating outline is particularly noticeable when the object moves in relation to its background. In this case every part of the object is moving at one uniform speed while every part of the background is moving at some other uniform speed. An analogous situation with brightness replacing speed would be a black object on a white background. In our world it seems to be the case that the environment is full of these local uniformities. All organisms capitalise on this special kind of redundancy. They ignore the uniformity and pay

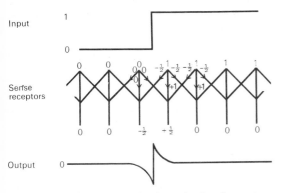

Figure 2.2 Diagram of a simple mechanism for contour extraction. When stimulated each receptor inhibits its neighbour. When the stimulation is uniform this mutual inhibition cancels out any signal from the receptor. However, where there is a change in stimulation (an edge), there will be receptors which are not inhibited by their neighbours and which will therefore transmit signals to the next stage in the perceptual system

particular attention to the parts of the environment that show a lack of uniformity. This helps them to distinguish an object from its background. In the case of simple visual perception this process is *contour extraction*. A black square on a white background is transformed into the outline of a square. This is achieved by a very simple mechanism called *lateral inhibition*. This means that in a grid of sense receptors each receptor when stimulated inhibits the responses of its neighbours (Figure 2.2) (von Bekesy, 1967).

Where the stimulation is uniform this mutual inhibition prevents any response. Only where there is a change in stimulation will a response occur. This ability of perceptual systems to emphasise change and

ignore uniformity occurs in both space and time and in most modalities. It allows the organism to describe the environment more economically by assuming that it has a particular kind of structure. This is the essential principle underlying all perceptual mechanisms whether they are automatic, i.e. 'wired into' the nervous system, or whether they result from learning.

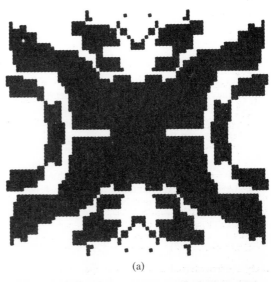

(a)

(b)

Figure 2.3 The components of the two pictures are equally 'predictable' in the sense that they are constructed largely of only one type of element. Picture (a) contains mostly clusters of black or white elements. Picture (b) contains mostly horizontally or vertically striped elements. However we expect pictures to contain mostly clusters and thus find picture (b) much more complex than picture (a)

Because all these systems make assumptions about the structure of the environment they will break down, or at least behave in a peculiar way when these assumptions are not met. Much psychological research on perception (e.g. the study of optical illusions) has depended on discovering and investigating situations in which the perceptual mechanisms break down in this way.

So far I have not properly defined terms such as structure, redundancy and economic description. There follows a simple and concrete example in which these terms are used and quantified:

xxxxxxxxoooooooo   xoxoxoxooxoxoxox

Both these sequences have equal numbers of xs and os, yet they are different and both are clearly highly structured. If the xs and os are taken in pairs both the sequences can be described very economically. The first has only one mixed pair (xo) in the middle, the second has only one unmixed pair (oo) in the middle. Thus each sequence can be described by stating the position of one type of pair. However the human perceptual system expects sequences of the first type and therefore pays attention to mixed pairs (ox) even when this results in descriptions that are far from economical (ignoring uniformity and noticing change). The evidence for this is that people find sequences of the first kind easier to remember and can find the rules to describe them more quickly (Figure 2.3) (Restle, 1967).

This example shows that contour extraction constitutes a basic perceptual process. Because contour extraction is a peripheral process 'wired into' the

nervous system, the amount of contour becomes a basic property of visual stimuli akin to brightness. Certain very highly contoured figures seem to overload the receptors and appear dazzling (Figure 2.4). Furthermore the camouflage adopted by various animals is clearly aimed at breaking up their contour lines.

THE PERCEPTION OF OBJECTS
Feature detection

By contour extraction we can reduce a black square on a white ground to an outline of a square. However there are regularities in this figure which allow us to give an even more economic description of it. The lines making up the square are straight, they are horizontal and vertical, they are equal in length and joined by 90 degree angles. These aspects of a figure, straightness, orientation and so on, are referred to as features. It is hypothesised that there are perceptual mechanisms which extract such features from an object thus describing the object in terms of a catalogue of features. These features are abstract entities, yet their extraction from the scene presented is carried out at a relatively low level in the perceptual system. Neurophysiologists have discovered single cells in the nervous system of cats and monkeys which respond to features such as lines of a certain orientation in any part of the visual field, lines moving in certain directions, and so on (Hubel, 1963).

It is clear that from a hierarchy of such feature detectors we could ultimately obtain single cells that responded to entities of any degree of abstractness or specificity required. This would only be useful for certain important objects that occurred very frequently in the organism's environment. In the case of humans this might, perhaps, apply to letters of the alphabet.

If feature extraction is to give an economic description of the environment then only some of the multitude of possible features will be extracted. Which features are chosen will depend on the properties of the environment. There is some evidence that this choosing occurs during early infancy as well as during the millions of years of evolution. Thus if kittens have experienced only horizontal lines during the first five months of life they will not respond to vertical lines (Blakemore and Cooper, 1970).

It has also been shown that this early visual experience must be active rather than passive (Held, 1965). If one kitten is pulled round by another in a carriage, thus having the same visual experience, the kitten with the passive experience is much inferior to the other in various visual discrimination tasks.

Feature analysis as a perceptual process is not necessarily tied to single cell mechanisms. It can be used to explain human performance in many quite complex situations. Shepard (1963) studied the learning of morse code. From the confusions people

Figure 2.4 There is so much regular contour in this figure that we find it 'dazzling' to look at and see illusory movements in it. (From Mackay, 1957, by courtesy of *Nature* (*London*))

made between letters he was able to show that two features of the symbols were being attended to. In the early stages of practice these features were the number of elements in the symbol (varying from   (E) to · · · · · (5)) and the kind of element in the symbol (varying from · · · (S) to --- (O)). In later stages of practice people attended not to the kind of element in the symbols, but the heterogeneity (varying from · · · (S) or --- (O) to · · · (R) or · · · (K)). This example demonstrates that even with a simple stimulus like a morse code letter there are a number of alternative features that can be attended to, and that people select only a small proportion of these.

Depth perception

In the study of depth perception we find that many of the various hypothetical perceptual processes are involved: feature extraction, assumptions about the environment and model building. Depth is perceived most directly through the subtle differences between the pictures presented to the two eyes. Having identified an object in the two pictures then the greater the discrepancy between the two views of that object the nearer it is. This is a very simple mechanism except that it depends on identifying an object as the same from two different points of view. Julesz (1965) has shown that this is done at a relatively peripheral level and even with random arrays of dots.

If we look at the world with only one eye or consider objects more than a few feet away then this direct perception of depth is no longer possible. In these cases the impression of depth depends on the use of special features and expectations about the environment. One of the most important is a 'texture gradient' (Gibson, 1966). As it gets further and further away from us the fine structure of the environment gets (retinally) closer and closer together ultimately becoming blurred and indistinguishable. The idealised form of this texture gradient is a pair of railway lines which meet in the distance and whose sleepers become closer and closer together until they can no longer be distinguished. Such a gradient is interpreted as indicating depth. This interpretation is of course quite arbitrary. An example is shown in Figure 2.5.

The slanting lines elicit an expectation of depth. The three vertical posts are the same length, but the one on the right appears longest because the depth interpretation makes us believe it is farther away. Other cues are *overlap*, (nearer objects are expected to overlap farther ones) and *movement parallax* (e.g. in a train the nearby objects move past faster than the farther ones). All these expectations about the environment can be falsified, giving rise to illusions. Of particular interest are the depth cues provided by the shape of objects.

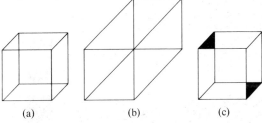

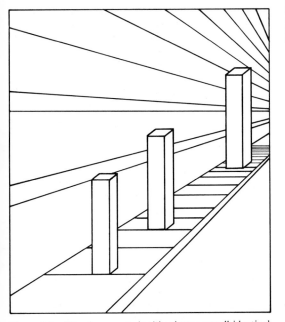

Figure 2.5 The three posts in this picture are all identical in size. However the one on the right looks considerably larger than the one on the left. This is because the slanting lines create an impression of depth

Figure 2.6 (a) This figure is seen as a three-dimensional wire cube rather than as an irregular two-dimensional object. However there are two three-dimensional interpretations of the figure and our perception spontaneously fluctuates from one to the other.

(b) This figure could be a particular view of a wire rectangle, but also forms a regular two-dimensional figure. We are less likely to see it in depth.

(c) Shaded areas have been added to figure (a). These additions make more sense in terms of the two-dimensional figure and so we are less likely to see it in depth.

(After Hochberg and McAllister, 1953)

Object (a) in Figure 2.6 tends to be seen as a cube in depth rather than as a complicated two-dimensional object. However, the figure is ambiguous as a representation of a cube, since we do not know which is the front and which the back. As we look at the picture we see the cube spontaneously alter from one form to the other. Why do we see this picture in depth? One possibility is that by seeing it as a cube in depth we can achieve a more economic description of the figure, since a cube is a very simple and regular object. Some evidence in favour of this notion is given by the sequence of objects in Figure 2.6 (Hochberg and McAllister, 1953).

Object (b) presents a very unusual view of a cube in which the two-dimensional representation also has a very simple and regular structure. This object is less likely to be seen in depth. By shading in areas, as in object (c), we can produce a figure that is simpler in two dimensions than in three, since, in terms of a cube, the shaded areas would be in irregular and unexpected places. This figure is also seldom seen in depth.

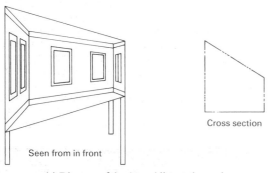

Seen from in front

Cross section

(a) Diagram of the Ames 'distorted room'

The expectation that the environment will provide simple and familiar objects can also give rise to striking illusions. The Ames room is an extremely distorted room which is interpreted as being rectangular. As a result people standing in it appear to be of impossibly different sizes (Figure 2.7). It is interesting that in this demonstration the expectation of rectangular rooms overrides the expectation that people remain the same size and do not grow when they walk across a room at the same distance from us. Perhaps this is because the size of an object is not very important to us (as long as we can recognise what it is) except as an indication of distance. Normally the position of an object in a room gives a better indication of distance than its size.

Constancies

Closely related to depth perception is the phenomenon of size constancy. We know that objects do not actually change size as they move away from us, and we use our knowledge of distance based on depth cues to compensate for this change and keep the apparent size of the objects constant. All this is done more or less automatically and so our view of the world might show people all more or less the same size sitting in a rectangular room even though the image on our retina

(b) Drawing of the appearance of the Ames 'distorted room'

Figure 2.7 We prefer to see this as a picture of a square room containing people of the wrong size rather than a distorted room with people of normal size. (From Vernon, 1962, *The Psychology of Perception*, by courtesy of Penguin, London)

would not be in the least like this. That is why perspective drawing was discovered so recently in art and is best achieved, not by looking at the scene, but by knowing the rules about vanishing points and so on, or stretching strings through a frame as shown in the picture by Dürer (Figure 2.8).

People are very good at estimating the real sizes and distances of objects, but very bad at estimating their apparent or retinal size. At art classes they used to teach students to hold their pencils at arms length to measure the size of things precisely to overcome this difficulty.

There are other aspects of objects that we expect to remain constant: colour, shape and brightness, for example. The mechanisms involved in these constancies are, in principle, the same as for size constancy. We compensate for changes in illumination, orientation etc. so that an object retains a constant identity. Thus a piece of white paper in shadow will appear lighter than a piece of black paper brightly illuminated even though the white paper may be objectively darker. However, this effect will only occur if we already know that one piece of paper is

white and the other black. If we do not know, then the objective brightness will be seen. Similarly, a round table top appears round, even when seen from a very acute angle making it truly an ellipse. All these compensatory mechanisms are unconscious and instantaneous yet clearly very sophisticated. Recent research (Bower, 1966) suggests that they are partially innate, being already present in infants of 36 days.

FIGURE PERCEPTION

All the constancy phenomena depend on first identifying objects and recognising them as the same in all circumstances: at different distances, from different points of view, in different illuminations, etc. The Gestalt psychologists (Koffka, 1935) suggested a number of rules which determined how a scene would be grouped into objects or figures (Figure 2.9). One of these was *common fate* which I have already mentioned in the section on contour extraction. If a number of points tend to have common movement which is different from that of the rest of the scene, these points will tend to be seen as a single object. Other rules are *closure*, *good continuation* and *proximity*.

Figure 2.8   A mechanical aid for making perspective drawings. The need for such an aid illustrates the difficulty we have in drawing what we 'see' rather than what we 'know'. (From *The Complete Woodcuts of Albrecht Dürer*, 1963. (W. Kurth, editor) by courtesy of Dover, New York)

It has been suggested (Hochberg and McAllister, 1953) that all these effects result from perceptual mechanisms that seek economic descriptions and capitalise on expected properties of the environment. An object is defined as something that has invariant properties when compensations for various transformations due to distance, illumination and so on have been allowed for. The object is important and is noticed. The various effects for which compensations have been made are not important and are ignored once they have been used to construct the object. The perceptual system seeks invariance and develops more and more sophisticated ways to compensate and transform the scene to produce invariance. This

method of describing the world is carried over into science. Water is conceived as an invariant substance although heat may transform it from ice into steam.

Most of the perceptual mechanisms discussed so far developed during the course of evolution or early infancy. Thus abnormalities in these mechanisms occur only through gross brain damage or severe drug intoxication. Certain drugs, such as LSD and mescaline, seem to affect the perception of space, perhaps

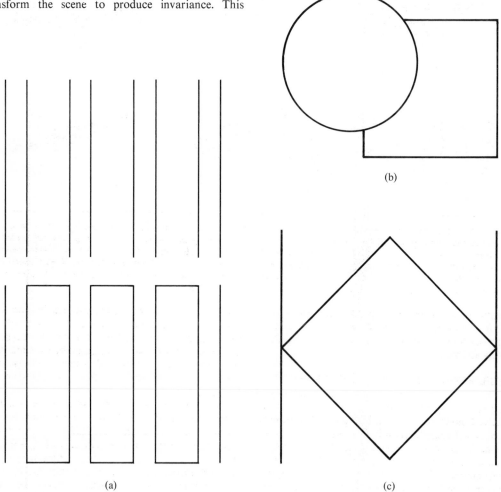

(b)

(a)   (c)

Figure 2.9 Gestalt principles of perceptual organisation
   (a) The upper figure is seen as four thin posts (grouping by proximity). However, by joining the tops of the lines as in the lower figure, three thick posts are seen instead (grouping by closure).
   (b) This figure is seen as a circle in front of a square, although the missing part of the 'square' could be any shape. We choose the 'simplest' interpretation of the situation, and that influences what we 'see'.
   (c) This figure is seen as a diamond between two parallel lines rather than as a W and an M. The figure is perceived in terms of components with maximum regularity, symmetry and hence simplicity even though W and M have frequently been seen before.

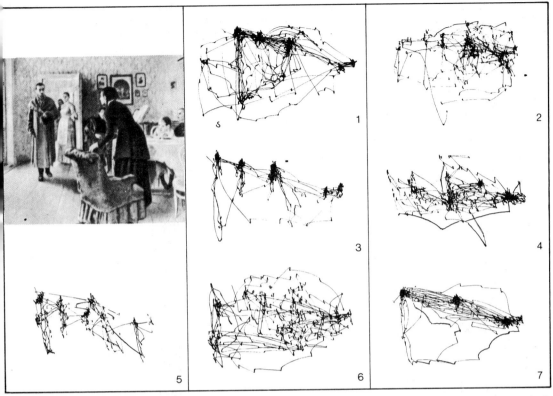

Figure 2.10   Seven records of eye movements by the same subject. Each record lasted 3 minutes. The subject examined the reproduction with both eyes. (1) Free examination of the picture. Before the subsequent recording sessions, the subject was asked to: (2) estimate the material circumstances of the family in the picture; (3) give the ages of the people; (4) surmise what the family had been doing before the arrival of the 'unexpected visitor'; (5) remember the clothes worn by the people; (6) remember the position of the people and objects in the room; (7) estimate how long the 'unexpected visitor' had been away from the family. (From Yarbus, 1967, by courtesy of Plenum Press)

by making the subject more aware of his retinal image through failure to make use of size and depth cues. Other constancies, such as that conserving colour, also break down.

THE PERCEPTION OF COMPLEX OBJECTS
So far we have considered perceptual mechanisms which apply to general aspects of the environment. In contrast I now want to consider particular aspects, aspects which are relevant only at a particular moment and which cannot therefore be picked out by evolution or learning during infancy. The observer has already transformed his scene into a space containing objects. However there is still an enormous amount of information in this transformed scene and he must make his description of it still more economic. He therefore tries to discover patterns and structures specific to this particular scene that are relevant to his needs at that particular moment.

Eye movements
The simplest way of cutting down the information in

a scene is to look only at the important aspects. We can see this happening if we study a person's eye movements. Yarbus (1967) invented an ingenious technique for doing this, which allowed the experimenter to observe the successive fixations of the eye of the subject and relate them to the scene being studied (Figure 2.10).

These fixations are far from random. They tend to follow the contours of the picture and pick out 'important' and 'interesting' details. Yarbus showed his subjects a picture, 'the unexpected visitor', and asked them various questions about it. Different questions induced different patterns of eye movements which showed that the subjects were looking only at the features relevant for answering the particular question. When schizophrenic and brain-damaged patients were shown the same picture their eye movements were not regular and structured, their fixation points seemed to be scattered randomly over the picture. It appeared that they were unable to pick out the important features. O'Connor and Hermelin (1967) found a similar effect with autistic children. The children looked into a box containing three displays on a matt black background. The autistic children spent more time looking at the background than either the normal or the subnormal control groups whatever was shown in the displays. It seems that autistic children, like schizophrenic adults, fail to pay attention to the important aspects of a scene. This could account for their apparent avoidance of the eyes of other people, since the face and eyes are the most important feature of a person and therefore receive a relatively large amount of attention from normal people.

Selective attention

It is clear that by moving our eyes we can switch our attention from one part of a scene to another. However we can also direct our attention in other modalities (e.g. hearing) where the sense organs can not so obviously be directed. A classic example of this kind of selective attention has come to be known as 'the cocktail party problem' (Cherry, 1957). At a party we are likely to be bombarded with loud music and several conversations going on simultaneously. Nevertheless we can attend to one of these conversations and ignore the rest.

There are thus two linked properties of our ability to attend: we can direct our attention and our attention span is limited. Thus our ability to selectively attend is both advantageous (we can pick out one conversation among many) and disadvantageous (we can only attend to one conversation at a time). The limits of our attention span are determined by the *information* content of the messages we are attending to. Mowbray (1953) had subjects read one prose passage while at the same time listening to another. With easy passages subjects could take in both quite well, but with difficult passages they did much worse than when dealing with one passage at a time. Cherry (1957) had subjects attend to a prose passage played into one ear and than asked them what they had heard in the other ear. He found that they could tell him nothing at all about the verbal content of the unattended passage, but could report certain physical characteristics such as whether it was a man or a woman's voice or a pure tone.

In order to select one message and ignore another we must initially attend to both messages in order to make the selection. Broadbent (1958) has called such a system a 'filter' selecting between different 'input channels'. This filter performs a classification of this input on the basis of simple physical characteristics such as sight *v.* sound, male *v.* female voice, words coming from the left rather than the right and so on. However this filter cannot pick out messages purely on the basis of meaning (Treisman, 1961). The filter does not eliminate the unattended channel completely. When the subject's own name is presented in the unattended channel it is usually heard whereas a neutral word is not (Moray, 1959).

It is probable that there is another, less efficient filter at a later stage in the system which classifies on the basis of more abstract features like word meaning rather than physical characteristics. Thus we can attend to colour names and ignore numbers even when they are alternating between the two ears (e.g. left ear: four red eight, right ear: green seven blue) (Yntema and Trask, 1963).

Pattern detection

The problem with studying natural scenes is that we do not know what the patterns and rules in the scene may be and so we cannot judge whether people successfully find them or not. One solution to this problem is to make up scenes containing special patterns and see whether people can find these. Such artificial scenes tend to be extremely simple. Frith (1970) presented binary sequences to children. These consisted of two words or two coloured counters following one another in various patterns: e.g. horse spoon horse horse spoon horse horse spoon horse. This is a fairly simple pattern. The triad *horse spoon horse* is repeated three times and so it is possible to code the pattern into a more economic form. Other patterns were presented which were more complex and could not be described so economically. Normal children clearly perceived these rules because they could remember the simple patterns better than the complex ones, and made errors of the kind expected if they were reconstructing the sequences on the basis of the rules they had discovered in them. Autistic children on the other hand appeared to have difficulty in perceiving the rules and remembered the simple sequences no better than the complex ones. They made errors which suggested that they were constructing their remembered sequences on the basis of rules that had not been present in the original sequences.

If you present children or adults with completely random sequences for which no economic description can be found then they will impose their own patterns upon them (Yacorzynski, 1941). For example you can ask someone to guess the colours of successive cards presented in random order. A young child will tend to guess alternatively black and red. An adult will guess, wrongly, that if a number of black cards have occurred in succession the next one is very probably going to be red.

Here we have two complementary processes in the perception of complex stimuli: the *discovery* of patterns and the *imposition* of patterns. As the difficulty or randomness of the stimuli increases people will tend to impose their own patterns. Autistic children much of the time seem to impose their own idiosyncratic patterns on their perception of the world suggesting that they find the world random and meaningless.

More complex sequences with which we are very familiar are written and spoken language. Here some of the underlying rules are the rules of grammar. If we are presented with a text in which every other word is missing we could make a fairly good job of reconstructing it, by making use of our knowledge of these rules. However if the text was a transcription of the speech of a schizophrenic patient this task of reconstruction would be much more difficult (Silverman, 1972). Thus these patients are not using the expected rules properly or perhaps are using idiosyncratic rules of their own. We say that a normal passage of writing contains constraints in the sense that each word is partially determined by those before and after it. We can also construct unconstrained word lists by selecting words at random from a dictionary. As you would expect, normal people can remember much longer sequences of text than they can of random word lists, since they make use of the rules of language. However, neither adult schizophrenics nor autistic children gain as much from the constraints provided by the rules of language (Lawson *et al.*, 1964; Hermelin and O'Connor, 1967). This does not appear to be due to a specific language deficit, but to a general difficulty of perception, a difficulty in finding rules and patterns.

Multidimensional stimuli

Another way of constructing economic descriptions of complex stimuli is to combine many low order features into a few high order concepts. The human face provides us with an overabundance of information. It contains many features: eyes, mouth, hair, etc. all of which vary along many dimensions. We can describe it in terms of a few higher order concepts such as attractiveness, intelligence and so on. One of the most tractable of these higher order concepts (which appears in all police descriptions of wanted men) is age. We presumably arrive at an estimate of a person's age from many cues although we are unaware of most of them. Some of the more obvious cues are amount of hair and number of wrinkles. This single concept, age, clearly carries a large amount of information about the appearance of a face. One of the phenomena that help us to arrive at such a concept is the correlation between the various features involved. For example people with grey hair will tend to have wrinkles, and most of the other signs of age.

It is difficult to study the perception of real faces since we do not know what their important dimensions

of variation are. Artificial stimuli of such complexity are difficult to produce and the schematic faces that have been studied are rather far from reality. Grodin and Brown (1967) constructed schematic faces with three variable features: length of chin, distance between eyes and length of forehead (Figure 2.11).

They demonstrated that when people judged the faces for degree of friendliness they combined the three features in a consistent manner. Thus, knowing the state of the three features, one could predict how friendly a particular person would find that face. Paranoid schizophrenic patients failed to combine the features in this consistent way. Bannister and Fransella (1966) have also shown that thought disordered schizophrenics have difficulty in assigning concepts such as friendliness, kindness, etc. consistently to photographs of unknown people. It has been suggested that schizophrenic patients suffer from a kind of perceptual overload (Payne, 1973). They appear to behave as if bombarded with more information than they can cope with. This suggests that some of the perceptual processes concerned with constructing economic descriptions of the environment have broken down. The schizophrenic patient is unable to discover patterns in the environment and has lost many of the expectations about the environment that 'normal' people have. Thus they will have to impose idiosyncratic patterns and expectations of their own. Creativity too depends on seeing novel patterns and relationships in the world. The difference between creativity and madness is perhaps merely that the patterns seen by the creative person are eventually also seen by a sizeable minority of other people.

Hallucinations

Little is known about hallucinations, but it is tempting to suggest that they result from the imposition of patterns and meaning on random inputs. Thus they tend to occur when people are deliberately put in minimally structured environments as in sensory deprivation experiments. It has also been suggested that drugs such as LSD produce entirely novel sensory experiences on which the observer tries to impose meaning. Auditory hallucinations found in alcohol withdrawal have been found to result from attempts to impose meaning on noises produced by a pathological state of the middle ear (Sarayay and Pardes, 1967).

However, the important dimension of hallucinations is the extent to which the observer believes in their reality, and this aspect is somewhat removed from the topic of perception.

SOCIAL PERCEPTION AND PREJUDICE

The economy achieved by perceptual processes depends on having expectations about the environment. When this principle is applied to the perception of people it seems synonymous with prejudice. To

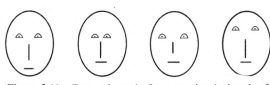

Figure 2.11 Four schematic faces varying in length of nose, height of eyes, height of mouth and distance apart of eyes. Normal people can use these features systematically to arrive at ratings of 'friendliness' for the whole face

treat every individual as a unique entity would put an impossible load on information processing and memory. We assume that certain verbal and non-verbal cues are important for communication and understanding and ignore the rest. Which particular cues we select for attention may vary on the basis of expectations about race, sex, class and other, finer classifications. Clearly if our expectations are false and we pay attention to the wrong cues communication will be difficult.

These expectancies are not quite the same as those associated with terms such as race prejudice and class prejudice. The latter prejudices must involve largely negative expectations about the behaviour of the individuals or groups being judged. That there is a close relation between such attitudes and perception is demonstrated by an experiment of Allport and Kramer (1946). These workers found that people with strong anti-Semitic prejudice were able to distinguish Jews from non-Jews more accurately than unprejudiced people. Presumably anti-Semites consider the division of people into Jews and non-Jews of vital importance in their world. They therefore pay attention to the cues indicating Jewishness (whatever they may be) and ignore other features. Another characteristic of the person having race prejudice is that he must be able to classify every person he is in contact with as either a member of the 'good' race or of the 'bad' race. Such a strict division is objectively impossible

and so attempts to apply it involve the denial of the existence of people on the boundaries of the categories. The occasionally ludicrous state of affairs that such denial can lead to is seen in the apartheid system of South Africa, by which the Japanese are classified as white, and the Chinese as coloured.

The denial of objects at the boundaries of well-defined classes is a feature of normal perception, for by assuming that objects fall into discrete groups we have an economic and convenient description of the world. Bruner and Postman (1949) briefly presented playing cards to people. Among the real cards were some with black hearts and red spades. The subjects failed to notice these, reporting that they were normal cards. Sometimes the denial was less complete and subjects reported 'purple' spades and hearts.

My theme in this chapter has been that perception is a process whereby we construct economic descriptions and models of the environment. This is done by 'discovering' relationships and patterns in the environment. The question as to whether these patterns actually exist in the world probably has no meaning. All that is required is that each person's model of the world (composed of his expectations and the patterns he sees) should be similar to the models of the people he comes into contact with. Thus necessarily our perception of the world is very much determined by our culture and our society (Douglas, 1973).

References

Allport, G. W. and Kramer, B. M. (1946). Some roots of prejudice. *J. Psychol.*, **22**, 9–39

Bannister, D. and Fransella, F. (1966). A grid test of schizophrenic thought disorder. *Brit. J. Soc. Clin. Psychol.*, **5**, 95–102

Blakemore, C. and Cooper, G. F. (1970). Development of the brain depends on the visual environment. *Nature (London)*, **228**, 477–478

Borges, J. L. (1964). Funes the Memorious. In: *Labyrinths* (New York: New Directions)

Borges, J. L. and Casares, A. B. (1971). *Extraordinary Tales* (New York: Herder and Herder)

Bower, T. R. G. (1966). The visual world of infants. *Sci. Amer.*, **215**, 6, 80–92

Broadbent, D. E. (1958). *Perception and Communication* (Oxford: Pergamon Press)

Bruner, J. S. and Postman, L. J. (1949). On the perception of incongruity: a paradigm. *J. Person.*, **18**, 206–223

Cherry, E. C. (1957). *On Human Communication* (London: Chapman & Hall)

Clark, W. C. (1969). Sensory decision theory analysis of the placebo effect on the criteria for pain and thermal sensitivity (d'). *J. Abn. Psychol.*, **74**, 363–371

Douglas, M. (1973). *Rules and Meanings* (London: Penguin)

Frith, U. (1970). Studies in pattern detection in normal and autistic children: I. Immediate recall of auditory sequences. *J. Abnorm. Psychol.*, **76**, 412–420

Gibson, J. J. (1966). The Senses considered as Perceptual Systems (Boston: Houghton-Mifflin)

Grodin, M. and Brown, D. R. (1967). Multivariate stimulus processing by normal and paranoid schizophrenic subjects. *Psychonomic Sci.*, **8**, 525–526

Held, R. (1965). Plasticity in sensory-motor systems. *Sci. Amer.*, **213**, 84–94

Hermelin, B. and O'Connor, N. (1967). Remembering of words by psychotic and subnormal children. *Brit. J. Psychol.*, **58**, 213–218

Hochberg, J. E. and McAllister, E. (1953). A quantitative approach to figural 'goodness'. *J. Exp. Psychol.*, **46**, 361–364

Hubel, D. H. (1963). The visual cortex of the brain. *Sci. Amer.*, **209**, 5, 54–62

Julesz, B. (1965). Texture and visual perception. *Sci. Amer.*, **212**, 2, 38–48

Koffka, K. (1935). *Principles of Gestalt Psychology* (London: Kegan Paul)

Lawson, J. S., McGhie, A. and Chapman, J. (1964). Perception of speech in schizophrenia. *Brit. J. Psychiat.*, **110**, 375–380

Luria, A. R. (1969). *The Mind of a Mnemonist* (London: Jonathan Cape)

Mackay, D. (1957). Moving visual images produced by regular stationary patterns. *Nature (London)*, **180**, 849–850

Milner, B. and Teuber, H.-L. (1968). Alteration of perception and memory in man. In: *Behavioural Change* (L. Weiskrantz, editor) (London: Harper & Row)

Moray, N. (1959). Attention in dichotic listening: Effective cues and the influence of instructions. *Quart. J. Exp. Psychol.*, 11, 56–60

Mowbray, G. H. (1953). Simultaneous vision and audition: comprehension of prose passages with varying levels of difficulty. *J. Exp. Psychol.*, 46, 365–372

O'Connor, N. and Hermelin, B. (1967). The selective visual attention of psychotic children. *J. Child Psychol. Psychiat.*, 10, 259–274

Restle, F. (1967). Grammatical analysis of the prediction of binary events. *J. Verb. Learn. Verb. Behav.*, 6, 17–25

Sarayay, S. M. and Pardes, H. (1967). Auditory elementary hallucinations in alcohol withdrawal psychosis. *Arch. Gen. Psychiat.*, 16, 652–658

Shepard, R. N. (1963). Analysis of proximities as a technique for the study of information processing in man. *Human Factors*, 5, 33–48

Silverman, G. (1972). The psycholinguistics of schizophrenic language. *Psychol. Med.*, 2, 254–259

Tanner, W. P. Jr and Swets, J. A. (1954). A decision-making theory of visual detection. *Psychol. Rev.*, 61, 401–409

Treisman, A. M. (1961). *Attention and Speech* (Oxford University: D. Phil. Thesis)

von Bekesy, G. (1967). *Sensory Inhibition* (Princeton: Princeton Univ. Press)

Yacorzynski, G. K. (1941). Perceptual principles involved in the disintegration of a configuration formed in predicting the occurrence of patterns selected by chance. *J. Exp. Psychol.*, 29, 401–406

Yarbus, A. L. (1967). *Eye Movements and Vision* (New York: Plenum Press)

Yntema, D. B. and Trask, F. P. (1963). Recall as a search process. *J. Verb. Learn. Verb. Behav.*, 2, 65–74

Chapter 3

EMOTIONS

Irene D. Martin

In the study of human emotions it is important that we distinguish carefully between the scientific observation of behaviour and the beliefs and faiths based on personal experience, however beguiling and convincing these may seem. Our ancestors could understand the mysterious existence of rocks, rivers, mountains, sun and stars by populating them with gods and spirits, whose purposes were similar to man's, and who were benign or hostile to him. Primitive animism formulated this hypothesis with complete credulity, filling nature with myth-figures which continue to engage us in our literature.

Such a subjective interpretation is not limited to inanimate nature: it extends to all kinds of animal life. Virtues of persistence and generosity have been attributed to forms of animal life from spiders to chimpanzees. Our pets are seen as understanding and 'knowing' our feelings. The cunning of Brer Rabbit, the homeliness of country mice, the wisdom of owls, form the entertaining and almost inescapable themes of nursery years.

It would be hasty to assume that modern culture has really given up these subjective interpretations of nature. It is still remarkably easy to see the actions of people around us in terms of our own perception and feelings; and remarkably difficult to consider alternative and more objective evidence.

Vocabulary of emotions

Literally hundreds of words are in everyday use which describe the emotions. An exhaustive search of the literature has shown the range to be very wide and in fact so extensive that one may be unaware of the precise shades of meaning involved. Consider depression and allied feeling states: sadness, melancholy, low-spirits, unhappiness, despair, misery. The distinctions may be far from clear and we often tend to use them synonymously. Conversely, we speak of love of people, love of home, of country, of beauty, but these feelings are distinguishably different. We therefore need to ask such questions as: How meaningful are these distinctions? How do we come to label different emotions? Is it that they relate to different physiological states, or to the context in which we experience them?

The evidence of the emotions

To apply the term 'emotional' either to ourselves or to other people generally subsumes a complex set of observations. So far as others are concerned there is much evidence from overt behaviour. Facial expressions involving change in eyes, lips and muscles can produce quite a different visage which in extreme emotion we can judge fairly accurately. Voices alter in pitch and intensity. Overt activity may occur, either simple running or fighting or a range of more subtle postural and gestural signals.

Another broad category of evidence comes from physiological change. This is one of the least disputed concomitants of many emotions. All writers, whether literary or scientific, have agreed on the observation of increased physiological activity: flushed face, accelerated heart rate, raised blood pressure, trembling and increased muscle tension, dilated pupils, shallow breathing, goose-flesh and visceral stirrings.

A final category of great, but essentially private, significance is that of our own internal feelings and perceptions. How we judge ourselves to feel, the intensity and the quality, can be communicated to others only through words.

These three broad categories are those to be considered and evaluated in any assessment of emotional states. To them a category of another kind must be added: the context or situation surrounding the individual, and which he judges to be provocative of particular types of feeling, whether of fear, anger or love.

Distinguishing emotion from other states

Before we distinguish among emotional states it is appropriate to consider how we distinguish the state of being emotional from other states. This raises the question of definition—whether we can specify that this state is 'emotional' and another state is not. In practice this has proved to be extremely difficult: outright emotions blend and blur with non-specific states of excitement, interest, arousal and involvement such as are experienced in activities like solving a puzzle, listening to a talk, engaging in conversation. In these states it can be shown that physiological activity is elevated: EEGs may show all the signs of arousal, there may be sweating, high heart rate, raised levels of muscle tension. Yet some of the components which would lead to a label of 'emotion' are missing. The individual with high physiological activation does not necessarily interpret this as 'feeling emotional'; this interpretation would seem instead to relate to subjective appraisal of the situation, whether for example it is perceived as threatening and whether the individual feels able to cope.

The transition from arousal to emotion can be illustrated in the behaviour of the young child and in playful, exploratory animals who will approach novel objects to examine them. This approach is cautious but does not seem to indicate fear; however, the dividing line between exploration and fearful behaviour is very fine, and the young child may suddenly run away screaming and in apparent terror if the object makes a sudden movement or noise. Presumably the evaluation of context as 'something to be explored' has shifted to 'something to be avoided'. Strictly speaking, we cannot say that his feelings have shifted from curiosity to fear because we have no access to internal states; the observations rest with external behaviour.

Differentiating one emotion from another

It follows from this that in observational studies of animals and children it is possible to differentiate *types of behaviour* which can be classified in terms of fighting, defence, feeding, exploring and so on, but it is not possible to differentiate *types of emotion* because part of the total pattern of valid emotional responding is subjective experience. Without this evidence we can only speak of emotional behaviour, and this falls short of the total concept of emotion. It might be the case that preverbal children and some species of animals experience something like adult emotion but this is very doubtful. It would imply that different emotions are innate and fixed in quality, whereas the argument to be presented is that a lengthy process of learning and differentiating internal states takes place throughout life, and that it is this process which leads to the diversity of adult subjective experience. That emotions are innate and fixed in quality is, however, a viewpoint which from time to time finds an exponent.

One of the first attempts to specify and list different kinds of emotions was based on the then current instinct theories (McDougall, 1912). McDougall assumed a long list of instincts each with its own associated emotion that was believed to be innate, ready made to serve the instinct by providing the appropriate driving force. Such assumptions do not lend themselves to experimental verification. Another influential view was that different emotional states relate to a differential pattern of physiological activation. An attempt has been made to test this empirically, with results suggesting that fear and anger produce different cardiovascular patterns. However, the evidence is relatively slight and very few convincing studies have emerged, not surprisingly, for if emotion is expressed in the components of the overt-motor, physiological and cognitive–verbal systems, the resulting response configuration could permit some very subtle permutations. It still remains a possibility that one day specific physiological patterns, specific cognitive patterns, and specific behavioural patterns, in association with given eliciting conditions, will be identified and shown to be organised in such a way as to clearly distinguish one emotional state from another (Lazarus, 1968).

MEASUREMENT OF EMOTION
1. Methods of assessing overt behaviour

One of the most common though rather global methods is that of rating overt behaviour in terms of some general criterion, for example, anxiety, depression, affection, hostility. Teachers are often required to assess a child's degree of emotional disturbance, assertiveness, sociability or co-operativeness. This kind of general assessment presumably makes use of a complex of observed items of behaviour, usually in a rather limited range of situations, and it involves complex judgements on the part of the rater. It is an occupation we all take part in, whether professionally or socially, and it is essential that anyone required to assess the behaviour of another person be aware of the factors which can influence the assessment. These have been described in detail by Eysenck (1969) and will be briefly mentioned here. They are:

(i) Differential understanding of trait names. For example, do the terms persistence, kindness, anxious and depressed mean the same to different judges?

(ii) The Halo effect. Whether we like (or dislike) someone, admire or despise them, is likely to colour all the judgements made of their behaviour—we may unwittingly attribute all the virtues to our friends and vices to our enemies.

(iii) Differences in rating ability. Persons who rate others may differ with respect to their ability to carry out this task.

(iv) Influence of unconscious bias. Biases for or against certain traits in others may be deeply rooted in the personality organisation of the rater.

(v) Influence of acquaintanceship. Contrary to common belief, relatively superficial knowledge seems to give better predictive accuracy than more thorough knowledge.

(vi) Raters' preconceptions. Kendell (1968) has shown how psychiatric ratings of clinical features of depression are significantly affected by raters' preconceptions about the classification of depressive illnesses (whether there are two distinct entities or only one) in such a way as to conform with, and so confirm, these opinions.

With so many factors influencing the rating it is not surprising that reliability between ratings, either made by the same person at different times or by different people on the same occasion, tends to be rather low. It also seems to be the case that self-ratings, e.g. of anxiety or depression, are not always highly concordant with ratings by observers: we do not always see ourselves as others see us.

The judgement of whether a person or child is 'affectionate' or co-operative is obviously a highly complicated one and limited to the samples of behaviour which we are able to observe. It is simpler to measure more specific components of behaviour such as smiling, amount of time spent in playing, crying, vocalisation, and so on. These can be fairly precisely defined among a group of observers, criteria decided on, and checks made on the measures obtained. This indeed is the position which contemporary ethologists have moved towards in their detailed observation of animal behaviour in natural surroundings. The more general (i.e. non-specific) observational studies which characterised the earlier work and which have been described in a number of popular books (e.g. Tinbergen, 1953, on the herring gull; Lorenz, 1967, on geese and fish and Jane van Lawick-Goodall, 1971, on chimpanzees) have since been much elaborated into careful and detailed monitoring of specifiable elements of behaviour.

Ethologists frequently draw analogies from animal to human behaviour on the grounds that humans are, after all, members of the animal kingdom and are descended through evolutionary processes from animals, and possess the same or similar sensory and neural equipment. Quite naturally they tend to emphasise the role of innate mechanisms—the view that organisms come into the world already equipped with behaviour programmes. This would mean that they have been programmed in the course of their phylogeny (the evolution of the species) and that their behaviour patterns are innate just like the physical structures they are born with. With this assumption in mind, it is a short step to apply the findings and explanations based on sex and aggression in fish, birds and apes, to man. Lorenz, for example, in discussing aggressive behaviour in the defence of territorial rights and pointing out the various inhibitory mechanisms which restrain aggression when animals live together in social groups, comments as follows:

'Every fish knew the owners of neighbouring territories very exactly and tolerated them peacefully at closest quarters, while he immediately attacked every stranger which approached his spawning hollow even from farther away.'

This peacefulness, it is postulated, is dependent on individual recognition of their fellows, and this non-aggressive pact of neighbours 'resembles true friendship'. Lorenz then continues with a beguiling analogy from human behaviour:

'Among human beings this phenomenon can regularly be observed in railway carriages, incidentally an excellent place in which to study the function of aggression in the spacing out of territories. All the rude behaviour patterns serving for the repulsion of seat-competitors and intruders, such as covering empty places with coats or bags, putting up one's feet, or pretending to be asleep, are brought into action against the unknown individual only. As soon as the newcomer turns out to be even the merest acquaintance they disappear and are replaced by rather shamefaced politeness.'

Ethological studies are fascinating to read and it is an intriguing exercise to make comparisons between human and animal behaviour. They have made us sensibly aware of the many comparable situations which we share in common with other animals. Analogies have an important role in science, but they require careful handling; vital differences must not be glossed over. To use these examples as complete explanations of human behaviour is to ignore many other factors, not the least being the possession of language and the role of thinking, which make any simple-minded use of analogies exceedingly misleading.

The technique of detailed behavioural sampling used by ethologists is, however, a valid and informative approach to the study of behaviour, especially when its elements can be carefully defined. It has been successfully applied to human studies, especially of young infants and children. Fears in infants are particularly interesting since they throw light on emotional, cognitive and social development. Fear of strangers (which in human infants usually appears in the second half of the first year of life and may extend long into the second year) can be studied by measuring such elements as the infant's facial expression (smiling, frowning, etc.), visual fixation, vocalisation, and motor activity in response to different types of strangers. In a controlled environment it is possible to examine analytically the effects of various factors on the child's fears, for example the size of the stranger, the sex, the proximity to the infant. One such study found, for example, that whereas the facial response was positive to the self (viewed in a mirror), and to mother and a strange child, it was negative to a strange male and female; further, the intensity of the reactions (either positive or negative) increased with closeness (Lewis and Brooks-Gunn, 1972).

One modern interpretation of the fear of strangers phenomenon is in terms of the massive learning and cognitive development which takes place in the young child. As we proceed along the phylogenetic scale learning becomes more important for the survival of the organism. The child has to learn to differentiate self from non-self, to discriminate the strange and the novel from the familiar. Hebb (1946) has suggested that fear occurs when an object is seen which is like familiar objects in enough respects to arouse habitual processes of perception, but in other respects arouses incompatible processes, and there is considerable evidence in infant studies (reviewed by Zegans and Zegans, 1972) to support the hypothesis that cognitive conflict affects emotional behaviour. This cognitive approach stresses the interaction between the infant's past and present experience; it stresses that the child's response to the 'strange' is a part of its larger emerging cognitive functions.

A point worth making in connection with some of these psychological studies is the methodological sophistication of the data analyses which are carried out. In infant/mother studies, for example, it is essential to study the interaction within the 'dyad' as this two-person relationship is termed. This matrix of maternal and infant behaviours involves the effect (for example) of vocalisation by A on vocalisation by B; or of vocalisation by A on the emotional response of B and the effect of this response back on A. Appropriate statistical analyses of this communication network are possible. The value of this approach is that a genuine two-way interaction can be assessed (Lewis and Freedle, 1972).

Some ethologists have extended their naturalistic approach to human behaviour in different societies and cultures. It becomes evident in human groups that social interactions and the means of smoothing social relationships assume great importance. These have been examined under such headings as territoriality, aggression, sexual, affiliative and group behaviour; Eibl-Eibesfeldt (1971), for example, illustrates the variety of greeting behaviours which are observed in different nations and interprets them in terms of their role in establishing a bond and appeasing aggression.

Posture and gesture are seen in this context as forms of expressive behaviour which are useful in social interaction as non-verbal means of conveying information. It is argued that the role of certain postures such as bowing, curtsying, falling to one's knees, etc. is that of making oneself small and thereby appeasing. This is the precise opposite of threatening behaviour and as such, ethologists suggest, is a central function of social rites. Threatening postures typically involve making oneself larger, often by raising the shoulders. Among primates for example, those small muscles are tensed which make the hairs on arms, back and shoulders stand erect. This in the chimpanzee leads to bristling of the fur which strikingly alters its appearance.

These field studies are interesting and useful reminders that social behaviour may have innate origins. They are supplemented by a quite independent set of studies which have been carried out on factors influencing social interaction, largely within the laboratory or controlled environment. Argyle (1969) has presented in a very readable and comprehensive way the varieties of non-verbal behaviour which occur in social situations such as meeting a strange person, being interviewed, performing before an audience, and in social structures such as being in prison or hospital. These behavioural elements include bodily contact, proximity, posture, facial and gestural movements, direction of gaze, and non-verbal aspects of speech. They are related not only to the type of situation, but the organisation of the group and the individual's perception and personality, and Argyle illustrates how they are modified by the different kinds of social encounter.

(a)

(b)

Figure 3.1 (a) The display face is shown by aggressive chimpanzees, especially during their charging displays or when attacking others.

(b) A full closed grin (upper and lower front teeth showing, but with jaws closed), is the expression of a chimpanzee who is probably less frightened or excited than one showing an open grin (upper and lower front teeth showing, jaws open). 'If the human nervous or social smile has its equivalent expression in the chimpanzee it is, without doubt, the closed grin' (Jane van Lawick-Goodall, 1971). (From Jane van Lawick-Goodall, 1971, by courtesy of Collins)

Facial expression

Can the face provide accurate information about emotion? This simple question, the answer to which may seem patently obvious on an intuitive basis, has baffled investigators for many decades. Earlier studies suffered from many methodological deficiencies and technical problems, and a variety of approaches has been tried out and discussed, e.g. the relative merit of motion (film or videotape) and still (photograph) records of facial behaviour; whether ratings should be made for specific *types* of emotions (fear, anger, sadness, disgust, etc.) or should aim to distinguish *dimensions* of feeling (such as pleasant/unpleasant, attention/rejection, positive/negative social attitude). Recent reviews of this area (Ekman *et al.*, 1972) conclude that when people look at the faces of other people, they can obtain information about happiness, fear, anger, disgust/contempt, interest and sadness. They can also describe the information they obtain in terms of dimensions such as pleasant-to-unpleasant, active-to-passive, and intense-to-controlled. Impressions about whether someone is angry, happy, sad, etc. can be related to particular movements and positions of the face.

Darwin was one of the earliest writers to draw attention to expressive movements of the face and ethologists since then have shown that these facial expressions are meaningful in that they convey accurate information of intention to other members of the species (Figure 3.1). Signs of threat, attack and submission seem well-understood and have been discussed in terms of 'sign stimuli' which are instantly recognised and activate the appropriate kind of strategic reaction (van Lawick-Goodall, 1971).

However, the study of facial behaviour in man in naturalistic settings has many difficulties: we wear our own masks in most social situations, and typically inhibit the direct expression of feeling. Ekman *et al.* (1972) hypothesise that there are culture-specific display rules, which dictate how facial behaviour is to be managed in particular social settings; and that this masking can be achieved in a variety of ways, by fragmenting the facial behaviour so that movements are seen in only one facial area rather than the whole; by time reduction, so that facial behaviour is visible for a brief instant; or by a miniaturisation, so that the excursion of the facial muscular movements is lessened.

Vocalisation: non-verbal aspects of speech

Much of the communication involved in speech goes on at a non-verbal level: how it is said rather than what is said. To take an extreme case: 'Yes' can be voiced to mean 'No'! Emotional tone is one of the most primitive aspects of speech; animals communicate their emotional states by sounds, and so in effect do humans. This is not the main conscious purpose of speech, in adults at least, but it is an important part of the message that gets across. These vocal characteristics can be described in terms of physical characteristics such as rate, pitch and timing; more elaborate measures include frequency distribution, and voice quality (e.g. resonant, breathy, quavery). Counts of speech errors can be made, but it is difficult to find a standard measuring situation since they are sensitive to audience effects and difficulty of material.

While research into vocalisation and emotion is continuing, the assumption that it would be possible to translate emotions into non-verbal cues has been proved difficult in practice. Much of this kind of research is reviewed by Argyle (1969) and Davitz (1964).

Eye contact

Eye contact behaviour, that is to say the duration of eye gaze, has been studied as part of the expressive

Figure 3.2 Flirting Samburu girl. She makes contact with the eyes, lowers her eyelids, then looks away. The ritualised flight is confined to the eye movements. It is no more than hinted at in the head movements. (From Eibl-Eibesfeldt, 1971, by courtesy of Methuen)

movements occurring in social interaction. Several differing processes seem to be involved in gaze-direction. In the first place A may look at B to try to establish a relationship, and will look more if he or she wants to establish a closer relationship of some kind (Figure 3.2).

In this case eye contact is sought, but too much of it creates anxiety. A prolonged stare seems to be interpreted as threatening and is rated as being very discomforting (Exline, 1971). It may also be used to try to establish a dominant relationship.

Argyle (1969) has outlined the ways in which looking at another person, together with other signals, can be used to establish different kinds of relationship. These other signals include facial expression (smiling, frowning, etc.), pupillary changes and physical proximity. Research at the Institute of Psychiatry in London has shown that anxious people tend to minimise eye contact by looking away from the experimenter. This is only evident under the stressful condition of a prolonged stare by the experimenter, and not during a relaxed period of conversation.

This section has illustrated some of the studies using observational techniques of overt behaviour in naturalistic settings and also some of the laboratory research which has aimed to measure behaviour more analytically. It raises a number of methodological and interpretative problems, some of which can be summarised as follows.

The biases of raters have been discussed, and there is considerable evidence that these biases significantly affect judgement. We should do well to be aware of our own! A more difficult factor to come to terms with is the great selectivity of perception which narrows informational input to the individual. What dimensions or categories are relevant will depend on the culture, the situation, the motivation and personality of the perceiver. Thus a religious enthusiast wants to know if people are saved or not, a political enthusiast which side they are on, a snob which class they belong to, and so on.

In this section there have also been examples of analogies of behaviour from different species of animal to man. These must be scrutinised carefully, as much for what they omit as for what they include. The dangers of anthropomorphism—of attributing to others (especially animals) the kinds of feelings and motives we experience ourselves—are ever present.

Quite obviously all the elements of behaviour which have been discussed convey signals and information, both to other animals of the same species and to the observer. Some of this information—the way it is given and the way it is interpreted—seems largely innately determined. But there is overwhelming evidence for the role of learning. Adults have been exposed to a very long learning process in which different elements of overt behaviour may be inhibited. Thus behaviour becomes fragmented—fear and anger may be experienced but perhaps rarely or never expressed in direct fearful and aggressive behaviour. Grief may be great, yet no tears allowed.

Whether overt reactions occur or not, there seems little doubt that underlying the behavioural signals there is a substratum of physiological activity which bears a complex and significant relationship to emotional experience.

2. Physiological concomitants of emotion

In considering this type of measurement we move to a set of studies which in general are characterised by complete objectivity of recording methods, a high degree of technical skill, and which are typically laboratory-based and involve controlled experimentation.

The fact of bodily involvement in emotion is widely recognised. Its manifestations are diffuse. 'Researches

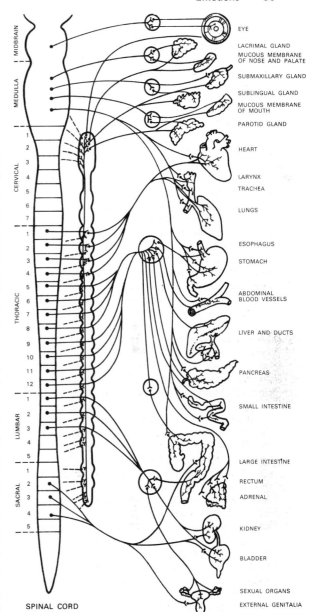

Figure 3.3 The autonomic nervous system is represented in this diagram. Parasympathetic fibres arise from the brain and sacral vertebrae. The sympathetic branches arise from the thoracic and lumbar vertebrae

. . . have shown that not only the heart, but the entire circulatory system, forms a sort of sounding-board, which every change of our consciousness, however slight, may make reverberate. Hardly a sensation comes to us without sending waves of alternate constriction and dilation down the arteries of our arms. The blood-vessels of the abdomen act reciprocally with those of the more outward parts. The bladder and bowels, the glands of the mouth, throat and skin, and the liver, are known to be affected gravely in certain severe emotions, and are un-questionably affected transiently when the emotions are of a lighter sort. That the heart-beats and the rhythm of breathing play a leading part in all emotions whatsoever is a matter too notorious for proof.' This quotation is from James (1890) and illustrates a pre-experimental viewpoint which has proved amply justified.

Many experiments have since provided data for the hypothesis that emotionality is related to excitability of the autonomic nervous system. Its role in emotional states was intensively examined by Cannon (1929). He recognised that the extensiveness and wide distribution of sympathetic nerve fibres permit diffuse action throughout the body, whereas the cranial and sacral divisions of the parasympathetic system with their restricted distributions allow for more specific action (Figure 3.3). He assigned to the cranial division the role of conserver of bodily energies; to the sacral division a group of mechanisms for emptying, while to the antagonistic sympathetic division he assigned an 'emergency' function. Pain, the major emotions fear and rage, and also intense excitement, are manifested in the activities of the sympathetic nervous division. When in these states, impulses are discharged over the neurones of this division to produce all the changes typical of sympathetic excitation.

Cannon also showed how closely related are the effects of the sympathetic nervous system and adrenal secretion. Epinephrine, secreted from the adrenal medulla, is extraordinarily effective in minute amounts and affects the structures innervated by the sympa-thetic division of the autonomic nervous system just as if they were receiving nervous impulses. Emotional excitement thus results in sympathetic (neural) dis-charges both to peripheral structures and to the adrenal medulla. This leads to the secretion of hormones, in particular adrenaline (or epinephrine as it is sometimes called) which has similar effects to the neural stimulation of sympathetic fibres, but on a longer time base. Thus sympathetic effects are auto-matically augmented and prolonged through direct chemical action on the organs themselves.

To summarise, the importance of Cannon's work was his experimental approach in linking emotional behaviour with precisely measured physiological effects. The utility of these bodily changes was discussed in terms of mobilising the organism for prompt and efficient struggle.

The relevance of sympathetic activity to emotional experience becomes evident when we review the effects of sympathetic activity on end organs. Sali-vation is reduced or stopped; movement of the stomach, secretion of gastric juices and peristaltic

movements of the intestines are all inhibited. These effects together slow down digestion. They also interfere with normal parasympathetic functions, giving rise to defaecation and urination. Changes in the circulatory system also take place. Sympathetic impulses to the heart make it beat faster. They also cause constriction of the blood vessels of the gut and control blood flow in such a way as to direct more blood to brain and skeletal muscle mass. The impulses of the sympathetic neurones, as indicated by their dominance over the digestive process, are capable of readily overwhelming the conditions established by the parasympathetic division of the autonomic nervous system.

Many of the bodily effects of sympathetic arousal can be detected from the surface of the body by means of appropriate transducers and high gain amplifiers. Active brain, muscles, heart, sweat glands

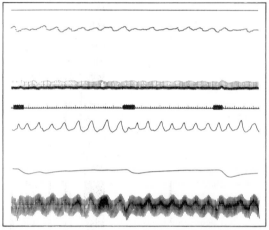

Figure 3.4 Sample of psychophysiological recordings. From top to bottom: tachograph (heart rate changes), EKG, event marker (stimulus = a tone), respiration, palmar skin resistance, and plethysmograph (blood volume change in the ear lobe). A respiratory rhythm can be seen super-imposed on the latter

and many other structures produce small voltages which can readily be picked up by means of appropriately situated electrodes placed on the skin. These small impulses are amplified to produce the recordings illustrated in Figure 3.4.

One of the most popular measures of the psycho-logical laboratory is palmar skin resistance. This is closely associated with sweat gland activity and is extremely sensitive to changes in level of arousal, and to novelty and stress. Polygraph recordings of this and other physiological measures are becoming reasonably commonplace in psychological labora-tories and are increasingly contributing to our understanding of human emotions, especially anxiety. It should be possible in the near future to employ existing techniques of telemetric recording (usually radio transmitted signals from individuals in free situations, i.e. not confined by wires and leads to apparatus in the laboratory) in psychological and psychiatric studies. It would then be possible to record from an agoraphobic patient, for example, in the real setting of his fear. As yet, however, psychophysiological studies are virtually confined to the laboratory, and this necessarily introduces an element of artificiality into the situation. Since it is not possible to induce strong emotions such as fear in those who volunteer to be subjects, experiments are carried out in 'analogue' situations, i.e. those of mild fear or unpleasantness, by using unpleasant sensory stimuli such as harsh tones, or by comparing groups of anxious subjects with non-anxious subjects in certain mildly stressful situations like solving problems, coping with distraction, etc. Physiological reactivity in the two groups (anxious *v.* non-anxious, stressed *v.* unstressed) can then be compared. Results of various psychophysiological studies in the context of psychiatric disorders have been reviewed by Martin (1973), and in the context of treatment by desensitisation by Mathews (1971).

In recent years, other classes of compounds have been implicated in various affective states, including normal and pathological anxiety, depression, elation and anger. These include the catecholamines, epinephrine and norepinephrine, and the indole amine, serotonin. While norepinephrine functions as a chemical transmitter substance at the terminals of the peripheral sympathetic nervous system, the role of this and other amines in the central nervous system is far from clear. It has been suggested that norepinephrine and serotonin may each function directly as a transmitter substance in the central nervous system, though none of the biogenic amines has yet been definitely established as a chemical neurotransmitter in the brain (see Schildkraut and Kety, 1967, for a review of this area).

Many of the experiments mentioned above (and all of Cannon's) were carried out on infra-human animals, often cats. The results of decades of experimental work with human subjects, while confirming time and time again the involvement of physiological reactivity in emotion, have nevertheless increased rather than reduced the puzzles and the problems. The dissociation mentioned earlier between behaviour and emotion (that an emotion might be felt strongly but not expressed in any way) is also found between physiological variables. It had been expected on the basis of the 'mass action' of the sympathetic division of the autonomic nervous system that all measures of sympathetic activity would relate highly with one another, i.e. an increase in one measure would be reflected by increases in others. Contrary to this assumption, the physiological reaction shows idiosyncratic patterning, one person responding more in one specific measure (say increased blood pressure) and relatively little in other measures, while another person evinces a high degree of sweating, and yet another elevated levels of muscle tension. It is possible that this patterning of reaction is a function of the relatively stress-free atmosphere of the laboratory, and that all systems would be equally elevated in a real-life stress. It is also possible that some degree of patterning really does exist and is related to specific symptom areas as found in psychosomatic illnesses. Research which has been carried out on symptoms such as backache and headache seems to suggest a fairly localised muscle tension: muscles in the symptom areas are excessively tense while other muscle groups remain relatively relaxed.

Another factor to be briefly mentioned is the nature of the measurements which are made from the physiological recordings. It is usual to refer to 'elevated' physiological reactivity, i.e. to the intensity or amplitude of a particular reaction, but there are other characteristics which can be measured but which are often ignored. In a given situation people may react physiologically at different latencies (short or long) for different durations, and they may take a longer or shorter time for the physiological reaction to subside. This persistence of reaction is not perhaps very meaningful in the laboratory situation, but differences in timing have been noted in the few real-life stress studies which have been carried out. Experienced *v.* inexperienced parachutists differ, for example, in their temporal patterning of heart-rate reactions prior to jumping (Epstein, 1967).

Another limiting factor in psychophysiological studies is their failure to take account of the role of pituitary–adrenal involvement in the stress response of human subjects. Measurement problems are of course formidable, but it should be recognised that not only the adrenal medulla but the adrenal cortex has been discussed in the context of emotion and stress (see, for example, Selye 1956). Thus the overall physiological pattern occurring in emotion and prolonged stress is likely to be very complicated indeed; and, within any general pattern which may eventually be elucidated, it will certainly be the case that individuals will differ in many characteristics. Eysenck (1967) has postulated that neurotic/anxious subjects tend to inherit a more reactive sympathetic nervous system, and hence personality characteristics which determine stress thresholds and stress tolerance; a similar case has been made out for biochemical individuality (Williams, 1956). These factors, combined with the effects which learning may have on the individual elements of the overall emotional response, suggest that we are far from an adequate measurement of the physiological response pattern of emotion.

Granted that physiological changes occur, how does the individual perceive them within himself?

Results of research in this area suggest, perhaps surprisingly, that people do not judge their internal states very precisely. Even physiological events which might seem obvious, like a markedly increased heart rate or level of muscle tension, are not always accurately rated. The evidence suggests that perception of bodily change and actual bodily change are not perfectly related, and that individuals may be hyporesponsive or hyperresponsive to particular kinds of change. It has been postulated that obese individuals, for example, may be unresponsive to hunger-induced bodily changes in the sense of not using them to define hunger or to initiate eating.

This concern with the perception of bodily changes gives rise to an interesting set of questions. What does an individual do when he does perceive bodily change? That is to say, what does he do with this information? Common sense tell us that novel information about ourselves is not disregarded. We think about it and attempt to understand it. This evaluative process is a crucial factor in recent cognitive theories of emotion. In an effort to deal with the inadequacies of a purely visceral or physiological formulation of emotion, several researchers have proposed that cognitive factors may be major determinants of emotional states. Given a state of physiological arousal it has been suggested that one labels, interprets and identifies this stirred-up state in terms of the characteristics of the precipitating situation. Thus it is argued that emotional experience is jointly determined by the *perception* and *labelling* of bodily changes.

3. Verbal methods: questionnaires, scales, self-reports

Any adequate account of human emotion must take into account the individual's description of his subjective feelings. These are often freely described in the clinical interview situation, but for experimental purposes methods of categorising and quantifying the verbal material have been devised. These include questionnaire responses, adjective check lists and mood scales, as well as some of the structured interviews which typically occur in many experiments.

In mood scales the subject is usually required to describe his feelings by endorsing from a large list of adjectives (angry, bored, tired, relaxed, etc.) those that apply to him. Even quite simply the subject may be asked to rate himself along a hypothetical continuum. For example, a mood scale of depression might include a scale ranging from 'feeling cheerful, on top of the world' at one end, to 'feeling unhappy and utterly miserable' at the other end. A scale of fear might ask the subject to rate a particular fear along a continuum of 0 as no fear at all to 100 as the most frightened he has ever been. The idea behind these scales is that of a standardised format, to help the subject describe his own feelings. They have been used in demonstrating changes in attitude with forms of psychotherapy, change in emotional responsiveness to frightening films and in reflecting the effects of drugs.

The typical questionnaire contains fairly specific statements about the individual's behaviour. An anxiety scale, for example, might contain such questions as: Do you suffer from sleeplessness? Do you worry about your health? Items in such scales usually refer to typical behaviour, to *generally* feeling tense, *often* having difficulty in sleeping, etc. In this sense they are used to refer to a personality *trait*, i.e. a relatively persistent, long-lasting aspect of a person's nature. We may also need to know how a person is feeling *now*. Granted that he has a trait of anxiety, that is to say he tends to be an anxious person and this tends to be manifested in many different situations, does he feel anxious *right now*. Such a question refers to the individual's current *state*. Trait and state aspects of personality measurements do not always coincide; however anxious in general, we may *right now* feel relaxed. Many personality scales have been designed with the 'state' measure in mind, and they require answers concerning the individual's current state of feeling.

There have been many criticisms of these methods of assessing emotional states. Many of the items included in these lists are selected quite arbitrarily. A person who scores high on an anxiety scale may also score high on a depression scale or a scale of hysteria, simply because the scales include haphazardly grouped items which were just guessed at in the first place. The *a priori* construction of questionnaires and the naive notion that because a questionnaire is given a particular label it therefore measures that particular trait have had to be abandoned. Very careful validation techniques and statistical analyses are required to sort out this kind of problem.

Eysenck (1969) has tried to structure the whole field of personality in terms of independent dimensions. Three major dimensions have been described to date: neuroticism, introversion–extroversion and psychoticism. Items which characterise neuroticism (or emotional instability) include nervousness, depression, inferiority feelings, etc. The neurotic is hypochondriacal, worried, excitable and impatient. Differentiated emotional states are seen within this dimensional framework: the introverted neurotic, for example, is predisposed to suffer anxiety and depression.

Other criticisms which have been raised concern subjects' biases (e.g. the tendency to answer 'yes' or 'no' to all questions), age and sex factors, and the observation that subjects may deliberately fake their answers. Modern questionnaires have gone a long way towards coping with these difficulties. A great deal of statistical and experimental expertise have gone into their construction, their reliability and validity. Nevertheless, questionnaire responses must be interpreted with care; they provide useful information, but this is probably most profitably considered alongside other sources of information, especially the physiological and the behavioural.

Cognitive/perceptual factors

The preceding section has dealt with relatively straightforward questions and responses concerning the subject's typical behaviour and his immediate feeling states. We move now towards a set of cognitive/peripheral factors which while of undeniable significance are more elusive of definition and measurement.

It is apparent that human subjects not only selectively perceive the world around, but make judgements and evaluations, deliberate about alternative solutions to problems, make plans, and try to cope with difficult situations by means of different plans and strategies. A number of studies have been carried out to examine how these factors affect behaviour.

Several writers have discussed emotion in terms of the individual's perception and appraisal of his situation. Arnold (1960) defines emotion as the felt tendency toward anything intuitively appraised as good (beneficial) and away from anything intuitively appraised as bad (harmful); this attraction or aversion is accompanied by a pattern of physiological changes organised toward approach or withdrawal. The appraisal process is described as direct, immediate and intuitive, not the result of reflection or deliberation.

This view that one of the primary evaluations of a stressful situation is in terms of the *threat* which it poses the individual has also been proposed by Lazarus (1968), who has carried out a long series of studies on this basis. He distinguishes a primary and a secondary appraisal, the first based on the immediate situational confrontation and the evaluation by the individual of its harmful or beneficial significance; the second within the context of the coping strategies which are employed. These are illustrated in Table 3.1

Meichenbaum (1972) illustrates the relationship between the individual's self-evaluatory statements and his level of anxiety in a situation of public speaking, during which some members of the audience walk out of the room, on two different speakers, both possessing essentially the same speaking skills.

This exodus elicits different self-statements from high v. low speech-anxious speakers. The high speech-anxious individual is more likely to say to himself: 'I must be boring. How much longer do I have to speak? I knew I never could give a speech' and so forth. These self-statements engender anxiety and become self-fulfilling prophecies. On the other hand, the low speech-anxious individual is more likely to view the audience's departure as a sign of rudeness or to attribute their leaving to external considerations. He is more likely to say something like: 'They must have a class to catch. Too bad they have to leave; they will miss a good talk'.

Such self-statements are often implicit, and may need to be made explicit in order for retraining of more positive attitudes to take place. A related aspect of performance is the individual's judgement of how he feels he has coped with a stressful situation, once he has acted. Was it well done? Does he feel a failure? Many appraisals and reappraisals take place as we think over past actions. The wider problem is often what constitutes coping adaptive behaviour in relation to the values which are held.

One extreme of coping behaviour (its absence) has

Table 3.1   Sources of information contributing to primary and secondary appraisal. (From Lazarus, 1966, by courtesy of McGraw-Hill)

	Primary appraisal *(based on nature of harmful confrontation)*	*Secondary appraisal* *(based on consequences of action tendencies)*
	Threat or non-threat	Coping
Factors in stress configuration contributing to appraisals	1. Balance of power between harm and counterharm resources 2. Imminence of confrontation 3. Ambiguity of stimulus cues concerning harm	1. Location of agent of harm 2. Viability of alternative coping actions 3. Situational constraints *Degree of threat
Factors within physiological structure contributing to appraisals	1. Motive strength and pattern 2. Several belief systems concerning transactions with environment 3. Intellectual resources, education, and sophistication	1. Motive strength and pattern (because of potential sacrifices entailed in any action) 2. Ego resources 3. Coping dispositions

* Belongs neither in stimulus configuration nor physiological structure but is a complex, intervening product of both.

been illustrated in studies carried out on dogs. When a dog receives traumatic electric shock which cannot be predicted and from which there is no escape it eventually seems to give up and passively accept the shock. Seligman *et al.* (1971) refer to this form of passive behaviour as 'learned helplessness'. Many of these dogs who are subsequently given the opportunity to escape from shock fail to learn to do so, and Seligman argues that these animals become passive in the face of trauma. Extending his argument on learned helplessness to human behaviour, he suggests that depressive patients feel helpless, hopeless and powerless because they have learned (or believe) that they cannot control those elements of their lives which relieve suffering and bring gratification. In short they believe they are helpless. The detailed analogy which Seligman offers is couched in learning theory terms, and on this basis he has suggested various ways of modifying the 'helpless' behaviour.

The role of cognitive and coping factors is being increasingly explored in different kinds of therapeutic situations. There is a rapidly expanding group of studies in which the many attributes of fears, especially fears of fairly specific objects like small animals, are carefully investigated. Self-reports of fear are obtained, together with physiological recordings to phobic and neutral stimuli, and observations of the subject's overt response to the feared object (i.e. degree of approach/avoidance, etc.). The self-reports often include information concerning the subject's perception and evaluation both of the situation and the degree to which he feels he is coping with it (Lang, 1968). This group of studies is closely related to various kinds of therapies, and they have often attempted to evaluate the success of specific treatments in terms of their effects on the components of fear.

Some of the specifically cognitive-oriented research into emotion is primarily concerned with the nature of the stimulus or situational effects which are involved in producing emotional reactivity. It has frequently been observed that man and infra-human animals react negatively to events that deviate from what they have adapted or habituated to. Information conflict arises when a previously laid down neutral pattern is set against a stimulus similar to, but not the same as one experienced in the past. Explanations have been given in terms of the organism maintaining some more or less optimal level of arousal and cortical activity. Stimulus variables such as novelty, incongruity and surprise which are mild or moderate in degree are likely to elicit orienting/arousal reactions, interest and possibly exploratory behaviour. Extremely intense stimuli on the other hand usually provoke defensive reactions such as rigidity, startle and flight (Figure 3.5).

Most of the arousal level hypotheses are essentially theories of tension reduction. Deviations from optimal

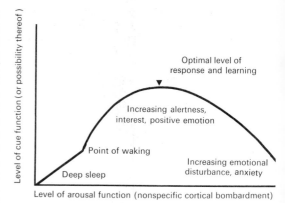

Figure 3.5 Relationship between the 'cue function' of stimuli which guide behaviour, and the general 'arousal function' of stimuli which energise behaviour. Cortical (cue) function is facilitated by the diffuse bombardment of the arousal system up to an optimum. Beyond this, as at the right, the greater bombardment may interfere with the delicate adjustments involved in cue function. Thus there will be an optimal level of arousal for effective behaviour. (From Hebb, 1955, by courtesy of *Psychol. Rev.*)

arousal levels create tension and discomfort which motivate the organism towards efforts at their removal. Such theories imply a kind of homeostatic or equilibrium principle.

Many specific problems along these lines have been examined by experimental research in this area, and the issue in the present context is the extent to which such cognitive factors affect an emotion like anxiety. Does a statement like 'I have failed' engender more anxiety and hence increased physiological arousal; and conversely a statement like 'I can convince myself to do it. I can reason my fear away' reduce anxiety and physiological arousal? The extent to which this type of modification can occur, and the type of learning procedures which it implies, will be dealt with in greater detail in the following chapter. The point to emphasise here is that the various systems, e.g. cognitive and physiological, appear to interact with each other in such a way as to augment or diminish general emotional responsivity.

RELATIONSHIP AMONG MEASURES OF EMOTION

The earlier naive assumption was that measures, e.g. of anxiety, would all relate to one another. It has become apparent, however, that this is far from true. As we have seen, the overall pattern of emotion contains many components: overt elements of behaviour, internal physiological changes, complex cognitions and perceptions; it leads the individual to act upon and to interact with his environment in ways which he interprets as 'coping' or 'failing', etc.

One group of studies has been concerned with the

cognitive activity which underlies the production and reduction of the stress reaction (Lazarus and Opton, 1966; Lazarus, 1968). This work has monitored physiological reactions and self-reports to frightening and threatening films involving death, mutilation, ostracism, etc. and has examined the effect of different types of instructions read concurrently with the showing of films. One set of instructions denied the harmful features of the events portrayed on the film. A second set encouraged detached, intellectualised modes of thought. A third emphasised the horror of the film. The key findings were that both denial and intellectualisation significantly reduced the stress reaction as measured via autonomic levels of arousal; and the results were interpreted as supporting the proposition that threat depends on the manner in which a situation is appraised or evaluated. 'Objectively' distressing stimulus events can be viewed without great stress reaction if these events are interpreted in non-threatening ways. These findings are illustrated in Figure 3.6 which shows how both denial and intellectualising instructions reduce skin-conductance (sweating) levels from those found in the control condition, when subjects are shown a film containing distressing accidents.

Lazarus' results also confirm previous findings in that the different measures yield different pictures of the emotional state of the individual. He discusses the reasons why divergence could well occur among major components without necessarily invalidating the inferences about a given emotion, suggesting that each response system has its own adaptive functions, i.e. it illustrates some special *transaction* between a person and his environment. 'Thus what the person reports to the observer and, to an extent, his instrumental actions, reflect intentions concerning the social being with whom he is interacting. At the same time, the physiological state should also reflect the direct action tendencies which are mobilised for dealing in some fashion with the appraised threat.' Such a view relates to the extensive learning processes which inhibit, augment, and in many ways 'shape' individual behaviour. (Chapter 4 reviews some of these forms of learning.)

Another set of studies in this area has been carried out by Schachter (1966) on the cognitive

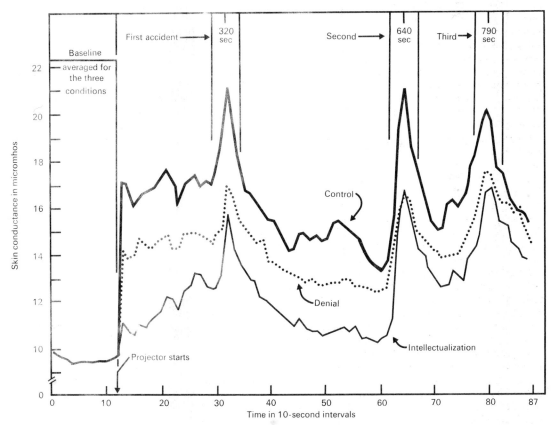

Figure 3.6 Group average skin conductance for three orientation treatments during a film showing distressing accidents. (From Lazarus *et al.*, 1965, by courtesy of *J. Personality*)

determinants of emotional states. Schachter accepts the evidence that a general pattern of sympathetic discharge is characteristic of emotional states. Given such a state of arousal, he suggests that one labels, interprets and identifies this stirred-up state in terms of the characteristics of the surrounding situation. 'It is the cognition which determines whether the state of physiological arousal will be labelled "anger", "joy" or whatever.' An experimental test of these propositions was carried out in which an injection of epinephrine was given to four groups: (1) informed about the nature of the injection and that they would probably feel physiological effects, (2) left totally ignorant about the injection except that it was harmless, (3) misinformed, and (4) a placebo group. To manipulate the emotional states of the subjects an actor was employed, trained to 'act euphorically' and to 'act angrily'. Results showed that in both euphoric and anger conditions, emotional level in Group 1 (epinephrine informed) was considerably less than the other two epinephrine groups, supporting the view that following the injection those subjects who had no explanation of their bodily state were readily manipulable into the disparate feeling states of euphoria and anger. Those subjects injected with epinephrine and told what they would feel and why proved relatively immune to the effects of the manipulated cognitions.

In addition to these experimental studies, some interesting reports have been made on the emotional life of paraplegics and quadriplegics. Hohmann (1966) conducted a structured interview with these patients about sexual excitement, anger, fear, grief and sentimentality; he noted that subjects with cervical lesions described themselves as acting emotional but not feeling emotional (Figure 3.7). A few typical quotes might be:

'. . . it's sort of cold anger. Sometimes I act angry when I see some injustice. I yell and cuss and raise hell, because if you don't do it sometimes, I've learned people will take advantage of you, but it just doesn't have the head to it that it used to. It's a mental kind of anger.'

'Seems like I get thinking mad, not shaking mad, and that's a lot different.'

These quotations are interestingly contrasted with those from subjects given injections of adrenaline (Marañon, cited by Schachter, 1966) and in whom physiological arousal is high. These people are conscious of a stirred up state but with no objective reason for emotionality they describe themselves *as if* frightened' but yet calm. Schachter (1966) describes these two sets of introspections as like opposite sides of the same coin. 'Marañon's subjects reported the visceral correlates of emotion, but in the absence of veridical cognitions did not describe themselves as feeling emotion. Hohmann's subjects described the appropriate reaction to an emotion-inducing situation but in the absence of visceral arousal did not seem to describe themselves as emotional. It is as if they were labelling a situation, not describing a feeling. Obviously, this contrasting set of introspections is precisely what should be anticipated from a formulation of emotion as a joint function of cognitive and physiological factors.'

THEORIES OF EMOTION

Up to this point we have been concerned with the concept of emotion, i.e. with the components of the emotional state and with the relationship among the components. Forms of measurement have been considered and a rough definition of emotion has been outlined in terms of the patterning of its parts in specific contexts.

However, we have concentrated on a relatively objective, testable and experimental approach to emotion. According to this view meaningful definitions of emotion, whether behavioural, physiological or clinical, must fulfil at least the requirements of verifiability and significance. 'The criterion of verifiability could be satisfied by defining the concept so that the laboratory manipulations could be repeated by any qualified investigator. The definition must then specify the relevant environmental, organismic and response variables. This first criterion is the procedure for defining scientific concepts "operationally" . . .'. The significance of a concept can be

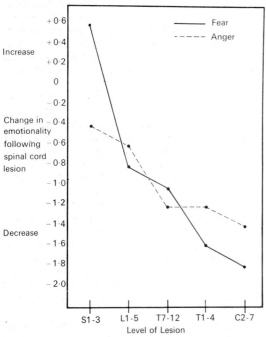

Figure 3.7   Changes in emotionality as related to height of spinal cord lesion. (Data from Hohmann, 1962, quoted by and reproduced from Schachter, 1966, by courtesy of Academic Press)

measured in terms of the extent to which it leads to the formulation of laws about the phenomena (Goldstein, 1968).

In considering theories of emotion it is evident that many lie outside the empirical approach which has been adopted in this chapter, which requires an agreed conceptual system and broad acceptance of experimental operations. Some theories, on the other hand, explicitly reject the experimental method, or phrase their hypotheses in ways which are not testable. Nevertheless they are of interest in that they are frequently ingenious and interesting, often exert considerable influence on our thinking and may possibly be rephrased in the future so that more direct tests of their hypotheses become possible.

Theories of emotion are enormously varied in content and scope and cover widely different aspects of emotion. It is probably true to say that no single comprehensive theory exists. Some are concerned with consciousness and the unconscious, some with the role of instinctual energies; some with the problem of how a single, primitive form of excitement becomes differentiated into specific emotions, others with the specification of innate emotions which appear ready made, as it were, to serve our purposes. The origin of emotional development in the young infant, in fact the whole genesis of emotional states, is a problem awaiting analysis. Some theories emphasise the essential subject–object interaction in emotion, i.e. the communicative aspects; others deal with those central nervous system structures which govern the physiological and behavioural concomitants of emotion. Obviously they are dealing with very different facets of the whole problem.

One of the earliest theories of emotion to appear was that of James (1890). This attempted to explain how emotional *behaviour* and emotional *experience* were interrelated. It stated that the physiological response comes first, following stimulation by an exciting event, and that the emotional experience is the result of that response. The essence of this view is the idea that the experience of emotion is based on the perception of sensations from the viscera. It seemed to be capable of experimental verification, in terms of investigating the role of visceral sensations in emotion. What would happen, for instance, if visceral connections were severed? Would we still experience emotion?

Reference has been made to the reports of Hohmann (1966) on patients suffering spinal cord lesions. In practice it is of course impossible to induce lesions in human subjects and much of the experimentation which purported to test James' theory was carried out on cats and dogs. The results of this work showed that total separation of the viscera from the central nervous system does not impair emotional *behaviour* but no conclusion could be reached concerning emotional experience. This can only be checked by asking the individual what he is feeling, hence only human studies are appropriate. Unfortunately, several theorists have failed to recognise that animal experimentation cannot be employed to test some of the major theories of emotion as they were originally formulated. Theories that consider emotional *experience* in their major postulates cannot be tested by animal experimentation.

As mentioned above, this means that different theories of emotion cover different aspects of the total phenomena. Theories of emotional *behaviour* are often based on instinct theories and the more sophisticated developments proposed by ethologists. Another approach to the study of emotional behaviour has been in terms of the neural structures and pathways which govern and organise physiological/behavioural reaction patterns. This is illustrated in the classic work of Hess (1954) who worked with electrodes implanted in diencephalic structures and observed autonomic and behavioural reactions to point by point stimulation of the diencephalon. The general field of physiological theories of emotion has been well-reviewed by Grossman (1967).

Quite a different set of theories emphasise the subjective, personal quality of human experience of emotion. This is especially the case in phenomenological and existential theories. Some existentialists, such as Sartre (1948) explicitly reject the experimental method; 'essences and facts are incommensurables and one who begins his inquiry with facts will never arrive at essences'. The analysis of conscious experience is not necessarily incompatible with an approach which would structure and assess the dimensions of such experience, but it must be admitted that there is no apparent solution to the measurement problems involved.

While such writers have emphasised the interrogation of consciousness, others have postulated emotions as psychic forces or tendencies independent of consciousness, so that the search for the essence of emotion leads to the unconscious or to unconscious psychic forces. Freud discussed the existence of unconscious emotions dating from early infantile experience, and for Jung an emotion is the intrusion of an unconscious personality. This group of theories frequently relates emotion to drives and instinct, to energy, conflicts and repression, and to a psyche structurally divided, e.g. ego, id and super-ego. Emotion is regarded as a phenomenon which bears witness to an unconscious zone of experience, and therapies of inadequate emotions therefore involve practices which investigate the unconscious and allow it to 'have its say'.

Certain schools derived from psychoanalytic thinking emphasise the role of emotion as energy which may be converted, for example into bodily symptoms. According to this view the job of psychosomatic therapy is to 'reverse' the flow of vital energy into appropriate channels of outlet before it causes permanent structural damage in those organs affected by the misdirected flow. A corollary to the theory of emotion as energy, and which does not involve transformation or conversion, is the idea that energy must be discharged or released. Therapeutic techniques of abreaction, catharsis, and release of organ-energy are relevant to the view that emotion is energy that must be 'let out', and they are applied to effect 'relief and harmony' within the individual.

Theories on the genesis of emotion are equally varied in their explanations. The view that innate emotions exist has already been mentioned, but there are also a number of viewpoints which postulate a primitive affectivity or excitement out of which the specific emotions develop. This 'genetic' theory of emotions states that the undifferentiated excitement present at birth becomes differentiated and associated with certain situations and motor responses to form the separate emotions of later life. The nature of the original feeling source has been much discussed.

In existential ontology it is *Angst*, and Freud, too considered *Angst* a fundamental emotion. Others have suggested a primary root of emotional experience in pleasure/unpleasure, sympathy, and a single fund of 'love-energy'. Therapy in this context can be seen as a process of development towards the differentiation of the emotions and away from their single, simple root or essence (Hillman, 1960).

The problem posed by these theories is that of explaining the qualitative variety of the emotions, their number and complexity, by referring to a single, simple source.

The differentiation of emotions is related to the development of language and its role in labelling the various kinds of personal experience. Relatively little is known about how the child acquires and applies verbal labels, and how such labels and more complex statements about emotional states are used by the adult to describe and explain his own feelings and behaviour.

Theories of emotion are necessarily linked with other areas of study in psychology—with motivation, memory, psychopathology, personality and learning—but relationships among these areas are often obscure and await clarification. The terms emotion and motivation, for example, may be treated as virtually synonymous by some writers, yet are differentiated by others. Such different viewpoints arise more from the separate traditions and research interests within psychology than from logical analysis.

Traditionally, the phenomena classified as motivational include activities such as eating, drinking, escaping from pain, attacking, exploring, care of the young and the like. It is these and similar activities that are labelled 'drive behaviours' and that have traditionally been interpreted in terms of 'instincts', 'drives' or some other primary motive. They are obviously more conveniently studied in animals like fish, birds and rats.

The concept of emotion has also been linked with drives and instincts but in a less satisfactory way, at least in human subjects. While fear, anger, love-attachment, etc. may be *inferred* from the behaviour of animals, they are directly *experienced* by human subjects and the perception and evaluation of this experience plays a prominent role in theories of human emotion, personality and psychopathology. Concern with subjective experience represents a different kind of emphasis from that placed on drive behaviour, but it does not necessarily imply an incompatibility of ideas. To attempt to explain behaviour from insect to man necessarily involves a variety of motivational processes, ranging from purely biogenic hypotheses, in which behaviour unfolds from a series of innate drives and instincts, to highly sociogenic theories which emphasise the flexibility of behaviour into patterns determined by cultural forces. Few of the available theories deal adequately with human subjective experience, either cognitive or emotional.

Motivation and drive

The concept of drive is central to most theories of motivation, and during the past few decades it has been extensively and ingeniously linked with theories of learning. These have mainly dealt with animal laboratory experiments but they have also been extended to human behaviour and human emotions. One of the advantages of the 'drive' concept over earlier instinct concepts was its precise definition in terms of factors like hours of deprivation (of food or water), the intensity of an unpleasant stimulus, or the level of organismic arousal as indexed by measures of autonomic or cortical activity. Deprivation, for example, was conceived as resulting in deficits (as in hunger) which provided stimuli that goaded the organism into activity. Thus deprived animals became restless and active; crossed obstructions to obtain incentives; learned a variety of appropriate responses which resulted in varieties of consummated behaviour.

This conception of drive as 'energy' impelling an organism to action has parallels in several analyses of human emotion. Classical psychoanalysis also developed a model in which drive energy was seen to accumulate and to require discharge, again with the implication of an inexorable accumulation of energy which stirs the organism into regulatory activity. Deprivation in Freud's model arises from the failure to discharge the accumulated tension rather than from the depletion of tissues (as in hunger); it was believed that widely varied behaviours had their ultimate motivational origin in libido, aggressive drives, and anxiety.

The model implied in these various views is that behaviour is an attempt to preserve organismic integrity by 'homeostatic' restorations of equilibrium. Some form of equilibrium concept occurs in instinct and drive theories, theories of emotion, analyses of conflict and stress and even in socially derived motivation (see Cofer and Appley, 1964). The term homeostasis was originally coined by a physiologist (Cannon, 1932) to describe the steady states attained at any particular moment by the physiological processes at work in living organisms. Since then the term has been applied to many psychological conditions. The homeostatic position in general is that the organism (and each of its subsystems) tends to resist changes in its environment that are of a magnitude large enough to upset its equilibrium or threaten its survival as a stable system. The theory does not require that a disturbed system return to its prior state of equilibrium; by assuming that biological systems are *open* and have continuous energy exchange with the environment it allows for a variety of means and states through which stability can be reached.

The learning theorist Clark Hull (1943) assumed that all behaviour is motivated by homeostatic drives or secondary drives based upon them. He also assumed that all *rewards* are ultimately based on the reduction of a primary homeostatic drive. A reward of food reduces the homeostatic imbalance produced by hunger: and all animals will rapidly learn quite difficult responses to get a reward. Secondary rewards, such as social approval, are effective because they have been associated with food and other primary rewards in the past. In this sense drive is conceived as arising from a tissue need and having the general function of arousing or activating behaviour. Direct tension reduction becomes the critical reinforcement factor in the process of learning.

The essence of the drive doctrine can perhaps be summarised (and oversimplified) in the form of two propositions:

(i) Organisms act only to reduce their drives; thus all activities are interpreted as direct or indirect attempts at drive reduction.

(ii) Activities that are accompanied by a reduction in drive are strengthened, and such drive reduction is a necessary condition for learning to occur.

Drive theory, in one form or another, still stands at the centre of modern thinking about motivation and learning, and has been extended to the analysis of emotional states such as fear and anxiety, aggression and dependency. These emotional states are considered within the theory as logically equivalent in status, character and function to such drives as hunger and thirst. Attempts have been made, for example, to treat frustration as a drive which has particular patterns of behaviour associated with it, typically anger and attacking behaviour. Aggression may be directed toward the frustrating agent or turned against some other object or person, including the self. Although the early suggestion was that aggression always results from frustration and that frustration always leads to aggression, the second half of this hypothesis has been modified to acknowledge that a number of other reactions to frustration, in addition to aggression, are possible. Included among these alternatives are regression, repression, and fixation (Maier, 1949).

Conflict can be regarded as a special case of frustration, often arising from two or more equal but incompatible response tendencies. In a sense it is equivalent to a condition of double frustration, each of the competing tendencies serving as the barrier to the completion of the other. As in the case of other frustrations, conflict is a state of increased tension, but by its very nature it is characterised by vacillation, hesitancy, fatigue and often complete blocking (Miller, 1944). In both clinical observations and experimental studies conflict has been shown to be an emotional response to a situation requiring incompatible responses, e.g. those involving approach to and those involving avoidance of a goal.

Perhaps the most widely discussed emotion in the context of learning and emotion is fear or anxiety. One influential view is that anxiety is a learned response occurring to signals that are premonitory of situations of injury or pain (Mowrer, 1939). According to this view, anxiety is basically anticipatory in nature and has great biological utility in that it adaptively motivates living organisms to deal with traumatic events in advance of their actual occurrence, thereby diminishing harmful effects.

It is in this general biological sense that both 'emotion' and 'motivation' can be viewed as a complex integration of behaviour involving selective attention to certain events, a heightened physiological state of excitement, and certain probable patterns of action. These patterns of action are common to most higher species of animals and have a clear biological utility in coping with environment and survival. Both are linked to environmental stimuli which act as incentives or triggers of behaviour, and to internal organismic conditions. Neither the external incentive nor the physiological state is in itself sufficient for producing any species-typical action: an interplay between them is necessary. This interplay can be illustrated in accounts of sexual arousal which emphasise that sexual behaviour depends on two conditions: adequate hormonal levels *and* adequate external stimulation.

Over the years it has become increasingly clear that our existing theories of motivation and learning, while retaining a certain heuristic value, are thinly stretched when it comes to human experience. Various social needs relating to achievement, power, affiliation, etc. have been postulated which do not readily fit into existing drive theories, and in the development of which early emotional experiences seem to be particularly relevant. There is, nonetheless, a very substantial and impressive set of studies attempting to analyse the many aspects of motivation, emotion and learning which have been outlined. The present chapter has considered some of this evidence in relation to the complex experience and reaction pattern which we label 'emotional'. This pattern is not fixed but alters as it encounters the stresses and demands of the environment, and as we learn to interact with the environment more or less successfully. Whatever innate emotional mechanisms there may be, they are modified and shaped by the individual's transactions with the outer world. It is the nature of these learning mechanisms which must now

be examined.

Animal laboratory studies of conditioning and learning have been of importance in psychology since the beginning of the century. It is only in the last decade or two that there has been a growth of interest in the application of conditioning principles to human problems and human retraining. The combination of laboratory-based experiments and applied clinical therapies provides a rich, diverse array of evidence which is contributing to a re-shaping of the older style theories of learning. The next chapter will first discuss some of the basic paradigms of learning and then consider their role in the analysis of human emotional behaviour.

References

Argyle, M. (1969). *Social Interaction* (London: Methuen)

Arnold, Magda B. (1960). *Emotion and Personality* (2 vols.) (New York: Columbia University Press)

Cannon, W. B. (1929). *Bodily Changes in Pain, Hunger, Fear and Rage*, 2nd Ed. (New York: Harper and Row)

Cannon, W. B. (1932). *The Wisdom of the Body* (New York: W. W. Norton)

Cofer, C. N. and Appley, M. H. (1964). *Motivation: Theory and Research* (New York: Wiley)

Davitz, J. R. (1964). *The Communication of Emotional Meaning* (New York: McGraw-Hill)

Eibl-Eibesfeldt, I. (1971). *Love and Hate* (London: Methuen)

Ekman, P., Friesen, Wallace, V. and Ellsworth, Phoebe (1972). *Emotion in the Human Face* (New York: Pergamon Press)

Epstein, S. (1967). Toward a unified theory of anxiety. In: *Progress in Experimental Personality Research*, Vol. 4 (B. A. Maher, editor) (New York: Academic Press)

Exline, R. (1971). Visual Interaction: The glances of Power and Preference. In: *Nebraska Symposium on Motivation* (J. K. Cole, editor) (Lincoln, Nebraska: University of Nebraska Press)

Eysenck, H. J. (1967). *The Biological Basis of Personality* (Springfield: Thomas)

Eysenck, H. J. (1969). *The Structure of Human Personality*, 3rd Ed. (London: Methuen)

Goldstein, M. L. (1968). Physiological theories of emotion: a critical historical review from the standpoint of behaviour theory. *Psychol. Bull.*, **69**, 23–40

Grossman, S. P. (1967). *A Textbook of Physiological Psychology* (New York: Wiley)

Hebb, D. O. (1946). On the nature of fear. *Psychol. Rev.*, **53**, 259–276

Hebb, D. O. (1955). Drives and the CNS (conceptual nervous system). *Psychol. Rev.*, **62**, 243–254

Hess, W. R. (1954). *The diencephalon: Autonomic and Extra-Pyramidal Functions* (London: Heinemann)

Hillman, J. (1960). *Emotion. A Comprehensive Phenomenology of Theories and their Meanings for Therapy* (London: Routledge & Kegan Paul)

Hohmann, G. W. (1966). Some effects of spinal cord lesions on experienced emotional feelings. *Psychophysiology*, **3**, 143–156

Hull, C. L. (1943). *Principles of Behaviour* (New York: Appleton-Century Crofts)

James, W. (1890). *Principles of Psychology* (London: Macmillan)

Kendell, R: E. (1968). *The Classification of Depressive Illnesses* (London: Oxford University Press)

Lang, P. J. (1968). Fear reduction and fear behavior: Problems in treating a construct. In: *Research in Psychotherapy*, Vol. 3 (J. M. Shlien, editor) (Washington: American Psychological Association)

Lazarus, R. S., Opton, E. M., Jr., Nomikos, M. S. and Rankin, N. O. (1965). The principle of short-circuiting of threat: Further evidence. *J. Personal.*, **33**, 622–635

Lazarus, R. S. (1966). *Psychological Stress and the Coping Process* (New York: McGraw-Hill)

Lazarus, R. S. and Opton, E. M. Jr. (1966). The study of psychological stress: A summary of theoretical formulations and experimental findings. In: *Anxiety and Behavior*, Chap. 10 (C. D. Spielberger, editor) (New York: Academic Press)

Lazarus, R. S. (1968). Emotions and adaptation: conceptual and empirical relations. In: *Nebraska Symposium on Motivation*, 175–266 (W. J. Arnold, editor) (Lincoln, Nebraska: University of Nebraska Press)

Lewis, M. and Brooks-Gunn, Jeanne (1972). Self, other and fear: the reaction of infants to people. Princeton, N. S. : Education Testing Service. *Res. Bull.*, May

Lewis, M. and Freedle, R. (1972). Mother-infant dyad: the cradle of meaning. Paper presented at a symposium on *'Language and Thought: Communication and Affect'* (Erindale College, University of Toronto)

Lorenz, K. (1967). *On aggression* (London: Methuen)

Maier, N. R. F. (1949). *Frustration: The study of behaviour without a goal* (New York: McGraw-Hill)

Martin, Irene (1973). Somatic Reactivity: Interpretation. *Handbook of Abnormal Psychology*, 2nd Ed., Chap. 11 (H. J. Eysenck, editor) (London: Pitman)

Mathews, A. (1971). Psychophysiological approaches to the investigation of desensitization and related procedures. *Psychol. Bull*, **76**, 73–91

McDougall, W. (1912). *An Introduction to Social Psychology* (Boston: Luce)

Meichenbaum, D. (1972). Clinical implications of modifying what clients say to themselves. *University of Waterloo, Research Reports in Psychology:* Waterloo, Ontario: Research Report, No. 42

Miller, N. E. (1944). Experimental studies in conflict. In:

Personality and the Behaviour Disorders (J. Hunt, editor) (New York: Ronald Press)

Mowrer, O. H. (1939). A stimulus–response analysis of anxiety and its role as a reinforcing agent. *Psychol. Rev.*, **46**, 553–565

Sartre, J. P. (1948). *The Emotions: Outline of a Theory* (New York: Philosophical Library)

Schachter, S. (1966). The interaction of cognitive and physiological determinants of emotional state. In: *Anxiety and Behavior*, Chap. 9 (C. D. Spielberger, editor) (New York: Academic Press)

Schildkraut, J. J. and Kety, S. S. (1967). Biogenic amines and emotion. *Science*, **156**, 21–30

Seligman, M. E. P., Maier, S. F. and Solomon, R. L. (1971). Unpredictable and uncontrollable aversive events. In: *Aversive Conditioning and Learning*, Chap. 6 (F. R. Brush, editor) (New York: Academic Press)

Selye, H. (1956). *The stress of life* (New York: McGraw-Hill)

Tinbergen, N. (1953). *The Herring Gull's World* (London: Collins)

van Lawick-Goodall, Jane (1971). *In the Shadow of Man* (London: Collins)

Williams, R. J. (1956). *Biochemical Individuality* (New York: Wiley)

Zegans, Susan and Zegans, L. S. (1972). Fear of strangers in children and the orienting reaction. *Behavioral Sci.*, **17**, 407–419

Chapter 4

CONDITIONING

Irene D. Martin

There is firm and substantial evidence for the view that conditioning processes play an important role in the acquisition of human emotional responses, attitudes and values, social skills, conscience, and even some aspects of language. This is not always apparent from the traditional, zoöcentric approach of learning theorists. It is now almost a hundred years since basic conditioning paradigms began to be explored, largely with infra-human animals and almost entirely under strictly-controlled laboratory conditions. An outline of these basic conditioning paradigms and principles will be given in this chapter; they represent the fundamental groundwork of conditioning theory and practice.

More recently, however, there has been an expansion in human-oriented studies, both laboratory and clinical, and this has forced investigators to broaden their view of conditioning and to adopt a more flexible approach to some of the basic assumptions of traditional studies. Older assumptions have had to make way for a loosening of definitions: a conditioned response is not necessarily a reflex, a stimulus not necessarily defined in physical terms but in terms of salience and significance for the individual. Perceptual/cognitive factors may alter the typical learning curve, and their effects have to be taken into account.

Learning is a process occurring continuously in the transactions which living organisms have with their surroundings. The varieties of learning in a lifetime's experience are many: we have learned to use our hands; we have learned languages; we have learned a whole range of social skills and attitudes.

It is debatable how many basic types of learning there are, and whether one or more theories is required to account for them. Categories of human learning include conditioning, probability learning, motor skill learning, and problem solving, among others. While certain theoretical issues remain obscure there is fairly general agreement about some of the principles of learning, i.e. on those factors which determine whether or not learning is likely to occur, how efficient and rapid the learned response will be, and how well it will be retained. High on the list of relevant principles is the role of motivation. The motivational state of the organism, whether in a more primitive 'drive' sense (hunger, thirst, sex, etc.) or in a more general arousal sense (level of general emotionality or autonomic activation) is known to affect the rate and kind of learning. Another important and related factor is that of reward and punishment. This can be used very effectively to control behaviour, and learning is more easily accomplished when explicit programmes are adopted. Thus the 'schedules of reinforcement' frequently described in the literature relate to the way in which the organism's specific responses are linked with specific rewards and punishment in a highly controlled way.

Conditioning is one of the categories of learning which has been studied in all kinds of species of animals. The process of conditioning refers to a change in responsiveness; first, to the occurrence of new responses, and second to a change in the response over time, often to some criterion such as increased efficiency or economy of effort. Typically the conditioning experiment involves the successive occurrence in time of two stimuli: the first a mild stimulus producing little or no reaction, and the second a significant or salient stimulus which produces a clear-cut reaction.

Typical examples of experimental sequences of pairs of stimuli are: a buzzer followed by an electric shock; a tone followed by food; a dim light followed by an airpuff into the eye. These sequences are illustrated in Figure 4.1 which also shows the kinds of reactions which are measured in laboratory conditioning experiments.

TERMINOLOGY

Pavlov called the presentation of food the unconditioned stimulus (UCS) and the salivation which it evoked the unconditioned response (UCR). The repeated pairing of the buzzer with the food turns the originally neutral stimulus into a conditioned stimulus (CS) which now evokes salivation as a conditioned response (CR). Thus conditioning experiments are essentially concerned with a simple temporal-relational property between two stimuli: A followed by B. Note that B must be the more intense or significant stimulus if conditioning is to occur. If this situation is reversed and the more intense stimulus B precedes A, we have a situation of 'backward conditioning' which has different and less profound effects than the usual forward conditioning situation. Note also that several important requirements must be met in order for conditioning to take place:

1. Contiguity of CS and UCS: the distance in time between the two stimuli is usually of the order of 0.5 seconds up to several seconds.

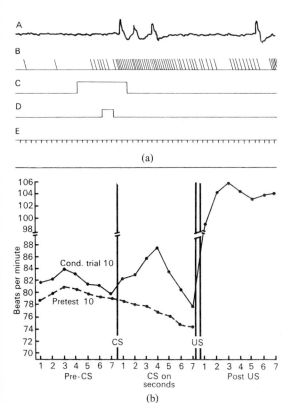

(a)

(b)

(Decrease in resistance = upward deflection)

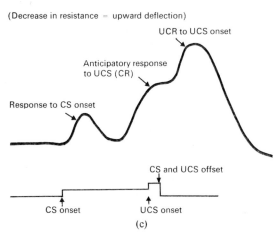

(c)

Figure 4.1 (a) A salivary conditioning trial. (A) swallowing and gross tongue movements (B) salivary record (C) CS, a 10-second tone (D) UCS, 2 ml 2% citric acid (E) time in seconds. From Feather (1967) by courtesy of Appleton-Century-Crofts.

(b) Second-by-second cardiac activity on last CS pretest trial compared with a later conditioning trial. From Westcott and Huttenlocher (1961) by courtesy of *J. Exp. Psychol.*

(c) Skin resistance responses occurring on a conditioning trial. The most common measure of conditioning is the anticipatory CR occurring just prior to UCS onset.

2. The relative strength and significance of the two stimuli (CS and UCS) have to be balanced in such a way that the CS is fairly weak (strong CSs have an interfering effect) and the UCS fairly strong (a weak ineffective UCS may produce little in the way of conditioning; indeed, rapid adaptation of the unconditioned response may occur instead).

3. The pairing of CS and UCS on one occasion constitutes a 'trial' in conditioning terminology. It is sometimes necessary to give many trials, i.e. CS–UCS pairings, for conditioning to take place.

The presentation of a series of trials (which may vary from very few to hundreds) constitutes the *acquisition* phase of conditioning. Very often the experiment then continues with an *extinction* phase during which the UCS is omitted and the CS is presented singly. When this is done a process of 'unlearning' seems to take place in that the previously acquired conditioned response which may have been occurring with strength and regularity on each trial now begins to lessen in strength and probability until, with sufficient presentations of the CS alone, the conditioned response will cease to occur.

Experimental extinction should not be equated with forgetting, if the term forgetting implies a complete loss of material once known. If subjects whose CRs have been extinguished return to the conditioning situation an hour or two later, it is found that the presentation of the CS causes the CR to occur again. This process is called *spontaneous recovery*—spontaneous in that it occurs following extinction and without further conditioning trials. This recovery of the conditioned response is not a robust phenomenon, however; it is dependent upon a number of factors: number of previous extinction trials, type of subject, etc., and the CR may be smaller in amplitude than it was prior to extinction.

Another phenomenon in this category has been termed *incubation*. Although the application of CSs without reinforcement normally gives rise to extinction, i.e. a decrement of the CR, it has sometimes been observed to produce an increment in the size of the CR. This phenomenon is more likely to occur following traumatic conditioning of pain/fear reactions, when the UCR is exceptionally strong (Eysenck, 1968).

Suppose the CS in our experiments is a tone of 1000 cps; and a strong CR is developed. What happens if the CS is altered to 800 cps or 200 cps? It is likely that the CR will be given to the 800 cps since it is not far removed from the original 1000 cps tone, but it is less likely to occur to the 200 cps tone. This process is called *stimulus generalisation* and is an important property of learning. In effect an organism learns to respond not to a single, specific stimulus but to a *class* of stimuli. Generally it can be said that CR strength will vary over the range of the class of

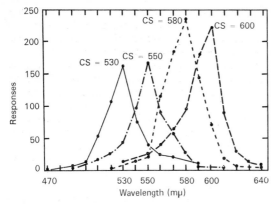

Figure 4.2   Mean generalisation gradients for four groups of pigeons (six to the group), trained to peck at different wavelengths of the colour spectrum. (From Guttman and Kalish, 1956, by courtesy of *J. Exp. Psychol.*)

stimuli, from zero at the extremes of the range to a maximum at the point where the CS is located. The spread or range of effective stimuli is referred to as a *generalisation gradient*. These gradients are illustrated in Figure 4.2 on data from pigeons taught to peck for food following the onset of a spectral colour (e.g. 530 mμ) and not to peck when the box was dark. The figure shows the extent to which the pigeon reacts to lights of other hues than the one it was trained on.

Closely related to generalisation is the process of *differential conditioning* or *conditioned discrimination*. Though the same response to a gradient or class of stimuli may be given as in stimulus generalisation, there is a point when it is undoubtedly more efficient to differentiate among similar stimuli. If we find that a red light and an orange light of equal intensity are capable of producing a conditioned response (CR) we may ask whether it is possible to train an animal to respond to the red light but not to the orange.

If trials of the red light (CS₁) followed by the UCS are given repeatedly, while on alternate blocks of trials the orange light (CS₂) is given alone, i.e. with no UCS following, the response to the red light will continue while response to the orange light will extinguish (assuming the animal can discriminate red from orange). Thus through a process of differential reinforcement (UCS occurring to CS₁ but not to CS₂) the discrimination can be learned.

MEASURES OF CONDITIONING
The process of conditioning refers essentially to *response* change, and in this section we will consider the nature of the changes which can occur. In the simpler reflex conditioning studies the nature of the response (UCR) is closely determined by the kind of

stimulus (UCS) applied: an airpuff to the eye produces a blink, acid placed on the tongue produces salivation, a shock to the footpad produces foreleg flexion, and so on.

Stimuli such as electric shock on the other hand, produce generalised pain–fear reactions which are accompanied by a wide range of skeletal and autonomic responses. Many of these reaction components are transferred to the CS during the course of acquisition, and the overall pattern of responding (both conditioned and unconditioned) can be extremely complicated. Few conditioning studies, however, measure the whole response range and it is usual to record only one or two representative responses in these pain–fear experiments, typically such responses as heart rate, sweating, vasomotor activity and (in infra-human studies) the animal's skeletal motor activity. Changes in the response being recorded are observed throughout the course of acquisition and extinction.

For obvious practical reasons, most types of conditioned and unconditioned responses are recorded from the body surface. However, there are quite a few studies which describe interoceptive conditioning. Interoceptive refers to sensory receptors in the internal organs or viscera, e.g. in the stomach, intestines and heart. Interoceptive conditioning, therefore, refers to CRs in which one or both of the stimuli (CS and UCS) are applied to the viscera rather than to an exteroceptor, i.e. an external receptor.

The most commonly used measure of a CR is *frequency*, that is, the occurrence or non-occurrence of the response on each conditioning trial. This measure is usually highly related to the trial number on which the first CR occurs (the more CRs, the earlier CR appearance). In addition, certain characteristics of the response are often recorded, for example the *amplitude* of the CR, its *duration*, and certain temporal characteristics such as *onset* and *peak*

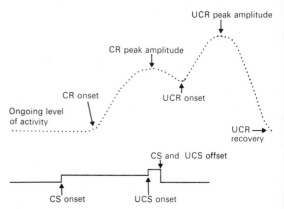

Figure 4.3   Schematic representation of CR and UCR characteristics

(a)

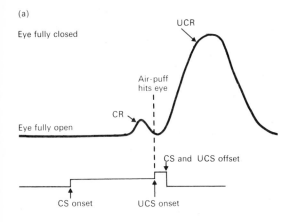

(b)

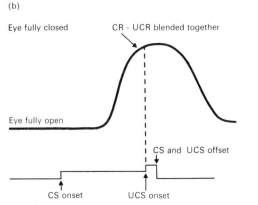

Figure 4.4 (a) Small, poorly-placed CR, which leaves the eye almost completely open at air-puff (UCS) impact.

(b) Large 'blended' CR and UCR, with eye fully closed at air-puff (UCS) impact

latency. These are illustrated in Figure 4.3. The frequency with which the CR is given, and occasionally its amplitude, are often referred to as measures of the *strength* of conditioning. Another and possibly independent measure of conditioning is its *efficiency* with respect to certain endpoints. Figure 4.4 illustrates conditioned eyelid responses of different amplitudes and placements. It can be seen (a) that at the point of UCS onset (dotted line) the eye is almost completely open and will therefore receive the full impact of the UCS airpuff; whereas (b) illustrates a large amplitude CR, completely joined with the UCR, placed in time so that the impact of the airpuff is on the fully closed eye. The latter CR can be described as efficient in that it successfully avoids the impact of the noxious UCS on the cornea, and it is in this sense that the CR can be described as adaptive.

Examples (paradigms) of basic conditioning experiments are as follows:

1. Classical conditioning

In the original Pavlovian experiment the sound of a bell was repeatedly presented shortly before food was given to the dog. Originally the sound of the bell produced a mild reaction such as looking toward the source of sound and pricking up the ears. When the food was presented it was ingested, producing the usual alimentary reflexes including salivation. After repeated paired presentation of bell and food the sound of the bell came to evoke salivation and orientation movements towards the feeding dishes. The new response of salivation to the CS is called the CR, and Pavlov stated that the CS serves as a signal that the food is about to be presented.

This experimental situation represents a simple form of learning which applies to a wide variety of responses and may well occur in the natural environment. Pavlov's contribution was to recognise that conditioning represents a mechanism by which the animal can deal more efficiently with events in its environment, by anticipating the consequences, beneficial or harmful, of the stimuli it encounters. He worked largely with simple physiological reflexes at a time when all behaviour was believed to be based on combinations of inborn reflexes, but the principle of conditioning can readily be extended to other classes of responses, and the reflex concept *per se* is no longer considered essential. Pavlov showed, however, how an organism can *adapt* more finely to its environment through the simple mechanism of conditioning, and provided a methodology for the quantitative study of this behaviour.

Interoceptive conditioning

As an example of one type of interoceptive conditioning, let us assume that volunteer human subjects have agreed to swallow inflatable tubes. If warm water is injected into the tube a recording will indicate vasodilation, whereas if cold water is used the record will show vasoconstriction. Following the classical conditioning paradigm, a neutral CS is given, for example, the word 'white' followed by the UCS, say an injection of warm water. Soviet investigators have reported several successful studies in which a conditioned vascular response of internal organs was developed, as in the present example, with an external CS and a UCS presented to the viscera. The conditioned response will resemble the pattern of the UCR, i.e. will reflect vasodilation or vasoconstriction.

In the classical conditioning paradigm emphasis is placed on the temporal arrangement of CS and UCS. The experimenter controls delivery of CS and UCS and chooses to observe one (perhaps of many) reactions elicited by the UCS. The subject in these experiments have little or no control over the situation, that is, the environment is not brought under the organisms control as a result of its responses. Hence the organism is 'passive' inasmuch as the organism's responses do not interact with the environment to alter the UCS. The experimenter retains control over the onset, duration, and offset of the UCS.

This kind of paradigm is contrasted with those of instrumental conditioning, presented in the following section, where the subject is free to 'act on' and thereby modify his environment, perhaps by seeking and obtaining rewarding stimuli or avoiding noxious ones.

2. Instrumental conditioning

A real-life example of this form of conditioning occurred in London during the last war. A siren was quite often used pre war as a signal to factory workers that the work-shift was ending. Hence, if it signalled anything it was probably relief. This same kind of signal was then used during the war to herald air raid attacks, and often in the early days the siren would be followed within a few minutes by the sound of aeroplanes and bombs dropping. This sound of course evoked strong fear reactions and quick action in seeking shelter. After very few repetitions of the siren–bombs combination the sound of the siren alone was eliciting the same or similar strong fear reactions and shelter-seeking activity. In this example the stimulus 'bomb' was a strong and effective unconditioned stimulus, fear and shelter-seeking a strong unconditioned response. Following the pairing of the siren–bomb combination the warning stimulus (siren) quickly came to act as a conditioned stimulus and to elicit strong conditioned responses, similar in kind to those of the unconditioned response. It is in this sense that fear is conditionable, i.e. can be learned as a response to previously neutral cues.

In the example just cited, two kinds of shelter-seeking behaviour were frequently observed. Some individuals would do nothing until bombs were actually falling about them: then they would seek air raid shelter to 'escape' from the effect of the bombs. Others, however, would act promptly upon hearing the siren: they would 'avoid' (or be more likely to avoid) the effect of bombing by seeking immediate shelter. This notion of 'escape' or 'avoidance' behaviour is one which occurs repeatedly in the conditioning literature. In real-life situations human subjects 'choose' whether to escape from the unpleasant situations when they judge they cannot stand any more, or to avoid them by never putting themselves in the position where they encounter the unpleasantness. In laboratory situations, experimenters usually determine whether or not their experimental subjects can avoid noxious UCSs, and also how they can avoid or escape from them, i.e. by running mazes, jumping barriers, pressing levers, etc. Quite understandably the laboratory experiment is devised so that control can be exercised over the animal's behaviour in order that the experimenter can observe the effects of his own experimental manipulations. Thus certain

illustrative experiments or 'paradigms' of instrumental conditioning have been evolved and provide relatively standard techniques for studying different kinds of learning in relatively restricted environments. The kinds of learning which can be motivated by an aversive UCS, or by a CS which elicits conditioned anxiety, are frequently described as either escape or avoidance. An escape response is one which results in UCS-termination (i.e. escape from the UCS). An avoidance response is one which prevents the effects and frequently the occurrence of the UCS (i.e. UCS-avoidance).

Escape/avoidance paradigm

The following is an example of the way in which this form of conditioning can be experimentally produced:

The subject, a dog, is harnessed into a rubber hammock, his chest, abdomen and chin firmly supported, and his legs hanging down. On either side of his head are two aluminium panels mounted on a wooden framework which surrounds the dog's head. Strapped to his hind toe pads are two large electrodes. Behind him is a loud-speaker. After a ten-minute period of adaptation, during which he initially struggles a little and then later remains almost motionless, he appears alert, orients towards sounds, may bark intermittently, and often wags his tail. Then the experimenter, who is controlling the experimental apparatus in an adjoining room and watching the dog through a one-way mirror, presents a tone through a loud-speaker behind the dog who pricks up his ears and looks around. The tone lasts for five seconds after which an intense electric stimulus is applied to the dog's rear toe pads. He is immediately thrown into a great surge of activity which includes skeletal and autonomic responses. He thrashes about, waves his legs, hunches his back against the harness straps, bites at the rubber hammock beneath his chin, screeches, defaecates, urinates, shows pupillary dilation, piloerection, and profuse salivation. After a period of struggling and thrashing a violent turn of the head ends in his pressing the aluminium panel to his right. Both tone and shock are terminated immediately by this act. The dog has finally *escaped* from both tone and shock.

During this whole sequence the dog's heart rate has been recorded. Before the tone went on, the resting heart-rate level was 100 beats/minute. This did not change during the five-second period between tone onset and shock onset. When the shock went on the rate climbed abruptly to 240 beats/minute, and maintained this level until the panel-press stopped the shock. Then the EKG became erratic and dropped precipitously to an average rate of 70 beats/minute, characterised by great irregularity of heart action. Even after the overall rate returned to normal, the beat-by-beat rate was at first more variable. Three minutes later the variability had disappeared.

On succeeding presentations of the tone–shock

sequence the dog escapes more quickly. His escape latencies decrease. After, say, 16 presentations the dog turns his head quickly after the onset of the tone and pushes the right-hand plate with his nose. This terminates the tone and prevents the shock from being applied: this is the first short-latency avoidance response, and after this the dog goes on to avoid shock perfectly, trial after trial. (This description is of an experiment by Black (1956) which is discussed by Solomon and Brush (1956).)

Thus the typical behavioural outcome of this type of training procedure is the gradual emergence of short-latency escape responses and the gradual increase in frequency of occurrence of avoidance responses. Several experiments have aimed to compare the effects of avoidance v. non-avoidance procedures, as follows:

A guinea-pig is placed in a revolvable cage and after a conditioned stimulus (CS-buzzer) it is given a shock which elicits running behaviour. One group of animals is shocked whether or not they run. Another group trained according to the principles of avoidance learning, are not shocked if they run. Learning begins similarly in both groups but reaches a much higher

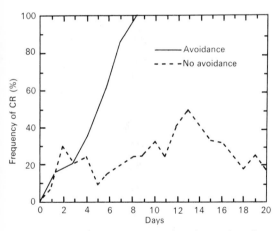

Figure 4.5 Learning curves showing the results of an experiment in which shock-avoidance and non-avoidance procedures were compared. The erratic lower curve is indicative of the conflict generated by the non-avoidance procedure. (From Brogden *et al.*, 1938, by courtesy of *Amer. J. Psychol.*)

level of performance in the second group. The results are shown in Figure 4.5. Guinea-pigs which are shocked whether or not they run continued to show anticipatory agitation at the sound of the buzzer but after the first few trials the tendency to run did not increase. Those shocked only if they did not run developed the habit of running promptly at the sound of the buzzer. Thus avoidance learning is better in an avoidance procedure compared with a procedure

where avoidance is not possible. In both cases, however, fear conditioning occurs.

Many theorists have considered that this paradigm involves much of relevance to conditioned human fears, and have suggested that both classical and instrumental conditioning processes are involved in the following sequence:

1. the subject learns to be afraid when the buzzer sounds (classical conditioning).
2. the subject learns what to do about his fear (instrumental conditioning).

According to this model, the development and maintenance of an instrumental avoidance response is assumed to depend heavily upon the development of conditioned anxiety reactions which serve a motivating function. The classical conditioning component, i.e. the straightforward pairing of CS and UCS without avoidance, is assumed to be responsible for the appearance of emotional responses elicited by the CS. Some of the attributes of the original unconditioned response to the noxious stimulus are transferred to the once-neutral CS by this process of classical conditioning. The animal then appears to be emotionally upset or anxious, exhibiting a wide variety of reactions to the CS that include autonomic, visceral and skeletal components. The reinforcement of learned instrumental avoidance responses comes about through drive reduction in the following fashion. Early in the learning process when the animal is escaping from shock, the instrumental act removes the UCS as well as the CS. Drive reduction then consists of reduction in the intensity of both pain and emotional upset. Later, when the animal is avoiding the shock, drive reduction consists of reducing the intensity of the emotional upset by removing the CS.

This two-process theory of conditioning involves the development first of conditioned fears and then of conditioned avoidance behaviour. The establishment of classical conditioning requires that:

(i) The intensity of the UCR and initial pain–fear reaction must be great.
(ii) There must be a reasonable temporal contiguity between CS and UCS.
(iii) The CS–UCS sequence may need to be repeated several times, although very rapid learning (even on one trial) may occur if the trauma is very severe.

The establishment of avoidance conditioning requires that:

(i) The skeletal act can terminate both the CS (which is the 'signal' of approaching trauma) and the UCS. Further, the skeletal act can terminate the CS before the UCS is presented and it can *prevent* the occurrence of the UCS.
(ii) The skeletal act must be followed by either pain–fear reduction (when the organism is escaping

from the UCS) or by anxiety reduction (when the organism is escaping from the CS and avoiding the UCS).

Avoidance is by and large, a remarkably persistent behaviour. Animals will commonly respond for hundreds of trials without receiving a shock: indeed experimenters have often given up trying to extinguish the animal before the animal has given up responding. Once the instrumental avoidance response is occurring regularly in the presence of the CS, then of course the animal is no longer receiving the UCS and this is the condition usually believed to be required for the *extinction* of a classically conditioned response. That is, the CS is no longer followed by the UCS and so one would expect according to Pavlovian laws that the conditioned anxiety reaction would gradually extinguish. If extinction of the classically conditioned anxiety response occurred then we would ordinarily expect the appropriate instrumental avoidance response to extinguish sooner or later. Yet extinction does not seem to occur in traumatic avoidance learning. Even with relatively long CS–UCS intervals, dogs undergoing avoidance learning will settle down to short-latency responses for many hundreds of trials after the last shock has been administered during acquisition.

We will return to a further consideration of this type of conditioning when we consider its significance for human conditioning studies. There is one further conditioning paradigm of importance which must be described. This goes under various names, but most commonly, 'operant conditioning' or Skinnerian conditioning after B. F. Skinner, who drew attention to its form and implications. The term 'operant' is used to describe a class of responses which 'operate' upon the environment to generate consequences.

3. Operant conditioning

Skinner distinguished between two kinds of responses: respondents and operants. Responses which are elicited by known stimuli are classified as *respondents*. Pupillary constriction to light, salivation to food, hand withdrawal from sudden heat, are examples of this type of response and they include the conventionally described reflex reactions. However, there is another class of responses which need not be elicited by any specific stimulus: these might be popularly referred to as spontaneous or ordinary ongoing responses. Skinner illustrates this as follows: 'We select a relatively simple bit of behaviour which may be freely and rapidly repeated, and which is easily observed and recorded. If our experimental subject is a pigeon, for example, the behaviour of raising the head above a given height is convenient.' Food is given whenever the pigeon's head rises above the specified height. If the experiment is conducted according to specifications, the result is invariable: an immediate change in the frequency with which the pigeon raises its head

is observed. The behaviour called 'raising the head' is an operant, and the process of operant conditioning is the 'strengthening' of an operant in the sense of making a response more probable, or more frequent. This is achieved by pairing a reinforcer with the animal's response. In the pigeon experiment, food is the *reinforcer* and presenting food when a response is emitted is the *reinforcement*. The *operant* is defined by the property of behaviour on which reinforcement is contingent—in this example the height to which the head must be raised. The change in frequency with which the head is lifted to this height is the process of *operant conditioning*. 'While we are awake, we act upon the environment constantly, and many of the consequences of our actions are reinforcing. Through operant conditioning the environment builds the basic repertoire with which we keep our balance, walk, play games, handle instruments and tools, talk, write, sail a boat, drive a car, or fly a plane' (Skinner, 1953).

These feats of performance are achieved by *reinforcing* the required behaviour. In another demonstration provided by Skinner the bird is conditioned to strike a marble placed on the floor. This may be done in a few minutes by reinforcing the pigeon's successive approximations: food is first presented when the bird is merely moving near the marble, later still when it moves its head toward the marble, and finally when it pecks it. What is specified in these illustrations is a procedure for altering the probability of a chosen response. By these means it has been possible to train an animal to do very much what the experimenter wishes by 'baiting' each step in the training. Skinner and his collaborators have demonstrated great skill and ingenuity in animal training through the use of this method. Some of the reports show a rat using a marble to obtain food from a vending machine, another shows pigeons playing a modified game of table tennis, and in yet another a dog learns to retrieve a bone from a pedal-operated rubbish bin. The animal-training possibilities are extremely varied.

This technique by which Skinner trains animals to perform complex acts that are outside their normal range of behaviour is known as shaping. The behaviour is shaped through a series of successive approximations, each made possible by selectively reinforcing certain responses and not others. Thus behaviour is gradually brought closer and closer to the desired pattern.

Schedules of reinforcement are of great importance in these animal-training demonstrations. In order to quantify both the amount and occasion of reinforcement in relation to specific operant responses, Skinner has designed a special apparatus suitable for use with white rats. It consists essentially of a darkened sound-resistant box in which the rat is placed. There is a small lever within the compartment which, if pressed, delivers a pellet of food. The lever is connected with a recording system which produces a graphical tracing of the number of lever pressings plotted against the length of time that the rat is in the box.

Such demonstrations have been criticised as mere technological applications of simple principles, contributing nothing to our scientific understanding of the principles themselves. However, they serve to demonstrate the power of reinforcement in shaping behaviour, and this demonstration is Skinner's object. Skinner has shown much interest in the application of learning to complex practical situations. He has analysed language as a system of operant responses. He has pointed to the various forms of reinforcement used in political, social and economic control, e.g. describing ordinary wages as fixed-ratio schedules for the control of economic behaviour. More ambitiously, he has described a Utopian community called Walden II, in which the principles of learning are used to create a more ideal form of social organisation.

Some of Skinner's applications, however, have gone far beyond the realm of speculation. One of these is the treatment of behaviour disorders. Whether the problem is a minor misbehaviour on the part of a relatively normal child or a psychosis that has kept a patient hospitalised for many years, Skinner's approach to treatment is quite straightforward. Rather than focussing on early childhood, current psychodynamics, or possible organic abnormality, Skinner simply asks what this person is doing that we don't like and what we would like to have him do instead. Once this is decided, we can proceed to extinguish the undesirable behaviours and reinforce desirable ones. In other words, we can change the contingencies of reinforcement, the specific relationships according to which reinforcement is contingent on one or another aspect of behaviour. This approach forms one of the behaviour modification techniques of behaviour therapy, and the techniques have been used in mental hospitals to deal with the deviant and undesirable forms of behaviour which occur. From the point of view of more traditional therapies the behaviour modification approach is open to criticism as too superficial, with its effects lasting only as long as the new contingencies of reinforcement are in effect. However, as long as the proponents of behaviour modification can point to rapid, measurable, and sometimes dramatically large changes in behaviour they are not likely to be greatly troubled by this criticism.

MOTIVATION AND REINFORCEMENT
Motivation

Many theories centre on the conception that learning takes place only as a consequence of reinforcement. Reinforcement is assumed to interact with some need within the animal—a need for food, water, activity, and additionally, in the case of human beings, needs for attention, affection and success. Theories of motivation frequently have their origins in a biological/ evolutionary view of animal behaviour. We observe animals to be active and exploring, looking for food and water; avoiding cold, heat and pain; engaging in sexual and social behaviour. The activity which leads up to these interactions may be intense and persistent, apparently purposive and goal seeking. The goal having been achieved (and this frequently involves the performance of consummatory actions) activity sharply decreases and a period of quiescence occurs.

Early theories postulated that animals were driven by a variety of instincts; without them it was assumed that organisms would not act in any significant way. Motivation tended to be identified with drives, conceived as changes in the internal physiological state, leading to ceaseless and restless activity which is terminated by various types of consummatory activity.

The biological viewpoint that bodily need is the ultimate basis of motivation has been supplemented by other theorists who stress the fact that many animals (infra-human as well as human) will work to obtain rewards that do not reduce any known biological drives. These theorists have been more likely to discuss such motivational tendencies as exploration, uncertainty, interest and ambition and a variety of factors which have no immediately apparent physiological basis. The long-range, complex, goal directed behaviour of higher species and especially of man— the delayed, involved and sometimes seemingly self-defeating behaviours he engages in—seem unlikely to be entirely accounted for on the basis of biological need-dominated responding.

Attempts have been made to explore motivation factors in the conditioning laboratory. Inevitably the greatest amount of work has been done on the motivating effect of basic needs—food, water, air, and also basic sexual/social interactions. Most experiments use animals who have, for example, been deprived of food for specified periods of time, or to a specifiable degree of weight loss. Thus the animal can be brought to a hypothetical level of motivation or drive and this can then be related to factors of learning such as speed, number of errors, efficiency, etc. Another method of manipulating drive level is to present varying intensities of stimuli such as loud noises, air deprivation, or electric shock to different groups of animals. These experiments have led to the general conclusion that the higher the drive level (produced by number of hours of food deprivation or by different intensities of unpleasant stimulation) the better, i.e. the speedier, the learning which occurs. They have led to the formulation of relationships between the *antecedent* stimulus conditions and the *consequent* response changes, which at one time, it was hoped, could form the basis of learning theories by specifying the role of motivational or drive factors in classical conditioning situations.

Attempts have also been made to explore other motivating factors in the laboratory. One 'drive' which has received attention experimentally is that which is satisfied by new experience. It is variously called curiosity, exploration, manipulation or novelty seeking, and is quite obviously a 'desirable' state in that monkeys, for example, will rapidly learn to press a lever to open a window so that they can look out and around. The tenacity and rapidity with which monkeys work at the task indicate that the activities seen through the window (they may be only everyday laboratory routine) are extremely interesting to them.

Another kind of 'drive' is satisfied by activity. A rat will run in an activity wheel just to get exercise by running, but no exploration need be involved since the wheel just goes round and round without getting anywhere. Studies have shown that if animals are deprived of these activities before being exposed to them they press or run more, indicating higher drive following deprivation. If the lever no longer opens the window or the wheel no longer turns, the animal's activity drops in the way expected in extinction.

Harlow (1958) in an interesting series of studies with baby monkeys, has illustrated an apparent 'need for contact' which characterises much of the infant's attachment to its mother. Baby monkeys were reared with surrogate mothers, wire models that gave milk like real mothers. He found that monkeys not only preferred a 'mother' covered with terry cloth to one made of bare wire, but ran to the terry cloth 'mother' when frightened. They did so even if the wire 'mother' supplied milk and the cloth 'mother' did not. These and other findings suggested to Harlow that 'contact hunger' as exemplified by the baby monkey's need for the cloth surrogate mother is an important factor in personality development.

These illustrations show how a range of 'needs' other than the obviously biological motivates animal behaviour. Various acquired drives have also been postulated as alternatives to unlearned motives. Cultural and class variations in behaviour related to motivation support the idea that much of human motivation is learned. Motives may be seen to be pushed by urges, drives and instincts, or pulled by goals, purposes and values.

There are various theories which consider how motivation has its effects on learning. For example:

1. Do drives simply energise behaviour? When sated, the animal is unmotivated and inactive. According to this view, drives produce restless activity, and the animal which moves about restlessly will generally travel over a wider area and consequently will be more likely to encounter food. When an animal has learned where to go for food, motivation activates the organism which actually goes to the feeding place only when it is hungry. It is in this sense that motivation acts as a switch or trigger, activating or energising behaviour patterns the animal already has.

or 2. Do drives in addition *direct* behaviour? Do they lead to specific, directed behaviour before the animal has learned the specific directions?

This problem centres on the distinction which is often made between learning and performance. We have learned to do many things, but actually perform them only in response to specific motivational triggers.

Another important factor in motivation theory is homeostasis. Behaviour is conceived as being motivated to restore a balance, to seek a state of equilibrium. This view of physiological homeostasis conceives of the organism as an open biological system which is in contact with its external environment, but which maintains a relatively stable state within its own internal environment. This can be achieved through a complex co-operation between the internal organs, the nervous system and the endocrine system. In addition, some psychologists have spoken of a psychological homeostasis leading the organism to resist changes in the environment which will upset its equilibrium or threaten the stability of the system. The overall view is that the organism seeks physiological and psychological quiescence from physiological and psychological disturbance.

Such disturbances may be viewed as drive stimuli. While pain is an example of drive produced by an external stimulus, hunger and thirst are drives produced by internal stimuli. In like manner, some drives are produced by stimuli accompanying emotions; when we are angry or afraid physiological changes take place in our bodies and these are stimuli which arouse the individual and which frequently impel action.

If the drive is pain produced by heat, moving away from the heat source will reduce the pain. A reduction in the strength of the drive is believed to have the property of reinforcing whatever response came just before. Thus, whatever response serves to reduce a drive is reinforced and tends to be learned. Drive or tension reduction is believed by some theorists to be a basic operation in learning. This view has been proposed very strongly by Miller (1963) among others. He is well aware of the problems which it leaves unanswered and both he and Pribram (1963) discuss the role of motivation and learning from a critical viewpoint.

Recent discussion and analysis of the motivation concept illustrate an awareness of the many shortcomings which exist in relation to learning. (Cofer and Appley, 1964, provide a comprehensive review of this area.) One of the major problems concerns the relative contributions of internal states (which act as internal stimuli) and external stimuli both before and after learning. Bodily conditions such as those caused by organic deprivation seem to be important in creating a *readiness* to behave in specific ways. Nevertheless, appropriate environmental cues are necessary if the responses are actually to occur. Such may be the case, for example, in sexual behaviour.

Stimulation is necessary to elicit sexual behaviour in an organism that is hormonally 'ready' for it. Cofer and Appley (1964) argue that it is anticipation which arouses the organism, alerts it and enhances its responsiveness to the available stimuli. They further stress that stimuli, including any coming from internal features of the deprivation state, may have a double function: they come through learning to evoke anticipations (and thus arousal) and they serve after learning as cues for responses.

Finally, mention should be made of a state which has sometimes been referred to as a 'negative' drive or motivation and which represents a form of response suppression. This was categorised by Pavlov under the concept of inhibition, and much of his early work was concerned with its study. Thus in very general terms it can be said that motivation may be either positive or negative. In the former category are those factors which actively motivate and facilitate behaviour; in the latter category those factors which tend to suppress it. Pavlov assumed that inhibition had a physiological reference point in the cortex, but these speculations have not been substantiated and in this context inhibition usually refers to a process which reduces efficiency of learning, conditioning, memory, and thinking. The role of inhibition will be further discussed in a subsequent section on individual differences.

Although few learning theorists actually dismiss the role of motivation in learning, some do not emphasise it. This arises, for example, in theories which deal solely with the external behaviour and which make no attempt to analyse the internal state of the organism. Skinner, for example, is not interested in the inner 'drive' determinants of behaviour. He may work with animals on a food deprivation schedule, but his emphasis is almost entirely on the environmental events which follow certain types of responses, and which by following them closely in time increase their probability of occurrence. For Skinner a reinforcer is a stimulus or environmental event which reinforces, that is, strengthens a response, and his experiments illustrate dramatically the importance of schedules of reinforcement. There are positive and negative reinforcers: if presentation of food achieves an increase in response rate we have a positive reinforcer. If response rate changes with removal of stimulus (like shock) we have a negative reinforcer. There are primary reinforcers (like shock) and secondary reinforcers (like money).

Reinforcement

Whereas animal experiments frequently deal with primary biological reinforcers such as food, sexual contact, water, painful stimuli, etc. it is apparent that a great many objects in our environment come to be generalised reinforcers, such as words, money, clothing, cigarettes, alcohol, cars, etc. This concept of *secondary reinforcers* is a necessary supplement to that of primary reinforcers. Stimuli which are regularly associated with primary reinforcement and which acquire the power to strengthen behaviour are called secondary reinforcers. Thus food for a hungry dog would be considered a primary reinforcer while the food dish might become a secondary reinforcer.

A token reward study of secondary reinforcement by Wolpe (1936) was carried out as follows. Chimpanzees were taught to obtain food by inserting poker chips into a machine which Wolpe constructed. The chimpanzees quickly learned to associate the chips with the receipt of food. They would work at a task when a poker chip was the reward for their effort. The chips would then be inserted into the machine for food. Other investigators have also found that chimpanzees would solve new problems when the only reinforcement was a token.

Skinner (1953) has described several generalised reinforcers which are acquired through social reinforcement of behaviour, including such important behavioural processes as attention, approval and affection.

Schedules of reinforcement

There are a number of parameters of reinforcement

Effect of Random Alternation of Reinforcement

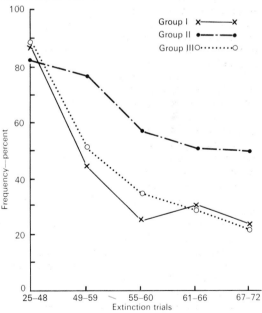

Figure 4.6 Course of extinction frequency of the conditioned eyelid response.

The similarity of Groups I and III (100% reinforcement) is readily apparent, while Group II (50% reinforcement) responds at a consistently higher level throughout. (From Humphreys, 1939, by courtesy of *J. Exp. Psychol.*)

over and above the simple fact of its occurrence. In the situation characterised by 'A followed by B', B may occur always, sometimes, or rarely. The rules which determine when and how often define what Skinner has called 'schedules of reinforcement'. Thus we can arrange that reinforcement B is provided on every occasion following A, i.e. continuous reinforcement, or intermittently, i.e. partial reinforcement, or only after a certain number of responses have been made. The deliberate use of these different schedules has been highly successful in developing, maintaining and controlling simple animal behaviour.

Other important parameters include the quantity and the quality of the reward, and time of its presentation. It is widely known that the effectiveness of a reinforcer is greater when it occurs immediately following the response than when it is delayed.

The effects of reinforcement are observed not only during acquisition but also during extinction. Figure 4.6 illustrates the effects of different kinds of reinforcement schedules on the conditioned eyelid response. The significant comparison is between Group II, given 50% reinforcement, and Group I and III given 100% reinforcement. Contrary to expectation but consistent with all the findings in this area, partial reinforcement is shown to extinguish more slowly. Explanations of this effect have been put forward in terms of subjects' expectancies of reinforcement. The rapid extinction following continuous reinforcement (Group I and III) is explained as a shift from the expectation of uniform reinforcement to that of uniform non-reinforcement. The subjects of Group II on the other hand may continue to expect reinforcement, since reinforcement has often previously followed non-reinforcement.

Skinner has explored extensively two main classes of intermittent reinforcement, called *ratio reinforcement* and *interval reinforcement*. In the ratio reinforcement schedule the animal is reinforced as a function of the number of responses given. In a *fixed-ratio* (FR) schedule the reinforcement follows a fixed number of responses, perhaps every tenth response, and such a schedule would be symbolised as FR 10. Thus with an operant training apparatus for teaching a child to learn to discriminate the letters of the alphabet, the investigator might reward with one piece of candy following each four responses, that is FR 4. This indicates that the child has to press a key under a correct letter four times before the candy is received. Continuous reinforcement would be an FR 1 schedule, that is, a schedule in which each response was followed by reinforcement.

In a variable ratio (VR) schedule of reinforcement, the reinforcer is systematically related to the number of responses; however, instead of occurring after a fixed number, the reinforcing stimulus occurs after a *variable* number of responses. In a VR 10 schedule, the organism would receive a reinforcement for every tenth response *on the average*. This means that in practice the reinforcement might occur following any number of unreinforced responses from zero to fifty or more, but it must occur following ten responses on the average.

The *interval reinforcement* refers to reinforcement given at certain intervals of time. Again, interval schedules may be fixed or variable. These types of reinforcement are described more fully by Hilgard (1956) who discusses theories of learning, and also by Smith and Moore (1966) in a useful self-instruction programme of conditioning and instrumental learning.

The technical characteristics of schedules of reinforcement are included since they have been shown to be a very significant factor in both the theory and practice of psychology. They have been applied to various therapeutic and educational programmes (see for example Krasner and Ullman, 1965; Skinner, 1971). They are frequently used as explanations of puzzling elements of human behaviour. For example, any one who observes devoted gamblers . . . 'will find it very difficult to explain why extinction of the gambling behaviour fails to occur. By recognizing that games of chance involve single or double variable-ratio schedules, it is possible to predict strong resistance to extinction' (Smith and Moore, 1966).

Reinforcement and learning

In spite of the success which schedules of reinforcement may have in controlling behaviour, there is no clear agreement about how reinforcement 'works' in relation to learning. Skinner's position is largely non-theoretical, but even those who have been concerned with reinforcement theory present a variety of viewpoints. The hypothesis that reinforcement accompanies drive reduction is one major view, but this has well-recognised difficulties. It does not specify which kinds of stimuli or responses are crucial to drive reduction and which are irrelevant. More needs to be known about temporal effect such as the onset *v.* offset of rewards and punishment; and about the different effects of peripheral (e.g. motor consummatory) responses *v.* central (e.g. cognitive) responses. We are still uncertain about the effects of reinforcers on *performance* as distinct from learning.

During the past few decades interest has been centred on electrical excitation of central regions of the brain and the possible relationship with mechanisms of reinforcement. A series of studies initiated by Delgado *et al.* (1954) and Olds and Milner (1954) have shown that electrical stimulation of certain areas of the brain has all the functional characteristics of a satisfier or reward. Olds and Milner placed the experimental animal in a 'do-it-yourself' situation in which it could press a lever to stimulate its own brain (see Figure 4.7). Left to itself in the apparatus the animal stimulated its own brain regularly about every five seconds, taking a stimulus of a second or so every time. Localisation experiments showed that when

Figure 4.7 The brain self-stimulation circuit. When the rat presses on the lever it triggers an electrical stimulus to its brain, and simultaneously records its action via the wire on the left.

electrodes were implanted in the classical sensory and motor systems response rates stayed at the chance level of 10–25 lever presses an hour. In most parts of the midline system, the response rates rose to levels of from 200 to 5000 lever presses an hour, indicative of a rewarding effect of the electric stimulus. Electrical stimulation in some of these regions actually appeared to be more rewarding than food.

It is uncertain as yet why electrical stimulation is so rewarding. One hypothesis is that brain stimulation in these regions may excite some of the nerve cells that would be excited by satisfaction of the basic drives—hunger, sex, thirst, etc. The possibility that there are identifiable reward and aversion systems that can be reliably differentiated by anatomical or physiological techniques may significantly advance our understanding of how reinforcement mechanisms operate.

HUMAN CONDITIONING STUDIES
The extensive work which was carried out in animal conditioning studies held the promise of general and clear-cut 'laws' of learning. The most influential theorists spoke in terms of stimulus–response (S–R) behaviour. They aimed to relate the course of learning (frequently referred to as 'habit strength' and assumed to be a strengthening of neural connections somewhere

in the nervous system) to factors under experimental control such as level of drive, number of paired presentation of CS and UCS, amount and nature of reinforcement. In Hull's system (Hull, 1943) the development of habit strength was largely dependent on certain specifiable factors of reinforcement. Theories of learning were developed which attempted to incorporate the factors affecting rate of learning and link them directly to observed conditioning curves. These were often assumed to be regular growth curves (as typified in Figure 4.8) an 'increment' of learning taking place on every trial.

It was recognised that the regularity of the typical learning curve might be affected by a number of factors. With highly intense and traumatic UCSs, learning in a very few trials (even one trial) had been observed. Some theorists in addition, maintained that learning curves displayed certain 'discontinuities' which could be explained in terms of the animal having a 'hypothesis' or strategy which resulted in sudden quite marked improvements in learning. This view seemed to imply that there is a symbolic level of activity in animals which results in 'hypotheses' which are tried out and if objectively unsuccessful are soon discarded for new ones. A 'hypothesis' thus arises from the animal's interpretation of the data and not simply from the direct effects of external stimulation. How such plans, ideas or insights could occur in rats or monkeys seemed an insoluble problem, and the issue of whether such factors were relevant or not to learning was shelved.

As interest shifted from animal to human conditioning studies, however, the question of subjective experience (feelings, ideas and thoughts) could no longer be ignored. Many of the paradigms and procedures used in animal conditioning studies have involved severe deprivation or painful stimuli, and the learning of escape–avoidance reactions. These are excluded from human studies and the emphasis has inevitably shifted from the intense emotional/motivational aspects of conditioning to milder anxiety-producing situations. But if in human studies only slight to moderate degrees of fear and pain are involved, the role of cognitive and verbal factors becomes far greater.

When exposed to a conditioning paradigm the human subject does not passively await the experimental stimuli and their contingencies. 'More often than not, he comes to the experiment as a human being with thoughts, feelings, attitudes, beliefs and expectations which play a major and critical role in the behaviour we observe' (Lockhart, 1973).

Thus human subjects will verbalise their awareness of contingencies between experimental stimuli; adopt positive or negative sets towards them and the experimenter, will develop expectancies, become involved or bored with the experiment. All these factors are known to affect conditioning, and most particularly conditioning of autonomic responses like skin resistance, peripheral blood volume and heart rate. For reasons which are not yet clear, simple reflex responses like the blink response to a puff of air remain relatively (though certainly not entirely) uninfluenced by cognitive factors. Autonomic responses, on the other hand, are very strongly affected.

A number of experimental studies have tried to show how cognitive factors affect the course of learning by examining their effects on learning curves. During the course of acquisition, human subjects frequently become aware of the CS–UCS relationship. At the point where this awareness occurs there may be a sudden change in the subject's response, reflected in the acquisition curve as a sharp increase in responding. This was recognised by Mowrer (1938) who observed that an apparent conditioned autonomic response can be suddenly established and equally suddenly abolished in human beings merely by controlling the subject's state of expectancy or preparatory set. There were subsequent debates as to whether these sudden changes in responding were 'true' conditioned responses or not. A classic study in this area (Cook and Harris, 1937), in which subjects appeared to condition simply when they were *instructed* about CS–UCS relationships, concluded that conditioning the skin resistance response in human subjects differs from the customary conditioning procedure in that it is established by *verbal* means and not via actual presentation of the CS–UCS pairings.

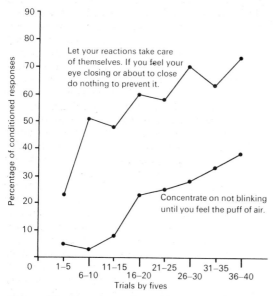

Figure 4.8 Percentage of conditioned responses as a function of trials for subjects conditioned with facilitatory and inhibitory instructions. Except for sentences on the two curves, instructions were the same for both groups. (From Nicholls and Kimble, 1964, by courtesy of *J. Exp. Psychol.*)

Some authors have preferred to distinguish two types of learning, calling one (without awareness) 'true' conditioning and those situations involving perception of stimulus relations as 'relational' learning. Unfortunately, such a distinction is difficult to maintain.

A long series of studies has investigated the effects of cognitive factors in conditioning. These factors include the perception of stimulus relationships and the effects of attitude, set and expectancies. Frequently the instructions of the experiment are manipulated, for example informing one group of subjects in advance of the precise nature of the stimulus relationships (that a red light will always be followed by a loud tone, a green light never) and comparing conditioned responses with those of a control group given no information. Alternatively, the true nature of the conditioning experiment may be masked by a variety of distracting tasks.

Figure 4.8 illustrates the effect of facilitatory and inhibitory instructions on the conditioned eyelid response. Conditioning curves are plotted as percentages of CRs against trials in blocks of five. It is apparent that the subjects in the group with facilitative instructions ('Let your reactions take care of themselves') performed much better than those conditioned with inhibitory instructions ('Concentrate on not blinking until you feel the puff of air'). The two curves separate and then become parallel, which suggests the operation of two interacting processes. The first is a facilitatory or inhibitory set which has achieved its full strength in something less than ten trials and from then on has a fairly constant effect on performance. The second is the conditioned eyelid reflex that requires much longer to establish.

The question has been raised as to whether conditioning can occur at all without awareness in human subjects (*cf.* a recent symposium on this topic: Classical conditioning and the Cognitive Processes, Psychophysiology, 1973). On the whole, current opinion is that verbalised awareness of stimulus relationships is not necessary for conditioning to occur, even though a strong causal relationship has been established between cognitive variables and rate of classical conditioning and extinction. It seems unlikely in the case of interoceptive conditioning that either the CS or UCS is symbolically mediated: contingencies are undoubtedly operating below the threshold of awareness. In the case of strongly-conditioned fears, the effects of cognitive variables (self-instruction, etc.) can be minimal.

If in certain situations verbal instructions can produce apparent conditioned responses in the absence of direct experience of the conditioning stimuli and their effects, the further question which can be raised is whether emotional responses can be conditioned 'vicariously' by simply observing another person being conditioned. A vicarious learning event is defined as one in which new responses are acquired as a function of observing the behaviour of others and its reinforcing consequences, without the modelled response being overtly performed. Emotional responses of others are conveyed through auditory cues, facial expressions and postural changes, and have the capacity to arouse empathetic emotional responses in observers. In the case of vicarious classical conditioning, the observers' vicariously elicited emotional responses became conditioned through contiguous association to formerly neutral stimuli.

Some experiments by Berger (1962) provide evidence for vicarious conditioning. This is labelled 'no-trial learning' since the observer does not engage in any *overt responding trials*, although he may require multiple observational trials in order to reproduce the modelled stimuli accurately. It seems likely that the development of mediational responses in the form of imaginal and implicit verbal representations of the perceived stimulus events plays a critical role in the vicarious learning process. Autonomic and instrumental classes of responses can not only be acquired but also extinguished on a vicarious basis. There is evidence that behavioural inhibitions can be removed by modelling procedures and these are discussed by Bandura (1965, 1971) with special reference to fearful and aggressive behaviour.

Although powerful conditioned fears are unlikely to be produced in the laboratory (see, as an exception, a study by Campbell *et al.*, 1964, in which fear conditioning was powerfully established with a single trial by means of Scoline inhibited respiration) the role of fear and anxiety is of central significance to several aspects of human conditioning. One concerns its relationship to personality. A second concerns the application of conditioning principles to explain and to modify the maladaptive emotional reactions which occur in real-life situations. Here the problem is usually a therapeutic one, i.e. extinguishing persistent fears and anxieties which, it is assumed, have been acquired in the life-history of the individual through a process of conditioning. A third is how the concept of fear can be incorporated in conditioning theories of fear acquisition and extinction.

Individual differences

The classic operation for establishing a motivational or drive state is deprivation. With rare exceptions, deprivation has not been employed in studies of human motivation. Assessment of the subject's drive state has more frequently been in terms of anxiety level, either by means of a questionnaire or by the experimental manipulation of arousal via threat of shock, stress, or failure.

Several theories have selected one aspect of motivation as a major source of individual variation, the difference between them lying mainly in the choice of specific motivational components. For Eysenck, the major emphasis has been on the negative drive represented by the concept of central inhibition, and referred to the activity of the reticular activating system (Eysenck, 1967). For Spence (1956) the major emphasis has been on positive drive components, particularly emotionality, referred to the activity of the autonomic nervous system.

A central concept in Eysenck's theory is that differences in learning capacity, more specifically in conditionability, account for the major aspects of human behaviour. This concept has been of particular importance in applying the theory to social problems, like neurotic behaviour and crime. In its simplest terms it proposes that individuals high on extroversion are impaired in utilising learned patterns of behaviour. Individuals high on extroversion are said to be less able to learn from experience (like criminals and psychopaths) whereas individuals low on extroversion are said to be more easily socialised.

It has been proposed that the characteristics of extroversion/introversion could be explained in terms of differences in cortical excitation/inhibition balance. In Pavlovian terms, this means that inhibition of cortical function is greater in the extrovert than in the introvert. Inhibition (of behaviour) by the cortex and inhibition (in function) of the cortex must be differentiated. In the extrovert, inhibition of cortical control leads to disinhibited behaviour. In the introvert, a chronically higher level of cortical excitation, together with less susceptibility to inhibition of cortical control, leads to more inhibited behaviour (Eysenck, 1967, p.75 elaborates this point). Although the role of the cortex in conditioning is now in doubt, the concept of an inhibition/excitation balance is not necessarily invalidated. However, the balance may be more complex than Pavlov imagined. Inhibition, though more active than excitation, is held in essential balance with excitatory processes within the nervous system and the concept of the inhibition/excitation balance in part defines CNS activity. Thus inhibition is a central process which at all times governs ongoing activity.

The general relationship between personality and inhibition was postulated as follows: 'Human beings differ with respect to the speed with which excitation and inhibition are produced, the strength of the excitation and inhibition produced and the speed with which inhibition is dissipated. These differences are properties of the physical structures involved in making stimulus–response connections' (Eysenck, 1967, p.79). It follows from this postulate that conditioning will be demonstrated more quickly in introverts than extroverts in experimental conditions which generate significant but not maximal amounts of inhibition. In the eyelid conditioning experiment which was employed to test this hypothesis the specific conditions relate to UCS (airpuff) intensity, reinforcement schedule (partial *v.* continuous) and the interval of time between CS and UCS (Levey, 1972). Extroverts, through their greater susceptibility to central inhibition, are impaired under the unfavourable

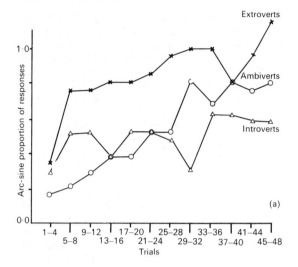

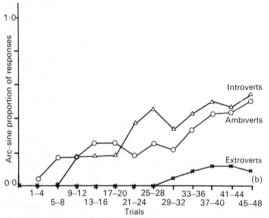

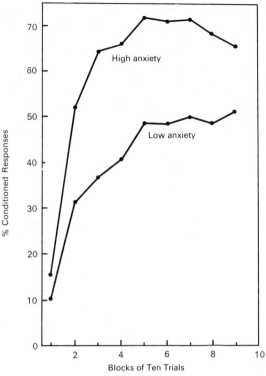

Figure 4.10 Frequency of conditioned eyelid responses for subjects with high and low anxiety. (From Ominsky and Kimble, 1966, by courtesy of *J. Exp. Psychol.*)

Figure 4.9 Conditioned eyelid response curves over trials.

(a) Acquisition curves for levels of extroversion under continuous reinforcement, long CS–UCS interval and strong UCS intensity

(b) Acquisition curves for levels of extroversion under partial reinforcement, short CS–UCS interval and weak UCS intensity. (From Levey, 1972, by courtesy of University of London)

conditions (low intensity UCS, short CS–UCS interval and partial reinforcement) but do well under favourable conditions (strong intensity UCS, long CS–UCS interval and continuous reinforcement). Introverts tend to condition well in both favourable and unfavourable conditions (Figure 4.9).

Spence's theory states that anxious people condition more rapidly than non-anxious, and he has suggested that emotionality, defined essentially as sympathetic autonomic arousal, acts as a drive. He argues that anxiety is an example of such a drive and offers this explanation of the role of individual differ-

ences in conditioning. The Taylor Manifest Anxiety Scale was developed as a means of identifying differences in anxiety, and has been used in many studies in relation to levels of conditioning (Figure 4.10).

Both the theories mentioned above present the motivational aspects of conditioning in terms of personality variables, with inhibition being the major factor in one and anxiety drive in the other. They are not in conflict, and are examples of two well-developed theories in the field with precise predictions and specification of the experimental conditions which will lead to rapid conditioning.

Extinction of conditioned fears

The basic fear conditioning paradigm as discussed earlier in connection with animal experiments simply involves the pairing of a neutral CS with an aversive UCS. Many investigators believe that essentially the same type of conditioning paradigm is responsible for the learning of fear reactions in humans. Furthermore, human methods of dealing with anxiety-provoking situations essentially follow the same strategy as the rat, i.e. to escape as quickly as possible from the presence of the feared CS.

In this situation the CS although unaccompanied

by the usual reinforcer (the UCS) continues to evoke strong avoidance responses for very long periods of time. Indeed, the term incubation has been used to describe the increment in CR strength which may occur in neurotic fears even though the usual conditions for extinction are present. Eysenck (1968, 1974) has suggested that the unreinforced CS elicits sympathetic fear responses (CRs) which are unpleasant to experience and thus lead to a strengthening of the CS/CR connection. What is being suggested is that conditioning sets in motion a positive feedback cycle in which the CR itself provides reinforcement for the CS. This is not an uncommon pattern, often described as 'having nothing to fear but fear itself' and with the implication that each of the fears may in some way exacerbate the other.

The physiological responses to the unreinforced CS in the case of pain/anxiety may often be identical to,

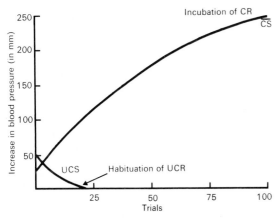

Figure 4.11 Illustrates the growth of blood pressure CR to an unreinforced CS (CS) from 30–40 mm on early trials to 190–230 mm on later trials, following a single conditioning trial. (From Eysenck, 1974 from data provided by Napalkov, 1963)

or even greater than, those to the primary UCS. Napalkov (1963) working with dogs found that repeated administration of the CS alone following a single conditioning trial brought about large increases in blood pressure as illustrated in Figure 4.11. In some cases the hypertensive state which was produced lasted over a year. Eysenck (1974) discusses evidence for the possibility that under certain circumstances, which might well occur in real life conditioning situations, the CR unlike the UCR is protected from extinction.

The failure to extinguish avoidance responses has also been discussed by Seligman and Johnston (1973) who offer an explanation in terms of expectancies. They argue that CSs which have been paired with the

absence of shock become 'safety signals'. Thus an animal may continue to respond to unreinforced CSs because the safety signals positively reinforce responding; in this situation it develops expectancies that some responses lead to shock while other responses lead to avoidance of shock. Their theory has two components: one, the cognitive element just mentioned by which the organism stores information about contingencies between responses and outcomes in a given situation. The second is an emotional element in which the animal 'prefers' one outcome (e.g. no shock) to another outcome (e.g. shock), or 'prefers' a state of no fear to one of fear.

It should be added here that although many conditioning theories recognise only fear and pain as the UCR which occurs in the conditioning situation there is good evidence that 'frustrative non-reward' (i.e. frustration which arises when a previously occurring reward no longer occurs) has very similar effects as punishment and that punishment may be functionally and physiologically related to the state of fear (Gray, 1971). Thus the extension of the paradigm from animals to humans in part coincides with the extension of the UCR from simple physical pain to frustrative non-reward; the difficulties which people face seldom involve actual pain, but they do very often involve frustrations of one kind or another, disappointed expectations or frustrated hopes, as the case might be.

Detailed accounts of the Eysenck, Gray, and the Seligman and Johnston theories are given in their papers. They are briefly mentioned here simply to illustrate the progress which is being made towards a more adequate though more complex version of two-process aversion theory. Eysenck has consistently argued that methods of treatment of neurotic disorders must take their place within a theoretical framework of anxiety extinction and preservation, and it is often argued that phobias and certain neurotic symptoms can be viewed as avoidance behaviour which is reinforced because it successfully helps the individual to escape from cues which elicit anxiety. Thus avoidance behaviour is an attempt to protect the person from a conditional fear, acquired in his life history and which continues to evoke intense anxiety.

In order to really test the situation, i.e. to check whether or not the undesirable UCS is or is not occurring, the subject has to be exposed to the total CS–UCS stimulus complex which he has previously learned to avoid. Since the testing of this hypothesis will result in a substantial increase in anxiety, it is not put into operation voluntarily. Treatment involves applying some of the well-established laboratory methods known to produce extinction of fear. These include such techniques as exposing the animal or person to the CS and forcibly restraining avoidance responses so that he can test the non-occurrence of the shock-UCS or feared object. Several investigators have found this to be an effective procedure, resulting in rapid extinction of the avoidance response and of the fear. Subjects appear to be highly anxious during the first few presentations of the total CS complex but after repeated extinction trials the anxiety dissipates quickly.

Another technique for reducing conditioned fear reactions is that of counterconditioning or systematic desensitisation, which aims to develop a new response which is inhibitory to the fear reaction, and which will gradually weaken and replace it (Wolpe, 1961). It has been hypothesised that anxiety and phobias consist of conditioned *sympathetic* reactions, and that treatment consists of conditioning *parasympathetic* reactions which, being antagonistic to the sympathetic ones, will weaken and then extinguish them.

In implosion or flooding techniques the patient is fully and intensively exposed to all the cues which elicit his anxiety. The therapist first tries to establish the exteroceptive and interoceptive conditioned stimuli that the patient is avoiding. Many of these will be situational or environmental cues which are highly correlated with the occurrence of the patient's symptom. These cues are then verbally described in detail, while the patient is encouraged to visualise them in imagery. Scenes are described to the patient which will produce a maximal level of anxiety: he might be asked to imagine himself climbing the stairs of feared tall buildings, or handling feared animals. The patient is maintained at this high level of anxiety until some signs of spontaneous reduction (extinction) in the anxiety produced by the stimuli takes place. Thus the therapist forces the patient to expose himself to some of the anxiety arousing situations which he would try to avoid outside the treatment session, and if these cues elicit the anxiety response in the absence of primary reinforcement, the anxiety response will eventually extinguish.

Finally, operant conditioning procedures may be employed, the therapist in this instance applying appropriate reinforcements contingent on the behaviour of the individual (Krasner, 1971).

These techniques raise many practical and theoretical problems, among them being the manner in which they operate. There seems to be fairly reasonable agreement that some form of extinction process is involved, and Wolpe (1961) has postulated that this is due to inhibition. The essence of his theory is that if a conditioned fear response is wholly or partially prevented from occurring by antagonistic responses, the accumulation of conditioned inhibition tends to prevent anxiety responses to the original stimulus when encountered again. Recent critics of desensitisation treatment have tended to discard terms such as reciprocal and conditioned inhibition, working on the practical problems of accelerating extinction and utilising only the empirical fact that competing conditioned responses interfere with each other. In the case of implosion and related techniques it has been

tentatively suggested that they operate by bringing about a type of 'exhaustion' of the patient's ability to respond emotionally and that during this refractory phase he is able to habituate to the formerly fear-evoking stimuli.

The concept of a conditioned fear

Although conditioning studies typically handle only one response measure at a time, a complex human emotion like fear comprises many response elements. These form a complex pattern of autonomic, skeletal-motor and cognitive-perceptual factors which are partially independent of one another. One individual may avoid feared objects and display heightened autonomic arousal, but verbally deny that he feels afraid. Another may admit to feeling afraid but be willing to approach and touch a feared object because he does not want to appear cowardly. Thus the individual components may have different kinds of interactions with the environment, and to some extent are capable of independent change. That is to say, they may have been acquired as a result of different conditioning processes occurring at different times in the history of the individual; and they may be 'shaped' (i.e. modified) by separate conditioning treatments. In re-training a complex reaction of fear it may well be necessary to apply a variety of extinction or counter-conditioning techniques to modify autonomic, behavioural and verbal response components.

To state the case simply, one could devise a programme of modification which would seek to lower an elevated physiological arousal by means of relaxation or desensitisation techniques, or by one of the bio-feedback operant methods in which the person is trained to control certain aspects of his physiological responding; it could seek to modify overt avoidance behaviour with a retraining programme offering more adaptive types of response strategies, e.g. by learning social skills instead of avoiding social situations. And the individual's attitudes and verbalisations about his fears could similarly be modified by various learning techniques (Staats, 1972).

It would be expected that training or modifying one component, say the verbal, would have some effect on the physiological. Conversely, retraining the physiological, say in terms of learning to relax, should affect the individual's verbalisations ('I feel more relaxed)' and his behaviour. The extent to which these interactions occur remains an empirical problem. We need to measure responses in all systems, and discover the laws that determine their interaction. Treatment programmes may have to be tailored to each response system, in the light of known principles of modification. 'Thus, a patient who reports anxiety, fails to cope or perform effectively under stress, and evidences autonomic activity that varies widely from the practical energy demands of the situation, needs to receive treatment for all these disorders. He should be administered a treatment directed simultaneously at shaping verbal sets (so as to reduce reported stress over the variety of situations in which it appears), assisted in building effective coping behaviours and practising them in appropriate contexts, and finally, administered a programme for attenuating autonomic arousal and excessive muscle tonus, with the goal of reducing the distraction and interference of peripheral physiological feedback' (Lang, 1971). In short, behaviour modification may need to incorporate a multisystem training program tailored to the unique behavioural topography presented by the patient.

Conditioning attitudes, values and language

The conditioning of fears has been discussed at some length because of its obvious theoretical and practical importance. Less obvious but perhaps equally significant is the evidence on the conditioning of attitudes, values, feelings other than fear, and language.

Razran (1940) for example asked subjects to rate sociopolitical slogans in terms of personal approval and social effectiveness (America for America; Workers of the World Unite!) and then divided the slogans into two sets. One set was always presented while the subjects were enjoying a free lunch and the other while they were required to inhale a number of unpleasant, 'putrid' odours. After five to eight conditioning sessions the original rating procedure was repeated. He found that slogans associated with the lunch showed increases in ratings for personal approval etc. while those combined with unpleasant odours showed decreases in ratings. Elsewhere Razran (1938) has discussed techniques for conditioning away social bias by presenting the social stimuli while subjects are enjoying a pleasant lunch.

Yet another approach to attitudes via the conditioning of verbal meaning has been described by Staats and Staats (1958). In the child, for example, stimuli that elicit negative emotional responses are often paired with the word 'bad', which then itself comes to elicit a negative emotional response. The classical conditioning of emotional responses to words has been well-demonstrated, and there is considerable evidence that words eliciting positive or negative emotional meanings have a high frequency in many languages.

The emotion eliciting and reinforcing functions of words are closely linked; and a large class of positive emotional words exist that can function as positive (enjoy, laughter, fun) or negative (ugly, die, sick) reinforcers. That is to say, in instrumental (Skinnerian, operant) conditioning, the presentation of such words contingent upon some type of behaviour has been shown to strengthen or weaken it. A common example in social situations is the use of the word 'Good!' following behaviour of which we approve and which we may wish to increase.

Other workers have pointed to the multiple effects of the stimuli used in conditioning. Along with the gustatory stimulation of sugar solutions, for example, there is also positive affective arousal. Some stimuli are preferred to others, some liked and some disliked. A neutral stimulus, like an auditory click, can arouse positive affective responses by being conditioned to a positively valued stimulus (like food). The general conditioning principle is that any neutral stimulus which occurs consistently and contiguously with primary affective arousal will tend to elicit a similar affective arousal (Young, 1961). These affective processes regulate and direct behaviour according to the principle of maximising the positive and minimising the negative. Thus they lead to the development of motives and evaluative dispositions that become relatively stable and permanent determinants of behaviour.

The multiple effects of stimuli therefore include not only observable motor and autonomic responses but also a range of cognitive–attitudinal–emotional responses. Very little is known about the significance of these responses. Available evidence suggests that the transfer of value (liking, disliking) can be achieved quite readily in human subjects with simple visual stimuli by means of a conditioning paradigm. Pictures originally rated as neutral (CSs) were paired with liked or disliked pictures (UCSs) and subsequently found to have shifted toward the value of the UCS, i.e. the neutral pictures were now liked or disliked (Levey and Martin, 1975). It is of interest that in this experiment transfer of liking/disliking occurred in the absence of strong autonomic/emotional activation or overt responding.

It has long been recognised that one of the components of an intense feeling like fear is an appraisal both of the external situation and of the fear/anxiety response itself. Field studies suggest, for example, that men may report being afraid but do not necessarily avoid participating in combat missions. It is apparently possible to tolerate and even to 'enjoy' fear. If a man should lose confidence or seem to lose control of the situation, however, as could occur in an unexpected accident, a general reappraisal takes place. The external situation may be evaluated as more threatening, coping strategies as ineffective, and the experience of fear now becomes intensely negative in quality.

In its simplest formulation the conditioning process refers to the association in time between well-defined stimuli and responses, but when complex attitudinal and evaluative processes are considered the definitions of stimulus and response become more and more obscure. A stimulus not only has physical characteristics but also conveys information and meaning to the individual. A response may be specified in terms of physiological change or skeletal activity, but it, too, becomes less clear-cut when it is considered as personal experience with connotations of good and bad, desirable or undesirable. Which of all the many attributes of a 'stimulus' or 'response' become associated in the conditioning process has yet to be established.

SOME PROBLEMS IN CONDITIONING THEORY

People will be interested in conditioning from different points of view: some from more academic and theoretical interests and others from clinical and applied needs. These two areas will no doubt be more closely linked in the future than they are at present, but any existing looseness between theory and practice is probably inevitable and should stimulate attempts to integrate them.

The problems of conventional learning theory are many. They include the effects of motivation and reinforcement on learning, and how these factors operate on different measures of learning and performance. One approach is typified by the work of Skinner, who has tried to establish the explanatory power of the reinforcement concept by an intensive operational analysis of reinforcement. He has not sought a unifying link that underlies different reinforcing events, but seeks instead for the empirical link between praise for a child and corn for a pigeon in terms of the similarity of the behavioural consequences. Other approaches have examined the brain structures which are involved in reinforcement. Early studies suggested the interesting possibility of a 'pleasure centre' in the CNS (central nervous system) acting to maintain behaviour through reward, and extensive work since has shown that there are many reward areas scattered through the limbic system and rhinencephalon. A full discussion of problems of motivation and reinforcement is provided by Cofer and Appley (1964).

Many attempts have been made to study the role of the CNS in learning. It should be borne in mind that there is no single type of conditioning, but a diversity of situations in which different types of conditioning occur. There is no final agreement about the logical distinction between the paradigms of conditioning (classical, instrumental, operant) which have been discussed in this chapter. Possibly they will be re-evaluated in the future and classified in different ways. This might be in terms of experimental operations, as has been done in the past, but it could also relate to different strategies of the organism, or to different reinforcing factors.

We should not expect to find a single neurophysiological explanation of learning (e.g. a 'learning centre') which would cover all cases. Many studies have been concerned with speculations about events in the cerebral cortex. Theorising in this area has been dominated by the view that some form of new pathway must be formed, directly or indirectly, between centres receiving the CS (e.g. in the sensory cortex) and those effecting the response (e.g. in the motor cortex). This is a plausible notion, but one which has received very little experimental support. Crude conditioned responses can be formed in partially or completely decorticate animals, but they cannot be differentiated or refined without the presence of all or most of the cerebral cortex. Many lines of investigation suggest that the first signs of electrical activity in the brain are in fact subcortical (see Grossman, 1967, for a full discussion of neurophysiological theories of learning).

A novel influence in conditioning theory has recently come from the studies of ethologists. These workers have most commonly observed the behaviours of individual species in their natural habitat and have tended to emphasise the role of instinctive factors. This approach is to be contrasted with the typical learning experiment in which the animal is isolated from all the stimuli available in his natural environment and is expected to attend to the artificial laboratory-type contingencies imposed on him. It is often tacitly assumed that the animal comes to the laboratory as a virtual **tabula rasa**, that species differences are not important, and that all responses are about equally conditionable to all stimuli. Ethologists argue, on the other hand, that an animal may learn some things much more readily than others. That is to say, some parts of the entire behavioural pattern may be changed by learning while others seem to be so rigidly fixed that no learning is possible. For example, herring gulls learn immediately to recognise their own chicks but never their own eggs. Presumably individuals of each species are predisposed to modify those aspects of their behaviour which are relevant to survival in natural conditions. In spite of these differences, however, the ethological and learning theory approaches are not in conflict, but have a great deal to offer one another.

The implications of such views on learning theory have been discussed in relation to the ease with which certain CS–UCS connections can be formed (Seligman and Hager, 1973). Using the term 'biological preparedness' these authors point out that an animal may be more or less prepared by the evolution of its species to associate a given CS and UCS or a given response and reinforcer. It has also been suggested that phylogenetic mechanisms in man may make certain stimuli prepotent over others in the production of phobias, e.g. the avoidance of perceived depth, fear of strangers and of objects and animals which move suddenly (Marks, 1969).

Finally, a recurring problem is that of what is 'really' learned in the conditioning process. Different theorists have maintained a variety of viewpoints, some arguing that it is an isolated reflex response, others that it is expectancy, and some again that it is a 'cognitive map'. Thus the simple view of a mechanical sequence of responses has been modified to include a number of 'mediation' processes, i.e. processes of thought and feeling which intervene in the stimulus–response connection. These are empirical problems, however; the essential requirement of a learning theory is that whatever intervening variables are introduced, they must always be related to observed antecedent and consequent conditions.

Traditional laboratory conditioning paradigms (and theories) have had a zoöcentric bias which is ill-suited to contemporary interests in individuals and therapy. Indeed, the application of behaviour modification techniques to human problems has acted as a search-light on the inadequacies of existing learning theories.

Eysenck and Beech (1971) provide a useful discussion on the connection between learning theory and the practices of behaviour therapists, dealing with many of the points frequently raised by critics. Yet the basic principles seem to hold with surprising strength, and what seems to be required is a corrective on previous biases and an incorporation of previously neglected factors (like human cognitions). At least it is a positive outlook to see how far such enrichment can benefit and accelerate the growth of a more satisfactory learning theory.

References

Bandura, A. (1965). Behavioral modifications through modelling procedures. In: *Research in Behavior Modification. New Developments and Implications*, Chap. 15 (L. Krasner and L. P. Ullman, editors) (New York: Holt, Rinehart and Winston)

Bandura, A. (1971). Psychotherapy based upon modelling principles. In: *Handbook of Psychotherapy and Behavior Change: An Empirical Analysis* (A. E. Bergin and S. L. Garfield, editors) (New York: Wiley)

Berger, S. M. (1962). Conditioning through vicarious instigation. *Psychol. Rev.*, **69**, 450–466

Black, A. H. (1956). *The Extinction of Avoidance Responses under Curare.* (Harvard University: Unpublished Ph.D. thesis)

Brogden, N. J., Lipman, E. A. and Culler, E. (1938). The role of incentive in conditioning and extinction. *Amer. J. Psychol.*, **51**, 109–117

Campbell, D., Sanderson, R. E. and Laverty, S. G. (1964). Characteristic of a conditioned response in human subjects during extinction trials following a single traumatic conditioning trial. *J. Abn. Soc. Psychol.*, **68**, 627–639

Cofer, C. N. and Appley, M. H. (1964). *Motivation: Theory and Research* (New York: Wiley)

Cook, S. W. and Harris, R. E. (1937). The verbal conditioning of the galvanic skin reflex. *J. Exp. Psychol.*, **21**, 202–210

Delgado, N. M. R., Roberts, W. W. and Miller, N. E. (1954). Learning motivated by electrical stimulation of the brain. *Amer. J. Physiol.*, **179**, 587–593

Eysenck, H. J. (1967). *The Biological Basis of Personality* (Springfield: Thomas)

Eysenck, H. J. (1968). A theory of the incubation of anxiety/fear responses. *Behav. Res. Ther.*, **6**, 309–321

Eysenck, H. J. and Beech, H. R. (1971). Counter conditioning and related methods. In: *Handbook of Psychotherapy and Behavior Change: An Empirical Analysis* (A. E. Bergin and S. L. Garfield, editors) (New York: Wiley)

Eysenck, H. J. (1974). *Anxiety and the Natural History of Neurosis*

Feather, B. W. (1967). Human salivary conditioning: a methodological study. In: *Foundations of Conditioning and Learning* (G. A. Kimble, editor) (New York: Appleton-Century-Crofts Inc.)

Gray, J. A. (1971). *The Psychology of Fear and Stress* (London: Weidenfeld and Nicolson)

Grossman, S. P. (1967). *A Textbook of Physiological Psychology* (New York: Wiley)

Guttman, N. and Kalish, H. I. (1956). Discriminability and stimulus generalisation. *J. Exp. Psychol.*, **51**, 79–88

Harlow, H. F. (1958). The nature of love. *Amer. Psychol.*, **12**, 673–685

Hilgard, E. R. (1956). *Theories of Learning*, 2nd Ed. (New York: Appleton-Century-Crofts, Inc.)

Hull, C. L. (1943). *Principles of Behaviour* (New York: Appleton-Century-Crofts, Inc.)

Humphreys, L. G. (1939). The effect of random alternation of reinforcement on the acquisition and extinction of conditioned eyelid reactions. *J. Exp. Psychol.*, **25**, 141–158

Krasner, L. and Ullman, L. P. (Editors) (1965). *Research in Behavior Modification. New Developments and Implications* (New York: Holt, Rinehart and Winston)

Krasner, L. (1971). The operant approach in behavior therapy. In: *Handbook of Psychotherapy and Behavior Change: An Empirical Analysis* (A. E. Bergin and S. L. Garfield, editors) (New York: Wiley)

Lang, P. J. (1971). The application of psychophysiological methods to the study of psychotherapy and behavior modification. In: *Handbook of Psychotherapy and Behavior Change: An Empirical Analysis* (A. E. Bergin and S. L. Garfield, editors) (New York: Wiley)

Levey, A. B. (1972). *Eyelid Conditioning, Extraversion and Drive: An Experimental Test of Two Theories* (University of London: Unpublished Ph.D. thesis)

Levey, A. B. and Martin, Irene (1975). Conditioning of a human evaluative response. *Behaviour Research and Therapy*, **13**, 221–226

Lockhart, R. A. (1973). Chairman: Classical Conditioning and the cognitive processes: A Symposium. *Psychophysiology*, 74–122

Miller, N. E. (1963). Some reflections on the law of effect produce a new alternative to drive reduction. *Nebraska Symposium on Motivation* (M. R. Jones, editor) (Lincoln: University of Nebraska Press)

Mowrer, O. H. (1938). Preparatory set. *Psychological Review*, **45**, 62–91

Napalkov, S. V. (1967). Information Process of the Brain. In: N. Wiener and J. C. Schade (Eds.) *Progress in Brain Research*, **Vol. 2**, 59–69 (Amsterdam: Elsevier)

Nicholls, Margaret F. and Kimble, G. A. (1964). Effect of instructions upon eyelid conditioning. *J. Exp. Psychol.*, **67**, 400–402

Olds, J. A. and Milner, P. (1954). Positive reinforcement produced by electrical stimulation of septal area and other regions of rat brain. *J. Comp. Physiol.*

Psychol., **47**, 419–427

Ominsky, M. and Kimble, G. A. (1966). Anxiety and eye-lid conditioning. *J. Exp. Psychol.* **71**, 471–472

Pribram, K. H. (1963). Reinforcement revisited: a structural view. *Nebraska Symposium on Motivation.* (M. R. Jones, editor) (Lincoln: University of Nebraska Press)

Razran, G. H. S. (1938). Conditioning away social bias by the luncheon technique. *Psychol. Bull.*, **35**, 693 (Abstr.)

Razran, G. H. S. (1940). Conditioned response changes in rating and appraising sociopolitical slogans. *Psychol. Bull.*, **37**, 481 (Abstr.)

Seligman, M. E. P. and Hager, Joanne L. (Editors) (1972). *Biological Boundaries of Learning* (New York: Appleton-Century-Crofts)

Seligman, M. E. P. and Johnston, J. C. (1973). A cognitive theory of avoidance learning. In: *Contemporary Approaches to Conditioning and Learning* (F. J. McGuigan and B. Lumsden, editors) (New York: Wiley)

Skinner, B. F. (1953). *Science and Human Behavior* (New York: Macmillan)

Skinner, B. F. (1971). *Beyond Freedom and Dignity* (New York: Knopf)

Smith, W. I. and Moore, J. W. (1966). *Conditioning and Instrumental Learning. A Program for Self-Instruction* (New York: McGraw-Hill)

Solomon, R. S. and Brush, Elinor S. (1956). Experimentally derived conceptions of anxiety and aversion. In: *Nebraska Symposium on Motivation* (M. R. Jones, editor) (Lincoln: University of Nebraska Press)

Spence, K. W. (1956). *Behaviour Theory and Conditioning* (New Haven: Yale)

Staats, A. W. and Staats, Carolyn K. (1958). Attitudes established by classical conditioning. *J. Abn. Soc. Psychol.*, **57**, 37–40

Staats, A. W. (1972). Language behaviour therapy: a derivative of social behaviourism. *Behavior Ther.*, **3**, 165–192

Westcott, M. R. and Huttenlocher, J. (1961). Cardiac conditioning: the effects and implications of controlled and uncontrolled respiration. *J. Exp. Psychol.*, **61**, 353–359.

Wolpe, J. B. (1936). Effectiveness of token-rewards for chimpanzees. *Comparative Psychol.*, *Monographs*, **12**, No. 60

Wolpe, J. (1961). The systematic desensitisation treatment of neuroses. *J. Nervous Mental Dis.*, **132**, 189–203

Young, P. T. (1961). *Motivation and Emotion* (New York: Wiley)

Chapter 5

MEMORY AND LEARNING

Elaine A. Drewe

Without memory we would have no knowledge of past events and hence be unable to adapt fully to changes in our environment. The record we have of preceding events provides a basis for analysing and interpreting ongoing ones, for seeing relationships between them and for planning appropriate action. At the risk of over-inclusion the study of memory and learning may be regarded as research into how past events are able to affect information processing and the resultant performance.

Studies of learning tend to concentrate on the acquisition of knowledge about events and those of memory on how retention or retrieval of information is affected with time. To the extent that the retention of past information affects the processing of new material the two are inextricably linked. They represent differences in orientation rather than subject matter investigated. The approach taken in this chapter is to consider the rate and nature of acquisition of knowledge and its loss over time as a function of the utilisation of three storage systems, each being defined primarily by how long information is able to be retained. Controversies inevitably arise such as how many systems are needed to account for all the evidence (Melton, 1963), how these are related (Shallice and Warrington, 1970) and what the bases of the differences between them may be (Tulving, 1970; Craik and Lockhart, 1972; Norman, 1973). These, and other issues are considered in later sections, although in the interests of clarity it is beyond the brief of this chapter to discuss them in the detail that they merit.

STORAGE SYSTEMS
Preperceptual memory

If, after being shown something for a fraction of a second, we did not retain an impression of it in a fairly literal fashion for a longer time we would not in most cases be able to adequately understand it. We process information both from the stimulus itself and from the memory we have of it afterwards. It appears that we have large capacity storage systems which are able to retain all that is encountered in a relatively unanalysed form for 1–2 seconds. After this time any information not attended to and processed further is forgotten. A number of such systems, each seemingly modality specific, have been investigated experimentally.

In the visual modality, Sperling (1960, 1963) found that if a 4×3 matrix of letters is shown for 50 ms then a subject (S) will be able to correctly identify and report an average of 4.3 letters. Although S may say that more than this number were 'seen', by the time four letters have been reported, the others have been forgotten. One way to test this is to randomly sample what can be identified immediately after seeing the letters and also after various delays. Sperling did this by asking S to report only one line of the matrix; the line chosen for this test was indicated by prearranged tone signals presented after the letters had been shown. Selection and report of the correct line must therefore be completely based on memory. By randomly sampling the line to be remembered each time, Sperling found that an average of just over three letters/line could be reported indicating that at least nine items altogether (three on each of three lines) were in fact retained. Thus more information is available immediately than is able to be reported, and from this material the selection of that which is specially relevant can be made. Selection may be on the basis of size or colour of items as well as position (von Wright, 1968) so the range of information available for a short period is considerable. Although enforced delay in reporting does not affect the amount recalled (Dick, 1969) delaying the tone guiding selection does, such that after one-third of a second from the offset of the array only six items on average are available and after one second there is no advantage in this guided partial report over a whole report (about four items in each case). Useful retention for this type of processing (naming) must therefore last approximately two seconds if the time taken to report the items is taken into account (Mackworth, 1963a). However there may be sufficient information available for a longer period to allow less complex analysis to be undertaken (Clark, 1969; Dick, 1969).

This 'iconic' sensory memory (Neisser, 1967) seems to be specifically visual. Subjects report 'seeing' the image for longer than the exposure duration (Sperling, 1967). Sensory manipulations such as stimulus duration (Mackworth, 1962, 1963b), stimulus brightness (Neisser, 1967) and brightness of the field following presentation (Sperling, 1960) affect the effective duration of the icon. In addition, a flash of light given shortly after the stimulus presentation prevents (or considerably reduces, Neisser, 1967) continued preperceptual retention. This only occurs however if the flash is to the same eye as that to which the stimulus was presented; flashes to the opposite eye having very little effect. However, such a masking effect is considerable to both eyes if patterns rather than just flashes follow the array (Schiller, 1965; Jacewitz and Lehmann, 1972). Auditory stimuli do not mask visual (Sperling, 1960). Retention in this preperceptual memory system (P.P.M.) therefore seems to take place on at least two levels and specifically within the visual modality.

Auditory retention has also been found to occur at a number of levels, some of which seem to correspond to the preattentive visual processes. Broadbent (1958) has shown that after presenting a series of pairs of digits simultaneously, one to each ear, which digits were correctly reported could be affected by post-stimulus indication of which ear stimuli to recall first. The effect of post-stimulus selection is not, however, so marked as is found on a similar task in the visual modality (Posner, 1967), a finding which may be a result of a longer storage duration for items presented in the auditory modality. A delay time similar to that found for visual material has, however, been found by Triesman (1964). In Triesman's dichotic listening experiment, if the same material was played to both ears but staggered in time and S was instructed to attend to and repeat that to one ear only then the similarity between the 'messages' was only recognised if the material to the attended ear lagged less than $1\frac{1}{2}$ seconds behind that of the unattended one. This was regardless of type of material used. Thus information to which attention is not paid seems able to be retained unanalysed for up to $1\frac{1}{2}$ seconds in this experiment. After this time only analysed material is remembered, for the unattended message could lag up to $4\frac{1}{2}$ seconds behind the attended (i.e. analysed) one and still be recognised. A similar but much shorter duration store has been indicated by Massaro (1970). He found that identification of a 20 ms tone as high or low in pitch was poor when another (masking) tone was presented immediately after it. However, recognition improved as the time between the tones was increased up to 250 ms. A presentation time of 20 ms may thus be insufficient for adequate analysis of the tone and processing must go on, on the basis of an auditory representational store, in the following 250 ms. The masking stimulus confounded the stored information (as is found in the visual modality) thus making further processing difficult.

A non-perceptual retention seems to be implicated in Massaro's study, for although varying the frequency of the masking tone did not alter the amount of blocking (therefore indicating that material specificity is not important), masking was effective to the ear opposite to that hearing the tone to be recognised as well as to the same ear. Stores based on type of information have also been indicated. If, after reading a list of words for recall, a suffix 'zero' is added, performance on the memory task is impaired even though the 'zero' is redundant (Crowder, 1967). Morton, Crowder and Prussin (1969) (see Morton, 1970) have found that the magnitude of this interfering effect depends on the similarity of the masking stimulus 'zero' to the rest of the list. Thus if it is spoken by a different voice or with a different loudness the disruption is less. White noise had no masking effect, although this suffix presented to the same ear as the list was more disrupting than when it was to the opposite ear. Thus, as in the visual modality, retention may be at various levels (peripheral or more central) and for material at different stages of analysis (by sensory qualities or speech/non-speech distinction) although the relationship between these is as yet poorly determined.

In the tactile modality, Bliss *et al.* (1966) have shown that there is more information available immediately after receiving blasts of air to the knuckles than is able to be recalled directly.

The differences between the properties of stimuli in each modality make comparability of these storage processes difficult to determine. For instance, the long retention shown for stimuli presented in the auditory modality (Erikson and Johnson, 1964, suggest a 10 second store) may be due to the fact that little information is needed to make some types of response (e.g. presence or absence of a tone). Processing may be faster or more effective for some types of material so that more information may be gained from similarly protracted storage systems or a longer term storage mechanism may be utilised. Thus, although general characteristics of initial sensory retention can be defined, the limits of these storage processes, how many there are, and the interaction between them, are not clearly able to be discerned.

There has been little study of the pathological breakdown of such storage systems. The research performed indicates that deficits are more likely to be a result of defective processing of information from such systems rather than impaired P.P.M. (Inglis and Sanderson, 1961; Kinsbourne and Warrington, 1962, 1963; Oscar-Berman *et al.*, 1973).

Primary memory

After material has been processed or analysed to some extent it may be retained in a buffer for a short time (usually a matter of seconds) where it is available for immediate use. This information may have come directly from P.P.M. processes or may have been retrieved from a longer term storage system to enable it to be available for immediate use. Unlike preattentive memory input, we have some control over selection of this material and the length of its retention although the limited capacity of the system restricts the amount that can be handled. We use this primary memory (P.M.) storage mechanism when we retain a telephone number whilst dialling, a complex short sentence whilst we comprehend it fully or try to hold numbers

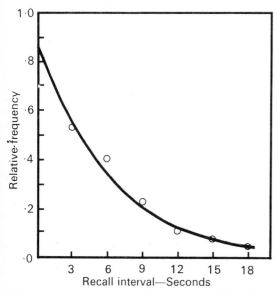

Figure 5.1 Frequency of recall as a function of time since presentation when the retention interval is filled with a distracting task. The height of the curve at the 18-second asymptote can be used to estimate the S.M. component in this task (here it is less than 10%). (From Peterson and Peterson, 1959, by courtesy of *J. Exp. Psychol.*)

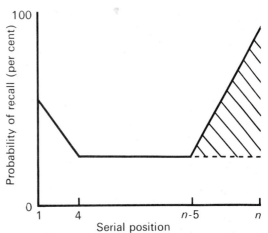

Figure 5.2 Schematic serial position curve for free recall of a list of length n. Immediate recall results are indicated by the solid line. Recall of the items in the last serial positions after 30 seconds delay is represented by the dotted line, recall of items in the preceding positions after this interval remaining the same. The shaded area can be used to estimate P.M. capacity. (From Shallice and Warrington, 1970, by courtesy of *Quart. J. Exp. Psychol.*)

in our heads whilst doing mental arithmetic. It is often called short-term memory but, as information can be held for a considerable time, and as not all retention over short periods involves this system, such a term is confusing (Waugh and Norman, 1965). There are however a number of short-term memory (S.T.M.) *procedures* which have been used to investigate the properties of this P.M. system.

One technique, investigated initially by Peterson and Peterson (1959), is particularly useful in showing the rate of forgetting material in P.M. Peterson and Peterson measured how well a small amount of material (e.g. 3 consonants) is retained by a S for varying lengths of time when a distracting task (e.g. counting backwards in threes) is performed in the interval. The results of such investigations usually follow the pattern shown in Figure 5.1. Thus even with very small amounts of material, if attention is drawn away from it, 90% is forgotten in 15–20 seconds. The remaining 10% is considered to be able to be retained over a longer period as it is processed by a different system—secondary memory (S.M.).

Capacity of the P.M. process, in addition to rate of forgetting, may be investigated by a free recall technique (Glanzer and Cunitz, 1966). If a list of about 20 items is presented one at a time and S is asked to recall as many as possible in any order, then the probability of remembering any item depends on its position in the list (Figure 5.2). The S will typically recall those items from the end of the list first and, no

matter how long the list (Murdock, 1962), will tend to get more of these correct than items presented earlier. This is known as the *recency effect*. Glanzer and Cunitz hypothesise that the short time between presentation and recall gives the last items the advantage of being able to be retained by a P.M. system whereas earlier items, because of the longer delay, must be retained exclusively by S.M. This is supported by a finding that asking S to recall the beginning of the list first attenuates the recency effect (Craik, 1969). Also imposing a delay of 30 seconds before recall eliminates it completely (Figure 5.2) whereas it does not significantly affect the probability of recall of earlier items (Glanzer and Cunitz, 1966; Craik, 1970). This forgetting within half-a-minute is consistent with results obtained from the Peterson task. A limit on the capacity of P.M. is indicated by the fact that regardless of presentation rate, only about the last five items in the list are susceptible to delay.

If instead of recalling the complete list, knowledge is sampled by a request to report only one specific item, then interference from the response itself is minimised and processing capacity can be more accurately estimated. This 'probe' technique has been utilised by Waugh and Norman (1965) who presented an item, which had occurred once before at the end of the list and S was requested to remember which item had followed it on the previous occasion. By varying the speed of presentation and the position in the list of the item to be reported, the effects of both time and number of items between presentation and recall may be assessed. Waugh and Norman found that the speed of presentation of items (1 or 4/second) did not significantly affect recall probabilities whereas the position in the list of the 'probed' item did affect likelihood of recall, such that the probability of a correct response decreased as the number of items between presentation and recall increased. With an interval containing 10 intervening items the recall probability was reduced to almost zero. If an 'intervening item' is taken as either perceiving a stimulus or responding in some way the results on Peterson and free recall tasks may be regarded as similar (Waugh and Norman, 1966). Thus university student subjects may process up to about 10 items in P.M. regardless of how quickly or slowly this takes place.

Digit Span is probably the best known of the S.T.M. tasks and, as in all span tasks, indicates the number of items S can recall immediately in the correct order after one presentation. This number is remarkably constant, averaging about seven (Miller, 1956) although it does vary with intelligence (Wechsler, 1955), nature of material (Miller, 1956), meaningfulness or pronounceability of items (Laughery and Pinkus, 1968) and redundancy (Waugh, 1970). An intelligent person may for instance easily be able to retain a 25-word sentence. The amount of information conveyed may therefore be of less importance than the number of 'chunks' into which the material can be grouped (Miller, 1956). The mechanisms behind this are not fully understood but it obviously implies a fairly complex level of analysis involving the use of information from S.M. before this stage of retention is implemented. Word span may in fact correlate more with other measures of S.M. recall than with that of P.M. and, if the capacity of P.M. is calculated from results of performance on tasks previously described, a limit of about three items recalled is derived (Craik, 1971). This assumes independence of S.M. and P.M. and that for most S.T.M. tasks some information is held by P.M. processes, some by S.M. and some by both, the proportions of each being determined by the nature of the task. How we are able to integrate these processes and to use them effectively together to remember over short periods is, however, unclear.

The finding that pronounceability of letter strings is more important in span tasks than their meaningfulness (Laughery and Pinkus, 1968) reflects another P.M. characteristic. This is because in most cases retention of verbal material is based on an acoustic representation regardless of modality of input or meaning. Conrad (1964) for instance found that the mistakes made in recalling sequences of letters presented visually were similar in nature to those made when identifying letters from a noisy tape, that is between letters that sound alike (e.g. TBV). Similarly lists of acoustically similar words (e.g. can, man, cap, map) are more poorly recalled than those which are comprised of words having similar meanings (e.g.

great, huge, big) or non-alike words (Baddeley, 1966, 1970; Kintsch and Buschke, 1969). There is controversy over the relative importance of acoustic and articulatory similarity (Wickelgren, 1969) although it is likely that the effects of both may be significant (Levy, 1971). This similarity interference is, however, only found if correct order of information needs to be retained, there being no 'acoustic factor' in the P.M. component of free recall tasks (Baddeley, 1968; Craik and Levy, 1970).

There is evidence of parallel S.T.M. processes which are not dependent on acoustic-articulatory coding. Semantic factors may have S.T.M. effects (Schulman, 1971) but this may well be a result of S.M. as well as P.M. being assessed. Visual representation on the other hand does seem to be possible in post-perceptual retention. The shape characteristics of letters can be memorised and used for 1.5 seconds if a visual match only is required and, unlike visual P.P.M. processes, this retention is not affected by visual masking but only by the non-specific interference of adding digits (Posner, 1969). It has also been found that recall of visually presented letters over 25 seconds is not susceptible to auditory similarity interference and that they are recalled better than auditory presented letters when an auditory verbal (repeating) task is used as a distractor (Kroll et al., 1970). Visual coding may be affected, then, when it is advantageous to do so. Similarly deaf people whose acoustic analysing ability is impaired do not show the normal auditory confusional errors (Conrad, 1970) thus indicating a different sort of coding system.

'Non-verbal' memory processes have been less well studied although there is evidence that significant losses of information may occur over short-time periods for some non-easily verbalisable auditory, visual and kinaesthetic information such as tones (Wickelgren, 1968), position of a cross on a line and positioning movements (Posner, 1967). Verbal acoustic processing of this material seems unlikely. However kinaesthetic information appears not to be susceptible to distractions in the same way as is other material (Adams and Dijkstra, 1966; Posner, 1967) and thus may involve a completely different processing system.

The existence of separate, parallel processing systems has been confirmed by analysis of performance of patients with memory disorders. A case with auditory, but little visual, P.M. loss has been described by Shallice and Warrington (1970) and Warrington and Shallice (1969, 1972). This patient (K.F.) had an auditory digit span of 1–2 and a visual of 2–4 items. The recency effect in free recall and probe tasks with auditory presentation was found to be limited to 1–2 items and, although confusions between acoustically similar letters with auditory presentations occurred, those from ordered recall visually presented letter lists tended to be of a visual nature. It seems then that this patient was able to process fewer than the normal number of items in an auditory S.T.M. system and tended not to use acoustic coding on the occasions in which it is typically found. Evidence for an increase in rate of loss of information from this system is less good. Although forgetting of auditory material was shown to be greater than that of visual on a Peterson task the asymptote was lower, implicating poor S.M. The reason for and nature of the auditory impairment is unclear and, as visual memory was also shown to be defective, the degree of independence of different modality systems is not completely established. Although K.F., who had a left supramarginal angular gyrus lesion (Warrington *et al.*, 1971), was tested only with verbal material, Samuels *et al.* (1972) have found that right or left temporal lobe damage may give rise to poor retention of auditory verbal material but not visual verbal or visual 'non-verbal' (geometric patterns) on a Peterson task.

Conversely, visual but not auditory S.T.M. losses have also been described. Patients with left posterior cortical lesions are poor at reporting letters, digits or non-symbolic lines from a 5-item visually presented display (Warrington and Rabin, 1971) and a limitation in simultaneous perception of more than one form has been described in patients with left occipital lesions (Kinsbourne and Warrington, 1962). These impairments were found to be independent of poor auditory digit span and thus seemingly restricted to the visual modality. It is unclear how far these are disorders of processing from visual P.P.M. rather than a limit on visual P.M. retention although these may well be intimately related. However, the right hemisphere has also been implicated in specifically visual processing. The rate of forgetting using a Peterson procedure has been reported to be greater in 'normal' people for visual material presented in the right-half visual field than for that in the left-half field, and this difference is accentuated in patients with right parietal lesions (Samuels *et al.*, 1971a). Again this impaired visual retention is found in the presence of apparently normal auditory retention (Butters *et al.*, 1970; Samuels *et al.*, 1971b). There may therefore be different modality systems, although the type of material used may also determine how it is processed and consequently how it may be disrupted.

Verbal material in the visual modality may be retained better when presented to the right-half field as compared with the left-half field in 'normal' people (Hines *et al.*, 1973) and in the auditory modality better when presented to the right ear as compared with the left ear (Goodglass and Peck, 1972). Retention rather than coding seems to be implied in both cases as the laterality difference was not found with immediate recall (auditory) or shorter processing time (visual). Consistent with these associations of retention of verbal material with left hemisphere function, Butters *et al.* (1970) have shown that forgetting of verbal material in both auditory and visual modalities

on a Peterson task is greater after left frontal and left parietal lesions, although immediate recall may also be impaired. No difference in visual pattern perception or retention was evident. Conversely, recognition of 'non-verbalisable' complex nonsense figures after a 10–20 second delay may be superior after presentation to the left-half field compared with presentations to the right whereas no difference is found at 0–5 second delays (Dee and Fontenot, 1973), and whilst S.T.M. for picture names is impaired with electrical stimulation of the cingulum, pulvinar or ventrothalamic regions on the left side of the brain (Ojemann and Fedio, 1968; Fedio and Ommaya, 1970; Ojemann *et al.*, 1971), right mammillothalamic stimulation impairs S.T.M. for only visual non-verbal material (Ojemann, 1971). Memory over 15–60 seconds, but not matching of nonsense shapes presented tactilely is similarly impaired when the right hand but not the left hand is used in patients with callosal sections (Milner and Taylor, 1972). Corsi (see Milner, 1970, 1971) has shown greater forgetting of a position of a cross on a line in patients with right hippocampal as compared with right non-hippocampal or left hippocampal lesions whereas verbal material was most poorly retained after left hippocampal damage.

Processing and retention of information over a short period may therefore be intimately related to the modality of input and the type of material involved, although some systems may rarely be apparent-being utilised only in cases of pathology of one system or when there is a very restricted form of input or expectation of use. It is not really known how these systems are interrelated and how far processing differences reflect S.M. rather than P.M. If P.M. is more associated with acoustic coding than semantic then the verbal/non-verbal distinction would be unexpected. However, as most of the findings have been from Peterson-type procedures on which amount of forgetting (to a lowered asymptote) rather than rate of forgetting (to a normal asymptote) has been assessed, it may well be S.M. deficits rather than P.M. ones which produce these apparent dissociations.

Secondary memory

We clearly have the ability to retain more than a small number of items of information for longer than a few seconds. A processing and storage system which is separable from P.M. seems to be evident. This secondary memory (S.M.) system, unlike that of P.M. seems not to have a limited capacity, can retain material for a considerable time if not indefinitely and has different types of processing/encoding capabilities.

S.M. is typically measured by assessing retention of supra-span amounts of material over long periods of time. However, as discussed previously, small quantities of information may be processed by S.M. and this may be utilised within a very short period of time. As a measure of this, the asymptote of the forgetting curve derived from the results of a Peterson type procedure and the central part of the curve derived from results of a free recall task are considered to give an estimate of the probability of immediately recalled material being processed by S.M. rather than P.M. (see Figures 5.1 and 5.2). Recall after a filled interval of 20–30 seconds may entirely be a function of S.M.

By comparing the factors which affect specific portions of these curves it is possible to assess the relative importance of different variables for each type of memory process. Thus delaying recall or asking for the early items to be reported first negatively affects only the recency part of the free recall curve (Glanzer and Cunitz, 1966; Craik, 1969). Slow rates of presentation increase recall probabilities for earlier presented parts of a list (Murdock, 1962; Glanzer and Cunitz, 1966) whereas the recency effect is, if anything, accentuated by fast presentation (Craik, 1969; Murdock and Walker, 1969). Slow presentation rate similarly raises the probability of recall at the longer delay times in a Peterson paradigm, but does not alter that at shorter retention intervals (Peterson, 1963). The asymptote of a Peterson curve is also increased by repetition of material, although the P.M. component is not affected (Hellyer, 1962; Peterson, 1963; Waugh and Norman, 1968) and the length of a free recall list affects the S.M. but not the P.M. components of recall (Waugh and Norman, 1968).

In S.M. it is the meaning of the material which primarily determines the efficiency of remembering. Thus, unlike P.M., words that have a similar meaning are recalled less well than non-alike words or words that are acoustically related (Kintsche and Buschke, 1969; Baddeley, 1970) and words that are used often in normal speech are remembered better than infrequently used ones or nonsense syllables (Raymond, 1969). Material that is highly related conceptually (e.g. north-south-east-west) is also beneficial to S.M. recall whilst it does not affect the contribution made by P.M. (Craik and Levy, 1970). Acoustic relationships, e.g. the use of rhymes can improve recall from S.M. however, if these are possible or stressed (Brown and McNeill, 1966; Craik and Levy, 1970; Bower, 1970) or if semantic ones are not possible (Baddeley and Levy, 1971). It is clear that we can remember voices, tunes etc. over a long period, which presumably are acoustically coded, and also faces, scenes, skills etc., which are difficult to process verbally. The mechanisms involved and how they are related to those of long-term verbal memory on the one hand and P.M. processes on the other are little understood, although analyses of further breakdowns of memory processes may help to clarify the situation.

Patients with unilateral temporal lobe lesions in the hemisphere dominant for speech have difficulty in remembering verbal material or information that can easily be described in verbal terms, e.g. delayed recall of passages, paired associate or list learning in both auditory and visual modalities. They are not impaired, however, in learning or retaining over long periods material that is not easily identified verbally, e.g. nonsense figures presented in the visual or tactile modality, faces, melodies or routes through visual or tactile mazes. The reverse seems to be the case for patients with non-dominant temporal lobe damage— they can retain verbal but not non-verbalisable material (Milner, 1967; Milner and Teuber, 1968). Memory systems for these types of material seem therefore to be separable and to some extent independent. Further divisions made on the basis of type of information may also be possible, e.g. although face recognition and maze learning are related negatively to amount of right hippocampal damage, memory for complex designs is not (Milner, 1971). Also, patients who have severe generalised amnesia and are unable to carry out any of the above tasks may be able to learn and retain certain motor skills, e.g. manual tracking tasks, learning to draw whilst only seeing the results in a mirror, playing a particular tune on the piano (Corkin, 1968; Starr and Phillips, 1970). We do not yet know how far these represent retention differences over and above encoding ones or separate retrieval mechanisms.

The validity of the distinction between P.M. and S.M. processes has been questioned on the grounds that similar processes, for example repetitions and spacing of material, affect recall on both S.T.M. and long-term memory (L.T.M.) tasks. If, however, the results of the S.T.M. tasks can reflect the operation of both S.M. and P.M. then the finding of an overlap of important variables is not surprising. The results of analyses of performance of patients with memory deficits have been regarded as evidence for separability of P.M. and S.M. Thus K.F., the patient with a low digit span described by Shallice and Warrington, was apparently unimpaired on L.T.M. tasks such as list or paired associate learning. Moreover on free recall, although the recency effect was attenuated, the rest of the obtained recall curve was found to be normal. The relationship between P.M. and S.M. is less clear from K.F.'s performance on a Peterson task for the asymptote of recall for auditory material was lower than that obtained for visual. The greater short-term loss for auditory material need not therefore be independent of longer term recall and could even be a consequence of it.

On the other hand patients with a severe amnesic (Korsakoff) syndrome may have an S.M. but not P.M. deficit. Whereas learning or recall of short stories, word lists, supra-span digit lists, faces, mazes etc. is very impaired in these patients, understanding of short sentences and span for digits or light positions is normal (Talland, 1965; Drachman and Arbit, 1966; Whitty and Zangwill, 1966; Milner *et al.*, 1968). Also, on a verbal free recall task, Baddeley and Warrington (1970) find that recall of the last items is

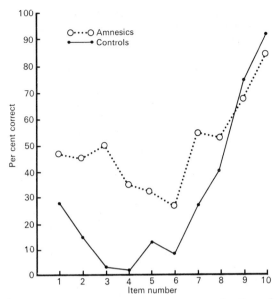

Figure 5.3   Mean percentage correct as a function of order of presentation on a free recall task for amnesic and control subjects with immediate recall. Amnesics are not impaired in recall of the last serial positions but are in the preceding ones. (From Baddeley and Warrington, 1970, by courtesy of *J. Verb. Learn. Verb. Behav.*)

unimpaired in these patients but the rest of the list is poorly reported (Figure 5.3). This indicates that the P.M.–S.M. distinction may be a valid one. However some points still need clarifying. If span tests involve S.M. as well as P.M. processes then Korsakoff patients (as well as those with unilateral temporal lesions) should be impaired on them. On the Peterson task forgetting curve the asymptote level obtained does not always correspond with that expected. Using verbal material it is similar for Korsakoff and control patients although for non-verbal material there is some indication of a lower end point for amnesics (Baddeley and Warrington, 1970; Warrington and Weiskrantz, 1973). On the other hand the suggestion of intact P.M. processes in these patients has not gone uncontested (Cermak *et al.*, 1971; Samuels *et al.*, 1971a; 1971b). These experimenters find that the amount of forgetting over 18 seconds with a Peterson procedure is greater in Korsakoffs than controls using verbal material and simple geometric patterns. Butters *et al.* (1973) claim that the impairment is a verbal one as, except in one condition, no deficits were found for any delays for auditory, visual or tactilely presented non-easily verbalisable material (random shapes or piano notes). Such an S.T.M. deficit, like those found after unilateral temporal lesions, may be reflecting the S.M. component of the Peterson task, but the finding is still difficult to reconcile with both the lack of S.T.M. deficit, e.g. digit span found in these patients

and the profound deficit for non-verbalisable material found in L.T.M. tasks (Milner and Teuber, 1968). The interaction of these processes and consequently the results of a breakdown are thus poorly understood.

CONTROL PROCESSES

Individuals are not passive recipients of information but have considerable control over what material is processed, how it is retained and under what circumstances it is remembered. Although storage processes have been considered in temporal order this does not imply that all must always be used. Preperceptual storage appears essential. Information may thence be processed and retained by P.M. followed by S.M. However it is obvious that not all material reaches S.M. Not so obvious is that P.M. may be bypassed, information entering S.M. directly perhaps only later to be subjected to P.M. processes. We have control to some extent over this.

Coding

Information that is received must be transformed or interpreted so that it is meaningful to the individual. This may be at a very simple level of perceptual analysis or a very complex semantic conceptualisation. Coding may function to reduce the amount of material stored by eliminating irrelevant or redundant information or by providing a way of utilising experience to make both storage and retrieval more efficient. The rate of forgetting may be related to how information is represented in memory (Craik and Lockhart, 1972): sensory coding may be more susceptible to temporal factors than semantic coding, visual more than auditory, verbal more than imaginal. Which type of storage process is utilised and how long material is successfully retained may therefore depend on how it is coded. Type of coding also determines what is retained. If two different patterns are given the same label any variation between these may be forgotten.

Coding takes time. As we have seen the 'read off' from P.P.M. must be rapid for most of the information is only available for a matter of milliseconds. During this time a perceptual analysis must be executed and important information must be extracted and organised, relevance or importance being determined by referral to a longer term storage system. For instance, an important and common method of coding material from sensory memory is by verbal naming or description; recall of a wide range of types of information being proportional to how easily it can be labelled verbally (Glanzer and Clark, 1963). However, the name, its associations and the important constituents of a perception, that must be encountered before the name is given, must be retained by S.M. processes. The complexity of the analysis that has to be made and the availability of the coding device for the individual determines how quickly information can be transformed and thus how much has a chance of being remembered. Mackworth (1963a) has found that the amount of material able to be recalled from a short stimulus exposure is proportional to reading rate and varies with type. For example, rate of recognition is quicker for digits than for letters and quicker for letters than for colours, even though the time it takes to actually report them is the same. It is assumed that the variation's reflect processing time requirements. The length of time needed to complete different levels of analysis (e.g. sensory, semantic) also varies although depth of processing is not always related to speed (as a well-integrated 'rule' may lead to rapid but complex analysis). Posner (1969) has investigated this extensively. He typically presents two stimuli (usually letters) at a time and finds how long it takes for S to make a decision about them and react on the basis of this decision. The level of analysis needed before a decision can be made varies, e.g. 'Are two letters the same?' (AA +); 'Are two letters the same even though they may have a different physical representation?' (Aa +); 'Are they both vowels?' (AE +). Although in each case a stimulus AB would require a 'no' reaction, the time taken to respond to this decision ranged from 450–800 ms. Physical matching is quickest and seems not to require access to a verbal system. The reaction time for decision about letters is the same as that for nonsense forms or line slants, and that for familiar pictures the same as that for unfamiliar ones. Requiring basic perceptual analysis only, physical matching may involve an early and quick processing utilising little longer term memory. Reaction time to name matching requires 70–100 ms longer than that to physical matching and is similar for stimuli in the same modality (e.g. Aa) and in different modalities (e.g. visual A and auditory A). This, and the even slower higher classification matching, must require rapid access and retrieval from S.M. The nature of the analysis may therefore be flexible and be a function of the type of material, the use to which it must be put, and the time available. Although visual retention is possible for verbal material (Posner, 1967; Kroll et al., 1970) acoustic P.M. processing is more common. It is not clear whether this is a result of conversion to an auditory form being quicker or easier than to a visual form (Sperling, 1963; Norman, 1966) or for some reason retention is better for acoustically represented material (Murdock, 1967). Even though S.M. is involved in the simple naming process as well as in higher order categorisation (e.g. meaning) the former is quicker and, for some reason, less resistant to forgetting with time than the latter.

Speed of access to longer term storage systems depends on the hemisphere predominantly involved in processing, retaining or retrieving the relevant information. Thus, when naming can be or is required, recognition of verbal material is faster or more accurate if the material is presented to the right-half field or right ear as opposed to the left-half field or left

ear. The left half field or ear is, however, superior for the perception of non-verbal material such as melodies, pitch, faces or dot patterns (Kimura and Folb, 1968; Milner and Teuber, 1968; White, 1969; Darwin, 1971; McKeever and Gill, 1972; Oscar-Berman et al., 1973). In some cases, however, this laterality effect for verbal material may not be shown or recognition of verbal items may be superior when analysed by the sense organ intimately related to the right hemisphere. Perception by the left ear may be better than that by the right when many vowel sounds, all from the same vocal tract, are presented (Darwin, 1971). Also, when vowel-varied syllables are given in the context of verbal material a right ear superiority is shown, whereas when the same syllables are given in a non-verbal context left ear recognition is better (Spellacy and Blumstein, 1970). As might be predicted from Posner's results, Gibson et al. (1972) found that, when words have to be matched but not named, accuracy with short exposure times is greater for material to the left half field. Interestingly, although able to match correctly with such rapid presentations (40 ms), subjects were unable to *name* the word.

Lesions of the right or left hemisphere also affect perception differently. Thus left hemisphere damage leads to impaired processing of material able to be labelled verbally, such as words or objects, and right damage to impairment for melodies etc. (Milner and Teuber, 1968; Warrington and Rabin, 1970). Right hemisphere lesions also affect the processing of the sensory qualities of verbal material as evidenced by the finding of disruption of perception of consonant–vowel sounds in patients with right pathology (Zurif and Ramier, 1972). Similarly De Renzi et al. (1969) have shown that right hemisphere lesions affect a patient's ability to discriminate and match objects, shapes or faces on the basis of perceptual information whereas conceptual comparisons (e.g. matching a doll with a picture of a different sort of doll) were impaired in patients with left lesions. Although in these studies patients without brain damage have not always been tested and so it is not known if either hemisphere impairs both sets of abilities to some extent, there does seem to be neurological evidence for separate coding processes based on the verbal or sensory qualities of material. Non-verbal coding appears less strongly hemisphere related than verbal (Shankweller, 1966; Dimond et al., 1972; Oscar-Berman et al., 1973). How far this then represents an earlier rather than parallel system is unclear.

Pathology of coding of both verbal and non-verbal material has been implicated for Korsakoff patients as they need an increased processing time, in terms of length of stimulus exposure or length of time before a masking stimulus is given, for both word naming and nonsense figure matching (Oscar-Berman et al., 1973). The impairment found was however greater for the verbal material. Evidence from dichotic listening tasks indicates that elderly people may also have a fairly generalised processing difficulty (Inglis and Sanderson, 1961; Broadbent and Gregory, 1965).

Coding may affect retention as well as speed of processing. As P.M. has a limited capacity and as the 'chunks' may be simple or complex, the more information that can be coded into one chunk the more that can be processed within the limited system. Thus it may be possible to retain seven isolated letters after seeing them once but if these are grouped into words we may easily remember 50. 'Rules' for encoding and decoding may be learned throughout life or specifically for a certain task. In all cases, however, they are retained in S.M. whilst being able to be used rapidly and efficiently. For instance, a morse code expert may recognise a series of dots and dashes very quickly, be able to make a sentence from them and then be capable of turning the sentence back into morse from his knowledge of the system. A novice on the other-hand may be very slow and perhaps miss some of the message because readout is inefficient and the words he does recognise may be wrongly decoded again when he transcribes them back to morse. This type of coding, which reduces the amount to be retained is utilised in S.M. as well as P.M. However, in each case we must retain the rules of encoding and decoding as well as the reduced 'message'. If any of these are forgotten then we shall be unable to reconstruct the original message from that remembered.

Unlike morse or reading, for most material formal or rigorous rules of translation are not available. We reduce the amount to be retained by the selection of important points or summarise the data such that, with the use of less precise systems, we may reconstruct it later. Bartlett (1932) has vividly demonstrated this in serial reproduction experiments in which stories or messages are passed from one person to another or recalled after various delays. Information tended to be extracted and embellished by each person or at each recollection in turn such that the final result often resembled in only minor ways that which was initially presented. Carmichael *et al.* (1932) have shown similar distortions, as a result of coding, for pictorial material. They asked subjects to remember 12 line drawings of the type shown in Figure 5.4 and then to reproduce them from memory. The drawings were named as they were shown thus providing a ready-made code for each item. One group of subjects were provided with one set of names and another group heard a completely different set. A third group were not given names as ready-made codes. When drawn from memory the distorted reproductions in the first two groups tended to look more like the label than the original, each group distorting it in different ways (Figure 5.4). The label had determined how the S had coded the material, how it had been retained and probably also how it was reconstructed. Note that some characteristics of the original were still main-

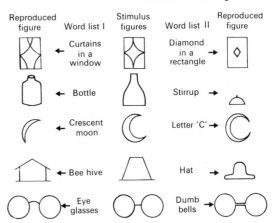

Figure 5.4 Effect of labelling on the perception and reproduction of figures. Centre figure was the stimulus and the outside ones examples of reproductions. (From Carmichael *et al.*, 1932, by courtesy of *J. Exp. Psychol.*)

tained in the reproductions so that not just the code is retained. Physical characteristics as well as meaning may be coded, the weighting of each depending on the material and task requirements.

Reducing the amount to be retained is not the only way of improving efficiency of remembering for it is often beneficial to increase the memory load in a systematic way. This may involve coding it in a variety of forms so that there is multiple representation and associations with many other types of material. If one code is forgotten then this redundancy means that others may provide a way of remembering and, as discussed later, retrieval of information is aided by the provision of a number of access routes. Thus information is filed into an organised structure which has been built up by prior experiences and learning in much the same way as books in a library are grouped together and then labelled and indexed to enable them to be found later. Books may be classified according to author, subject matter, size, date etc. and may be retrieved via knowledge of any of these together with information concerning the indexing systems used. In general, the more organisation that is possible the greater the chance of retention and retrieval. Associating in imagery is a very powerful mnemonic and used a great deal by mnemonists (e.g. Luria, 1969). Thus lengthy lists of words may be remembered if a street scene is imagined and then each item in the list is placed along the street in a strategic place. When recalling, an imaginal 'walk' along the street will enable each word to be remembered in turn and in the correct order. Wallace, Turner and Perkins (in Miller *et al.*, 1960) have found that if subjects who are naive with regard to memory experiments are asked to imagine pairs of objects in an interacting scene, then after one presentation, 95%

of 700 pairs may be successfully recalled. A common verbal elaboration mnemonic utilising organisation is the reciting of the 'Thirty days hath September' rhyme when attempting to recall the number of days in any month. Categorisation by sensory or semantic groupings is a related mnemonic. For instance, Bower *et al.* (1969) have found that a list of 112 words could be learned in 3–4 trials if the subject was able to organise the words into a hierarchical scheme such that recall of the highest code (e.g. minerals) would facilitate recall of others (e.g. stones, metals) which in turn would provide a prompt for even lower categories (e.g. gold, silver). Material including a possible structure of which S has no knowledge does not help; the code has to be actively utilised. On the other hand, organisation by imaginal or other means without attempts to memorise aids recall as much as intention to remember and more than intention without organisation (Mandler, 1967; Bower, 1972).

How material is organised and retained and consequently what is retained, is therefore flexible. If time is short, then sensory coding may be the only type possible, whereas over longer periods more complex organisation may be implemented (Baddeley, 1970). Some types of information encourage certain coding principles: rules or methods of organising principles may already be in our repertoire of knowledge (e.g. reading, speaking) or are easily adapted (e.g. easily imagined words). The use to which material is to be put often enables some specific sorts of coding (e.g. by shape or by the first letters of words) or a particular organisation may be suggested by how input is arranged (e.g. similar sounding words are grouped together). Set or expectation also affects how an item is retained. For instance, Restle (1970) demonstrated that, if it was expected that words would have to be retained only for a short interval (12 seconds) and subjects were than tested over a longer period (60 seconds), words were recalled less often than if a longer retention period had been led to be expected. Perhaps reflecting the same factor, Sperling and Speelman (1970) found that some subjects reported actively organising letters in lists, when these had to be retained, whilst others just attempted to rehearse them. The latter made acoustic confusional mistakes whereas the former did not. Thus the same material can be coded in different ways involving different systems and hence different degrees of retention.

The ability of patients with memory deficits to develop and use associations has recently been extensively investigated. Although patients with temporal lobe lesions are able to recall more words if they are semantically associated than if there is no association in a free recall task, there is no beneficial association effect on serial recall (Weingartner, 1968). Weingartner suggests that unilateral temporal lesions of either hemisphere may impair the ability to organise and thus retain. Patients with left temporal lesions are however much slower than those with right lesions in finding associations between words, although doing so greatly improves later learning of the words (Blakemore, 1969). Thus it seems that organisation or association may be a difficult procedure for these patients, although it is able to be utilised in the retention–retrieval process.

Some associative impairment has also been found in Korsakoff patients. Although they are able to use acoustic and, to a lesser extent, semantic similarity groupings to improve word learning, any imaginal associations fail to act as a mnemonic (Warrington and Weiskrantz, 1971; Baddeley and Warrington, 1973). Cermak *et al.* (1973) similarly find that, compared to alcoholics, Korsakoffs are impaired in their ability to use semantic but not acoustic prompts and that they make more homonym and associative errors but not more synonym errors in recall. Attempts to use semantic coding to remember short lists of words hindered recall of Korsakoffs although it aided that of alcoholics. It seems that Korsakoffs may be better able to use sensory coding than semantic. When, in S.T.M. tasks, acoustic coding is adequate they show little or no task impairment but when semantic coding is required, primarily in L.T.M. tasks, they show a considerable deficit, with degree of difficulty depending on type of coding utilised.

Breakdown of coding processes of a different type has been investigated by Corsi (see Milner, 1971) who found that lesions of the frontal lobes disrupt ability to discriminate events by recency of occurrence. Unlike those with temporal lobe lesions, these patients are not impaired if required to say whether or not they have seen material previously, but are impaired if they are presented with two items and have to decide which they have seen most recently. Time codes appear to be material-related, for left frontal lesions disrupt the ability to discriminate relative recency of verbal material (words) and right frontal lesions disrupt that of non-verbal (designs).

Attention—rehearsal

It has been suggested that sensory memory is preattentive but that attention is crucial in determining which information is selected for retention. Continued attention or rehearsal may also affect the amount and length of storage. Rehearsal is generally regarded as the recycling or maintenance of information in a system which is limited in capacity. Subjectively, it seems to be mostly verbal in nature and in the form of covert speech. However its seeming effectiveness in enhancing retention may not just be a function of verbal repetition, for Glanzer and Meinzer (1967) have found that subjects who were required to repeat items aloud retained less than those who were allowed a similar period for silent rehearsal. Covert rehearsal is, however, difficult to study for it is possible that S is not just repeating material in the delay period but may be actively recoding it into a different form. It seems likely that non-verbal rehearsal also occurs, perhaps in the form of motor movements or programs (Norman, 1973) or regeneration of activity in the perceptual system (Posner, 1967; Kroll *et al.*, 1970). Rehearsal is generally thought to be prevented by requiring performance of another non-specific task which would involve a limited capacity system, e.g. adding digits, but if rehearsal is visual (Kroll *et al.*, 1970) or non-verbal such as remembering tones (Deutsch, 1970) or involves kinaesthetic information (Posner, 1967) then this may not be effective.

The opportunity to rehearse seems to lead to maintenance of items which would otherwise be lost in a P.M. system (Brown, 1958). An amnesic patient (H.M.) described by Milner (1970) was able to remember a three-figure number for 15 minutes by maintaining his attention on it continuously. When distracted it was forgotten. If rehearsal is intimately involved with P.M. systems then the capacity of a system should limit the number of items able to be rehearsed. Why then we seem to be able to rehearse seven items is unclear. Perhaps S.M. or P.P.M. systems are also involved.

Allowing time to rehearse also seems to increase the likelihood of S.M. storage. Thus, number of repetitions affects the asymptote of a Peterson curve (Hellyer, 1962) and repetitions or increased spacing between items (enabling rehearsal) increases recall probabilities for the beginning and middle positions of a free recall but not for those at the end (Glanzer and Cunitz, 1966) The fact that there is greater recall for items at the beginning of a list compared with those in the middle has been attributed to easier rehearsal of earlier items and, if rehearsal is not possible, this 'primacy' effect does not occur (Bernbach, 1967). Expectations are important in producing the primacy effect. Crowder (1969) has found that if S expects a nine-word list the primacy effect is evident (possibly because S thinks it is worth rehearsing) whereas if he expects a much longer list it does not. Again, the distinction between coding and repetition is unclear, for rote rehearsal seems to make memories susceptible to acoustic confusions (and therefore probably only maintaining information in P.M.) whereas further recoding does not (Sperling and Speelman, 1970). Also unlike organisation, repetition without intention to learn does not enhance retention (Miller *et al.*, 1960). It seems likely therefore that more than overt repetition is necessary to enable information to be held for a longer period of time.

It is clear that S has choice in the processing of information and the mechanisms used will depend on what information S considers important, whether he thinks it worth trying to retain and for how long he thinks he will be required to hold it.

FORGETTING
Not only is information transformed but it is also lost. This is a result of the effects of a number of interacting factors.

The passage of time
Generally the longer the period of retention needed the more we forget. Why this happens has been a major source of controversy. With time alone the memory 'trace' could become less effective or decay and this seems to be particularly important in P.P.M. Even if nothing else happens in the interval, within about two seconds the record of the information in P.P.M. is lost and, unless very simple information is needed, the impression is too weak for read-off to take place. Similarly in P.M., Brown (1958) concluded that, as material is forgotten over a few seconds regardless of the sort of task carried out in the interval (providing it stops S rehearsing), the trace decays passively. The loss of the recency effect over 30 seconds on a free recall task could also reflect this.

However it may not be time itself that is important but what happens during this interval. Even in P.P.M. backward masking effects do decrease the time for which the information is available. In P.M. however interference may be the major if not exclusive cause of forgetting. Thus Waugh and Norman (1965) have shown that it is the number of items between presentation and recall that determines forgetting and not the rate of presentation (i.e. the length of time held). Glanzer and Cunitz (1966) likewise find that speed of presentation has no significant effect on the number of items in the recency part of a free recall curve. Delay on its own therefore may have little or no effect. As Waugh and Norman found that forgetting was proportional to number of intervening items over a wide range of tasks, they suggest that there is a system of limited capacity and we forget because new items are continually displacing old, which are then lost. Rehearsal maintains the same items in the processing system thus blocking the entry of other information and preventing forgetting. In free recall verbal tasks, number of intervening items between presentation and recall also seems to be more important in determining forgetting than either the difficulty of this distracting material or its similarity to that which is to be retained (Glanzer *et al.*, 1969). Acoustic similarity may, however, negatively affect order information although not item information and, in some tasks utilising non-verbalisable material, interference seems to be either less important or of a very specific nature (Posner, 1967; Deutsch, 1970). Why these should differ is not as yet understood.

Interference between items to be remembered and other material encountered either before (proactive inhibition) or after (retroactive inhibition) learning them has also generated much attention in the analysis of forgetting from S.M. For instance Jenkins and

Dallenbach (1924) found that less forgetting of verbal information occurs during sleep than occurs if subjects are awake during a retention interval. Sleeping, it was assumed, reduced the amount of material that might potentially interfere retroactively. Underwood (1957) showed that list learning deteriorates with 'practice'— a typical proactive interference effect. These types of interference may be demonstrated on both L.T.M. and S.T.M. tasks (Melton, 1963), a finding that has been regarded as mitigating against the S.M.–P.M. dichotomy. This view neglects the possibility of an S.M. component in S.T.M. tasks.

In general, and unlike that found for P,M., for verbalisable material in S.M. semantic similarity of the interfering items to the learned ones is important—the greater the similarity the more likely it is that the extraneous events will intrude in the recall process (Osgood, 1949). If we are trying to remember events which are similar to ones that have occurred in the past then, unless the old irrelevant memories are suppressed or extinguished (Barnes and Underwood, 1959) or unless we can learn to successfully discriminate the two occasions and which material is appropriate to each, then attempting to recall one source of memories will bring both to mind with a consequent confusion.

Interference does therefore seem to be important in the forgetting process, although how far it is a cause of forgetting rather than a result of it (a less well-defined trace leading to similar material being confused) is still unclear. Also, interference produced in the experimental setting cannot account for the total amount of material lost. For instance, in the Jenkins and Dallenbach study the sleepers also forgot and poorer recall with time in a Peterson procedure is found on the *first* set of items given (Baddeley and Scott, 1971). This may be due to an exclusively time-related decay or to sources of interference that have not been controlled in the experiment (e.g. noises in the room, what happened to subjects whilst they were trying to get to sleep).

Loss of information from P.P.M. or P.M. may not however necessarily mean 'forgetting'. As we have seen, material lost from P.P.M., if it has been attended to, can be retained in a longer term storage system. Similarly, S.M. processes may make available information lost from P.M. and P.M. may process material stored permanently by S.M. if it is needed for current utilisation. Loss from one may not then affect loss from the other (Posner, 1967).

Pathological loss of material from memory, as opposed to poor acquisition, is difficult to study. The impaired recall with shorter processing times found in Korsakoff patients by Oscar-Berman *et al.* (1973) could reflect a more rapid decay of the icon but, as increase in time available improved recall, the deficit is more likely to be a coding difficulty. Similarly, faster forgetting of material in P.M. has not convincingly

been demonstrated in patients with memory disorders. The patient described by Warrington and Shallice (1969, 1972) was shown to have a low capacity auditory verbal P.M. system and increased forgetting of a small number of items over a short period. It has not been shown however that there was faster decay for similar amounts of material and overall loss, i.e. the same amount of loss but at a faster rate. In fact slow presentation of items in span tests led to an improvement in this patient's recall.

Figure 5.5   Example of incomplete word stimuli in descending order of presentation. (From Weiskrantz and Warrington, 1970, by courtesy of *Neuropsychologia*)

Comparison of rate of forgetting in S.M. across groups has been confounded by the difficulty of equating initial levels of learning, for amount of loss may well vary with degree of learning. Fortunately, there are some tasks which Korsakoff patients are able to learn (see Warrington and Weiskrantz, 1963, for review). One such task involves learning to accurately perceive incomplete words or pictures such as those shown in Figure 5.5. Fragmented words (or pictures) are shown initially in the most incomplete form and the patient is required to recognise them by naming. Failing this the words are again shown but in a more complete form and this continues until the patient manages to recognise a complete set of words. Unlike that found in normal list learning paradigms, Korsakoffs are, over a number of trials, able to learn these words until they may finally recognise the most incomplete version of each. The ability to learn such tasks enables similar initial levels of performance to be obtained for Korsakoffs and controls and thus forgetting may be validly compared. Weiskrantz and Warrington (1970) showed that Korsakoffs forget more over 1–72 hours than patients without memory deficits although they do retain some information, as evidenced by a reduced number of trials to relearn as compared with initial learning.

A heightened susceptibility to interference has been indicated in Korsakoffs by Cermak and Butters (1972). They found that in conditions which might be expected to increase interference effects on a Peterson task, that is a task utilising similar material given beforehand and short inter-trial intervals between tasks, Korsakoffs showed a greater relative decrement in retention than did alcoholic controls. Also the intrusion of previously learned items (proactive inhibition) seems to be a feature of recall in Korsakoff patients (Warrington and Weiskrantz, 1968; Starr and Phillips, 1970). Weiskrantz and Warrington (1970) suggest that the reason why fragmented material procedures, or alternatively giving the first letters of words as prompts, aids recall in Korsakoffs is due to the restriction of the number of interfering intrusions that are possible. In support of this, the number of words that can be formed from the initial letters presented is proportional to scores on a first letters prompt task for both Korsakoffs and controls. Also, nonsense trigrams, which are not so specifically defined by a 'prompt', are poorly learned by amnesics (Warrington and Weiskrantz, 1973).

Selection

When there is too much information to be retained selection must occur. Information not so chosen is forgotten. Subjects select crucial material from P.P.M., that which is most important to process in the limited capacity of P.M., what to maintain attention to or rehearse, and how and what to code. These involve decisions about which information to forget as well as which to retain. Semantic coding implies likely forgetting of the syntactical structure of sentences; emphasis on order of events affects recall of item information detrimentally. Selection of a coding procedure that is inefficient or fails to be precise enough with the passage of time or intervening events means that less can be encoded and thus more forgotten.

Selection and attention are active processes. Thus not all that is presented will be processed any further than P.P.M. What is important to one person will not be to another, what is relevant in one state of mind will not be in another. Thus memory for particular events will depend on the motivation or expectation of the subject at the time, how much material he is willing or able to process and what information will be retained. Biases occur which may reflect previous learning, expectation of the situation or subjects estimated probability of certain events occurring (Broadbent, 1969, 1970). Any situation which affects these variables will alter how much is remembered and what is forgotten.

Retrieval

In any large scale storage system there is a problem of retrieval of information. If access to material is required quickly then systematic search through the complete contents is not feasible. Instead there must be access routes and an organisation on which search strategies can be based. Retrieval is therefore intimately tied to input of information—how material is coded, organised and how well association or coding cues are retained. 'Forgetting' in the sense of not recalling material at the appropriate time may not be due to 'loss' of the information. It may be an inability to retrieve it as the indexing system guiding search is lost or inefficient or because material has been classified in an inappropriate way so that the normal cues for retrieval are not effective (Tulving, 1968, 1970). Thus a library filing system may not be organised in the way that is required for a particular need, it may be totally disorganised, cards being misplaced or lost so that books cannot be found, or books could be put into the wrong stack so that even an efficient indexing system fails to lead us to them. In all cases books are in the library but cannot be found. Similar inability to 'find' information in memory, although it is retained (as evidenced by later retrieval), has been shown. The 'tip of the tongue' condition (Brown and McNeill, 1966), in which we know we have a knowledge of a fact or name but cannot think of it at the moment, is typical. We may know some things about the word— the number of letters, word shape, the sound or semantic content but these may be too vague or too few to retrieve the word at the right time. In general the more associations material has when retained, i.e. the more links it has with other stored information, the greater the chance of retrieving it. If some retrieval cues are lost then others may be used, and more contextual 'prompts' will be effective in recall.

Fast recognition of material, for example of a letter or picture, indicates that information must be indexed in terms of sensory qualities as well as semantic, for knowledge of meaning can only come from an organisation of the perceptual properties. Tulving (1970), in fact, has argued that the difference between P.M. and S.M. is in the type of retrieval cues used and not from where information is retrieved. Circumstances determine the effectiveness of different types of cue and he postulates that semantic ones are available for longer than sensory. There are a multitude of problems in viewing memory in terms of retrieval systems (Norman, 1973), e.g. how we retain the retrieval cues or associations which must, if they are to be effective, be more easily recalled than the material itself; how we select the right answer from the large number of possibles associated with each cue, how we recognise an answer as correct. These must be solved if we are to have a full understanding of this complex system.

Retrieval difficulties have provided a focus for the analysis of memory defects. The forgetting of events preceding a trauma (retrograde amnesia) may well be due to such impairments. Firstly, we must assume that storage took place at the time of the event and secondly, this amnesia is to some extent reversible. Thus patients, when recovering from injury, remember things not recalled in the initial post-trauma period. This must mean information was retained but is not, for some reason, accessible. Retrograde amnesia may occur after injection of sodium amytal into a carotid artery unilaterally (Milner, 1966) but this is reversible, unlike forgetting of events occurring after the injection (anterograde amnesia). Bickford *et al.* (1958) have likewise shown that stimulation of the medial temporal areas of the brain causes a reversible retrograde amnesia, the duration of which (few minutes–weeks) and the rate of recovery (10–120 min) being proportional to the length of stimulation (2–10 seconds).

This greater difficulty of access to information occurring in close temporal proximity to the trauma has been a common finding in clinical practice. However it has also been disputed. Warrington and Silberstein (1970), Warrington and Sanders (1971) and Sanders and Warrington (1971), using an information questionnaire for public events happening over 40 years, find that older people and Korsakoff patients are not more impaired in recalling recent events than they are more remote ones. They conclude that all memories are equally unavailable and that the forgetting of pretrauma and post-trauma events may have a similar explanation. A retrieval deficit is postulated by Warrington and Weiskrantz (1970) to be the basis of anterograde amnesia as well as retrograde because (a) as intrusion of previously learned material is a feature of Korsakoff learning, some information must be retained but just produced at the wrong time, and (b) the amount recalled depends on how memory is assessed. Thus Warrington and Weiskrantz (1970) found that high retention scores over a one-minute interval were only obtained if partial information techniques (fragmented words or initial letters) were used, no matter whether original learning was by a partial information technique or by presenting a list of

words in the usual way. Straight recall of words was poor however after rote learning and after partial information learning. If an optimal technique is used some retention can therefore be shown. Warrington and Weiskrantz postulate an inability to suppress or eliminate retained but inappropriate information which thus interferes. Partial information techniques would then aid retrieval by reducing the number of possible wrong alternatives. Motor-skill retention, also found to be preserved in these patients, may have similar characteristics for it seems that this type of material is less affected by the usual sort of interference tasks than are other types of information. The place and nature of the breakdown in the organisation–search–recognition procedure is yet to be determined but it is clear that it can at least be separated from one of storage.

CONCLUSIONS

Memory is thus a complex process which is the culmination of many interacting systems. The nature of each system and how they interact are as yet little understood, although analyses of different types of breakdown have furthered our knowledge considerably. These have been considered from a psychological viewpoint only, for although there is a considerable body of knowledge on the physiological basis of memory this is as yet poorly integrated with the behavioural aspects of normal and abnormal processes. The study of memory in humans has been concentrated in the main on verbal learning and retention. This is partly a function of ease of experimentation and partly due to the importance of language for human memory and learning processes. However, it is clear that this is very restricting. Even though perception, skill learning and even language comprehension and expression are intimately related to retention they are rarely integrated into models of memory and learning. Perhaps with further analytic studies of the psychological aspects of agnosia, apraxia and aphasia, together with the positive as well as negative attributes of 'amnesics' of all types, this will be remedied.

References

Adams, J. A. and Dijkstra, S. (1966). Short-term memory for motor responses. *J. Exp. Psychol.*, **71**, 314–318

Baddeley, A. D. (1966). Short-term memory for word sequences as a function of acoustic, semantic and formal similarity. *Quart. J. Exp. Psychol.*, **18**, 362–365

Baddeley, A. D. (1968). How does acoustic similarity influence short-term memory? *Quart. J. Exp. Psychol.*, **20**, 249–264

Baddeley, A. D. (1970). Effects of acoustic and semantic similarity on short-term paired associate learning. *Brit. J. Psychol.*, **61**, 335–342

Baddeley, A. D. and Warrington, E. K. (1970). Amnesia and

the distinction between long- and short-term memory. *J. Verb. Learn. Verb. Behav.*, **9**, 176–189

Baddeley, A. D. and Levy, B. A. (1971). Semantic coding and short-term memory. *J. Exp. Psychol.*, **89**, 132–136

Baddeley, A. D. and Scott, D. (1971). Word frequency and the unit sequence interference hypothesis in short-term memory. *J. Verb. Learn. Verb. Behav.*, **10**, 35–40

Baddeley, A. D. and Warrington, E. K. (1973). Memory coding and amnesia. *Neuropsychologia*, **11**, 159–166

Barnes, J. M. and Underwood, B. J. (1959). 'Fate' of first list associations in transfer theory. *J. Exp. Psychol.*, **58**, 97–105

Bartlett, F. C. (1932). *Remembering: A Study in Experimental and Social Psychology* (London: Cambridge Univ. Press)

Bernbach, H. A. (1967). The effect of labels on short-term memory for colors with nursery school children. *Psychonomic Sci.*, 7, 149–150

Bickford, R. G., Mulder, D. W., Dodge, H. W., Svien, H. J. and Rome, H. P. (1958). Changes in memory function produced by electrical stimulation of the temporal lobe in man. *Res. Pub. Ass. Res. Nerv. Ment. Dis.*, 36, 227–243

Blakemore, C. B. (1969). Psychological effects of temporal lobe lesions in man. In: *Current Problems in Neuropsychiatry* (R. N. Herrington, editor) (Brit. J. Psychiat. Spec. Pub. No. 4)

Bliss, J. C., Crane, H. D., Mansfield, P. K. and Townsend, J. T. (1966). Information available in brief tactile presentations. *Perception Psychophys.*, 1, 273–283

Bower, G. H., Clark, M. C., Lesgold, A. M. and Winzen, Z. D. (1969). Hierarchical retrieval schemes in recall of categorised word lists. *J. Verb. Learn. Verb. Behav.*, 8, 323–343

Bower, G. H. (1970). Organisational factors in memory. *Cognitive Psychol.*, 1, 18–46

Bower, G. H. (1972). Mental imagery and associative learning. In: *Cognition in Learning and Memory* (L. W. Gregg, editor) (Toronto: Wiley)

Broadbent, D. E. (1958). *Perception and Communication* (New York: Pergamon Press)

Broadbent, D. E. and Gregory, M. (1965). Some confirmatory results on age differences in memory for simultaneous stimulation. *Brit. J. Psychol.*, 56, 77–80

Broadbent, D. E. (1969). Communication models for memory. In: *The Pathology of Memory* (G. A. Talland and N. C. Waugh, editors) (New York: Academic Press)

Broadbent, D. E. (1970). Recent analyses of short-term memory. In: *Biology of Memory* (K. H. Pribram and D. E. Broadbent, editors) (New York: Academic Press)

Brown, J. (1958). Some tests of the decay theory of immediate memory. *Quart. J. Exp. Psychol.*, 10, 12–21

Brown, R. and McNeill, D. (1966). The 'tip of the tongue' phenomenon. *J. Verb. Learn. Verb. Behav.*, 5, 325–337

Butters, N., Samuels, I., Goodglass, H. and Brody, B. (1970). Short-term visual and auditory memory disorders after parietal and frontal lobe damage. *Cortex*, 6, 440–459

Butters, N., Lewis, R., Cermak, L. S. and Goodglass, H. (1973). Material specific memory deficits in alcoholic Korsakoff patients. *Neuropsychologia*, 11, 291–299

Carmichael, L., Hogan, H. P. and Walter, A. A. (1932). An experimental study of the effect of language or the reproduction of visually preceived form. *J. Exp. Psychol.*, 15, 73–86

Cermak, L. S., Butters, N. and Goodglass, H. (1971). The extent of memory loss in Korsakoff patients. *Neuropsychologia*, 9, 307–315

Cermak, L. S. and Butters, N. (1972). The role of interference and encoding in the short-term memory deficits of Korsakoff patients. *Neuropsychologia*, 10, 89–95

Cermak, L. S., Butters, N. and Gerrein, J. (1973). The extent of the verbal encoding ability of Korsakoff patients. *Neuropsychologia*, 11, 85–94

Clark, S. E. (1969). Retrieval of color information from preperceptual memory. *J. Exp. Psychol.*, 82, 263–266

Conrad, R. (1964). Acoustic confusions in immediate memory. *Brit. J. Psych.*, 55, 75–84

Conrad, R. (1970). Short-term memory processes in the deaf. *Brit. J. Psychol.*, 61, 179–195

Corkin, S. (1968). Acquisition of motor skill after bilateral medial temporal-lobe excision. *Neuropsychologia*, 6, 255–265

Craik, F. I. M. (1969). Modality effects in short-term storage. *J. Verb. Learn. Verb. Behav.*, 8, 658–664

Craik, F. I. M. (1970). The fate of primary memory items in free recall. *J. Verb. Learn. Verb. Behav.*, 9, 143–148

Craik, F. I. M. and Levy, B. A. (1970). Semantic and acoustic information in primary memory. *J. Exp. Psychol.*, 86, 77–82

Craik, F. I. M. (1971). Primary memory. *Brit. Med. Bull.*, 27, 232–236

Craik, F. I. M. and Lockhart, R. S. (1972). Levels of processing: a framework for memory research. *J. Verb. Learn. Verb. Behav.*, 11, 671–684

Crowder, R. G. (1967). Prefix effects in immediate memory. *Canad. J. Psychol.*, 21, 450–461

Crowder, R. G. (1969). Behaviour strategies in immediate memory. *J. Verb. Learn. Verb. Behav.*, 8, 524–528

Dale, H. C. A. and McGlaughlin, A. (1971). Evidence of acoustic coding in long-term memory. *Quart. J. Exp. Psychol.*, 23, 1–7

Darwin, C. J. (1971). Ear differences in the recall of fricatives and vowels. *Quart. J. Exp. Psychol.*, 23, 46–62

De Renzi, E., Scotti, G. and Spinnler, H. (1969). Perceptual and associative disorders of visual recognition. *Neurology*, 19, 634–642

Dee, H. L. and Fontenot, D. J. (1973). Cerebral dominance and lateral differences in perception and memory. *Neuropsychologia*, 11, 167–173

Deutsch, D. (1970). Tones and numbers: specificity of interference in immediate memory. *Science*, 168, 1604–1605

Dick, A. O. (1969). Relations between sensory register and short-term storage in tachistoscopic recognition. *J. Exp. Psychol.*, 82, 279–284

Dimond, S. J., Gibson, A. R. and Gazzaniga, M. S. (1972). Cross field with field integration of visual information. *Neuropsychologia*, 10, 379–381

Drachman, D. A. and Arbit, J. (1966). Memory and the hippocampal complex. *Arch. Neurol.*, 15, 52–61

Erikson, C. W. and Johnson, H. J. (1964). Storage and delay characteristics of non-attended auditory stimuli. *J. Exp. Psychol.*, 68, 28–36

Fedio, P. and Ommaya, A. (1970). Bilateral cingulum lesions and stimulation in man with lateralized impairment in short-term verbal memory. *Exp. Neurol.*, 29, 84–91

Gibson, A. R., Dimond, S. J. and Gazzaniga, M. S. (1972). Left field superiority for word matching. *Neuropsychologia*, 10, 463–466

Glanzer, M. and Clark, W. H. (1963). The verbal loop hypothesis: binary numbers. *J. Verb. Learn. Verb. Behav.*, 2, 301–309

Glanzer, M. and Cunitz, A. R. (1966). Two storage mechanisms in free recall. *J. Verb. Learn. Verb. Behav.*, 5, 351–360

Glanzer, M. and Meinzer, A. (1967). The effects of intralist activity on free recall. *J. Verb. Learn. Verb. Behav.*, 6, 928–935

Glanzer, M., Giantusos, R. and Dubin, S. (1969). The removal of items from short-term storage. *J. Verb. Learn. Verb. Behav.*, 8, 435–447

Goodglass, H. and Peck, E. A. (1972). Dichotic ear order

effects in Korsakoff and normal subjects. *Neuropsychologia*, **10**, 211–217

Hellyer, S. (1962). Frequency of stimulus presentation and short-term decrements in recall. *J. Exp. Psychol.*, **64**, 650

Hines, D., Satz, P. and Clementino, T. (1973). Perceptual and memory components of the superior recall of letters from the right visual half fields. *Neuropsychologia*, **11**, 175–180

Inglis, J. and Sanderson, R. E. (1961). Successive responses to simultaneous stimulation in elderly patients with memory disorder. *J. Abn. Soc. Psychol.*, **62**, 709–712

Jacewitz, M. M. and Lehmann, D. (1972). Iconic memory, dichoptic interference and short-term consolidation. *Neuropsychologia*, **10**, 193–198

Jenkins, J. G. and Dallenbach, K. M. (1924). Obliviscence during sleep and waking. *Amer. J. Psychol.*, **35**, 605–612

Kimura, D. and Folb, S. (1968). Neural processing of backwards speech sounds. *Science*, **161**, 395–396

Kinsbourne, M. and Warrington, E. K. (1962). A disorder of simultaneous form perception. *Brain*, **85**, 461–486

Kinsbourne, M. and Warrington, E. K. (1963). A study of visual perception. *J. Neurol. Neurosurg. Psychiat.*, **26**, 468–475

Kintsch, W. and Buschke, H. (1969). Homophones and synonyms in short-term memory. *J. Exp. Psychol.*, **80**, 403–407

Kroll, N. E., Parks, T., Parkinson, S. R., Bieber, S. L. and Johnson, A. L. (1970). Short-term memory while shadowing: recall of visually and of aurally presented letters. *J. Exp. Psychol.*, **85**, 220–224

Laughery, K. R. and Pinkus, A. L. (1968). Recoding and presentation rate in short-term memory. *J. Exp. Psychol.*, **76**, 636–641

Levy, B. A. (1971). Role of articulation in auditory and visual short-term memory. *J. Verb. Learn. Verb. Behav.*, **10**, 123–132

Luria, A. R. (1969). *The Mind of a Mnemonist* (London: Jonathan Cape)

McKeever, N. F. and Gill, K. M. (1972). Visual half-field differences in masking effects for sequential letter stimuli in the right and left handed. *Neuropsychologia*, **10**, 111–117

Mackworth, J. F. (1962). The visual image and the memory trace. *Canad. J. Psychol.*, **16**, 55–59

Mackworth, J. F. (1963a). The duration of the visual image. *Canad. J. Psychol.*, **17**, 62–81

Mackworth, J. F. (1963b). The relation between the visual image and post-perceptual immediate memory. *J. Verb. Learn. Verb. Behav.*, **2**, 75–85

Mandler, G. (1967), Organisation and Memory. In: *The Psychology of Learning and Motivation: Advances in Research and Theory*, **Vol. I** (K. W. Spence and J. T. Spence, editors) (New York: Academic Press)

Massoro, D. W. (1970) Preperceptual auditory images. *J. Exp. Psychol.*, **85**, 411–417

Melton, A. W. (1963). Implications of short-term memory for a general theory of memory. *J. Verb. Learn. Verb. Behav.*, **2**, 1–21

Miller, G. A. (1956). The magical number seven, plus or minus two: some limits on our capacity for processing information. *Psychol. Rev.*, **63**, 81–97

Miller, G. A., Galanter, E. and Pribram, K. H. (1960). *Plans and the Structure of Behaviour* (New York: Henry Holt)

Milner, B. (1966). Amnesia following operation on the temporal lobes. In: *Amnesia* (C. W. M. Whitty and O. L. Zangwill, editors) (London: Butterworths)

Milner, B. (1967). Brain Mechanisms suggested by studies of temporal lobes. In: *Brain Mechanisms underlying Speech and Language* (F. L. Darley, editor) (New York: Grune and Stratton)

Milner, B., Corkin, S. and Teuber, H. L. (1968). Further analysis of the hippocampal amnesic syndrome: 14-year follow-up study of H.M. *Neuropsychologia*, **6**, 215–234

Milner, B. and Teuber, H. L. (1968). Alteration of perception and memory in man: reflections on methods. In: *Analysis of Behavioral Change* (L. Weiskrantz, editor) (New York: Harper and Row)

Milner, B. (1970). Memory and the medial temporal regions of the brain. In: *Biology of Memory* (K. H. Pribram and D. E. Broadbent, editors) (New York: Academic Press)

Milner, B. (1971). Interhemispheric differences and psychological processes. *Brit. Med. Bull.*, **27**, 272–277

Milner, B. and Taylor, L. (1972). Right hemisphere superiority in tactile pattern recognition after cerebral commissurotomy: evidence for non-verbal memory. *Neuropsychologia*, **10**, 1–15

Morton, J. (1970). A functional model for memory. In: *Models of Human Memory* (D. A. Norman, editor) (New York: Academic Press)

Murdock, B. B. (1962). The serial position effect of free recall. *J. Exp. Psychol.*, **64**, 482–488

Murdock, B. B. (1967). Auditory and visual stores in short-term memory. *Acta Psychologica*, **27**, 316–324

Murdock, B. B. and Walker, K. D. (1969). Modality effects in free recall. *J. Verb. Learn. Verb. Behav.*, **8**, 665–676

Neisser, U. (1967). *Cognitive Psychology* (New York: Appleton-Century-Crofts)

Norman, D. A. (1966). Acquisition and retention in short-term memory. *J. Exp. Psychol.*, **72**, 369–381

Norman, D. A. (1973). What have the animal experiments taught us about human memory? In: *The Physiological Basis of Memory* (J. A. Deutsch, editor) (New York: Academic Press)

Ojemann, G. A. (1971). Alteration in non-verbal short-term memory with stimulation in the region of the mamillothalamic tract in man. *Neuropsychologia*, **9**, 195–221

Ojemann, G. and Fedio, P. (1968). Effect of stimulation of the human thalamus and parietal and temporal white matter on short-term memory. *J. Neurosurg.*, **29**, 51–59

Ojemann, G., Blick, K. I. and Ward, A. A. Jr (1971). Improvement and disturbance of short-term verbal memory with human ventrolateral thalamic stimulation. *Brain*, **94**, 225–240

Oscar-Berman, M., Goodglass, H. and Cherlow, D. G. (1975). Perceptual laterality and iconic recognition of visual materials by Korsakoff patients and normal adults. *J. Comp. Physiol. Psychol.*, **82**, 316–321

Osgood, C. E. (1949). The similarity paradox in human learning. *Psychol. Rec.*, **56**, 132–143

Peterson, L. R. and Peterson, M. J. (1959). Short-term retention of individual verbal items. *J. Exp. Psychol.*, **58**, 193–198

Peterson, L. R. (1963). Associative memory over brief intervals of time. *J. Verb. Learn. Verb. Behav.*, **2**, 102–106

Posner, M. I. (1967). Short-term memory systems in human information processing. *Acta Psychologica*, **27**, 267–284

Posner, M. I. (1967). Representational systems for storing information in memory. In: *The Pathology of Memory*

(G. A. Talland and N. C. Waugh, editors) (New York: Academic Press)

Raymond, B. (1969). Short-term storage and long-term storage in free recall. *J. Verb. Learn. Verb. Behav.*, **8**, 567–574

Restle, F. (1970). Training of short-term memory. *J. Exp. Psychol.*, **83**, 224–226

Samuels, I., Butters, N. and Goodglass, H. (1971a). Visual memory deficits following cortical and limbic lesions: effect of field of presentation. *Physiol. Behav.*, **6**, 447–452

Samuels, I., Butters, N., Goodglass, H. and Brody, B. (1971b). A comparison of subcortical and cortical damage on short-term visual and auditory memory. *Neuropsychologia*, **9**, 293–306

Samuels, I., Butters, N. and Fedio, P. (1972). Short-term memory disorders following temporal lobe removal in humans. *Cortex*, **8**, 283–298

Sanders, H. I. and Warrington, E. K. (1971). Memory for remote events in amnesic patients. *Brain*, **94**, 661–668

Schiller, P. H. (1965). Monoptic and dichoptic visual masking in patterns and flashes. *J. Exp. Psychol.*, **69**, 193–199

Schulman, H. G. (1971). Similarity effects in short-term memory. *Psychol. Bull.*, **75**, 399–415

Shallice, T. and Warrington, E. K. (1970). Independent functioning of verbal memory stores: a neuropsychological study. *Quart. J. Exp. Psychol.*, **22**, 261–273

Shankweiler, D. (1966). Effects of temporal lobe damage on perception of dichotically presented melodies. *J. Comp. Physiol. Psychol.*, **62**, 115–119

Spellacy, F. and Blumstein, S. (1970). The influence of language set on ear preference in phoneme recognition. *Cortex*, **6**, 430–439

Sperling, G. (1960). The information available in brief visual presentations. *Psychol. Monogr.*, **74**, Whole No. 498

Sperling, G. (1963). A model for visual memory tasks. *Human Factors*, **5**, 19–36

Sperling, G. (1967). Successive approximations to a model for short-term memory. *Acta Psychologica*, **27**, 285–292

Sperling, G. and Speelman, R. G. (1970). Acoustic similarity and auditory short-term memory: experiments and a model. In: *Models of Human Memory* (D. A. Norman, editor) (New York: Academic Press)

Starr, A. and Phillips, L. (1970). Verbal and motor memory in the amnestic syndrome. *Neuropsychologia*, **8**, 75–88

Talland, G. (1965). *Deranged Memory* (New York: Academic Press)

Triesman, A. M. (1964). Verbal cues, language and meaning in selective attention. *Amer. J. Psychol.*, **77**, 206–219

Tulving, E. (1968). Theoretical issues in free recall. In: *Verbal Behavior and General Behavior Theory* (T. R. Dixon and D. L. Horton, editors) (New Jersey: Prentice Hall)

Tulving, E. (1970). Short- and long-term memory: different retrieval mechanisms. In: *Biology of Memory* (K. H. Pribram and D. E. Broadbent, editors) (New York: Academic Press)

Underwood, B. J. (1957). Interference and forgetting. *Psychol. Rev.*, **64**, 49–60

von Wright, J. M. (1968). Selection in visual immediate memory. *Quart. J. Exp. Psychol.*, **8**, 62–68

Warrington, E. K. and James, M. (1967). Tachistoscopic number estimation in patients with unilateral cerebral lesions. *J. Neurol. Neurosurg. Psychiat.*, **30**, 468–474

Warrington, E. K. and Weiskrantz, L. (1968). A study of learning and retention in amnesic patients. *Neuropsychologia*, **6**, 283–291

Warrington, E. K. and Shallice, T. (1969). The selective impairment of auditory verbal short-term memory. *Brain*, **92**, 885–896

Warrington, E. K. and Rabin, P. A. (1970). A preliminary investigation of the relation between visual perception and visual memory. *Cortex*, **6**, 87–96

Warrington, E. K. and Silberstein, M. (1970). A questionnaire technique for investigating very long-term memory. *Quart. J. Exp. Psychol.*, **22**, 508–512

Warrington, E. K. and Weiskrantz, L. (1970). Amnesic syndrome: consolidation or retrieval? *Nature*, (*London*), **228**, 628–630

Warrington, E. K., Logue, V. and Pratt, R. T. C. (1971). The anatomical localisation of selective impairment of auditory verbal short-term memory. *Neuropsychologia*, **9**, 377–387

Warrington, E. K. and Rabin, P. (1971). Visual span of apprehension in patients with unilateral cerebral lesions. *Quart. J. Exp. Psychol.*, **23**, 432–431

Warrington, E. K. and Sanders, H. I. (1971). The fate of old memories. *Quart. J. Exp. Psychol.*, **23**, 432–442

Warrington, E. K. and Weiskrantz, L. (1971). Organisational aspects of memory in amnesic patients. *Neuropsychologia*, **9**, 67–73

Warrington, E. K. and Shallice, T. (1972). Neuropsychological evidence of visual storage in short-term memory tasks. *Quart. J. Exp. Psychol.*, **24**, 30–40

Warrington, E. K. and Weiskrantz, L. (1973). An analysis of short-term and long-term memory deficits in man. In: *The Physiological Basis of Memory* (J. A. Deutsch, editor) (New York: Academic Press)

Waugh, N. C. and Norman, D. A. (1965). Primary memory. *Psychol. Rev.*, **72**, 89–104

Waugh, N. C. (1970). Primary and secondary memory in short-term retention. In: *Biology of Memory* (K. H. Pribram and D. E. Broadbent, editors) (New York: Academic Press)

Wechsler, D. (1955). *Manual for the Wechsler Adult Intelligence Scale* (New York: The Psychological Corp.)

Weingartner, H. (1968). Verbal learning in patients with temporal lobe lesions. *J. Verb. Learn. Verb. Behav.*, **7**, 520–526

Weiskrantz, L. and Warrington, E. K. (1970). A study of forgetting in amnesic patients. *Neuropsychologia*, **8**, 281–288

White, M. J. (1969). Laterality differences in perception: a review. *Psychol. Bull.*, **72**, 387–405

Whitty, C. W. M. and Zangwill, O. L. (Editors) (1966). *Amnesia* (London: Butterworths)

Wickelgren, W. A. (1968). Sparing of short-term memory in an amnesic patient: implications for strength theory of memory. *Neuropsychologia*, **6**, 235–244

Wickelgren, W. A. (1969). Auditory or articulatory coding in verbal short-term memory. *Psychol. Rev.*, **76**, 232–235

Zurif, E. B. and Ramier, A. M. (1972). Some effects of unilateral brain damage on the perception of dichotically presented phoneme sequences and digits. *Neuropsychologia*. **10**, 103–110

Chapter 6

THINKING AND PROBLEM SOLVING

P. D. Slade

INTRODUCTION

'Thinking' has long been considered the essential and most important ingredient of mental activity. The philosopher Aristotle, for example, selected the 'capacity to think' as the defining attribute of Man: while another philosopher, Descartes, used the same concept to distinguish mind from matter. The term itself has come to be one of the most widely used in common parlance yet, despite its privileged position in our everyday vocabulary, it is not without ambiguity. It is essentially a descriptive label for certain internal processes and behaviours which cannot be directly observed in the same way as eating or drinking can be. Of course, it shares this feature in common with many other internal processes which are the rightful subject matter of psychology.

The basic ambiguity of the term 'thinking' can best be illustrated by considering just a few of the many internal behaviours to which the label is sometimes applied:

1. 'I am trying to think where I left my pen.' Here the term is used synonymously with *remembering*.
2. 'I am trying to think what my new job will be like.' Its use in this context is synonymous with *imagining*.
3. 'I wasn't thinking what I was doing.' Here the behaviour described would seem to be that of *concentration*.
4. 'I think everyone should be paid more money.' Synonymous terms in this context would be *belief*, *attitude*, or *opinion*.
5. 'I am thinking about how to write this chapter.' The internal behaviour referred to here involves working out the details of organisation: or more simply *reasoning*.

It is this last use of the term, often referred to as 'reflective thinking', which most (but not all) psychologists have taken as the subject matter for a scientific study of thinking.

From the discussion so far it will be apparent that an unambiguous, readily acceptable, scientific definition of thinking will be hard to achieve. One attempt has been to render it synonymous with problem-solving behaviour. Humphrey (1951), for example, defined thinking as 'what happens in experience when an organism, human or animal, meets, recognises and solves a problem'. Many psychologists have found this too limiting a definition, preferring the wider and much looser one of thinking as simply 'the internal representation of events' (e.g. Osgood, 1953). For our purposes we shall begin with a consideration of facts and theories assembled under the narrower banner of problem-solving behaviour and then move on to a coverage of work and ideas within the wider definition.

ANIMAL PROBLEM SOLVING: TRIAL-AND-ERROR v. INSIGHT

E. L. Thorndike in his book *Animal Intelligence* published in 1911, reported on his findings from laboratory studies of animals, mainly cats. His primary research tool consisted of the Puzzle Box, a cage in which the animal was confined and from which it could escape to obtain a food reward only by activating levers or pulling strings to open the door (Figure 6.1a). From his observations of the behaviour of cats and other animals in these puzzle boxes Thorndike came to the conclusion that problem solving, at least in lower animals, involves a slow, gradual and at times tortuous trial-and-error process. There appeared to be no reasoning underlying the process of discovery exhibited by his animals. As a result Thorndike came to conceive problem solving as a gradual 'stamping-in' of correct responses and a gradual 'stamping-out' of incorrect responses. For Thorndike this trial-and-error process was guided by two basic principles—the law of repetition or exercise and the law of effect. The latter states that any response which is followed by a pleasurable state of affairs (reward) will tend to become associated with the existing stimulus situation and will be repeated in that situation; while a response which is followed by an annoying state of affairs (punishment) will tend to become weakened in that situation and tend not to recur. One can see in Thorndike's law of effect the forerunner of modern-day reinforcement principles.

A very different approach to problem solving in animals was employed by Wolfgang Köhler, a leading proponent of the Gestaltist approach. He criticised the experimental techniques and findings of Thorndike on the basis that they require unnatural behaviour on the part of the animal and also that they impose essential limitations on the kinds of behaviour the animals can manifest. As he pointed out, cats do not escape from

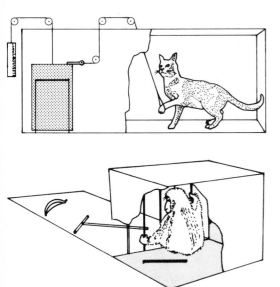

Figure 6.1 Problem-solving situations used by Thorndike and Köhler.

(a) A 'puzzle box' of the type used by E. L. Thorndike (1911). To open the door of its box the cat must claw at a loop of string which, outside the box, releases the catch of the door via a pulley system. A separate weight-and-pulley system raises and holds open the door when released.

(b) A problem situation of the type used by Köhler (1925). The chimpanzee cannot reach its food with the short stick inside its cage; but it can use the short stick to rake the long stick into reach, and then use the long stick to draw in the fruit. (From Wright *et al.*, 1970, *Introducing Psychology*, by courtesy of Penguin Books, London)

traps by manipulating levers or pulleys; they push, claw and scratch at obstacles and try to squeeze through openings or climb or jump to freedom. In fact they do all the things which Thorndike's set-up discourages. The correct response is bound to be reached by trial-and-error behaviour and stamped in by repetition simply because it is an unfamiliar sort of accomplishment for a cat to have to learn.

Köhler's own studies were carried out on a colony of apes and chimpanzees on the island of Tenerife while he was isolated there during the first world war. His observations and conclusions on their problem-solving behaviour is described in his classic book entitled *The Mentality of Apes* (1925). Köhler's technique involved setting the animals a series of food-getting problems and then sitting back and observing their behaviour. In one experiment a chimpanzee is placed in a cage and chained to a tree. A stick is placed within its reach. The animal handles the stick, gnaws at it, and eventually loses interest and drops it. After an interval a banana is placed on the ground out of reach. After futile attempts to grasp the fruit with hands or feet, the chimpanzee seizes the

stick, looks at the fruit, and then suddenly, clumsily, but quite deliberately, drags the fruit within reach. In another experiment (Figure 6.1b) the chimpanzee is again caged. Outside the cage and beyond arm's-reach lies a bunch of bananas. Inside the cage and directly opposite the fruit is a short stick which is not long enough to reach the fruit. At the other end of the cage and outside the bars is a long stick. At first the chimpanzee uses the short stick in a vain attempt to reach the fruit. Failure is followed by behaviour suggesting frustration and anger—the animal makes a wild attempt to pull down the strong bars. After a period of wandering round the cage, the animal suddenly seizes the short stick, runs deliberately to the point opposite the long stick, pulls it in with the aid of the short stick and then uses the long stick to reach the fruit. Other problem situations studied by Köhler required the animals to fit together two short sticks to reach fruit and to assemble packing cases into a vertical structure in order to reach fruit too high to reach by jumping alone.

Köhler claimed that the intelligent behaviour displayed by his chimpanzees involves a capacity to 'think' or 'reason'. Furthermore, he argued that their behaviour could not be described in terms of a trial-and-error process but rather that it reflected an 'insightful' problem-solving capacity. For Köhler, the essential features of 'insight' solutions, which distinguish them from trial-and-error learning, are: (1) Suddenness: the appropriate solutions appear to occur with dramatic suddenness and, having occurred, tend to persist as permanent acquisitions. (2) Smoothness: once the animal has apparently 'seen' the correct solution, the appropriate sequence of behaviour is executed in a continuous, smooth manner. (3) Solution precedes execution: according to Köhler, in many of his situations it is apparent that the animal has mentally solved the problem before it initiates the actual behaviour.

Learning-set formation: A compromise account
Perhaps the most telling criticism that has been made of Köhler's work was that he had no knowledge of the previous life-history and experience of his animals. He simply assumed that insightful behaviour, such as the use of a stick as a reaching implement, was a novel response determined by the immediate perceptual situation quite independently of the previous experiences of the animal. A study by H. G. Birch (1945) suggested that this is not the case. He used six young chimpanzees reared under nearly continuous observation in the Yerkes Laboratories of Primate Biology in Florida. Prior to the experiment proper, only one of these naive animals (Jojo) had been observed using a stick regularly as a tool: and on preliminary testing with a stick problem, Jojo was the only one to solve it directly and smoothly within a 30-minute work period. The six animals were then

allowed three days of spontaneous play with short, straight sticks, which were placed in their enclosure. The use of sticks as poking, shovelling and prying instruments was seen to develop gradually during this period. The animals were then. retested on the stick problem. All of them now solved it smoothly and quickly, the slowest animal taking a mere 20 seconds. The conclusion seems inescapable that past experience played a role in the insightful solution of problems, both in preparing the animals to perceive sticks as tools and in refining the skill with which they used them.

The most comprehensive attack on the role of past experience in problem-solving ability has been made by Harry F. Harlow. He began by setting monkeys a simple discrimination problem. In front of their cage he placed two food-wells, one of which contained a food reward. The two food-wells were covered by two objects which differed in colour, size and shape. If the monkey picked up the correct object, it was rewarded by finding the food beneath. The position of the two objects and the food was shifted in a random fashion from one trial to the next and the trials were continued until the monkey learned to choose the correct object consistently. The problem was then repeated with a second pair of objects until consistent correct performance was achieved, and then repeated again with a third pair of objects, and a fourth pair, and so on, with several hundred different pairs of objects being used in all. On each occasion, therefore, the basic problem set the monkey was the same (i.e. discover which of the two objects was associated with

the food), while the task stimuli (i.e. the pair of objects) were changed from one problem to the next.

The initial performance of the monkeys on these problems reflected a slow, laborious 'trial-and-error' process (see the. lower curve for problems 1–8 in Figure 6.2), correct performance increasing gradually over the first six trials. But as the monkeys solved more and more problems of the same basic kind, their behaviour changed in a most dramatic way. Each new problem was solved with progressively greater efficiency, until a stage was reached at which the monkeys appeared to show 'insight': they solved the problems in a single trial. If they chose the correct object on the first trial, they rarely made mistakes subsequently. If they chose the incorrect object on the first trial, they simply shifted to the correct one on the second trial (see the upper curve for problems 257–312 in Figure 6.2). Harlow repeated this study with other types of learning problems with monkeys, and also applied them to young children, with similar results. One of the main conclusions Harlow drew from this work was that 'trial-and-error and insight are but two different phases of one long continuous process. They are not different capacities but merely represent the orderly development of a learning and thinking process' (1949). Harlow was suggesting that when animals or humans are first faced with an entirely novel problem they are forced to use a trial-and-error approach: but that after having had experience with many similar problems they are able to use apparently 'insightful' methods. The intervening process Harlow referred to as 'learning to think' or 'learning set formation'. To quote Harlow again:

'We have called this process of progressive learning the formation of a "learning set". The subject learns an organised set of habits that enables him to meet effectively each new problem of this particular kind. A single set would provide only limited aid in enabling an animal to adapt to an everchanging environment. But a host of different learning sets may supply the raw material for human thinking' (Harlow, 1949).

HUMAN PROBLEM SOLVING

The investigation of problem-solving processes in humans has proved more difficult and complicated than that in animals and has evoked the development of a wide-ranging and diverse series of problem situations to cope with it. Before turning to a consideration of some of the variables that affect human problem-solving, let us briefly describe two of the classic problem-situations that have been studied.

Duncker's radiation problem

The problem which was studied most intensively by Duncker, a German psychologist, in his investigations of human problem-solving was the 'radiation' problem. The problem he set his subjects was as follows: 'Given a human being with an inoperable

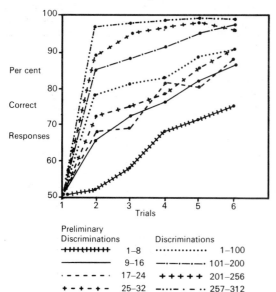

Figure 6.2   Discrimination learning curves on successive blocks of problems. (From Harlow, copyright (1949), *Psychol. Rev.*, 56, 51–65, by permission of the American Psychological Association)

Preliminary Discriminations		Discriminations	
++++++++++	1–8	············	1–100
——————	9–16	—·—·—·—	101–200
· - - - - - ·	17–24	+ + + + +	201–256
+ - + - + -	25–32	—··—· - —··	257–312

stomach tumour, and rays which destroy organic tissue at sufficient intensity, by what procedure can one free him of the tumour by these rays and at the same time avoid destroying the healthy tissue which surrounds it?'

Duncker was especially interested in the stages a subject would go through in his attempts to find a solution to this problem rather than in the number or type of subjects who could solve it. In order to get information on the solution process he asked his subjects to verbalise freely throughout their attempt. From the large number of records he obtained in this way, he selected a protocol which he felt was 'particularly rich in typical hunches' and therefore probably reflected most clearly the kind of solution process that subjects went through.

Protocol
1. Send rays through the oesophagus.
2. Desensitise the healthy tissues by means of a chemical injection.
3. Expose the tumour by operating.
4. One ought to decrease the intensity of the rays on their way; for example—would this work?—turn the rays on at full strength only after the tumour has been reached. (Experimenter: False analogy; no injection is in question.)
5. One should swallow something inorganic (which would not allow passage of the rays) to protect the healthy stomach-walls. (E: It is not merely the stomach walls which are to be protected.)
6. Either the rays must enter the body or the tumour must come out. Perhaps one could alter the location of the tumour—but how? Through pressure? No.
7. Introduce a cannula. (E: What, in general, does one do when, with any agent, one wishes to produce in a specific place an effect which he wishes to avoid on the way to that place?)
8. (Reply:) One neutralises the effect on the way. But that is what I have been attempting all the time.
9. Move the tumour toward the exterior. (Compare 6.) (The E repeats the problem and emphasises, '. . . which destroy *at sufficient intensity*'.)
10. The intensity ought to be variable. (Compare 4.)
11. Adaptation of the healthy tissues by previous weak application of the rays. (E: How can it be brought about that the rays destroy only the region of the tumour?)
12. (Reply:) I see no more than two possibilities: either to protect the body or to make the rays harmless. (E: How could one decrease the intensity of the rays en route?) (Compare 4.)
13. (Reply:) Somehow divert . . . diffuse rays . . . disperse . . . stop! Send a broad and weak bundle of rays through a lens in such a way that the tumour lies at the focal point and thus receives intensive radiation. (Total duration about half an hour.)

As Duncker noted, all the suggestions in this protocol are both concrete and also far from being random. In fact he felt that they could be neatly classified into three groups of proposals, namely: (1) proposals emphasising the avoidance of contact between the rays and the healthy tissue (2) proposals emphasising the desensitising or immunising of the healthy tissue, and (3) proposals emphasising the

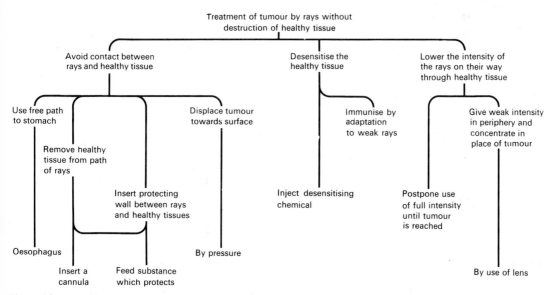

Figure 6.3 Classificatory tree of solution proposals. (From Duncker, copyright (1949), *Psychol. Rev.*, 58, by permission of the American Psychological Association)

reduction of radiation intensity on the way. Duncker took this classificatory analysis a stage further by erecting a classificatory tree to describe the lines of approach taken by the subject. This is reproduced in full in Figure 6.3. From this analysis, Duncker concluded that each step towards a correct solution involves a development or reformulation of the problem. As Dunker put it: 'It is therefore meaningful to say that what is really done in any solution of problems consists in formulating the problem more productively' (Duncker, 1945). This emphasis by Duncker on the 'development of the problem' receives support from some of the more experimentally oriented work to be dealt with later.

Maier's two-string problem

A very different type of problem was developed and used by Maier (1931). The problem situation consisted of a large room which contained many objects such as poles, ringstands, clamps, pliers, extension cords, tables and chairs. Two cords were hung from the ceiling, and were of such length that they reached the floor. One hung near a wall, the other from the centre of the room. The subject was told, 'Your problem is to tie the ends of those two strings together'. He soon learned that if he held either cord in his hand he could not reach the other. He was then told that he could use or do anything he wished. The problem situation is illustrated diagrammatically in Figure 6.4.

The correct solution, or at least the one which Maier defined as the correct one, involved the subject tying a weight to one of the strings and then using it as a pendulum. The subject could then catch the swinging pendulum while holding onto the other string and thereby tie the two strings together. Maier was interested principally in the time required for solution, the nature of errors, the effects of hints and the subjects' conscious awareness of the effects of hints on their performance. We shall return to the results of his studies in the next section.

Variables affecting human problem solving

As mentioned previously a large number of different

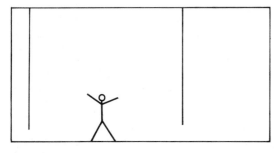

Figure 6.4 Maier's two-string problem. (After Maier, 1931).

problem situations have been used in the study of human problem solving. In consequence the effects of a wide range of variables on performance have been investigated. A number of the more important ones will now be considered prior to a presentation of the main theoretical formulations of the problem-solving process.

Effects of instructions

The way in which the problem is presented and the amount of information given has been found to be a potent factor affecting the attainment of the correct solution. This variable seems to have its effect both by limiting the number of possible alternatives (i.e. by limiting the size of the problem) and by providing the problem solver with direction. For example, in a study of anagram solving by Safren (1962), it was found that telling the subjects to look for animal names led to much quicker solutions than when no such information was given. In a related study, Maltzman et al. (1956) presented subjects with anagrams having more than one possible solution (e.g. EHROS has two solutions, HORSE and SHORE). Subjects told to look for animal names were much more likely to find the first solution than they were to find the alternative one.

A rather more subtle effect of instructions involves the expectations for success which they can engender. In one study, Aronson and Landy (1967) gave subjects a task which could be completed in five minutes. Subjects who were told that they had 15 minutes to complete the task took longer than subjects who were told that they only had five minutes. Similar results have been obtained in other studies in which subjects have been told that some tasks are very difficult and that others are very easy.

Priming of solutions

The familiarity of the correct solution to the subject enhances his chances of solving the problem quickly. In a number of studies it has been shown that this solution-familiarity can be increased by manipulating the subject's immediately preceding experiences. For example, in a study of anagram solving Dominowski and Ekstrand (1967) had subjects learn word lists including the correct anagram solutions prior to doing the task. The effect of this manipulation was to cause the subjects to achieve speedier solutions to the anagram problems.

In a similar type of study using Maier's two-string problem, Judson et al. (1956) found that having subjects learn a word list containing a critical sequence (rope, swing, pendulum) facilitated their performance on the two-string problem. However, this latter result has not always been replicated and it seems that this type of priming manipulation is more effective in a structured problem situation (such as that reflected in anagram solving) than in the less structured situations involving 'insight' problems (such as the two-string problem).

Effects of hints

In one study using his two-string problem, Maier (1931) provided 'hints' for subjects failing to solve the problem correctly after a period of at least ten minutes. The first hint involved the experimenter walking across the room and, apparently accidentally, knocking against the centre string causing it to swing backwards and forwards. Of 23 subjects who had failed to solve the problem up to this point in time, 19 solved it within seconds of this hint being given. Interestingly enough, when questioned afterwards most of these subjects denied that this hint had affected their behaviour, although from observations of their performance it blatantly had.

In a more recent study of the effects of direct hints of this type on the solution of practical problems, Burke *et al.* (1966) were able to replicate this finding with similar kinds of problem situations. Moreover, they found that the facilitatory effect of hints was far greater when they were provided at the beginning of the subject's performance than when provided half-way through. The mechanism involved would seem to be akin to that of 'mental set', which will be considered shortly.

Functional fixedness and functional value

As well as having a positive, beneficial effect on performance, past experience can have a negative, detrimental effect. This was first highlighted by Duncker who used the term 'functional fixedness' to refer to a special type of interference effect from previous experience. He found that if a subject had to use a particular object in a specific way to solve a problem and then was presented with another similar problem in which the same object had to be utilised differently, the subject's performance on the second task was impeded. This effect has been replicated and confirmed in a number of independent investigations and is particularly well-demonstrated in a study by Birch and Rabinowitz (1951). They used a modification of Maier's two-string problem in which only two objects were provided as potential pendulum weights, an electrical relay and an electrical switch. Prior to being set the problem, subjects were divided into three groups. Group S were given a pretest task of completing an electrical circuit using the electrical switch. Group R were given a pretest task of completing the electrical circuit using the electrical relay: while Group C, the control group, were given no pretest experience. The dependent variable investigated was the number of subjects using either the switch or the relay as a pendulum weight in the two-string problem. The results are presented in Table 6.1.

Table 6.1 No. of subjects using the switch or relay in the two-string problem

	Relay	*Switch*
Group S	7	2
Group R	0	10
Group C	3	3

Although the number of subjects studied is small, there is clear evidence in the two experimental groups of subjects using the alternative object as a pendulum weight from the one they had used for a different purpose on the pretest.

This type of finding led Sangstad and Raaheim (1960) to talk about the 'functional value' of objects and the 'availability of these functions' to subjects. They found that if subjects, prior to being given the problem situation, were able to specify the appropriate functions for objects or were shown the appropriate functions, they were able to solve the tasks without difficulty.

Mental set

The concept of 'mental set' is closely related to that of 'functional fixedness'. Whereas the latter refers to a degree of rigidity in the utilisation of objects, the term 'mental set' is reserved for describing rigidity in the solution process itself. Perhaps the earliest and most outstanding attempt to bring this phenomenon under experimental control was that made by Luchins and Luchins (1950). In their experiments they used water-jar problems. Subjects were told to imagine they had three empty water-jars of varying capacities: that by using these three jars in different combinations they were to work out how to obtain a stipulated amount of liquid. The actual problems they posed their subjects are presented in Table 6.2. The first problem in fact involves only two jars and is to be solved by applying the formula $a-2b$. Problems 2–6 are the 'Einstellung' or set-inducing problems: they can only be solved by using the formula $b-a-2c$. Problems 7–11 are the 'critical' problems: they can be solved either by applying the laborious Einstellung method (i.e. $b-a-2c$) or by the use of easier, more direct methods (i.e. either $a-c$ or $a+c$). The aim of the studies was to see to what extent subjects would continue to use the Einstellung method with the 'critical' problems rather than the more direct methods. The finding was that most adults and nearly all the children tested do show such rigidity. Luchins and Luchins went on to try out various instructional manipulations to try to reduce this tendency, but without much effect. They concluded that mechanisation in thinking, or the development of a mental set, posed serious problems which were especially pertinent to educational practices, such as the teaching of mathematics.

Table 6.2   Luchins and Luchins' water-jar problems. (From Luchins and Luchins, 1959, by courtesy of *J. Gen. Psychol.*)

Problem	Containers given Capacity in Quarts			To get	
	a	b	c		
1	29	3		20 quarts	
2	21	127	3	100 quarts	
3	14	163	25	99 quarts	Einstellung or
4	18	43	10	5 quarts	set-inducing
5	9	42	6	21 quarts	problems
6	20	59	4	31 quarts	
7	23	49	3	20 quarts	
8	15	39	3	18 quarts	Critical
9	28	76	3	25 quarts	or
10	18	48	4	22 quarts	test problems
11	14	36	8	6 quarts	

THEORETICAL FORMULATIONS OF PROBLEM SOLVING

Gestalt theory approach

The Gestalt approach to psychology originated in Germany in the early 1900s under the auspices of three men: Max Wertheimer, Kurt Koffka and Wolfgang Köhler. Their main tenet was that psychological processes are essentially indivisible and can only be understood in terms of the total organism: the whole or Gestalt is greater than the sum of the parts. Their main preoccupation was with perceptual processes but, as we have seen, Köhler attempted to apply similar principles to an understanding of problem solving. The most distinctive features of the theory developed in this vein are:

1. The emphasis on 'insightful' solutions.
2. The characterisation of solution processes as involving perceptual reorganisation and development of the problem (*cf.* Duncker).
3. A general de-emphasis on the role of past experience in favour of the idea of 'direction' determined by the presenting perceptual situation.

Although this theoretical approach has given rise to some interesting concepts and research, such as that of 'functional fixedness', it has proved to be too loose and inadequate as a scientific description of the problem-solving process and work along these lines has lapsed in recent years.

Associative theory approach

The associative theory approach may be depicted as the attempt to apply the principles of classical and operant conditioning to an understanding of the processes involved in problem solving. This approach has generated by far the most theorising and research during recent years and many associative models of the problem-solving process have been postulated. The main distinctive features in these various models have been:

1. Description of stimulus/response connections in terms of reinforcement and extinction principles.
2. Description of unobservable internal processes in terms of mediating responses.
3. An emphasis on response hierarchies to explain the differential probability of different responses occurring.

Although most of the work stimulated by this approach has been concerned with structured problem situations, such as anagram solving, a number of attempts have been made to account for 'insightful' problem solving within the same theoretical context. Davis (1966), for example, proposed a distinction between Type O or overt problem solving and Type C or covert problem solving. In the former the organism cannot predict the outcomes of the various response alternatives open to him and must therefore carry them out 'overtly' in a trial-and-error fashion: in the latter situation the organism, as a result of past experience, can successfully predict the outcomes for various responses and therefore need only choose 'covertly' the appropriate one for the given situation: his performance is likely to appear 'insightful'. The parallel between this formulation and that of Harlow in terms of 'learning set formation' is an obvious one.

Information theory approach

In the past decade, considerable effort has been made to programme computers to simulate human problem-solving processes. It is argued, for example by Newell and Simon (1963), that if a close analogue of human problem-solving can be produced by a computer programme this will allow us not only to predict the behaviour of a human being in a problem situation but will also provide a good theory of the subject's problem solving behaviour. The main distinctive features of this approach are:

1. An emphasis on the human problem-solver as an active, information processing unit.
2. A major concern with selection processes implicit in the concepts of 'searching' and 'scanning'.
3. An emphasis on the role of feedback or regulatory mechanisms whereby the organism's behaviour is continuously monitored and modified.

At the present time the main difficulties appear to be those of accounting for the discontinuities and failures in human problem-solving rather than their successes. However, many psychologists feel that these problems can be overcome and that the approach holds out great promise for the future in the development of a satisfactory and sufficiently sophisticated account of problem solving, at least at the behavioural level.

CREATIVITY AND DIVERGENT THINKING

Closely allied to the field of human problem-solving is that of original or creative thinking. Although traditionally of interest to psychologists it is only in fairly recent years that the subject of creative abilities has stimulated a considerable amount of attention and research. Two distinct lines of attack on the problem of creativity can be discerned. The first, and historically older approach, is concerned with the nature of the creative process. How do eminent composers, artists, scientists and mathematicians produce original and inventive ideas? The second, and newer approach, is concerned with the nature and measurement of individual differences in creativity. What are the characteristics of creative individuals and how do such individuals differ from less creative ones? We shall now briefly consider each of these two approaches in turn.

The nature of the creative process

Most of the observations and ideas on the nature of the creative process have come from introspective accounts of eminent men generally recognised to be inventive in their field of speciality. Thus we have available, among others, the introspective accounts of Mozart and Tchaikovsky on the creation of musical compositions; the accounts of A. E. Housman and Stephen Spender on poetic creation; the accounts of Balzac and Proust on literary creation; and the account of Poincaré on mathematical invention. As an example of this type of first hand, introspective report, Poincaré's account of his discovery of Fuchsian functions is given below:

'It is time to penetrate deeper and to see what goes on in the very soul of the mathematician. For this, I believe, I can do best by recalling memories of my own. But I shall limit myself to telling how I wrote my first memoir on Fuchsian functions. I beg the reader's pardon; I am about to use some technical expressions, but they need not frighten him, for he is not obliged to understand them, I shall say, for example, that I have found the demonstration of such a theorem under such circumstances. This theorem will have a barbarous name, unfamiliar to many, but that is unimportant; what is of interest for the psychologist is not the theorem but the circumstances.

'For fifteen days I strove to prove that there could not be any functions like those I have since called Fuchsian functions. I was then very ignorant; every day I seated myself at my work table, stayed an hour or two, tried a great number of combinations and reached no results. One evening, contrary to my custom, I drank black coffee and could not sleep. Ideas rose in crowds; I felt them collide until pairs interlocked, so to speak, making a stable combination. By the next morning I had established the existence of a class of Fuchsian functions, those which come from the hypergeometric series; I had only to write out the results which took but a few hours.

'Then I wanted to represent these functions by the quotient of two series; this idea was perfectly conscious and deliberate, the analogy with elliptic functions guided me. I asked myself what properties these series must have if they existed, and I succeeded without difficulty in forming the series I have called theta-Fuchsian.

'Just at this time I left Caen, where I was then living, to go on a geologic excursion under the auspices of the school of mines. The changes of travel made me forget my mathematical work. Having reached Coutances, we entered an omnibus to go some place or other. At the moment when I put my foot on the step the idea came to me, without anything in my former thoughts seeming to have paved the way for it, that the transformations I had used to define the Fuchsian functions were identical with those of non-Euclidean geometry. I did not verify the idea; I should not have had time, as, upon taking my seat in the omnibus, I went on with a conversation already commenced, but I felt a perfect certainty. On my return to Caen, for conscience' sake I verified the result at my leisure.

'Then I turned my attention to the study of some arithmetical questions apparently without much success and without a suspicion of any connection with my preceding researches. Disgusted with my failure, I went to spend a few days at the sea-side, and thought of something else. One morning, walking on the bluff, the idea came to me, with just the same characteristics of brevity, suddenness and immediate certainty, that the arithmetic transformations of indeterminate ternary quadratic forms were identical with those of non-Euclidean geometry.

'Returned to Caen, I meditated on this result and deduced the consequences. The example of quadratic forms showed me that they were Fuchsian groups other than those corresponding to the hypergeometric series; I saw that I could apply to them the theory of theta-Fuchsian series and that consequently there existed Fuchsian functions other than those from the hypergeometric series, the ones I then knew. Naturally I set myself to form all these functions. I made a systematic attack upon them and carried all the outworks, one after another. There was one however that still held out, whose fall would involve that of the whole place. But all my efforts only served at first the better to show me the difficulty, which indeed was something. All this work was perfectly conscious.

'Thereupon I left for Mont-Valerien, where I was to go through my military service; so I was very differently occupied. One day, going along the street, the solution of the difficulty which had stopped me suddenly appeared to me. I did not try to go deep into it immediately, and only after my service did I again take up the question. I had all the elements and had only to arrange them and put them together. So I wrote out my final memoir at a single stroke and without difficulty.' (Excerpt from H. Poincaré, 1924, *The Foundations of Science*, translated by G. B. Halstead, Science Press.)

Using such introspective material psychologists have attempted to analyse and describe the various and successive stages of creative innovation. Although there have been many disagreements, the four-stage model suggested by Wallas (1926) has achieved a fairly general acceptance. His four stages are as follows; (1) preparation (2) incubation (3) illumination and (4) verification. The 'preparation' stage includes recognition that a problem exists, acquisition of the necessary skills and background knowledge, and appropriate attitudes and motivation. The term 'incubation' is used to describe the phase of apparent quiescence when the creator is not actively working on his problem. 'Illumination' refers to the creative experience, the point at which the solution occurs to the creator. The term 'verification' is used for everything that follows; the scientist testing his hypothesis, the musician writing out his composition, the mathematician working out the minor but perhaps intricate details of his discovery, etc. Although Wallas' scheme provides no more than an inadequate descriptive framework, it is perhaps the nearest psychologists have yet managed to get to understanding the nature of the creative process.

Individual differences in creativity and divergent thinking

Earlier investigations of individual differences in creativity concentrated their attention on studies of especially eminent or gifted individuals. Galton in his classic book, *Hereditary Genius*, reported results obtained from the study, largely from biographical and historical records, of eminent judges, statesmen, soldiers, men of letters, poets, musicians, painters and scientists. His main finding concerned the high frequency of above average abilities in the families of these distinguished men and the implication for a genetic basis for such talents. A similar, more recent type of study was conducted by Anne Roe (1952) on sixty-four eminent, living American scientists, using more sophisticated psychometric techniques. But it was another psychologist, L. M. Terman, who has carried out the most intensive studies of gifted individuals. In one study, Terman and Cox investigated the biographies of the 300 most eminent men in history from the year 1450 onwards. In another more intensive, complementary study·Terman in 1922 selected the top one per cent, as determined by conventional intelligence tests, of a school population of more than a quarter of a million and compared them with their peers on a battery of achievement, personality, character and interest tests. He found that they were generally superior in all respects (educational, social and emotional) to their peers. Terman has since turned this into a truly prospective study by following up the bulk of his sample, by means of questionnaires, interviews and tests, through their adolescence, adulthood and even into early middle life. In this way he has succeeded in documenting a monumental wealth of material on the longitudinal development of gifted individuals. However, as Terman himself noted, while his sample of children did exceptionally well in later life, none of them has apparently reached the heights of genius such as that exemplified by Darwin or Einstein.

A different type of approach to the problem of creativity has gained recent impetus following the work of J. P. Guilford. In a paper delivered in 1950 he pointed out that nearly all intelligence and attainment tests used by psychologists and educationalists required a single correct answer to each item: that is, they required 'convergent' thinking abilities. He argued that there may be a whole range of imaginative, creative, 'divergent' thinking abilities, which are untapped by such tests. Moreover, he suggested that such 'divergent' thinking abilities may be continuously distributed in the population and not simply the qualities associated with a few, highly-select gifted individuals. Accordingly, in developing his multifactorial 'model of the intellect' Guilford included a series of 'divergent thinking' abilities and constructed tests to measure them. These tests include, for example, the following two:

(a) Unusual uses. The subject is asked to list as many uses as he can for an object such as a brick. His performance is then scored for number and unusualness of uses offered.

(b) Plot titles. Two story plots are presented and the subject is asked to write as many titles as he can think of for each plot. The titles are then scored for number and cleverness.

Many subsequent investigators have adopted the ideas and tests of Guilford in their studies of creativity. The popular research paradigm has been to compare and contrast highly 'intelligent' children, as selected by conventional intelligence tests, with highly 'creative' ones selected on the basis of divergent thinking tests. The two selected groups are then compared on a range of achievement, personality, social, attitudinal and interest variables. In general, marked differences have been found on most of the variables investigated. One study along these lines by Getzels and Jackson (1962), which has aroused particular attention, will be briefly described. Subjects were selected for the two contrasting groups from a school adolescent population on the basis of a single I.Q. test and five creativity tests. Two groups were formed: high intelligence, low creativity and high creativity, low intelligence. Comparison on a series of measures revealed among other things:

1. No difference in terms of school achievement. The high creativity group, although having much lower I.Q.s, were just as successful scholastically.
2. The high intelligence group were preferred by their teachers over the high creativity group.
3. The high intelligence group rated highly the qualities they thought important for being liked by the teachers and for adult success; the high creativity group rated these qualities low.
4. The high creativity group indicated a much wider choice, and a more unconventional choice, of career aspirations.

While this study has been criticised by other workers, it has helped to stimulate a lot of the ensuing research. At the present time controversy surrounds the question of whether the abilities tapped by creativity tests are in fact independent of general intelligence or whether they represent no more than another facet of the structure of intelligence not previously mapped out in such detail. The validity of creativity tests in current use have also been questioned on the grounds of their frequent failure to separate people who have actually produced creative works from those who have not. Some investigators, however, continue to feel that such tests represent a useful and welcome adjunct to existing test batteries.

CONCEPT ATTAINMENT AND CONCEPT FORMATION

We live in a world, both physical and psychological, in which we are confronted with a vast array of individual stimuli in the form of objects, events and people. In order to cope with such a world we have to classify and categorise such stimuli, to reduce the enormous number of single elements into a smaller, more manageable set of categories. The categories we erect for such purposes are referred to as 'concepts'. For example, we use the concept of flowers to refer to such things as roses, lilies, chrysanthemums, daisies, etc. and each of these is a separate concept in its own right. Thus it is clear that a concept is any means of categorising a particular set of stimuli on the basis of common attributes. Concepts are also hierarchically arranged in terms of the degree of generality they entail. The concept of flower is of a higher order than that of rose, while the concept of plant is of a higher order still.

One concept which has been introduced in the foregoing discussion and requires further elaboration is that of 'attribute'. An 'attribute' is usually defined as any discriminable feature of an event that is susceptible of some discriminable variation from event to event. The attributes of a stone, for example, are its shape, size, weight, colour, and also its beauty and its throwability. The attributes of a person include all those discernible features of his outward physical appearance together with all the discernible features of his ideas, attitudes and behaviour. In the Personal Construct Theory of G. A. Kelly (1955) the term 'construct' has a similar meaning to that of attribute.

Concepts are clearly basic to all our thinking, whether it be that involved in specific problem-solving experiments or that utilised in more general real-life situations. Research into the processes underlying concept development has been confined to two areas primarily:

1. Research on the development of new class concepts in adults, referred to as 'concept attainment' studies, and
2. Research on the development of basic concepts in children, referred to as 'concept formation' studies.

Studies of concept attainment

The major pioneering work in this field was conducted by J. S. Bruner *et al.* and reported in their book entitled *A Study of Thinking* (1956). Bruner begins by elaborating the three main types of class concept which people use, namely: conjunctive, disjunctive and relational. A conjunctive concept is one defined by the joint presence of several attributes. Thus the concept 'red pencil' is conjunctive in so far as it is only used when the single attributes of 'redness' and the various attributes of 'pencil' co-exist. A disjunctive

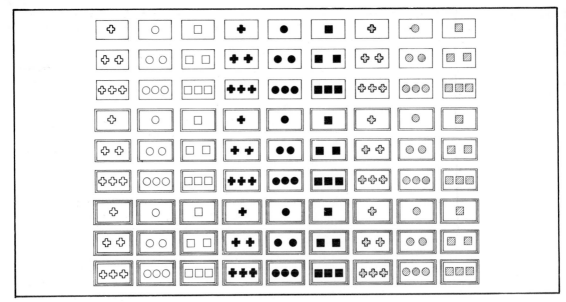

Figure 6.5   An array of instances comprising combinations of four attributes, each exhibiting three values. Plain figures are in green, striped figures in red, solid figures in black. (From J. S. Bruner, J. J. Goodnow, and G. A. Austin *et al.*, by courtesy of Wiley)

concept is one defined by the presence of one or more of a number of attributes. The traditional concept of 'schizophrenia' is disjunctive, in so far as the concept is applied whenever any two or three defining attributes are present, although no single one is obligatory. A relational concept is one defined by a specifiable relationship between defining attributes. For example, income tax levels are defined in terms of the relationship between number of dependants and other variables and level of income.

In order to study experimentally the ways in which people attain new concepts of these three kinds, Bruner developed a set of cards such as that displayed in Figure 6.5. Eighty-one cards are shown in the figure, representing combinations of four attributes, each exhibiting three values, namely:

1. Colour: green, red, or black.
2. Type of figure: cross, circle, or square.
3. Number of figures: one, two, or three.
4. Border: single, double, or treble.

Bruner then distinguished two types of research paradigm for studying concept attainment, namely 'selection' and 'reception' paradigms. In the former, subjects are allowed to select cards, one at a time, and then told whether they are or are not instances of the concept the experimenter has in mind, the subject's task being to find the correct concept. In the latter, the experimenter picks out the cards, one at a time, for the subject and informs him of whether or not they entail the correct concept. In the former paradigm the subject can actively test out his own

hypotheses by selecting appropriate cards, while in the latter he is the passive recipient of certain kinds of information which he must then use. Bruner compares these two paradigms to those employed by the 'animal' and the 'human' neuropsychologist. The former can study the effects of any surgical intervention he likes to make, the latter is limited to the study of only operations performed of necessity.

We shall turn now to the results of Bruner's studies utilising the 'reception paradigm' in the attainment of conjunctive concepts. Bruner's approach is to work out ideal strategies for the task and then to study the correspondence between the performance of his subjects and these ideal strategies. Bruner distinguishes two main ideal strategies that an individual can use, namely:

1. A focussing or wholist strategy.
2. A scanning or part strategy.

With the 'focussing' strategy the subject takes the first positive instance and makes it *in toto* his initial hypothesis, e.g. four red circles with a single border. Succeeding presentations of cards are then used to rule out systematically the attributes which are not relevant to the correct concept (e.g. redness or single border). With the 'scanning' strategy, on the other hand, the subject begins with part of the first positive instance as his hypothesis (e.g. red circles) and tests this out with succeeding cards. As soon as he meets a positive infirming instance, he must change his hypothesis and test a new one (e.g. red figures with a single border). From a purely logical point of view

Bruner argues that the 'focussing' strategy is the better one as it involves less cognitive strain for the subject: at any one point the 'focusser' has to remember less than the 'scanner'.

As the result of studying the performance of groups of undergraduate students on the task, Bruner came to the following conclusions:

1. More subjects use a 'focussing' than a 'scanning' strategy.
2. Subjects are markedly consistent in the strategies they employ from one task to another.
3. The complexity of the task, in terms of the number of attributes in the array, does not affect either the preference for the 'focussing' strategy or the consistency of subjects.
4. 'Focussers' are more successful than 'scanners', especially with more difficult tasks and when time-pressure is introduced.
5. Failures occur with both types of strategies, mainly because subjects are unable to adhere strictly to the rules of the two ideal strategies.
6. However, adherence to the strategy rules was far in excess of what would be expected if subjects were behaving in a purely random fashion.

As a comment on Bruner's approach and its implications, I can do no better than quote his own words: 'We have examined in these pages the manner in which a human being deals with the task of sorting out events that come to him in a haphazard sequence, finding out which of the events are significant and which are not. The experiment has utilised highly stylized materials—slips of cardboard with designs varying in certain properties printed on them—but the task is not so different from the task of the traveller learning what type of inn can be trusted by its externals and without the pain of sampling the service, or any person who must learn what something is by means short of trying it out directly' (Bruner *et al.*, 1956, p. 153).

Studies of concept formation

The investigation of concept formation in children is most closely associated with the name of Piaget, a Swiss psychologist. His work has involved in the main an intensive, longitudinal study of small numbers of children from birth to adolescence employing both passive observation and simple experiment. His primary contribution has been in the delineation of stages of conceptual development, through which he believes all children pass, not necessarily at the same chronological ages but in the same order. Before describing these developmental stages it is necessary to consider some of his basic concepts.

Piaget argues that, in order for a child to learn to adapt appropriately to his environment, he requires two basic functions, namely 'assimilation' and 'accommodation'. 'Assimilation' involves the active manipulation of objects and stimuli in the environment: the young infant explores, probes, shapes, grasps and sucks. In contrast, 'accommodation' involves a passive adjustment to these external stimuli: objects and people resist, move, hurt, reward and punish the infant. By employing these two functions the child builds up 'schemas' which represent his picture of the outside world. At a later date the child develops 'operations', by which Piaget means actions which are internalised and reversible. An 'operation' enables a child to think about certain actions without having to carry them out; enables him in fact to plan his behaviour.

Piaget has described four main stages in concept formation, namely: (1) sensorimotor period (2) pre-operational thought (3) period of concrete operations and (4) period of formal operations.

Sensorimotor period (birth to 2 years)

During this early period, the infant is limited to sensation and motor action. By using his functions of assimilation and accommodation, the infant starts to organise his external sensory stimulation and to form concepts of stable objects. The infant learns to recognise that an object, seen from different angles, remains the same object and does not become a different one. He also acquires the concept of the 'permanence' of objects. At five months, if an object is hidden, the infant behaves as if it no longer exists or perhaps never existed. (The mother who leaves her five months old baby outside a supermarket may be a mother who ceases to exist). While at eight months the infant will search for and attempt to find the object.

Preoperational thinking (2 to 7 years)

This phase spans the widest period of development. It begins with the child developing primitive representational abilities, such as that of imitation, and then gradually the more sophisticated symbolic representational systems provided by language. Closely linked to this 'representational' development is that of the concept of 'conservation', the most important and influential of all Piaget's notions. Piaget uses the term 'conservation' to refer to the concept of invariance in the mass, weight or volume of a substance over transformations in its appearance. Let us see what this means.

In a study of the conservation of 'mass', a child is given two plasticine balls which he agrees are the same size. One of the balls is then rolled out in full view of the child until it looks like a sausage. If the child is then asked whether the ball or the sausage now contains more clay, the typical four year old will say that the sausage one does. Only at a somewhat later chronological age will the child have learned to 'conserve' mass and say that they are the same.

In order to study conservation of weight, the two

original plasticine balls might be balanced at the two ends of a set of scales and thereby shown to be equal in weight. One of the balls is then turned into the sausage shape and the child quizzed as to which will weigh more. The ability to conserve weight, which would be reflected in the answer 'neither', is independent of and more difficult than that of mass and is typically achieved at a later date.

Finally, the classical experimental situation for studying the conservation of volume is depicted in Figure 6.6. The young child is first presented with two beakers and told to pour exactly the same amount of water into each one. The water from one of the beakers is then poured into another glass of a different shape, and the child asked if there is still the same amount. If the second beaker is thinner, the child will usually say there is more water because the water level is higher: while if the second glass is thicker, the child will usually say the opposite because of the lower water level. In the case in which the water is poured into six small beakers, he will usually say that the little beakers have more because there are more of them.

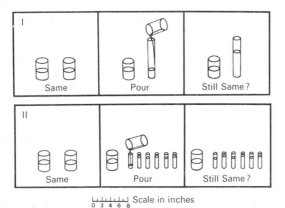

Figure 6.6   Conservation tests. (From Bruner *et al.*, 1966, by courtesy of Wiley)

Piaget claimed from his studies that conservation of mass is typically achieved at age 7, of weight at age 9, and of volume at age 11. Many replications of his basic experiments have been performed, which, while confirming his developmental sequence, have generally suggested somewhat lower average levels for the various conservation achievements. Bruner *et al.* (1966) have been concerned with the essential processes underlying 'conservation'. Their experimental results suggest that two factors contribute to a child's failure to 'conserve': firstly, a tendency to concentrate on a single perceptual dimension at a time (e.g. height of the water in the beaker) to the exclusion of other perceptual dimensions (e.g. dia-

meter of beaker). Bruner and his colleagues have shown that the most difficult concepts for a child to achieve are the ones involving relationships between a number of different perceptual dimensions, e.g. relative 'fullness' or 'emptiness' of a glass. A second factor is a failure on the part of the child to match his language with his organisation of the experience to which it must be applied. The verbal labels 'same' and 'more' do not mean the same thing to the child as they do to the adult.

Concrete operations (7 to 11 years)
The ability to 'conserve' which begins to develop during the latter part of the pre-operational phase emerges gradually as a stable conceptual structure during the period of concrete operations. Other allied operations are also built up during this phase, including those of classification (the inclusion of one class within another) and seriation (the ability to order stimuli on the basis of continuous variation in their appearance). Operations fundamental to the development of number concepts such as composition, reversibility, associativity, identity and tautology, are also said to emerge in a stable form during this period.

Formal operations (11 to 15 years)
Whereas in the previous phase the child's operations are limited in their application to concrete situations, the child now develops the ability to use them in an abstract way. This enables the child to think beyond the present situation, to form hypotheses and theories which he can test. To clarify the kind of change that Piaget imputes to this fourth stage, the following verbal problem could only be solved correctly by a child who had reached it: 'Edith is fairer than Susan: Edith is darker than Lily, who is the darkest of the three?'

Piaget's work and ideas have aroused considerable interest among both theoretical psychologists and practising educationalists during recent years. In fact, in the field of education generally, and in the teaching of mathematics specifically, Piaget's concepts have achieved a position of supreme importance.

CONCEPTUAL MEASUREMENT IN THE INDIVIDUAL
Finally, turning to the problem of measuring the individual concepts a person has and uses, a number of different techniques have been evolved. These include free description, word association tests, sorting tests and ranking and rating methods. For present purposes we shall limit ourselves to a brief consideration of the two most widely used techniques, namely the Osgood Semantic Differential and the Kelly Repertory Grid techniques.

The Osgood Semantic Differential
The Semantic Differential technique, which was

developed by C. E. Osgood, stemmed from his studies and those of other people on the nature of synaesthesia. This latter term refers to 'a phenomenon characterising the experiences of certain individuals, in which certain sensations belonging to one sense or mode attach to certain sensations of another group and appear regularly whenever a stimulus of the latter type occurs'. For example, people often describe the effect of music on them (auditory stimulation) in terms of colours (visual experience) or in terms of heaviness or sharpness (tactile sensations). Such experiences and descriptions are extremely common. Taking this as his starting point Osgood, together with his co-workers, went on to explore the range of application of bipolar adjectival scales of various types in determining the connotative meaning of concepts relating to the physical world, to people and to emotions.

In a series of studies Osgood asked groups of individuals to rate the meaning of concepts such as 'lady', 'boulder', 'sin', 'father', 'lake', 'symphony', etc. on seven point scales such as, 'rough–smooth', 'good–bad', 'large–small', 'beautiful–ugly', 'yellow–blue', etc. He found that his subjects could do this reasonably easily even when the adjectival scale being rated was not one which is normally associated with a particular concept. As a result of this work Osgood elaborated a theory of meaning which has essentially two aspects. In the first place, meaning is seen as a set of 'mediating responses' stemming from initial pairings of stimuli and responses but which have become separated from these and relatively autonomous. In the second place, the meaning of a word or concept is viewed as being 'multidimensional' in the sense of being determined by its relative position on a set of meaning dimensions.

In order to determine the number and type of meaning dimensions, Osgood carried out a series of factor-analyses of ratings of concepts, by groups of individuals, on large numbers of bipolar adjectival scales (factor-analysis is a statistical technique which helps one to isolate groups of items or scales which intercorrelate highly with each other—see Chapter 7). These studies suggested the existence of a number of meaning dimensions, the three most stable being 'evaluation', 'potency', and 'activity'. The *evaluative* factor, invariably the largest, is defined by such scales as 'good–bad', 'wise–foolish' and 'beautiful–ugly': the *potency* factor is defined by such scales as 'potent–impotent', 'hard–soft', 'strong–weak': while the *activity* factor is defined by such scales as 'active–passive', 'excitable–calm', 'fast–slow'. However, there is now some evidence that these factors are not as clear-cut and stable as Osgood's work suggested, especially when the scales are being applied by a single individual to a set of personal concepts.

In practice, the Semantic Differential involves presenting an individual or group of individuals with a

Scale	1	2	3	4	5	6	7	
Cruel	:	:	:	:	:	:	:	: Kind
Hard	:	:	:	:	:	:	:	: Soft
Active	:	:	:	:	:	:	:	: Passive
Good	:	:	:	:	:	:	:	: Bad
Masculine	:	:	:	:	:	:	:	: Feminine
Excitable	:	:	:	:	:	:	:	: Calm
Beautiful	:	:	:	:	:	:	.	: Ugly
Strong	:	:	:	:	:	:	:	: Weak
Fast	:	:	:	:	:	:	:	: Slow
Wise	:	:	:	:	:			: Foolish
False	:	:	:	:	:	:		: True
Potent	:	:	:	:	:	:	:	: Impotent

Figure 6.7 Semantic differential format. Concept self

set of concepts to rate on a series of bipolar scales. An example of the format normally used is presented in Figure 6.7. Both the concepts and the scales have to be selected by the investigator to suit the requirements of his particular study. For example, if the investigator was interested in studying the meaning of architectural features to a group of people, the concepts he would select would probably be buildings while the scales might be of the kind 'beautiful–ugly', 'strong–weak', 'angular–rounded'. On the other hand, an investigator interested in studying the meaning of mental illness to a group of lay people would obviously choose very different concepts and scales. In this sense the Semantic Differential, as also the Repertory Grid, is a technique and not a standardised test. For further information the reader is referred to Osgood *et al.* (1957).

Repertory Grid technique

Repertory Grid technique was developed by George Kelly as a means of quantifying relationships implicit in his theory of personal constructs (Kelly, 1955). This theory treats all men as scientists who are concerned with anticipating and predicting events, both physical and psychological, in their respective environments. Each individual is seen as developing his own personal and idiosyncratic system of bipolar constructs by means of which he conceptualises and interprets his world. Repertory Grid technique is a means of sampling the individual's construct system and of specifying the relationships inherent therein.

The earliest form of this technique required an individual to dichotomise a set of elements (e.g. people) in terms of a construct such as 'friendly–unfriendly'. The individual would then be asked to repeat this procedure using a different construct such as 'kind–unkind'. The relationship between these two constructs for the individual could then be determined by calculating a matching score. For example, if the individual sorted the same elements (people) he considered 'friendly' into the category 'kind', and vice versa, there would be a perfect match and the two constructs would be perfectly correlated. More recent use of the technique has employed a ranking method: the individual is asked to rank the elements from 'most friendly' to 'least friendly' and similarly for other constructs. This enables a more powerful statistical analysis of relationships to be made. A rating method is also possible but has not been widely used as yet.

There are two methods of obtaining the constructs to be used with a given individual. Constructs can be selected and supplied by the investigator to suit his particular requirements. Or they can be elicited from the individual in the manner suggested by Kelly. He developed a triadic method in which the individual is presented with elements, three at a time, and asked to state some important way in which two are alike and different from the third. This process can be repeated over and over again until an adequate sample of meaningful constructs have been elicited. Many developments and sophistications in Grid methodology have occurred in recent years. For further details the interested reader is referred to Bannister and Mair (1968).

There are of course many similarities between Repertory Grid and Semantic Differential techniques and some differences. The biggest difference is perhaps in the nature of the theoretical frameworks that underlie the two methods. The greatest similarity would seem to lie in the essential flexibility and individual-centred focus that both techniques share.

SUMMARY

This chapter has been a wide-reaching one. After a brief discussion of the thorny problem of definition, consideration was given to animal studies of problem solving, emphasising the contrasting theories of 'trial-and-error' and 'insightful' behaviour. An attempt to reconcile these two approaches in terms of a 'learning set' model was then described. The chapter moved on to outline some of the variables that have been found to affect human problem-solving and to an all-too-brief account of the three major theoretical approaches which have emerged: namely, Gestalt theory, Associative theory and Information theory.

Consideration was next given to the allied problem of creativity which has stimulated a resurgence of interest during the past two decades. The description focussed on the older work on the nature of the creative process, about which we still know very little, and on the more recent studies of individual differences in creativity which are posing promising lines of attack.

Attention was then turned to the role of concepts in thinking and to the question of how people develop concepts. Two areas were dealt with; namely, the development of concepts in adults (concept attainment studies) and the development of conceptual thinking in children (concept formation studies).

Finally, a brief discussion was given over to methods of concept-measurement in individuals, the two most widely used techniques being described (the Semantic Differential and the Repertory Grid).

References

Aronson, E. and Landy, D. (1967). Further steps beyond Parkinson's Law: a replication and extension of the excess time effect. *J. Exp. Soc. Psychol.*, 3, 274–85

Bannister, D. and Mair, J. M. M. (1968). *The Evaluation of Personal Constructs* (London, New York: Academic Press)

Birch, H. G. (1945). The relation of previous experience to insightful problem-solving. *J. Comp. Psychol.*, 38, 367–383

Birch, H. G. and Rabinowitz, H. S. (1951). The negative effect of previous experience on productive thinking. *J. Exp. Psychol.*, 41, 121–125.

Bruner, J., Goodnow, J. J. and Austin, G. A. (1956). *A Study of Thinking* (New York: Wiley)

Bruner, J. S., Oliver, R. R. and Greenfield, P. M. (1966). *Studies in Cognitive Growth*, 184 (New York: Wiley)

Burke, R. J., Maier, N. R. F. and Hoffman, L. R. (1966). Functions of hints in individual problem-solving. *Amer. J. Psychol.*, 79, 389–399

Davis, G. A. (1966). Current status of research and theory in human problem solving. *Psychol. Bull.*, 66, 1, 36–54

Dominowski, R. L. and Ekstrand, B. R. (1967). Direct and associative priming in anagram solving. *J. Exp. Psychol.*, 74, 85–86

Duncker, K. (1945). On problem-solving. *Psychol. Monogr.*, 58, Chaps. 1 and 3

Galton, F. (1869). *Hereditary Genius* (London: Macmillan and Appleton)

Getzels, J. W. and Jackson, P. W. (1962). *Creativity and Intelligence: Explorations with Gifted Students* (New York: Wiley)

Guilford, J. P. (1950). Creativity. *Amer. Psychol.*, 5, 444–454

Harlow, H. F. (1949). The formation of learning sets. *Psychol. Rev.*, 56, 51–65

Humphrey, G. (1951). *Thinking* (London: Methuen)

Judson, A. J., Cofer, C. N. and Gelfand, S. (1956). Reasoning as an associative process: II. 'Direction' in problem solving as a function of prior reinforcement of relevant responses. *Psychol. Reports*, 2, 501–507

Kelly, G. A. (1955). *The Psychology of Personal Constructs*, Vols. I and II (New York: Norton)

Köhler, W. (1925). *The Mentality of Apes* (London: Routledge and Kegan Paul, 1925; Pelican Books, 1957)

Luchins, A. S. and Luchins, E. H. (1950). New experimental attempts at preventing mechanisation in problem solving. *J. Gen. Psychol.*, 42, 279–297

Maier, N. R. F. (1931). Reasoning in humans: II. The solution of a problem and its appearance in consciousness. *J. Comp. Psychol.*, 12, 181–894

Maltzman, I., Eisman, E. and Brooks, L. O. (1956). Some relationships between methods of instruction, personality variables, and problem-solving behaviour. *J. Educ. Psychol.*, 47, 71–78

Newell, A. and Simon, H. A. (1963). GPS, a program, that simulates human thought. In: *Computers and Thought*, 279–293 (E. A. Feigenbaum and J. Feldman, editors) (New York: McGraw-Hill)

Osgood, C. E. (1953). *Method and Theory in Experimental Psychology* (New York: Oxford Univ. Press)

Osgood, C. E., Suci, G. J. and Tannenbaum, P. H. (1957). *The Measurement of Meaning* (Urbana: Univ. of Ill. Press)

Roe, A. (1952). A psychologist examines sixty-four eminent scientists. *Sci. Amer.*, 187, 21–25

Safren, M. A. (1962). Associations, sets and the solution of word problems. *J. Exp. Psychol.*, 64, 40–45

Sangstad, P. and Raaheim, K. (1960). Problem-solving, past experience and the availability of functions. *Brit. J. Psychol.*, 51, 2, 97–104

Terman, L. M. (1947). Psychological approaches to the study of genius. *Papers on Eugenics*, No. 4, 3–20

Thorndike, E. L. (1911). *Animal Intelligence* (London: Macmillan)

Wallas, G. (1926). *The Art of Thought* (London: Jonathan Cape)

Suggested Reading

Bourne, L. E., Ekstrand, B. R. and Dominowski, R. L. (1971). *The Psychology of Thinking* (New Jersey: Prentice-Hall)

Flavell, J. H. (1963). *The Development Psychology of Jean Piaget* (Princeton: Van Nostrand)

Thomson, R. (1959). *The Psychology of Thinking* (England: Penguin)

Vernon, P. E. (1970). *Creativity: Selected Readings* (England: Penguin)

Wason, P. C. and Johnson-Laird B. (1968). *Thinking and Reasoning: Selected Readings* (England: Penguin)

INDIVIDUAL DIFFERENCES

Chapter 7

PSYCHOMETRICS: ✓

THE STATISTICAL BASIS FOR THE STUDY OF INDIVIDUAL DIFFERENCES

H. J. Eysenck

Psychometrics is the name given to the application of statistical methods to the study of psychological phenomena, just as biometrics is the name given to the application of statistics to the study of biological phenomena. Students of pyschology often have little background in statistics, or mathematics and exposure to courses in psychometrics may produce traumatic reactions including a revulsion from the subject altogether. They may question the necessity of learning about statistical methods and theories, and doubt the relevance of such knowledge to their main area of concern—human beings and their behaviour. It will be the purpose of this chapter to explain the reasons why psychometrics is so important in the study of psychology (as well as in the study of psychiatry, or sociology, both of which share many problems with psychology), and to give a simple explanation of the main problems and methods the student is likely to encounter. These explanations will be mainly verbal; I believe that the logical basis of psychometrics can be understood even by the innumerate, and that such an understanding will be sufficient to follow the remaining chapters of this book. This chapter, then, does not pretend to be an introduction to statistics; many good, elementary textbooks are available for that purpose, and will be mentioned at the end of the chapter. If the reader emerges with some understanding of why psychologists do what they do in their use of such things as correlation coefficients, analysis of variance and factor analysis, that is all that is aimed at here; such understanding is basic to any comprehension of psychological books and articles, but it is of course not sufficient to enable the reader to judge the appropriateness or correctness of statistical treatment in a given report, or to carry out the statistical treatment of a set of data himself.

WHY STATISTICS?

Why do psychologists use statistics? The first and most obvious use is simple *description*. Let us suppose that we have measured the I.Q.s (intelligence quotients) of a random sample of 10 000 12-year-old children; how can we describe the main results of our study other than by printing in detail the 10 000 I.Q.s themselves? We can plot them on graph paper, as shown in Figure 7.1; along the abscissa are given the I.Q.s in question, and along the ordinate we would plot the actual numbers of children in each I.Q. group. This simple graph would show us that 50% of the

children have I.Q.s between 90 and 110; that 2% have I.Q.s between 130 and 140, or between 60 and 70, and so forth. This contributes greatly to our understanding of the meaning of a given I.Q.; if a child has an I.Q. of 120, say, we see roughly where he fits into our picture—in other words, we can compare his performance with a standardisation group. We know that he is brighter than 90% of his peers; that is an important bit of information. If he has an I.Q. of 140, we know that there is only one child in 200 (roughly) brighter than he is; this gives meaning to the bare statement of an I.Q.

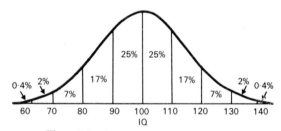

Figure 7.1 A normal frequency distribution

But we can go further. The distribution of I.Q. scores follows a curve that has been studied for many years by mathematicians; it is the so-called 'normal' or Gaussian curve (after the famous mathematician Johann Gauss, who first investigated it), also known as the curve of error (because chance errors tend to follow a similar distribution). One of the most important properties of such a curve is that we can describe it completely by simply stating two figures: the *mean* (which is the arithmetical average, 100 in the case of our I.Q. distribution), and a variable called the *standard deviation* (S.D.), which measures the spread of scores. Looking at Figure 7.1 we see that on either side of the mean the curvature changes from convex to concave; if we connect the point at which this happens with the line drawn across from the mean, then the length of that line tells us what the S.D. is for this distribution. Inspection will tell us that it must be about 15, and calculation tells us that it is indeed exactly 15 (the change in curvature occurs at I.Q. 115 and I.Q. 85). If we know simply that I.Q.s in our population have a mean of 100 and a S.D. of 15, we could recreate all the information in Figure 7.1; these two numbers accurately inform us of the main contents of our countless sheets listing the 10 000 I.Q.s we measured to start with. Thus we can describe our original data with much parsimony; two figures instead of 10 000!

There is another great advantage to having a variable such as the S.D. to deal with; such variables are not bound to the particular measure used. We can translate our statement: This child has an I.Q. of 130 into another statement: This child is two S.D.s above the mean. This second type of statement does not contain any mention of I.Q. and is therefore more general. Suppose we also measured our 10 000 children's height, and found that these measures also showed a normal (Gaussian) distribution, with a mean of 60 inches and a S.D. of two inches. We could then say that in some meaningful way a child 64 inches tall was equivalent in height to a child with an I.Q. of 130 in intelligence. In other words, we can now define a person's score in terms of the distribution itself, and make comparisons across different types of measures. This becomes crucial when we come to the very important concept of *correlation*.

THE CORRELATION COEFFICIENT

Suppose we wish to know whether or not tall children are brighter than small children. Many people have a mental picture of the 'swot' at school as being non-athletic, small, with glasses, sitting bent over his books, rather than out playing football with the boys. If this were true, then small children might be brighter than tall ones. Suppose we had data on the height and I.Q.s of 100 boys attending a particular school; we could write these down in two columns, one for height (in inches), the other in I.Q.s (for intelligence) with a given child thus having two figures after his name. If our theory were right, then high I.Q.s should be accompanied by below-average inches, and vice versa. Inspection of the data is too subjective to make such a comparison reliable; we need something more objective. We cannot directly compare inches with I.Q.s, but we can turn both into S.D.s from their respective means, thus giving us dimension-free values which can be put into a formula. This is the well-known product–moment correlation formula, which reads:

$$r_{xy} = \frac{\Sigma(xy)}{N\sigma_x \sigma_y}$$

In this formula, r stands for the correlation coefficient, x and y for the two variables which are being correlated (height and I.Q.). The Greek letter stands for summation, i.e. it tells us to sum the values which appear after it, i.e. x and y; these are the deviations from their respective means of height and I.Q. σ_x and σ_y are the S.D.s of height and I.Q.; the small Greek letter σ is often used in formulae to represent the standard deviation. The correlation coefficient, r,

ranges from $+1$ through 0 to -1; $+1$ indicates complete agreement (i.e. the tallest boy is the brightest, the shortest the least bright, and so on through the whole list). A zero correlation ($r=0$) simply means that there is no relation at all between the two variables; a tall boy could just as likely be bright as dull, or average. A correlation of -1 means that there is perfect inverse correspondence, with the tallest the dullest, and the smallest the brightest. Observed correlations do not usually get anywhere near unity; in the case of height and I.Q. one might find correlations around $+0.2$—possibly lower, almost certainly not much higher. Thus the data would contradict our hypothesis; empirical studies tend to show that our stereotype of the 'swot' is in fact inaccurate and that tall children tend to be just slightly brighter than small ones.

A few typical correlations may make the meaning of such coefficients clearer. If you were to give a group of persons an I.Q. test today, and another, similar one next week, the I.Q. scores would correlate something like 0.95, or possibly a little lower—this would depend on the actual tests used. If you gave schoolchildren I.Q. tests and correlated these with achievement tests in English, or History, the correlations would be anywhere from 0.5 to 0.8; this would depend very much on the accuracy of the achievement tests, the samples of children studied, and other factors. Height and weight would correlate around 0.5 or 0.6, possibly a little higher. If an expert ranked the football teams in the first division, or the major baseball teams, in order of excellence, and correlated this order with the final order emerging at the end of the season, the correlation would be only 0.3 or thereabouts; not enough to justify one in betting any money on it! Note that these correlations are all positive; it is customary to leave out the $+$ sign in front of the correlation which strictly speaking should accompany it.

THE PROBLEM OF SAMPLING

These examples will alert the reader to certain difficulties and complexities which arise in practice when we calculate correlations, or other statistics. The first of these relates to the sample tested. Our generalisations in psychology always pertain to a given population –all Englishmen, all Europeans, all Humans, all Mammals or whatever. But we never test all Englishmen, or all Europeans, leave alone all Humans or all Mammals; we test only a very small sample of whatever our population may be. It is very important that this sample should be carefully chosen; if it is not representative of the population in which we are interested, then our generalisation may be completely false. There are many different ways of sampling a population; the least satisfactory, and at the same time the most widely used, is the method of accidental sampling. If you look at papers published in the leading American journals of psychology, you will see that the subjects used are almost invariably rats, lunatics or sophomores; none of these are perhaps entirely representative of the population about which experimentalists are really concerned, i.e. the average human person. The particular samples chosen are not even representative of all rats, lunatics or sophomores. The rats are usually of a particular strain (Wistar or albino); the lunatics are neurotics in treatment or psychotics under drugs; and the sophomores are students of psychology acting as subjects for experiments under duress—doing this is part of their course requirements.

A truly representative sample is difficult to achieve; studies of attitudes and of intelligence come nearest to achieving this aim, particularly when children are involved. Such a sample should be made up in such a way that every member of the population has an equal chance of being chosen, and the choice should be made on a purely random basis. We might have a list of all the inhabitants of Great Britain, or the United States; we could then number all the people concerned and ask a computer to print out a list of random numbers, choosing our subjects in accordance with the output. This would clearly present us with an impossible problem, having to travel all over the country, chasing up subjects in isolated cottages as well as in city centres. In practice we might have to settle for a quota sample, i.e. a sample which in make-up (age, social class, proportion of the sexes) resembled the population in which we were interested. This is the practice of most polling organisations, and for many purposes it is probably not too inexact.

For experimental purposes, however, a rather different type of sample might be preferable. Suppose we are interested in the effects of nutrition on intelligence, and one of our queries related to the possibility that white–black differences in I.Q. were related to differences in nutrition. If we carried out our study on a quota sample of the population we would end up with a sample in which nine out of ten were white, and only one was black. We might be better off to design a sample in such a way that we first of all list the variables in which we are interested; this might be, in this case, race, sex and social class. There would be two races, two sexes and say, six social class notations, giving $2 \times 2 \times 6 = 24$ cells. Our most parsimonious use of interviewer time would be if there were equal numbers in each cell; statistically, this gives us the greatest amount of information. This would be an artificially created sample, but one which would have many advantages. Its construction is based on the hypothesis that perhaps a quota sample hides certain inhomogeneities, i.e. that what is true of men may not be true of women, or that what is true of whites may not be true of blacks, or that what is true of middle-class people may not be true of working-class people. Such a design, which is called an analysis of variance design, enables us to answer the questions raised in this manner; it also enables us to tell whether these different variables interact. Thus diet may affect I.Q. in working class blacks, but not in middle-class whites, etc.

Sometimes investigators study a whole population, say all the children in a particular school, or even a whole school district. This does not necessarily constitute a good sample if we want to generalise our conclusions to all children; schools may differ profoundly and so may different school districts. Our conclusions are much more firmly based if we take a few children from each of a large number of schools, than if we take many children from each of a small number of schools. Principles of sampling are well worked out, and should be understood by the reader of a report before coming to any conclusions about the applicability of the results. How do the investigators using rats, or sophomores, counter the implied criticisms of this discussion? They would say that there are certain uniformities in the behaviour of all humans, say, or all mammals, and that in the study of such invariances the choice of subject is relatively immaterial. This answer should not be accepted uncritically, nor should it be rejected categorically. There are certain uniformities which link rat behaviour with human behaviour; much can be learned from rat experiments that will carry over to human conduct. After all, evolution teaches us that there are important links between species; rats, like humans, have a central nervous system, and a cortex, as well as an autonomic nervous system which mediates emotion. But results from mammals can only be suggestive as far as human behaviour is concerned; before the results are transferred from one species to another, it has to be demonstrated that such transfer is permissible. Neither wholesale acceptance nor wholesale rejection of the results of animal experiments in their application to humans is justified; each case must be examined on its merits.

THE SIGNIFICANCE OF STATISTICAL DATA

A sample, however carefully chosen, does not give us results which are identical (except by chance) with those we would have obtained had we tested the whole population; chance makes the values obtained from different samples vary around the 'true' (population) mean. It will be intuitively obvious that our values will be more accurate if the sample is larger; if we want to know the average height of Englishmen we could measure random samples of 10, 100, 1000 or 10000 people. Clearly, the larger samples would give more accurate estimates than the smaller ones. Unfortunately the gain in accuracy is not proportionate directly to the increase in numbers; accuracy increases not as the number of the people in the sample, but rather as the square root of that number. In other words, accuracy can be doubled only by having four times as many subjects in your sample, not by having twice as many. This rule governs the economics of research design; large numbers are less efficient than they seem at first. Fortunately we can calculate the limits of accuracy achieved by a given sample fairly accurately, and predict how many people we need in our sample for any given degree of accuracy; this is another function of statistics which requires little more than a knowledge of the mean and the S.D. of the sample we have tested.

The second difficulty in calculating, or evaluating statistics arises directly out of the fact that we always deal with samples, and that the means and S.D.s derived from samples are not exactly right, but contain a certain amount of error. This difficulty leads us directly to the second function of statistics in psychological research, namely the analysis of *significance*. Suppose we test a group of 100 men and 100 women with a typical I.Q. test, and we discover that the men have a mean of 102, while the mean of the women is 97. Can we argue from this difference of five points that men are brighter than women? If we tested another sample of 100 men and women, can we anticipate with any degree of confidence that the men would again have the higher score, or that the difference would again be five points? It is possible to quantify the vague expression 'degree of confidence' by relating it to probability. It is customary (although quite arbitrary) in statistics to say that a difference is 'significant' if it could have arisen by chance once in 20 trials; another way of stating this is to say that the probability of the obtained difference being due to chance is less than 5% (< 0.05, as the statistics books would print it). Similarly, a difference is 'very significant' if chances are 100:1 in favour of discovering it again; in this case $p < 0.01$. Thus we identify the confidence we have with the probability that our result is not due to chance; the greater this probability (the smaller the p value), the greater our confidence. This probability varies with the number of people in the samples tested, the S.D.s of the distributions, and the size of the difference observed. Statistical significance does not guarantee psychological significance; a result may be statistically significant but psychologically trivial.

Without going into details, let us return to our example of male–female differences in I.Q. If we test samples as described, their I.Q.s will roughly follow a normal distribution, with an S.D. not far removed from 15. Chance alone will ensure that the mean of a given sample will not be exactly 100, nor the S.D. exactly 15. If we tested 100 samples of men and 100 samples of women, each sample containing 100 men (or women), and calculated the means for each sample, we would find that these means would be distributed in the form of a normal curve, around a

mean of 100; the S.D. of these means would of course be much less than 15, because means of 100 people are much less likely to deviate from each other than are the scores of individuals. The S.D. of the means of our 100 samples would in fact be 1.5, rather than 15; this follows from the formula for the S.D.$_M$, which reads: $\sigma/\sqrt{N}$. In our case, this means 15 divided by the root of 100, which is of course 10; $15/10 = 1.5$. Thus 68% of our samples of 100 men or women would deviate from 100 by no more than 1.5; only 5% would lie above 103 or below 97. Samples of this size therefore do seem to give us pretty accurate information, although hardly accurate enough to conclude that men are intellectually superior to women! Starting out with the 'null hypothesis' (i.e. the hypothesis that there are in truth no differences between our samples of men and women), we could easily discover whether or not the observed differences were too large to have arisen by chance. This is a very important function of statistics; we constantly want to compare groups with respect to intelligence, personality, attitudes, or what not, and our measurements are always affected by chance sampling errors which make it impossible to take our results too seriously. Statistics tell us with some degree of exactitude just how likely our results are to be replicable, how 'significant' they are in a formal sense. This can be done with differences: it can also be done with correlations. If we find a correlation of 0.2 between height and I.Q. in a sample of 100 boys, can we assume that this (or a similar correlation) will be found in another sample? The p value is exactly 0.05; in other words, our chances of discovering a positive correlation in another sample of 100 boys is 20:1—our result is significant (barely!)

Figure 7.2 shows the values of r which are required for significance at the $p = 0.05$ and the $p = 0.01$ levels for different sizes of sample. It will be seen how these values fall as the number in the sample increases. When there are 20 in the sample, the r values required for significance are 0.43 and 0.55 respectively; when there are 150 in the sample, they are 0.16 and 0.21. It will be seen from Figure 7.2 that increasing the sample produces a marked drop in the required values of r when the numbers are small, but that this drop becomes much less marked as the numbers get larger. This is in part a function of the fact, already mentioned, that it is the *square root* of the number of subjects in the sample which is directly proportional to the increase in accuracy of the values obtained by measurement. It is also important, however, to note that correlation coefficients have a peculiar property which is somewhat misleading. This might be expressed by saying that they are not percentages; to say that x and y correlate 0.50 is not to say that 50% of x is caused by y, or vice versa. When there is a causal relation such that x causes y, or y causes x, we may say that the percentage of overlapping elements in x

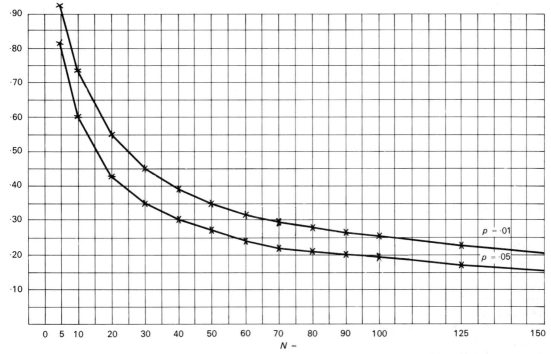

Figure 7.2 Values of the correlation coefficient required for significance at the 5% and 1% levels for different sample sizes

and y is proportional to the square of r (r^2). Thus one might say that half of a perfect correlation ($r = \pm 1$) is $r = 0.71$, and not 0.50; the square of 0.71 is 50%, while the square of 0.50 is only 25% In other words, a correlation of $r = 0.50$ is indicative of only 25% of common elements shared by x and y. It is important to bear this fact in mind, as otherwise one will tend to *exaggerate* the importance of low correlations, and *undervalue* the importance of high correlations. A correlation of 0.30 may sound quite impressive, but it indicates only 9% of common elements between x and y.

THE PROBLEM OF CAUSATION

Another problem which arises in connection with correlations is the question of causation. The discovery of a correlation, even a very sizeable one, between x and y does not imply necessarily any direct causation between the two variables. It is of course possible that x may have caused y, or that y may have caused x; however, in the absence of additional information it is not safe to make either of these assumptions. A well-known example to illustrate the danger of such hasty generalisations is the famous correlation of 0.93 between the number of registered prostitutes in Yokohama, and the number of iron ingots exported from Pittsburgh during the first half of this century. It is difficult to see how either event could have caused the other in any meaningful sense.

However, this does not mean that there is no causal nexus at all; there are many other possibilities. Thus z could cause both x and y; in our case there is a particular variable, z, which is indeed responsible for both the increase in the number of prostitutes (x) and in the number of ingots (y). This underlying variable is the population explosion which took place during this time, doubling and trebling the number of people in all major cities, and thus also increasing the numbers engaged in almost any activity, from prostitution to metal smelting. It is an underlying sin of psychologists (and even more of psychiatrists and sociologists) that they tend to interpret observed correlations as evidence of direct causation, even though there are many alternative hypotheses.

Suppose that we find a correlation between delinquency and broken homes, in the sense that delinquents come more frequently from broken homes than do non-delinquents. It is inviting to argue that this proves that broken homes *cause* delinquency, but this would be mistaken. This causal interpretation is only one of many possible explanations. It could be that people with bad genes more easily break up their marriages, and also hand these genes on to their children, who then are genetically predisposed to criminality. It could be that potential criminals, as children and adolescents, are so troublesome that they produce an intolerable strain on their parents' marriage. These, and many other possible hypotheses could be true singly or jointly; the simple fact of correlation tells us nothing about which of these alternative explanations might be true. We would need a much more analytic experimental design to throw light on the causal question. All that such an experiment as that described would tell us is that there is some connection; it tells us nothing about the causal nature of this connection. If readers of this chapter learn nothing but this one fact, namely that extreme caution is needed in interpreting correlation coefficients, and that correlation does not imply direct causation, the reading of it will have been well worth while—many eminent psychologists and sociologists have made this error time and time again!

RELIABILITY AND VALIDITY

Of particular concern to psychometrists is the application of statistics to mental testing. Tests have to be reliable and valid in order to be of much use, and these terms require careful definition in terms of psychometrics. Each term in fact can be used in two main ways which differ markedly from each other. Let us consider *reliability* first. A test is said to be reliable if it gives similar results on being applied several times. If we give a test of I.Q. today to a group of subjects, and give it again in a week's time, we might consider the correlation between the two sets of scores the reliability of the test; this is often called the *test–retest* reliability. There are difficulties associated with this definition; perhaps our subjects remember their previous answers on being retested? One alternative would be to give one form of the test on the first occasion, another form on the second; many tests have been constructed in this way, i.e. having two forms which are interchangeable, in order to assess the influence of intervening treatments on the subjects. A rather different form of reliability is the so-called *odd–even* reliability; here we might give a test consisting of, say, 100 items and correlate the sum of the odd items passed with the sum of the even items passed. This would tell us how consistently the test measured whatever it was measuring. One might consider the odd items as one form of the test, and the even items as another; this makes this form of reliability rather similar to our test–retest reliability with alternate forms.

Validity is at the same time more important than reliability, and also much more difficult to measure. By the validity of a test we mean simply the degree to which the test measures what it is supposed to measure. There are two main ways of measuring this; the first is *external validity*, in which we correlate our test with some external criterion. Suppose that we have constructed a battery of tests of flying ability, i.e. measuring those characteristics of a person which predispose him to succeed in learning to fly quickly and competently. We could give this to a sample of 100 candidates for training in the Air Force, and then put them through a uniform course of training. At the end we could test their flying ability; if our test battery was valid, then scores on it should correlate with success on the final test of flying ability. This would be an external criterion.

There are two difficulties with this course of action. In the first place, we have no criteria for most of the psychological qualities which we wish to measure. What would we use as a criterion for intelligence, for instance? School success? Amount of money earned in one's life? Social class reached? Ratings by teachers? Obviously all these criteria would be expected to correlate with intelligence, but none would make a proper criterion. Or what would our criterion be for extroversion? For aesthetic ability? Clearly there are enormous difficulties here in finding a reasonable criterion. But even when there seems to be a good criterion in existence, it often turns out that this criterion is in fact faulty. During the second World War the U.S. Air Force carried out experiments such as that just described, using as the criterion ratings made by an experienced flying instructor of the performance of the students on a set of exercises carefully defined—loops, rolls and other aerobatics they had to execute. It turned out that the battery of tests used did not correlate at all with the criterion—not because the tests were bad, but because the criterion was worthless! It was discovered that the criterion had zero reliability; when the same set of manoeuvres was rated by two independent instructors, their ratings did not correlate with each other at all! It proved more difficult, in fact, to construct a proper criterion than to construct the original battery of tests. When this was achieved, the battery was shown to be highly valid; it was in use throughout the remainder of the war, and is still in use. Examinations of all kinds are often used as criteria, but psychologists are somewhat wary of such 'criteria' and like to make sure that they are in fact highly reliable, and possess validity in turn. It is well-known that school examinations of English, for instance, are not very reliable; when the same papers are graded by different examiners, the correlation between the examiners is often quite low. The same is true of many other school subjects which depend on subjective judgements. Much work is required to make the 'criteria' anything like as reliable as the tests used to predict them.

FACTOR ANALYSIS

Psychologists, impressed with these difficulties, have concentrated more and more on a rather different type of validity, which may be called *internal validity*. This type of validity depends on the construction of a nomological network of theories and facts within which a particular concept is enshrined; validity then consists in the degree to which this network makes possible successful prediction. A statistical technique which is often used in connection with internal validation is *factor analysis*; in view of the wide-ranging usefulness of this technique a brief explanation will now be attempted, using the measurement of intelligence as our example.

Let us begin by assuming that there is a general quality, possessed in differing degree by different people, called intelligence; let us also assume that this is measured to different degrees by various mental tests, and that these tests measure nothing else in common, except *g* (which letter we will use to denote general intelligence). In addition, imagine that we have a perfect criterion of *g*, and that we have correlated our six tests with this criterion; the resulting correlations, for the purpose of our example, are 0.9, 0.8, 0.7, 0.6, 0.5, and 0.4. Given these assumptions, then we can construct a table listing the correlations between the various tests; this table is given below (Table 7.1). Note how this table is constructed. Tests 1 and 2 correlate with *g* 0.9 and 0.8 (these correlations are called 'factor saturations' in the table, for reasons which will become apparent). The correlation between tests 1 and 2 is the product of their factor saturations, i.e. $0.9 \times 0.8 = 0.72$. All the other correlations in the table are constructed in a similar fashion; thus the correlation between tests 2 and 5 is $0.8 \times 0.5 = 0.40$. Note the values in brackets; these denote the correlations of a test with itself, i.e. its reliability. However, we could not use ordinary estimates of reliability because these would introduce factors other than *g*, consequently these values are not empirically testable, and this is the reason they are put in brackets. Numerically, they are quite easy to discover; they are simply the squares of their factor saturations, i.e. that for test 1 is $0.9 \times 0.9 = 0.81$, etc. If we know the factor saturations, then we know these 'reliabilities'—and conversely, if we know the 'reliabilities', then we also know the factor saturations (which are the square roots of the 'reliabilities'). Consider this table carefully, because we shall now turn the whole example around and try to derive the factor saturations from a table of observed correlations.

This of course is what would happen in actual fact; we would administer the six tests to a large group of children, compute the intercorrelations between the tests, and end up with a table like Table 7.1 (with the values in brackets missing, of course, because these are not empirically derived) and without knowledge of the factor saturations. Let us assume that we were faced with a table such as this; what could we deduce from it? Note first of all that there are certain interesting regularities in the table. It is of the superdiagonal form, i.e. the correlations get smaller as we go from the top left corner either to the right, or down. If we take a group of correlations, such as those between tests 1 and 2, and 4 and 5, we find that they are proportional; 0.54 divided by $0.45 = 0.48$ divided by 0.40. On thinking it over, this must of course be so; we obtain the correlations in column 4 and 5 by multiplying our factor saturations by 0.6 and 0.5 respectively, consequently all the values in column 4 must be six-fifths of those in column 5! Putting it in another way, $0.54 \times 0.40 = 0.45 \times 0.48$. A mathematician would say that this matrix (any rectangular array of figures is a matrix in mathematics) has a rank of unity; this is a very unlikely thing to happen by chance, and many important consequences follow from it. One of these is that we can immediately calculate our 'reliabilities', and knowing these, our factor saturations. What is the 'reliability' of test 1? Call it *x*, and form equations such as those given a few lines above.

Let us take tests 1 and 2; all the values in column 1 are nine-eighths of those in column 2. Thus $x = 9/8$ of 0.72, which is 0.81! There are literally hundreds of such equations in the table from which we can find the 'reliabilities', and consequently the factor saturations. But that means that from a table of observed correlations we can obtain correlations between our tests and our hypothetical perfect criterion of g! The validity of our six tests is as given in the table of factor saturations; that for test 1 is 0.9, that for test 2 is 0.8, and so on. By a little statistics we can even discover the validity of the whole battery of tests, which turns out to be over 0.95.

Table 7.1 Intercorrelations among six ability tests

	1	2	3	4	5	6	*Factor saturation*
1.	(0.81)	0.72	0.63	0.54	0.45	0.36	0.9
2.	0.72	(0.64)	0.56	0.48	0.40	0.32	0.8
3.	0.63	0.56	(0.49)	0.42	0.35	0.28	0.7
4.	0.54	0.48	0.42	(0.36)	0.30	0.24	0.6
5.	0.45	0.40	0.35	0.30	(0.25)	0.20	0.5
6.	0.36	0.32	0.28	0.24	0.20	(0.16)	0.4

Table 7.2   Intercorrelations among Thurstone's 'primary mental abilities'

	R	W	V	N	M	S	Factor saturation	
R	(0.71)	0.48	0.55	0.54	0.39	0.39	0.84	Reasoning
W	0.48	(0.48)	0.51	0.47	0.39	0.17	0.69	Word fluency
V	0.55	0.51	(0.46)	0.38	0.39	0.17	0.68	Verbal ability
N	0.54	0.47	0.38	(0.36)	0.19	0.22	0.60	Numerical ability
M	0.39	0.39	0.39	0.19	(0.22)	0.15	0.47	Rote memory
S	0.39	0.17	0.17	0.26	0.15	(0.12)	0.34	Spatial ability

APPLICATIONS OF FACTOR ANALYSIS

So much for theory; Table 7.1 looks nice and orderly, but of course it was drawn up precisely to illustrate certain principles of orderliness. Do actual empirical observations support the general theory? Professor C. Spearman, of the University of London, was the first to draw attention to the orderly appearance of matrices of intercorrelations between intelligence tests, and to formulate the general theory we have been dealing with Sir Cyril Burt, also of the University of London, added a proviso which we will return to in the next. chapter, namely that in addition to *g* there are a number of special abilities (group factors, in the language of factor analysis), such as verbal ability, memory, numerical ability, perceptual ability, etc.; these make the pattern more complex, but they do not destroy the case for *g*. This is made clear when we look at the results of an actual empirical study, carried out by Professor L. L. Thurstone and his wife, Thelma, both of the University of Chicago. Table 7.2 lists the intercorrelations they found between six sets of intelligence tests, grouped into sets according to the special abilities they measured. It will be seen that the pattern is very similar to that shown in Table 7.1, although of course the inevitable chance errors make the orderliness of the matrix less impressive*. It is possible to test statistically whether the departure from complete orderliness is significant, or due to chance, and the calculation shows that it is not significant. Empirical data, then, bear out the general theory first put forward by Spearman, always provided we also take into account group factors.

The whole procedure may seem a piece of statistical legerdemain at first, but consider the rationale. Theory tells us that the intercorrelations between carefully chosen tests of intellectual ability should assume a certain pattern, very unlikely on *a priori*

*Note that tests of 'reasoning' are much better measures of general intelligence than tests of rote memory, the respective factor saturations being 0.84 and 0.47; this is what one would expect on common sense grounds

grounds; the observed matrices tend to fall into precisely the predicted pattern. This does not prove the theory to be right; it merely strengthens it, and justifies us in accepting it provisionally until a better theory comes along which predicts the same organisation of correlation coefficients, and also succeeds in predicting other phenomena which Spearman's and Burt's theories do not predict. In this factor analysis follows the usual dictates of the scientific method.

The case where there is only one factor is of course the simplest, and has been chosen especially to illustrate the workings of the method of factor analysis. Suppose we had two factors? Table 7.3 lists 12 questions, six of which (keyed N) were chosen as measures of the personality dimension of neuroticism–stability, while the other six (keyed E) were chosen as measures of the personality dimension extroversion–introversion; these two dimensions are conceived of as independent (uncorrelated). When correlations between the 6 E questions, and zero for large samples of the population, the resulting matrix had an appearance quite different from that given in Table 7.1, or Table 7.2; there were uniformly high correlations between the 6 N questions, high correlations between the 6 E questions, and zero correlations where N questions were correlated with E questions. Table 7.4 gives the actual correlations, and the factor saturations. We may regard saturations below 0.10 as quite insignificant; Table 7.4 shows that N items have saturations only with the N factor, E items only with the E factor. Again, such a pattern could not have resulted from chance accidents, and in so far as it is in good agreement with prediction, it confirms the theory according to which the items were chosen originally.

It is often convenient to graph factorial patterns, and Figure 7.3 illustrates how this can be done. Geometrically, correlations can be represented as cosines of an angle; the cosine of a right angle (90 degrees) is of course zero, and consequently two lines at right angles to each other can represent the two factors (N and E) which are conceived of as indepen-

Table 7.3 Personality questionnaire items

		Key
A.	Do you sometimes feel happy, sometimes depressed, without any apparent reason?	N
B.	Do you have frequent ups and downs in mood, either with or without apparent cause?	N
C.	Are you inclined to be moody?	N
D.	Does your mind often wander while you are trying to concentrate?	N
E.	Are you frequently 'lost in thought' even when supposed to be taking part in a conversation?	N
F.	Are you sometimes bubbling over with energy and sometimes very sluggish?	N
G.	Do you prefer action to planning for action?	E
H.	Are you happiest when you get involved in some project that calls for rapid action?	E
I.	Do you usually take the initiative in making new friends?	E
J.	Are you inclined to be quick and sure in your actions?	E
K.	Would you rate yourself as a lively individual?	E
L.	Would you be very unhappy if you were prevented from making numerous social contacts?	E

dent, and which emerged from the analysis as independent. We can now mark off our factor saturations on these two factors, and mark with crosses the positions of our 12 items; this has been done in Figure 7.3. The resulting diagram shows clearly how there are two quite independent clusters of items. The two lines drawn to represent E and N are usually given the neutral name 'axes'; when they represent personality factors, as in this case, it is convenient to label them 'dimensions of personality'.

THE NATURE OF FACTORS

There could of course be more than two axes or dimensions; mathematically, the number is limited only by the number of tests and subjects used in a study, although of course it is difficult to imagine more than three dimensions at right angles to each other. What does the term 'factor' imply? Some people have suggested that factors are causal agencies, others that they are principles of organisation, others still that they are statistical artefacts. The simple

Table 7.4 Factor analysis of twelve personality questions

	Intercorrelations												*Factor saturations*	
	1	2	3	4	5	6	7	8	9	10	11	12	E	N
1	—	0.65	0.48	0.38	0.29	0.50	−0.04	0.08	−0.04	0.09	−0.07	0.01	0.01	0.75
2	0.65	—	0.60	0.35	0.27	0.46	0.01	0.02	−0.10	−0.11	−0.10	0.05	−0.06	0.74
3	0.48	0.60	—	0.30	0.25	0.45	−0.04	0.02	−0.06	−0.15	−0.15	0.08	−0.09	0.71
4	0.38	0.35	0.30	—	0.50	0.31	0.03	−0.08	−0.04	0.17	−0.04	0.06	0.02	0.58
5	0.29	0.27	0.25	0.50	—	0.32	−0.04	−0.09	−0.14	−0.14	0.17	0.02	−0.06	0.58
6	0.50	0.46	0.45	0.31	0.32	—	0.02	0.12	0.04	−0.02	0.07	0.13	0.09	0.63
7	−0.04	−0.04	0.04	0.03	−0.04	−0.02	—	0.40	0.12	0.17	0.20	0.16	0.48	0.00
8	0.08	0.02	0.02	−0.08	−0.09	0.12	0.40	—	0.19	0.38	0.26	0.21	0.59	0.04
9	−0.04	−0.10	−0.06	−0.04	−0.14	0.04	0.12	0.19	—	0.08	0.44	0.53	0.59	−0.06
10	0.09	0.09	−0.15	0.17	−0.14	−0.02	0.17	0.38	0.08	—	0.42	0.13	0.49	−0.04
11	−0.07	−0.10	−0.15	−0.04	0.17	0.07	0.20	0.26	0.44	0.42	—	0.41	0.68	−0.02
12	0.01	0.05	0.08	0.06	0.02	0.13	0.16	0.21	0.53	0.13	0.41	—	0.64	0.09

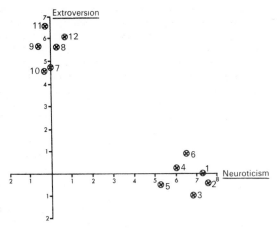

Figure 7.3   Relative position in two-dimensional space of six neuroticism and six extroversion questionnaire items

answer is that they could be any of these, or all three; the meaning attached to a factor depends crucially on the original theories which led the investigator to carry out his study, the tests used, the populations studied, and the outcome of the analysis. No general answer is possible, except perhaps that factors are suggestive of concepts, and usually support (or fail to support) some conceptualisation or other. They are artefacts in the same way that scientific concepts are always artefacts; intelligence, like gravitation, is not something 'out there' which we can see and touch, but a concept which may be useful or useless. It is pointless to ask whether extroversion, or neuroticism really exists; concepts never 'really' exist, whatever that might mean. Factor analysis is one of many methods to test the applicability of certain concepts to certain types of material; it is particularly suited to certain psychological problems, but has also been used in physics (particularly in rheology) and in other 'hard' sciences. It is no panacea; bad data, collected without any particular theory in mind, will not give rise to elegant and meaningful factors. Factor analysis, like all other methods of statistics, is a good help maiden; it is not a good mistress. Much of the criticism which has been directed at factor analysis is really meant for psychologists and others who have used it improperly; mathematically, the method has received impressive support from professional statisticians, and in fact it was invented by Karl Pearson, who also invented the product–moment method of working out correlations. It cannot be condemned wholesale as a method, although particular applications of this method may be criticised as faulty.

Psychologists have to go one step further than statisticians in the applications of factor analysis. Statisticians are concerned entirely with the descriptive value of the method; there is a tremendous economy when you can describe a whole matrix of 36

correlations (as in Table 7.1) in terms of six factor saturations, or a matrix of $12^2 = 144$ correlations (as in Table 7.2) in terms of 24 factor saturations. When we have to deal with matrices of $150 \times 150 = 22\,500$ correlations, the saving in space and effort can be very marked indeed. But the psychologist, in addition, has to be concerned with the meaning of the resulting factors; they may be convenient descriptively, but are they psychologically useful?

THE ROTATION OF FACTORS

Let us return to Figure 7.3. The pattern created there by the positions of the 12 crosses, representing the 12 items in the questionnaire, is invariant; in a mathematical sense it represents the best description of the relations (correlations) between the items possible in a two-dimensional space. But the position of the two axes is to some extent arbitrary; we could rotate these in the two-dimensional space without disturbing the relative positions to each other of the 12 items. To the extent that we use these axes in our description, our description is arbitrary. Sometimes the position of the items is so clear-cut that the arbitrariness is not very apparent; given the position of the origin (where the axes cross) and the 12 crosses, most people would probably have placed the axes where they actually occur. But this is not always so, and Thurstone has elaborated certain rules which help us in objectively deciding on an optimal position. He looks for something called 'simple structure'; this might be defined (not entirely correctly, but near enough) as a position

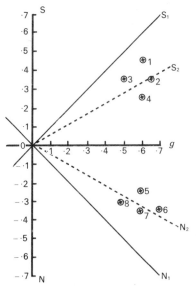

Figure 7.4   Alternative axis placements for describing the relationship among eight ability tests

of the axes in which there is the largest possible number of zero factor saturations. It will be seen that in our Figure 7.3 this is indeed so; however you may shift the axes, you cannot obtain a larger number of zero saturations than the $6+6=12$ shown there, and detailed in Table 7.3. (Remember that because of chance errors any saturation below 0.10 is considered as a zero saturation.) This rule is objective, and works surprisingly well, but it is not a law of nature, and may occasionally misfire. The most interesting difficulty occurs when this rule comes into conflict with the rule that factors should be independent, uncorrelated or orthogonal (at right angles to each other).

Consider Figure 7.4. It represents the pattern of correlations between four tests of spatial ability (tests 1, 2, 3 and 4) and four tests of numerical ability (tests 5, 6, 7 and 8). The various axes drawn represent several different ways in which we can conceptualise the observed pattern. Taking the right-angled axes marked g and S–N, we might say that we have two major factors; first there is general intelligence, with both spatial and numerical tests having saturations on that factor, and second there is a factor which contrasts spatial and numerical ability—perhaps because some people have a spatial bent, others a numerical one. This is the kind of solution which Burt might have preferred in the early days of his work. Thurstone would have rotated the axes into the position indicated by the right-angled axes labelled S_1 and N_1. He would have said that there is no evidence here of a general factor of intelligence at all; there are simply two 'primary factors', namely spatial and numerical ability. This indeed was his original contention when he began working in this field; however, this interpretation came into conflict with the principle of 'simple structure', which would lead us to place the axes as indicated by the broken lines. We again have two factors, S_2 and N_2, which can be conceptualised as verbal and numerical ability; in addition, we have the

advantage that these factors obey the principle of simple structure, and are therefore defined objectively, and not arbitrarily. We do, however, have the difficulty that now the axes are not at right angles; they are oblique, and as the cosine of the angle indicates the correlation between the axes, the factors are not independent. Actually the angle happens to be 75 degrees, of which the cosine is 0.26; in other words, spatial and numerical aptitude in this sample correlate 0.26! As Table 7.2 shows, this is precisely what Thurstone did in fact find, although the particular data in Figure 7.4 have not been drawn from his work. The finding that Thurstone's 'primary factors' are intercorrelated (as shown in Table 7.2) means that we must postulate some 'higher-order factors' to account for these correlations in turn, and Thurstone himself suggested that in his analysis Spearman's g emerges as such a second-order factor, from the intercorrelations of his primaries.

Which of these different interpretations of the data in Figure 7.4 is correct? The simple answer of course is that they are all correct; mathematically, these solutions are interchangeable—in other words, you can write a transformation equation which will turn the one set into either of the others. But from the practical, psychological point of view Thurstone's second conception (oblique factors whose intercorrelations give rise to higher-order factors like g) has many advantages, particularly that of objectivity; furthermore, it gives rise to a hierarchical picture of intellectual abilities which is very attractive. At the bottom of this picture we have individual tests of mental abilities; these are correlated to form primary factors, such as verbal aptitude, numerical ability, rote memory, etc. These in turn are correlated and define a general factor, g, of intellectual ability. Figure 7.5 shows such a picture, which is of course much simplified, but nevertheless gives a good picture of the organisation of mental abilities.

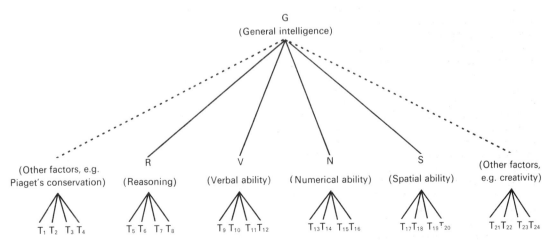

Figure 7.5   The hierarchical model of abilities

In this chapter we have dealt rather more in detail with factor analysis than with other -methods; the reason is simply that no other statistical method interacts so closely with the substantive aspects of psychological research as does factor analysis. As a consequence, other methods have not become identified to the same degree as factor analysis with substantive results, such as the hierarchical representation of mental abilities shown in Figure 7.5, or the dimensional analysis of personality shown in Figure 7.3. It is hoped that enough detail has been given to enable the student to understand the logic of the approach; for a detailed understanding or application, this introduction is of course quite inadequate. Below are given a few suggestions of books which the reader may wish to consult in his search for further enlightenment.

Suggested readings

A long list of books on statistics would be quite inappropriate here. A. E. Maxwell's *Basic Statistics in Behavioural Research* (Harmondsworth: Penguin, 1970), is an excellent brief introduction. So is J. T. Spence, B. J. Underwood, C. P. Duncan and J. V. Cottons *Elementary Statistics* (New York: Appleton-Century-Crofts, 1968). References given in these books will introduce a wider range of writings. C. Burt's *The Factors of the Mind* (London: University Press, 1940) is probably the best introduction to factor analysis and its logic.

Chapter 8

INTELLIGENCE

H. J. Eysenck

The notion that people can be divided into more or less bright, clever or 'intelligent' groups is not a new one; the very term 'intelligence' goes back to Cicero, something like 2000 years ago, and the distinction between 'cognitive' and 'emotional' aspects of human nature was clearly drawn by Plato, even earlier. Emotion as the driving force in human affairs, reason as the charioteer; pictures of this kind are found in many ancient writers on human nature. In modern times, it was Sir Francis Galton and the father of sociology, Herbert Spencer, who introduced the term into popular consciousness; for them it referred to an ability which enabled its owner to adjust himself more effectively to a complex and ever-changing environment. Galton considered this ability to be strongly determined by heredity, and was the first to draw attention to the possibility of using twins to investigate this suggestion. He also devised mental tests of various kinds, but these bore little relation to modern intelligence tests. Cyril Burt defined intelligence in the early years of this century as *innate, general, cognitive ability*; he explicitly based his definition on the conceptions of Galton and Spencer, but pointed out that there was much empirical work to support such a view. Leaving the question of heredity aside for the moment, we may with advantage consider what is meant by the other two terms.

INTELLIGENCE AS A GENERAL COGNITIVE ABILITY

We have already considered the meaning of 'general' in the chapter on psychometrics (Chapter 7); the hypothesis here is that all sorts and types of cognitive, problem-solving, abstract mental activity require one and the same mental ability, although they may do so to varying degree; some activities depend more on intelligence than do others. We have also considered the evidence required for such an assertion, and the methods used in order to test the hypothesis of 'generality'; it will be remembered that it is a universal finding that all tests of cognitive ability correlate positively together, and that these correlations, provided certain precautions are observed, fall into a particular kind of pattern which corroborates the theory. There is now no doubt that in addition to general ability (often referred to as *g*) there are several more specialised abilities (verbal, numerical, visuo-spatial, perceptual, memory, etc.), giving rise to a hierarchical model of intelligence; nevertheless, to crown this hierarchical model there is the Plato–Cicero–Spencer–Galton–Burt–Spearman concept of *g* or general intelligence. Thus Burt's definition is correct as far as *generality* of mental ability is concerned.

When we turn to the term 'cognitive' in his definition, we may have some difficulty in coming to an agreed conception of what this word implies. Clearly it refers to mental activity concerned with thinking; *cogitare* is the Latin word for thinking, as in Descartes' famous saying: *Cogito ergo sum*. Involved in cognition are such things as awareness of external reality, processing of information, problem solving, and the eduction of relations and correlates. Spearman laid down three laws of cognition which he thought completely defined the whole field. His first law was one of 'apprehension', stating that a person has more or less power to apprehend outer reality, and inner states of consciousness; in more modern language this might be rephrased to read that a person has the power to encode and transmit information. That people differ in this apparently very elementary 'ability', and that this correlates with intelligence, has been shown in a very simple experiment. We can measure reaction time very simply; a light goes on, setting off an electronic timer, and the subject of the experiment depresses a key, stopping the timer. The time elapsed (usually something like 1/5th of a second or thereabouts) is the reaction time of the subject. We can complicate this experiment, introducing two, four, or even eight lights, and asking the subject to press the key underneath the particular light that goes on. With two lights we have what is technically known as one 'bit' of information, with four lights we have two 'bits', and with eight lights we have three 'bits'. With each 'bit' of information added, reaction time increases linearly, but this progression differs for bright and dull subjects. There is no difference between them when we are simply testing their raw reaction time; introduce 'bits' of information which require to be processed, and the reaction time of dull subjects increases disproportionately, as compared with that of bright subjects.

Spearman's second law relates to the eduction of relations. 'When a person has in mind two or more ideas (using this word to embrace any item of mental content, whether perceived or thought of) he has more or less power to bring to mind any relations that essentially hold between them.' Thus looking at the words: Black–White, or High–Low, the relation of oppositeness is brought to mind. His third law relates to the eduction of correlates: 'When a person has in mind any idea together with a relation, he has more or less power to bring up into mind the correlative item.' Thus looking at the typical intelligence test problem: Black is to White as High is to ——, we would argue that the relation implied in the first pair of words is one of opposition (according to the law of eduction of relations), and that when this relation is applied to the word High, the correlative word Low should spring to mind, and be written down on the test form. Relations and correlates can be discovered between words, numbers, shapes, and indeed in many different ways; typically, intelligence tests consist of items explicitly calling for the discovery of relations and correlates. Below are given typical items exemplifying Spearman's three laws.

For examples see below, also page 117.

Intelligence test items: Examples

(1) Tall:Short=Up: _____ (Write in the missing word)
(2) Car Train Violet Buses (Underline the odd man out)
(3) a d g j m _____ (Write in the missing letter)
(4) 4 9 19 39 _____ (Write in the next number)

Relations can be very obvious, and usually (certainly in tests designed for school children) the answer is pretty obvious. But of course quite complex relations can be dealt with in problems of this kind. Consider the following:

Beethoven:Schoenberg=Dickens:?
Select the correct answer from the following:
    Hemingway, Joyce, Mann, Hesse, Amis, Priestley.

Here the correct answer is of course James Joyce, but the process of reasoning which leads to this answer is much more complex than in the 12 examples given on this page. Indeed, the complexity of relations involved can be as intricate as the maker of the test

Select the correct figure from the six numbered ones.

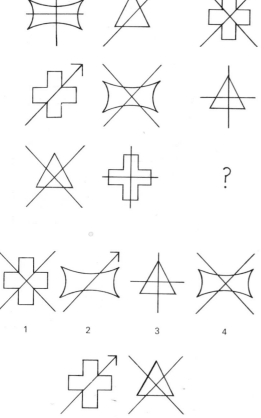

Select the correct figure from the six numbered ones.

chooses; usually many less complex problems are preferred to a few very complex ones because chance always plays a part, and this part is reduced by having many different problems. But this is a choice of convenience, dictated by the fact that usually only an hour or so is available for testing; given unlimited testing time one might prefer the more complex type of test, particularly for highly educated and very intelligent subjects.

THE MEANING OF I.Q.

With children, of course, simple test items are usually mandatory, and practically all I.Q. tests make use of such items. Most of the test items used in this connection go back to the work of A. Binet, who was the first man to construct an intelligence test that actually agreed with external criteria, such as school achievement, teachers' ratings, etc. He introduced some of the concepts, such as mental age, which are still central to the measurement of intelligence, and a brief look at his contribution may serve to clarify

many of the problems we shall encounter later on.

Working at the psychological laboratory of the Sorbonne in Paris, Binet spent 10 years trying out various mental tests on children from the schools of Paris and its suburbs. This choice of children as subjects turned out to have been a lucky accident, and it is responsible for the very term 'I.Q.'. If we wish to distinguish between bright and dull people, nature gives us a good yardstick in children—as they get older, they also, on the average, get smarter. The 10-year-old can do things, intellectually, that the five-year-old cannot do. Nor is this a simple function of learning. The 10-year-old has learned more than the five-year-old, but that is not all. Consider Figure 8.1 below; this is the Figure Copying Test which was developed at the Gesell Institute of Child Study at Yale University. The test consists of the ten figures depicted, arranged in order of difficulty; the child is simply instructed to copy them on paper with a pencil. Young children succeed only with the first one or two items; as they get older, they succeed with more and more difficult items. This is not a function

Select the correct figure from the six numbered ones.

Select the correct figure from the six numbered ones.

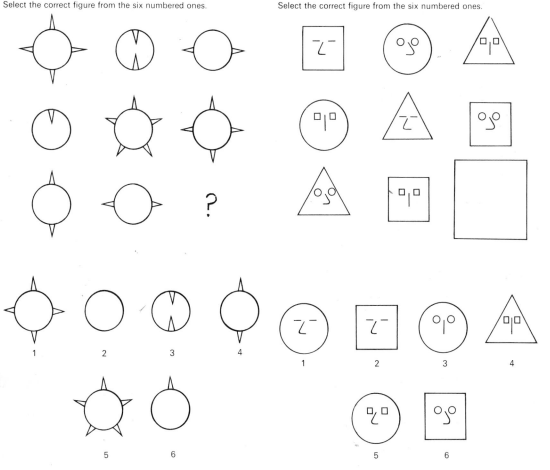

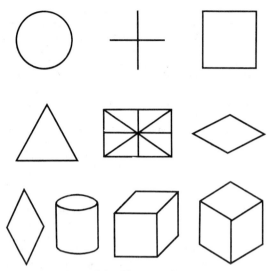

Figure 8.1   Figure copying test

of teaching; it is practically impossible to coach a young child to succeed with an item which is beyond his ability. This test correlates very well with other tests of intelligence, and is much less influenced by cultural and environmental factors than most. Binet did not use this particular test, but he employed a rather similar verbal one—he would read a simple sentence to the child, and ask him to reproduce the content of the sentence. On this 'sentence reproduction test' older children succeeded in producing more of the contents of the sentence than younger children, and the same was found with other tests of mental functions which Binet devised.

In 1904, the Minister of Public Instruction turned to Binet with a request to devise a test which would spot mentally subnormal children in the Parisian schools, so that they could be put into special groups and provided with special schooling. In devising a proper measuring scale, as opposed to simple tests, Binet had to find some way of expressing the relative brightness or dullness of each child, and the observation that each child increased in intelligence as he got older gave him his cue. He developed the concept of 'mental age', i.e. the age level which a given child's performance equalled, regardless of the actual, chronological age of the child. If, on the Figure Copying Test, the average seven-year-old can draw the rectangle, while the average six-year-old cannot, then the mental age of any child who can draw the rectangle, but not the next more difficult figure is seven— whether the chronological age of the child is five or 10, or whatever. Of course a five-year-old child with a mental age of seven is bright, while a 10-year-old child with a mental age of seven is dull; thus by relating mental and chronological age we can tell something of the relative intelligence of each child.

Obviously one would never rely on a single test in this connection; Binet used a great variety of different tests. At first, Binet and his collaborator, Simon, drew up a progression of thirty tests which they thought covered the range of mental capacity. For very young babies the examiner simply noted eye– head co-ordination as a lighted match was moved across the field of vision. A little more advanced were the making of grasping movements, the imitation of gestures, the following of instructions to touch various parts of the body, the naming of familiar objects, the repetition of sentences, the construction of sentences which included three given words, and at the very top the ability to distinguish between abstract words such as 'liking' and 'respecting'. Binet and Simon established the age at which the average child could first succeed with each test, and defined his 'mental age' accordingly. This still left the problem of how to bring together mental and chronological age. Binet used the simple difference between the two, but this is unsatisfactory. A difference of two years between M.A. and C.A. (the abbreviations commonly used for mental and chronological age) is much more diagnostic at the age of six, say, than at the age of 12; at the early age one child is obviously brighter than one whose M.A. equals his C.A., while at the age of 12 no-one could say for sure whether there was any difference at all. We would have to look at the *proportional* rather than the *absolute* difference between M.A. and C.A.

This important step was taken by W. Stern, a German psychologist; he suggested dividing the M.A. by the C.A., giving a quotient which would be more invariant than a simple difference score. Later on it became customary to multiply this quotient by 100, in order to get rid of the decimal point, and this figure became known throughout the world as the Intelligence Quotient, or I.Q. By definition, the average person has an I.Q. of 100; a bright person has an I.Q. higher than 100, and a dull one has an I.Q. lower than 100. Consider two children, both with a mental age of eight; one is actually six years old, the other 12. The I.Q. of the former would be 133; that of the latter 67. Intelligence quotients show a distribution in the population rather similar to that of height, or weight, most people being centred on the middle range, with few extremes either way. In the chapter on psychometrics (Chapter 7) there is a diagram which illustrates the distributions of I.Q.s in the population; it will be remembered that something like 50% of the population have I.Q.s between 90 and 110; only $\frac{1}{2}$% have I.Q.s of 140 or over, or of 60 or below.

THE SOCIAL IMPORTANCE OF THE I.Q.
What do different I.Q. levels mean, in terms of everyday experience? Table 8.1 shows the mean I.Q.s recorded for members of different professions and occupational groups; these values are very similar for

different countries, and have been repeatedly found in many different investigations. Roughly speaking, there is a difference of some 50 points of I.Q. between the upper middle class and the semi-skilled and unskilled working class; these of course are only average figures. There is also much overlap; there are many working class people with high I.Q.s, and there are some middle class people with low I.Q.s. The overlap is greater in the lower social classes; it is easier to have a high I.Q. and lose out in the occupational stakes for reasons of bad luck, bad health, lack of persistence, or mental illness, than it is to get past the many hurdles, educational and otherwise, which bestrew the path to middle class success, with a low I.Q. It is sometimes suggested that it is not I.Q. which determines social class, but rather the reverse; the environmental advantages of the middle class child are responsible for his high I.Q. and the disadvantages of the working-class child for his low I.Q. This is not so; when children within a given family are tested, it is found that the bright ones move up in the social scale, while the dull ones move down. There is considerable social mobility in our social system, with only a minority of children found in the same social class as their parents, and it is the child's intelligence which determines whether he will go up, down, or stay where he is.

Table 8.1 Mean I.Q. of different professional and occupational groups

140	Higher Professional; Top Civil Servants; Professors and Research Scientists.
130	Lower Professional; Physicians and Surgeons; Lawyers; Engineers (Civil and Mechanical).
120	School Teachers; Pharmacists; Accountants; Nurses; Stenographers; Managers.
110	Foremen; Clerks; Telephone Operators; Salesmen; Policemen; Electricians; Precision Fitters.
100+	Machine Operators; Shopkeepers; Butchers; Welders; Sheet Metal Workers.
100−	Warehousemen; Carpenters; Cooks and Bakers; Small Farmers; Truck and Van Drivers.
90	Labourers; Gardeners; Upholsterers; Farmhands; Miners; Factory Packers and Sorters.

Table 8.1 demonstrates that it is possible to measure the I.Q.s of adults. This involves certain difficulties, but these are not connected with the construction of tests; intelligence tests are equally easy to construct for adults as for children. The problem arises because the M.A. ceases to grow after the age of 16 or so; that means that if we take the I.Q. formula seriously a person's I.Q. would seem to drop as he gets older! (The M.A. remains the same after 16, but his C.A. grows; this makes the quotient smaller and smaller.) Psychologists use a statistical method of calculating I.Q.s for adults; these adult I.Q.s are not really quotients at all, but the term has been retained in order not to complicate the picture.

Are I.Q.s constant, or do children have a high I.Q. at one time, a low one at another? The answer seems to be that I.Q.s are not very accurate when measured in very young children; it is only when children are six years old that a reasonable estimate of their final (adult) I.Q. can be obtained. By the time they reach the age of eight or so the I.Q. value obtained is not subject to much change; after this age the I.Q. may be said to remain pretty steady—omitting of course cases of brain damage, or other external interference with the intactness of the organism. After the age of 60 or so there is a deterioration in mental ability which is much more precipitate in some people than in others; these differences are probably due to arteriosclerosis and other physical changes in the brain. The constancy of the I.Q. depends of course on two presuppositions: that a properly constructed test has been used in the measurement, and that the measurement has been carried out by a properly qualified psychologist. When eager amateurs use badly constructed tests, anything can happen; in this, psychological measurement is no different from measurement in the physical sciences.

It is sometimes suggested that the I.Q. is not a measure of intelligence at all, but merely some sort of educational achievement test. I.Q. does of course correlate quite highly with educational achievement; you need intelligence to benefit from educational instruction. But the notion that I.Q. tests are simply arbitrary riddles constructed by white, middle class testers for the benefit of white, middle class children is wide of the mark. Just to take one example— Canadian Eskimos do slightly better than white Canadians on I.Q. tests; yet they hardly qualify as middle class whites! Similarly, many working class children do better than middle class children. We shall see later on that the main determinant of I.Q. performance is heredity, and that environment plays only a rather minor part. Furthermore, you cannot teach people how to do I.Q. tests; there is a minor effect derived from doing a few tests as practice, but that is all. A dull person cannot be coached to come up with a high I.Q.—unless of course you know what test is going to be used, and make him learn by heart all the answers! The evidence is pretty conclusive that I.Q. tests are fairly good measures of human intelligence; they are not perfect, but the I.Q. is by far the best estimate of a person's innate intelligence that we have.

THE GENETIC BASIS OF I.Q.
We have defined intelligence as the innate, general, cognitive ability a person possesses; in so far as it is innate, clearly it cannot be increased. We can increase a person's knowledge, or his effectiveness in particular situations, by special teaching, but we can do little to improve his capacity-for-learning. At first sight, therefore, the situation seems remarkably gloomy; a

second look, however, may change the prospect somewhat. In the first place, there may be physiological methods for increasing intelligence by drugs and in other ways which directly affect the biological basis of intellect; in the second place intelligence, as measured by intelligence tests, is not identical with the intelligence that is inherited. It is merely an estimate, even though quite a good estimate, of biological intelligence, and to the extent that our measure of intelligence is influenced, as it undoubtedly is by environmental factors, to that extent we can claim that intelligence can be increased.

Before discussing these points, we must look at the claim that differences in intelligence are in fact largely due to heredity. There are many different types of proof; these lead to numerical estimates of the relative contribution of nature and nurture which are in remarkably good agreement. The total amount of variation in intelligence which can be found in the population is called the 'variance', and there is now good agreement that 80% of this variance is contributed by heredity, 20% by environment.

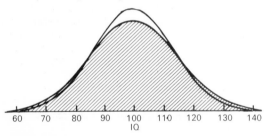

Figure 8.2 Shaded curve is distribution of I.Q.s in the population. Unshaded curve is hypothetical distribution if all environmental variance were removed. (From Jensen, 1973, by courtesy of Methuen)

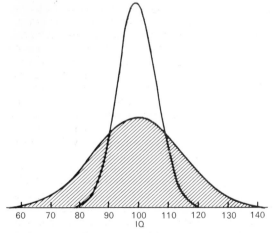

Figure 8.3 Shaded curve is distribution of I.Q.s in population. Unshaded curve is hypothetical distribution if all genetic variance is removed. (From Jensen, 1973, by courtesy of Methuen)

This leaves to environment a definite, though small, influence, and I.Q. can certainly be improved to an extent corresponding to this figure. Just what is meant by these estimates can be seen in Figure 8.2, in which the shaded curve shows the existing distribution of I.Q.; the unshaded curve shows the kind of curve that would exist if all environmental effects on I.Q. were removed. It will be seen that the difference would be quite small. On the other hand, consider Figure 8.3, which shows what would happen if all genetic factors could be removed as by magic. The unshaded curve shows how I.Q.s would be distributed in the population if this were done; now there is a most marked difference from the situation as it exists at present, which is indicated again by the shaded curve.

There are ten main indications of the importance of heredity in determining I.Q.; the first two make use of the phenomenon of twinning. Identical twins share a common heredity; when such twins are brought up in separation from an early age, any similarities they may show with respect to I.Q. are almost certainly due to heredity—after all, their environments are quite different. There have been observations made of 122 pairs of such twins, and they have been found remarkably alike. When a person is tested today, and again next week, the results are never quite identical; there are errors of measurement, accidental factors like a pencil breaking, or the person having a headache on one occasion and not the other, and so on. On the average, under these circumstances, a person's score on one occasion will differ from his score on another occasion by 4.5 points of I.Q. The I.Q.s of identical twins, brought up in separation from each other, differ on average by only 6.6 points—in other words, the twins are almost as much like each other as a person is to himself on two occasions. If we subtract this amount of 'error', the twins only differ by 2.1 points of I.Q.—in spite of having been brought up in entirely different circumstances, by different persons! This is a truly remarkable result. It has been suggested that perhaps there is a critical period, early in life (say during the first year or two) when environment is particularly important; later separation might be unimportant once this critical period had been passed. When identical twins were compared who had been separated very early (after two months), and who had been separated rather later (after 24 months on the average), it was found that those separated early on were in fact more alike than those separated late, disproving this hypothesis.

The second twin method makes use of comparisons between identical twins, on the one hand, and fraternal twins, on the other. Fraternal twins only share 50% heredity; hence for any trait or ability which depends very largely on heredity identical twins should be more nearly alike than fraternal twins. This has been found to be so; on the average identical twins correlate 0.86, fraternal ones only 0.55. This

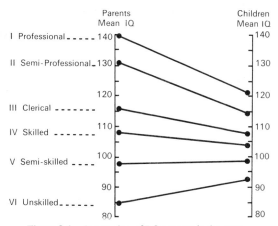

Parents
Mean IQ

Children
Mean IQ

I Professional
II Semi-Professional
III Clerical
IV Skilled
V Semi-skilled
VI Unskilled

Figure 8.4 Regression of I.Q.s towards the mean

large difference makes it clear that heredity plays a very important part in causing individual differences in intelligence.

A third method of proof involves kinship correlations. On a genetic hypothesis, one can predict the correlations to be found between different members of a family. Thus second cousins should correlate 0.14; the observed value was 0.16. Uncles and aunts, on the one hand, should correlate with nephews and nieces, on the other, 0.32; the observed value was 0.34. Kinship correlations have always supported the genetic hypothesis very strongly. So have the effects of inbreeding, which constitute our fourth proof. Inbreeding should produce a lowering of I.Q. in the offspring, and studies of cousin marriages have shown the predicted effect.

Of particular interest is the fifth proof; this depends on the well-known genetic phenomenon of regression to the mean. Very tall parents have tall children, but the children are not quite as tall as their parents; they have regressed towards the mean of the whole population. Similarly, very short parents have short children, but these too have regressed towards the mean, and are taller than their parents. Exactly the same happens in the case of intelligence; Figure 8.4 gives results from some very large-scale studies carried out by Professor Sir Cyril Burt. Fathers who are members of the professions have mean I.Q.s of 140, but their children have regressed towards the mean; their I.Q.s average only just above 120. On the other hand, fathers in the unskilled group average something like 85 points of I.Q.; their children regress upwards, and have I.Q.s on the average which are well above 90. Thus the children of parents who can provide the best environment go down in I.Q.; the children of parents who can only provide the very worst environment go up in I.Q. It would be very difficult to explain these effects in environmentalistic terms.

ENVIRONMENTAL STUDIES OF I.Q.

These five proofs have been based on genetic postulates; the remainder come from studies in which environmental factors have been varied. Figure 8.2 has shown the effects theoretically expected if environmental factors could be eliminated completely, so that all variation in intelligence was due only to heredity We can try to carry out an experiment coming close to this situation by taking children whose mothers, for one reason or another, are incapable of or unwilling to look after them, and bringing them up in an orphanage from a very early age; conditions in an orphanage are such as to expose the children to pretty much the same environment—same teachers, same food, same companions, same excursions, same books, same buildings. No doubt the environments are not identical, but they are as similar as it would be humanly possible to go—certainly no egalitarian government could legislate for greater environmental equality than that experienced by these children. Under these conditions believers in the importance of environment would have expected a considerable decrease in the variation in I.Q. observed; if these variations are produced by good or bad environmental influences, then eradicating these excesses should produce pretty uniform I.Q.s. In fact this did not happen; there was hardly any change in the variance of I.Q.s. Very much as indicated in Figure 8.2, the elimination of environmental influences made practically no difference to the variation in I.Q.; there was an effect of this kind, but it was minimal, amounting to less than 10%.

Foster children provide another interesting avenue of approach. We can measure the I.Q. of foster children when they are grown up, and correlate this with the I.Q.s of their true (biological) mothers, and with the I.Q.s of their foster mothers. If heredity is important, children's I.Q.s should correlate with their true mothers' I.Q.s; if environment is important, children's I.Q.s should correlate with foster mothers' I.Q.s. Empirical studies show that the former is true; foster children's I.Q.s correlate with the I.Q.s of their biological mothers to almost the same extent as do the I.Q.s of children brought up by their own mothers. The home environment of the foster parents seems to make little or no difference in this case. Correlations with foster mothers' I.Q. are low or non-existent, in spite of the fact that the children have lived with their foster parents practically all their lives.

In the fostering situation it is possible to correlate a child's I.Q. with measures of the various features in the foster home which might be assumed to determine the child's success or failure on the intelligence test—socio-economic status, number of books, amount of time devoted to the child by the mother each day, pressure for education, and so on and so forth. When this is done, the correlations are found to be remarkably low; taking all these, and many other factors together, and combining them in such a way as to get the optimum correlation, it is found that all these environmental factors add up to only 17% of the total variance—just about what our original estimate of 20% amounted to.

We must next turn to efforts at direct manipulation of the I.Q., i.e. attempts to raise the I.Q. above the level reached at an earlier age. Many such attempts have been made, and many successes claimed; this is a difficult field to survey because most of the studies in question have made experimental errors in conducting the experiment, and statistical errors in analysing the results. A typical error of the first kind is that of 'teaching the test'. Let us assume that we have given I.Q. test A to a group of children, and that we now proceed to split this group in two—the experimental group is given special tuition, the control group is not. At the end of several years, both groups are again tested with I.Q. test B. Now the attempt made by the experimenter has been to improve the intelligence of the children in the experimental group; what often happens, instead, is that he teaches them specifically the contents of test B! The experimental children now do very well on test B, but if you gave them test C it is very doubtful whether they would differ from the control group of children. Incredible as it may seem, this sort of error, though often in a milder form, has in the past been made by experimenters whose results have then received wide coverage in the press as evidence of the possibility of improving the I.Q.! When we eliminate experiments of this kind, and restrict ourselves to those where both the conduct of the experiment and the statistical analysis could be said to have been adequate, we find that I.Q.s can indeed be raised, but that these increases always remain well within the limits set by our allocation of 20% of the total variance to environmental factors. In other words, the formula says that environment plays a part, though a rather less important one than heredity, in the determination of I.Q. differences, and efforts to increase the I.Q. produce effects well within the limits of these environmental influences.

The last proof pertains to the existence of two kinds of mental defect. Children with I.Q.s between 50 and 70 are in most cases the bottom end of the normal distribution of I.Q.s; they tend to come from homes where the parental I.Q. is very low, and where often there are other mental defectives in the family. Imbeciles with I.Q.s below 50 are suffering, in the majority of cases, from a single gene disorder which over-rides all other influences; these children may come from any sort of family, and the I.Q.s of their parents are not different from the average. Such disorders are usually recessive, which means that the genes in question may have been handed on by parents and grandparents who never themselves showed any trace of the disease. It is this group that provides a 'hump' at the bottom end of the I.Q.

distribution, making it less 'normal' than indicated in the diagram in Chapter 7.

Having now looked at the sort of proof advanced for the proposition that differences in I.Q. are largely determined by heredity—genetic factors—we can see why it is so very difficult to improve a child's I.Q.

When claims are made to the effect that something of the kind has been accomplished, it is usually found that things have gone seriously wrong in the experimental setup—either in the design of the experiment, or else in the analysis of the data. As an example, consider the claims recently made by Dr O. S. Heyns for his technique of 'abdominal decompression'. In this technique, a kind of close-fitting tent is erected over a structure surrounding the abdomen of the prospective mother, and this is then decompressed by suction, changing the shape of the womb and allowing greater amounts of oxygen to reach the cortex of the developing foetus. Heyns used the Gesell tests of intelligence on children of mothers so treated, and found that their mental age was advanced by something like 30%; moreover, he found that the rise in I.Q. was proportional to the number of decompression sessions the mother had undergone. At the time of testing the children were only two years old, and it is well-known that I.Q.s measured at that age are very poor prognosticators of terminal I.Q. for any given child; the correlation between I.Q. measured at the age of two, and that measured at the end of adolescence is practically zero. (The reason for this is that infant tests are mainly tests of physical development, and such development has little to do with intelligence.) Nevertheless, the claims aroused considerable interest, and obviously had to be tested. When such tests were carried out, it was found that it was inadvisable to rely on volunteers for the experiment; mothers who volunteered were nearly all of high I.Q., good education, and middle class origin! No wonder their babies scored reasonably well, and better than average. When this design error was eliminated, children born of mothers who had decompression treatment showed no difference in I.Q. from children born of mothers not receiving this type of treatment. Tests were carried out until the age of three, but no differences were observed at any stage. Sad though it is, decompression does not provide an easy way of raising the I.Q. level of the population by 30 points!

THE BIOLOGICAL BASIS OF I.Q.

Rather more positive have been studies using glutamic acid. When it was claimed, some 25 years ago, that this acid could improve I.Q.s by 10 or more points there was a rush to test the claim on human subjects, mostly mental defectives, and on rats. (Rats can be given intelligence tests, too; usually the psychologist makes them learn to run mazes, and counts the number of errors made until they have mastered the maze.) The results were very confusing, and it was thought that perhaps this, too, was just a lost cause. But the facts seem to support a rather more complicated conclusion. Glutamic acid does nothing for the child (or rat) of average or above-average intelligence; it does, however, raise the performance level of dull children (and rats), and of mental defectives. There are now too many positive results to discount the possibility that here we may have an approach to the raising of I.Q. levels which promises well. Obviously what is needed is a more thoroughgoing experimental approach; we need to know what are the optimal doses of glutamic acid, how these should be spaced to get optimum results, and with what type of child positive results can be obtained. We would then want to go on to find out, by physiological and neurological research, just where in the brain the drug acts, and what structures or processes it acts upon; there are already some reasonable hypotheses regarding this problem. And finally we would want to find out what it is in the glutamic acid that produces the effect; biochemists would then be able to take the drug apart and perhaps improve its principle of action. Exciting developments are ahead along these lines, provided that society can be turned away from idle and doomed-to-failure attempts to improve I.Q. by educational and other environmental manipulations, and can be made to support rather biological approaches based on the principle that human beings are fundamentally biological organisms, developed through the process of evolution well beyond anything previously existing, but nevertheless still showing the same physiological, anatomical and neurological structures which characterise our forefathers.

There is direct evidence of the biological determination of I.Q. It is possible to record on the electroencephalograph brain waves produced by sudden sounds (the so-called evoked potentials).

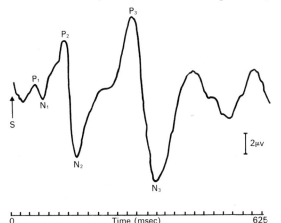

Figure 8.5 Illustration of evoked potential in the EEG. P = positive component. N = negative component. S = stimulus onset. (The S was a tone delivered over earphones)

Figure 8.5 shows a typical curve of this type, with three positive and three negative components. These reactions are very consistent indications of a person's reactivity; identical twins show very similar reactions, as compared with fraternal twins, demonstrating a strong genetic component. Several studies have shown that I.Q., as measured by ordinary pencil-and-paper tests, correlates quite well with the evoked potentials, in the sense that bright subjects show smaller latencies (shorter waves) and greater amplitude (bigger waves) than do dull subjects. Other types of EEG activity have also been found to correlate significantly with I.Q., and there seems to be no doubt that we can measure with some degree of accuracy the physiological activity underlying intelligence, as shown in our pencil-and-paper tests. This work, which is just beginning, fills an important lacuna; previously, efforts to find a biological basis for I.Q. measurement had been unsuccessful.

SEX DIFFERENCES IN I.Q.

In view of this biological determination of I.Q., can we say that men and women (who after all differ profoundly at the biological level), also differ at the level of intelligence? In the days before the suffragette movement and 'women's lib' it used to be taken for granted that men were superior to women with respect to intellect; laws were framed in such a way as to protect women against their assumed foolishness, putting a male (father, husband, brother) in charge of her affairs at all times. The apparent absence of female genius in any important sphere—science, sculpture, mathematics, drama, painting, politics, war, but with the possible exception of novel writing—seemed to support this argument, and remnants of this attitude still linger; we still speak of women successful in business, or in academic careers, or in medicine, as having a 'masculine mind'. Objective facts were hard to come by until the turn of the century, and alternative theories, such as the fairly obvious one that women were culturally and socially so handicapped that whatever intelligence they had might be prevented from manifesting itself in outstanding achievement, were seldom considered. The development of intelligence tests changed the position drastically, and we now have clear-cut evidence to show that these old-fashioned views are quite wrong. From the very first, girls and women were found to be equal to boys and men on any of the most widely used intelligence tests; when slight differences were found, usually among younger children, girls if anything were superior to boys. To some extent this exact equality may be an artefact; the makers of intelligence tests, finding that on the whole there were few differences between the sexes, tended to avoid items which did show such differences; if they did not omit such items, they tended to balance an item favouring the males by another item favouring the females. Such equalisation could not have happened had not the sexes been approximately equal in any case, but the equality in average I.Q. between the sexes hides two important differences which may have far-reaching consequences.

The first major difference between men and women relates to the spread of intelligence. This is not equal; there are more very bright men, just as there are more very dull men. There are more women with average I.Q.s, shading into the bright and dull regions. The position is pictured in Figure 8.6, although the differences apparent there are somewhat exaggerated; in actual fact, they are somewhat less than those shown in the figure. The cross-hatched area at the top of the Figure shows the surplus number of females in

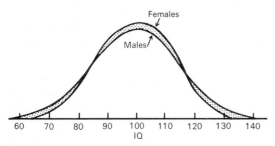

Figure 8.6   Diagram to illustrate the greater dispersion of male I.Q.s

the middle range of I.Q.s, i.e. roughly between 90 and 110; the cross-hatched areas at both ends show the surplus number of males in the extreme ranges of I.Q., i.e. roughly above 120 and below 80. Thus men are more *variable* with respect to I.Q., women more *uniform*; the differences are slight, but nevertheless they may have much social importance.

It has been suggested that this difference in distribution of I.Q. may be responsible for the remarkable fact that men are greatly over-represented both among the mentally defective and among the geniuses. The argument is attractive. If there are more men with very low I.Q.s, and if very low I.Q.s are closely identified with mental defect, then an explanation of the predominance of men in the mentally defective category seems obvious. Similarly, genius requires a high I.Q.; there are more men with high I.Q.s, and consequently we may have here an easy explanation of the otherwise rather puzzling predominance of men among the outstanding persons of every age. But inviting as these speculations may be, there are reasons for distrusting such an obvious and convenient explanation. The act of certification of a person as mentally defective is a social act which takes into account many factors quite independent of I.Q.; indeed, intelligence testing in mental defective institutions has unearthed individuals with quite high I.Q.s—the highest to date was 125! Youngsters with

psychopathic personalities are sometimes sent to mental institutions for want of a better place to send them; they are often of average or even superior intelligence—and nearly always male! Furthermore, men are required in our society to earn a living; low I.Q. may make this extremely difficult, and thus finally results in their being certified. Women are not equally likely to be required to earn a living; they may live at home until married, and after marriage their low I.Q. may impose a burden on their husbands, but not lead to certification. There are thus all sorts of reasons of a purely social and administrative nature which may account for the observed excess of males among the mentally defective.

The same is true of genius. There are thousands of people with high I.Q.s; there are very few geniuses. Without a doubt, there are enough women with very high I.Q.s to provide a quota of geniuses; the reason for their failure to do so must lie elsewhere. Two possible causes spring to mind. The first is the obvious social disability which still makes it much more difficult for women, particularly women who wish to marry and have children, to compete successfully with men—men can devote themselves much more single-mindedly to the pursuit of a career than can women. The second cause is the greater aggressiveness, dominance, assertiveness and sheer bloody-mindedness of men—all qualities often shown by the budding genius, and probably necessary to carry him to success. These personality qualities are closely linked with male hormones, and are consequently not accidental accompaniments of the male state; without them outstanding success is not likely in a very competitive society.

PATTERNS OF ABILITY IN MEN AND WOMEN

The second major difference between men and women relates to the pattern of abilities which go to make up their respective I.Q.s. Binet was insistent that problems as varied as possible should be included in his test; thus he used different modalities (verbal, numerical, spatial), as well as different mental mechanisms (reasoning, memory, suggestion, etc.). The I.Q. in a sense is the average of all these different types of mental abilities, applied to all these different materials; though two people may achieve the same total I.Q. score, one may have better verbal ability, another better numerical ability. One may have outstanding reasoning ability, the other excellent memory. Thus the possibility arises that men and women, although equal in total score, are yet different with respect to certain strengths and weaknesses; men might be better with respect to one type of ability, women with respect to another. This indeed seems to be the case, and the particular pattern of abilities, as related to sex, has received much attention from psychologists in recent years.

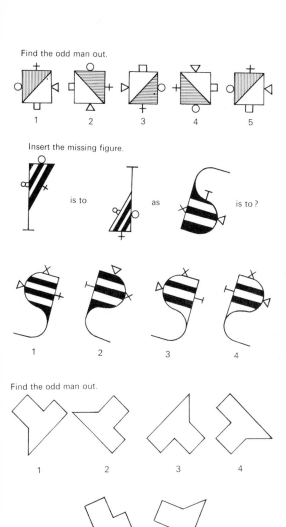

Find the odd man out.

Insert the missing figure.

is to   as   is to?

Find the odd man out.

Find the odd man out.

We may begin with very elementary abilities which are related to Spearman's law of apprehension. Women have lower touch and pain threshholds than men; this greater sensitivity to touch and pain has been observed from birth, and is characteristic of the female sex. Women also have better auditory discrimination; men, on the other hand, are better at visual discrimination. These differences, too, are found very early in life; when only a few weeks old, girls show more interest in tonal patterns, while boys are more concerned with visual stimuli. Studies of sexual stimulation bear out this differentiation—men are more responsive than women to visual erotic stimuli, as any pornographer will testify. Women are more dependent on tactile stimulation. These differences, as well as the related one of greater female susceptibility to, and sensitivity towards olfactory stimuli (odours), seem related to the presence of sex hormones; in other words, they are not accidental concomitants of social conditioning, but are genetically linked with sex.

When we turn to more complex abilities, we find that men excel in spatial ability, i.e. in the visuo-spatial skills required to organise and relate visual stimuli to their spatial contexts, and quite generally to manipulate (e.g. rotate) visual material imaginatively. A number of typical items from a test of visuo-spatial ability are given below; they will illustrate the sort of thing that psychologists talk about in this connection.

Spatial ability is also better developed in males in other species than the human; in rats and chimpan-

Find the three odd men out.

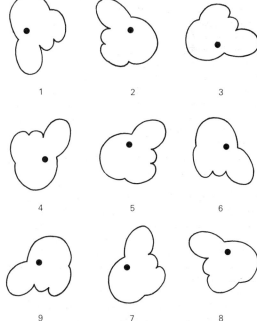

zees we find the same superiority. We now know that there is a genetic link between a person's sex, and his visuo-spatial ability; if social customs and habits exert an influence, it cannot be very large or decisive. It has been suggested that there may be evolutionary reasons for these differences. Males (at least within the mammals) are required to roam around for the purpose of hunting, defence and aggression; they therefore require good visual acuity, as well as visuo-spatial ability. Females, sitting at home and tending to offspring, do not require equal acuities and abilities. Whether this speculation is true or not is impossible to say at the moment; the fact that other mammals besides ourselves show this feature makes it likely that evolution has in fact played a part in causing these differences.

If females are inferior with respect to visuo-spatial ability, they come into their own with respect to verbal skills. Girls learn to talk earlier than boys; they have a better vocabulary than boys of comparable age, and they articulate better. Altogether, they are superior with respect to all aspects of language usage—writing, spelling, grammar and sentence construction show girls ahead of boys. Furthermore, their particular ability at even quite early ages predicts well their final I.Q.s when they reach adolescence or adulthood; this is not so with boys, whose development is much more erratic. Typical of tests on which girls are superior is the so-called synonym-antonym test. It is required to indicate which of the two words printed on each line means the same, or opposite of the first word.

Nonchalant	zealous	melancholy
Quandary	dilemma	quadrant
Incursion	encroachment	disaster
Diabolical	ridiculous	satanic
Chagrin	vexation	sneer
Obdurate	intractable	vigilant
Sang-froid	composure	climax
Intrepid	silent	dauntless

Women are thus superior to men with respect to the executive aspects of language; this superiority does not apply to verbal reasoning, i.e. to reasoning in which the problem is stated in words, and where the process is most likely carried out verbally. On a test like the following, women would not have an advantage over men. Here the testee is required to formulate the relation that is implied between the first two words, and then formulate the correct correlate for the third word, and finally select the word nearest to this correlate among the five choices given in brackets.

Haughty—pride : quivering—(quake, fool, shivering, fear, shaking)

Warrant—arrest : license—(swim, dog, automobile, certificate, wed)

Chapel—cathedral : ward—(room, insane, hospital, hoard, patient)

Innocence—acquittal : guilt—(error, crime, police, guild, conviction)

Clock—time : scales—(fish, scalp, beam, weight, balance)

Obesity—ridicule : grace—(face, grant, ovation, kindness, admiration)

Muscle—contraction : nerve—(expansion, serve, fibre, monkey, conduction)

Another ability in which women excel is rote memory. They are able to hold in their memory store various unrelated and personally irrelevant facts, for short periods of time, where men tend to remember only coherent and/or personally relevant material. In school work, girls often learn by committing material to memory, while boys tend to try to master the underlying principles. It is not known whether this difference is really sex-linked in a biologically meaningful fashion, or whether it is due to differences in upbringing, social expectations, and the like. On the other hand, boys and men tend to do better on tests of numerical and mathematical abilities, although not necessarily when dealing with simple problems of 'mechanical' arithmetic; it is when more complex mathematical reasoning and the manipulation of abstract numerical entities are called for that this superiority becomes apparent.

Men tend to be superior to women at mechanical tasks, probably because of their proficiency in visuo-spatial abilities. This superiority is particularly marked when a task calls for the comprehension of mechanical relationships; as far as manual dexterity is concerned women tend to perform better. These differences may be responsible for the different sorts of careers into which men and women tend to drift; men predominate in technical, constructive and motor repair jobs, while women predominate in secretarial jobs, and assembly jobs requiring deft use of their hands. There may of course be social forces determining these different careers in part, but it would not be reasonable to forget the underlying, biologically determined abilities which make such differentiation meaningful.

With regard to the primary asymmetry between the sexes, visuo-spatial versus linguistic skills, it is interesting to note that this may be related to a similar cerebral asymmetry. The right hemisphere is more concerned with perceptual, motor, spatial and quite generally non-linguistic skills; the left hemisphere, on the other hand, is concerned almost entirely with language. (This is true of most right-handed people.) Now there is some evidence that in young children, myelination and the growth of neuronic dendrites in various areas is more advanced in the left hemisphere in girls, and in the right hemisphere in boys. Possibly this may be regarded as evidence for the biological determination of such differences in ability as have been observed.

CRITICISMS OF INTELLIGENCE TESTING

We may conclude this chapter by looking at certain

criticisms which are often made of intelligence testing. Thus it is said that environment and heredity are so intimately interwoven that it is impossible to tease them apart. All I.Q. tests make use in part of skills and information previously acquired through contact with the environment; how can we ever hope to equalise these contacts? The problem is similar to that encountered by Galileo and Newton in putting forward their laws of motion; these laws only apply properly in a complete vacuum, and cannot be tested anywhere on earth, where friction and air resistance are ever present (even in the most perfect vacuum we can produce nowadays.) There are many ways out of this difficulty. We can calculate the effects of air resistance; or we can measure the fall of different types of bodies in different vacua, forming a regression equation and calculating the effect on having a complete vacuum. Similarly, in psychology we can construct tests depending to a greater or lesser extent on environmental factors; tests least dependent on such factors are often called 'culture fair', to indicate that they rely less than most tests on cultural knowledge. Test items on pages 117 and 118, are examples of 'culture fair' tests; the test items on page 126 would be examples of strongly culture-dependent items. Such diverse items measure slightly different aspects of *g*; these are sometimes called 'fluid' and 'crystallised' ability. Fluid ability comes nearest to the genotype of intelligence; it refers to a person's 'potential energy', as yet uncommitted to any particular expression. Crystallised ability is 'kinetic energy', i.e. the result of the application of fluid ability to a particular set of items of knowledge. These two types of ability correlate quite closely under most ordinary circumstances, but it is of course conceivable that occasionally one might find a culturally very handicapped child with high fluid ability, but little crystallised ability. Such a child could only be tested properly with a 'culture fair' type test. Racial comparisons also require 'culture fair' tests. We have already mentioned that Eskimos score well, compared with white Canadians, on such tests; they do not do quite so well, for obvious reasons, on culture-bound tests.

Another type of criticism is often directed at the format of test items; looking back at those quoted as examples in this chapter, it will be seen that they are all 'convergent'—in other words, the correct solution is unique, and completely prescribed by the relations obtaining between the parts of the problem. It is sometimes suggested that 'divergent' tests might give a better indication of a person's originality and creativeness—such tests are scored in terms of how many solutions to a problem the subject can put forward. A typical problem might be: Think of as many as possible uses of a brick. It has been suggested that such tests measure something entirely different from I.Q., but this is not true; correlations between the two types of tests are in fact quite high. Nor is there any evidence that truly creative people do any better on 'divergent' tests than on 'convergent' tests. There is some evidence that extroverts do better on divergent tests; this is probably due to the fact that introverts are more critical of their solutions, and suppress the sillier ones. Solutions are evaluated in terms of quantity, not quality; hence such reticence is penalised. School children who go in for science tend to do better on convergent tests, those who go in for arts on divergent tests; this may be related to the extrovert–introvert distinction. On the whole the available evidence does not suggest that divergent tests would add anything of lasting value to I.Q. measurement, although further research may unearth something of importance.

Another criticism which is often raised against I.Q. tests suggests that there is much arbitrariness about the selection of items. This, as we have seen, is not so. Items are selected in accordance with certain objective psychometric principles; their survival depends on the pattern of intercorrelations found in relevant populations. It is interesting to note that types of items which are particularly highly correlated with *g* tend to be types of items which best incorporate Spearman's three cognitive laws; this suggests that we may be dealing here not with arbitrary generalisations, but with true and testable scientific laws. Many people have tried to construct tests which would eliminate observed I.Q. differences between different groups, but without any success; item selection is not an arbitrary business which by design or accident has resulted in such results as are shown in Table 8.1 or Figure 8.4, but a lawful procedure the results of which have scientific meaning.

One last point may be worth making. It is often objected that intelligence tests are not a measure of a man's worth; this is obviously true, but then no psychologist has ever suggested that intelligence has any such wide-ranging function. Science, as we have seen in the first chapter, always abstracts from the rich web of experience; only in this way can we carry out measurement at all. We can isolate a certain class of invariant events which we label 'intelligent'; this class of events is not identical with the class of events we label 'compassionate', or yet another class we label 'altruistic', or yet a third one we label 'brave'. There are many desirable virtues; intelligence is only one among many, and a person possessing high intelligence can of course be lacking in any or all of the other virtues. Very intelligent men have been cowards, self-seekers, sadists, exploiters of others, criminals, hypocrites, adulterers, and every bad thing you can conjure up in the imagination; I.Q. tests have nothing to say about these other aspects of personality. All that a high I.Q. score means is that the person in question has a marked ability to solve problems, think abstractly, and generally act intelligently. He may not always be able to employ his high gifts to the best advantage; many neurotics are intelligent, but their emotional problems interfere with the proper exercise of their ability.

It is easy to exaggerate the importance of this abstract ability we call 'intelligence'; it is equally easy to underrate its value. It is only possible for 60 million people to live on this island, which is not blessed with many natural riches, by the exercise of a high degree of intelligence; only the use of their great abilities enables them to import enough food and raw materials to survive. We are sometimes told that we over-rate intelligence in the upbringing of our children; but if we fail to help them reach the highest level of achievement their innate endowment permits, the whole nation will be sufferers. All our plans for improving the level and style of living of the poorer sections in our society are dependent utterly on our intelligence, and its proper use; without this we would all starve. No society can restrain those who possess the highest ability, and hope to survive; this simple biological fact is not always taken into account in discussions of intelligence. Intelligence is not all there is to man; nevertheless, intelligence is an important and, socially, extremely useful part of man. Our ability to measure this variable with some degree of precision means that we can control it and use it to the general advantage of society.

References

For the purpose of this book, it seemed best to omit primary references to the large number of facts mentioned; instead, we give here a list of secondary sources in which the reader can discover references to all the points discussed. The titles of these books are a good indication of the ground covered by each.

Butcher, H. J. (1968). *Human Intelligence: Its Nature and Assessment* (London: Methuen)

Cattell, R. B. (1971). *Abilities, their Structure, Growth and Action* (Boston: Houghton Mifflin)

Eysenck, H. J. (1973). *The Inequality of Man* (London: Temple Smith)

Eysenck, H. J. (1973). *The Measurement of Intelligence* (Lancaster: Medical and Technical Publishers)

Guilford, J. P. (1967). *The Nature of Human Intelligence* (New York: McGraw-Hill)

Jensen, A. R. (1973). *Educability and Group Differences* (London: Methuen)

Spearman, C. (1927). *The Abilities of Man* (London: Macmillan)

Vernon, P. E. (1961). *The Structure of Human Abilities* (London: Methuen)

Vernon, P. E. (1969). *Intelligence and Cultural Environment* (London: Methuen)

Chapter 9

PERSONALITY

G. D. Wilson

WHAT IS PERSONALITY?

The layman uses the term 'personality' in two senses: sometimes he describes an acquaintance as having a 'good' or 'strong' personality, meaning that he has qualities enabling him to 'win friends and influence people'. At other times he describes people in terms of their most striking characteristics—submissiveness, impulsiveness, aggressiveness, etc. This latter usage corresponds fairly closely with the way that psychologists use the term. Broadly, the psychology of personality is concerned with important individual differences between people. Traditionally, however, the field has been further delimited: individual differences in abilities and aptitudes are not usually included in the realm of personality; nor are attitudes and beliefs. These areas have separate chapters devoted to them.

A distinction worth noting at the outset is that between traits and states. Nearly all of the adjectives that can be used to summarise people's behaviour—anxious, aggressive, talkative, depressed, sober, etc.—can refer either to characteristic differences between people (traits) or to temporary fluctuations or moods within the same individual (states). Personality is mainly concerned with enduring characteristics of the individual, i.e. traits rather than states.

Trait names are useful for describing people. If we say that Smith is 'sociable', we have suggested a great deal about his characteristic behaviour in one word. It is then likely that Smith would enjoy meeting people, going to parties, talking with his friends, and that he would be unhappy if deprived of the company of others for any length of time. There are thousands of situations in which his 'sociability' could be manifested, and knowing this about him we could predict how he would probably behave. We do not, however, know anything about the causes of his behaviour. It would be circular to say that he likes parties because he is sociable; we have described him as sociable after observing his characteristic behaviour including, perhaps, his enjoyment of parties. So trait names are purely descriptive; causal analysis is a more complex further step that will be attempted later.

MEASUREMENT OF PERSONALITY

If we describe Smith as 'sociable' some amount of information may be conveyed to another person who has not met Smith. A scientist would wish to take this further by establishing precisely what is meant by 'sociability' and where Smith stands on this attribute compared to other people. These are the two major purposes of measurement: to provide operational definitions of variables (definitions expressed in terms of the operations that must be performed in order to observe variations in the behavioural attribute in question), and to attach numbers to objects and events in such a way that mathematical manipulations can be performed upon them (e.g. calculation of averages, measures of variance, etc.—see Chapter 7).

Direct observation

Any measure of an individual's personality is actually a sample of his behaviour. Therefore its validity will depend upon the representativeness and importance of the behaviour that is sampled. Some attempts have been made to measure personality by direct observation of ongoing behaviour, but there are distinct practical problems. It is not generally possible to shadow a person at all times like a private detective and observe his behaviour in all important and relevant circumstances—time and respect for human privacy forbid. Direct observation 'in the field' is most often used with children and subhuman species; for example, children might be observed in the school playground and rated on characteristics such as gregariousness, dominance and aggressiveness. Sometimes it is helpful to use a time-sampling technique in which a note is made of what a particular child is doing say every 10 minutes. Other kinds of behaviour can be measured by a simple count, e.g. how many times does the child perform certain predefined fidget movements during a one-hour session in the classroom?

Questionnaires

Probably the most straightforward and useful method of measuring personality is to have the individual report on his own characteristic behaviour by filling out a questionnaire or inventory. Examples of the kinds of items used in a typical personality inventory are shown in Table 9.1. (The meaning of the three traits assessed by these items will be discussed below.) This is clearly a very easy way of getting at an individual's personality traits, but it depends upon the assumption that the person filling out the questionnaire is able and willing to report accurately on his characteristic behaviour. 'Ability' implies that he understands the meanings of the items and can 'place'

Table 9.1   Examples of the type of item in the Eysenck Personality Inventory

Are you a very talkative person?
Do you like plenty of excitement going on around you?
Would you enjoy a lively party?
Do you often do things on the spur of the moment?

Are you worried by awful things that might happen?
Do you suffer from 'nerves'?
Are you often tired and listless for no good reason?
Would you describe yourself as 'moody'?

Would you take drugs that have strange effects on you?
Do you think insurance schemes are a waste of time?
Did you tend to dislike your parents?
Do you sometimes tease animals?

Note: 'Yes' answers would tend to be obtained to the first 4 items by the extrovert, to the second 4 by the neurotic (emotional) person, and to the last 4 by the person high on psychoticism (tough-mindedness)

himself relative to other people with respect to the types of behaviour involved. For example, if he is asked whether he is 'very talkative' he has to decide whether he is more or less talkative than most other people, or about the same. Of course, the response to each individual item is not critical since it is the overall pattern emerging that is the basis of scoring traits. There is, in fact, fairly satisfactory evidence that people are able to report accurately on their own characteristics. As regards 'willingness', it is possible that some respondents might fill out a questionnaire so as to appear in what they imagine will be a favourable light; or they might wish to appear as neurotic as possible in order to gain sympathy, treatment or attention of some kind. The evidence suggests that under certain motivational situations, e.g. in applying for a job, distortions of this kind can affect the measurement of personality. There are ways of combating these motivational influences, notably the inclusion of 'lie scales' to assess the extent to which 'faking good' has occurred, but they cannot be regarded as effective under all conditions of admin-

istration. Despite this limitation, however, the self-report technique has proved the most generally useful of all personality measures.

Before going on to discuss other personality measures it is worth distinguishing some of the major approaches to the construction of questionnaires and inventories by reference to their best known examples. The first method is called *empirical keying* and it is typified by the Minnesota Multiphasic Personality Inventory, abbreviated (thank goodness) to M.M.P.I. This questionnaire was originally developed as an aid to diagnosis of psychiatric disorder. Its authors began with a set of several hundred statements covering psychiatric symptoms, physical health, general habits, domestic, occupational and social affairs. Score keys were then developed according to the power of each item to discriminate various criterion groups, regardless of the content or apparent meaning of the statement. For example, a schizophrenia scale was constructed by comparing the responses of a group of individuals diagnosed as schizophrenic with normal controls and selecting questionnaire items which showed maximum discrimination between these groups. In this manner a large number of scales have been constructed—hypochondriasis, depression, hysteria, psychopathy, paranoia, masculinity–femininity, etc. (Table 9.2). A number of 'control keys' have also been designed to detect and allow correction to be made for biases such as 'faking good', evasiveness and carelessness. Some clinicians claim to be able to tell a great deal about an individual on the basis of his profile on all of these scales; but validation checks have often shown that their confidence is not completely justified. An interesting recent development is the availability of computer scoring and interpretation (Figure 9.1). Any similarity to a horoscope is coincidental!

The M.M.P.I. has so many items, covering such diverse areas, that theoretically it could be used to measure any attribute for which an outside criterion is available just by following the empirical keying procedure. To take a mildly ridiculous example, a key of 'baldness' could be devised by noting which items

Table 9.2   Some scales on which the M.M.P.I. is frequently scored

Hs	Hypochondriasis	Concern over bodily functions, concern about health, tendency toward physical complaint.
D	Depression	Depression, dejection, discouragement, despondency.
Hy	Hysteria	Immature, unrealistic, amenable to group ideas, kindly, courteous, naive, needs social acceptance.
Pd	Psychopathic deviate	Irresponsible, undependable, impulsive, egocentric, defiant, asocial, individualistic.
Pa	Paranoia	Aggressive, critical, irritable, moody, sensitive, sensitive to criticism.
Mf	Masculinity–femininity	Masculinity or femininity of interests.
Pt	Psychasthenia	Apprehensive, tense, hesitant, insecure, self-conscious, feelings of inadequacy.
Sc	Schizophrenia	Bashful, withdrawn, oversensitive, secretive, cautious.
Ma	Hypomania	Confident, hypersensitive, not persistent, aggressive, charming, expansive.
Si	Social introversion	Tendency to avoid social contacts, little dependency upon people.

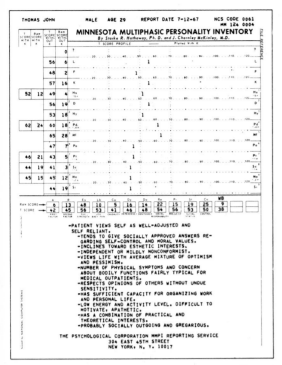

Figure 9.1 Computer printout of an MMPI profile and interpretation. This is derived from 14 basic scales: those described in Table 9.2 and the four 'control keys,' question (?) lie (L), validity (F) and correction for 'caginess' (K). Various multiples of K are added to the Trait Scale Scores before they are entered onto the profile sheet. (From Hathaway and McKinley, 1967, by courtesy of Psychological Corporation)

are answered differently by bald and hirsute men (if in fact any items do so discriminate). At least 100 supplementary keys for scoring various attributes from the M.M.P.I. have appeared in the literature since the test was originally published; they include scales for measuring socio-economic status, prejudice, responsibility, dominance and academic achievement.

There are certain dangers attached to the empirical keying method. For example, items might discriminate, but for trivial reasons that would not transfer to other uses of the test. Thus the item, 'Are you in a mental hospital?' would discriminate hospitalised schizophrenics from normals but would not detect them elsewhere. A more important criticism of the M.M.P.I. as a personality test is that the selection of scales is fairly arbitrary and based on traditional diagnostic labels rather than factor analysis. Research has shown that the scales lack factorial purity and independence. It appears that the M.M.P.I. permits diagnosis in terms of the broad categories 'neurotic' and 'psychotic' only and not in terms of more specific types.

Another widely used personality questionnaire is the Edwards Personal Preference Schedule, which is designed to measure the relative strength of Henry Murray's list of supposed 'psychological needs'—abasement, affiliation, achievement, aggression, autonomy, etc. Items are arranged as pairs of statements referring to various activities and goals, and the respondent has to give his preference for one of the two. This is called the *paired comparisons* method. The scales in the Edwards test were not determined by any empirical method like that used with the M.M.P.I.; instead a simple *content analysis* method was employed. That is, the items in the questionnaire were drawn up so that intuitively they could be supposed to tap the personality dimension in question.

British psychologists as well as some Americans (notably Cattell and Guilford) favour the use of *factor analysis* in the construction of personality questionnaires (see Chapter 7). This is a statistical classification technique which not only provides information as to which items should be scored on each scale, but also suggests the number and nature of scales that may be usefully derived from the set of items in the questionnaire. Increasingly, factor analysis is being recognised as an important step in the development of questionnaires even if elements of other methods are also employed. The question of the structure of personality as revealed by factor analysis will be discussed in the next section.

Other-person ratings

A third method of measuring personality incorporates aspects of the previous two. A standard rating scale (or set of scales) is given to people who know the subject well (teachers, supervisors, doctors, nurses, parents, or peers) and they are asked to assess his characteristic behaviour. This by-passes some of the practical limitations of the direct observation method and the problem of subjects trying to impress by 'faking good' on the questionnaire. Unfortunately, many other biases are known to occur. Some raters tend to be over-generous, giving ratings toward the favourable end of the scale to nearly everybody. The term 'halo effect' refers to the tendency for ratings of an individual on specific traits to be influenced by the overall impression that he gives. Other sources of error are ambiguity of the attributes upon which subjects are to be rated and the fact that raters usually have limited information about the people they are rating. As Eysenck (1970) points out, 'rating cannot be taken strictly as a description of the person rated; it is always quite inevitably an interaction between rater and ratee'.

Some standardised rating scales are available, and they have found particular application in the psychiatric field. For example, the Wittenborn Psychiatric Rating Scales consist of a series of scales relating to symptoms and ward behaviour which have been sorted by factor analysis into twelve major clusters: anxiety, hysterical conversation, manic state, depres-

sive state, schizophrenic excitement, psychotic belliger-
ence, paranoia, hebephrenia, compulsive–obsessive,
intellectual impairment, homosexual dominance, and
ideas of grandeur. These scales have usually been
found to show reasonable reliability and separation
although; of course, they are far from independent.
Since they refer to temporary conditions as well as
diagnostic categories they may be used to monitor
changes in the illness, such as progress towards
recovery, as well as more enduring characteristics.

Projective tests

Another major group of techniques is designed to get
at the more hidden, perhaps 'unconscious', aspects of
the personality (the so-called 'deeper recesses') by
analysis and interpretation of fantasy material generated in response to vague or ambiguous stimulus
configurations. One classic approximation to the
projective method is the *word association* procedure
invented by Francis Galton and popularised by C. G.
Jung. In this test, the subject is presented with a series
of words and is asked to react to each with the·first
word that comes into his head. This method is supposed to be useful for diagnosing various kinds of
thought disorder apart from revealing the person's
major 'unconscious' motives. Also notorious as a
diagnostic test is the *Rorschach Inkblot Test*, in which
the patient has to say what he 'sees' in each of a
standard set of inkblots. The *Thematic Apperception
Test* developed by Henry Murray and colleagues uses
slightly more structured material. The subject has to
tell a story about each of a series of drawings depicting
shadowy and sometimes genderless characters in
various ambiguous situations and interactions. In
theory, he identifies with one of the characters in the
picture and projects his own interests, needs, motives
and conflicts into the story that he writes.

In the clinical setting these tests have usually been
used impressionistically—that is, no scoring system is
employed, and the clinician interprets the pattern of
responses purely on the basis of his own experience
and intuition. Although clinicians are often highly
confident about the meaningfulness and validity of
judgements arrived at in this manner, controlled
research has shown that projective tests interpreted
'holistically' perform poorly in terms of reliability and
validity. Objective scoring methods have been attempted with projective personality tests, but these
have added little predictive validity to the method (e.g.
see Jensen, 1958). The status of projective tests, then,
is at present highly dubious.

Objective behaviour tests

Since personality is the study of individual differences,
differential performance on almost any laboratory
task may be of interest in the study of personality,
and may in fact be found useful as a personality
measure. Among the numerous laboratory paradigms

**Table 9.3   A selection of objective behaviour tests
widely used in studies of personality**

1. The Stroop Test—interference between words for
   colours and the colours in which these words are
   printed.
2. Rod and Frame Test—adjustment of a rod to the
   vertical within the context of a tilted frame.
3. The Lemon Drop Test—amount of salivation in response to a drop of lemon juice placed on the tongue.
4. Body sway suggestibility—response to suggestions that
   one is swaying backwards when standing with eyes
   closed.
5. Level of aspiration—extent to which stated goals exceed
   actual performance.
6. Pursuit rotor—performance on a tracking task in which
   the subject pursues a rotating target with a stylus.
7. Tapping—amount of fatigue shown in attempting to
   maintain a constant rate of tapping on a finger key.
8. Dark adaptation—speed with which ability to see in the
   dark is acquired.
9. Conditioning—acquisition of conditioned responses in
   classical and operant situations.
10. Vigilance—detection performance on a long-term
    watch-keeping task.
11. Figural after-effects—extent to which exposure to one
    visual pattern affects perception of spatial relations in
    a subsequently presented visual pattern.
12. Illusions—extent to which one is subject to common
    visual illusions (e.g. Muller–Lyer).
13. Colour-form dominance—relative interest shown in
    colour versus shape aspects of the environment.
14. Speed—e.g. speed of tracing when instructed to be both
    quick and accurate.
15. Persistence—e.g. holding breath for as long as possible.
16. Manual dexterity—e.g. assembling and disassembling
    pegs and washers on a 'form board'.

that have been shown to have relevance to personality
are perceptual tasks, motor tasks, learning phenomena
and response to drugs. A list of typical behavioural
tests that have been investigated in connection with
personality is given in Table 9.3. These tests have in
common the fact that they are samples of behaviour
than can be observed under laboratory conditions and
which allow objective (unambiguous and highly
reliable) scoring. All of them can be studied from the
point of view of general processes and laws that apply
to all members of the species (or·at least an average
member) or they can be studied with interest focussed
on the difference between individuals in their manner
of responding. That these individual differences are
relevant to personality is shown by the often striking
relationships between them and other measures of
personality such as the questionnaire.

Physiological measures

Individuals also vary in their physiological responses,
whether spontaneously emitted or evoked by specific
test stimuli. Once again, these might not seem to be
central to the popular concept of personality, yet they

have been shown to relate to scores on personality questionnaires, and they represent one of the most satisfactory ways of getting at the 'inner world of experience' (which many argue is the proper concern of psychology) without relying solely on introspective reports from the subject. In Chapter 1, it was shown how men's reports of feeling different degrees of sexual arousal could be checked against measurements of penis volume obtained with a penile plethysmograph. It will be seen shortly that the physiological measures are also of particular theoretical interest because of the hypothesised biological basis of personality. Among the physiological indices that have been frequently studied are the galvanic skin response (G.S.R.; a measure of electrical skin conductivity related to action of the sweat glands), blood pressure, heart rate, respiration rate, the E.E.G. ('brain waves'), salivary output, muscular relaxation/tension. and pupillary dilation/contraction. Most of these measures can be recorded as chronic 'resting' levels, or the extent of change in response to selected stimuli can be studied. Some of them are almost purely indicators of the state of the autonomic (visceral nervous system); others are more closely connected with activity in the central nervous system (e.g. arousal in the cerebral cortex).

Physique

People also vary greatly with respect to physique, and there are popular stereotypes suggesting connections with personality (e.g. the jolly fat man, the thoughtful, introspective thin man, the bull-necked, arrogant and conceited operatic tenor). The relevance of physique to the study of temperament has in fact been supported by scientific investigations. Theories in this area date from at least the time of Hippocrates, but the most famous contribution is probably that of Kretschmer (1921). He distinguished four types of body build; the *pyknic* (short and fat), *leptosomatic* or *aesthenic* (tall and thin), *athletic* (intermediate and muscular) and *dysplastic* (an incongruous mixture of different types in different parts of the body). These body types he showed to be related to the three major psychoses: schizophrenia, manic-depression, and epilepsy (Table 9.4). Although his results have been subject to some methodological criticism, his finding

of a tendency for schizophrenics to be taller and thinner than manic-depressives has received some support; his findings concerning characteristic physiques of epileptics are less well substantiated.

A similar three-way classification of body types was popularised in the U.S. by Sheldon. He adopted the terms *endomorphy*, *ectomorphy* and *mesomorphy* to apply roughly to fat, skinny and muscular body types respectively—the terms being derived from a supposed link-up with the three germinal layers in the embryo: endoderm, ectoderm and mesoderm. Figure 9.2 shows a diagrammatic representation of these body types with the names that have been applied to them by various theorists, many of whom preceded Sheldon. Sheldon scored his subjects on three 7-point scales corresponding to the three components, making use of a photographic technique in which each person was photographed three times from different angles (the three poses being the same for each subject). Sheldon reported some very high correlations between his body types and three theoretically matched temperamental types called: *viscerotonia*—relaxed posture, love of physical comfort, slow reaction, amiability, deep sleep etc.; *cerebrotonia*–restraint and tightness of posture, fast reactions, inhibited social responses, poor sleep habits, chronic fatigue, etc.; and *somatotonia*—assertiveness of posture, love of physical adventure, competitive aggressiveness, etc. Unfortunately there is reason to believe that Sheldon's temperament ratings were influenced by his knowledge of the subjects' physiques and in subsequent better controlled studies Sheldon's correlations have shrunk considerably.

Sheldon's system has also been criticised on the ground that the variation in physiques can be summarised by a smaller number of factors. Rees and Eysenck (1945) conducted a factor analysis of a great variety of body measurements and found the structure illustrated in Figure 9.3. From this diagram it can be seen that there is first of all a general factor relating to overall body size (the horizontal axis); then there is a second bipolar factor which separates the thin elongated individual from the rotund person (the vertical axis). These two types were dubbed 'leptomorphs' and 'eurymorphs' respectively in order to distinguish them from the tripartite classification schemes and to avoid

Table 9.4 Distribution (in per cent) of body type for schizophrenic, manic-depressive, and epileptic groups
(From results of Kretschmer, 1921, by courtesy of Harcourt-Brace)

	Schizophrenics: 5233 cases	Manic-depressives: 1361 cases	Epileptics: 1505 cases
Pyknic	13.7	64.6	5.5
Athletic	16.9	6.7	28.9
Leptosomatic	50.3	19.2	25.1
Dysplastic	10.5	1.1	29.5
Doubtful	8.6	8.4	11.0

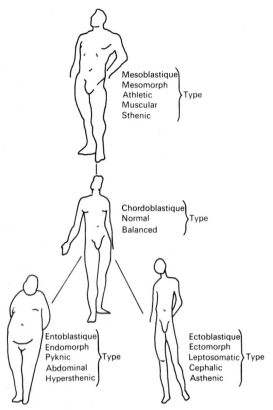

Figure 9.2 Diagrammatic representation of three main body types derived according to the hypothesis of embryological development. (From Martiny, 1948, by courtesy of Peyronnet)

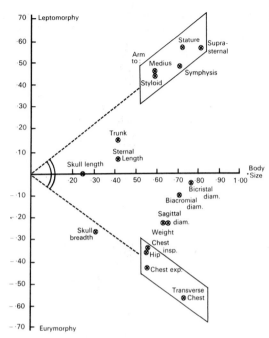

Figure 9.3 Saturation of anthropometric measurements with general and type factors (men). (From Eysenck, 1970, by courtesy of Methuen)

the theoretical assumptions underlying some of the other naming systems. Although this study used men only, the same factor structure has been repeatedly observed using women and other samples ranging widely in age, race and social class. Rees and Eysenck have found that for purposes of typing physique the body can be conveniently represented as a height × chest-width rectangle. Multiplying these together gives a measure of overall size (the general factor); dividing height by chest-width gives a measure of leptomorphy versus eurymorphy (now commonly known as the Rees–Eysenck index). Research on the relationships between these two physique factors and personality has produced two fairly reliable findings: (1) People with generally small bodies tend to be mentally as well as physically 'poor specimens', with a tendency to be lower in social class and intelligence, poor in physical health, sexually inhibited, hypochondriacal, anxious, depressed, submissive, etc. (2) Leptomorphs tend to be introverted and neurotic compared to eurymorphs who are relatively stable and extrovert. These findings are consistent with those of Sheldon insofar as com-

parison between the two systems is possible, although the correlations are much less spectactular than those initially reported by him, usually being of the order of around 0.30. In the light of Kretschmer's finding it also seems probable that leptomorphy is associated with schizophrenia and eurymorphy with manic-depressive illness; and there are well-established links between physique and criminality (Chapter 16). However, enough has been said to indicate the relevance of physique to personality study and to justify the inclusion of body measurements in personality research.

STRUCTURE OF PERSONALITY

One of the earliest theories of personality was that of Hippocrates, which was extended and popularised by Galen in the second century A.D. They supposed that there are four temperamental types corresponding to four 'humours' (a bit like hormones); the names given to these types—melancholic, choleric, phlegmatic and sanguine—still survive in common usage. The descriptive part of this theory is an oversimplification in that people cannot be pigeon-holed into four clear-cut categories. Most of us exhibit some mixture of these characteristics. Therefore the German psychologist, W. Wundt, suggested that the Greek system could be accommodated by two major dimensions of individual emotional response: *strength* of emotions, and *speed of change*. Factor analytic studies of the structure of personality using all of the different measurement techniques described above have repeatedly confirmed the broad descriptive usefulness of this two-dimensional scheme. Different names have been applied to them, but probably the most widely accepted are those used by Eysenck—*extroversion versus introversion* (equivalent to quick–slow in the Wundt system) and *neuroticism versus stability* (strong–weak emotions) (Figure 9.4). The typical extrovert is sociable, lively, outgoing, carefree, changeable, impulsive, assertive, physically active and optimistic, in contrast to the typical introvert who is quiet, passive, careful, thoughtful, reliable, mentally active, and pessimistic. People high on neuroticism tend to be nervous, anxious, moody, touchy, restless, excitable, and generally emotionally changeable, as against stable people, who are placid, even-tempered, reliable and calm. The advantage of a dimensional system over the categorical system of the Greeks is that individuals can be located at any point within the space defined by the two factors, thus allowing a much greater range of discriminable personalities. Most people of course fall in the middle range on each of these dimensions, with only a few tending towards the extremes.

We have said that Eysenck's two dimensional descriptive system is widely accepted. Yet America's leading factor analyst, Raymond Cattell, is known to favour description of personality in terms of no less than sixteen factors. A list of these 16 factors together with the names and code letters assigned to them by

Cattell are given in Table 9.5. If there is in fact little disagreement in this area, how can such a discrepancy be reconciled? The answer has been anticipated in our discussion of factor analysis (Chapter 7). Cattell's 16 factors are at a lower level than Eysenck's two; because they are intercorrelated (oblique), they can be refactored and thus collapsed back to Eysenck's two factors, or at least something closely approximating them.

The relationship between these different levels may be clarified by reference to Figure 9.5, which shows a hierarchical model of the structure of personality much like that given for abilities in Chapter 7. At the lowest level of generalisation we can observe a *specific response*, e.g. Mr Smith approaching a stranger at a cocktail party. If Smith is repeatedly observed approaching strangers then we can describe it as a *habitual response*. Now willingness to approach strangers is known to correlate quite closely with many other habitual responses such as liking parties, having lots of friends, being talkative, etc., which together comprise the trait of sociability. Finally, the empirical discovery that sociability is in turn correlated with certain other traits such as impulsiveness, activity, liveliness, and excitability leads us to the type level concept of extroversion (neuroticism is another type level concept). Note that 'type' is used here to distinguish an order of generality above that of 'trait'; it does not imply exclusive categories.

Eysenck prefers to deal mainly with the type level because the two major factors are much better established; they are reliably identified in factor analytic studies that vary greatly in terms of the personality measures and subject samples employed. There is even an indication that the intercorrelations among many of Cattell's sixteen primary factors are as high as could be expected given the limits on the reliability of the individual factors (Eysenck, 1972a). This being the case, there is apparently very little information lost in reducing Cattell's factors down to the two Eysenck factors. In actual fact, though, the comparison is not really between 16 and 2 factors, but between 16 and 5. This is because one of Cattell's 16 factors is intelligence, and another is conservatism–radicalism; the importance of both these as major factors underlying human variation is fully endorsed by Eysenck and the British school—but they have followed convention in treating abilities and attitudes as separate domains not falling under the heading of personality. Another major dimension of personality which has been gaining increasing attention by Eysenck and his colleagues in recent years is that called 'psychoticism' or 'tough-mindedness'. Subjects scoring high on this 'P'-factor are described as cold, aggressive, cruel, and given to bizarre, antisocial behaviour. Although the psychoticism factor is not held to be synonymous with the clinical usage of the term, schizophrenics, manic-depressives, psychopaths and criminals all show fairly high P scores.

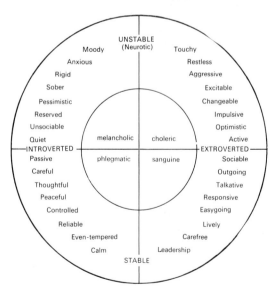

Figure 9.4   Two major dimensions of personality revealed by factor analysis compared with the four Greek categories (From Eysenck, 1964, by courtesy of London University Press)

Table 9.5   Cattell's sixteen primary factors (From Cattell, 1963, by courtesy of Institute for Personality and Ability Testing)

High- score description	Factor	Low-score description
Outgoing, warmhearted, easy-going, participating (Cyclothymia)	A	*Reserved*, detached, critical, cool (Schizothymia)
More intelligent, abstract thinking, bright (Higher scholastic mental capacity)	B	*Less intelligent*, concrete thinking (Lower scholastic mental capacity)
Emotionally stable, faces reality, calm (Higher ego strength)	C	*Affected by feelings*, emotionally less stable, easily upset (Lower ego strength)
Assertive, independent, aggressive, stubborn (Dominance)	E	*Humble*, mild, obedient, conforming (Submissiveness)
Happy-go-lucky, heedless, gay, enthusiastic (Surgency)	F	*Sober*, prudent, serious, taciturn (Desurgency)
Conscientious, persevering, staid, rule-bound (Stronger superego strength)	G	*Expedient*, a law to himself, by-passes obligations (Weaker superego strength)
Venturesome, socially bold, uninhibited, spontaneous (Parmia)	H	*Shy*, restrained diffident, timid (Threctia)
Tender-minded, dependent, over-protected, sensitive (Premsia)	I	*Tough-minded*, self-reliant, realistic, no-nonsense (Harria)
Suspicious, self-opinionated, hard to fool (Protension)	L	*Trusting*, adaptable, free of jealousy, easy to get on with (Alaxia)
Imaginative, wrapped up in inner urgencies, careless of practical matters, bohemian (Autia)	M	*Practical*, careful, conventional, regulated by external realities, proper (Praxernia)
Shrewd, calculating, worldly, penetrating (Shrewdness)	N	*Forthright*, natural, artless, sentimental (Artlessness)
Apprehensive, worrying, depressive, troubled (Guilt proneness)	O	*Placid*, self-assured, confident, serene (Untroubled adequacy)
Experimenting, critical, liberal, analytical, free-thinking (Radicalism)	Q^1	*Conservative*, respecting established ideas, tolerant of traditional difficulties (Conservatism)
Self-sufficient, prefers own decisions, resourceful (Self-sufficiency)	Q^2	*Group-dependent*, a 'joiner' and sound follower (Group adherence)
Controlled, socially precise, self-disciplined, compulsive (High self-concept control)	Q^3	*Casual*, careless of protocol, untidy, follows own urges (Low integration)
Tense, overwrought, fretful (High ergic tension)	Q^4	*Relaxed*, tranquil, torpid, unfrustrated (Low ergic tension)

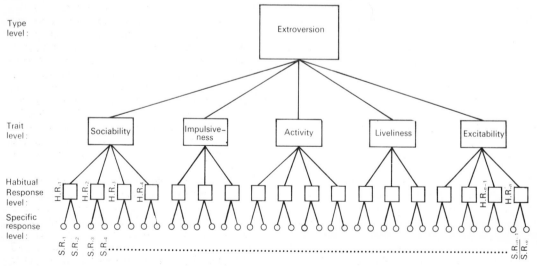

Figure 9.5   Diagrammatic representation of hierarchical organisation of personality. (From Eysenck, 1970, by courtesy of Methuen)

It seems useful, then, to consider five major dimensions of individual variation:

1. Extroversion–introversion (called exvia-invia by Cattell).
2. Neuroticism (emotionality, anxiety, instability).
3. Psychoticism (tough-mindedness, psychopathy, aggressiveness).
4. Intelligence (general ability).
5. Conservatism (*v.* radicalism or liberalism).

Although this might seem an incredibly small number of factors with which to describe the enormous range of personalities that may be observed making their peculiar ways about the world, it should be remembered that each individual can be located at any point along each of these dimensions (i.e. anywhere in the five-dimensional space). This leaves a tremendous amount of scope for individual variation. To take an analogy from psychophysics, there are about 25 000 discriminable colours in the visual world, but any one can be almost perfectly specified by giving its co-ordinates on just three dimensions: hue, saturation and brightness. The three dimensions with which the rest of this chapter is concerned (E, N and P) probably do not tell the whole story about human temperament; consideration of other additional factors would no doubt give greater precision for certain purposes. As will be seen, however, they do give a broad and generally useful description of the field of personality.

Some critics of the trait approach have insistently objected that each personality is totally unique and therefore classification in this area is misleading or impossible. To say this is to misunderstand the nature of scientific thought. It is true nobody is perfectly duplicated, not even by their identical twin, but such a statement is utterly unhelpful. Every banana is also unique; this does not render the concept of bananas (as distinct from apples and oranges) useless, nor the validity of grouping them according to whether they are green, ripe or bad, large or small, bent or straight. The unique individual may be of interest to the novelist or dramatist, possibly even to the practising clinician; science is concerned only with concepts and generalisations, without which our thinking would be impotent indeed.

PERSONALITY AND ABNORMAL BEHAVIOUR

The three primary personality factors have been found useful in the classification of abnormal behaviour as well as the normal range of behaviour. In fact, to a large extent, the distinction is found to be arbitrary—most kinds of abnormal behaviour are simply extremes of, and continuous with, normal behaviour (although certain others, e.g. epilepsy and mongolism, are better thought of in terms of the traditional disease model—see Chapter 15). In *The*

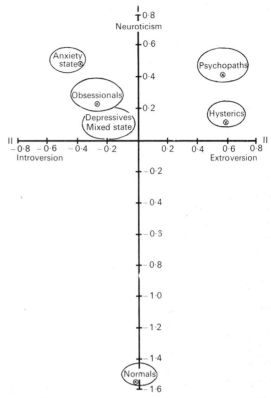

Figure 9.6 Position of one normal and six neurotic groups in two-dimensional framework determined by canonical variate analysis of objective test performances.

Dynamics of Anxiety and Hysteria (1957), Eysenck showed that neurotics could be classified according to their position on the introversion–extroversion dimension. A great deal of subsequent research has confirmed that introverted people tend to develop 'dysthymic'-type neuroses (e.g. anxiety, obsessionality, and depression) while extroverted people are more likely to exhibit psychopathic and hysterical symptoms (Figure 9.6). Another way of viewing these differences is to say that the introvert turns his neurosis inward and inflicts it on himself, while the extrovert turns it outwards and inflicts it on society. Some theorists have described the same distinction in terms of 'personality problems' versus 'behaviour problems', but this practice is likely to lead to terminological confusion.

The picture becomes slightly more complicated when the psychoticism dimension is considered in addition to E and N. As might be expected, schizophrenics and manic-depressives are separated from all of the groups shown in Figure 9.6 mainly on the basis of this dimension. So too are psychopaths and criminals (Chapter 16); not only are they high on E and N, they are also considerably higher on P than normals. This provides a way of distinguishing psychopaths from hysterics; psychopaths are high on all three dimensions, hysterics are high only on E and N. It would be nice to offer a three dimensional diagram showing the relationships among these various diagnostic groups, but this would be very diffcult to draw clearly on two-dimensional paper.

This question of diagnosis and the classification of abnormal behaviour is dealt with fully in Chapter 15. At this point it is sufficient to note: (a) that in the main abnormal behaviour is continuous with normal behaviour, albeit sometimes rather extreme, and (b) both abnormal and normal behaviour can be fairly well-described in terms of the same three major dimensions of personality: E, N and P.

SOME FURTHER CORRELATES OF PERSONALITY

The broad descriptive usefulness of this three-factor system is seen in its power to predict behaviour in many other areas in addition to mental disorder and criminality. A particularly interesting example concerns an epidemic of overbreathing among schoolgirls in a Lancashire school reported by Moss and McEvedy (1966). Apparently it began with one or two girls complaining of dizziness and fainting, and by late morning 'they were going down like ninepins'. Eighty-five of the most severely affected were taken to hospital by ambulance, and the school was closed; twice it was reopened and each time a repetition of the episode occurred. No physical cause was discovered but since this behaviour seemed classically 'hysterical' it was hypothesised that the girls most affected would be higher on E and N than those unaffected. This predic-

tion was clearly supported by the data collected by the investigators (Figure 9.7).

This same personality constellation (high E, high N) has been shown in other studies to be associated with careless, erratic driving and accident proneness on the road, the likelihood of becoming an unmarried mother, contracting V.D., and a high frequency of absence from work. Other fields of social activity in which the E and N factors have provided verifiable predictions include the board-room, where successful managers were shown to be stable introverts. and the armed forces, where commando trainees and para-chute-jumping volunteers were found to be nearly always stable extroverts (Eysenck, 1970). Most of these studies have dealt only with E and N; it is only recently measures of psychoticism have been widely employed in studies of personality correlates.

One area where the implications of psychoticism were investigated, and which we will take as a final example, is that of sexual attitudes and behaviour. On the basis of what is known about the nature of people at various locations along the E, N, and P dimensions, Eysenck (1972b) made a number of predictions about the likely relationships between personality and sexual behaviour. For example, it was expected that extroverts would lead a more active and varied sex life and would be less inhibited where socially proscribed sexual behaviour is concerned. Neurotics were thought likely to feel more guilt and anxiety about sex and suffer more problems such as impotence and frigidity. High P scorers were expected to incline towards impersonal, exploitative sex, sadism and other 'perversions'.

A questionnaire concerning sexual habits and attitudes was distributed to a group of 423 unmarried male and 370 unmarried female students, along with a revised Eysenck Personality Inventory containing a P scale. Results showed that the three personality types were associated with quite different patterns of sexual attitudes and habits, and in a manner consistent with prediction. Extroverts emerged as happy philanderers, being promiscuous and free from nervousness and prudishness. They tended to have had intercourse earlier in life, more frequently (about twice as often as introverts), with more different partners and in a greater variety of positions. Female extroverts claimed to experience orgasm more frequently than introverts. The sexual attitudes of high N scorers were characterised by excitement, nervousness, hostility, guilt, inhibition and lack of satisfaction; in general they showed a high level of sex drive but for various reasons failed to find adequate outlets or achieve satisfaction. High P scorers showed an even higher degree of 'libido' but were better able to act out their promiscuous and 'perverted' (e.g. oral) desires. Despite their participation in a great variety of sexual practices, however, they too remained generally unhappy with their sex lives. Apparently, they can

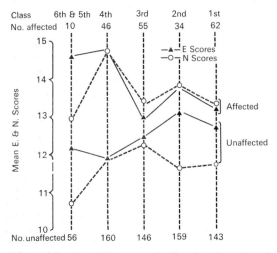

Figure 9.7 E and N scores of affected and unaffected children by school class. (From Moss and McEvedy, 1966, by courtesy of *Brit. Med. J.*)

'never get enough'. Results pertaining to the attitude items from the sex questionnaire are summarised in Table 9.6.

Table 9.6   Sexual attitudes related to personality
(From Eysenck, 1972b, by courtesy of Library Press)

Factors	E	N	P
1. Satisfaction	+	− − −	−
2. Excitement	+	+ +	+
3. Nervousness	− − −	+ +	0
4. Curiosity	0	+	+ +
5. Premartial sex	+	0	+ +
6. Repression	0	0	−
7. Prudishness	− −	+	+
8. Experimentation	+	0	0
9. Homosexuality	0	+	+
10. Censorship	−	0	-
11. Promiscuity	+ +	0	+ + +
12. Hostility	0	+ + +	+ + +
13. Guilt	0	+ + +	0
14. Inhibition	0	+ + +	+
Summary factors			
A. Sexual pathology	−	+ + +	+ +
B. Libido	+	+	+ + +

N.B.: +, 0, and − signs indicate positive, zero, and negative relationships respectively. The strength of the relationship is indicated by the number of signs

These examples have been selected as representative of a vast literature which demonstrates that personality as assessed in terms of positions on the major dimensions will permit testable predictions to be made in a wide variety of areas. Even if some of these relationships seem tautological in the sense that they may be regarded as following naturally from the self-reported traits, they do illustrate the broad social significance of the descriptive system. We have seen in Chapter 1 that psychology comprises the link in the reductive ('causal') chain between social behaviour and biology; we will therefore now extend the system back in the biological direction.

THE GENETIC BASIS OF PERSONALITY

Having established a reasonably stable and widely agreed descriptive system of personality, the next question that arises is that of its origins. Do differences along these three dimensions reflect variations in experience or are they determined genetically from the moment of conception? Support for both of these propositions is found in folk wisdom and also in the evidence.

The evidence for the importance of heredity in human personality is thoroughly reviewed by Shields (Chapter 10) so there is no need to discuss it in detail here. Mainly it depends upon twin studies. For example, the influence of the environment can be estimated from a comparison of identical twins (twins who share the same genes because they result from a

zygote which split after conception) reared together in the same household, with others reared separately in different environments. Surprisingly, it has sometimes been found that identical twins reared apart are even more like one another than identical twins reared together. This extraordinary finding can best be explained by supposing that when identical twins are reared together they react against each other in such a way as to accentuate the natural differences between themselves. Another interesting comparison is that between the personality similarities of identical and non-identical (fraternal) twins. Studies adopting this tactic have revealed significantly higher correlations between identical twins than between fraternal twins regardless of whether they are reared together or apart. This finding also suggests that personality is strongly influenced by hereditary factors. It is not possible to be precise about the proportion of variance due to heredity, but for the major personality factors it seems to be in the range of 40% to 70%.

It is useful to distinguish between personality *genotypes* and *phenotypes*. The genotype of, say, extroversion, refers to a position on this dimension that is programmed by the genes and which is the best predictor of extroversion scores at the moment of conception. Extroversion, as observed and measured in the fully developed human being, is always phenotypic, however. That is, it inevitably reflects various environmental influences and measurement artifacts in addition to the genotypic level of extroversion. Although we might seek a measure of the pure personality genotype, this is unlikely to be possible. Physiological measures and performance on various laboratory tests probably come closer to the genotype than questionnaires, and a combination of measures might allow an even closer estimate. Nevertheless, the phenotypic measure always remains an approximation to the genotype.

The above discussion implies that personality is either genetic or a result of various kinds of measurement error, effects of the environment being classified with the latter. This view may appear radically hereditarian, but the problem is to a large extent conceptual. Obviously the environment does affect our behaviour: it determines whether we speak French, English, or Chinese, whether or not we wear cuffs on our trousers, and whether we eat with our fork in our left or right hands. To the layman these may all be important behaviours and integral to the concept of personality; to the personality psychologist they are of little interest. He is concerned with generalised modes of responding to the environment which are relatively independent of what the environment actually dishes up. Thus 'neuroticism' is ideally the tendency to react with anxiety, nervousness, etc. in response to environmental stress, whatever the actual source or nature of that stress. An individual subjected to an unusually high degree of environmental stress throughout life is probably more likely to 'break down' and be diagnosed as 'neurotic', but his position on the N dimension would theoretically remain unchanged. The point is that to a large extent environmental influences are ruled out by definition from the concept of personality, since it is concerned with stable and enduring temperamental traits that determine characteristic reactions to the environment.

EYSENCK'S THEORY

Eysenck (1967) has put forward a theory regarding the biological basis of the E and N factors. Briefly, he suggests that individual differences in extroversion–introversion reflect variations in the nature of the ascending reticular activating system of the brain (A.R.A.S.), while emotionality–stability (neuroticism) is related to characteristics of the visceral brain (i.e., hippocampal structures, amygdala, cingulum, septum and hypothalamus). The rough anatomical location and relationships between these structures is shown in Figure 9.8.

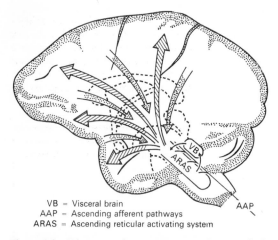

VB = Visceral brain
AAP = Ascending afferent pathways
ARAS = Ascending reticular activating system

Figure 9.8 Diagrammatic representation of anatomical–physiological structures postulated by Eysenck as responsible for differences in E (ARAS) and N (VB). (From Eysenck, 1967, by courtesy of C. C. Thomas)

The reticular activating system is believed by neurophysiologists to be responsible for producing non-specific arousal in the cerebral cortex in response to external stimulation. Eysenck postulates that this state of arousal is higher in introverts than extroverts given identical conditions of external stimulation. This differential in arousal is held responsible for all of the experimentally observed differences between extroverts and introverts, for example the relative speed with which introverts acquire conditioned reflexes compared with extroverts (Chapter 4). The difference in conditionability is in turn held responsible for the different types of abnormal behaviour to which introverts and extroverts are respectively prone:

emotional introverts show dysthymic symptoms such as obsessions and phobias because of their over-ready conditioning to normally neutral stimuli, while the hysterical and psychopathic behaviour typical of emotional extroverts results from a failure of the conditioning which constitutes the normal socialisation process in childhood.

How can this differential arousal theory of extroversion–introversion be tested? Perhaps the most direct way is to compare questionnaire scores on this dimension with physiological measures that are supposed to reflect arousal. Here it is necessary to distinguish clearly between cortical arousal and autonomic arousal, because many, in fact, most physiological measures that are widely used in psychological laboratories (e.g. heart rate, blood pressure, respiration rate) are really indices of the latter (see Chapter 3). It has been suggested that some confusion might be avoided if the term 'activation' was used consistently to refer to high autonomic activity, leaving 'arousal' to mean high cortical excitation.

There are a few physiological variables which are dependent on cortical activity more than autonomic, most notably the E.E.G. Eysenck (1967) has reviewed a number of studies of personality links with E.E.G. responses. Results collected under optimal conditions offer some support for the hypothesis that introverts are generally higher in arousal than extroverts, but problems of measurement and interpretation are

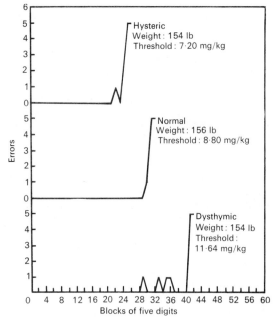

Figure 9.9 Typical sedation threshold curves of extroverted and introverted neurotics: one subject from each group. (From Claridge and Herrington, 1963, by courtesy of Pergamon Press)

considerable and the matter cannot be said to have been finally settled.

Other fairly direct evidence for the theory has been sought in studies of drug effects. For example, if introverts are more aroused than extroverts we would expect them to be more difficult to sedate with a drug such as sodium amytal, and this is precisely what is found. The sedation threshold may be measured by E.E.G., slurring of speech, or perhaps most objectively in terms of a sudden loss of facility in a simple arithmetical task (adding digits). Some typical results using the latter measure are shown in Figure 9.9. Although hysterics and dysthymics are both neurotic groups, they are distinguished, as we have noted, along the extroversion–introversion dimension; thus dysthymics, who are introverted neurotics, are the most difficult to sedate, and hysterics (extroverted neurotics) the easiest, with the normals falling in between.

Another hypothesis which is logically derived from the introversion/arousal theory is that stimulant drugs (which increase arousal) should shift a person's behaviour in the introverted direction and depressant drugs (which lower arousal) should shift behaviour in the extrovert direction. These effects should occur regardless of the normal placement along the E–I continuum except that subjects who are already 'pushing the poles' would have less latitude for further movement away from the centre. An enormous body of research is of course relevant to this hypothesis and it is not possible to detail it here, but a review by Eysenck (1967) reveals considerable support for the theory. To take but one example, Franks and Trouton (1958) demonstrated that a stimulant drug (dexamphetamine sulphate) facilitated eye-blink conditioning, while a depressant drug (amobarbital sodium) decreased the amount of conditioning observed relative to a placebo control, in a manner exactly parallel to the demonstrated association of E–I with conditioning. Other experimental tests that are affected by drugs in a manner predictable from the differing performance of extroverts and introverts on them include vigilance, perceptual after-effects, rote learning, flicker fusion, visual-masking phenomena and risk-taking. Some anomalous findings have also been reported but these can usually be explained by taking account of the Yerkes–Dodson law (increases in arousal generally facilitate task performance only up to a certain point after which they become debilitatory—see Chapter 4).

Apart from the physiological and drug studies, which bear fairly directly on the biological basis of personality, there are numerous other predictions which can be made from Eysenck's theory. For example, consider the area of personality in relation to verbal recall. It is now very well-established that high drive or arousal interferes with immediate memory but is beneficial to longer-term memory. This is apparently because arousing experiences, normally being more important, are given priority of transfer from temporary to permanent memory banks. During this 'consolidation' process the material is less available for immediate use and is therefore harder to recall on demand; it is, however, better remembered in the long run. Experiences that are low in motivational significance, on the other hand, are comparatively well-recalled in the short-term and forgotten in the long-term. Extending these facts about learning to personality differences we would predict that introverts (being chronically more aroused) would show better long-term memory than extroverts and poorer short-term memory. Experimental results confirm this prediction rather strikingly (Figure 9.10). Elsewhere Eysenck has observed that the contradictory proverbs: 'Absence makes the heart grow fonder' and 'out of sight, out of mind' might be reconciled if the former is held to apply to introverts and the latter to extroverts. Perhaps the Howarth and Eysenck study could be viewed as experimental confirmation of this idea.

Another example may be taken from the field of sensitivity to external stimuli. Eysenck's theory suggests that a stimulus of standard intensity will have a greater impact on the introvert than on the extrovert because of the introvert's higher arousal level. A simple way of testing this hypothesis is to measure the

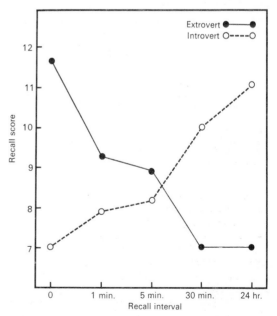

Figure 9.10 Recall scores of five groups of extroverts and five groups of introverts after different recall intervals. Introverts show reminiscence as recall interval increases; extroverts show forgetting. (From Howarth and Eysenck, 1968, by courtesy of *J. Exp. Res. Personal.*)

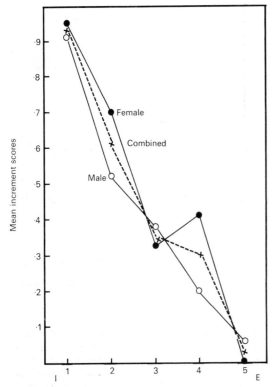

Figure 9.11   Mean salivation increments of five groups of male and female subjects, ordered according to degree of introversion, after placing four drops of lemon juice on tongue. (From Eysenck and Eysenck, 1967, by courtesy of *Percept. Mot. Skills*)

amount of saliva produced in the mouth during a short period after a few drops of lemon juice have been placed on the tongue. The results from such a study, using 50 men and 50 women split into five levels of extroversion are shown in Figure 9.11. As expected the introverts showed a much greater increase of salivation, the correlation between introversion and salivary output being as high as 0.7. Many other experiments confirm that the introvert is more sensitive to stimuli throughout the range from threshold to painful intensity.

The greater sensitivity of introverts to stimuli is matched by their relative dislike of strong stimuli. The general preferences of introverts and extroverts for gentle and sensational stimuli respectively are illustrated in Figure 9.12. Here it can be seen that there is an optimal level of stimulation for all persons, but that it is lower for introverts than extroverts. Experiments confirm that introverts have lower pain thresholds while extroverts are more susceptible to the adverse effects of sensory deprivation. The 'stimulus hunger' of extroverts has also been demonstrated in an experiment which showed them willing to expend considerable effort in order to obtain a 'reward' of loud jazz music and bright lights—stimuli that introverts in the same experimental situation would work to avoid (Weisen, 1965).

We have concentrated on Eysenck's theory concerning the biological basis of extroversion because this has been better researched than the other dimensions and the findings are more clear-cut. Nevertheless there has been a substantial amount of research related to Eysenck's theory of neuroticism also—the

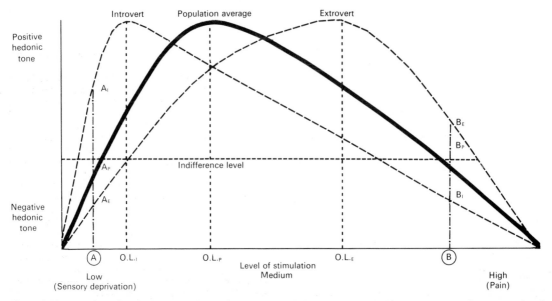

Figure 9.12   Relation of hedonic tone to level of sensory stimulation, showing relative displacement of extroverted and introverted subjects from population mean. (From Eysenck, 1970, by courtesy of Methuen)

idea that high neuroticism reflects a labile (changeable and responsive) autonomic nervous system—most of which appears confirmatory (Eysenck, 1967). The biological basis of the psychoticism (tough-mindedness) factor is less clear. Perhaps a clue is to be found in the fact that males are higher on P than females, and 'super-males' (the XYY syndrome) higher still. It would be interesting to see if it relates to male sex hormone levels within groups of normal men and women; if so, one simple biological basis at least will have been established. Also of interest in this connection is the ease with which certain psychotic symptoms such as hallucinations and delusions can be simulated by biochemical intervention in the nervous system (e.g. with drugs such as LSD and mescaline).

As noted, personality traits observed in everyday life, and more systematically in ratings and questionnaires, are always phenotypic. That is, they result from the interaction of a genotype with the environment. Laboratory experiments probably get closer to the genotype but they remain theoretical constructs which cannot be directly observed (Figure 9.13). The actual biological structures underlying these personality dimensions are far from being perfectly established and understood. Some modifications of Eysenck's theory have already appeared, e.g. those of J. A. Gray (1972) and G. S. Claridge (1967), and Eysenck has himself modified his theory in certain ways over the years. This is not the place to go into the details of these modifications or the reasons why their authors considered them necessary. Our purpose has been simply to illustrate the kind of theorising that is possible in this area: theory that lends itself readily to empirical investigation. Eysenck regards his theory

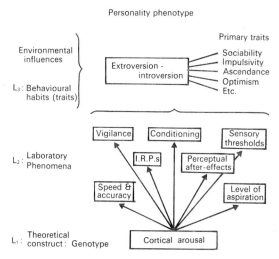

Figure 9.13 Diagrammatic representation of genesis of extrovert–introvert phenotype through interaction of genotype and environmental influences. (Modified from Eysenck, 1970, by courtesy of Methuen)

as being of primarily 'heuristic' value, i.e. he considers it less important that it be 'true' than that it serve as a guide to the direction of experimentation. Parts of it have received such frequent and reliable confirmation, however, that it is unlikely at this point to be overturned in its entirety. More probably it will evolve in the light of further experimentation, becoming progressively comprehensive and detailed in the predictions of which it is capable. This is the natural history of most scientific theories.

References

Cattell, R. B. (1963). *The Sixteen Personality Factor Questionnaire*. (Illinois: Institute for Personality and Ability Testing)

Claridge, G. S. and Herrington, R. N. (1963). Excitation–inhibition and the theory of neurosis: A study of the sedation threshold. In: *Experiments with Drugs* (H. J. Eysenck, editor) (New York: Pergamon Press)

Claridge, G. S. (1967). *Personality and Arousal* (Oxford: Pergamon Press)

Eysenck, H. J. (1957). *The Dynamics of Anxiety and Hysteria* (London: Routledge and Kegan Paul)

Eysenck, H. J. and Eysenck, S. B. G. (1964). *Manual for the Eysenck Personality Inventory* (London: Univ. Press)

Eysenck, H. J. (1967). *The Biological Basis of Personality* (Springfield, Illinois: C. C. Thomas)

Eysenck, S. B. G. and Eysenck, H. J. (1967). Salivary response to lemon juice as a measure of introversion. *Percept. Mot. Skills*, 24, 1047–1053

Eysenck, H. J. (1970). *The Structure of Human Personality* (London: Methuen)

Eysenck, H. J. (1972a). Primaries or second-order factors: a critical consideration of Cattell's 16PF battery. *Brit. J. Soc. Clin. Psychol.*, 11, 265–269

Eysenck, H. J. (1972b). *Psychology is About People* (New York: Library Press)

Franks, C. M. and Trouton, D. (1958). Effects of amobarbital sodium and dexamphetamine sulphate on the conditioning of the eyelid response. *J. Comp. Physiol. Psychol.*, 51, 220–222

Gray, J. A. (1972). The psychophysiological nature of introversion–extroversion. A modification of Eysenck's theory. In: *Biological Bases of Individual Behaviour* (V. D. Nebylitsyn and J. A. Gray, editors) (New York: Academic Press)

Hathaway, S. R. and McKinley, J. C. (1967). *M.M.P.I. Manual* (New York: Psychological Corporation)

Howarth, E. and Eysenck, H. J. (1968). Extroversion, arousal, and paired associate recall. *J. Exp. Res. Personal.*, 3, 114–116

Jensen, A. R. (1958). *The Reliability of Projective Techniques: Review of the Literature and Methodology* (Amsterdam: North Holland Pub. Co.)

Kretschmer, E. (1936 trans.). *Physique and Character* (New York: Harcourt-Brace, orig. pub. 1921)

Martiny, M. (1948). *Essai de Biotypologie Humaine* (Paris: Peyronnet)

Moss, P. D. and McEvedy, C. P. (1966). An epidemic of overbreathing among schoolgirls. *Brit. Med. J.*, Nov. 26, 1295–1300

Rees, L. and Eysenck, H. J. (1945). A factorial study of some morphological and psychological aspects of human constitution. *J. Ment. Sci.*, **91**, 8–21

Weisen, A. (1965). Differential reinforcing effects of onset and offset of stimulation on the operant behaviour of normals, neurotics, and psychopaths (Univ. Florida: unpub. Ph.D. thesis)

Chapter 10

HEREDITY AND ENVIRONMENT

J. Shields

DEVELOPMENTAL PATHWAY FROM GENES TO BEHAVIOUR

Both seed and soil are essential for development. This is a truism, whether we are concerned with a purely physical characteristic like height or with a psychological disposition like proneness to anxiety, a mental disorder like schizophrenia, or socially defined behaviour like crime. In the strictest sense it is only the genes and chromosomes that are inherited—the DNA with its encoded sequence of amino acids. Everything else is acquired by the individual in the course of his development. The pathway between an individual's inherited constitution and his standing height as an adult will be one of immense complexity and will depend on an intricate web of interactions between factors in the individual and factors in his prenatal and postnatal environment. Here and there, the scientist may be able to implicate genetic differences in growth hormone or social class differences in nutrition in his attempts to account for individual or group differences in stature. Not being omniscient, he will refrain from trying to explain the precise role of innumerable influences which enter into the reasons for individual variation. But for a particular population he may be able to see whether the genetic factors are uniform or whether individuals differ from one another genetically in ways which, other things being equal, will affect their eventual height. If they do, he can estimate the contribution of genetic differences to variation in the population relative to the effects of such environmental differences as are operative at the time.

Psychological traits and social behaviour depend on intricate mental processes and social learning. This does not rule out the importance of genetic factors any more than the intricate hormonal and nutritional relationships do in the case of height. The pathway from genes to behaviour will be even more intricate in psychology; but in principle it is just as possible that genetic factors may differ within human populations in ways which affect mental abilities and behaviour, and not merely that they differentiate man from other species.

Man is a very varied creature genetically and hence biochemically. In the last resort, every individual with the exception of genetically identical twins will, according to Harris (1970), be found to have a unique enzymatic constitution. This will be reflected in a great number of ways in his physical, neurochemical and physiological characteristics, and hence in some of his personality traits and his relative susceptibility or imperviousness to different stresses. It is through their influence on patterns of growth and on ways of responding to the environment that the genes will produce their effects on behaviour.

CHROMOSOME ABNORMALITIES, SINGLE MAJOR GENES, AND POLYGENIC INHERITANCE

This chapter summarises various attempts to evaluate the genetic contribution to individual differences in personality and abnormal behaviour. There are three ways in which genetic factors may enter the picture. The first two—chromosome abnormalities and mutant genes of major effect—need only concern us briefly, since they are relatively rare and their effects are usually medical rather than psychological.

A small extra chromosome (No. 21, a small autosome) is the cause of mongolism or Down's syndrome, which accounts for about 25% of admissions to hospitals for the mentally severely subnormal. Missing or extra sex chromosomes have a less gross effect on mental function. Females with a missing X chromosome (45, XO; Turner's syndrome) have been reported to suffer from a relative difficulty in spatial perception. Among high-grade subnormal patients with behaviour abnormalities there is a significant excess of males with an extra X chromosome (47, XXY; Klinefelter's syndrome). It might be argued that this could be the consequence, direct or indirect, of the sexual abnormality of XXY individuals. However, when XXY cases were compared with a similar group of subfertile, hypogonadal males who did not have the extra chromosome, the XXY men were found to have more psychological abnormality (Theilgaard et al., 1971). This was despite a similar family background in the controls. Males with an extra Y chromosome (47, XYY) are generally found to excess in institutions for the hard-to-manage, persistent criminal. In a special hospital in Scotland for such cases one patient in 35 was found to have an extra Y chromosome, compared with about one in 700 among new-born males in Scotland. Probably most XYYs are psychologically normal, however.

Examples of single genes with a major and specific effect on behaviour are those which cause Huntington's chorea, phenylketonuria and colour blindness. The first two conditions are rare. Huntington's chorea is a disease which leads to mental deterioration and usually comes on in middle life: inheritance is dominant. Phenylketonuria is one of the recessively inherited inborn errors of metabolism. With appropriate dietary treatment early on, the gross effects on intelligence are preventable. Red—green colour blindness, a sex-linked recessive trait in which carrier mothers pass the trait to half their sons, affects about 8% of males. Inability to taste the chemical phenylthiocarbamide (P.T.C.) is another common minor perceptual variation of which a recessive gene is the primary cause and is a further example of how the same environmental stimulus is experienced differently by individuals of different genetic make-up.

The effects of chromosome abnormalities and single mutant genes account for only a small proportion of the total individual variation in psychological traits. For graded characters, physical or psychological, one does not think of single causes, genetic or environmental, but rather of multifactorial origins. Far from 'one gene—one trait' (as in Huntington's chorea), one thinks of the secondary effects of many genes combining with many environmental causes. The polygenic model assumes that both genetic and environmental variations play a part. If we assume that the model holds for a trait like musical ability (and there is some evidence that it does), then on average the more musical will have more genes predisposing to musicality than the unmusical and will be more likely to produce musical offspring for genetic reasons. But at any given point on a scale of musicality individuals will not all be alike in their innate musicality, since environmental factors such as music lessons will also influence the trait. Similarly in the case of anxiety, if the model holds, an individual's reactions will depend partly on his constitution and partly on his experience. This is the so-called diathesis—stress theory (Rosenthal, 1970). Both the genetic and the environmental contributing factors are regarded as multiple and a matter of degree. The polygenic diathesis—stress theory may also apply to traits or disorders which for one reason or another are usually defined as present or absent—crime or epilepsy, for example. Here the predisposing factors are still graded or dimensional, but manifestation of the trait depends on a threshold or cutting point being passed.

Among the ultimate hopes of the behaviour geneticist in studying a polygenic variable are the identification of some of the contributing genetic and environmental factors and the discovery of how they interact in development. More often we must be content with attempts to establish whether the genes really make any appreciable difference. The answer will depend on how far the facts fit a genetic-interactionist model or various purely environmental hypotheses.

METHODS FOR DISTINGUISHING THE EFFECTS OF HEREDITY AND ENVIRONMENT

Family, twin and adoption studies help us to infer the existence of genetic factors. If the genes make any difference there should be some degree of family resemblance. If this can be shown to be non-existent or illusory, the genetic hypothesis is refuted. If, however, there is a family resemblance in respect of a particular measure, one can go on to see how far it parallels the proportion of genes shared by relatives of different kinds. On average, parent and child, brother and sister, and dizygotic (genetically dissimilar) twins, all have half their genes in common. These are called first-degree relatives. Uncle and nephew, grandparent and grandchild and half-brother and half-sister share a quarter of their genes and are termed second-degree relatives. First cousins share an eighth of their genes (third-degree relatives). Methods of biometrical analysis enable one to see how far resemblance fits various genetic and environmental hypotheses about the mode of inheritance and the extent of environmental influence. The different kinds of first- or second-degree relative do not share the same kind of environment. Half-sibs are often brought up together in the same home. An uncle and a niece are brought up in different homes a generation apart.

For practical reasons family studies are concerned mainly with resemblance between parents and children and brothers and sisters. In the case of a behavioural trait acquired in the home resemblance could, in whole or in part, be due to the shared family environment. Twin studies are important because they attempt to test the non-genetic hypothesis. If resemblance is due to the social, cultural or physical environment and the genes make no difference, then dizygotic (DZ) pairs of twins of like sex should be about as similar in the trait as monozygotic (MZ) pairs of twins who are identical in all their genes. As previously noted, DZ pairs have on average only half their genes in common. If on the other hand MZ pairs are significantly more alike than DZ pairs the hypothesis that the genes make a difference receives support.

There are various problems concerned with carrying out and interpreting the results of twin studies. Care needs to be taken to avoid a sampling bias in favour of MZ pairs that are alike in respect of the trait. Twins are unusual, and it is sometimes objected that resemblance in respect of certain abnormal traits including schizophrenia might be largely because twins, and MZ twins in particular, are especially liable to be affected on account of the hazards, biological or psychological, of being a twin. When this possibility is investigated, for instance by looking at the proportion of schizophrenics who are twins, the objection is generally found to be invalid. MZ pairs are more alike than DZ pairs not only in respect of their genes. They also may be more alike in certain environmental respects. They may be treated more alike by parents. They may select more similar environments for themselves (partly for genetic reasons), and they may influence each other more. Such factors may be more relevant for some traits—juvenile delinquency, possibly—than for others. But when attempts have been made to evaluate the influence of these micro-environmental factors on personality resemblance and mental illness it has usually been shown to be minimal. When parents were mistaken as to whether their twins were identical or not, resemblance tended to accord with their actual zygosity and not with their assigned zygosity (Scarr, 1968). Those twins who were most closely attached to one another were not more alike in personality or neurosis than those who were less closely attached (Shields, 1954; Parker, 1964). Twins reared apart in different homes by different parents and without the opportunity of influencing one another still tended to show extensive personality resemblance, indicating that such resemblance is not dependent on similarities of the within-family environment which are more similar for MZ than DZ twins (Shields, 1962).

Some of the biases in twin studies work in the opposite direction and may lead to an underestimation rather than an overestimation of the importance of genetic factors compared with the postnatal environment. Random errors in classifying twins as MZ or DZ would have this effect. Perhaps more important are prenatal factors. MZ twins may differ in the cytoplasm which surrounds the nucleus of the egg cell and in the share of the placental circulation which they receive, leading to differences in birth weight. Also, possibly for prenatal reasons, they can differ in cerebral dominance and handedness.

Studies of twins reared together aim, as we have seen, to hold the environment constant and vary the genotype. To complete the picture we need to hold the degree of genetic resemblance constant and vary the environment. The study of MZ twins reared apart is one way of doing this. It can show the effect or lack of effect of the different environments which the twins experienced. On its own it tells us nothing directly about genetics. Adoption and fostering studies fall into the same class. They aim at separating out the effects on a child of parental genes and parental environment, as in the recent adoption studies in schizophrenia and crime to be described later. If heredity and environment both have effects on a trait (as the model assumes), the method should permit the identification of environments which are harmful or advantageous for persons genetically at risk for disorders of a particular kind.

A further method which can be instructive is animal breeding. Such studies have shown that in other mammals, such as dogs and rats, there is considerable genetic variability influencing perfor-mance on tasks analogous to tests of intelligence, emotionality, aggression and social behaviour. Animal genetic studies also show the importance of specifying the environment in any statement about the effects of genetic differences. Inbred strains of 'maze bright' and 'maze dull' rats did not reveal the same differences under grossly restricted or grossly enriched environments that they did in their normal environment. It is easier to study the genetic aspects of some biological processes in animals than it is in man. But no animal analogues have been found for schizophrenia, and there are difficulties in extrapolating from one mouse strain to another, let alone from mouse to man.

Intellectual ability has been quite extensively studied using all the methods mentioned—family, twin and adoption studies in man, and selective breeding animals. This work has been discussed by Eysenck in Chapter 8. Except perhaps in the case of schizophrenia, the work on personality variation, normal and abnormal, is on the whole less extensive.

PERSONALITY

Apart from twins there has been little work on family resemblance in personality traits. Most of the genetic evidence comes from the several comparisons of MZ with DZ twins, and a few comparisons of MZ twins brought up apart with those brought up together. There are two lines of approach, sometimes combined in the same study. The first is the observational, clinical, life-history method, based on interviews with the twins and their parents, on school reports, medical and criminal records and the like. Besides comparing groups, studies using this method also attempt to uncover possible environmental reasons for the differences observed in the individual pair—for instance, why only one of MZ twins has suffered from depression. They can also examine whether the findings bear out any particular environmental or developmental hypothesis—for example, did the twin with the lower birth weight do less well at school? The second method is to use a personality questionnaire or other mental test which aims at greater objectivity than the interview, but which is usually given on one occasion only. If more than one test is given, the degree of resemblance on different tests can then be examined to see how the various traits may be structurally or biologically related.

MZ and DZ twins

The present writer's study of 62 pairs of 12–15 year old London twin schoolchildren (Shields, 1954) may be used as an illustration of an MZ *v.* DZ comparison using the first method. MZ twins were far from being carbon copies of one another psychologically, but they were assessed as being considerably more alike than same-sexed DZ pairs in so-called neurotic traits (e.g. enuresis) and in their outstanding personality characteristics. Their differences often seemed to be related to the tendency in some pairs for one twin to take the lead socially. Differences in DZ pairs were more far-reaching. Typical is a pair where one twin was nicknamed 'the terror', the other 'the professor'. Antisocial behaviour, however, was not much more similar in MZ than DZ pairs in this study, and the presence of behaviour problems was associated with ratings of the social environment as favourable or unfavourable. Environmental factors were thought to have a relatively greater influence on the presence or absence of problems and constitutional factors a relatively greater influence on the kind of reaction an individual is likely to show in response to stress. In a parallel psychometric study of the same twins (Eysenck, 1956) the degree of extroversion–introversion was found to be significantly more similar in MZ than DZ pairs, which was in accord with the impression given by the histories.

The findings in twin studies using personality questionnaires were discussed and tabulated a few years ago by Vandenberg (1967). Most of the studies were carried out in the U.S.A. Typically, attempts were made to locate all twins in the schools (usually high schools), and all co-operative pairs whose zygosity could be reliably determined by blood groups would then be studied. Vandenberg's table comprises 785 MZ and 908 DZ pairs. Eleven tests purported to measure personality traits, needs, attitudes and factors of many kinds, e.g. those labelled Energetic conformity, Masculinity–feminity, Dependency needs, Punitive attitude, Responsibility, etc. In all but eight

of the 101 variables MZ pairs were more alike than DZ pairs, but in only about half was the difference statistically significant, 29 times at the 0·01 level and 22 times at the 0·05 level. The kinds of variable that most readily showed a significant MZ:DZ difference in these studies were those that seemed to measure the degree of sociability and energy (i.e. extroversion). The only investigation of twins and their parents is that by Elston and Gottesman (1968), which confirmed the strong genetic component in social introversion (heritability=70%, if sexes are combined). The (harder to measure?) neuroticism factor also showed up in some studies as likely to be under some degree of genetic influence. Lindzey *et al.* (1971) considered that in the studies of adolescent twins using personality and interest inventories, a correlation coefficient of 0·46 for MZ pairs and one of 0·28 for DZ pairs is not unrepresentative. However, as they admit, there is a good deal of variation between studies.

One problem that frequently arises with personality tests is that of considerable but inconsistent sex differences in correlation coefficients. Findings also seem to depend on the sample studied and on the particular test used. It would be interesting to know how far differences remain stable over time. In some studies a significant MZ:DZ difference is obtained with only a moderate MZ correlation and a zero or negative DZ correlation. Similar problems have arisen with both clinical assessments of personality and some objectively measured physiological traits.

Table 10.1 shows the results of studies on a large

Table 10.1   Resemblance between twins on Eysenck's dimensions of personality. (Unpublished data of H. J. Eysenck, Judith Kasriel and L. J. Eaves, 1973 by courtesy of the authors)

			MZ	DZ
Number of pairs completing each of 2 tests				
Personality inventory (P.I.)		Male	98	38
		Female	303	173
Personality questionnaire (P.Q.)		Male	78	50
		Female	240	132
Within-pair correlation coefficients				
Extroversion	P.I.	Male	0.49	0.30
		Female	0.49	0.14
	P.Q.	Male	0.70	0.17
		Female	0.50	0.17
Neuroticism	P.I.	Male	0.48	0.17
		Female	0.52	0.14
	P.Q.	Male	0.53	0.07
		Female	0.37	0.10
Psychoticism	P.I.	Male	0.33	−0.09
		Female	0.35	0.22
	P.Q.	Male	0.56	0.35
		Female	0.47	0.32

The subjects were adult volunteers. Most of the pairs who completed the P.I. also completed the P.Q. after an interval of about two years.

sample of adult twins from the U.K. who completed two of the Eysencks' recent personality tests. The relative excess of MZ female and scarcity of DZ male pairs is a frequent occurrence in studies that have to rely on volunteers. A significant MZ:DZ difference in resemblance is not always found in more moderate-sized samples (e.g. Canter, 1973, who gave the P.I. to 40 MZ and 45 DZ pairs).

With further developments in test construction—whether with questionnaires or with performance tests or measures of a more biological kind remains to be seen—it may be possible to obtain more valid measures of personality which, in samples of a practical size, will reliably give high MZ correlations and DZ correlations which are significantly different both from those of MZ twins and from those of unrelated pairs of individuals. Though we should at present not put too much weight on the precise correlation or heritability estimate for particular traits or dimensions, we can nevertheless state with some confidence that in several studies MZ twins are more alike than DZ twins over a range of personality measures.

Resemblance in one trait compared with that in another can be studied by the methods of multivariate analysis (e.g. Vandenberg, 1968) in order to see what statistically higher order factors emerge, or it can be used to test hypotheses about the relationship between dimensions such as extroversion or neuroticism as measured by questionnaires, on the one hand, with theoretical constructs such as cortical inhibition as assessed by E.E.G. readings, psychophysiological measures or behavioural response to sedative drugs. Claridge *et al.* (1973) have recently attempted to test their theories based on Pavlov's nervous typology by examining the responses of twins tested on various personality, cognitive and physiological measures, including a test of sedation threshold. It may be of some interest that this last variable showed much greater within-pair resemblance in 11 MZ than in 10 DZ pairs.

MZ twins brought up apart
Personality variables in MZ twins reared apart (MZA) have been studied in the U.S.A. by Newman *et al.* (1937, 19 pairs), in the U.K. by Shields (1962, 44 pairs), and in Denmark by Juel-Nielsen (1965, 12 pairs). There have also been some further single case reports, including that of a pair where one twin was brought up as a Jew, the other as a Roman Catholic (Lindeman, 1969). Findings were based on tests and interviews. Table 10.2 shows the results of the personality questionnaires administered by Newman *et al.* and Shields to their MZA pairs, MZ twins reared together (MZT) and DZ twins. The MZT pairs were schoolchildren in the Newman study and matched adult controls in the Shields study. Juel-Nielsen did not compare his sample with other twins. It will be seen that MZA pairs showed a resemblance in the tests of the same order as that of MZT pairs in these and other studies. As previously noted, this shows that MZ:DZ differences are not accounted for by subtle within-family environmental factors of the kind which are more alike for MZT than for DZT. Indeed, correlations are slightly higher in the MZA pairs of Table 10.2. Though the difference is not statistically significant, Shields speculated that differences in MZT acquired as a consequence of their close proximity, such as the tendency for one to take the lead, may have obscured the effect of the different environments in the MZA pairs.

In this study, as in the others, age at separation did not have a major effect on the personality differences in MZA pairs. Those separated at birth were about as alike as those separated later. Some pairs were reared in homes that were similar in many respects, such as a pair who were brought up by different aunts in the same street, but in other pairs the twins had very different experiences. In one pair, one twin was brought up by a rich doctor in a South American city, the other by a psychopathic ship's carpenter in rural Scandinavia. In another pair, one was adopted by a middle-class builder and his warm emotional wife in the Home Counties, the other by his cool, reserved grandmother who was married to a Chinese cook in Limehouse. There were generally

Table 10.2   Twins reared apart: resemblance on personality questionnaires

	MZ pairs		DZ pairs reared together (mostly)
	Reared apart *r*	Reared together *r*	*r*
Newman *et al.* (1937) Neuroticism (Woodworth-Mathews)	0.583	0.562	0.371
Shields (1962) Self-rating questionnaire (Eysenck) Neuroticism	0.53	0.38	0.11
Extroversion	0.61	0.42	−0.17

considerable differences in the personalities and occupations of the parents and in the structure of the family, even in pairs where the twins were brought up by different branches of the same family. Of course it cannot be claimed either that the twins were farmed out into homes chosen at random, or that the findings would be the same if it were possible to study only twins exposed to extremes of environmental deprivation and enrichment. The main point was that the family environments of the twins could vary considerably without obscuring basic similarity in a pair of genetically identical twins. On the environmental side, the case histories suggested several ways in which the environment might have led to personality differences in MZA pairs. However, MZT pairs could differ quite widely too. A somewhat higher proportion of pairs with relatively large personality differences was found in the MZA than the MZT group, but the proportion of pairs rated as extremely alike was close to 20% in both MZ groups. The findings in Juel-Nielsen's intensive investigation of the lives of his MZA twins, many of them elderly, also brings out the importance for personality of both genetics and environment. Most of his pairs were obtained from a register of all twins born. His results suggest that the findings in the other two MZA studies were not seriously biased by having been based on volunteers.

NEUROSIS AND PERSONALITY DEVIATION

'The aetiology of all neuroses is a mixed one . . . Generally there is a contribution of the two factors: the constitutional and the accidental. The stronger the constitutional factor the more readily will a trauma lead to fixation, with its sequel in a disturbance of development; the stronger the trauma the more certain is it that it will have injurious effects even when the patient's instinctual life is normal.' The above formulation of a diathesis–stress theory for neurosis was by Freud (1937), who in the same paper made it clear that by constitutional he meant genetic. It was Eliot Slater (1943) who was the first to attempt to put such a theory on a quantitative basis and relate it to genetic theory. He studied the symptoms and diagnoses and outcome of 2000 soldiers admitted to a Neurosis Centre during World War II and found a clear relationship between the degree of military stress undergone and background factors such as family history and previous personality: the poorer the constitution the less stress was required to cause breakdown. With his brother (Slater and Slater, 1944) he proposed the theory that the neurotic constitution was predominantly determined by a large number of genes of small effect, partly similar and partly different in their effects. 'The neurotically predisposed man is then to be regarded as a man who has a more than average susceptibility to environmental stresses of one or a number of kinds; he represents one of the extremes of normal human variation.'

Though neurosis and personality disorder are generally regarded as matters of degree, much of the work is still carried out on psychiatric patients, their families and their twins, categorised as either having or not having particular conditions such as anxiety neurosis, obsessional neurosis, reactive depression or psychopathic personality. Attempts to assess patients and their relatives quantitatively on psychometric tests have not so far led to any positive results genetically. For example, the relatives of neurotics did not score highly on the neuroticism scale of the Maudsley Personality Inventory (M.P.I.) and correlation between patient and relative was generally low (Coppen *et al.*, 1965). This may partly be because many psychiatric disorders are transient or escalate out of previously fairly normal personalities. Recovered neurotics were found to score similarly to normals on the M.P.I. (Ingham, 1966).

Despite different standards of psychiatric diagnosis, there is some evidence from twin and family studies (reviewed by Slater and Shields, 1969) that anxiety proneness is to a considerable extent dependent on inherited factors. Work on animals, and physiological and psychometric studies of normal human twins supported this conclusion. About 15% of parents and sibs of anxiety neurotics are reported as being similarly affected. There have been six twin studies which give some support to the genetic interactional hypothesis. In these authors' own study of neurotic and personality disordered twins from the Maudsley Hospital, the precaution was taken of diagnosing the twin without knowing the diagnosis of the patient or whether the pair was MZ or DZ. According to Slater's diagnostic practice, the MZ pairs where both twins had a psychiatric diagnosis were considerably more alike than the DZ pairs. In 47% of 62 MZ pairs both twins had a psychiatric diagnosis, compared with 24% of 84 DZ pairs. In 29% of the MZ pairs the diagnosis was the same, compared with only 4% of the DZ pairs. A genetic influence of some specificity was suggested particularly in the case of anxiety neurosis and personality disorder. For example, if both MZ twins had a personality disorder they tended to be described in similar terms, e.g. both antisocial, both obsessional personalities, or both schizoid. However, other kinds of neurosis such as neurotic depression showed no evidence of genetic determination. The rate of abnormality was similar in twin partners of both kinds, and when abnormal the MZ co-twin did not receive the same diagnosis as the patient. In an earlier twin study (Slater, 1961) hysteria as it is frequently diagnosed, e.g. in the case of fits labelled 'hysterical' because no organic cause could be found, was considered to be a symptom which could occur in a number of different disorders and as such had no genetic specificity.

Many types of socially deviant behaviour have

been studied by the twin method, including male homosexuality (Heston and Shields, 1968) and alcoholic abuse (Kaij, 1960). Normal drinking habits have also been studied in a comprehensive twin study from Finland (Partanen *et al.*, 1966). The usual finding is that MZ twins are by no means always identical in their behaviour but are significantly more alike than DZ twins. In other words, genetic predisposition and environmental experience can both to some extent be implicated. Exceptions to this general conclusion are therefore of some interest. To judge from twin studies, juvenile delinquency may be one such exception. In 1941 Rosanoff and his colleagues in California found that, given one twin as delinquent, the other twin generally got into trouble too, and it made little difference whether they were MZ (40 out of 41 pairs) or DZ (21 out of 26 pairs). Among the DZ female pairs both twins were delinquent in all nine pairs found. The case histories contained many phrases such as 'Father, in Penitentiary, had encouraged the twins to steal'. Two smaller studies, one from the Maudsley Hospital Childrens Department, the other from Japan (see Shields, in press) also failed to show an MZ:DZ difference in juvenile delinquency.

The position is different for crime in general. In a Danish study (Christiansen, 1970) based on matching police records and records of all twins born 1870–1910, both male twins were criminals in 35% of 71 MZ pairs, compared with 12% of 120 DZ pairs. Crime here corresponds approximately to indictable offences in this country and so includes offences of many different kinds, committed no doubt for a variety of reasons. The findings suggest that these include genetic influences. In studies that have been concerned in the main with persistent offenders, often diagnosed as having psychopathic personality disorders, the role of genetic factors appears to be relatively greater than in the case of crime as a whole. Since most persistent criminals start early, juvenile delinquents may therefore be a mixed group. A larger part may be situationally determined and relatively uninfluenced by constitutional factors. A small core group may go on to contribute to persistent crime and so partly on account of polygenic influences on characteristics such as impulsiveness and low intelligence.

Robins (1966) found that sociopathic boys seen in a child guidance clinic tended to become sociopathic adults* and tended to have sociopathic fathers, but

---

*Adult sociopathy in Robins' study was defined as 'a gross, repetitive failure to conform to societal norms in many areas of life, in the absence of thought disturbance suggesting psychosis'. Sociopaths were required to show poor social adjustment in at least five out of 19 defined life areas, such as work or marital history, financial dependency, arrests, alcohol, and (difficult to establish) lack of guilt. (Only 6% of sociopaths had symptoms in the minimum five areas; the median number was 11 areas.) (Robins, 1966, pp. 79–81.)

was cautious about invoking a definite genetic component in the transmission. Although the sociopathy rate remained high when the boys had no contact with their sociopathic fathers, many were reared by mothers in homes that were very inadequate in other respects. But clearly genetic influences could not be excluded either.

ADOPTION STUDIES OF SOCIOPATHIC DISORDERS

MZ twins who in adolescence go around together may be exposed to similar temptations, to the effects of mutual influence and to increased risk of detection, which might inflate concordance rates for criminal behaviour. Parents may provide their children with unfavourable environments as well as unfavourable genes. For these reasons adoption studies are of particular importance for the further evaluation of genetic and environmental influences in areas such as crime, sociopathy and psychopathic personality. In such studies a child does not receive his genes and his environment from the same source. There have been recent adoption studies on crime, alcoholism and psychopathy, and on schizophrenia (see pages 155–6).

Crime

Hutchings (1972; Hutchings and Mednick, 1975) had access to the names of all 1145 male nonfamilial adoptees from the Copenhagen area, born 1924–47, and to those of their biological and adoptive parents with the exception of some fathers. He also had access to the files of the Danish Police Record Office on all persons known to the police. As many as 30·8% of children placed for adoption had a criminal biological father. It is also surprising that 12·6% of adoptive fathers had a criminal record. The rule which was generally applied by the adoption agencies at that time was that persons adopting children should have been free from a criminal record for at least five years. There was evidence of selective placement of the adoptees in that the social class of the biological and adoptive fathers tended to be similar, but the biological children of criminal fathers were not more often placed with criminal adoptive fathers than would be expected by chance. The sample was large enough to apply a cross-fostering design, comparing the incidence of a criminal record in cases where the adoptive father was criminal but the biological father not known to the police, with the incidence in cases where the biological father was criminal but the adoptive father not known to he police. To make the picture clearer the analysis omitted cases where either parent was known to the police for a non-criminal offence only. The results are shown in the middle two rows of Table 10.3. The Table suggests that hereditary effects may have been more important than environmental ones in this

Table 10.3   Criminality of adoptees, including results of a crossfostering experiment. (Data of Hutchings, 1972)

	Number of adoptees	Percentage with criminal record
Neither father known to police	333	10.4%
Adoptive father criminal, biological father not known to police	52	11.2%
Biological father criminal, adoptive father not known to police	219	21.0%
Adoptive and biological fathers both criminal	58	36.2%

particular analysis: but both factors played a part, and the highest rate of criminality (36·2%) was found when the adoptive and biological father both had a criminal record. The criminality rate of 10·4% in adoptees where neither father was criminal is on the high side. Only 8·8% of 1145 non-adoptees were criminal in a control group matched with the total adopted sample for occupational status of the home in which they were brought up.

Hutchings went on to make a more detailed study of the 143 criminal adoptees with identifiable biological fathers born 1890 onwards, comparing them with the same number of control adopteees not known to the police, matched for age and adoptive father's occupation. Median age of transfer to the adoptive homes (6–7 months) did not differ between the groups, indicating that age at placement was not of vital importance in relation to subsequent criminality among adoptees. Once again the findings demonstrated the apparent influence of both genetic and environmental effects (Table 10.4): compared with the control adoptees the criminal adoptees had more biological fathers and also more adoptive fathers who were criminal.

Very little of the genetic effect could be explained by associations with mental illness in the families. Nor was there a correlation between subsequent criminality and pregnancy or birth complications of the adoptees, as recorded on the midwife's records. Hutchings considered that genetically transmitted characteristics of the autonomic nervous system might to a certain extent explain the inheritance of criminal behaviour, placing certain individuals at greater risk of succumbing to crime.

Crowe (1972) reported the provisional results of a study of the children of 41 female offenders from Iowa who had given up their babies for adoption. The

Table 10.4   Fathers of criminal and non-criminal adoptees. (Data of Hutchings, 1972)

	No. of criminal fathers	
	Biological	Adoptive
143 Criminal adoptees	70	33
143 Control adoptees	40	14

offences of the mothers were not such as to make one think that Crowe was dealing with a particularly psychopathic type of offender. However, by the age of 25 there were significantly more arrests and criminal convictions among these offspring than in a control group of adoptees. Further investigation (Crowe, 1974) showed that the children in the experimental group had not been placed in less favourable conditions than the controls. However, within the experimental group, the antisocial adoptees generally had a criminal biological father; and, compared with normal adoptees in the same group, they spent more time in temporary care or orphanages before final adoption. The findings were interpreted as showing the importance of interaction between genetic endowment and environmental factors in the development of antisocial personality.

Alcoholism

An early adoption study on this subject (Roe *et al.*, 1945) was of interest because it suggested that a favourable foster home environment could have a protective effect. None of the 36 fostered children of alcoholic biological parentage was known to be alcoholic at a mean age of 31, and only three used alcohol regularly; unfortunately there was no information about the drinking habits in seven cases. On the other hand, ten of the children of alcoholics had been in 'serious trouble' during adolescence, compared with only two in the control group of normal parentage; but the children in the alcoholic group had been placed for adoption significantly later than those of the control group, so nothing can be inferred about genetic influences in this study.

Two recent studies may be mentioned. Goodwin *et al.* (1973), using the same Danish adoptee registers as Hutchings, studied the children of alcoholics placed for non-familial adoption and found a higher prevalence of alcohol problems and divorces than in a group of control adoptees. Psychiatric illnesses unassociated with drinking did not differ significantly between the groups. Schuckit *et al.* (1972) studied the half-sibs of alcoholics from a poor area in Iowa. Some had a biological parent who was alcoholic, others not. Some were reared by an alcoholic parent or step-parent, others not (Table 10.5). Presence of

Table 10.5   Incidence of alcoholism in half-sibs of alcoholics under different conditions of biological parentage and upbringing. (Data of Schuckit *et al.*, 1972)

	Biological parent alcoholic	
	Yes	No
Brought up by alcoholic parent or step-parent	Proportion of alcoholics:	
Yes	11/24=46%	2/14 =14%
No	11/22=50%	9/104= 8%

alcoholism was found to be associated with the biological parentage rather than with the presence of an alcoholic parent in the home. Since the half-sibs were about as often alcoholic as were the full sibs in these families, too much genetic influence should not be inferred.

These studies, together with the more conventional family and twin studies (reviewed by Slater and Cowie, 1971) and experimental work on alcohol preference in strains of rats and mice suggest that genetic variation plays a part in addiction, as well as more obvious social factors such as availability of alcohol and social drinking habits. The relevance of biological factors is likely to differ from group to group. In a community where heavy drinking is the social norm, a chronic alcoholic is less likely to be a biological deviant than in a community where heavy drinking is exceptional. Little can be said at present about how far biological influences on drinking habits are secondary to those on personality or how far they may involve some pharmacological specificity for alcohol preference or response.

Psychopathic personality

The Copenhagen register of non-familial adoptions was also used by Schulsinger (1972) in his genetic–environmental investigation of psychopathy—or at least of that kind of psychopathy which comes to psychiatric attention. Adoptees on the register who were psychopathic were identified through the Danish psychiatric register. Psychopathy was defined as inappropriate, non-psychotic, impulse-ridden, or acting-out behaviour, persisting after the age of 19—a definition which secured good agreement between three psychiatrists who rated the records blindly. The incidence of mental disorder in the adoptive and biological relatives of 57 psychopathic adoptees and 57 matched control adoptees was investigated. Cases of psychopathy, of doubtful psychopathy and of criminality, alcoholism and hysterical character disorder were found most frequently among the biological relatives of the psychopathic adoptees. Table 10.6 shows the findings for psychopathy itself (which is mainly a disorder of the male sex) among the fathers in Schulsinger's study.

Table 10.6   Fathers of psychopathic and non-psychopathic adoptees. (Data of Schulsinger, 1972)

	Percentage of fathers who were psychopaths	
	Biological	Adoptive
57 Psychopathic adoptees	9.3	1.9
57 Control adoptees	1.8	0.0

Normal adoptee children

Bohman (1970) studied all 168 children adopted early through a Stockholm adoption society within a two-year period and followed up at the age of 10 or 11. The adoptees had more conflict with their peers than did a group of control children, a finding which Bohman thought might have been connected with the adoptive situation itself. Certainly his study showed no clear-cut effects of either heredity or family environment. 38 biological fathers were registered abusers of alcohol and 40 were on the Swedish criminal register, both rates being higher than would be expected. However, the children of these abusers of alcohol and criminals were not found to excess among those with school adjustment problems. It is possible that the carefully selected adoptive homes may have protected them from manifesting behaviour disorders, or it may be that some of these children will be at risk in adolescence or later. As regards the adoptive homes, the education of the adoptive parents showed no correlation with the children's school performance; nor did adoptive mothers treated for mental illness have more than their share of maladjusted children.

In a further study of fostered—not adopted—children Bohman (1971) found a positive association between criminal or alcoholic biological fathers and maladjustment in the child, but this applied to girls only and not to boys. If boys are more susceptible to psychological as well as biological stresses (Rutter, 1970), it will take more to cause disorder in a girl than in a boy. Bohman did not consider his findings could be explained by negative expectations of foster parents knowing the history of the biological father, since this would have affected the boys.

From the adoption and fostering studies on crime, alcoholism and psychopathic personality it seems clear that the involvement of genetic factors in behavioural abnormalities defined by social criteria cannot be dismissed, even though the hypothesis needs to be refined. Tasks ahead are to try to identify the constitutional bases on which sociopathic behaviour most easily develops; to find means of distinguishing the situational juvenile delinquent from those at risk of developing chronic personality disorder; and to discover the best means of protecting them from such a development.

PSYCHOSIS

We now turn to heredity and environment in disorders classified as psychotic (see Chapter 15), in particular the so-called functional psychoses. We shall not discuss the genetic aspects of psychosis associated with epilepsy or with growing old, though there are of course aspects of these disorders which are of as much concern to the psychologist as are manic-depressive psychosis and schizophrenia.

Depression

The classification and causes of the depressions and other disorders of mood are topics about which there is a diversity of opinion. Views differ as to how many categories or dimensions there are and, on the genetic side, as to the role of single and multiple determinants in each. Genetic studies support the hypothesis that there is more than one kind of depression. The commonest is so-called *reactive* depression, for which genetic factors may be of little or no importance (or, if one prefers, may be universal) or at least non-specific for depression (see p. 150). In depressions classified as *endogenous* or *psychotic*, internal biological factors affecting mood regulation play a bigger role, though they are not infrequently precipitated by physical stresses or by events such as bereavement. There is a tendency for similar conditions to occur in other members of the family. They are about five times as frequent in parents, siblings and children of patients as they are in the general population; approximately 15% and 3% are the respective risks, according to recent estimates (Slater and Cowie,

1971). MZ co-twins are similarly affected in about 67% of pairs (average of eight studies, comprising 103 pairs). The polygenic hypothesis fits the data rather better than the older hypothesis of a single dominant gene. According to the latter hypothesis all persons with the disorder must possess the same rare gene, though all those with the gene do not develop the disorder. According to the polygenic hypothesis the genetic predisposition is graded.

Recent work suggests that the genetic basis may well be different in cases in which phases of manic excitement occur as well as depression (i.e. bipolar disorders) from that in most cases of recurrent unipolar endogenous depression without mania. A Swedish study by Perris found a strong tendency for the two types to breed true (Table 10.7), and there was a higher risk of mood disorders in the families of bipolar than unipolar disorders. In Switzerland Angst obtained similar though not quite so clear-cut results (see Angst and Perris, 1972, for a comparison of the two studies). Analyses of the twin data and work at other centres offer further support for the hypothesis of genetic differences among the psychotic depressions. Proposals to subdivide the unipolar and bipolar psychoses still further are for the present probably best treated with caution. The psychotic depressions carry an increased risk of suicide, but the risk for suicide is no greater for relatives of depressed patients who have committed suicide than for the relatives of depressed patients who have not.

While more than one overlapping polygenic dimension is probably involved in the depressions, it may well be that there are some genes with relatively major effect which account for some of the specific family resemblances. From time to time an abnormal dominant gene on the X chromosome is suggested as playing a major part in one or another type of depressive disorder. This, it is claimed, would account for the observation that females (who have two X chromosomes) are more often affected than males (who have one only). However, the findings are not consistent from study to study and not always consistent with the principles of sex-linked inheritance. Hormonal sex differences rather than sex-linked genes may be involved in the differing sex incidence.

Table 10.7   Specificity of inheritance within the depressive psychoses. (Data of Perris, 1966)

	Relatives of 138 bipolar patients ($n=1077$)	Relatives of 139 unipolar patients ($n=1203$)
Bipolar psychosis	58	2
Unipolar psychosis	3	44
Unclassifiable affective disorder	14	16
Suicide	32	24
Total	107	86

Schizophrenia

Though much more work has been done on schizophrenia than on manic-depressive psychosis, there is still a widespread tendency to regard schizophrenia as essentially a learned disorder of thought or a style of life in which the genetic constitution is irrelevant.

Perhaps the strongest argument against this extreme position is the fact that so far no environmental factors have been found which will predictably raise the incidence of schizophrenia in persons unrelated to a schizophrenic. Scharfetter (1972) studied persons in whom a schizophrenic-like psychosis had been induced (*folie à deux*). He found a raised incidence of schizophrenia among the blood relatives of these cases similar to that found among the relatives of schizophrenics, and this was so even when the inducer of the psychosis was not a blood relative. A group working on the Danish registers, which we have previously mentioned in connection with studies of sociopathy, succeeded in finding persons who had been adopted *by* schizophrenics, but they were not found to have more abnormality than a group of suitable controls, and none of them had a schizophrenic-like psychosis (Wender *et al.*, 1974). Birley and Brown (1970) have demonstrated that events such as moving house had occurred during the past three months more often among acute schizophrenic admissions than among controls, but the life events which they studied were in no way specific for schizophrenia. In this respect schizophrenia differs from, say, anxiety neurosis or depression in that there are threatening situations or events such as bereavement which can be shown in general to make an individual more anxious or depressed. The fact that, as we shall see, the MZ twins of schizophrenics are often not schizophrenic themselves points to the existence of environmental factors, but it seems that these are likely to be chance combinations of nonspecific factors acting idiosyncratically on individuals predisposed to a schizophrenic reaction by their biochemical or neurophysiological make-up (Gottesman and Shields, 1972).

The genetic hypothesis receives support from family, twin and adoption studies which refute different alternative environmental explanations. Differing diagnostic standards, particularly between Europe and the U.S.A., make the comparison of some studies difficult, but according to work based on European standards the risk for developing schizophrenia some time during life is about 1% for a person in the general population; it is about 3% for a second-degree relative such as a niece or nephew of a schizophrenic; and it is about 10% for the children, ordinary siblings and DZ co-twins. (The rate for parents is lower, but the marriage rate is low for schizophrenics: many schizophrenics do not become parents.)

The genuine familial aggregation of cases cannot be entirely due to the shared family environment, because MZ twins reared together are at least three times more often both affected than DZ twins reared together. This is still true in the recent studies which have allowed for the sampling and diagnostic biases which may have influenced some of the older studies. There have been 11 systematic studies from seven different countries, comprising more than 1300 pairs. Recent studies from Norway (Kringlen, 1967) and Denmark (Fischer, 1973) matched national registers of all twins born with psychiatric registers, and also included extensive personal investigation. Gottesman and Shields's study (1972) comprised all twins from consecutive admissions to in-patient and out-patient departments at the Maudsley Hospital over a 16-year period and used psychological tests as well as psychiatric assessments. Final diagnosis was based on the consensus of six judges who did not know the zygosity of the pair or the diagnosis of the other twin. Both twins were schizophrenic in 50% of 22 MZ pairs and 9% of 33 DZ pairs. These figures are fairly representative when differences in diagnostic standards are taken into account.

The higher concordance of MZ pairs is not due to hazards of monozygosity, such as an alleged weak ego formation, since there is no excess of MZ twins in populations of schizophrenics. If MZ concordance were attributable to subtle similarities within the same family environment, as is often claimed, it should virtually disappear in twins brought up apart. There have now been reports of 25 MZA pairs where at least one twin was schizophrenic. Some cases are not as well documented as one would wish; some of the twins spent part of their lives together; and sometimes both were reared in homes which were far from ideal. In 15 of the 25 pairs both twins had schizophrenia or a similar psychosis. This rate of 66% may not be the best estimate of concordance in general, but at least it refutes a frequent objection to the genetic hypothesis.

Even before the results of adoption studies were reported, it seemed clear from the MZ and DZ twin studies that genetic factors played a part. But it could be argued that the twin studies gave a misleading idea of their importance: schizophrenia might be the result of a chaotic family environment with irrational modes of communication—which, it has been claimed, is provided by the parents of many schizophrenics—in interaction with the constitution of the more genetically predisposed children. But the findings in four studies employing the strategy of the adoption method showed that the environment shared with a person suffering from a schizophrenic-like disorder is certainly not a major cause of breakdown in schizophrenic families, and may not be relevant at all. For instance, Heston (1966) studied 47 offspring of schizophrenic mothers, reared from birth away from their mothers or their mothers' families. He found five of them to be schizophrenic at a mean age

Table 10.8   Relatives of schizophrenic and non-schizophrenic adoptees. (Data of Kety *et al.*, 1968)

	Relatives* with schizophrenia spectrum disorder†	
	Biological	*Adoptive*
33 Schizophrenic adoptees	13/150 (8.7%)	2/74 (2.7%)
33 Control adoptees	3/156 (1.9%)	3/83 (3.6%)

* Parents, full sibs, half-sibs.
† Schizophrenia (incl. borderline schizophrenia), certain or doubtful; and inadequate personality.

of 36, a similar proportion to that reported in the children of schizophrenics not so separated, and he found no cases of schizophrenia in his control group of foster children.

It has been argued that Heston's findings could be accounted for as the result of a self-fulfilling prophecy. Some of the foster mothers might have known that the real mother was schizophrenic; these mothers might have looked for and thought they found symptoms in the child; this in turn might have induced genuine schizophrenic symptoms in the child or have led psychiatrists to diagnose them. But this is an example of the kind of *ad hoc* conjectural objection that can always be raised. A different explanation would have to be given for a similar study with similar results (Rosenthal *et al.*, 1968), because here most of the parents were diagnosed schizophrenic only *after* the legal, non-familial adoption of the child. The adoptive parents would not have known.

It was Rosenthal and his colleagues who first used the Danish register of adoptions for research on abnormal psychology, and who also first employed the strategy of comparing biological and adoptive relatives of abnormal and control adoptees already illustrated in Tables 10.4 and 10.6. Table 10.8 shows the original findings of Kety *et al.*, (1968) in respect of schizophrenia and possible borderline disorders. The excess of what they termed 'schizophrenia spectrum disorder' among the biological relatives held just as strongly when the study was restricted to adoptees who had been removed from their biological parents within the first month. These findings, based on records only, held up when the relatives were interviewed (Kety, 1974).

Though the majority of psychologists and psychiatrists now accept the evidence that genetic factors play a part in causing schizophrenia, there are differences of view about the specificity of the genes, since other psychological disorders besides schizophrenia are found in the families and twins of schizophrenics. However, what stands out is the fact that, when the relative of a psychotic is likewise psychotic, he tends to have the same kind of psychosis and often the same subtype—for example, catatonic schizophrenia or bipolar manic-depressive psychosis, both quite rare disorders. This is more impressive than the

fact that numerically there may be more relatives with less severe but commoner neuroses or personality problems. It is unlikely that this resemblance in the form of the psychosis is environmental, since stresses do not predict one type of reaction rather than another, and resemblance in precise symptomatology is not close enough for it to be the result of imitation.

The way one envisages the interplay of genetic and environmental factors depends on the genetic model preferred. There are some who prefer a single gene theory, according to which one relatively rare gene is necessary but not sufficient for virtually all schizophrenias. Until the existence of such a gene can be demonstrated biochemically, others prefer a multifactorial model according to which many genetic and environmental factors contribute to the predisposition or liability; schizophrenia occurs once a threshold in liability has been passed. This model can be tested from the incidence of schizophrenia in the general population and in the relatives of schizophrenics, and it can be shown that it fits the data as well as the single gene theory (Gottesman and Shields, 1972). Substantial estimates of heritability—around 80%, according to one method—are consistently obtained, derived independently from relatives sharing different kinds of environment. Genetic factors, some more specific than others, and environmental factors are each necessary but insufficient for the development of schizophrenia, but it seems that genetic factors are the most uniformly potent cause.

According to the Gottesman and Shields model, the whole population varies in degree of genetic predisposition. Only those individuals towards the tail of the normal distribution are at serious risk of developing schizophrenia—say, the top 10%. A very few at the extreme tail might be regarded as almost certain to become affected; but the majority of schizophrenics within the high risk group would be in the zone most sensitive to environmental stresses, which over time can tip the individual's total liability over the threshold. On this model we do not see the social, psychodynamic and learning theories of schizophrenia as necessarily conflicting with the genetic theory but potentially as complementing it.

Figure 10.1 illustrates some of these points. It shows the imaginary life curves of four persons with an above average genetic predisposition to schizo-

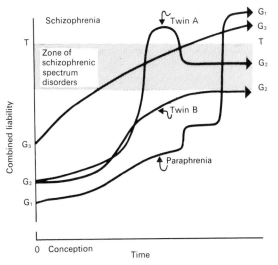

Figure 10.1 Schematic proposal of how diathesis interacts with stress in the development of schizophrenia. (From Gottesman and Shields, 1973, by courtesy of *Brit. J. Psychiatry*)

phrenia. Two of them are a pair of discordant MZ twins. With age and environmental experiences of various kinds their total genetic-cum-environmental liability varies over time so that sometimes they cross the threshold of diagnosable schizophrenia. At other times they show subthreshold manifestations such as odd personality traits or borderline psychotic features, shown here as a zone of schizophrenic spectrum disorders. G3 has the highest genetic liability. He develops a schizoid personality and becomes a chronic schizophrenic without remission. Twins A and B start with the same, lesser loading of genetic liability (G2). Twin A encounters stresses which result in an overt schizophrenic illness. This ameliorates with treatment, but he remains an impoverished, eccentric personality. Twin B, at the time of observation, has got by without detectable abnormality, though his total liability may have brought him close to the zone of spectrum disorders. G1 is intended to indicate the trajectory of a person with a lower genetic liability than most schizophrenics. Over time, environmental contributions to liability, say, first the death of a spouse and then the onset of deafness, lead to the development of an acute late onset paranoid schizophrenia or 'paraphrenia' in a previously normal personality.

In principle, pairs of MZ twins where only one is schizophrenic (discordant pairs) should be able to throw light on environmental factors in a way which might be important for prevention, but so far the results of such studies have been disappointing. Findings tend to focus on small relative differences in birth weight and submissiveness. It is the relatively more submissive twin who tends to be the schizo-

phrenic in discordant pairs, but this finding is not specific for schizophrenia and it is uncertain how relevant it is outside the twin situation. As noted earlier, a twin's fate may depend largely on chance—on the simultaneous occurrence of minor stresses to which he is personally sensitive. Perhaps more hopeful (and more basic) is the approach which looks for ways, relevant to schizophrenia, in which the affected and unaffected twins are *alike*. Though psychological tests of thought disorder have not proved to be a stable marker of the genetic predisposition, it is possible that physiological, pharmacological or biochemical measures may fare better.

To summarise the nature–nurture relationship in schizophrenia as outlined here, the genes are the most uniformly potent cause. The genetic, developmental predisposition is graded. Most of those at high risk are sensitive to various stresses, but these are less specific than the genetic factors. So far no environmental factor has been found which successfully predicts schizophrenia in persons unrelated to a schizophrenic.

CONCLUSIONS

Further references to the work described in this chapter will be found in the writer's chapters in the *Handbook of Abnormal Psychology* (Shields, 1973) and Rutter and Hersov's *Recent Developments in Child Psychiatry* (Shields, in press), and in *Schizophrenia and Genetics* (Gottesman and Shields, 1972). The area of abnormal behaviour genetics in man is one on which it used to be difficult to recommend a comprehensive textbook. Fortunately the situation is now improved. *Genetic Theory and Abnormal Behavior* (Rosenthal, 1970) by an American clinical psychologist and *The Genetics of Mental Disorders* (Slater and Cowie, 1971) by two British psychiatrists are two recent textbooks which can be recommended, as can the multi-author volume *Genetics and Mental Disorders* edited by the behaviour geneticist Erlenmeyer-Kimling (1972). The salient papers of Eliot Slater were recently published under the title of *Man, Mind, and Heredity* (ed. Shields and Gottesman, 1971). Twin studies in psychology have been well dealt with by Mittler (1971) and by Claridge *et al.*, (1973). The whole field of human population genetics is expertly covered in Cavalli-Sforza and Bodmer's (1971) large book.

The aim of the chapter has been to present the main evidence about whether genetic differences account for any of the wide range of individual differences observed in personality, neurosis and psychosis. It should be clear that they do, and equally clear that it is a question of heredity and environment, not heredity or environment. The question of heritability, or how much of the variance of a trait in a particular population can be accounted for by genetic variation, has not been a central issue. This is partly because of the problems of finding reliable, valid measurements of a trait. A particular aspect of this general problem is to find a measure which is sufficiently independent of variations in an individual's mental state at different times for it to be useful when comparing relatives. Tests which are suitable for assessing response to treatment may not be the best ones for genetic studies. But assuming a test measures a stable trait and it can be given to appropriate strategic groups, various methods of biometrical analysis are available which can provisionally estimate not only the heritability of a trait but also how much of the variance is due to the effect of common family environment, to the correlation between heredity and environment, and to interaction effects of environment with different genotypes. They can attempt to elucidate the genetic 'architecture' of the trait, and even decide whether natural selection in the past has favoured those who are high or low in respect of the trait. Jinks and Fulker (1970) recently subjected the available data on intelligence and personality to such an analysis. Sir Cyril Burt was one of the pioneers. As he pointed out himself (Burt, 1958), all such estimates of hereditary, environmental and 'error' variance depend on the test used and the population studied. They also depend on the method. A further point that needs to be stressed is that the finding that genetic factors are important does not imply that treatment is impossible, any more than the fact that an environmental cause (such as accidental brain injury) is all-important means that treatment is easy.

One of the main problems in the area is how far different kinds of behaviour have the same or different causes. We know enough to eschew the extremes of genetic specificity and generality. It is clearly not a case of one pair of genes determining degree of intelligence, another anxiety, a third criminality, a fourth schizophrenia, and so on. Equally discredited is the theory of a global neuropathic taint according

to which one or a number of similar genes determine degree of 'abnormality' and whether this manifests itself as ineducability, sexual irregularities, epileptic fits or certifiable psychosis depends on other factors. What we generally find when we look at twins and families is some degree of both generality and specificity. Depression and schizophrenia occur in the same family more often than would be predicted by the theory that they are quite separate diseases with causes each of which produces only its distinctive effect. On the other hand there are sufficiently close resemblances in families to make it unlikely that schizophrenia and depression are merely different manifestations of a dimension of psychoticism where all the predisposing genes have the same effect. Within the psychotic depressions, as we have seen, there may be genetic distinctions too. The investigator can put forward and test various hypotheses about the degree of homogeneity or heterogeneity of a given class of behaviour and how far its causes overlap with those of other classes.

Since the genes exert their effects on behaviour indirectly, in the first place by determining different biochemical reactions, it may well be that advances in understanding the genetic aspects of psychology will depend on genetic studies of biological variables and on a firmer knowledge about how they are related to personality and mental disorder (Eysenck, 1967). Advances in the understanding of genetic–environmental interaction should come from comparing the effects of different 'treatments' (social, pharmacological or whatever) on persons of different basic personality.

Continued scientific attention to behaviour genetics in a developmental context focusses attention on the individual and his needs. It does not imply a fatalistic attitude. It should avoid misunderstandings such as blaming a parent for causing schizophrenia in his child by faulty upbringing. Any account of psychological differences which ignores either the genetic or the environmental dimension will be a partial one.

References

Angst, J. and Perris, C. (1972). The nosology of endogenous depression. In: *Genetics and mental disorders* (L. Erlenmeyer-Kimling, editor). *Int. J. Mental Health*, 1, 145–158

Birley, J. L. T. and Brown, G. W. (1970). Crises and life changes preceding the onset or relapse of acute schizophrenia: clinical aspects. *Brit. J. Psychiatry*, 116, 327–333

Bohman, M. (1970). *Adopted Children and their Families* (Stockholm: Proprius)

Bohman, M. (1971). A comparative study of adopted children, foster children and children in their biological environment born after undesired pregnancies. *Acta Paediat. Scand.*, Suppl. 221,

Burt, C. (1958). The inheritance of mental ability. *Amer. Psychol.*, 13, 1–15

Canter, S. (1973). Personality traits in twins. In: *Personality Differences and Biological Variations: A Study of Twins* (G. Claridge, S. Canter and W. I. Hume, editors) (Oxford: Pergamon Press)

Cavalli-Sforza, L. L. and Bodmer, W. F. (1971). *The Genetics of Human Populations* (San Francisco: W. H. Freeman)

Christiansen, K. O. (1970). Crime in a Danish twin population. *Acta Genet. Med. Gemellologiae*, 19, 323–326

Claridge, G., Canter, S. and Hume, W. I. (1973). *Personality Differences and Biological Variations: A Study of Twins* (Oxford: Pergamon Press)

Coppen, A., Cowie, V. and Slater, E. (1965). Familial aspects of 'neuroticism' and 'extroversion'. *Brit. J. Psychiatry*, 111, 70–83

Crowe, R. R. (1972). The adopted offspring of women criminal offenders. *Arch. Gen. Psychiatry*, 27, 600–603

Crowe, R. R. (1974). An adoption study of antisocial personality. *Arch. Gen. Psychiatry*, 31, 785–791.

Elston, R. C. and Gottesman, I. I. (1968). The analysis of quantitative inheritance simultaneously from twin and family data. *Amer. J. Human Genetics*, 20, 512–521

Erlenmeyer-Kimling, L. (editor) (1972). Genetics and mental disorders. *Int. J. Mental Health*, Vol. 1, Nos. 1–2

Eysenck, H. J. (1956). The inheritance of extroversion–introversion. *Acta Psychologica*, 12, 95–110

Eysenck, H. J. (1967). *The Biological Basis of Personality* Springfield, Illinois: C. C. Thomas)

Fischer, M. (1973). Genetic and environmental factors in schizophrenia. *Acta Psychiatr. Scand.*, Suppl. 238,

Freud, S. (1937). Analysis terminable and interminable. *Collected Papers*, 5 (London: Høgarth)

Goodwin, D. W., Schulsinger, F., Hermansen, L., Guze, S. G. and Winokur, G. (1973). Alcohol problems in adoptees raised apart from alcoholic biological parents. *Arch. Gen. Psychiatry*, 28, 238–243

Gottesman, I. I. and Shields, J. (1972). *Schizophrenia and Genetics: A Twin Study Vantage Point* (New York: Academic Press)

Gottesman, I. I. and Shields, J. (1973). Genetic theorizing and schizophrenia. *Brit. J. Psychiatry*, 122, 15–30

Harris, H. (1970). *The Principles of Human Biochemical Genetics* (Amsterdam: North-Holland Publ.)

Heston, L. L. (1966). Psychiatric disorders in foster home reared children of schizophrenic mothers. *Brit. J. Psychiatry*, 112, 819–825

Heston, L. L. and Shields, J. (1968). Homosexuality in twins: a family study and a registry study. *Arch. Gen. Psychiatry*, 18, 149–160

Hutchings, B. (1972). Environmental and genetic factors in psychopathology and criminality (University of London: Unpublished M.Phil. Thesis)

Hutchings, B. and Mednick, S. A. (1975). Registered criminality in the adoptive and biological parents of registered male criminal adoptees. In: *Genetic Research in Psychiatry* (R. R. Fieve, D. Rosenthal and H. Brill, editors) (Baltimore: Johns Hopkins Press)

Ingham, J. G. (1966). Changes in MPI scores in neurotic patients: a three year follow-up. *Brit. J. Psychiatry*, 112, 931–939

Jinks, J. L. and Fulker, D. W. (1970). A comparison of the biometrical genetical, MAVA and classical approaches to the analysis of human behavior. *Psychol. Bull.*, 73, 311–349

Juel-Nielsen, N. (1965). Individual and environment. A psychiatric–psychological investigation of monozygotic twins reared apart. *Acta Psychiatr. Scand.*, Suppl. 183,

Kaij, L. (1960). *Alcoholism in Twins* (Stockholm: Almqvist and Wiksell)

Kety, S. S., Rosenthal, D., Wender, P. H. and Schulsinger, F. (1968). The types and prevalence of mental illness in the biological and adoptive families of adopted schizophrenics. In: *The Transmission of Schizophrenia* (D. Rosenthal and S. S. Kety, editors) (Oxford: Pergamon Press)

Kety, S. S. (1974). From rationalization to reason. *Amer. J. Psychiatry*, 131, 957–63

Kringlen, E. (1967). *Heredity and Environment in the Functional Psychoses* (London: Heinemann)

Lindeman, B. (1969). *The Twins Who Found Each Other* (New York: William Morrow)

Lindzey, G., Loehlin, J., Manosevitz, M. and Thiessen, D. (1971). Behavioral genetics. In: *Annual Review of Psychology*, Vol. 22 (P. H. Mussen and M. R. Rosenzweig, editors) (California: Annual Reviews Inc.)

Mittler, P. (1971). *The Study of Twins*. Penguin Science of Behaviour (London: Penguin)

Newman, H. H., Freeman, F. N. and Holzinger, K. J. (1937). *Twins: A Study of Heredity and Environment* (Chicago: University of Chicago Press)

Parker, N. (1964). Close identification in twins discordant for obsessional neurosis. *Brit. J. Psychiatry*, 110, 496–504

Partanen, J., Bruun, K. and Markkanen, T. (1966). *Inheritance of Drinking Behavior* (Helsinki: The Finnish Foundation for Alcohol Studies)

Perris, C. (1966). A study of bipolar (manic-depressive) and unipolar recurrent depressive psychoses. *Acta Psychiatr. Scand.*, Suppl. 194,

Robins, L. N. (1966). *Deviant Children Grown Up* (Baltimore: Williams and Wilkins)

Roe, A., Burks, B. and Mittelmann, B. (1945). Adult adjustment of foster-children of alcoholic and psychotic parentage and the influence of the foster-home. Memoirs of the Section on Alcohol Studies, Yale University, No. 3, *Quart. J. Studies on Alcohol*, New Haven

Rosanoff, A. J., Handy, L. M. and Plesset, I. R. (1941). The etiology of child behavior difficulties, juvenile delinquency and adult criminality with special reference to their occurrence in twins. *Psychiatric Monographs (California)*, No. 1. (Sacramento: Department of Institutions)

Rosenthal, D., Wender, P. H., Kety, S. S., Schulsinger, F., Welner, J. and Østergaard, L. (1968). Schizophrenics' offspring reared in adoptive homes. In: *The Transmission of Schizophrenia* (D. Rosenthal and S. S. Kety, editors) (Oxford: Pergamon Press)

Rosenthal, D. (1970). *Genetic Theory and Abnormal Behavior* (New York: McGraw-Hill)

Rutter, M. (1970). Sex differences in children's responses to family stress. In: *The Child in His Family* (E. J. Anthony and C. Koupernik, editors) (New York: Wiley-Interscience)

Scarr, S. (1968). Environmental bias in twin studies. In: *Progress in Human Behavior Genetics* (S. G. Vandenberg, editor) (Baltimore: Johns Hopkins Press)

Scharfetter, C. (1972). Studies of heredity in symbiontic psychoses. In: *Genetics and mental disorders* (L. Erlenmeyer-Kimling, editor). *Int. J. Mental Health*, 1, 116–123

Schuckit, M. A., Goodwin, D. A. and Winokur, G. (1972). A study of alcoholism in half siblings. *Amer. J. Psychiatry*, 128, 1132–1136

Schulsinger, F. (1972). Psychopathy: heredity and environment. In: *Genetics and mental disorders* (L. Erlenmeyer-Kimling, editor). *Int. J. Mental Health*, 1, 190–206

Shields, J. (1954). Personality differences and neurotic traits in normal twin schoolchildren. *Eugenics Review*, 45, 213–246

Shields, J. (1962). *Monozygotic Twins Brought Up Apart and Brought Up Together* (London: Oxford University Press)

Shields, J. and Gottesman, I. I., (editors) (1971). *Man, Mind, and Heredity: Selected Papers of Eliot Slater on*

Psychiatry and Genetics (Baltimore and London: Johns Hopkins Press)

Shields, J. (1973). Heredity and psychological abnormality. In: *Handbook of Abnormal Psychology*, 2nd Ed. (H. J. Eysenck, editor) (London: Pitman Medical)

Shields, J. Polygenic influences in child psychiatry. In: *Recent Developments in Child Psychiatry* (M. Rutter and L. Hersov, editors) (London: Blackwell Scientific Publications Ltd., in press)

Slater, E. (1943). The neurotic constitution: a statistical study of two thousand neurotic soldiers.* *J. Neurol. Psychiatry*, 6, 1–16

Slater, E. and Slater, P. (1944). A heuristic theory of neurosis.* *J. Neurol. Psychiatry*, 7, 49–55

Slater, E. (1961). The thirty-fifth Maudsley Lecture: 'hysteria 311'.* *J. Mental Sci.*, 107, 359–381

Slater, E. and Shields, J. (1969). Genetical aspects of anxiety. In: *Studies of anxiety* (M. H. Lader, editor). *Brit. J. Psychiatry Spec. Publ.*, No. 3. (Ashford, Kent: Headley)

Slater, E. and Cowie, V. A. (1971). *The Genetics of Mental Disorders* (London: Oxford University Press)

Theilgaard, A., Nielsen, J., Sørensen, A., Frøland, A. and Johnsen, S. G. (1971). *A Psychological–Psychiatric Study of Patients with Klinefelter's Syndrome, 47, XXY.* (Publication of the University of Aarhus, Copenhagen: Munksgaard)

Vandenberg, S. G. (1967). Hereditary factors in normal personality traits (as measured by inventories). In: *Recent Advances in Biological Psychiatry*, Vol. 9 (J. Wortis, editor) (New York: Plenum Press)

Vandenberg, S. G. (1968). Primary mental abilities or general intelligence? Evidence from twin studies. In: *Genetic and Environmental Influences on Behaviour* (J. M. Thoday and A. S. Parkes, editors) (Edinburgh: Oliver and Boyd)

Wender, P. H., Rosenthal, D., Kety, S. S., Schulsinger, F. and Welner, J. (1974). 'Cross-Fostering': A research strategy for clarifying the role of genetic and experiential factors in the etiology of schizophrenia. *Arch. Gen. Psychiatry*, 30, 121–128

* Reprinted in: *Man, Mind, and Heredity* (1971). (J. Shields and I. I. Gottesman, editors) (Baltimore and London: Johns Hopkins Press)

DEVELOPMENTAL AND SOCIAL PSYCHOLOGY

Chapter 11

DEVELOPMENTAL PSYCHOLOGY

Valerie E. Labrum

Developmental psychology is the study of the development of different patterns of behaviour as they emerge through the process of maturation and learning; it is concerned with the unfolding of genetic potential under the stimulation and modification of environmental forces; it is about growth, differentiation and the acquisition of learned responses. As in other branches of human psychology the aim is (1) to observe, (2) to explain, (3) to predict and (4) to control human behaviour.

OBSERVATION IN DEVELOPMENTAL PSYCHOLOGY

Observation is a necessary first stage of scientific enquiry; on the basis of observed 'facts' and perceived 'causal connections' we form hypotheses and theories whose validity can be tested experimentally. Unfortunately, our expectations and prejudices tend to make us selective in our observations, so that we often only notice what we want to notice, and theories based on biased data will themselves be biased. The perpetuation of old wives' tales is the price we pay for sloppy observational techniques, and developmental psychologists spend a great deal of time checking the validity of 'motherhood myths' which have been uncritically accepted. To illustrate, John and Elizabeth Newson, two research child psychologists, became very aware of the amount of conflicting advice (often based on very dubious premises) offered to young mothers. In a well-planned questionnaire survey of 709 Nottingham mothers of one-year-old children (Newson and Newson, 1963), they decided to find out, not whether childbearing happens as theorists think it 'ought' to occur, but what in fact happens, how often and with what result. They found, for example, that the average daily sleeping time (13.6 hours), though compatible with the figures obtained from similar studies, was considerably less than the sleep requirement figures given in widely-read baby manuals. They also found that the use of dummies (comforters) during the first year (apparently in excess of 72%) was considerably more than one might expect (and a follow-up study showed that some children were still sucking dummies at four years of age), though the mothers were reluctant to admit to using a dummy to health visitors, which suggests that they had been made to feel guilty about this very common practice.

The process of human development cannot ethically be investigated by experimental manipulation. We cannot deliberately set out to interfere with genes or make fundamental alterations to important aspects of the environment in order to assess the effect of their influence on the developmental process. We can, however, adopt the quasi-experimental approach in which we identify groups of children which differ from other groups in important respects, and then observe the differential effect that these variables have on the development of their behaviour. The success of this latter method requires skilled sampling, skilled observation and skilled evaluation; it also requires sensitivity of approach to ensure that these processes of investigation do not themselves interfere with the natural course of development.

Cross-sectional and longitudinal studies

Two main approaches have been used to trace the pattern of human development through the life-cycle—the normative cross-sectional method and the longitudinal method.

In the *normative cross-sectional approach*, information is collected from observations, surveys, questionnaire or retrospective studies, at one point in time, and from a large number of children of different ages. The normative cross-sectional approach studies different groups at different ages at the same time; it yields information about the range of individual differences, and gives a 'vignette' of the characteristics of an age-group by comparison with other age-groups. Comparison between data of, for example, a sample of three-year-olds with data from samples of four-year-olds and five-year-olds enables us to develop norms for each age level, and so (by extrapolation) to study age trends from three to five years. The normative cross-sectional approach is the method used in the large-scale standardisation of intelligence tests.

In the *longitudinal approach*, a representative sample is taken from the population, a description of the sample is made, baseline measurements are taken, and developmental progress is monitored continuously or by follow-up assessments at predetermined intervals using the same sample of children, each measured against himself at an earlier age. The longitudinal approach studies the same group at different times; it is the method of choice in the study of developmental processes, growth increments and the effect of individual differences on maturation and learning. This method has the advantage that the subjects act as their own controls. For example, Smith (1952) studied the persistence of personality characteristics from childhood through to adulthood and old age in the same six individuals, and found that when they were rated on 35 personality traits 50 years after their mother had recorded judgments about them in her diary, there was a 70% persistence in these traits after half a century of individual development had elapsed. The constancy of personality traits in both well-adjusted and poorly-adjusted individuals was found to be greater in adulthood, and all showed 'improvement' in both 'desirable' and 'undesirable' aspects of their personality (suggesting, perhaps, that it took them a half-century of maturation and learning to acquire consistent patterns of socially-acceptable behaviour!)

The cross-sectional approach has the disadvantage that it studies different children at each age-group so that it cannot give a good picture of different kinds of developmental processes, nor can norms based on cross-sectional studies tell us what is normal for an individual child. The cross-sectional approach tells us nothing about the effect of individual characteristics (such as personality variables) on the course of development, and tells us nothing about the aetiology of developmental disorders (only their prevalence). Furthermore, it is misleading in some cases to look for the typical characteristics of an age-group. For example, a sample of 13-year-old girls will consist of some prepubertal girls and some pubertal girls, each group being accompanied by different stages of emotional development and neither group giving a truly 'typical' picture of 13-year-old girls. The longitudinal approach has its disadvantages too. To follow up a group of children over a number of years is a costly business; it requires considerable preplanning including a great deal of sophisticated knowledge about the variables under study if the resulting data are to be meaningful. It requires a great deal of co-operation from all concerned if the total sample (including those children who have moved away from the district) is to be traceable over the years for follow-up study. It is also difficult to know whether changes in the variable under study are really due to developmental processes, or whether they are due to changes (such as war, educational reform and re-housing programmes) in the social, cultural or economic environment in which the children are growing up.

Recently there has been a great deal of interest in another approach to collecting data—the *cohort method*. This method is really a combination of the cross-sectional and longitudinal methods, and helps to control and minimise many of the disadvantages described above. By this method, samples of children from different age-groups (as in the cross-sectional method) are followed up over a number of years (as in the longitudinal method) until the youngest 'cohort'

overlaps with the next cohort. This method has the advantage that experience gained in studying an older age-group can be used to refine measures and answer more questions when a younger cohort reaches the same age (Rutter *et al.*, 1970; Davie *et al.*, 1972). Figure 11.1 shows how, in a three-year cohort study, age samples of four to ten-year-olds can be followed up, with cross-checks at ages six and eight to ensure that the samples contain similar groups of children.

Figure 11.1   Plan of three-year cohort study

	Sample I	Sample II	Sample III
First year of study	4 years	6 years	8 years
Second year of study	5 years	7 years	9 years
Third year of study	6 years	8 years	10 years

EXPLANATION IN DEVELOPMENTAL PSYCHOLOGY

When we have gathered together data from carefully-controlled observations, surveys, questionnaire studies and retrospective enquiries, patterns begin to emerge which suggest lawful relationships and causal connections. Testable hypotheses are formed, their validity is checked and a theoretical framework is established. In this way data from a variety of sources are drawn into a unified whole and given meaning within the context of the theory.

Behaviour may be defined as the response of an organism to its environment; from this it follows that any piece of behaviour is under the dual influence of heredity and environment, governed by nature and nurture. The development of behaviour consists of two interacting processes: maturation, or the realisation of preprogrammed inbuilt mechanisms progressively through the life-cycle, and learning, or the modification of habit patterns resulting from exposure to environmental influences. These two processes are mutually dependent in the sense that normal development can only proceed in an adequately-stimulating environment and features of the environment only act as stimuli when the organism is sufficiently mature to respond to them. What we try to do is explain why limited maturational potential or restricted opportunities for learning distort the chain reaction, producing anomalies of development.

The critical or sensitive learning period

Much of our knowledge and understanding of inbuilt behaviour is derived from the study of instinct in animals. However, extrapolation from animal behaviour to human psychology is often a risky business, and theories based on evidence collected during the study of animals must usually undergo considerable modification when we attempt to apply them to man.

In ethology, the term 'critical learning period' refers to a strictly delineated period within the life-cycle of an organism during which it is particularly sensitive to (or orientated towards) a specific environmental stimulus capable of triggering off innately programmed patterns of complex behaviour which have high survival value to the species. Implicit in this concept is the idea that once these behaviour patterns have been acquired during the appropriate developmental phase they are irreversible and continue to have considerable influence on future behaviour. Furthermore, the acquisition (or learning) of these behaviour patterns cannot take place after the critical period has passed.

The paradigm case for the theory of critical learning periods is the 'imprinting' of waterfowl. This consists of the social attachment and following behaviour of the young bird to the nearest large moving object (usually its mother), which is rapidly learned as a conditioned response during a strictly delineated period of time (e.g. for an hour within the range of 12–17 hours of age in the case of the mallard duck). Such behaviour has the biological value of providing the young bird with the ready availability of a protector, example and social reinforcer, and has a fundamental influence on social attachments throughout its development to maturity (Lorenz, 1937).

It is still a matter of debate whether (and, if so, in what sense) the concept of critical learning periods applies to man. It seems unlikely, in the strict sense, that in response to very specific environmental stimuli and during strictly delineated periods of the child's life, preprogrammed and irreversible complex behaviour patterns are elicited which cannot be learned at a later stage. However, as Illingworth and Lister (1964) show, a good case can be made for the existence of less strictly defined *sensitive learning periods*, each specific to a particular type of behaviour, during which the child is developmentally ready to learn, particularly sensitive to the appropriate environmental stimuli, and optimally orientated towards making the appropriate response. These authors use the concept of sensitive learning periods to explain their observation that if a baby is not given solid foods shortly after he has learned to chew, there is often considerable difficulty in getting him to take solids later; he tends instead to refuse solid food, refuse to chew it, or regurgitate and vomit the unchewed food. They quote several examples of children who had not learned to chew at the appropriate developmental age because of physical problems associated with feeding and digestion, delayed weaning due to overanxiety and overprotection in the feeding situation, or because the appropriate stage for the introduction of solids had passed by unrecognised due to the child's subnormality. In each of these cases there was considerable difficulty in teaching the child to chew at a later stage. Illingworth and Lister also quote other evidence in support of sensitive learning periods: delay in starting to train a deaf child beyond the first three years of life increases his difficulty in learning the auditory discrimination required for speech; postponement of the operation for repair of cleft palate beyond two years of age may lead to extreme difficulty in teaching the child to speak; delay in removing congenital cataracts or correcting a squint may result in permanent impairment of visual perception.

The onset of the sensitive learning period may be due to maturation of the nervous system (as in sphincter control), maturation of the endocrine system (as in sexual behaviour), arrival at the appropriate stage of cognitive development to be 'ready' to learn (as in language skills), or the acquisition of sufficient previous learning for the new piece of learning to be easily acquired by positive transfer (as running ability is dependent on the skill of walking). The offset or close of the sensitive learning period (while not so clearly demarcated) may result from atrophy and decay (e.g. athletic ability), negative transfer or competition from the development and acquisition of a more complex but incompatible skill (e.g. purposeful hand-movements blocking the more primitive grasp reflex), possible change in motivation or change of interest (e.g. exploration of objects by smelling and mouthing). The end of a sensitive learning period may also occur because of the existence of optimum stages for learning to inhibit pieces of behaviour which no longer have biological survival value to the individual (Thorpe and Zangwill, 1961; Foss, 1965).

As Illingworth and Lister point out, if the evidence for the existence of sensitive learning periods is valid it has important implications for child-rearing and educational practices; parents and teachers should be aware of the onset of sensitive learning periods so that the acquisition of important pieces of behaviour can be facilitated at the optimal stage before the opportunity is lost. In fact, the Montessori method of preschool and primary teaching, established at the turn of the century, is based on the principle that in the development of the preschool child there are periods when he is particularly interested (and therefore optimally sensitive to instruction) in speech, temporal and spatial sequencing, sensory impressions of all kinds, and even the acquisition of good manners.

PREDICTION IN DEVELOPMENTAL PSYCHOLOGY

An understanding of developmental stages, developmental sequences and the range of individual differences in development means that in general we can predict development sufficiently to plan ahead to provide clothes, toys and educational facilities adequate to the needs of a child. Indeed, in looking at a group of normal children one is as much impressed by the similarities between individuals as by their differences.

Schedules of development

Traditionally, developmental psychology has devoted a great deal of effort to the attempt to chart out a temporal plan of the phases and milestones in the development of behaviour. These schedules have been used to study the overall principles and trends of development, and also to act as standards against which the developmental progress of an individual child can be assessed. This provides a useful 'early warning system' to identify children who are 'at risk' for slow, uneven, deviant, impaired or maladjusted development (Egan *et al.*, 1969).

Developmental schedules are designed to give the average age at which a milestone is achieved; the more sophisticated schedules also give the 'normal' range limits. Group norms often prove to be of limited value in the study of the individual case; however, very late milestones in all spheres of development, extreme developmental patchiness, or unusual sequence of development do seem to be useful alerting signals that all is not well.

Principles of development

Development is a function of maturation and learning. Physical maturation, including maturation of the central nervous system, consists of increase of size and greater complexity of structure, and leads to greater functional capacity. This allows for more complex differentiation and finer discrimination, generalised mass activity is replaced by specific individual responses, and a wider range of behaviour patterns results. The mature individual possesses a wide repertoire of available behavioural skills so that in response to relevant stimuli he may select the response which is most appropriate to the situation. This holds true for interpersonal situations too; the healthiest individual is the one who possesses the widest repertoire of behavioural responses together with sufficient flexibility to choose the most appropriate response.

Some skills (called *phylogenetic*) are common to all members of the species and are 'preprogrammed' to emerge without training at the appropriate maturational stage. Other skills (called *ontogenetic*) are special to the individual; they need to be learned and their development can be speeded up by training. Phylogenetic skills are affected very little by special stimulation or deprivation of experience, within fairly wide limits, though they require at least some exercise during the sensitive learning period if permanent impairment of function is to be avoided. McGraw (1939) reports a study of the motor development of a pair of twins, one of whom was trained on motor skills from three weeks of age while the other was allowed to develop at his own pace. By the age of two years the trained twin was found to be superior on ontogenetic skills such as roller skating, but showed negligible superiority on phylogenetic skills such as

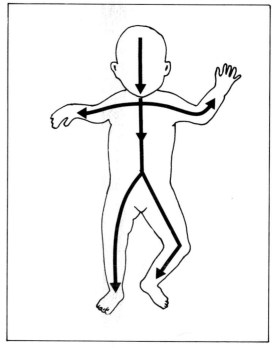

Figure 11.2 The laws of developmental direction. (Adapted from E. L. Vincent and P. C. Martin, Copyright © 1961, *Human Psychological Development*: The Ronald Press Company, New York)

walking. In a similar twin-study experiment, the twin who was potty-trained from the age of one month showed little superiority in bladder control at the age of two years two months compared with his twin whose potty training began at the age of two years, suggesting that the acquisition of bladder control is a phylogenetic skill with a strong genetic component (McGraw, 1940); this finding is supported by Bakwin (1971) who found the concordance rate for enuresis after the fourth birthday to be twice as high in monozygotic twins (with the same genetic endowment) as in same-sex dizygotic twins (with partly-different genetic endowment).

Development follows a predictable pattern; general statements can be made about the sequence of development that hold true for all individuals. It is generally recorded, for example, that growth and voluntary control of function in the foetus and infant progresses in a cephalocaudal/proximodistal direction; that is, growth of the head and control over head movement develops before growth and control of the limbs (Figure 11.2). It is interesting to note that this directional trend is reversed during the adolescent growth spurt when growth takes place in the following order: feet, calves and thighs, hips and chest, shoulders (Tanner and Taylor, 1970).

The sequence of development is similar for all, but

Table 11.1   Piagetian developmental stages

Developmental stages	Approximate age ranges	Examples of adaptive style
Sensori-motor includes six substages	Birth to 18 months	Mainly motor reactions to sensory experiences (initially purely reflexive)

Preoperational
  (a) Symbolic and prelogical
  (b) Intuitive
	1½ years to 4 years
	4 years to 7 years
		Learning by analogy
		Beginning of insightful problem-solving (e.g. use of tools)

Concrete operational	7 years to 11–12 years	Manipulation of number concepts, serial order, etc., based on concrete symbols and mechanical application of rules
Formal operational	11–12 years onwards	Formation of logical rules, deductive reasoning from abstract premises

the rate of development differs from child to child. Different areas of functioning develop at different rates, and in any one individual some areas of functioning (e.g. speech) may be delayed more than other areas (e.g. locomotor, perceptual).

Development is a continuous process, a progressive series of orderly coherent changes; but development proceeds in stages (or sensitive learning periods) with important qualitative differences rather than mere quantitative differences. For example, Piaget has distinguished a series of developmental stages of cognitive development (Table 11.1; Sandstrom, 1968; Woodward, 1970).

At each stage the child has a characteristic cognitive style, a characteristic mode of conceptualising and processing his percepts. Each of the earlier cognitive modes is in turn abandoned as the child develops a more sophisticated way of conceptualising which is more efficient in processing a wider range of stimuli. Some support is given for Piaget's developmental sequence of cognitive styles in an analysis by Hofstaetter (1967) of the loading of test items contributing to measured intelligence over the age range two months to 18 years (Figure 11.3). Three factors emerge which represent typical age trends in problem-

solving behaviour, and these have parallels in Piagetian theory. Hofstaetter's analysis shows that up to the age of 20 months the predominant factor accounting for achievement on 'intelligence' tests is a 'sensori-motor alertness' factor, which seems to parallel Piaget's 'sensori-motor stage'. Between 20 months and 40 months the 'persistence' factor predominates (a tendency to persist in using perceptual sets that have been proved useful and relevant in the past, rather than to modify these habits to accommodate unique aspects of the present stimulus situation) and this corresponds with Piaget's 'symbolic stage'. The third factor has a high loading on measured intelligence from the age of four years and is called 'manipulation of symbols' by Hofstaetter who comments that it resembles Spearman's 'g', or general factor of intelligence (see Chapter 8). Factor III would correspond with Piaget's 'intuitive', 'concrete operational' and 'formal operational' stages.

Individual differences in development

Given a reasonable level and quality of environmental stimulation (including reasonable behavioural reinforcement and interaction from loving care-takers), the course of development runs more or less unhindered for most individuals, though it is often difficult for clinicians (who frequently see the exceptions to the rule) to appreciate this.

It unfortunately remains true, as Tredgold (1952) postulated in his definition of 'psychopathic diathesis', that 'the majority of defectives occur in families in which there is an exceptional and sometimes a large amount of various kinds of mental abnormality'. Even earlier, Berry (1939), in his 'investigation into the mental state of the parents and sibs of 1050 mentally defective persons', stressed the variability of presentation of inherited proneness by concluding that 'what are inherited are altered potentialities for growth and not specific mental states'. More recently Oliver and Cox (1973) in their investigation of the aetiological factors leading to the battering of a nine-month-old baby, discovered multiple family pathology which included schizophrenia, neurosis, psychopathy, mental

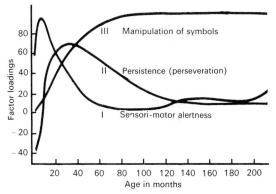

Figure 11.3 Factor loadings of measured intelligence from birth to maturity. (From Hofstaetter, P. R., 1967, by courtesy of Penguin)

subnormality, severe personality disorder, criminal and aberrant sexual behaviour, neurological and physical disease, child starvation, deprivation and neglect in a significant proportion of family members over four generations. It seems that just as many normal parents are passing on normal genes to their normal children in normal environments, so it is equally true that some pathological families in pathological circumstances are prone to pass on pathological experiences to children who can genetically least afford these stresses. Thus, while many children are genetically fitted to withstand a great deal of physical and psychological traumata, some children seem constitutionally fragile in that they are particularly vulnerable to even minimal exposure to adverse environmental influences.

In a study of normal neonates, Sander (1969) monitored activity, quiescence and crying under different conditions of care-taking. He concluded that there was considerable variation in the extent to which infants responded to changes in environmental conditions. Some babies quickly developed regular patterns of sleep, as though their sleep–wake cycles were governed by a 'biological clock', and these neonates appeared to be relatively unaffected by environmental changes; however, the sleep patterns of other babies, even in the first week of life, seemed to be easily disrupted by environmental factors such as substitution for the familiar care-taker. There is growing evidence that individual differences in reactivity existing from birth (and presumably of constitutional origin) are important factors in personality development.

Thomas *et al.* (1968), in a longitudinal study of 136 children, collected data on such behavioural indices as activity level, rhythmicity, approach to new situations and intensity of reaction, and identified three behavioural styles or types of temperamental organisation which remained relatively constant throughout early childhood and differentially affected later adjustment.

(i) *The difficult child*, with intense reactivity, irregular biological functions, negativism and withdrawal from new stimuli, seemed prone to develop behaviour disorders if he was not carefully handled with tolerant understanding;

(ii) *The easy child*, who was positive in mood and in his approach to new situations, regular in his biological functioning, less intense in his reactions, tending to adapt readily, was unlikely to develop behaviour disturbances unless great demands were made on him by the imposition of unrealistically high standards by parents and teachers, or by severe emotional trauma;

(iii) *The slow-to-warm-up child* was passive in early life, with negative moods and a tendency to withdraw; he was well-adjusted later, provided that he was not pushed beyond his limits but allowed to develop in his own good time.

Once again this study suggests that constitutional factors set the broad limits to behavioural development, while environmental factors influence the manifestation of genetic potential.

A study reported by Wilson (1972) also shows that individual differences in mental development are strongly determined by constitutional factors. The mental development of infant twins was followed up during the first and second years of life using the Bayley Scales. Monozygotic twins (having identical genetic blueprint) were more alike than dizygotic twins (having different genetic endowment) not only in their level of mental development, but also in their rate of mental development; monozygotic twins were concordant for the spurts and lags in their development, and thus showed more similar curves of mental growth.

While some genetic characteristics are manifest early in infancy, it seems likely that others do not exert their influence until later in childhood, and may become manifest, for example, as a progressive slowing down of development, early completion of intellectual growth, or late spurts of development in specific skills. The trend of increasing similarity between a child's intelligence quotient and the mean IQ of his parents is probably due partly to these late manifestations of inherited patterns of development, partly to the cumulative effect of environmental influences, and partly to artefacts of psychological testing (e.g. the older a child is, the more accurately and reliably are we able to sample the type of abstract conceptualisation measured by adult IQ tests) (Honzig, 1957).

Jensen (1967), commenting on observed properties of the distribution curve of intelligence in the general population as compared with the theoretical normal 'Gaussian' curve, claims that environment probably affects development as a threshold variable. Environment seems to be extremely important in the lower ranges of ability and in the less stable personalities, but, above a certain minimum of genetic endowment and given a basic level of environmental stimulation, development will tend to proceed unhindered at its own pace. Unfortunately, environmental influences on development are usually recorded as statistical trends in group data, rather than as causal quantifiable laws applying of necessity to the individual case to a measurable degree. The identification of these environmental influences is nonetheless important, as it gives us the information to enable us to design an environment which would allow maximal opportunity for those of poor genetic endowment to function to full capacity.

CONTROL IN DEVELOPMENTAL PSYCHOLOGY

In his novel *Walden Two*, Skinner (1948) describes a

fictional Utopia, which has been carefully designed using principles of 'behavioural engineering', where the individual's freedom is curtailed by a deliberate shaping of his behaviour to fit into a society based on theoretical ideals. In real life, it would be considered a despotic arrogance and an abuse of behavioural technology to attempt to control the lives of people in this way, even supposing we possessed the technical skills to do so. Instead, the search for methods of controlling human behaviour in psychology is directed towards harnessing and eliminating the factors which interfere with the individual's ability to perceive and interact with his environment in a meaningful and efficient way. In developmental psychology we aim to discover the optimal conditions for development so that maturation and learning may be facilitated, and to recognise, publicise and minimise the effect of noxious environmental stimuli, so that the child's development may proceed unhindered.

Prenatal influences on development

Early and late manifestations of genetic predisposition to developmental and psychiatric disorders are discussed elsewhere in this book (Chapter 10), but Chamberlain (1969) gives a detailed account of the physical hazards in the environment of the unborn child, including poor antenatal care, irradiation, maternal illness and diet, drugs and toxins, and it is worth noting that even from an early stage, the development of genetic potential is modified by environmental factors. It has even been suggested (Rorvik and Shettles, 1970) that the emotional state of a woman during intercourse may have a marginal influence on the pH (acid/alkali balance) of her cervical mucus which could differentially favour the survival and transport of gynosperms (larger, X-chromosome carrying, female-producing sperms) or androsperms (smaller, Y-chromosome carrying, male-producing sperms), and could therefore have an influence on the sex of her offspring. Furthermore, it seems likely that, during the early stages of cell multiplication and division, unusual uterine conditions can cause a misreading of the genetic 'blueprint' causing fundamental developmental aberrations including some of the chromosomal abnormalities of the mental subnormality syndromes.

The emotional state of a mother during pregnancy has been shown to have an effect on the unborn foetus; resentment of pregnancy, marital and family discord, anxiety and depression, and prolonged emotional strain during pregnancy can lead to physiological changes (notably endocrinal imbalance) in the mother which are transmitted to the foetus, causing increased foetal motility during pregnancy, and faulty physical homeostasis, motor and speech impairment, and particularly behaviour disturbance with hyperactivity in infancy and childhood (Dunbar, 1944; Sontag, 1944; Wallin and Riley, 1950; Stott, 1973).

In a study reported by Davids *et al.* (1961) and Davids and DeVault (1962), Taylor's Manifest Anxiety Scale, projective techniques, subjective ratings by mothers and objective ratings by psychologists were used to measure the anxiety of mothers attending a clinic during the last trimester of pregnancy. They found that highly anxious mothers had more variability in delivery time and more obstetric problems, and were more likely to have damaged and abnormal children, compared with mothers who were less anxious during the last trimester. Reassessment after childbirth showed that the anxiety of both groups of mothers was considerably reduced, though there was still a slight difference between the 'normal' group of mothers and the 'abnormal' group on their anxiety scores. On the available evidence it seemed unlikely that the higher anxiety of the 'abnormal' mothers during pregnancy was due to an informed suspicion that they were carrying an abnormal baby, and one wonders whether a third factor (causing both maternal anxiety and foetal abnormalities) was operating or whether there was a direct causal connection between maternal anxiety and the well-being of the foetus. Stott (1973) describes a longitudinal study in which 187 children were followed up from birth to four years to study the sequelae of prenatal stress. Maternal emotional stress was apparently most harmful to the foetus when it consisted of prolonged depression or continuous or repeated anxieties for which the mother felt she had some responsibility but which she was unable to remedy (such as marital and family discord). Even quite severe short-lived shocks and bereavement appeared to have little effect on the health of the foetus. However, direct genetic connections between the mother and child may have contributed to this result.

Longitudinal cohort studies, by Davie *et al.* (1972) provide evidence that the babies of mothers who smoke during pregnancy have a 30% greater risk of perinatal death, have lower than average birthweight (due to dysmaturity), are shorter in height at seven years, and have reading retardation at seven years (if the mother smokes 10 or more cigarettes a day during pregnancy her child is likely to be on average four months behind with his reading at seven years of age). Although contradictory results have also been produced in this field, the harmful effects of smoking during pregnancy are now fairly well-established.

There is also a risk to the foetus if the mother develops a virus illness during pregnancy, especially during the first trimester when the foetus is particularly vulnerable to physiological stress. Maternal rubella (German measles) during the first month of pregnancy is known to be associated with a high rate of spontaneous abortion, during the second month gives a high risk of heart lesions and eye defects, and during the third month is associated with deafness (Edmond, 1971). If rubella is contracted during the first two months of pregnancy there is a 100% chance of a defective foetus; if rubella is contracted during the third month 50% of the foetuses are defective (Minsky, 1957).

The gross deformities of children whose mothers took the drug thalidomide during a vulnerable stage of foetal development are sad reminders that some drugs and toxins which have a mild or unremarkable effect on the mother can cause severe damage to the foetus including limb and body deformities, and sensory defects (Taussig, 1962).

Perinatal and neonatal influences on development

It has long been recognised that there is a relationship between obstetric problems in the mother and abnormalities in her child; the classic paper by Little (1862) cited obstetric complications as causes of physical deformities, cerebral palsy and mental deficiency. It is by now becoming commonplace to refer to the birth history (for relevant factors such as length of gestation period, presenting position, prolonged and difficult labour, asphyxiation and foetal distress and neonatal jaundice) in the investigation of such childhood pathology as early death, physical deformity, cerebral palsy, epilepsy, mental subnormality, developmental delay, sensory defects, learning disorders and school underachievement, hyperkinetic syndrome and behaviour disorders. Sometimes there appears to be a direct cause–effect relationship between perinatal problems and later developmental disorders, but often birth abnormalities and subsequent childhood abnormality are both symptomatic of prenatal pathology.

The 1963 Ministry of Health Report on Congenital Malformations estimates that some significant abnormality is present in more than 1% of children surviving to the age of one year. A sizeable proportion of spontaneous abortions are deformed as are an estimated 20% of stillbirths. About 15% of children with congenital abnormalities are stillborn and a further 30% die in the first 12 months; about half survive over the age of five years.

Over the past twenty years there has been considerable interest in the long-term sequelae of low-birthweight babies (usually defined as those having a birthweight less than $5\frac{1}{2}$ lb or 2500 g). This group contains not only premature babies (born up to 38 weeks of gestation) but also dysmature (small-for-dates) babies. Drillien (1966; 1967) found that one-third of surviving low-birthweight babies exhibited moderate or severe handicaps at seven years. Half of these were a result of developmental defects originating early in gestation; their mothers frequently had a history of obstetric problems, and Drillien felt that better obstetric care was unlikely to make much difference except to raise the incidence of surviving defective children. In a quarter of these low-birthweight babies the foetus had

probably suffered cerebral damage resulting from intrauterine hypoxia caused by chronic disease or toxaemia in the mother. The aetiology of childhood handicaps was uncertain in the remaining quarter of cases, but most of these babies weighed less than 1500 g at birth and came from very poor homes.

In a follow-up study of premature babies with a birthweight of less than 3 lb (1360 g) Drillien found that at school age one-third were unsuitable for education in a normal school, over one-third of those in an ordinary school were educationally retarded, and less than one-third were doing age-appropriate schoolwork. Intelligence quotients fell steadily with decreasing birthweight. Of those with siblings, 76% were intellectually inferior to their full-term siblings. 70% of the sample of low-birthweight premature babies showed restlessness, overactivity and other behaviour problems at school age. Intellectual ability was also related to socio-economic status, but in each social class group low-birthweight babies were disadvantaged compared with normal controls from similar backgrounds (Figure 11.4).

Baird (1959) found that the intelligence of nine-year-old children with a birthweight of $4–5\frac{1}{2}$ lb at or near term (i.e. dysmature babies) was much lower than those in whom delivery occurred at 36 weeks or less (i.e. premature babies).

The intellectual deficits of premature low-birthweight children appear to be fairly specific. Harper

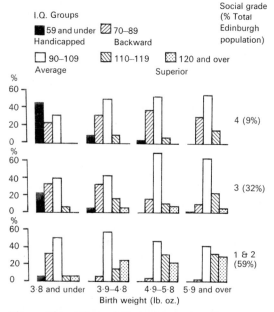

Figure 11.4   Effect of birthweight and environment on intellectual ability at age five to seven years. (Social Grade I—middle class; Grade II—superior working class; Grade III—average; Grade IV—poor.) (From Drillien, C. M., 1966, *Child Health and Development*, Ellis and Mitchell (eds) by courtesy of Churchill Livingstone)

and Wiener (1965) found that scores on perceptual items taken from the W.I.S.C. (Wechsler Intelligence Scale for Children) and on the Bender Gestalt Test (which measures perceptual–motor ability), given when the children were 6 years and 10 years of age, differentiated significantly between children of different birthweights rather better than the Terman-Merrill Scale (which is a verbally-loaded test of general intelligence). This result was obtained even controlling for social class differences and excluding those children with gross sensory, motor, emotional and intellectual handicaps.

Childhood influences on development

As a child develops we get an increasingly clearer picture. of his genetic endowment and the constitutional limits on his growth and maturation. We can also observe his behaviour patterns being modified by learning and we can gain some impression of the extent to which he reacts to and is conditioned by environmental forces. For most children development proceeds at its own pace, relatively unaffected by adverse environmental conditions; other children appear to need continual and prolonged protection from emotional and physical trauma. This variability between individuals in the extent to which they are affected by external forces is one of the most important reasons why studies of the influence on behaviour of differing environmental conditions have often proved inconsistent, insignificant or trivial. They are nonetheless of theoretical interest and sometimes have important and far-reaching implications for child-rearing practices.

The ordinal position of a child in his family probably affects his development mainly because it influences how he and others perceive his status within the family. Studies of intelligence show that there is a definite tendency for the IQ to increase progressively from the first-born child to the later-born child. However, 'genius' occurs more frequently among first-born siblings (Hurlock, 1964). Adams and Phillips (1972) perhaps give a clue to this paradox when they suggest that parents have higher expectations for their first-born children and inspire them with a higher level of motivation; their first-borns live up to parental expectations in intellectual superiority and a higher level of school attainment. In cases where first-borns show no difference in motivation compared with later-born children their intellectual and scholastic superiority is not demonstrated.

Lees and Stewart (1957) have shown that the more younger sibs a child has, the worse is likely to be his reading, which again suggests that superior school progress is helped by the parent who has time to motivate and reassure the child and reinforce his confidence in his abilities.

Children from large families tend to be lower in intelligence, particularly when this is measured on a verbally-loaded intelligence scale, and this effect appears to be cumulative up to the age of 12 years (Nisbet and Entwistle, 1967).

Studies on the relationship between socio-economic. class and the intelligence of children have consistently demonstrated the advantages of being born into a middle-class home rather than a lower-class home. Kagan and Tulkin (1971) attribute this to different styles of child care. Middle-class mothers were more attuned to their infants' needs; they had more face-to-face contact with them, talked more to them, entertained them more, were more adept at providing an appropriate level of stimulation for their infants, and they responded more quickly when their infants cried, thus ensuring that their infants quickly returned to a normal level of functioning. Thus middle-class mothers helped their babies to select and attend to relevant features of their environment. The advantages of this kind of upbringing were shown in a laboratory experiment in which middle-class infants were found to be superior to lower-class infants in differentiating the mother's voice from a stranger's voice, and differentiating between meaningful and non-meaningful speech. The type of speech used by a middle-class mother and her methods of child control have also been found to facilitate the child's understanding and use of abstract and emotional vocabulary (rather than the more concrete concepts used by the lower-class mother) and to facilitate the child's acquisition and internalisation of moral values and cultural prohibitions (Bernstein, 1961). These relationships seem to hold good even when parental intelligence has been matched between class groups, although better control for genetic effects would require matching of grandparents as well.

From an early age sex differences in behaviour emerge. Moss (1967) studied 30 first-born infants and their mothers and observed that the amount of contact a mother had with her child was directly related to the amount of time a baby spent crying. At the age of one month this was true of both males and females. By the age of three months sex differences were evident, boys were more irritable and spent more time crying without being pacified by extra attention from their mothers. Their mothers had become less responsive to their needs as their mothering activity had not been reinforced by their babies; this was in contrast to the responsive mothering of girls who were less fretful and more easily pacified by mother's attention.

By the age of seven years, sex differences in behaviour (both constitutional and acquired) are clearly in evidence. Davie *et al.* (1972) found that seven-year-old girls were better than boys at reading, oral expression and creativity, but boys were better at problem arithmetic. Boys were more accident-prone, hyperactive and clumsy, had more stammers, tics, headbanging, rocking and other habit spasms, but were less prone to abdominal pain and travel sickness.

The effect of early emotional and social deprivation on development is a subject of great controversy. Schaffer (1965) found that, in babies of about three months, maternal deprivation during hospitalisation caused apathy in the infants so that it was difficult to elicit age-appropriate behaviour during developmental testing. After a short period at home their test performance quickly caught up with that of control subjects. As the infant grew older his reaction to maternal deprivation became more specific. Schaffer (1958) found that after the age of about seven months, maternal deprivation during hospitalisation resulted in a disturbed mother–child relationship (shown in such behaviour as overdependent clinging) when the child was returned to maternal care. Perhaps the explanation for the different reactions of these two groups of babies lies in the development of attachment behaviour, the tendency for the infant to seek and maintain the proximity of his mother (or mother substitute). In a study of Ugandan infants, Ainsworth (1967) found that from around four to six months of age these babies would cry when their mother left the room or attempt to follow her. It is tempting to suppose that this early attachment behaviour is an important and necessary first step to the formation of all future emotional attachments.

O'Connor and Franks (1961) found no clear-cut evidence that the effects of emotional deprivation in infancy are permanent. Certainly the relationship between early deprivation and later adult personality adjustment is not straightforward. The simple presence or absence of a mother during the early years is not as significant as the quality of mothering the child receives. Warm, consistent and responsive attention from a single care-taker in the early years is preferable to childrearing by a natural mother if she is depressed, inconsistent, unresponsive or otherwise unable to maintain a caring relationship with her child.

There is evidence that early mothering patterns have an effect on the establishment of regular biological rhythms in the infant. Sander and Julia (1966) report a study in which infants who were kept in a neonatal nursery were compared with infants who 'roomed in' (i.e. stayed alongside their mothers and received individual care) with respect to activity and crying. At first there was no significant difference between the two groups, but by the third day, while the nursery neonates showed little evidence of an establishment of daily rhythms, the 'rooming in' neonates were beginning to show a higher proportion of daytime activity as their daily rhythms became established. However, physiological factors transmitted genetically to offspring have just as important an effect on later emotional adjustment as does the mothering received in childhood. Levy (1942) related favourable attitudes towards mothering to the duration of menstrual flow, and found that the longer the duration of menstrual flow, the greater the amount of 'mothering' behaviour such as childhood doll-play, baby-sitting, desire for a large family, anticipation of breast-feeding babies. This finding would suggest either that there are causative constitutional factors in operation or that motherly attitudes in potential mothers can bring about fundamental physiological changes.

Adulthood influences on development

Development is a continuous process and involves atrophy and decay of function as well as growth and differentiation. Performance on intelligence tests reaches a peak during the second or third decade of life and gradually changes in emphasis from the mental alertness and quick grasp of relationships at younger ages to the wise utilisation of past experience at older ages (Wechsler, 1961). There is a progressive slowing of performance partly because of sensory and neuromuscular handicaps, but mainly because the synthesis of information is less efficient in the ageing brain (Welford, 1958). Disease processes and lack of attention to diet add to the difficulties of older people. There is an increasing feeling in many older people that their useful life is over and that they no longer need or want to function to full capacity. Parkes *et al.* (1969) showed that bereavement over the death of a spouse can lead to physical disease which may even result in death; they found a higher incidence of disease and mortality among recently widowed men compared with the expected rate for married men of the same age. Hopefully the trend towards earlier retirement, better preparation for retirement, longer and healthier old age, and increasing awareness of the social and financial needs of older people will alleviate this problem.

CONCLUSION

The genetic endowment of an individual has a profound effect on the course of his development. Genes determine not only the raw material of the embryo, but also set limits on the individual's sensitivity to his environment and the flexibility with which he deals with the stresses of daily life and the threats to his viability. Although heredity is a constant factor, its effects will continue to emerge at appropriate stages of maturation in response to environmental triggers and will become modified by learning throughout the life cycle.

There are both moral and technical limitations on the extent to which we can prescribe the genetic raw material of our offspring; there are genetic limitations on the extent to which we can modify growth and development. What we can do is to facilitate learning at critical stages to ensure that appropriate environmental stimuli are available and accessible, so that full use can be made of sensitive learning periods. We can support the aim of educationalists (including parents) to bring out or actualise latent potential, to assist the maximisation of assets and to train to compensate for deficiencies. To achieve this efficiently we must be prepared to abandon misleading myths and substitute a scientifically-based body of knowledge about the development of behaviour.

References

Adams, R. L. and Phillips, B. (1972). Motivational and achievement differences among children of various ordinal birth positions. *Child Dev.*, 43, 155–164

Ainsworth, M. D. S. (1967). *Infancy in Uganda: Infant Care and the Growth of Attachment* (Baltimore: Johns Hopkins Press)

Baird, D. (1959). The contribution of obstetrical factors to serious physical and mental handicap in children. *J. Obstet. Gynecol.*, 66, 743–747

Bakwin, H. (1971). Enuresis in twins. *Amer. J. Dis. Childh.*, 121, 222–225

Bernstein, B. B. (1961). Social class and linguistic development: a theory of social learning. In: *Education, Economy and Society* (A. H. Halsey, editor) (Glencoe, Illinois: Free Press)

Berry, R. J. A. (1939). An investigation into the mental state of the parents and sibs of 1050 mentally defective persons. *Bristol Med.-Chir. J.*, 56, 1–12

Chamberlain, G. (1969). *The Safety of the Unborn Child* (Harmondsworth: Penguin)

Davids, A., DeVault, S. and Talmadge, M. (1961). Anxiety, pregnancy and childbirth abnormalities. *J. Consult. Psychol.*, 25, 74–77

Davids, A. and DeVault, S. (1962). Maternal anxiety during pregnancy and childbirth abnormalities. *Psychosom. Med.*, 24, 464–470

Davie, R., Butler, N. and Goldstein, H. (1972). *From Birth to Seven: 2nd Report of the National Child Development Study (1958 Cohort).* (London: Longman/National Children's Bureau)

Drillien, C. M. (1966). Prematurity and low birth weight. In: *Child Health and Development*, 4th Ed. (R. W. B. Ellis, editor) (London: Churchill)

Drillien, C. M. (1967). The long-term prospects for babies of low birth weight. *Brit. J. Hosp. Med.*, 1, 937–944

Dunbar, F. (1944). Effect of the mother's emotional attitude on the infant. *Psychosom. Med.*, 6, 156–159

Edmond, R. T. D. (1971). Rubella. *Brit. J. Hosp. Med.*, 313–320

Egan, D. F., Illingworth, R. S. and Mac Keith, R. C. (1969). *Developmental Screening 0–5 Years* (London: Spastics International Medical Publications/Heinemann)

Foss, B. (1965). The idea of sensitive learning periods. In: *The Teaching of the Cerebral Palsied Child* (J. Loring, editor) (London: Heinemann)

Harper, P. A. and Wiener, G. (1965). Sequelae of low birth weight. *Ann. Rev. Med.*, 16, 405–420

Hofstaetter, P. R. (1967). The changing composition of intelligence. In: *Intelligence and Ability* (S. Wiseman, editor) (Harmondsworth: Penguin)

Honzig, M. P. (1957). Developmental studies of parent–child resemblance in intelligence. *Child Dev.*, 28, 215–228

Hurlock, E. (1964). *Child Development*, 4th Ed. (New York: McGraw-Hill)

Illingworth, R. S. and Lister, J. (1964). The critical or sensitive learning period, with special reference to certain feeding problems in infants and children. *J. Pediat.*, 65, 839–848

Jensen, A. R. (1967). The culturally disadvantaged: psychological and educational aspects. *Educ. Res.*, 10, 4–20

Kagan, J. and Tulkin, S. R. (1971). Social class differences in child rearing during the first year. In: *The Origins of Human Social Relations* (H. R. Schaffer, editor) (London: Academic Press)

Lees, J. P. and Stewart, A. H. (1957). Family or sibship position and scholastic ability. *Sociol. Rev.*, 5, 173–190

Levy, D. M. (1942). Psychosomatic studies of some aspects of maternal behaviour. *Psychosom. Med.*, 4, 223–227

Little, W. J. (1862). On the influence of abnormal parturition, difficult labours, premature births and asphyxia neonatorum on the mental and physical condition of the child, especially in relation to deformities. *Trans. Obstet. Soc. London*, 3, 293

Lorenz, K. Z. (1937). Imprinting. *The Auk*, 54, 245–273

McGraw, M. B. (1939). Later development of children specially trained during infancy. Johnny and Jimmy at school age. *Child Dev.*, 10, 1–19

McGraw, M. B. (1940). Neural maturation as exemplified in achievement of bladder control. *J. Pediat.*, 16, 580–590

Ministry of Health (Standing Medical Advisory Committee) (1963). *Report on Congenital Malformations* (London: H.M.S.O.)

Minsky, L. (1957). *Mental Deficiency in Children* (London: Heinemann)

Moss, H. A. (1967). Sex, age and state as determinants of mother infant interaction. *Merrill-Palmer Quart.*, 13, 19–36

Newson, J. and Newson, E. (1963). *Infant Care in an Urban Community* (London: Allen and Unwin)

Nisbet, J. D. and Entwistle, N. J. (1967). Intelligence and family size, 1945–1965. *Brit. J. Educ. Psychol.*, 37, 188–193

O'Connor, N. and Franks, C. (1961). Childhood upbringing and other environmental factors. In: *Handbook of Abnormal Psychology* (H. J. Eysenck, editor) (London: Pitman Press)

Oliver, J. E. and Cox, J. (1973). A family kindred with ill-used children: the burden on the community. *Brit. J. Psychiatry*, 123, 81–90

Parkes, C. M., Benjamin, B. and Fitzgerald, R. C. (1969). Broken heart: a statistical study of increased mortality among widowers. *Brit. Med. J.*, 1, 740–743

Rorvik, D. M. and Shettles, L. B. (1970). *Your Baby's Sex: Now You Can Choose* (London: Cassell)

Rutter, M., Tizard, J. and Whitmore, K. (1970). *Education, Health and Behaviour* (London: Longman)

Sander, L. W. and Julia, H. L. (1966). Continuous interactional monitoring in the neonate. *Psychosom. Med.*, 28, 822–835

Sander, L. W. (1969). Regulation and organization in the early infant-caretaker system. In: *Brain and Early Behaviour* (R. J. Robinson, editor) (London: Academic Press)

Sandström, C. I. (1968). *The Psychology of Childhood and Adolescence* (Harmondsworth: Penguin)

Schaffer, H. R. (1958). Objective observations of personality development in early infancy. *Brit. J. Med. Psychol.*, 31, 174–183

Schaffer, H. R. (1965). Changes in developmental quotient under two conditions of maternal separation. *Brit. J. Soc. Clin. Psychol.*, 4, 39–46

Skinner, B. F. (1948). *Walden Two* (New York: Macmillan)

Smith, M. E. (1952). A comparison of certain personality traits as rated in the same individuals in childhood and fifty years later. *Child Dev.*, **23**, 159–180

Sontag, L. W. (1944). Differences in modifiability of foetal behaviour and physiology. *Psychosom. Med.*, **6**, 151–154

Stott, D. H. (1973). Follow-up study from birth of the effects of prenatal stress. *Dev. Med. Child. Neurol.*, **15**, 770–787

Tanner, J. M. and Taylor, G. R. (1970). *Growth* (Nederland N. V.: Time-Life International)

Taussig, H. B. (1962). The thalidomide syndrome. *Sci. Amer.*, **207**, 29–35

Thomas, A., Chess, S. and Birch, H. G. (1968). *Temperament and Behaviour Disorders in Children* (London: University Press)

Thorpe, W. H. and Zangwill, O. L. (1961). *Current Problems in Animal Behaviour* (Cambridge: University Press)

Tredgold, H. F. (1952) *A Textbook of Mental Deficiency* (London: Baillière, Tindall and Cox)

Wallin, P. and Riley, R. P. (1950). Reactions of mothers to pregnancy and adjustment of offspring in infancy. *Amer. J. Orthopsychiatry*, **20**, 616–622

Wechsler, D. (1961). Intelligence, memory and the ageing process. In: *Psychopathology of Ageing* (P. H. Hoch and J. Zubin, editors) (New York: Grune and Stratton)

Welford, A. T. (1958). *Ageing and Human Skill* (London: Oxford University Press)

Wilson, R. S. (1972). Twins: early mental development. *Science*, **175**, 914–917

Woodward, M. (1970). The assessment of cognitive processes: Piaget's approach. In: *The Psychological Assessment of Mental and Physical Handicaps* (P. Mittler, editor) (London: Tavistock/Methuen)

Chapter 12

INTERPERSONAL PROCESSES

J. F. Orford

ATTACHMENTS

It is not unreasonable to expect that a study of the attachments which human beings form towards other individuals, would be at the very heart of human psychology. Whether we use the term 'bond', 'relationship', 'friendship' or 'attachment', we are discussing matters which are of the utmost importance to nearly everyone. Most people possess a variety of attachments, including a small number of 'close' ones (children have parents, adults have sexual partners, and from early adolescence onwards most people have 'friends' to whom they are not related by 'blood' or in any very obvious sexual way). The closest attachments are often along kinship or marriage lines, carry a complex set of mutual obligations, and are fostered and protected by weighty, legal or cultural, rules and sanctions (see Fox, 1967, for an excellent discussion of kinship and marriage in various parts of the world).

Despite the importance of this topic, surprisingly little is known, in a scientific sense, about the number and nature of people's social contacts. However, some specific areas have been fairly heavily researched. A great deal is known about the development, and nature, of attachments between infants and their mothers (Bowlby, 1969; Maccoby and Masters, 1970); about adult sexual contacts (Kinsey *et al.*, 1948, 1953, are still the major references here); and about specific relationships such as that between a psychotherapist and his patient (e.g. Goldstein, 1971). The marriage bond, in particular, provokes a great deal of research, indeed at least one whole journal, the *Journal of Marriage and the Family*, is almost entirely devoted to research on this topic. But the emphasis has been upon research focussed towards specific age groups, or specific types of relationship, and there is a disappointing absence of general study of the phenomenon of interpersonal attachment.

Undoubtedly a wide variation would be found. There would probably be some people who have relatively few social contacts, others who have many. Some people would be found who had no special contacts other than those of a superficial kind. Lowenthal (1964) reported a study which concerned over 500 men and women, aged 60 or over, who were admitted to the psychiatric ward of a large general hospital. Almost 10% were, what Lowenthal calls, 'pure isolates'. In these cases, no relatives or friends were involved in the decision-making process leading to hospitalisation, and it turned out that no individual contacts had been made with any relative, nor anyone who could be called a 'friend', during the preceding three years. In a further 10% ('semi-isolates') only infrequent, or casual, recent social contacts were reported. Nor was isolation confined to the hospital-admitted sample. A degree of isolation was found for a number of members of a comparison sample of elderly people living in the community.

Amongst the 'pure-isolates' were some whose history of social contact appeared to warrant the term 'life-long alienated'. They were predominantly single men (women rarely came into this category), or men whose marital relationship had been terminated early; their occupational and residential histories were of the 'rolling stone' variety, and the term 'lone wolf' was often used as a self-description.

Some criteria of attachment

Many words, including 'close', 'superficial', and 'meaningful', can be used to qualify the word 'relationship'. However, there is relatively little agreement about the usage of these terms, for scientific study. Gewirtz (1972) has reviewed some of the criteria for 'attachment' and 'dependence' which have been used in studies of infant-mother pairs. Some of these criteria might be of more general relevance to all types of relationships.

1. *Approach responses*

One category of criteria, for example, is that of 'approach responses'. But approach responses are of various types and have a variety of relevant parameters. Approach may involve sexual contact, physical contact with no obvious sexual involvement, physical proximity without actual bodily contact, or talking and sharing information (sometimes at a distance, as on the telephone).

After a certain age infants spend less and less time within their mothers' reach (literally), and at a later age, older children or adolescents tend to spend less and less time within their parents' orbit. These changes are obviously related to processes of child maturation or learning. There is some evidence that a somewhat similar change occurs, but presumably for quite different reasons, in many marriage pairs. The spending of leisure time with the spouse may, for many marriages, be at its peak early in marriage, and

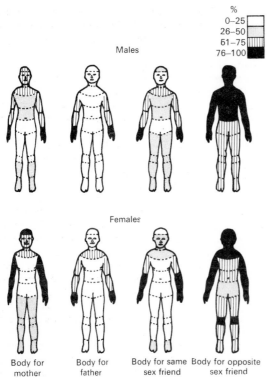

%
0–25
26–50
61–75
76–100

Males

Females

Body for
mother

Body for
father

Body for same
sex friend

Body for opposite
sex friend

Figure 12.1 The Ss' 'Body-for-Others', as experienced through amount of touching received from others. Percentages are based on $N = 168$ males and 140 females. The darkest portions signify that from 76–100% of the Ss reported being touched by the target-person in question on the body-region indicated. (From Jourard, 1966, by courtesy of *Brit. J. Soc. Clin. Psychol.*)

the time spent in extra-marital socialising may increase later. In infant–mother pairs, both partners play their role in preserving a balance between attachment and separation, but at any one time there are likely to be between-pair differences in the degree to which it is the infant, or the mother, who is displaying the greater degree of initiative in encouraging separation.

2. Body contact

One of the obvious factors constituting 'intimacy' is bodily contact, a factor which has been relatively ignored by students of human psychology. Jourard (1966) has begun to provide us with some basic descriptive data which is illustrated in Figure 12.1. College student subjects were asked to report which parts of their body were touched by their fathers, mothers, own-sex friends, and opposite-sex friends. Not surprisingly opposite-sex friendships turned out to be the most intimate, in terms of the total body area of contact criterion. The role which physical

touch plays in some of the currently fashionable psychotherapeutic techniques is of considerable interest in this context.

3. Separation distress

Another of the criteria for attachment, mentioned by Gewirtz, is that of 'distress on separation'. Many infants, of a certain age, react in a striking way when separated from their mothers (the words 'protest' and 'despair' have been used to describe the immediate and subsequent reactions which are frequently witnessed—see Maccoby and Masters, 1970, pp. 104–105, for example). Reactions to separation or loss, either actual or anticipated, probably also play a large part in most people's definitions of 'closeness' when applied to adult relationships ('Life has not been the same since I lost . . .', 'I know I shall miss . . . terribly', 'I don't know what I'd do without . . .').

4. Self-disclosure

Another important factor, which is unlikely to be amongst the criteria used by students of animals or infants, is that of personal information-sharing, or 'self-disclosure'. Taylor and Altman (1966) have scaled a variety of topics, in terms of the degree of intimacy which their disclosure indicates. People are relatively choosey about the people to whom they disclose details of their own sex life, feelings about parts of their own body (most people have opinions about the attractiveness of different parts of their body, and many people are very concerned about such matters, sometimes to a degree which others would consider to be 'unreasonable'), feelings about members of their own family, and details of financial affairs.

A very important finding of one study (Jourard and Lasakow, 1958) was that married subjects reported higher levels of self-disclosure to their spouses, than towards any other 'target' person (including parents and friends). These self-disclosure-to-spouse levels were higher than any levels reported by unmarried subjects. Sexual bonds are thus likely to be important for social, as well as for sexual, intimacy, and the absence of a satisfactory sexual relationship may deprive a person of the most favourable circumstances for the development of social intimacy.

5. Interpersonal attraction

An obvious criterion is that of interpersonal attraction or 'liking'. Liking and self-disclosure are related. In one experiment female subjects were grouped in fours. They got to know each other briefly first, and then rated the degree of liking which they each felt for each of the others. They then had the opportunity to decide how self-disclosing they would be, and to which of the other member(s) of the group they would make self-disclosing remarks. Finally, they re-rated the degree of liking they felt for each of the group members. Subjects were most likely to disclose to group members whom they liked, and in addition, subjects who made the more intimate disclosures were more liked subsequently (Worthy *et al.*, 1969).

A non-experimental survey of all faculty members of a college of nursing also demonstrated the relationship between self-disclosure and liking. Each member of the college was asked to report on the degree of their own self-disclosure to each of their colleagues, the degree to which each colleague disclosed to them, and their liking for each colleague. Self-disclosures tended to be reciprocated, and higher levels of disclosure were associated with greater liking (Jourard, 1959).

6. *Empathy, warmth, and genuineness*
Truax and Carkhuff (1967) suggested that the effective psychotherapist was someone who showed high levels of three 'conditions'. These were accurate empathy (i.e. the therapist should be sensitive to his client's feelings, and should be able to convey this understanding to the client), non-possessive warmth (i.e. he should accept the patient for what he is, and not for what the therapist would like him to be), and genuineness (i.e. the therapist should behave in a sincerely unselfconscious fashion, and not hide behind a professional facade). One might suppose that these would be the conditions making for good friendship in general. Truax and Carkhuff showed that they could successfully operationalise these concepts. They were able to train raters to make reliable judgments, from tape-recordings of therapy sessions, of the degree to which different therapists displayed these conditions. On the whole, research has suggested that higher levels of these therapist conditions are associated with greater therapeutic change.

Although there may be general associations between certain of these criteria (liking and self-disclosure, for example), we should not suppose that the different criteria of intensity of interpersonal relationship will always co-vary. Although many relationships are obviously 'superficial' in almost all senses, and others are 'close' by almost all criteria, there are numerous relationships which are only 'close' in particular ways. A psychotherapy patient is likely to be highly self-disclosing to his therapist, but the reverse is unlikely to be the case (despite Truax and Carkhuff's argument that the best psychotherapists reciprocate the patient's self-disclosure). Some marriages are characterised by long duration, joint residence, and a large amount of time in close physical proximity, but at the same time are characterised by low levels of sexual and physical intimacy, and even low levels of liking. Relationships with prostitutes are, almost by definition, likely to be unbalanced, high on sexual contact of a particular type, and low on almost all other criteria of intimacy.

Relationships with employers and teachers, amongst others, are often extremely 'important', but are likely to be high only on certain criteria of closeness.

Non-verbal behaviour
In the studies reviewed by Truax and Carkhuff (1967), the instructions normally given to those whose task it was to rate therapists emphasised therapists' verbal behaviour. Indeed the method of rating from tape-recordings excluded from consideration many of the possible non-verbal cues. However many, if not most, of the cues indicating greater affiliation or liking, are non-verbal in nature; they consist of such things as postures, gestures and tones of voice. It is therefore of considerable interest that Shapiro *et al.* (1968) were able to show that raters, who had been trained to use the linguistically-orientated scales of therapist conditions, were able to come to a considerable measure of agreement about the levels of therapist conditions being offered, when they were required to make their judgments simply on the basis of still photographs of the therapist. A further study showed a significant degree of positive relationship between ratings made from audio-only records and ratings made from video-only records.

It seems, therefore, that people who are most effective, in this special form of relationship, are likely to display a relatively high level of liking for, or affiliation with, their clients, and that they do this by a combination of verbal and non-verbal means.

Relationship defining cues
An idea that has been put forward many times, is that verbal aspects of interpersonal behaviour have, as their primary function, the conveying of information, whilst non-verbal aspects convey emotion. The verbal might be the channel of communcation most relevant to the carrying out of the task upon which A and B are engaged, whilst the non-verbal channel might be the primary means whereby the relationship between A and B (intimate, non-intimate, hostile, superordinate–subordinate etc.) might be established and expressed. Although the discussion above suggests that this idea is likely to be an oversimple one, there is some evidence that non-verbal cues are the ones which are most effective, in revealing the nature of the relationship between A and B. Argyle *et al.* (1970, 1971) conveyed messages to their experimental subjects which were ambiguous with regard to the degree of dominance, or of warmth, which they displayed. Dominance or warmth could be indicated by verbal content, or non-verbally by tone of voice, or by facial expression. By systematically varying the indications of dominance in the messages (in one experiment), or by systematically varying indications of warmth (in the second experiment), and by then having the subjects rate the degree of dominance or warmth which they felt the message as a whole

conveyed, it was possible to tell which cues were the most effective in conveying these aspects of relationship. The results showed that raters relied most heavily upon the non-verbal, and relied less upon verbal content. Of course in these experiments many of the messages were deliberately ambiguous or misleading (for example something very assertive might be said in a very mousey tone of voice) and in real life verbal or non-verbal signs are more likely to be congruent.

Double binds

These results are very relevant to the theory of the *double bind* which has been derived from close observation of families containing an adolescent or young adult 'schizophrenic' member (Bateson *et al.*, 1956). Briefly, the concept refers to situations in which one person receives contradictory communications from someone with whom he is involved in an intense emotional relationship. Usually one part of the communication is conveyed by verbal content (e.g. 'I love you, you ought to love me too'), another by non-verbal means (e.g. withdrawing from an embrace). The theory has it that repeated exposure to such contradictory communications is confusing, and even schizophrenogenic, if the person on the receiving end cannot escape the situation, is obliged to respond to the verbal part of the message, and is punished if he attempts to point out the contradiction. In fact, the evidence for its importance in the origins of 'schizophrenia' is not strong (even if 'schizophrenia' were not the very mixed bag which it is, a specific link between a form of interactional behaviour, and a particular form of individual behaviour, is scarcely to be expected). None the less double binds may well turn out to be 'micro' characteristics of many types of relationship which are characterised by indefiniteness or disagreement about the nature of the relationship.

Interpersonal conflict

Ferreira and Winter (1968) have outlined a number of other features of interaction which may be general to relationships which are breaking down, or which are characterised by low levels of liking, or high levels of conflict. Their studies are typical of the many, recent, semi-artificial studies of family interaction, which require that real families be observed interacting in a setting which is partially controlled, but which retains a fair degree of naturalness. For example, in their studies, families were asked to discuss amongst themselves, and come to a joint decision, regarding certain choices (e.g. choice of film viewing, of restaurant food, of car colour). Other similar studies have employed rather more personal issues (e.g. what to do when an adolescent child stays out late). Ferreira and Winter found that problem families, when interacting, were characterised by long decision-times, low individual choice fulfilment (i.e. the initial,

individual, preferences of family members were relatively unlikely to be represented in the final joint family decision), a relatively large total amount of silence, and relatively low levels of information exchanged (i.e. few instances of clear and explicit communication of preference from one family member to the rest). These researchers were led to propose the idea of a family pathology cycle, of self-perpetuating events leading the family into greater and greater breakdown of communication.

Such events are of course not confined to problem families. Essentially the same phenomena can be observed in interstaff relationships in large institutions, such as hospitals (e.g. Caudill, 1958), where conflict may lead to poor communication, misunderstandings and administrative mistakes; and also in the realm of international diplomacy where the 'breaking off of diplomatic relations' has obvious parallels in intra-family relationships (Kelman, 1965).

MONADIC CONCEPTIONS OF INTERPERSONAL BEHAVIOUR

Social skills

The concept of social skills is an example of a relatively 'monadic' concept of social behaviour. It assumes that an individual can be said to have a greater or lesser degree of some attribute, and that change can be brought about by training, retraining, or advising, the individual alone. It assumes that there are things that can be usefully said about the individual's social behaviour, irrespective of the behaviour of the other people with whom he interacts. Such an assumption may be quite useful in certain circumstances. For example, it leads to such procedures as assertive training for people who feel themselves to be handicapped in a wide range of circumstances which call for assertive behaviour (e.g. complaining about food in a restaurant, refusing to loan a book to a person who failed to return a previously loaned book, refusing to accept a bill which is too large). A combination of instruction, demonstration and opportunity for practice appears to be quite an effective combination in producing some change in the direction required by such people.

A quite different, but still monadic, approach to individual differences, involves the locating of an individual on an interpersonal behaviour 'map'. The 'maps' which have been produced for this purpose differ from one to another, but many take a basic two-dimensional format. There is in fact a great deal of evidence (reviewed for example by Carson, 1969, pp. 98–107) that when people are observed inter-acting socially, they differ amongst themselves most strikingly in terms of two major dimensions. Firstly, some people are relatively affectionate, pleasant, or co-operative, whilst other are relatively unpleasant, cool or unco-operative. Secondly, some people are

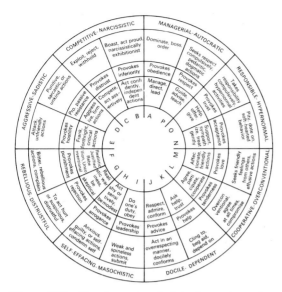

Figure 12.2 The interpersonal behaviour circumplex. (From Leary, 1957, by courtesy of Ronald)

relatively assertive, dominant or controlling, whilst others are relatively submissive, shy or dependent. There are of course many other ways of contrasting individuals' social behaviour, but these two factors emerge time and time again, whether the situation involves mothers interacting with their children, managers discussing joint tasks, or groups of students brought together for purely experimental purposes. Furthermore, these two dimensions are usually thought of as being independent, so that all possible combinations of the two dimensions are possible (dominant and affectionate; dominant and hostile; submissive and affectionate; submissive and hostile). Most of the relevant research has involved ratings of observed behaviour, so both verbal and non-verbal cues could have contributed. Research which has focussed on non-verbal aspects of behaviour alone has suggested the importance of a third variable or dimension, namely activation (Mehrabian, 1971). Irrespective of the degree of dominance or affection displayed, some individuals are more activated, aroused or involved than others.

The interpersonal behaviour circle

A somewhat different 'map', which has been highly influential, is the circular or circumplex scheme elaborated by Leary (1957), and shown here in Figure 12.2. This scheme preserves the two dimensions, but fills in the gaps between the poles of those dimensions, so that all points on the circumference of the circular map are represented by certain features of social behaviour. An important property of the circumplex ordering of interpersonal behaviour is that behaviour represented by any par-

ticular point on the circumference of the circle is highly correlated with behaviour represented by adjacent points; is less highly correlated with behaviour represented by points further removed on the circumference of the circle; and is most negatively associated with behaviour represented by a point on the opposite side of the circle. For example, rebellious–distrustful behaviour should correlate most positively with aggressive–sadistic or self-effacing–masochistic behaviour, and should correlate most negatively with behaviour in the responsible–hypernormal category. There is indeed some evidence for the correctness of this assumption.

Leary, who at that time worked as a Clinical Psychologist and probably saw many people whose behaviour was relatively extreme or unusual, used this map in monadic fashion, in order to categorise people. He thought that there were people whose 'personality disorder' consisted of inappropriate and rigid adherence to behaviour in a single part of the interpersonal behaviour circle. For example, he thought that there were 'autocratic personalities' whose preference was for managerial or controlling behaviour towards other people, irrespective of the situation or of the people with whom they were interacting. Other people were chronic rebels, confirmed conformists, and so on.

A management group

The work setting is one where one may be most

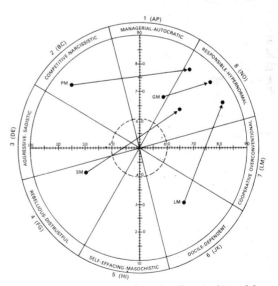

Figure 12.3 The reputations and self-perceptions of four members of a management group. The labelled point represents each member's reputation, and the head of the arrow his self-perception. PM—Production Manager; GM—General Manager; SM—Sales Manager; LM—Personnel Manager. (From Leary, 1957, by courtesy of Ronald)

forcefully persuaded of the aptness of this type of formulation (after all, who has not used this type of epithet in describing work colleagues!). Figure 12.3 shows some data presented by Leary which was gathered from a small group of managers who were asked to describe both themselves and each of their colleagues, in terms of the items of behaviour representing the different parts of the interpersonal behaviour circle. The data shows that each of the managers acquired a definite reputation for himself (e.g. the Personnel Manager a reputation as being a bit of a softy; the Production Manager a reputation for being a tyrant). It also demonstrates the lack of insight which each had about the effects of his behaviour upon others. Despite their reputations, each thought himself to be essentially responsible and 'hypernormal'. For example, Leary writes of the Sales Manager: 'He is seen by others as a bitter, suspicious, non-conventional member of the executive group. He, on the other hand, thinks of himself as a friendly, affiliative tolerant person. It is very easy to deduce the confusion and dissatisfaction which occurs when he communicates with the others' (Leary, 1957).

Marital aptitude
A monadic concept which was once much more fashionable than it is now, is that of 'marital aptitude'. In the 1930s, Terman stated that: 'What comes out of marriage depends on what goes into it . . . whether by nature or by nurture there are persons so lacking in qualities which make for compatibility that they would be incapable of finding happiness in any marriage' (Terman, 1938). Of course that is a predictive statement, and logically requires a prospective research design in order to prove it, a design which Terman himself did not employ. Later, Luckey (1964) reported that happily married couples tended to describe both themselves, and their spouses, as responsible—over-generous, co-operative—over-conventional and docile—dependent, in terms of the interpersonal behaviour circle. Unhappily married couples, on the other hand, described both themselves and their spouses as relatively sceptical—distrustful or blunt—aggressive. Other students of marriage have referred to 'marriage wrecking traits', irritability and moodiness being prominent amongst them.

Social role
A general limitation of the ideas outlined above, as a general scheme for describing, or predicting, how individuals behave, concerns the lack of reference to the important concept of social role. Different responsibilities, tasks, or roles invite, or even require, social behaviour of particular types. The manager is obliged to be managerial, the nurse to be nurturant, the pupil attentive and co-operative, the prison officer controlling and so on. This is not to say that the occupant of a particular role may approve of the social system which puts him in that position. However, the occupancy of some of these roles is very largely voluntary, and there must be a considerable degree of self-selection. On the other hand, many roles are entered largely accidentally, and many others come to most people at some time or other (pupil, parent, befriender etc.)

Role-occupancy may be a more important determinant of interpersonal behaviour than 'personality'. One demonstration of this involved subjects in 20-minute role playing sessions, during which either an assertive or a submissive role had to be played. Some of the subjects who took part were known, on the basis of previously held group discussions, to be relatively assertive, whilst others were known to be relatively submissive. Both this prior tendency, and the part which the subjects were required to play in the role playing session, influenced behaviour, but it was the latter which was the more influential (Borgatta, 1961). We may all know our places, and be able to play our parts, when the occasion demands.

A quite dramatic demonstration of the same thing, in a natural setting, was observed by Caudill (1958) during his study of staff conferences in a psychiatric hospital. There were consistent differences between the volumes of speech contributed by different members of staff. Amongst the doctors, for example, one particularly assertive male doctor spoke most on nearly every occasion, whilst a more retiring female doctor consistently spoke least. The same sort of thing was true amongst the nurses. However, the different role, or status, positions in the hospital were much more influential in this regard than were individual differences within role groups. The senior doctors spoke most, the junior doctors next most, supervisory nurses next, and junior nurses least. Even the most assertive nurse spoke less than the most retiring doctor!

DYADIC CONCEPTIONS OF INTERPERSONAL BEHAVIOUR

A feedback model
Of course interpersonal behaviour isn't as simple as either the 'personality predisposition' or 'role demand' hypotheses suggest. Figure 12.4 represents a crude outline of a more dynamic scheme.

This model contains a vital feedback element; whatever S's reaction to O, in any ongoing interaction, O's future action must, to some degree, be influenced by it. Watzlawick *et al.* (1968) point out: '. . . interpersonal systems—stranger groups, marital couples, families; psychotherapeutic or even international relationships—may be viewed as feedback loops, since the behaviour of each person affects, and is affected by, the behaviour of each other person'.

Crude though the scheme depicted in Figure 12.4 is, it is nonetheless beyond our present methods to test such a social feedback system in its entirety. It has,

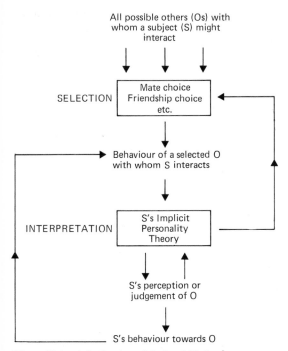

SELECTION → Mate choice
Friendship choice
etc.

All possible others (Os) with
whom a subject (S) might
interact

Behaviour of a selected O
with whom S interacts

INTERPRETATION → S's Implicit
Personality
Theory

S's perception or
judgement of O

S's behaviour towards O

Figure 12.4   A feedback model of social behaviour

on the other hand, been posssible to probe individual bits of the mechanism. If we take implicit personality theory (I.P.T.) to mean the whole collection of views, beliefs, pieces of knowledge, which S holds about categories of Os, or about all Os in general (e.g. 'no-one can be trusted', 'all men are childish', 'people who are like my mother are domineering') then there is plenty of evidence that how other people are perceived, and how they are responded to, depends upon aspects of the I.P.T. All sorts of experiments have been done: when low status boys make mistakes, these are likely to be accurately perceived, but when high status boys make mistakes they are more likely to be misperceived; when smartly dressed people offer to donate blood it is assumed that they do this of their own free-will, but when roughly dressed people offer to donate blood it is assumed that they were coerced; when people are described as warm, they are more likely to be thought humorous and sociable also; when people are seen briefly they are judged to be more intelligent if they are wearing glasses. Of course greater scope is given for the operation of these 'prejudices' if S is cut off from accurate information about O. A neat demonstration of this was provided by Argyle and McHenry (1971), who showed that Ss attributed significantly more intelligence to Os who were wearing spectacles, but only if they had no opportunity to talk to them. If they had the chance to interact with them, for only five minutes, this was sufficient to erase the effect of the prior assumption that glasses meant higher intelligence.

Reactions to evaluations of self

An important aspect of the I.P.T. concerns S's view of himself, and what he thinks other people think about him. There is a lot of evidence that S's self-attitudes, or his expectations about his own performance, influence his reaction to other people's assessment of him. In several relevant experiments it is arranged that an O, or several Os, make assessments of S, or comment upon his performance on some task. S is then allowed to give some reaction to this evaluation. The general finding is that Ss who are confident in their own abilities, who are of high self-esteem, or who have been led to believe that they are successful on the type of task being performed, react very differently to those who give them a bad, as opposed to a good evaluation. They are relatively well-disposed towards the latter O, and relatively badly disposed towards the former. On the other hand, Ss who are lacking in confidence, or have been led to believe that they are poor performers, show relatively little differentiation in their reactions to Os who give them good, or bad, evaluations.

Secord and Backman (1961) have proposed a two-factor theory to account for this sort of result. They suggest that everyone, other things being equal, likes to hear favourable things being said about them (the first factor). But in addition, everyone has a preference for hearing things said about them which are consistent with their own self-view (the second factor). If the self-attitude is highly positive, then these two factors summate, and result in a markedly stronger preference for receiving positive, rather than negative, evaluations. On the other hand, for someone whose confidence or esteem is low, the two factors tend to cancel out, resulting in a weaker, or non-existent, preference for positive evaluations.

This sort of effect doesn't always occur, but it has been demonstrated on a sufficient number of occasions to suggest that it may be of importance. The effect might be quite important in real life. Confident people might be expected to surround themselves with people who admire them; they might be expected to make a forceful rebuttal whenever they are attacked, and to use other mechanisms for minimising threats to their self-esteem. The person low in self-esteem would obviously be at a considerable disadvantage, if he lacked the motivation to minimise such threats.

Other experiments suggest that self-attitudes may influence the tasks which S attempts. People who are 'fearful of failure' or who are afraid of having their deficiencies shown up, may adopt low risk or low cost strategies. They may have a preference for 'tasks' which either carry a low risk of failure, or where the cost of failure is relatively low.

Other experiments demonstrate the way in which self-expectations can, under certain circumstances, lead people to behave in ways which appear not to be in their best interests. For example, Aronson and Carlsmith (1962) led subjects to believe, either that

Table 12.1 The effects of expectancy–performance discrepancy; details of the Aronson and Carlsmith experiment

Subject group		False scores given to subjects at end of round*					Mean number of trial responses changed when round 5 repeated†
Expectancy (rounds 1–4)	Performance (round 5)	1	2	3	4	5	
High	High	17	16	16	17	17	3.9
High	Low	17	16	16	17	5	11.1
Low	High	5	4	4	5	17	10.2
Low	Low	5	4	4	5	5	6.7

* Each round contained 20 trials. The chance of a correct answer on each trial was 50:50, so a score of 10 represented a 'chance' score

† Analysis of variance showed the expectancy–performance interaction effect to be significant ($p < 0.001$)

they were doing particularly well, or particularly badly, on a game-like task in which they had a 50% chance of being correct on each trial. After a number of 'rounds', half the subjects were led to believe that their performance on the next round was consistent with their previous performance, whilst the other half were led to believe that their performance was inconsistent (see Table 12.1). When all subjects were given a second chance to go through this same 'round' again, subjects who thought their performance had been consistent with previous performance (whether good or bad) changed relatively few of their responses, whilst subjects who thought their performance on that round had been inconsistent with the previous performance (whether good or bad) mostly changed half or more of their responses. This suggested that people who had been led to believe that their previous performance was poor were behaving in a maladaptive way. Those whose performance on the last round was initially good (despite previous poor performance) should have stuck with those responses, in order to maximise their score. Those whose performance on the last round was initially bad (and consistent with previous poor performance) should have changed as many responses as possible. In fact the reverse was the case, and these subjects with low expectations of their own performance engineered their own defeats.

Mate choice

Another aspect of the scheme shown in Figure 12.4, which has received much attention from psychologists, is the filter governing the selection of a limited number of Os from the total 'field of eligibles' (as Winch, 1958, called it). There have been many fanciful ideas put forward about mate choice, for example. These have particularly emanated from abnormal psychology, where it is often assumed that some people choose mates who 'fit' them personality-wise, even though this may sometimes result in a choice of mate who, by general standards, is deviant in some important respect (the word 'choose' is often used although it is not implied that the process is a conscious or deliberate one). It is then supposed that this

'complementary fit' makes it more difficult for the spouse to give up his/her deviance. It is sometimes claimed that there is some peculiar satisfaction, for some people, in being married to someone who drinks very heavily, or who displays symptoms of neurosis. Most of these ideas have stressed complementarity, or difference. For example, they suggest that a controlling person may marry a younger, or particularly submissive, partner, to assist the expression of their controlling nature. These ideas particularly concern the dominance–submissiveness dimension of interpersonal behaviour.

In fact, the research that has been done on mate choice, friendship choice, and interpersonal attraction in general, suggests that the general picture is rather more mundane than these ideas would suggest. The major determinants of who forms attachments with whom turn out to be propinquity and similarity. We tend to form attachments to people who are available, because they are near, and to people who are similar to ourselves in general social characteristics (such as race, social class, education, occupation), and values and interests. Even when it comes to more subtle 'personality' traits, the evidence is mainly in favour of similarity, rather than complementarity. However, it has to be said that theories of mate choice are becoming more sophisticated. For example, there are now a number of 'stage' theories, which allow the possibility that the factors governing choice at a relatively early stage in bond formation, are not the same principles upon which progress may be based at a later, more intimate, stage. Furthermore the evidence for similarity is much weaker when the traits examined have to do with dominance or submissiveness, than when they have to do with other dimensions of interpersonal behaviour. There must be many marital bonds characterised by considerable discrepancies between the partners in levels of assertiveness or dominance. There is some suggestion that such discrepancies may be relatively concentrated in marriages where one partner is in some way psychologically distressed or deviant.

The eliciting function of behaviour

A key link in the scheme depicted in Figure 12.4 is

that joining 'Ss behaviour' to 'O's behaviour'. It was one of Leary's most important contentions that social behaviour representing a particular part of the interpersonal behaviour circumplex would 'elicit', 'prompt' or 'pull' a particular type of social response from other people. Indeed he went so far as to state that: 'The reflex manner in which human beings react to others and train others to respond to them in selected ways is . . . the most important single aspect of personality' (Leary, 1957). In general he proposed that behaviour would elicit a reaction which was opposite to it along a vertical axis of the interpersonal behaviour circle (e.g. dominance would elicit submissiveness, and *vice versa*), and would pull similar behaviour along a horizontal axis (e.g. affection would be responded to with affection, hostility with hostility). These expectations are shown in Figure 12.2.

This aspect of interpersonal processes, concerned with the effects which elements of interpersonal behaviour have upon the behaviour of other interactants, would seem to be a crucial one, and ought to have a central place in social psychology. Strangely enough, though, it has been relatively little studied. There have been studies of the peer-group interactions of hyperaggressive and well-adjusted boys, and of groups of female college students in group discussion. There have also been experimental studies in which actors have played standardised client roles, and the effects upon interviewer behaviour have been observed. Each of these studies, whether naturalistic or experimental, shows that aggressive–rejecting behaviour is more likely to be followed by behaviour of this same type in other people, than is behaviour of other types. Similarly, friendly or co-operative behaviour is relatively likely to be reciprocated. There is also substantial support for the 'vertical axis' part of Leary's formulation. Docile–dependent or submissive behaviour is particularly likely to be followed by leading–advising or dominant behaviour, and the reverse also tends to be the case. There is some support, then, for the main hypotheses concerning behaviour at the poles of the main vertical, and the main horizontal, axes. Beyond that, it seems that Leary's suggestions may have been overprecise. The realities of social interaction are not so easily and systematically accounted for as he supposed. For example, in the study of female college students in group discussion (Shannon and Guerney, 1973) self-enhancing–competitive behaviour, which it was expected would elicit rebellious–distrustful behaviour, in fact tended to be followed by behaviour of its own sort.

Shannon and Guerney make the important suggestion that the picture will depend very much upon the particular demands of the setting. Firstly it is only to be expected that the frequency of behaviour in the different categories will differ between settings (in their study there was more leading–advising behaviour than anything else, a not unexpected finding, in view of the setting, which encouraged the voicing of opinions on a number of quite important university matters). In addition, it is a reasonable expectation that the categories of reaction which different types of behaviour elicit will also depend upon the setting. For example, they suggest that self-enhancing–competitive behaviour may have elicited further behaviour of that same type in this setting, where the groups were of one sex only, where there was no established authority hierarchy, and where there was no pressure to solve particular problems. They speculate that Leary's own hypothesis (that this behaviour would elicit behaviour of a more submissive variety from other people) might be true in a group where there is a 'socially sanctioned dominance discrepancy', and where a dominant member displays the self-enhancing–competitive behaviour. A whole range of complex hypotheses of this type remains to be tested.

Dyadic and compensation effects

The eliciting function of behaviour has also been demonstrated in relation to a variety of cues (sometimes called immediacy cues) which indicate affiliation or liking. As well as physical distance, topic of

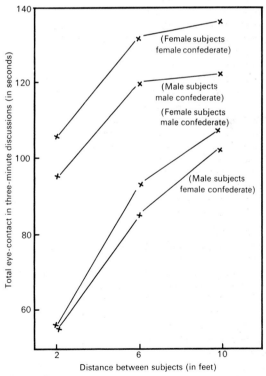

Figure 12.5 Relation between eye-contact and distance apart of subjects. (From Argyle, 1967, by courtesy of Penguin)

conversation, and physical touch, they include form of address (title and surname, first name, nickname etc.), body orientation, body lean, eye-contact, and smiling. People are likely to turn towards, lean towards, make eye-contact with, and smile at, other people whom they like most. And people who behave this way are more likely to be liked.

Under some circumstances, the production of these cues shows a dyadic effect (e.g. if you lean towards me, smile, and make some self-disclosing remark, then I am more likely to lean towards you, smile, and reciprocate). On the other hand there is much evidence in favour of a compensation effect in relationships between relative strangers. For example, Argyle and Dean (1965) found that subjects engaged in greater amounts of eye-contact when they were placed at a greater distance from partners who had been instructed to stare at the subject throughout a three-minute discussion period (see Figure 12.5). It was as if an intimacy equilibrium or balance was established: when the balance was disturbed (by increasing distance apart, for example), equilibrium was restored in some other way (by increasing eye-contact).

In the study just mentioned the interaction was very short, and the partners were strangers. In relationships of longer duration the equilibrium point may change gradually over time.

INTERPERSON PERCEPTION
Elements of implicit personality theories

A person's view of mankind (his 'implicit personality theory') may contain very powerful general rules, which govern his perception of a wide range of other people. The paranoid individual, for example, is generally suspicious; he sees threat where others see none. Raush (1965) suggested that part of the problem with hyperaggressive boys, whom he observed in group interaction, was that they interpreted other people's actions as hostile, even when it appeared clear to the observer that hostility was not intended. Kelley and Stahelski (1970) have reviewed research using the prisoners dilemma game (see Chapter 13 page 203 of this book for a description of this 'game'). They conclude that there is evidence that people who prefer to compete, rather than co-operate, when playing this game tend to believe that other people are generally competitive. Those who prefer co-operation, on the other hand, are more likely to believe that other people are heterogeneous.

There may well be a general optimism–pessimism or favourable–unfavourable dimension to social perception. Shrauger and Altrocchi (1964) concluded, from their review, that the evidence generally supported the hypothesis that people who had a favourable view of themselves, held a generally favourable view of other people. A recent study of delinquent boys in Glasgow (Bhagat and Fraser, 1970) showed that these boys had (in comparison with non-delinquent boys) negative views about themselves, members of their families, their teachers, their work, and the area in which they lived. Other studies suggest that people who have a reputation for being relatively 'well-adjusted' tend to look on the bright side of things, and have a generally optimistic view of human nature and personal relationships.

Projection

Other studies have looked at projection as a 'defence mechanism'. Early studies suggested that people tended to project their own characteristics onto other people (they attributed their own 'stinginess' to other people, for example) if they lacked insight about their own possession of a particular trait. Unfortunately there were some serious methodological difficulties in these studies, and later research has suggested that the matter is much more complicated. For one thing, situational factors are important. For example, boys who have been frightened by watching a film are more likely to attribute fear to other boys, and also to attribute hostility to older people. Other experiments suggest that the attribution of characteristics to other people depends on a complex combination of S's characteristics, O's characteristics, and the nature of the trait which might be projected. For example, in one experiment, subjects were more likely to attribute homosexual interest to another person if their own self-esteem had been given a recent boost, but even then only when the other person was evaluated relatively highly.

Self-deception

The availability of alternative defence mechanisms further complicates matters. An early study by Frenkel-Brunswick (1939) was extremely revealing. Subjects of this study were a number of advanced psychology students who had worked at a particular institute for a number of years. They each described themselves, and a number of colleagues, and answered a number of questions about their views. A variety of mechanisms of 'self-deception' seemed apparent. Sometimes a subject would just omit to mention a characteristic when describing himself, even though his colleagues had given considerable prominence to this same characteristic when describing him. In many cases there was even 'distortion into the opposite', whereby a subject described himself in terms quite opposite to those used by his colleagues in describing him. Subjects who displayed this particular mechanism were particularly likely to have a bad reputation. Some interesting things came to light when subjects were asked about their views and ideals. For example, subjects who valued 'sincerity' as an ideal were less likely to have sincerity attributed to them by their colleagues! Furthermore, the greater the number of ideals mentioned by a subject, the more likely he was to be rejected by colleagues.

Association rules

Many of the rules in an 'implicit personality theory' may be in the nature of association rules, taking the general form, 'people who are X, tend also to be Y'. In other words, they represent assumptions about what goes with what. Some of these assumptions may be widely shared (e.g. girls who wear short skirts have a high level of hetrosexual interest), others may be more contentious (e.g. people who vote Conservative are more reliable), and others may be idiosyncràtic and personal (e.g. men who are like my father are easy-going and likely to drink a lot). Following George Kelly's (1955) presentation of personal construct theory there has been considerable interest in examining the 'constructs' (e.g. 'like my father', 'reliable', 'easy-going') which people use, and the assumptions which they make about the way in which they are associated. Methods for examining individual implicit personality theories include the repertory grid methods (see Bannister and Mair, 1968) and other methods that have been reviewed by Rosenberg and Sedlak (1972). It is supposed, as shown in Figure 12.4, that the content of the implicit personality theory influences both interperson perception, and interpersonal behaviour, in important ways. However, for the moment, this is something that is taken for granted rather than something that is proved.

Cognitive structure

An alternative focus of interest has been the structure, rather than the content, of a person's implicit personality theory. Some people may use relatively few constructs in their descriptions or perceptions of other people, others may use relatively many. A construct may be finely graded in its use or, at the other extreme, may just be a matter of 'either/or'. One person may have a relatively 'monolithic' structure, in which nearly all the constructs used are strongly related to each other, and to some superordinate, probably evaluative (good–bad), construct.

Such a person would see the world largely in black–white, good–bad, terms, and almost all constructs would have implications for 'goodness' or 'badness'. Other people may have many, relatively independent, constructs, so that their system allows for a variety of combinations of characteristics. For example, intelligence might or might not be a good thing, depending upon whether it was associated with meanness; being devoutly religious might or might not be associated with kindheartedness; and so on.

These notions have led to the concept of cognitive complexity–simplicity (Crockett, 1965). It seems that people with a relatively 'simple' way of thinking about other people, are likely to form more confident, polarised, first impressions of other people. This might be functional in a situation which puts a premium upon decisiveness. On the other hand, confident first impressions may be wrong, and less open to modification. When people who are relatively cognitively simple are shown two films depicting the same character, the first showing the character in a favourable light, the second in an unfavourable light, judgments show a volte-face after the second film. The first impression is totally rearranged and displaced by a quite contrary new opinion. Subjects who are relatively cognitively complex, on the other hand, are better able to integrate the two impressions, and come to a rounded opinion of the film character, which provides an 'explanation' of the rather different behaviour displayed in the two films. It has to be admitted that research in this particular field is hampered by lack of agreement about the operational definition of cognitive complexity. The whole matter of cognitive structure is highly complicated, and some researchers prefer one definition (e.g. the number of constructs used by a person), whilst others prefer others (e.g. the independence of constructs).

The attribution of responsibility

Correspondent inferences

An important aspect of interperson perception or judgment concerns the circumstances under which one person attributes, to another person, responsibility for actions (Jones and Davis, 1965). It has been supposed by some that the individual person decides in much the same way as a court of law decides upon guilt. If it can be supposed that O had the ability to bring about certain consequences, had the knowledge that his acts would bring these consequences about, and intended these consequences, then he is likely to be held responsible. Under these circumstances, correspondent inferences are likely to be made by S about O. In other words, the inferences which S makes about O's character, are likely to correspond with the consequences of O's acts, for which S holds him accountable. Kindliness will be attributed to someone held to be responsible for a kind action, hostility attributed to the perpetrator of a hostile action, and so on.

Out-of-role behaviour

Other factors which might affect whether or not confident inferences will be made about O's character include whether or not behaviour was out-of-role. We are relatively unlikely to infer from a job applicant's claim that he has the right abilities for the job, that he really does have those abilities; but if he claimed not to have the appropriate abilities, we would be more likely to believe him. The former behaviour is appropriate to the situation whereas the latter is 'out-of-role'. Similarly, we are unlikely to infer a basic politeness from observing that someone is polite towards his boss.

Table 12.2   Some self and spouse-descriptions, and derived dyadic indices, used in studies of interperson perception and marriage

	Husband (H) as object of perception			Wife (W) as object of perception
Descriptions				
Self-description	H → H (i.e. H describes himself)			W → W
Description of spouse	W → H (i.e. W describes H)			H → W
Metaperception	H → W → H (i.e. H describes how he thinks W describes him)			W → H → W
Meta-metaperception	W → H → W → H (i.e. W describes how she thinks H thinks she describes him)			H → W → H → W
Derived dyadic indices				
Partner likeness	H → H	compared with		W → W
Agreement with spouse's self-description ('sensitivity')	{ H → W	,,	,,	W → W
	{ W → H	,,	,,	H → H
Understanding of spouse's perception of oneself	{ W → H → W	,,	,,	H → W
	{ H → W → H	,,	,,	W → H
Realisation of (mis)understanding	{ H → W → H → W	,,	,,	W → H → W
	{ W → H → W → H	,,	,,	H → W → H
Feeling (mis)understood	{ H → W → H → W	,,	,,	H → W
	{ W → H → W → H	,,	,,	W → H

Relevance and justification

Another factor is that of personal relevance. People are more likely to make extreme inferences when they have been personally affected. This is likely to be of great importance. If S and O are involved in a reciprocally contingent relationship (i.e. what S does is partly provoked by what O does, and *vice versa*) and if the behaviour of each is having considerable consequences for the other, then both are likely to be making extreme inferences. It may be supposed that the factor of justification is relevant here too. It may be generally true that people are particularly likely to view their own actions as 'justified'; can see some justification in the behaviour of both parties in an argument in which they are not involved; but are least likely to admit any justification for the behaviour of other people with whom they are personally involved in a squabble. The capacity for self-justification is probably very strong. Frenkel-Brunswick noted that self-justification was amongst the self-deceptions used by her subjects. For example, one subject with a reputation for aggressiveness explained: 'I don't let myself be intimidated'.

The importance of personal relevance for making extreme inferences about others, combined with self-justification and the unwillingness to see justification for the behaviour for an adversary, may have a great deal to do with the escalation of conflicts at family, social group, and international levels. Watzlawick

et al. (1968) have referred to the 'punctuating' of social sequences by those personally involved. The sequence: → A → B → A → B → A →, extended indefinitely, may best represent the true state of affairs between A and B. However, A may 'punctuate' the sequence, and see it as: B → A → B. In other words, B started it, and A is an innocent whose behaviour towards B is totally justified in terms of provocation. B, on the other hand, may punctuate the sequence rather differently.

Dyadic indices

For many years, social psychologists have been fascinated by the possibility of individual differences in 'sensitivity', 'understanding' or 'accuracy of interperson perception'. This has led to a great deal of research involving a variety of dyadic indices. These involve the comparing of two sets of perceptions. For example, how a husband describes his wife might be compared with how the wife describes herself. If the two sets of descriptions match, we might suppose that the husband is 'sensitive' to his wife. Some of the descriptions which have been used, and some of the dyadic indices derived from them, are shown in Table 12.2.

It can be seen that the method has been carried to considerable lengths. A number of researchers have asked husbands and wives to provide metaperceptions. For example, the husband would be asked to describe himself, as he thinks his wife describes him. Laing *et al.* (1966) have even carried the method one stage further, and required the couple to provide meta-metaperceptions. For example, a wife might be asked to describe her husband, as she imagines that he thinks that she describes him (i.e. W → H → W → H). It might be supposed that what is important in a marriage, or indeed in any relationship, is that each participant 'feels understood' or at least 'realises that he is misunderstood'.

Artefacts

Unfortunately this is a case of the researcher's imagination running rather ahead of his methods. As such, it represents a rather important demonstration of the dangers inherent in some types of social psychological investigation. Cronbach (1955) was one of the first to point out these dangers, and Wright (1968) has done the same, most cogently, recently. What it amounts to is that 'sensitivity', 'realisation of understanding', and the rest, may appear to be the case when two descriptions are compared, but may in fact have been produced by a variety of artefacts. Let us take a simple example: if a wife is asked to describe her husband on an adjective check-list, she may well describe him as loving and assertive, particularly if she is reasonably satisfied with her mate. After all, in many cultures that is exactly what husbands are supposed to be. If he describes himself in the same terms (which he is quite likely to do unless he is going out of his way to be self-condemnatory), then it will look as if his wife is very 'sensitive' to his view of himself. What has really happened is that both husband and wife have provided a description of the approved male sex-role stereotype. The 'understanding' is more artefactual than real, and at best is a form of stereotype accuracy.

That this sort of accuracy is not what it seems, can be neatly demonstrated by rearranging, or 'reshuffling', pairs of descriptions. This has been done in a variety of studies. When the results are first analysed, it looks as if happily married wives are more accurate about their husbands than are unhappily married wives; and that students who have close friendships are more understanding of their close friends than are pairs of students who are relative strangers. However, when happily married couples are shuffled around, so that the description of her husband provided by one wife is compared with the description which a quite different husband has given of himself, then the same result is still produced. Happily married wives turn out to be just as sensitive to other happily married wives' husbands, as they are to their own husbands! And students who have close friendships are just as sensitive to other students' close friends, as they are to their own close friends! So it looks as if the accuracy or 'sensitivity' which some people display has more to do with personal factors, than to do with interpersonal factors. It may have more to do with the way in which happily married people, and people with close friendships, describe themselves, and other people, than to do with differential accuracy in describing one particular other person.

SOCIAL INFLUENCE PROCESSES

Social power

Although human social psychology is currently short on basic descriptive data, it is by no means short of analytic concepts. One of the more useful of these concepts is that of 'social power'. The prostitute is dependent on her client's money, the client upon her services; the pupil is dependent on the teacher's expert knowledge, and the teacher is dependent upon the pupil's immaturity or ignorance; the employee is dependent upon his employer's good opinion and financial reward, whilst the employer is dependent upon his employee's labour. The dependence of A upon B affords B a certain amount of 'social power'. French and Raven (1959) have attempted to categorise the major types of social power: they refer to reward power (B has some power over A if B has the power to dispense, or withhold, rewards valued by A); coercive power (B can administer punishment to A or withhold it); referent power (A refers to, or identifies with, B); expert power (B is expert in a subject in which A is a non-expert); and legitimate power (B has an acknowledged right to control A, e.g. A is B's child). This form of analysis is relatively easy to apply when the 'resources' that pass between A and B are fairly tangible (goods or services for money, for example) or when there is a marked power differential between A and B, but it becomes more difficult to apply when social power is relatively intangible, or when power is more equally distributed, as in 'pure friendship'. However, attempts have been made to apply this type of social exchange analysis (see Thibaut and Kelley, 1959, and Homans, 1961, for basic formulations of this type of theory) to marriage and friendship relationships (e.g. Carson, 1969).

People in a position of 'social power' in relation to others are in a position to influence others. A parent has a great measure of control over his or her child, for example, by virtue of the parent's control over a wide range of reinforcements of value to the child. Nurses have a large measure of control over the behaviour of their patients, but this control is often only temporary.

Reward and coercive power

It is hardly surprising that under such high power conditions, behaviour is highly responsive to the administration of rewards or punishments, provided that these are carefully administered, so as to be contingent upon the behaviour which the high power

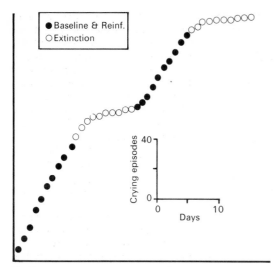

Figure 12.6 Cumulative record of the daily number of crying episodes of a four-year-old boy (N.B. the record is cumulative so a flattening of the record indicates a cessation or near cessation of crying episodes). (From Harris, *et al.*, 1972, by courtesy of Appleton-Century-Crofts)

Table 12.3   The first of Betty and Bill's contingency contracts. (From Patterson, and Hops, 1972)

Agreement No. 1

Betty's request for changes in Bill:

1. Discuss money only once a week for about 15 minutes.
2. Nag only once a month.
3. No nagging about the job unless the routine is changed.
   Consequence: If he slips up and does more nagging than agreed upon, then Betty can buy a dress on the household account ($20.00). However, if he nags more than three times in the week, this is not a down payment on a $100 dress.

Bill's request for changes in Betty:

1. No deviations from the present work routine. At present, this includes: M, 9–5.30; Tu, 5–9; W, off; Th, 5–9; F, 9–1; no Sat or Sun. Consequence: If the routine is broken, i.e., Betty comes home after the specified hours or works on a weekend, it will cost her $5 from her personal checking account.
2. When Bill can afford to give Betty $100 per month for herself then she quits working.

person wishes to see increased or decreased. There can be little doubt that this straightforward principle accounts for a great deal of human conformity. Of course, the nature of the rewards and punishments employed may be relatively crude (food, sexual satisfaction, the threat of a bullet in your stomach, electric shock) or relatively subtle (approval, attention, the opportunity to watch moving pictures, a bunch of flowers).

The principles of operant, or instrumental, conditioning (reward and punishment training) have been consciously applied, over recent years, to the modification of 'inappropriate' behaviour in a variety of situations characterised by a large power differential. For example, there have been applications in the nursery school, the classroom, mental hospitals, and in correctional institutions for delinquents.

The powerful, and immediate, effects of this sort of conditioning can be seen in the example, given in Figure 12.6, which shows the results of attempts to control the behaviour of a single nursery school child. This four-year-old boy displayed a number of crying episodes each morning, and observation suggested that this behaviour brought attention from the teachers, which he was less likely to receive at other times. It was therefore arranged that, during the 'extinction' period, his crying behaviour would be ignored, and he would instead be given 'approving attention' for talking and self-help behaviours. Ten days of this new regime reduced his crying almost to zero. Just to prove that it was teacher behaviour that was effective, the old regime was reintroduced for a further ten days, and as Figure 12.6 shows, the child

started once again to clock up a number of crying episodes each morning. After that, the reintroduction of 'extinction' reduced his crying once more to near zero (Harris *et al.*, 1972).

Marital coercion

In circumstances where the distribution of power is more equitable, as may be the case in the best marriages, no one person is in a position to deliberately engineer the behaviour of the other in quite this way. Even so, each probably has powerful weapons, in the form of rewards and punishments, which can be used to exercise some degree of control. Some sort of exchange, bargaining or unwritten contract formation process, is likely to be the result in such circumstances. Whereas nation states are likely to make the basis of their co-existence highly explicit, in the form of written pacts, agreements, and the like, husbands and wives are unlikely to do so. However, in Betty and Bill's case their relationship had deteriorated to the point where it was felt that the drawing up of a set of rules might be of assistance. Table 12.3 shows the first of a number of agreements which Betty and Bill entered into together at that time (Patterson and Hops, 1972).

Modelling

It should not be supposed, of course, that people only influence one another when they are in a position to control each other in this way. Much, maybe most, behaviour may be acquired by imitating, or by producing behaviour which matches behaviour modelled by others. Modelling may be an extremely pervasive process. It may serve to facilitate behaviour which is already in a person's repertoire. For example, people eat more when others are eating, drink more when others are drinking, clap more when others are clapping, and in general feel obliged to follow fads and fashions. Simply observing others breaking rules, or performing actions which are normally kept under control, may be sufficient to disinhibit behaviour. People drink from taps which have 'no drinking' signs on them if they see other people doing so, children are more likely to be aggressive towards large dolls when they have just witnessed adults doing the same, and people drop rubbish where others have done so before. Alternatively, behaviour may be inhibited as a result of seeing a model's behaviour produce punishing consequences.

Emotional reactions can be picked up by a similar process. Fears are contagious and probably run in families, and can sometimes be got rid of again by exposing the fearful person to models who display fearlessness in the presence of the relevant object(s). Parents and children often show remarkable similarities in terms of non-lexical aspects of speech, such as average speech length, or pause frequency. Attitudes, even of delusional proportions, can be infectious. The phenomenon of *folie à deux*, whereby a family member or close associate appears to pick up a psychotic delusion, has been known to psychiatrists for many years. Indeed, there have been reports of whole families affected by the same paranoid delusion.

Bandura (1971) has outlined the subprocesses that may mediate between modelled events on the one hand, and matching performances on the other. As Figure 12.7 shows, his scheme supposes that imitation depends upon the working of the processes of attention, retention, motor-reproduction, and motivation. Later matching performance will not occur if the modelled events were not sufficiently attended to in the first place, or if some record of these events is not retained in some way, or if the performance cannot be

correctly reproduced, or finally, if negative sanctions operate or unfavourable incentive conditions exist.

There is some evidence that people are more likely to be imitated, and therefore have more influence, if they are better liked or have relatively high status or power in a relationship. Probably more important, however, is the amount and length of exposure to different models. Parents are likely to be particularly effective models for their children by virtue of the lengthy, sustained, exposure which children have to them. In addition, particularly when children are young, the exposure to parents is fairly exclusive, and undiluted by exposure to a range of alternative models. The same is true of siblings, although the influence of siblings has been relatively ignored, in comparison with parents, in research on socialisation. None the less there is some evidence that siblings are important: for example, in one study, second-born boys were more likely to be thought 'kind' if they had older sisters, and second-born girls were more likely to be thought 'aggressive' if they had older brothers (Brim, 1958).

Reference has already been made to the association between similarity and interpersonal attraction. Adding to this the principle of modelling, we can begin to understand the force behind the saying 'birds of a feather flock together'. People who associate together are likely to start off somewhat similar, and during the course of their association their habits, attitudes, values, and emotions are likely to rub off on one another. Survey investigations of social habits, such as alcohol, tobacco and cannabis use, suggest a very strong association between such behaviours, and behaviour of close friends. People who smoke tend to have friends who smoke, for example. It is probably not just a matter of imitation of other people's behaviour; exposure to increased opportunity, and perhaps a certain amount of social coercion, must also be operating.

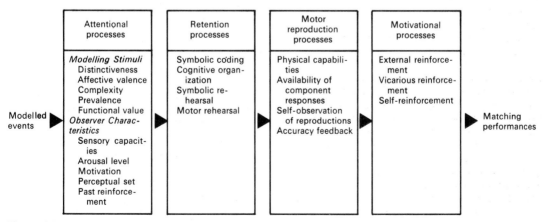

Figure 12.7   Subprocesses in the social learning view of observational learning. (From Bandura, A., 1971, by courtesy of Aldine-Atherton)

References

Argyle, M. and Dean, J. (1965). *Sociometry*, **28**, 289–304

Argyle, M. (1967). *The Psychology of Interpersonal Behaviour* (Harmondsworth, England: Penguin)

Argyle, M., Salter, V., Nicholson, H., Williams, M. and Burgess, P. (1970). *Brit. J. Soc. Clin. Psychol.*, **9**, 222–231

Argyle, M., Alkema, F. and Gilmour, R. (1971). *Eur. J. Soc. Psychol.*, **1**, 385–402

Argyle, M. and McHenry, R. (1971). *Brit. J. Soc. Clin. Psychol.*, **10**, 27–29

Aronson, E. and Carlsmith, J. M. (1962). *J. Abn. Soc. Psychol.*, **65**, 179–182

Bandura, A. (1971). In: *Psychological Modeling: Conflicting Theories* (A. Bandura, editor) 1–62 (Chicago: Aldine-Atherton)

Bannister, D. and Mair, J. M. N. (1968). *The Evaluation of Personal Constructs* (London: Academic Press)

Bateson, G., Jackson, D., Haley, J. and Weakland, J. (1956). *Behav. Sci.*, **1**, 251–264

Bhagat, M. and Fraser, W. I. (1970). *Brit. J. Psychiatry*, **117**, 381–387

Borgatta, E. F. (1961). *Sociometry*, **24**, 218–234

Bowlby, J. (1969). *Attachment and Loss: Vol. 1: Attachment* (London: Hogarth)

Brim, O. G. (1958). *Sociometry*, **21**, 1–16

Carson, R. C. (1969). *Interaction Concepts of Personality* (London: Allen and Unwin)

Caudill, W. (1958). *The Psychiatric Hospital as a Small Society* (Cambridge, Mass.: Harvard University Press)

Corckett, W. H. (1965). In: *Progress in Experimental Personality Research*, Vol. II (B. A. Maher, editor) (New York: Academic Press)

Cronbach, L. J. (1955). *Psychol. Bull.*, **52**, 177–193

Ferreira, A. J. and Winter, W. D. (1968). *Fam. Proc.*, **7**, 17–36

Fox, R. (1967). *Kinship and Marriage: an Anthropological Perspective* (Harmondsworth, England: Penguin)

French, J. R. P. and Raven, B. H. (1959). In: *Studies in Social Power* 118–149 (D. Cartwright, editor) (Ann Arbor, Michigan: University of Michigan Press)

Frenkel-Brunswik, E. (1939). *J. Soc. Psychol.*, **10**, 409–420

Gewirtz, J. L. (1972). In: *Communication and Affect: A Comparative Approach*, 19–49 (T. Alloway, L. Krames and P. Pliner, editors) (New York: Academic Press)

Goldstein, A. P. (1971). *Psychotherapeutic Attraction* (Oxford: Pergamon Press)

Harris, F. R., Wolf, M. M. and Bayer, D. M. (1972). In: *The Experimental Analysis of Social Behaviour*, 90–100 (R. Ulrich and P. Mountjoy, editors) (New York: Appleton-Century-Crofts)

Homans, G. C. (1961). *Social Behaviour: its Elementary Forms* (New York: Harcourt, Brace and World)

Jones, E. E. and Davis, K. E. (1965). In: *Advances in Experimental Social Psychology*, Vol. 2, 219–266 (L. Berkowitz, editor) (New York: Academic Press)

Jourard, S. M. and Lasakow, P. (1958). *J. Abn. Soc. Psychol.*, **56**, 91–98

Jourard, S. M. (1959). *J. Abn. Soc. Psychol.*, **59**, 428–431

Jourard, S. M. (1966). *Brit. J. Soc. Clin. Psychol.*, **5**, 221–231

Kelley, H. H. and Stahelski, A. J. (1970). *J. Personal. Soc. Psychol.*, **16**, 66–91

Kelly, G. A. (1955). *The Psychology of Personal Constructs: Vol. 1, A Theory of Personality* (New York: Norton)

Kelman, H. C. (editor) (1965). *International Behaviour: A Social–Psychological Analysis* (New York: Holt, Rinehart and Winston)

Kinsey, A. C., Pomeroy, W. B. and Martin, C. E. (1948). *Sexual Behaviour in the Human Male* (Philadelphia: Saunders)

Kinsey, A. C., Pomeroy, W. B., Martin, C. E. and Gebhard, P. H. (1953). *Sexual Behaviour in the Human Female* (Philadelphia: Saunders)

Laing, R. D., Phillipson, H. and Lee, A. R. (1966). *Interpersonal Perception: a Theory and a Method of Research* (London: Tavistock)

Leary, T. (1957). *Interpersonal Diagnosis of Personality: a Functional Theory and Methodology for Personality Evaluation* (New York: Ronald)

Lowenthal, M. F. (1964). *Amer. Sociol. Rev.*, **29**, 54–70

Luckey, E. B. (1964). *J. Counsel. Psychol.*, **11**, 136–145

Maccoby, E. E. and Masters, J. C. (1970). In: *Carmichael's Manual of Child Psychology*, Vol. 2, 3rd Ed. (P. H. Mussen, editor) (New York: Wiley)

Mehrabian, A. (1971). In: *Nebraska Symposium on Motivation*, Vol. 19, 107–161 (J. K. Cole, editor) (Lincoln, Nebraska: University of Nebraska Press)

Patterson, G. R. and Hops, H. (1972). In: *The Experimental Analysis of Social Behaviour*, 424–434 (R. Ulrich and P. Mountjoy, editors) (New York: Appleton-Century-Crofts)

Raush, H. L. (1965). *J. Personal. Soc. Phychol.*, **2**, 487–499

Rosenberg, S. and Sedlak, A. (1972). In: *Advances in Experimental Social Psychology*, Vol. 6 (L. Berkowitz, editor) (New York: Academic Press)

Secord, P. F. and Backman, C. W. (1961). *Psychol. Rev.*, **68**, 21–32

Shannon, J. and Guerney, B. (1973). *J. Personal. Soc. Psychol.*, **26**, 142–150

Shapiro, J. G., Foster, C. P. and Powell, T. (1968). *J. Clin. Psychol.*, **24**, 233–236

Shrauger, S. and Altrocchi, J. (1964). *Psychol. Bull.*, **62**, 289–308

Taylor, D. A. and Altman, I. (1966). *Psychol. Rep.*, **19**, 729–730

Terman, L. M. (1938). *Psychological Factors in Marital Happiness* (New York: McGraw-Hill)

Thibaut, J. W. and Kelley, H. H. (1959). *The Social Psychology of Groups* (New York: Wiley)

Truax, C. B. and Carkhuff, R. R. (1967). *Towards Effective Counseling and Psychotherapy* (Chicago: Aldine)

Watzlawick, P., Beavin, J. H. and Jackson, B. D. (1968). *Pragmatics of Human Communication: a Study of Interactional Patterns, Pathologies and Paradoxes* (London: Faber and Faber)

Winch, R. S. (1958). *Mate Selection: a Study of Complementary Needs* (New York: Harper)

Worthy, M., Garey, A. L. and Kahn, G. M. (1969). *J. Personal. Soc. Psychol.*, **13**, 59–63

Wright, P. H. (1968). *J. Exp. Res. Personal.*, **3**, 126–135

Chapter 13

GROUP PROCESSES

H. H. Blumberg

INTRODUCTION

There seems to be more agreement about the overall content of social psychology than about how the field is to be divided. One convenient subdivision has been into three parts—group dynamics, attitudes and communication, and interpersonal perception. However, two major areas of current research do not fit into any one of the parts. Studies of decision-making and conformity have been built on what is really the interface of all three subdivisions; and social change and contemporary issues have been receiving an increasingly large amount of attention, partly in the context of group dynamics but largely from eclectic sources. The present discussion covers group dynamics, incorporating some of the relevant material on conformity to group norms, on the ways that individuals and groups reach decisions, and on social change.

Research on group processes has been carried out in a wide variety of settings. Some studies have made use of animals or of computer simulations of social processes rather than directly involving people. Much work with people has been done 'in the laboratory' where specially formed groups might take part in elaborately contrived experiments or might simply be called upon to solve problems, carry out discussions, or make decisions. And some research has taken the form of 'field studies'; these can be experiments, as when some randomly-selected groups in a factory participate in deciding on work changes, or they can be naturalistic observations of committees, social movements, etc.

BACKGROUND CHARACTERISTICS

Physical situation

In spite of current interest in communal living arrangements, popular lore would probably still suggest a positive relationship between crowding and aggression. However, in one experiment (Loo, 1972), groups of children (each group having three boys and three girls, four to five years of age) were left to play either in a small room (high-density condition) or a large one, while observers in the next room rated their behaviour on a number of dimensions, including aggression and social interaction. The girls showed the same low levels of aggression in both room sizes, but the boys actually showed less aggression in the smaller room. 'Thus a spatially crowded condition

seemed to create physical and psychological restraints on children . . .' Other experiments (Freedman et al., 1971; cf. Freedman et al., 1972; Kutner, 1973) suggest that spatial density does not have much effect on people's ability to perform various tasks.

Even a straightforward variable such as 'room size' can present much complexity. Spatial density (the amount of space for a given group) has been distinguished from social density (in which additional people are introduced into a given space). Desor (1972) concluded that 'being crowded' is the 'reception of excessive social stimulation and not merely lack of space'.

Until recently not much systematic attention has been paid to the physical environment of groups, although studies of spatial arrangements of people have been carried out for some time. In a much-cited study, Sommer (1961) found, not surprisingly, that if a chair is located sufficiently far (over $5\frac{1}{2}$ feet) from a facing couch, two people will sit next to each other rather than across from each other.

The distance people choose to be from one another depends on the situation. Observing people in 'natural settings' (the Houston zoo!), Baxter (1970) found cultural differences related to ethnic group (closer together for Mexican–Americans than for Blacks or Caucasians), age (children closer), sex (male–female couples closer), and setting (Blacks closer indoors and Mexican–Americans closer outdoors).

Kuethe (1964 and other studies there cited) was able to measure what he calls 'social schemata' simply by having people remove felt figures from a board and replace them back onto the board. A child figure typically was replaced closer to a woman figure than to a man figure. People were replaced closer together than rectangles. And homosexual subjects replaced same-sex figures closer together than did heterosexual subjects. As with many social phenomena, cross-cultural differences have been found: subjects from Mediterranean countries (Greeks and Southern Italians) have shown closer doll placements than North European (Swedish and Scottish) subjects (Little, 1968). For all groups, distance varied with relationship (more distance from dolls representing authority figures) and specific content (closer for 'transactions of an intimate nature').

Systematic differences occur not merely in how physically distant people are from one another but also in the kinds of seating locations taken. Several studies—using discussion groups, 'mock juries', etc.—indicate that certain seating positions (e.g., the head of a table or a location central to communication) are associated with more talking and greater influence (Strodtbeck and Hook, 1961; Hare and Bales, 1963; Leavitt, 1965).

An increasing trend in the observation of physical variables is to try to look, not simply at single factors in isolation, but at a broad array of variables—i.e., at the entire ecology of human behaviour and its physical environment. Architecture and group dynamics are no longer totally separate fields (*cf.* Deasy, 1970).

In a study of men isolated in pairs, the investigators examined not just one or two variables but the interrelationships among (a) degree of privacy, outside stimulation, and expected time in isolation (all varied experimentally) (b) environmentally oriented behaviours such as social activities (c) territoriality for beds, chairs, and areas of the room and (d) performance on team and individual tasks (Altman *et al.*, 1971). One of the many interrelated findings was that successful groups showed more social interaction, which was necessary if they were to work out an interpersonally viable pattern of life.

Personality

The way a person acts in a group is related partly to the situation, partly to the person, and partly to random events. Some situations (or *roles*), such as being part of the audience at a concert, are highly 'structured' and leave little room for individual variance. Even at concerts, however, individual differences may be communicated to others by means of facial expressions, applause, other bodily movements (depending on the nature of the concert), and indeed by the fact that a particular person is or is not present in the first place.

A person may show consistent behaviour in a number of situations (e.g. often talking, or often smiling) and this is especially likely if the situations are similar to one another. This consistency may be partially a reflection of fixed social variables such as the person's age, sex, or place of birth. And it may be partly related to comparatively stable personality traits.

No two psychologists, it sometimes seems, derive quite the same list of 'major personality dimensions', but one list of four dimensions which emerged from work taking account of a large number of personality tests included extroversion, aggression, anxiety and authoritarianism (Couch, 1960). Verbal ability and interpersonal sensitivity have also received much attention. In general, one would expect a high-extroversion person to be comparatively dominant and positive in most groups—that is, to do more of the talking than someone scoring low on extroversion, and to seem friendly and show agreement. Aggression would be manifest in dominant-negative interaction

(behaviour such as more talking plus showing disagreement). Personality scores do typically provide a small but significant prediction of how a person will behave socially, and this predictability is increased if one also takes into account the scores of the other people who will be present. Although personality traits are stable enough to contribute to the prediction of behaviour (*cf.* Hall and Williams, 1971), they are not impervious to change and there is no logical bar to learning, say, how to increase one's interpersonal sensitivity (*cf.* Hare, 1962, Chapter 6; Shaw, 1971, Chapter 6).

Social characteristics and other variables

In many studies of group processes, several key variables—age, sex, socio-economic status, national or ethnic background, and degree of prior acquaintance—are either held constant or systematically varied or at least measured.

Effects due to age are generally considered in the context of developmental psychology. In some studies, such as those of mock-jury deliberations, older subjects and males have been found to be more dominant and more likely to emerge as leaders.

Social variables by no means have invariant effects. For instance, Atkinson (1968; *cf.* Johnson and Mihal, 1973) found that most of the differences favouring females over males in verbal ability tests did not appear among children receiving computerised instruction in reading rather than being in the normal classroom environment for this subject. This particular study focussed on education rather than group dynamics, but the results do suggest that subtle differences in the way people in groups are treated can 'cause' apparently 'basic' associations between intelligence and other key variables such as sex or race.

In fact, increasing attention has been paid to 'demand characteristics', or the ways that the outcome of a group experiment is affected by prior instructions and the experimenter's expectations. As we shall see in the next section, the mere presence of the experimenter or other observer in a laboratory discussion group can, for example, result in higher rates of task-oriented interaction and lower rates of task-irrelevant behaviour (Wilson, 1969).

PRESENCE OF OTHER PEOPLE

Social facilitation

The presence of the experimenter or other observer in a laboratory discussion group can have marked effects—resulting, for example, in higher rates of task-oriented interaction and lower rates of task-irrelevant behaviour (Wilson, 1969). When a task is sufficiently easy or familiar that one's dominant response is likely to be 'correct', the presence of others is likely to have a positive effect. One example is Triplett's (1898) experiment in which children turned fishing reels more rapidly when working together in the same room than when working alone. Similar results have even been found with a variety of non-human subjects: nest-moving ants move more earth (per ant) when other ants are working with them, chickens eat more in the presence of other chickens that are also eating, and pairs of rats copulate more if other pairs of copulating rats are in the same room (studies cited by Cottrell, 1972). However, the presence of other people may have a negative effect if a task involves unfamiliar responses—e.g., learning a list of nonsense syllables (Cottrell, 1972, evaluating a theory put forth by Zajonc).

When people actually work together in problem-solving groups, the resulting work, in a number of experiments, has been found to be superior to that of the average individual working apart. This is partly because the mean of several judgments is likely to be more accurate than any one given judgment and partly because of the greater chance that at least one person will have the 'right answer' and share it with other group members (see Argyle, 1969, page 255; Shaw, 1971, Chapter 3; Hare, 1962, Chapter 12).

Working with other people has 'social' as well as 'task' implications, a fact which task-oriented researchers sometimes lose sight of. In one study, American high school students who daily used co-operative groups for an entire academic year were compared with equivalent students from classes which used the traditional lecture-discussion method:

'Subjects in the co-operative groups experienced more peer pressure for involvement and assigned greater importance to their peers' expectations. The climate in the co-operative groups was perceived as being less "relaxed". However, the co-operative subjects appeared to be less "alienated" from the class. Co-operative subjects also viewed themselves as having lower levels of interpersonal competence. If a student filled a leadership position in the co-operative groups, he was much more likely to be affected by the treatment.'

(DeVries, Muse and Wells, 1971)

Group composition

Experimental comparisons *between* groups have usually made use of either background characteristics or such procedural differences as comparing co-operative groups with competitive ones. The most common question regarding background characteristics is whether it is better for group members to be diverse (heterogeneous) or similar (homogeneous) with regard to some particular trait such as dominance, warmth, or authoritarianism. In general, it has been found that a certain amount of variety yields increased productivity and satisfaction among group members, but too much heterogeneity may make it difficult for a group to work together (*cf.* Tuckman, 1967). The results depend on how a specific trait 'meshes' with itself. Heterogeneity of dominance may be preferable to situations where everyone is assertive or where nobody is. However, homogeneity of warmth may be better than some members wanting close relationships while others prefer to keep at a distance—an incompatible situation which is likely to have low productivity as well as dissatisfaction (Hare, 1962, Chapter 13). Furthermore it is best if a group leader and members are similar in degree of authoritarianism (*cf.* Argyle, 1969, page 219). Because given groups may become more homogeneous over time, a certain amount of turnover in membership has the value of preserving diversity (Ziller, 1972)

The question of co-operation *v.* competition is being researched systematically in the context of group decision-making, bargaining, and coalition formation (see below and see Wrightsman *et al.*, 1972). When a situation favours co-operation among individuals or groups (such as tasks that require different members' skills, and rewards that are equally shared), more cohesiveness is likely to result—i.e., more positive sentiment (friendliness, etc.) among members is likely to emerge. Whether *productivity* is also higher in co-operative groups depends on the norms of the group and whether the task lends itself to specialisation. For instance a group of repairmen in a factory may have a tacit norm or co-operative agreement as to what constitutes 'a day's work' and may discourage or even ostracise someone who produces too little or too much. Detailed analyses of group problem-solving have been presented by Hoffman (1965) and Kelley and Thibaut (1969).

Conformity

Mere exposure to the opinions and answers of other group members does have a profound effect on one's own expressed opinions and answers, as shown by studies on conformity (see also, the discussion of 'co-operation', below). If, for some reason, you find yourself looking at a small light in a dark room or on a cloudy night, the light will appear to move even though it is stationary (the 'autokinetic effect'). As early as the 1930s, Sherif (1965a; *cf.* Sherif, 1966) found that when individuals in groups were asked to make a series of judgments as to the apparent distance that such a light had moved, they would soon begin to take their cues from other group members, and each group would converge on its own narrow range of estimates.

Next, in one of social psychology's better known experiments (Asch, 1965), imagine that you are seated at a table with three other people, who are being shown a series of cards and being asked which of three lines (labelled A, B and C) on each card is the same length as a (fourth) 'standard' line on the card. For the first few cards all of you are agreed as to the correct answer. However, on one card (and for others later on) it appears to you that, say, 'line B' is the correct answer, but each of the three other people in the group answers, 'line A'. It is then your turn to answer. What do you say? In one study, subjects in your position agreed with the majority and gave a wrong answer about a third of the time (even though wrong answers were virtually non-existent in a control condition where subjects were answering without anyone else being present). In these experiments, the other three subjects are actually 'stooges' who have been instructed to give particular wrong answers on certain trials. The important finding is that people may conform to a wrong majority opinion even when the correct answer is plain. The more ambiguous the right answer, the greater the conformity to majority opinion. The larger the number of people who constitute the unanimous majority, the more likely one is to conform (Gerard and Conolley, 1972). However, the presence of even one other person giving correct answers will drastically reduce the conformity effect.

What kinds of social control lead to such conformity? A hint of the answer to this question comes from turning around the main Asch experiment and having a majority of naive subjects giving correct answers; the one stooge, who gives occasional obviously incorrect answers, is likely to find that the others will point out his errors and laugh at him (*cf.* Hare, 1962, Chapter 2).

Experiments on conformity have proliferated. Some of them have been cross-cultural; some have employed natural setting; still others have used electrically automated panels (instead of stooges) which make every subject appear to be the 'fourth' person to answer. Among Japanese subjects, Frager (1970) actually found instances of anticonformity, in which subjects would disagree with a correct majority. Anticonformity was found to be significantly correlated with alienation (measured by survey items dealing with rejection of modern society).

At Trinity College, Dublin, two humorous verbal recordings (Private Eye Christmas Record and Milligan Preserved) were each prepared in two ways—with and without dubbing onto the recording the laughter of a group of about twenty people. In the condition of dubbed laughter, subjects 'laughed longer, more frequently, and also rated the material as more amusing' (Smyth and Fuller, 1972). Furthermore when a crowd were looking up at a building on a busy American street, the larger the crowd the more likely were passers-by to join them and look up (Milgram *et al.*, 1969).

Some of the background and situational variables that have been found to be associated with higher conformity in at least one study are as follows: sex and age (higher conformity for females and younger subjects; Conger, 1972), higher authoritarianism (Moore and Krupat, 1971), co-operative orientation

of subjects and usefulness of information previously received (Crawford and Haaland, 1972), and attire of source-person (passers-by at a peace demonstration in Washington, D.C., were more likely to sign an antiwar petition, and to sign without reading it, if the woman soliciting signatures was dressed as a hippy; Suedfeld *et al.*, 1971).

Before the discussion turns to 'risky shift' it seems worth pointing out that conformity, in and of itself, is not necessarily good or bad. Conformity to inaccurate information or authoritarian values may hinder one's search for truth and freedom. However conformity to various norms and judiciously selected opinions forms a basis for 'productivity' and solidarity. As we have seen, group estimates are often closer to the truth than individual ones, and there is a good chance that at least one member of a group will have a valid answer. As regards solidarity, continual disagreement is seldom productive of friendships.

Risky shift

Risky shift has come to stand for much more than it initially meant. The first relevant studies were carried out by Stoner and others in the early 1960s; one of the first analyses was presented by Brown (1965, Chapter 13) in his widely read textbook on social psychology. In a typical experiment, each group of six people would be presented with a problem such as:

> 'A captain of a college football team, in the final seconds of a game with the college's traditional rival, may choose a play that is almost certain to produce a tie score, or a more risky play that would lead to sure victory if successful, sure defeat if not. If you were asked to advise the captain, what is the lowest probability of success that you would consider acceptable to make it worthwhile for the captain to choose the risky play?'
>
> (see Brown, 1965, page 658)

Subjects were asked to give initial individual answers. Then they discussed each problem in order to arrive at a unanimous group decision. Finally, they were asked to record their private judgments after the group decision had been made, it being understood that the individual and group judgments need not agree. The general finding has been that, for a variety of problems, the group and final individual recommendations are usually riskier than the initial individual judgments.

The subsequent flood of research has dealt, not merely with 'shift to risk', but with the overall process whereby other people influence one's decisions. Relevant explanations, and their evaluations on the basis of experimental evidence, are summarised in Table 13.1. By looking through this table one may be able to get a general idea of the *way that alternative hypotheses can be developed and evaluated*.

The main finding seems to be that, as a result of

Table 13.1   Explanations of risky shift

Theory	Contents	Evaluation
1. Diffusion of responsibility	Group experience reduces anxiety about the possible negative consequences of making the risky decision because the responsibility can be 'diffused' from one's own shoulders to those of other group members	Generally rejected. Dilemmas are hypothetical anyway; so guilt is unlikely; shifts persist for up to six weeks after discussion; does not account for the shifts toward caution that have occurred for some items
2. Familiarisation	Shift due simply to greater familiarity with the items	Generally rejected. Does not specifically account for shifts toward caution nor shifts on dimensions other than cautious-risky. Two studies showed that merely writing 'briefs' on the items produced risky shift, but eight subsequent studies failed to replicate this
3. Leadership theories	Shifts are in the direction of the most persuasive group members	
a. Inherent persuasiveness	Inherently high risk takers are more influential in group discussions than other people are	Disproved
b. Leader-confidence	The people who are most confident in their position, and therefore most assertive and influential on any given item, are those who, for that particular item, favour risk (or, for some items, caution)	Not strongly supported; may account for part of effect. On the choice-dilemma problems, positive correlation has been found between individual risk-taking and confidence. However, risky shift does disappear if high-risk member is low in confidence
c. Rhetoric of risk	Verbal arguments for risk are inherently more dramatic and persuasive than those for caution	Little evidence for or against; at best accounts for part of effect
d. Release theory	(See below, as this is also an example of value theory)	
4. Value theories	Groups shift in a direction toward which most members are already attracted	Largely supported. For instance, there are consistently high correlations across items between the average initial risk rating for an item and the amount of subsequent shift toward greater risk
a. Social comparison i. risk as value	Culturally prescribed (American) value is to be at least as risky as everyone else (but a value on caution where, e.g., safety of others is at stake)	Qualified support. Prior to group discussion, subjects thought others were *already* less risky than themselves. However, mere information about others' true levels produces only weak shifts in the absence of discussion
ii. multiple values	Same as 'risk as value', but degree to which risk is valued is item-specific	More general support than 'risk as value' because accommodates differences among items in degree of risky shift. There may be a general value for risk *plus* a correction for item-specific factors

Table 13.1 continued overleaf

Table 13.1 (*continued*)

Theory	Contents	Evaluation
b. Pluralistic ignorance	Initial response is a compromise between 'real preference' and 'assumed group standard'. On discovering that group standard is closer to ideal than might have been thought, subject will shift towards ideal	Same as 'social comparison, multiple values'—but specific evidence slightly weaker
c. Release (response polarisation)	Subject is released from assumed social constraints against risk (or other value felt as desirable) by observing someone behaving in the desirable way	Largely supported. Same as social comparison plus: presence of *single* other risky member produces about as much shift towards risk as *two* other risky members. Also supported by the evidence favouring leadership theories
d. Relative arguments	The dominant values adhering in a decision problem elicit persuasive arguments in group discussion	Supported as part of a two-process theory—i.e. combined with another 'value theory'. Accounts for finding that mere information about others' risk levels produces only weak shifts in the absence of discussion (*cf*. Moscovici and Lecuyer, 1972) Contents of discussion are heavily weighted with arguments in the direction of subsequent shift (which is not inconsistent with leadership theories)
e. Commitment	Discussion is a setting for individuals to commit themselves in a valued direction	Not strongly supported. Shift occurs when individuals passively witness discussion
5. Decision theories	Mechanisms are described whereby group discussion or relevant arguments can influence the utilities or values placed on different outcomes in the risky-shift problems	Insufficient evidence to conclude that changed utilities *cause* shifts
a. Majority rule and other principles	Various mathematical models	Conflicting evidence regarding prediction of overall shift. However, individuals may shift toward group mean *plus* other factors described above

Note.   This table has been compiled largely on the basis of material described by Pruitt (1971a and 1971b), by courtesy of *J. Personal. Soc. Psychol.*

exposure to group discussion, the entire group may shift in the direction toward which most members were already attracted, but that various factors may affect the group decision. The risky shift does seem to depend on a particular experimental framework (Castore, 1972), and laboratory results may differ from the 'real world' in content, if not in underlying principles. In one experiment, people who happened to be betting at a race track were each given '$2 Win Tickets' and were required, in groups of three people, to agree on the same horse (McCauley *et al.*, 1973). This field experiment produced a shift, but unlike its specific laboratory counterpart, the shift was toward caution (*cf.* McGrath and Altman, 1966).

In any event, not only do individuals sometimes conform to unusual group norms (as Asch demonstrated) but also, under specifiable circumstances, the group members as a whole are likely to shift their positions as a result of considering the norms (*cf.* Davis, 1973).

Helping and hurting

When will a person come to the assistance of someone else who is present? 'Only if there is not *too* much pressure to do so' is the unexpected answer emerging from various experiments. In general, the probability of giving help is proportional to the degree of prior help received (Wilke and Lanzetta, 1970; this is an example of the general principle that positive behaviour tends to be reciprocated—see Hare and Blumberg, 1968, page 520). However, in a study by Jackson (described by Berkowitz, 1973, page 312) an experimenter first did half of the subjects the favour of providing each with a soft drink.

'Then, some subjects were told that the experimenter was highly dependent upon them because he greatly needed "good" results from them, while other subjects were led to think he was much less dependent upon them. The performance was a verbal conditioning task. Jackson found that subjects . . . displayed more verbal conditioning the greater the experimenter's dependence upon them—but only if the experimenter had *not* done them the favor earlier.'

(Berkowitz, 1973, page 312, emphasis added)

Apparently, even the gift of a soft drink might be viewed as 'too much' pressure. However, if other people are present who might deal with an emergency, there might be 'not enough' pressure on any one person to help out by reporting the emergency (Latane and Darley, 1970; Schwartz and Clausen, 1970; *cf.* Lerner *et al.*, 1971; Berkowitz, 1973).

As if to complement the studies that describe when people are (or are not!) willing to help others, a series of experiments have dealt with the conditions under which people might harm others. In Milgram's (1965) prototypical studies, adult subjects (from a range of ages and occupations) were told that they were participating in an experiment on the effects of punishment on memory—one subject in each pair would be the 'teacher' and the other the 'learner'. Fortunately, the 'learner' in these experiments is in fact an accomplice of the experimenter and never actually 'learns' anything and does not receive any real shocks. The learner is strapped into a chair:

'The naive subject is told that it is his task to teach the learner a list of paired associates, to test him on the list, and to administer punishment whenever the learner errs in the test. Punishment takes the form of electric shock, delivered to the learner by means of a shock generator controlled by the naive subject. The teacher is instructed to increase the intensity of electric shock one step on the generator for each error. The learner, according to plan, provides many wrong answers, so that before long the naive subject must give him the strongest shock on the generator. Increases in shock level are met by increasingly insistent demands from the learner that the experiment be stopped because of the growing discomfort to him. However, in clear terms the experimenter orders the teacher to continue with the procedure in disregard of the learner's protests.'

(Milgram, 1965, page 245)

The overall level of shocks which subjects were willing to administer before refusing to go on was, in general, surprisingly high. In one experiment 75% of subjects administered 450 V 'shocks'. (Forty psychiatrists at a leading medical school predicted that most subjects would not go beyond 150 V.)

The level to which subjects did go was progressively higher for experimental conditions in which subjects were more distant from the victim. In the 'nearest' of four conditions, the victim only received a 'shock' when his hand rested on a shockplate and, after a point when he refused to place his hand there, would receive a 'shock' only if the naive subject obeyed the experimenter's instruction to force the victim's hand onto the plate; whereas in the most distant of the four conditions the victim was in an adjacent room and could not be heard or seen by the subject.

It was also found, however, that when the naive subject was given a 'teacher–partner' (another confederate) who refused to administer high shocks, 90% of the subjects followed suit and defied the experimenter. In the other direction, Liebert and Baron (1972; *cf.* Schuck *et al.*, 1971) found that children exposed to aggressive excerpts from T.V. programmes engaged in longer attacks against an ostensible child-victim. In yet another study, by Zimbardo (1973), 'So rapidly did normal and relatively homogeneous young men change their behaviour in conformity with their randomly assigned "guard" or "prisoner" status, that after six days of a projected two-week experiment, the experimenter-warden closed down his mock prison' (Helmreich *et al.*, 1973, page 343).

A number of authors have argued against the myth that man is innately aggressive (see, e.g. Montagu, 1968). One can at least hope that, if there is increased awareness of what makes people willing or unwilling to help or to harm others, this will enable people to act more sensitively and humanely.

NATURE OF GROUP

Up to this point we have dealt largely with background characteristics and group processes that can follow from observing other people who are present. Even the risky shift does not depend on a person being part of a group but can take place if one learns the positions taken by other group members and passively watches their discussion. The experiments on helping and hurting do not focus on the social interaction between the subject and the other person but are really concerned with conformity to norms. The present section deals more directly with the nature of the group. Our main concern is with relatively informal groups (in contrast with Cyert and MacCrimmon, 1968; Etzioni, 1969; Vroom, 1969).

Social interaction and task

The kinds of tasks that group members carry out (and the accompanying social interactions) are obviously

Table 13.2   Task effects on performance and member reactions. (Adapted from Hackman and Vidmar, 1970, by courtesy of *Sociometry*. See also Vidmar and Hackman, 1971)

Group product characteristics	Task type		
	Production	*Discussion*	*Problem solving*
Action orientation	2.96	3.17	6.22
Length	4.42	3.31	3.77
Originality	4.87	3.24	2.62
Optimism	3.49	3.77	5.06
Quality of presentation	4.34	4.26	3.61
Issue involvement	2.39	5.20	4.44
Creativity	4.35	3.85	3.88
*Member Reactions**			
1. Group too small	2.13	2.44	2.37
2. Group too large	3.23	2.90	2.66
3. Made best use of time	4.34	4.36	4.79
5. Too much competition	2.62	2.43	2.29
12. Group needed strong leader	3.56	3.21	2.98
13. Group was creative	4.94	4.05	4.26
14. I was inhibited	2.26	2.20	2.03
15. Was sufficient time	3.79	4.47	4.30
18. Not unified: subgroups	3.17	3.02	2.72
20. Group influenced me	2.90	2.62	2.65

Note. Higher figures represent higher scores on particular group product characteristics.
*Only items relating significantly to task type are included

different, e.g., for families, employment groups, encounter groups and experimental laboratory groups. In its widest sense, *task* is concerned with the basic purpose of a group (*cf.* Hare, 1962, Chapter 9; Shaw, 1971, Chapter 9). Even among experimental laboratory groups, differences in task (or basic purpose) are associated with striking differences in group performance and member reactions. Table 13.2 shows some of the significant differences, in one experiment, between production tasks (such as, 'Describe this mountain scene'), discussion tasks (such as, 'What makes for success in our culture?'), and problem solving (such as, 'How should you safely change a tyre on a busy road at night?').

Many investigators have attempted to quantify social interaction—to specify the differences either between groups or among the sessions or members of a particular group (*cf.* Leary, 1957; Bales, 1970; Hare, 1973). One efficient system uses four 'dimensions'. The first dimension has to do with degree of activity or *dominance*. Some discussion groups may show continual interaction, while the people on an underground train may be inactive to the point of not being a group. Within a group, leaders might be expected to show higher rates of interaction. The second dimension is evaluative—some acts are rated or felt as more *positive* than others. The third dimension is task-social: Some interaction deals seriously with the *task* at hand, while other interaction is more expressive and social. Finally, behaviour varies in the degree to which it *conforms* to group norms.

One system of rating interaction, 'interaction process analysis', provides information which can be translated into some of the dimensions just described. According to this system, developed by Bales and his associates, observers (of a group) rate every act of communication according to (a) who is speaking to whom and (b) which of twelve categories is appropriate—seems friendly, dramatises, agrees, gives suggestion/opinion/information, asks for information/opinion/suggestion, disagrees, shows tension, seems unfriendly (Bales, 1970, page 96; *cf.* Hare, 1962, Chapter 3). Different groups having their particular purposes will also have their own characteristic 'interaction profiles', i.e. amount of interaction and proportion of acts falling into each category (Bales, 1965). For example, in the typical problem-solving group over 60% of the interaction is in categories 3, 5 and 6 (shows agreement, gives opinion or information); whereas people who had just taken some L.S.D. showed relatively high frequencies of solidarity and tension-release; and in doll play among children there were high frequencies of giving information and showing tension (Hare, 1962, page 68; Bales and Hare, 1965; for further discussion relevant to 'group process' see Jim Orford's Chapter 12 and, below, the section on 'Processes').

The nature of interaction is also likely to vary in the course of a group's dealing with a particular situation and with the overall *group development*. One typical sequence of the kinds of problems and activities a group might have to deal with would be: agreeing on basic values, allocation of resources, interpersonal harmony, actual goal-directed behaviour, and final evaluation (see Hare, 1973).

Size. Some observations at present explained by various theories may be a function of basic variables such as size of group. For instance, something like an 'Oedipal situation' may be potentially present in all three-person groups (Lindsay, 1972). As another example, members of typical discussion groups have preferred five-person groups over smaller or larger ones (Hare, 1962, Chapter 8).

Special groups and reform of institutions. Attention has been paid to the social interaction in specific kinds of groups and institutions, and also to the kinds of reform which might be in order, in the family, schools, prisons, hospitals, political and corporate bodies, and other 'institutions' (see below, 'Social issues' and, under 'Recommended Reading', *Social Movements*). Encounter groups have been studied, partly in their own right, partly for their relevance to group dynamics, and partly to evaluate their usefulness in sensitivity training and for therapeutic settings (see Campbell and Dunette, 1968; Egan, 1970, 1971; and *Sociological Inquiry*, 1971—special issue on sensitivity training).

Communication networks

Particularly as a group becomes large, the chances diminish that everyone will have a chance to talk directly with everyone else. What are the effects of various communication patterns on people's performance and satisfaction? To illustrate a few possible communication networks, imagine first that you and several other people are seated around a formal dinner table such that each of you can comfortably talk only with two other people, one to your left and one to your right. This network, aptly called the circle, has low centrality—that is, for most conversational purposes no particular person has a central leadership position; it is also a restricted network in that only two of the several conceivable channels are actually open to each person. The wheel is the name given to the net in which one central person can talk with all of the other people, but they cannot talk with one another. This network calls to mind authoritarian groups, or at least some groups with clearly defined leaders. Approximate examples are 'typical classroom situations' and work groups where one person tells each of the others what to do (and answers questions). An elaboration of this centralised, restricted net occurs in hierarchies, where (except at the bottom) each person is 'above' several other people. A decentralised, unrestricted network (the comcon, or *com*pletely *con*nected net) is one where everyone can communicate with everyone else. Examples abound—for instance, almost any group of reasonably alert people sitting on the floor of a small room, where the record player is not overly loud, and no-one is 'talking too much'.

In a typical experiment, different groups are organised according to different patterns (e.g. the members within each group are separated from one another by partitions, and there are slots in the partitions to allow messages to be passed between particular people). The groups are given standard problems to solve or they perform other tasks, and afterwards the different 'structures' or communication networks are contrasted in terms of work quality, productivity and member satisfaction.

In Leavitt's (1965) classic study, which used simple problems of symbol-matching, 'leaders' were in fact more likely to emerge in highly centralised structures. No one kind of group did best, but the fastest solutions often came from the wheel (one central person). People in the circle were 'satisfied' more than those on the periphery of the wheel but less than those in the centre of the wheel.

Findings have been extended, and many subsequent studies reviewed, by Glanzer and Glaser (1961), Hare (1962, Chapter 10), Shaw (1964), Davis and Hornseth (1967), Burgess (1968), and Snadowsky (1972). For instance, the circle may take longer to reach a 'steady state' of organisation than the wheel, but differences are small once this steady state is reached (Burgess, 1968). One advantage of the comcon is that, if the situation demands, it is capable of functioning like any structure, including the wheel or the circle.

The communication network does not completely determine the style of leadership. In both the wheel and comcon, leaders can be either democratic or authoritarian (*cf.* Snadowsky, 1972; see also, below, the discussion of leadership).

Relevant research on the communication that passes through a network has typically dealt with one or more of the following components: sender, message, medium (e.g. face-to-face verbal, written), receiver, and effect (*cf.* Harary and Havelock, 1972). For instance, evaluations of people are known to be communicated freely among most friends, regardless of sender or receiver, but information tends to be withheld from the person being evaluated (Blumberg, 1972), at least among women.

Friendship

In most informal groups (but not necessarily in formal organisations!) the communication network is apt to be closely aligned with the friendship network. In general, most of the people we speak with ('interaction') are likely to be the ones we become friends with ('sentiment') and *vice versa*. Also, the people who are nearby ('proximity') and with whom we carry out various tasks are likely to be the ones we talk with and become friends with—and *vice versa* (*cf.* Homans, 1950). For example, in an experimental study of two housing projects ('Westgate' and 'Westgate West'), friendship choices tended to be made among people living very near to one another (Festinger *et al.*, 1950).

Pioneering work in sociometry, or the study of friendship networks, was carried out by Moreno (1953), who emphasised that people will be more satisfied and (for a given level of skill) more productive, if groups are constituted according to the preferences of the people concerned.

Friendship may result from a series of circumstances including (a) proximity plus (b) similarity or complementarity of individual characteristics, interests, values and personality (Newcomb, 1960; Hare, 1962, pages 139–141).

'Innovative' behaviour in a group (such as the prescription of a new drug by doctors in a large town) tends to start from member(s) who are relatively 'cosmopolitan' (in the particular context) and to spread via the social network (Katz *et al.*, 1963; see also, the discussion of 'modelling' in Chapter 12).

A puzzle. If interaction (talking) and sentiment (liking) really are associated with each other—if the people we speak with most are actually the ones we come to like best and *vice versa*—then it is something of a puzzle to explain why, in most actual tabulations of group interaction, the two main dimensions (how much a person talks and how positively that person is evaluated) are found to be uncorrelated. As part of the answer: probably, each person tends to talk most with those others whom that person knows best, but this does not have much systematic effect on the total amount of talking done by that person. Degree of acquaintance, which is often held constant in studies, also needs to be taken into consideration. In groups of strangers, the association between interaction and sentiment has not had much time to develop. In 'naturally occurring' groups of acquainted people, there may be a norm or widespread custom against speaking too exclusively with the people one knows or likes especially well—or indeed against making too conscious a point of liking some of those present much more than others. People who want to talk extensively with one another may simply go off by themselves. If there were no norm for trying to avoid 'excluding' anyone present, the 'face-to-face group' might lose its value as a 'plateau of stability' larger than the organism, organ, cell, . . . and smaller than the village, nation, . . .

STRUCTURE

Structure has to do with the ways in which different group members are interrelated. This is especially a question of 'roles' (including leadership roles) but also has already been dealt with in terms of the various kinds of communication and friendship networks that may be present.

Role

It is not merely the case that background variables such as sex, age, and social class might *affect* social interaction. In many cases, the nature of interaction in a group will be *largely determined* by the roles of the participants. Many roles have been studied in their own right, including sex roles, age roles (baby, teenager, etc.), family roles (mother, son, etc.), occupational roles, and other categories which carry with them a broad array of social expectations (*cf.* Brown, 1965, Chapters 3 and 4).

Even where a group does not have a built-in structure, one may emerge. The tasks of a group may lend themselves to a division of labour; and different people may come to fill different roles, possibly including leadership positions. Given any particular role differentiation, a group's resources and profits (defined broadly, so as to include things like 'affection' as well as finances) are likely to be distributed partly according to each person's contribution and status and partly according to each person's 'equal or needed share' (Burnstein and Katz, 1972).

Role devaluation. One effort in applied research has been (a) to document situations in which people are denied equality of opportunity because of their roles or membership in minority groups and (b) to discover how such equality might be achieved. Study of the 'authoritarian personality' (Adorno *et al.*, 1950; *cf.* Frenkel-Brunswick *et al.*, 1965) has been within this tradition, as has research on racial desegregation (Pettigrew, 1965), and, e.g., various experiments which document favourable changes in attitude which have followed when black and white people live in close proximity (Deutsch and Collins, 1965). More recently, to take but one example from 'a complicated area of research, Coleman and his co-workers have carried out large-scale surveys concerned with equality of educational opportunity in America (see *Equal Educational Opportunity*, 1969).

Many groups have received attention as regards deprivation of education, employment, or housing—or infringement of civil liberties. Such groups have been based, for example, on age (the young and the elderly), sex, sexual orientation, race, religious/national/ethnic origin, and social status. Enthusiasm in carrying out research can be sparked by the view that, in general, all people (and other forms of life) should be treated fairly and equally, and that at the very least, fixed roles (based on age, sex, race, etc.) should be devalued as a basis for prescribing what people ought to do. The same principles apply, at a different level, in the view that nations ought to be constrained from exploiting one another (see Etzioni, 1969).

Leadership

For a given situation there may be consensus about ideal leadership qualities. However, no one set of traits 'makes for a good leader' in all situations. Even within a particular state highway department, two different bureaus (Construction and Design) were characterised by differences in preferred leadership and also in actual leadership behaviour (Hunt and Liebscher, 1973). To draw comparatively general conclusions about leadership, one must consider: *input* variables such as how 'favourable' the group situation is and the leader's personal style of inter- action, the *process* of leadership in the particular situation (such as whether procedures are authori- tarian or democratic), and *output* measures such as member satisfaction (related to social concerns) and productivity (related to task matters).

Fielder (1972, 1973) and his associates have demonstrated a moderate relationship between leader- ship success and a person's 'L.P.C.' score (calculated on the basis of whether the person generally gives high or low ratings to his Least Preferred Co-worker). However, the relationship is a bit complicated. 'Low- L.P.C.' people are generally concerned with inter- personal relations and are successful leaders under very favourable or unfavourable circumstances; while 'High-L.P.C.' is associated with task orientation and predicts successful leadership in intermediate situ- ations. In this context, successful performance gen- erally refers to task productivity, and a 'favourable' situation is one in which: leader–member relations are good; leaders have the power to hire, fire, discipline and reprimand; and the task is structured, with the leader knowing in detail how it is to be carried out. Although Fiedler's findings have been replicated in a number of settings, a certain amount of controversy surrounds the procedures and results (Graen *et al.*, 1970), and a more complete explanation would be welcomed by everyone concerned.

Some of the earliest and best-known experimental work in social psychology, carried out by Lewin and others, has been to compare different styles of leader- ship. In one study (Lippitt and White, 1965) adults took the part of authoritarian, democratic and laissez- faire leaders in several boys' clubs. Each club had one leader at a time, the positions being rotated so that each adult took different parts in different clubs. Under authoritarian leadership (autocratic, giving orders), members got more done (in quantity) in the short run, when the leader was present, but dissatis- faction was high, and groups reacted either apatheti- cally or aggressively (*cf.* Tokuda and Jensen, 1968). In the democratic groups (where the leader actively provided guidance and information) morale was high, work was of good quality, and members kept working at the same rate when the leader left the room. (Related points are made in the discussions of com- munications networks, above, and of decision-making, below.) The laissez-faire leader did little other than give information on request: productivity was at an intermediate level (and was in fact highest when the leader was out of the room); the 'environmental unstructuredness' was interpreted by the investigators as inhibiting 'psychological freedom'. A group which is used to one style of leadership may experience difficulty in adjusting to another style (Hare, 1962, Chapter 11).

There have been a variety of instructive cross- cultural and other replications of this experiment. In diverse experimental conditions, authoritarian-led groups required less time for planning, but were less efficient in the actual solving, of problem tasks, as compared with democratic-led groups (Snadowsky, 1972). In one study, Hindu boys showed higher morale under authoritarian leadership (MacDonald, 1967). Also in India, men and women who were older, better educated, and from urban areas were more likely than others to prefer a democratic type of leadership (Bhushan, 1968)—a finding which is not completely unexpected, since authoritarianism has frequently (but not invariably) shown negative cor- relations with things like verbal ability, education and cosmopolitanism.

Task and social leaders. In the first meeting of a laboratory group, the same individual may wind up a leader in several different ways: being best liked, helping in the maintenance of social relations, and initiating task activity. However, in later meetings of the group (and this is true to a lesser extent for 'real' non-laboratory groups), these three functions tend to be uncorrelated. That is, there is no significant rela- tionship between scoring high on one of these areas and a person's scores on the other two. Therefore, the main leader, who deals with task (directing, summaris- ing, providing ideas, etc.), is likely to be a different person from the one who deals with social–emotional matters (alleviating frustrations, disappointments, tensions, etc.) (Bales, 1965; Burke, 1972).

PROCESSES

Simulation

In a much-publicised event, a spaceship team learned how to improvise a crucially needed part by following procedures worked out by a similar team on earth whose immediate environment and resources simu- lated those of the actual crew.

In simulated jury deliberations, in which the partici- pants were drawn from the regular jury pools, males and higher-status individuals showed disproportion- ately high participation and influence in the mock jury's decision-making (Strodtbeck *et al.*, 1965).

As the study of social activity becomes increasingly complex and simultaneously takes into account many interrelated variables, models of the processes in question become especially useful. One obvious kind of model is to be found in animal studies—e.g. of territoriality, dominance, and imprinted attachment of young to a mother (Brown, 1965, Chapter 1; Argyle, 1969, Chapter 2). Such studies are of interest in their own right and as a source of hypotheses (but not of direct conclusions) about human behaviour.

Sometimes a basic model or principle can, arguably, account for much of the variance in a particular dimension of social behaviour. Tarantino (1970) described much behaviour as: *approach* toward stimuli that are moderately deviant from adaptation level (what one is used to) and *withdrawal* from strongly deviant stimuli. Sorokin (1967) has concisely set forth the principle that 'like begets like'—i.e. positive or negative acts tend to be reciprocated with similarly positive or negative acts. The general validity of such a principle leads to fruitful research, in part to explain why the principle holds true, and in part to account for exceptions.

A model can be quite complex and can operate at a variety of different levels. For instance, the distribution of interaction for any one individual in a given session for a small group can be partially predicted from (a) the overall rates of interaction for each participant and (b) the overall distributions of different kinds of acts (e.g. 75% of all acts in a particular group are 'moderately positive'). Prediction can be improved if one also takes into account each participant's typical distribution of different kinds of acts, and improved further if one incorporates the probabilities of any one kind of act being followed by a particular other kind of act (*cf.* Hare, 1962, page 411–412; Leik, 1967; Gustafson, 1969; Kadane and Lewis, 1969; Lewis, 1970).

The interaction which is being simulated need not take place within the experimental laboratory (*cf.* McReynolds and Coleman, 1972). Spanhel (1971) has described a model of interpersonal relationships relevant to the formation and description of working collectives in Czechoslovakia.

When a simulation is based on a number of quantifiable factors, it may be advantageous or essential to employ computer programs. For example: if the model is partly probabilistic (e.g. specifies that under various circumstances each interaction category has a certain probability of being followed by each particular category), one can then 'run the program' innumerable times for each of a variety of sets of probabilities/circumstances and see which sets of results are most closely aligned with 'real' data.

Co-operation, competition and conflict resolution

A number of studies comparing co-operation and competition among groups and group members have been followed, more recently, by the systematic investigation of bargaining and related processes.

A set of experimental observations starting in 1927 at the Hawthorne works of the Western Electric Company suggested that productivity depended, not so much directly on physical working conditions, nor even on provisions for incentive payments, but more on interpersonal factors (see Homans, 1965). In spite of marked weaknesses in the 'methodology' of the original studies (small sample and lack of control groups, among others), subsequent work has borne

out the importance of paying attention to whether group members enjoy working with one another and to how they regard their work.

Essential but minor changes in work routines at an American pyjama factory and at a similar Norwegian factory were implemented much more successfully for groups that had a chance to participate fully in considering the need for change and the way to carry it out (Coch and French, 1965). When competing groups of young American summer campers found themselves working together for common goals (e.g. averting a 'water shortage' crisis), intergroup tensions were eased (Sherif, 1965b).

Mintz (1965) has suggested that the decisive factor in 'the non-adaptive behaviour of people in panic' is not primarily the emotional excitement of crowds but a situation in which there is competition for a scarce goal. In Mintz's experiments, group members had the task of pulling cones out of a narrow-mouthed glass bottle; each subject was given a piece of string to which a cone (in the bottle) was attached. All cones could be pulled out within the set time limit, provided that they were removed one at a time in a reasonably quick and orderly fashion. Failures were found to occur either when subjects were rewarded individually (rather than as a group) or when subjects did not have sufficient opportunity to arrive at a plan of action.

Other studies and reviews have verified that: subjects who anticipate working together show a more favourable attitude toward their group (Rabbie and Wilkens, 1971); groups that are well-acquainted produce better group decisions than *ad hoc* groups (Hall, 1971); and decisions are better accepted if decision-making is shared (Wood, 1973).

Merely providing a means for terminating an intense conflict by co-operative behaviour may be insufficient to reduce the conflict—if, for example, subjects have incompatible goals, limited communication, a need for complete trust in opponents, or the means to terminate a situation by conflict (Cole, 1972). Early co-operation may actually increase conflict if, for instance, it means that a later hostile act is particularly unexpected (*cf.* Teger, 1970).

However, retaliation may be less likely if there is an expectation of continuing interaction with the opponent, or if another person shares one's situation and can independently decide to retaliate (Friedell, 1968). Conflict resolution (see Smith, 1971) can be improved by a number of factors, sucn as intervention by a mediator (Pruitt and Johnson, 1970; *cf.* Johnson and Tullar, 1972), waiting for a 'respectable' amount of time to pass (*cf.* Tolor, 1970), fewer resources for carrying out conflict, increased co-operative interests and resources 'for recognising or inventing potential bargaining agreements and for communicating to one another . . .' (Deutsch and Krauss, 1960, page 181; see also: Etzioni, 1969; Deutsch, 1971; Pruitt, 1971c).

Prisoners' dilemma, bargaining and coalitions

Two persons who act in their own individual interests may both find themselves in a situation worse than what would have happened if they had been able to agree on an alternative. A prototype for such a situation—which is probably not too difficult to follow and worth the effort—comes from 'the prisoners' dilemma', a hypothetical paradigm attributed to A. W. Tucker:

'Two men suspected of a crime have been taken into custody and separated. The district attorney is confident that the two together have committed the crime but he does not have evidence that is adequate to convict them. He points out to each prisoner alone that each has two alternatives: to confess to the crime the police are sure they have committed or not to confess. If they both do not confess the district attorney states that he will book them on some minor charge such as illegal possession of weapons and each will get one year in the penitentiary. If both confess they will be prosecuted but the district attorney will recommend less than the most severe sentence; both will get eight years in the penitentiary. However, if one confesses and the other does not then the one who confesses will receive lenient treatment for turning state's evidence while the other will get the maximum penalty. The lenient treatment might mean six months in jail and the maximum might be twenty years.'

(Brown, 1965, page 738)

The essentials of the dilemma are diagrammed in Table 13.3.

Clearly, the best joint outcome is for neither prisoner to confess; if both confess, then both will be worse off than if neither does. However, each prisoner —looking at the diagram alone—could reason, 'If the other prisoner confesses, I will be better off if I confess than if I don't. If the other prisoner does not confess, I will still be better off if I confess than if I don't. Therefore, I will confess.' An altruistic prisoner, leaning toward not confessing, might still be afraid that the other prisoner would confess.

Games analogous to the prisoners' dilemma have been carried out in the experimental laboratory, typically using monetary incentives (subjects are given a certain amount of money from which they can be 'fined'), a series of problem trials, and a format which enables one to distinguish whether a player is maximising joint gain (co-operation), maximising own gain (individualism), or maximising relative gain (competition). In various studies the proportion of competitive responses has been found to vary with: trials (e.g. increasingly competitive over the course of a session; also, over time the members of a pair tend to become increasingly similar to one another), age (increasingly competitive for six, eight and 10-year olds), sex and verbal/numerical reasoning (more competition for males scoring higher and females scoring lower, among 14-year-old Czechoslovakians), culture, nature of the ratios of the monetary pay-offs, acquaintance (more competitive responses when players are strangers than when they are friends), sex pairing (more co-operation in mixed-sex pairs), the nature of the interaction (more competition if players are continually permitted to view the cumulative scores of every player; more competition from players who are behind than from those ahead; and less competition if one is confronted with a player who 'mimics one's own choices') and degree of isolation (most co-operation if players can both hear and see one another, least if they can do neither) (Wichman, 1970; McClintock, 1972; *cf.* Rapoport, 1965; Morley and Stephenson, 1970; Nemeth, 1972).

To investigate the more inclusive cases where people confront one another, a number of studies of bargaining in general have involved players in negotiating a 'sale' while using rather elaborate profit tables for sellers and for buyers. Such studies could be viewed as bearing limited analogy to, not only cases of real bargaining, but also general instances of people reaching agreement with one another. One typical bargaining strategy which players have been found to employ is: to explore successive (lower) levels of own profit until a mutually satisfactory agreement is reached (Kelley and Schenitzki, 1972). Happily, such agreement is likely to realise the 'maximum joint profit' even if only one player follows this strategy and even if both players are ignorant of the profits being made by the other player. A person's adaptation level, or level of aspiration, is determined in part by the level of reward she/he has come to expect. Players with

Table 13.3 Pay-off matrix for the prisoners' dilemma. (From Brown, 1965, by courtesy of Collier–Macmillan)

		Prisoner B	
		Not confess	Confess
Prisoner A	Not confess	1 year for A; 1 year for B	20 years for A; 6 months for B
	Confess	6 months for A; 20 years for B	8 years for A; 8 years for B

Table 13.4 The environments of an effective group assigned a structured task. (Adapted from Shaw, 1971, by courtesy of McGraw-Hill)

The task environment*	The personal environment	The social environment		The physical environment
		Composition	*Structure*	
Co-operation requirements: high	Five persons	Cohesive	Leader: strong, having task and social skills, motivated to be a leader	Work area: undifferentiated
Difficulty: moderate	Adults	Compatible with respect to interpersonal needs		Communication network: decentralised
	Physically sound			
Intellectual manipulative requirements: high	Intelligence: at least average	Heterogeneous with respect to abilities and personality	Followers: of equal status	
Intrinsic interest: moderate	Approach oriented		Decision structure: centralised	
	Socially sensitive			
Population familiarity: moderately high	Ascendant			
	Dependable			
Solution multiplicity: very low	Emotionally stable			

*The task environment is 'given'; i.e. when the task to be completed has the characteristics listed in this column, the characteristics listed in the other columns represent the 'best guess' about the other environments of an effective group.

high levels of aspiration wind up with larger profits and if both players have high levels of aspiration then, not surprisingly, 'the bargainers have a great deal of conflict and a low rate of agreement' (Kelley and Schenitzki, 1972, page 330). Results may differ for different numbers of bargainers, and some of the individuals in a group who are bargaining with one another may work together or form coalitions.

In general, coalitions occur when two or more people (or groups or nations) decide to pool their resources to achieve a scarce goal when, otherwise, another person or group would have enough resources/power to achieve the goal. Because people with very large resources may claim an especially large share of the goal (depending on the goal), coalitions may tend to be comprised of people who collectively have (a little more than) just enough resources to achieve the goal (Stryker, 1972).

CONCLUDING COMMENTS AND SOCIAL ISSUES

At this point (or earlier) one might well wonder whether concrete recommendations can in fact be made about the 'probable best form' for a group having a particular purpose. Prescriptions will depend on circumstance, but Shaw (1971, Chapter 10) does give an example of how a particular set of circumstances can lead to a list of preferred specifications.

His example is of a group that must decide which of four types of appliances a manufacturing company should produce for a given production year. After listing the 'scale values' for various dimensions (these values roughly correspond to the 'task environment' in Table 13.4), he compiled the recommendations shown in Table 13.4.

The study of group processes seems to be getting beyond the point where advances in understanding can be based largely on experiments which demonstrate the effects of one or two variables. The need for more 'real-world' field experiments, to complement laboratory work, is at last being met. However, the need remains for empirically—and theoretically—based studies which take account of many variables which may *all affect one another*, and the effects of which may change over time and different settings (McGuire, 1973; *cf.* Sorenson, 1971).

Social issues. Some of the relevant topics have already been discussed above—for instance, in the contexts of group ecology, reform of institutions, and role devaluation.

One approach to studying collective behaviour and other large-group processes is to treat them in part like extensions of small-group processes. Thus, Brown (1965, Chapter 14) analyses fads (e.g. a tulip-buying craze) and crowd behaviour partly in terms of prisoners'-dilemma-type pay-off matrices.

Blumer (1971) points out that social problems are typically not definable by purely objective standards but that the 'definition' of a problem is itself a product of collective behaviour, and he suggests that it is important to analyse the way in which societies label certain issues as 'problems' as well as studying the issues themselves. In his evaluation of a motivational approach to social movements, Zygmunt (1972) distinguishes (a) the motivational approach (which typically posits frustration of basic needs as leading to alienation from some part of the *status quo* and attraction to an alternative change-seeking programme) from (b) structural–functional theory (which focusses on the kinds of condition within a social system that make change-seeking movements likely to emerge) and (c) interactional theory (emphasising the actual processes of social interaction through which movements arise and develop).

The actual issues which are of most concern have varied from year to year and from place to place. If one looks through copies of the *Journal of Social Issues* from 1965 to 1974 one finds that some of the topics that have been of particular concern are: violence and conflict resolution, drug use, the New Left and the Old Left, poverty, and equality for women, blacks, and other groups. Some of the exciting methods of change which have received a fair amount of attention are the adoption of alternative life styles, community organising, and direct action.

The most useful role for 'social science' in the suggestion and evaluation of change is not completely clear. Campbell (1969) has described how effective evaluation can be built into many programmes of social reform. Caplan and Nelson (1973) call into question the view that the dissemination of social-science findings, with their current focusses, is by itself productive of improvement. In any event, there seems to be a growing consensus on the 'need for relevance in social science', if not on how this relevance is to be achieved. Those who are interested in group dynamics are being urged not only to maintain objectivity and a 'sense for theoretical rationale' but also to avoid losing touch with their environment and with people's needs.

Acknowledgment

The author wishes to thank A. Paul Hare and A. N. Oppenheim for their helpful comments on a draft of this chapter.

References

Abelson, R. P. (1968). Simulation of social behavior. In: *The Handbook of Social Psychology* (2nd Ed.), **Vol. 2**, 274–356 (G. Lindzey and E. Aronson, editors) (Reading, Massachusetts: Addison-Wesley, 1969)

Adorno, T. W., Frenkel-Brunswik, E., Levinson, D. J. and Sanford, R. N. (1950). *The Authoritarian Personality* (New York: Harper and Row)

Allen, V. L. (1965). Situational factors in conformity. In: *Advances in Experimental Social Psychology*, Vol. 2, 133–175 (L. Berkowitz, editor) (New York: Academic Press)

Altman, I., Taylor, D. A. and Wheeler, L. (1971). Ecological aspects of group behavior in social isolation. *J. Appl. Soc. Psychol.*. 1, 76–100

American Behavioral Scientist. (1971) (May), **14,** (5)

Apter, M. (1970). *The Computer Simulation of Behaviour* (London: Hutchison U. Library)

Argyle, M. (1969). *Social Interaction* (London: Methuen)

Asch, S. E. (1965). Effects of group pressure upon the modification and distortion of judgments. In: *Basic Studies in Social Psychology*, 393–401 (H. Proshansky and B. Seidenberg, editors) (New York: Holt, Rinehart and Winston)

Atkinson, R. C. (1968). Computerised instruction and the learning process. *Amer. Psychol.*, 23, 225–239

Back, K. W. (1971). Biological models of social change. *Amer. Sociol. Rev.*, 36, 660–667

Bales, R. F. (1965). Task roles and social roles in problem-solving groups. In: *Current Studies in Social Psychology*, 321–333 (I. D. Steiner and M. Fishbein, editors) (New York: Holt, Rinehart and Winston)

Bales, R. F. and Hare, A. P. (1965). Diagnostic use of the interaction profile. *J. Soc. Psychol.*, 67, 239–259

Bales, R. F. (1970). *Personality and Interpersonal Behavior* (New York: Holt, Rinehart and Winston)

Baxter, J. C. (1970). Interpersonal spacing in natural settings. *Sociometry*, 33, 444–456

Berkowitz, L. (1973). Reactance and the unwillingness to help others. *Psychol. Bull.*, 79, 310–317

Bhushan, L. I. (1968). Leadership-preference as related to age, education, residence, and sex. *Indian J. Soc. Work*, 29, 193–196

Blumberg, H. H. (1969). An annotated bibliography of serials concerned with the nonviolent protest movement. *Sociol. Abstr.*, 17, xxi–xlx

Blumberg, H. H. (1972). Communication of interpersonal evaluations. *J. Personal. Soc. Psychol.*, 23, 157–162

Blumberg, H. H. (1973). *Periodicals concerned with Social Change and Non-Violent Action; with Geographic, Organization, and Subject Indexes* (Haverford, Pennsylvania: Center for Nonviolent Conflict Resolution (Haverford College))

Blumer, H. (1971). Social problems as collective behavior. *Social Problems*, 18, 298–306

Brown, R. (1965). *Social Psychology* (London: Collier-Macmillan)

Buckhout, R. (editor) (1971). *Toward Social Change: A Handbook For Those Who Will* (New York: Harper and Row)

Burgess, R. L. (1968). Communication networks: an experimental re-evaluation. *J. Exp. Soc. Psychol.*, 4, 324–337

Burke, P. J. (1972). Leadership role differentiation. In: *Experimental Social Psychology*, 514–546 (C. G. McClintock, editor) (New York: Holt, Rinehart and Winston)

Burnstein, E. and Katz, S. (1972). Group decisions involving equitable and optimal distribution of status. In: *Experimental Social Psychology*, 412–448 (C. G. McClintock, editor) (New York: Holt, Rinehart and Winston)

Campbell, J. P. and Dunnette, M. D. (1968). Effectiveness of T-group experiences in managerial training and development. *Psychol. Bull.*, 70, 73–104

Campbell, D. T. (1969). Reforms as experiments. *Amer. Psychol.*, 24, 409–429

Caplan, N. and Nelson, S. D. (1973). On being useful: the nature and consequences of psychological research on social problems. *Amer. Psychol.*, 28, 199–211

Carter, L. F., Hill, R. J. and McLemore, S. D. (1967). Social conformity and attitude change within nonlaboratory groups. *Sociometry*, 30, 1–13

Cartwright, D. and Zander, A. (editors) (1968). *Group Dynamics* (3rd Ed.) (New York: Harper and Row)

Castore, C. H. (1972). Group discussion and prediscussion assessment of preferences in the risky shift. *J. Exp. Soc. Psychol.*, 8, 161–167

Clarkson, G. P. (1968). Decision making in small groups: a simulation study. *Behav. Sci.*, 13, 288–305

Coch, L. and French, J. R. P. (1965). Overcoming resistance to change. In: *Basic Studies in Social Psychology*, 444–460 (H. Proshansky and B. Seidenberg, editors) (New York: Holt, Rinehart and Winston)

Colby, K. M. (1967). Computer simulation of change in personal belief systems. *Behav. Sci.*, 12, 248–253

Cole, S. G. (1972). Conflict and co-operation in potentially intense conflict situations. *J. Personal. Soc. Psychol.*, 22, 31–50

Coleman, J. S. (1966). Introduction: in defense of games. *Amer. Behav. Sci.*, (October), 10(2), 3–4

Collins, B. E. and Raven, B. H. (1969). Group structure: attraction, coalitions, communication, and power. In: *Handbook of Social Psychology* (2nd Ed.), Vol. 4, 102–204 (G. Lindzey and E. Aronson, editors) (Reading, Massachusetts: Addison-Wesley)

Conger, T. W. (1972). The equivalence of group conformity measures: fact or fiction. *Diss. Abst. Int.*, 33, 2789–B

Cottrell, N. B. (1972). Social facilitation. In: *Experimental Social Psychology*, 185–236 (C. G. McClintock, editor) (New York: Holt, Rinehart and Winston)

Couch, A. S. (1960). Psychological determinants of interpersonal behaviour. (Harvard University: Unpublished Ph.D. Thesis)

Craik, K. H. (1973). Environmental psychology. *Ann. Rev. Psychol.*, 24, 403–422

Crawford, J. L. and Haaland, G. A. (1972). Predecisional information seeking and subsequent conformity in the social influence process. *J. Personal. Soc. Psychol.*, 23, 112–119

Cyert, R. M. and MacCrimmon, K. R. (1968). Organisations. In: *The Handbook of Social Psychology* (2nd Ed.), Vol. 1, 568–611 (G. Lindzey and E. Aronson, editors) (Reading, Massachusetts: Addison-Wesley)

Davis, J. H. and Hornseth, J. (1967). Discussion patterns and word problems. *Sociometry*, 30, 91–103

Davis, J. H. (1973). Group decision and social interaction: a theory of social decision schemes. *Psychol. Rev.*, 80, 97–125

Deasy, C. M. (1970). When architects consult people. *Psychology Today*, (March), 3(10), 54–57, 78–79

Desor, J. A. (1972). Toward a psychological theory of crowding. *J. Personal. Soc. Psychol.*, 21, 79–83

DeSoto, C. B. (1965). Learning a social structure. In: *Current Studies in Social Psychology*, 382–389 (I. D. Steiner and M. Fishbein, editors) (New York: Holt, Rinehart and Winston)

Deutsch, M. and Krauss, R. M. (1960). The effect of threat upon interpersonal bargaining. *J. Abn. Soc. Psychol.*, 61, 181–189

Deutsch, M. and Collins, M. E. (1965). The effect of public policy in housing projects upon interracial attitudes. In: *Basic Studies in Social Psychology*, 646–657 (H. Proshansky and B. Seidenberg, editors) (New York: Holt, Rinehart and Winston)

Deutsch, M. (1971). Toward an understanding of conflict. *Int. J. Group Tensions*, 1(1), 42–54

DeVries, D. L., Muse, D. and Wells, E. H. (1971). The effects on students of working in co-operative groups: an exploratory study. *Center for Social Organization of Schools Report (Johns Hopkins University)*, (December), No. 120

Egan, G. (1970). *Encounter: Group Processes For Interpersonal Growth* (Belmont, California: Brooks/Cole)

Egan, G. (editor) (1971). *Encounter Groups: Basic Readings* (Belmont, California: Brooks/Cole)

Equal Educational Opportunity (1969). (Cambridge: Harvard University Press)

Esser, A. H. (editor) (1971). *Behavior and Environment: The Use of Space by Animals and Man* (New York: Plenum Press)

Etzioni, A. (1969). Social–psychological aspects of international relations. In: *The Handbook of Social Psychology* (2nd Ed.), Vol. 5, 538–601 (G. Lindzey and E. Aronson, editors) (Reading, Massachusetts: Addison-Wesley)

Farr, G. and Leik, R. K. (1971). Computer simulation of interpersonal choice. *Comparative Group Studies*, 2, 125–148

Festinger, L., Schachter, S. and Back, K. (1950). *Social Pressures in Informal Groups: A Study of Human Factors in Housing* (New York: Harper)

Fiedler, F. E. (1972). Personality, motivational systems, and behavior of high and low LPC persons. *Human Relations*, 25, 391–412

Fiedler, F. E. (1973). The trouble with leadership training is that it doesn't train leaders. *Psychology Today*, (February), 6(9), 23–30, 92

Frager, R. (1970). Conformity and anticonformity in Japan. *J. Personal. Soc. Psychol.*, 15, 203–210

Freedman, J. L., Klevansky, S. and Ehrlich, P. R. (1971). The effect of crowding on human task performance. *J. Appl. Soc. Psychol.*, 1, 7–25

Freedman, J. L., Levy, A. S., Buchanan, R. W. and Price, J. (1972). Crowding and human aggressiveness. *J. Exper. Soc. Psychol.*, 8, 528–548

Frenkel-Brunswik, E. F., Levinson, D. J. and Sanford, R. N. (1965). The authoritarian personality. In: *Basic Studies in Social Psychology*, 670–679 (H. Proshansky and B. Seidenberg, editors) (New York: Holt, Rinehart and Winston)

Friedell, M. F. (1968). A laboratory experiment in retaliation. *J. Conflict Resolution*, 12, 357–373

Gerard, H. B. and Conolley, E. S. (1972). Conformity. In: *Experimental Social Psychology*, 237–263 (C. G. McClintock, editor) (New York: Holt, Rinehart and Winston)

Gibb, C. A. (1969). Leadership. In: *The Handbook of Social Psychology* (2nd Ed.), **Vol. 4**, 205–282 (G. Lindzey and E. Aronson, editors) (Reading, Massachusetts: Addison-Wesley)

Glanzer, M. and Glaser, R. (1961). Techniques for the study of group structure and behavior: II. Empirical studies of the effects of structure in small groups. *Psychol. Bull.*, **58**, 1–27

Goodman, P. and Goodman, P. (1960). *Communitas: Means of Livelihood and Ways of Life* (2nd Ed. revised) (New York: Vintage Books)

Graen, G., Alvares, K., Orris, J. B. and Martella, J. A. (1970). Contingency model of leadership effectiveness: antecedent and evidential results. *Psychol. Bull.*, **74**, 285–296

Gustafson, H. W. (1969). Model for the analysis of talk-spurt and silence durations in conversational interaction. *Proc. 77th Ann. Convention Amer. Psychol. Assoc.*, **4**, 43–44

Hackman, J. R. and Vidmar, N. (1970). Effects of size and task on group performance and member reactions. *Sociometry*, **33**, 37–54

Hall, E. T. (1966). *The Hidden Dimension* (New York: Doubleday)

Hall, J. (1971). Decisions, decisions, decisions. *Psychology Today*, (November), **5**(6), 51–54, 86–88

Hall, J. and Williams, M. S. (1971). Personality and group encounter style: a multivariate analysis of traits and preferences. *J. Personal. Soc. Psychol.*, **18**, 163–172

Harary, F. and Havelock, R. (1972). Anatomy of a communication arc. *Human Relations*, **25**, 413–426

Hare, A. P. (1961). Computer simulation of interaction in small groups. *Behav. Sci.*, **6**, 261–265

Hare, A. P. (1962). *Handbook of Small Group Research* (New York: The Free Press of Glencoe)

Hare, A. P. and Bales, R. F. (1963). Seating position and small group interaction. *Sociometry*, **26**, 480–486

Hare, A. P. and Blumberg, H. H. (editors) (1968). *Non-violent direct action: American cases, social-psychological analyses* (Washington, DC.: Corpus Books)

Hare, A. P. (1972). Bibliography of small group research 1959–1969. *Sociometry*, **35**, 1–150

Hare, A. P. (1973). Theories of group development and categories for interaction analysis. *Small Group Behavior*, **4**(3)

Helmreich, R., Bakeman, R. and Scherwitz, L. (1973). The study of small groups. *Ann. Rev. Psychol.*, **24**, 337–354

Hoffman, L. R. (1965). Group problem solving. In: *Advances in Experimental Social Psychology*, **Vol. 2**, 99–132 (L. Berkowitz, editor) (New York: Academic Press)

Hollander, E. P. and Julian, J. W. (1969). Contemporary trends in the analysis of leadership processes. *Psychol. Bull.*, **71**, 387–397

Homans, G. C. (1950). *The Human Group* (New York: Harcourt, Brace and World)

Homans, G. C. (1965). Group factors in worker productivity. In: *Basic Studies in Social Psychology*, 592–604 (H. Proshansky and B. Seidenberg, editors) (New York: Holt, Rinehart and Winston)

Hunt, J. G. and Liebscher, V. K. C. (1973). Leadership preference, leadership behavior, and employee satisfaction. *Organizational Behavior and Human Performance*, **9**, 59–77

Johnson, D. F. and Tullar, W. L. (1972). Style of third-party intervention, face-saving and bargaining behavior. *J. Exp. Soc. Psychol.*, **8**, 319–330

Johnson, D. F. and Mihal, W. L. (1973). Performance of blacks and whites in computerised versus manual testing environments. *Amer. Psychol.*, **28**, 694–699

Kadane, J. B. and Lewis, G. H. (1969). The distribution of participation in group discussions: an empirical and theoretical reappraisal. *Amer. Soc. Rev.*, **34**, 710–723

Katz, E., Levin, M. L. and Hamilton, H. (1963). Traditions of research on the diffusion of innovation. *Amer. Sociol. Rev.*, **28**, 237–252

Kelley, H. H. and Thibaut, J. W. (1969). Group problem solving. In: *The Handbook of Social Psychology* (2nd Ed.), **Vol. 4**, 1–101 (A. Lindzey and E. Aronson, editors) (Reading, Massachusetts: Addison-Wesley)

Kelley, H. H. and Schenitzki, D. P. (1972). Bargaining. In: *Experimental Social Psychology*, 298–337 (C. G. McClintock, editor) (New York: Holt, Rinehart and Winston)

Kuethe, J. L. (1964). Pervasive influence of social schemata. *J. Abn. Soc. Psychol.*, **68**, 248–254

Kutner, D. H. (1973). Overcrowding: human responses to density and visual exposure. *Human Relations*, **26**, 31–50

The Last Whole Earth Catalog. (1971). (Harmondsworth, Middlesex: Penguin)

Latane, B. and Darley, J. M. (1970). *The Unresponsive Bystander: Why Doesn't He Help?* (New York: Appleton-Century-Crofts)

Leary, T. (1957). *Interpersonal Diagnosis of Personality* (New York: Ronald Press)

Leavitt, H. J. (1965). Some effects of certain communication patterns on group performance. In: *Basic Studies in Social Psychology*, 577–592 (H. Proshansky and B. Seidenberg, editors) (New York: Holt, Rinehart and Winston)

Leik, R. K. (1967). The distribution of acts in small groups. *Sociometry* **30**, 280–299

Lerner, R. M., Solomon, H. and Brody, S. (1971). Helping behavior at a bus stop. *Psychol. Rep.*, **28**, 200

Levine, N. (1971). Emotional factors in group development. *Human Relations*, **24**, 65–89

Lewis, G. H. (1970). Bales' Monte Carlo model of small group discussions. *Sociometry*, **33**, 20–36

Liebert, R. M. and Baron, R. A. (1972). Some immediate effects of televised violence on children's behavior. *Develop. Psychol.*, **6**, 469–475

Lindsay, J. S. B. (1972). On the number in a group. *Human Relations*, **25**, 47–64

Lippit, R. and White, R. K. (1965). An experimental study of leadership and group life. In: *Basic Studies in Social Psychology*, 523–537 (H. Proshansky and B. Seidenberg, editors) (New York: Holt, Rinehart and Winston)

Little, K. B. (1968). Cultural variations in social schemata. *J. Personal. Soc. Psychol.*, **10**, 1–7

Loo, C. M. (1972). The effects of spatial density on the social behavior of children. *J. Appl. Soc. Psychol.*, **2**, 372–381

McCauley, C., Stitt, C. L., Woods, K. and Lipton, D. (1973). Group shift to caution at the race track. *J. Exp. Soc. Psychol.*, **9**, 80–86

McClintock, C. G. (1972). Game behavior and social motivation in interpersonal settings. In: *Experimental Social Psychology*, 271–297 (C. G. McClintock, editor) (New York: Holt, Rinehart and Winston)

MacDonald, W. S. (1967). Social structure and behavior modification in Job Corps training. *Perceptual and Motor Skills*, **24**, 142

McGrath, J. E. and Altman, I. (1966). *Small Group Research: A Synthesis and Critique of the Field* (New York: Holt; Rinehart and Winston)

McGuire, W. J. (1973). The Yin and Yang of progress in social psychology: seven koan. *J. Personal. Soc. Psychol.*, **26**, 446–456

McReynolds, W. T. and Coleman, J. (1972). Token economy: patient and staff changes. *Behav. Res. Ther.*, **10**, 29–34

Milgram, S. (1965). Some conditions of obedience and disobedience to authority. In: *Current Studies in Social Psychology*, 243–262 (I. D. Steiner and M. Fishbein, editors) (New York: Holt, Rinehart and Winston)

Milgram, S., Bickman, L. and Berkowitz, L. (1969). Note on the drawing power of crowds of different size. *J. Personal. Soc. Psychol.*, **13**, 79–82

Milgram, S. and Toch, H. (1969). Collective behavior: crowds and social movements. In: *The Handbook of Social Psychology* (2nd Ed.), **Vol. 4**, 507–610 (G. Lindzey and E. Aronson, editors) (Reading, Massachusetts: Addison-Wesley)

Mintz, A. (1965). Nonadaptive group behavior. In: *Basic Studies in Social Psychology*, 620–628 (H. Proshansky and B. Seidenberg, editors) (New York: Holt, Rinehart and Winston)

Montagu, M. F. A. (editor) (1968). *Man and Aggression* (New York: Oxford University Press)

Moore, J. C. and Krupat, E. (1971). Relationships between source status, authoritarianism, and conformity in a social influence setting. *Sociometry*, **34**, 122–134

Moreno, J. L. (1953). *Who Shall Survive?* (Revised Ed.) (Beacon, New York: Beacon House)

Morley, I. E. and Stephenson, G. M. (1970). Formality in experimental negotiations: a validation study. *Brit. J. Psychol.*, **61**, 383–384

Morris, C. G. (1970). Changes in group interaction during problem solving. *J. Soc. Psychol.*, **81**, 157–165

Moscovici, S. and Faucheux, C. (1972). Social influence, conformity bias, and the studies of active minorities. In: *Advances in Experimental Social Psychology*, **Vol. 6**, 149–202 (L. Berkowitz, editor) (New York: Academic Press)

Moscovici, S. and Lecuyer, R. (1972). Studies in group decision I: Social space, patterns of communication and group consensus. *Eur. J. Soc. Psychol.*, **2**, 221–244

Nemeth, C. (1972). A critical analysis of research utilising the prisoner's dilemma paradigm for the study of bargaining. In: *Advances in Experimental Social Psychology*, **Vol. 6**, 203–234 (L. Berkowitz, editor) (New York: Academic Press)

Newcomb, T. M. (1960). Varieties of interpersonal attraction. In: *Group Dynamics: Research and Theory*, 104–119 (D. Cartwright and A. Zander, editors) (Evanston, Illinois: Row, Peterson)

Pettigrew, T. F. (1965). Social psychology and desegregation research. In: *Current Studies in Social Psychology*, 508–519 (I. D. Steiner and M. Fishbein, editors)

(New York: Holt, Rinehart and Winston)

Proshansky, H. M., Ittelson, W. H. and Rivlin, L. G. (editors) (1970). *Environmental Psychology: Man and His Physical Setting* (New York: Holt, Rinehart and Winston)

Pruitt, D. G. and Johnson, D. F. (1970). Mediation as an aid to face saving in negotiation. *J. Personal. Soc. Psychol.*, **14**, 239–246

Pruitt, D. G. (1971a). Choice shifts in group discussion: an introductory review. *J. Personal. Soc. Psychol.*, **20**, 339–360

Pruitt, D. G. (1971b). Conclusions: toward an understanding of choice shifts in group discussion. *J. Personal. Soc. Psychol.*, **20**, 495–510

Pruitt, D. G. (1971c). Indirect communication and the search for agreement in negotiation. *J. Appl. Soc. Psychol.*, **1**, 205–239

Rabbie, J. M. and Wilkens, G. (1971). Intergroup competition and its effects on intragroup and intergroup relations. *Eur. J. Soc. Psychol.*, **1**, 215–234

Rapoport, A. and Chammah, A. M. (1965). *Prisoner's Dilemma: A Study in Conflict and Co-operation* (Ann Arbor: University of Michigan Press)

Sampson, E. (1970). *Social Psychology and Contemporary Society* (New York: Wiley)

Schuck, S. Z., Schuck, A., Hallam, E., Mancini, F. and Wells, R. (1971). Sex differences in aggressive behavior subsequent to listening to a radio broadcast of violence. *Psychol. Rep.*, **28**, 931–936

Schwartz, S. H. and Clausen, G. T. (1970). Responsibility, norms, and helping in an emergency. *J. Personal. Soc. Psychol.*, **16**, 299–310

Secord, P. F. and Backman, C. W. (1974). *Social Psychology* (2nd Ed.) (New York: McGraw-Hill)

Shaw, M. E. (1964). Communication networks. In: *Advances in Experimental Social Psychology*, Vol. 1, 111–147 (L. Berkowitz, editor) (New York: Academic Press)

Shaw, M. E. (1971). *Group Dynamics: The Psychology of Small Group Behavior* (New York: McGraw-Hill)

Sherif, M. (1965a). Formation of social norms: the experimental paradigm. In: *Basic Studies in Social Psychology*, 461–471 (H. Proshansky and B. Seidenberg, editors) (New York: Holt, Rinehart and Winston)

Sherif, M. (1965b). Superordinate goals in the reduction of intergroup conflicts. In: *Basic Studies in Social Psychology*, 694–702 (H. Proshansky and B. Seidenberg, editors) (New York: Holt, Rinehart and Winston)

Sherif, M. (1966). *The Psychology of Social Norms* (New York: Harper Torchbooks)

Sills, D. L. (editor) (1968). *International Encyclopedia of the Social Sciences* (New York: Macmillan and Free Press)

Smith, C. G. (editor) (1971). *Conflict Resolution* (Notre Dame, Indiana: University of Notre Dame Press)

Smyth, M. M. and Fuller, R. G. (1972). Effects of group laughter on responses to humorous material. *Psychol. Rep.*, **30**, 132–134

Snadowsky, A. M. (1972). Communication network research: an examination of controversies. *Human Relations*, **25**, 283–306

Sociological Inquiry (1971). (Spring), **41**(2)

Sommer, R. (1961). Leadership and group geography. *Sociometry*, **24**, 99–110

Sommer, R. (1967). Small group ecology. *Psychol. Bull.*, 67, 145–152

Sommer, R. (1969). *Personal Space: The Behavioral Basis of Design* (Englewood Cliffs, New Jersey: Prentice-Hall)

Sorenson, J. R. (1971). Task demands, group interaction and group performance. *Sociometry*, 34, 483–495

Sorokin, P. (1967). *The Ways and Power of Love: Types, Factors, and Techniques of Moral Transformation* (Chicago: First Gateway Edition)

Spanhel, J. (1971). Mezilidské vztahy jako vyznamny faktor tvorby uspesneho pracovniho kolektivu. *Sociologicky Casopis*, 7, 281–292

Strodtbeck, F. L. and Hook, L. H. (1961). The social dimensions of a twelve man jury table. *Sociometry*, 24, 397–415

Strodtbeck, F. L., Simon, R. J. and Hawkins, C. (1965). Social status in jury deliberations. In: *Current Studies in Social Psychology*, 333–342 (I. D. Steiner and M. Fishbein, editors) (New York: Holt, Rinehart and Winston)

Stryker, S. (1972). Coalition behavior. In: *Experimental Social Psychology*, 338–380 (C. G. McClintock, editor) (New York: Holt, Rinehart and Winston)

Suedfeld, P., Bochner, S. and Matas, C. (1971). Petitioner's attire and petition signing by peace demonstrators: a field experiment. *J. Appl. Soc. Psychol.*, 1, 278–283

Tarantino, S. J. (1970). Toward a conception of behavior based on concepts of approach–withdrawal and adaptation level. *Psychol. Rep.*, 26, 767–776

Teger, A. I. (1970). The effect of early co-operation on the escalation of conflict. *J. Exp. Soc. Psychol.*, 6, 187–204

Tokuda, K. and Jensen, G. D. (1968). The leader's role in controlling aggressive behavior in a monkey group. *Primates*, 9, 319–322

Tolor, A. (1970). The "natural course" view of conflict resolution. *Psychol. Rep.*, 26, 734

Triplett, N. (1898). The dynamogenic factors in pacemaking and competition. *Amer. J. Psychol.*, 9, 507–533

Tuckman, B. W. (1967). Group composition and group performance of structured and unstructured tasks. *J, Exp. Soc. Psychol.*, 3, 25–40

Vidmar, N. and Hackman, J. R. (1971). Interlaboratory generalizability of small group research: an experimental study. *J. Soc. Psychol.*, 83, 129–139

Vroom, V. H. (1969). Industrial social psychology. In: *The Handbook of Social Psychology* (2nd Ed.), Vol. 5, 196–268 (G. Lindzey and E. Aronson, editors) (Reading, Massachusetts: Addison-Wesley)

Vroom, V. H., Grant, L. D. and Cotton, T. S. (1969). The consequences of social interaction in group problem solving. *Organizational Behavior and Human Performance*, 4, 77–95

Wichman, H. (1970). Effects of isolation and communication on co-operation in a two-person game. *J. Personal. Soc. Psychol.*, 16, 114–120

Wilke, H. and Lanzetta, J. T. (1970). The obligation to help: the effects of amount of prior help on subsequent helping behavior. *J. Exp. Soc. Psychol.*, 6, 488–493

Wilson, S. R. (1969). The effect of the laboratory situation on experimental discussion groups. *Sociometry*, 32, 220–236

Wood, M. T. (1973). Power relationships and group decision making in organizations. *Psychol. Bull.*, 79, 280–293

Wrightsman, L. S., O'Connor, J. and Baker, N. J. (editors) (1972). *Co-operation and Competition: Readings on Mixed Motive Games* (Belmont, California: Brooks/Cole)

Ziller, R. C. (1972). Homogeneity and heterogeneity of group membership. In: *Experimental Social Psychology*, 385–411 (C. G. McClintock) (New York: Holt, Rinehart and Winston)

Zimbardo, P. G. (1973). The pathology of imprisonment. In: *Social Psychology* (E. Aronson and R. Helmreich, editors) (New York: Van Nostrand-Reinhold)

Zygmunt, J. F. (1972). Movements and motives: some unresolved issues in the psychology of social movements. *Human Relations*, 25, 449–467

Recommended Reading

Where possible, the discussion has been keyed to commonly available advanced sources (e.g. Brown, 1965, a fine textbook on social psychology). Secord and Backman (1974) provide exceptionally thorough coverage (excluding social movements). Where reference is made to Hare (1962) (a specific handbook on small groups), a list of relevant papers published in the 1960s can be found by consulting Hare (1972) under the section corresponding to the 1962 chapter number. The *International Encyclopedia of the Social Sciences* (Sills, 1968) provides reasonably thorough coverage under the following entries (and entries cross-referenced from them): groups, leadership, social change, and social movements. For subsequent and current material, consult *Psychological Abstracts*, *Sociological Abstracts* and *Cumulative Book Index*. References for a few selected topics (where it was not possible to cite all of the major references in the present text) are as follows.

Group ecology

The *Last Whole Earth Catalog* (1971) and books by Paul Goodman (e.g. Goodman and Goodman, 1960), Edward T. Hall (1966) and Robert Sommer (1969) have become 'undergraduate best sellers'. Major anthologies have been edited by Esser (1971) and Proshansky *et al.* (1970). Review articles have dealt with small group ecology (Sommer, 1967) and the larger field of environmental psychology (Craik, 1973).

Conformity

Additional relevant material has been presented by Allen (1965), Carter *et al.* (1967), Cartwright and Zander (1968; see Section III of this prominent textbook/selection of readings on group dynamics), and Moscovici and Faucheux (1972).

Group development

Hare, 1962, Chapter 3; Vroom *et al.*, 1969; Morris, 1970; Levine, 1971; Shaw, 1971, Chapter 4.

Structure

While attention here has been given mostly to experimentally-created structure (in the discussion of communication networks) and to leadership roles, one can learn more about structure in general by consulting: Brown (1965, Chapters 3 and 4), DeSoto (1965), Cartwright and Zander (1968, section VII), Collins and Raven (1969), Shaw (1971, Chapter 8) and Burnstein and Katz (1972).

Leadership
Cartwright and Zander (1968, Sections IV and V), Gibb (1969) and Hollander and Julian (1969).

Simulation of interpersonal behavior
Hare (1961), Coleman (1966), Colby (1967), Abelson (1968), Clarkson (1968), Apter (1970) and Farr and Leik (1971).

Social movements
Hare and Blumberg (1968), Milgram and Toch (1969), Sampson (1970), *American Behavioral Scientist* (1971), Back (1971), Buckhout (1971) and Blumberg (1969, 1973).

Textbooks
Although the following information was not received in time to be integrated within the present chapter, a paper by D. J. Stang (1975) (Student evaluations of twenty-eight social psychology texts. *Teaching of Psychology*, 2) suggests that three texts are to be especially recommended: CRM Books, (1974), *Social Psychology: Explorations in Understanding* (DelMar, California: CRM Books); Middlebrook, P. N., (1974), *Social Psychology and Modern Life* (New York: Knopf); Wrightsman, L. S., (1972), *Social Psychology in the Seventies* (Monterey: Brooks/Cole)

Chapter 14

ATTITUDES

G. D. Wilson

CONCEPT OF ATTITUDE

The attitude concept is of central importance in social psychology and basic to the understanding of today's most pressing social problems (wars, strikes, racial intolerance, etc.) because it is concerned with the disagreements amongst people that give rise to interpersonal and intercultural conflict. An attitude may be defined as *a relatively enduring evaluative orientation towards a particular object or class of objects*. In other words, it is a fairly persistent 'point of view' with respect to something, whether it be favourable unfavourable, or even neutral. The requirement that an attitude be fairly enduring is necessary to distinguish the concept from those of *set* and *expectation*, which normally refer to more temporary states of readiness. This does not mean that attitudes can never change; just that they are inclined to be very resistant to change. As we shall see, an important research area is concerned with the conditions under which attitudes can be expected to change.

Attitudes must show some degree of variation within or between cultures. Unless there is some amount of disagreement the concept of attitude is not relevant. This is the primary basis for distinguishing attitudes from various other concepts referring to characteristic behaviour and response predispositions such as *instinct* and *habit*. As Sherif *et al.* (1965) point out, 'the fact that we customarily walk downstairs instead of tumbling down does not require explanation in terms of an attitude, nor does the characteristic response of eating when a hungry person is offered food'. Such response tendencies have clear survival value and are therefore fairly universal; attitudes refer to varying modes of adaptation to the environment. This variation is often taken to imply that attitudes are learned rather than genetically determined, and some definitions actually include the condition that an attitude be learned. It seems feasible, however, that certain inherited temperamental dispositions such as aggressiveness and impulsiveness may influence the acquisition of certain attitudes. The evidence concerning the extent to which attitudes are based on learning experiences and genetic predispositions is dealt with later in the chapter.

Many popular definitions of the attitude concept list three components, called the cognitive, affective and conative. Table 14.1 describes these three components and gives an example of each relating to attitudes toward Jews. The *cognitive* component is concerned with evaluative beliefs about the nature and characteristics of the attitude object, e.g. the belief that Jews are 'shrewd and acquisitive'; the *affective* component refers to feelings and emotions, or 'gut reactions' to the objects ('Jews disgust me'); the *conative* aspect refers to behavioural tendencies or intentions ('I would not allow my daughter to marry a Jew'). Of these three components, the affective one is probably most central; but the three components are usually correlated in such a way as to exhibit some degree of consistency.

The conative or behavioural component of an attitude is not the same as actual behaviour that seems to have stemmed from an attitude, e.g. discrimination against Jews. Each of the three attitude components may be assessed by questionnaire. It is important to maintain this distinction between attitude as a hypothetical construct and overt behaviour, since behaviour is presumed to be determined by many different attitudes as well as many non-attitudinal factors. An attitude cannot be directly observed; it must be inferred from regularities in observable behaviour such as verbal statements of opinion, physiological changes occuring during exposure to the attitude object, or overt acts relating to the object. None of these observables should be equated with an attitude, although they may be used as indicators or even operational definitions.

The conative component is usually found to be the best predictor of the actual behaviour which is specifically referred to, but the affective component is of

Table 14.1 Three components of an attitude

Component	Concerned with:	Example
Cognitive	Evaluative beliefs	'Jews are shrewd and acquisitive'
Affective	Feelings and emotions	'Jews disgust me'
Conative	Behavioural tendencies	'I would not allow my daughter to marry a Jew'

broader psychological significance, and predictive of behaviour over a wider range of situations.

Beliefs and attitudes are so closely bound up together that they are frequently confused in everyday language. When our next-door neighbour tells us that she does not 'believe in' homosexuals, she does not mean to deny their existence; only to express disapproval. On the other hand, when she says that she 'believes in' ghosts, she is expressing faith in the existence of the phenomenon rather than a positive attitude towards it. Beliefs in this sense may be quite unrelated to attitudes, e.g. a person's belief that 'Negroes are tall' tells us little about his likely attitude toward Negroes. The distinction here is whether the belief would naturally lead to an evaluation (good/bad) or whether it simply reflects a fact or cognitive hypothesis that carries no affective significance.

It may be useful to say a word about the concept of 'prejudice' since this has been much misunderstood. A prejudice is an overly inflexible attitude that is self-defeating to the individual or unfair to others. We need to carry concepts and generalisations in our head in order to deal effectively with the environment, but we also need to be able to suspend judgement when dealing with specific cases that do not always conform to 'the rule'. To say that men are taller than women is not a prejudiced statement; it is true as a generalisation. However, to say that 'this five-foot man is taller than that six-foot woman' would be an error resulting from prejudice. Likewise, national and ethnic groups may vary or appear to vary on average in many valued attributes such as cleanliness, intelligence, honesty, aggressiveness, etc. Generalisations concerning differences between groups on these attributes may be made without prejudice necessarily being involved. Prejudice, however, might lead to a belief in incorrect generalisations or to discriminatory behaviour in dealing with the individual case. This point is mentioned because prejudice is often confused with a negative attitude. A negative attitude toward black people or Jews is often equated with prejudice, while a negative attitude toward war is seldom described in these terms. The assumption is that racial minorities are undeserving of negative evaluations, while war is not. Thus the concept of prejudice as it has often been used in social psychology reflects an attitude on the part of the psychologist himself (i.e. political liberalism). Questionnaire measures of prejudice are likely to err when they include statements that many people believe to be true as generalisations, e.g. 'The Jews are very shrewd when it comes to matters of business and finance'. It would be possible to endorse this statement without necessarily displaying prejudice when dealing with an individual Jew.

MAJOR VARIABLES OF AN ATTITUDE

An attitude may be analysed into three major parts: the object, the direction and the intensity (valence).

The object

The object of an attitude is that which it relates to: its topic, content, or 'target'. This may be a person (President Nixon), a group (the John Birch Society), an institution (marriage), a type of person (cripples) an idea (socialism), or an event (the assassination of Martin Luther King). In fact, the object of an attitude may be 'anything that exists for the individual' (Krech *et al.*, 1962). The qualification that it must exist for the individual is necessary because the range of attitudes held by a given individual is limited by his experience. Not everyone has an attitude toward Strontium 90; many people have never heard of it. Krech *et al.* suggest that failure to appreciate this point has led to the misinterpretation of results from many attitude surveys and opinion polls. They argue that before an attitude can be meaningfully measured it is first necessary to establish that the individual has an attitude toward that particular object.

Some interesting results have been obtained using content-free attitude scales in which respondents are asked to express an opinion about various objects that do not exist anywhere, let alone in their experience. For example, they may be asked whether or not they are in favour of some non-existent piece of legislation such as the 'Downtrodden Earthworms Act of 1927', or some more plausible equivalent. Apparently, many people are able to respond in a consistent way to questions such as this, presumably because they are able to interpret the content to themselves in some way. Perhaps they respond in terms of the general associations of the item, just as, for example, some housewives are intimidated by any lengthy chemical name appearing in the list of ingredients of a food product. On the other hand, consistency in this situation might reflect the influence of response bias or personality rather than true attitudes. Whatever the case, it must be agreed that Krech *et al.* are right in drawing attention to the possibility that lack of experience with an attitude object or failure to understand the items in an attitude questionnaire could lead to low validity in

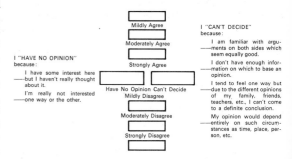

Figure 14.1 An attitude questionnaire response format allowing a fairly comprehensive set of alternatives. Note the variety of different neutral responses that may be given. (From Ehrlich, 1964, by courtesy of *Social Forces*)

attitude measurement, and thus invalidate some research results.

The best way of minimising the possibility of measuring attitudes which do not really exist is to allow some kind of neutral or indifferent response category rather than force a response in one direction or the other. This neutral position could have a variety of different psychological meanings and, if desirable, these could be discriminated using a more elaborate set of response alternatives such as that shown in Figure 14.1. This response format was used in a study of stereotyping by Ehrlich (1964). Persons choosing the 'no opinion' or 'can't decide' responses were required to indicate the basis for adopting such a position. Ehrlich concluded from his study that response formats which force a response in one direction or the other are likely to exaggerate the extent to which people agree with 'prejudiced' statements.

The direction

Our 'affective' definition of attitudes implies that an attitude normally involves a direction of evaluation, sometimes called the sign (+ or −). In Figure 14.1 the direction is represented as 'agreement' (above the neutral point) and 'disagreement' (below). A person may also be indifferent (sign of 0) on a number of issues, and it is a question of definition as to whether or not this should be regarded as an attitude at all. The problem is resolved when the intensity variable is taken into account and the various attitude 'positions' are arranged on a continuum running from extremely pro to extremely con, with a neutral point in between. This is called a bipolar scale.

The intensity

An attitude is also characterised by a certain level of intensity, degree or valence. More than being just favourable or unfavourable toward an object or issue we evaluate it with a certain level of extremeness. We may be mildly opposed to the death penalty or passionately against it, opposed to it under certain conditions and with reservations, or totally and unequivocably opposed to it under all circumstances. In Figure 14.1 this variable is represented by the neutral-mildly-moderately-strongly scale. Intensity is closely bound up with direction in that an extreme attitude must be held in one direction or the other.

MEASUREMENT OF ATTITUDES

Equal-appearing intervals

One of the earliest techniques developed for the measurement of attitudes is that described by Thurstone (1931). This was derived from certain psychophysical procedures for establishing an equal-interval scale. The main steps in the construction of a Thurstone-type scale are as follows:
(a) A large number of statements representing both favourable and unfavourable views on the topic in question are collected from a wide variety of sources. (b) This set of statements is given to a number of judges who are asked to place them into 11 categories. Category 1 represents the most unfavourable position with respect to the attitude object, Category 11 represents the most favourable position, and Category 6 is the intermediate or neutral position. The judges are further instructed to make the intervals between the adjacent pairs of categories equal (e.g. so that the difference between the 2nd and 3rd categories is apparently the same as the difference between, say, the 7th and 8th). (c) The scale value of each statement is taken as the median of the positions assigned to the statement by all the judges used. (d) A series of statements are chosen which provide a good range of scale values and which are relatively unambiguous. Ambiguity is operationally defined in terms of the inter-quartile range (Q) of the distribution of judgments obtained for the statement. A low Q indicates high agreement among the judges regarding the scale value of a statement. (e) Statements which pass the *criterion of ambiguity* are then presented to a second, usually larger, group of subjects who, this time, are asked to indicate whether or not they agree with the statement. An internal consistency check is then run to ensure that subjects who agree with a particular statement do not also endorse other statements with widely differing scale values. Statements which pass this test are said to meet the *criterion of relevancy*.

Table 14.2 gives an example of a Thurstone scale of attitudes towards war as used in a study by Peter-

Table 14.2   A Thurstone scale of attitudes toward war. (From Peterson and Thurstone, 1933, by courtesy of Macmillan). The scale values on the left do not appear on the actual form, and the statements are presented in random order. Respondents are asked to check each statement with which they agree, and their attitude position is taken as the mean scale value of all statements that they endorse.

(0.2) There is no conceivable justification for war.

(1.4) War is a futile struggle resulting in self destruction.

(2.4) War is an unnecessary waste of human life.

(3.2) The benefits of war are not worth its misery and suffering.

(4.5) We want no more war if it can be avoided without dishonour.

(5.5) It is hard to decide whether wars do more harm than good.

(6.6) There are some arguments in favour of war.

(7.5) Under some conditions war is necessary to maintain justice.

(8.5) War is a satisfactory way to solve international difficulties.

(9.8) War stimulates men to their noblest efforts.

(10.8) The highest duty of man is to fight for the power and glory of his nation.

---

son and Thurstone (1923). In this case 0.0 represents the extreme antiwar end of the scale and 11.00 the extreme pro-war end. When the scale is administered in practice the scale values do not appear, but the subject's score is calculated by averaging the scale values of all the statements with which he agrees.

The Thurstone method of constructing an attitude scale is very cumbersome, and the amount of effort expended is justified only if there is some kind of advantage to be gained. Unfortunately, its major advantage, the possibility that it does in fact provide an equal-interval scale, has been questioned following the discovery that the scale values assigned to statements are dependent upon the characteristics of the sample of judges. In particular, two biases are apparent:

(1) There is a tendency for judges with extreme attitudes to place statements in extreme categories.

(2) Judges tend to displace statements towards the end of the scale away from their own position.

There is another way in which the logic of the Thurstone technique must be treated with caution. Referring to Table 14.2 it is clear that the most antiwar score on the scale would be obtained by endorsing the first statement only. This means that a person who endorsed the following three statements also, would come out with a relatively pro-war score, even though these are also clear expressions of an antiwar attitude. The traditional Thurstone method of calculating an attitude position by averaging the scale values of all items endorsed must, then, be considered dubious so long as respondents are given freedom to decide how many statements they will endorse.

One way round this problem would be to ask respondents to choose the single statement that comes closest to representing their own position on the issue and take the scale score of this item as the measure of his attitude. Such a procedure is the basis of some modern elaborations on the Thurstone method, e.g. that described by Coombs (1964). In the *unfolding technique*, the respondent selects from a number of Thurstone-type statements the one he thinks is closest to his own position. He then selects the statement next closest to his own position, followed by the third nearest his position, and so on. In this way, all the statements are ranked on the basis of their discrepancy from the respondent's own position. At this point we are missing certain information, for the statements may be discrepant from the respondent's own position in either the favourable or unfavourable direction. What is needed is some method for 'unfolding' the scale at the pivotal point represented by the statement selected as nearest to the respondent's own position, i.e. so that some of the items fall on one side of the respondent's own position and some fall on the other side. Coombs describes a procedure which enables this to be achieved when the rankings are done by a large number of respondents. The mathematics of this procedure are too complicated to be described here, but it yields information concerning both the unidimensionality of the scale and the relative spacing between the individual items in the scale without recourse to the panel of judges required in the classical Thurstone method.

Summated ratings

The method of attitude scaling which is basic to most current attitude research is that devised by Likert (1932). The major steps in this procedure are as follows:

(1) A large number of attitude statements are gathered from various sources, an attempt being made to include an approximately even number of favourable and unfavourable items. (2) A rating scale is attached to each item such as that in Figure 14.1. Respondents are required to go through the statements selecting one of these rating categories as best representing their own position. (3) Numbers are assigned to each of the rating categories, e.g. 1–7 or 7–1, with the order depending upon the direction of wording (favourable or unfavourable) of the statement. (4) The total score on the attitude scale for each subject is calculated by adding the numbers assigned to all of the categories selected. (5) In the process of developing the scale individual items may be discarded if they fail to correlate in the predicted direction with the whole test score. Alternatively the concept of the scale as unidimensional may be abandoned and a multidimensional scoring system developed.

This is clearly a more convenient method of measuring attitudes than the Thurstone technique and many modifications of it are currently in use. There are certain criticisms to be made of it though, and these will be discussed below.

Scalogram analysis

Guttman (1950) argued that if a set of attitude statements form a 'true' scale then it should be possible to reproduce perfectly the responses of an individual to every item given a single score. In this case, we would have a *cumulative scale*, i.e. one in which endorsement of a given item implies endorsement of all items below it in the scale. Guttman scaling has also been called the method of 'successive hurdles', the analogy being that an athlete who is able to jump a hurdle of a given height should have no difficulty clearing lower ones.

One kind of cumulative scale which has been widely used existed before Guttman described his technique. This is the social distance scale (Bogardus, 1925) which was designed to assess the acceptability of various national or ethnic groups. Instructions given to subjects are: 'According to my first feeling reactions, I would willingly admit members of each race (as a class, and not the best I have known, nor the worst members) to one or more of the classifications under which I have placed a "cross".

1. To close kinship by marriage.
2. To my club as personal chums.
3. To my street as neighbours.
4. To employment in my occupation.
5. To citizenship in my country.
6. As visitors only in my country.
7. Would exclude from my country'.

It was intended that these should form a cumulative scale such that accepting one level of intimacy would imply acceptance of all the levels below. In the United States this has generally been found to hold true, very few reversals being observed, but there is evidence that the same order of intimacy of relationships may not hold good for Britain (Eysenck, 1954). Apparently in this country admission to citizenship and employment indicate a greater degree of acceptance of a group than admission to the same street as neighbours or to one's club as personal friends.

In terms of the tripartite classification of attitudes mentioned above, the Bogardus scale deals with the conative (behavioural intention) component of attitude. Therefore it is likely to be a relatively good predictor of overt behaviour such as racial discrimination; but by the same token it may be of less general psychological interest. One other slight limitation of the Bogardus scale—an extreme anti-attitude sometimes involves. more than a desire to maintain social distance; it may involve a desire for punishment, or even elimination of the group.

Factor analysis
The classical techniques for scaling attitudes are primarily concerned with the development of unidimensional scales, i.e. the object is classified in relation to one dimension only. With the advent of computer techniques for analysing data, they have been rendered obsolete to a large extent because there are statistical methods available for discovering the dimensionality of a field of attitudes (the number of important dimensions involved and the relationships among them) and for providing scores on each of these dimensions. The most widely used multidimensional scaling technique is factor analysis, which has been discussed in Chapter 7. The structure of social attitudes as it is revealed by factor analysis will be outlined in a later section.

Opinion polling
Opinion polling is a specialised kind of attitude research in which interest is focussed on the proportion of the population at large favouring different positions on various controversies. Thus, for example, concern is with whether or not a majority of people favour legalisation of marijuana rather than with the psychological basis of attitudes on this issue. Opinion pollsters are therefore particularly concerned about the representativeness of the sample of people that they question rather than with individual differences among the people in their sample.

There are various techniques used for approximating a representative sample. *Random sampling* means giving every individual in the population an equal chance of being selected. In practice this is very difficult to obtain. For example, if every 100th person listed in a telephone directory is selected for study, we have at best only a random sample of telephone subscribers in the area covered by the directory. Most simple procedures for obtaining a random sample involve some systematic form of bias which means that the sample can seldom be said to be more than an approximation to randomness. A more widely used procedure is *quota sampling* in which the proportions of people in each age, sex and occupational group, for example, are arranged in the sample so as to reflect the known proportions of these characteristics in the population at large. An effort is made to randomise selection within each demographic category.

Opinion polls are well known in connection with attempts to predict election outcomes. At this they have been fairly successful, although when parties have been closely matched some notable reversals on the prediction have occurred. They are also used by governments for guidance in policy-making and by consumer researchers in assessing attitudes to current or experimental products. Sociologists also use opinion polls to investigate the connection between opinions and various demographic factors such as age and social class.

It is well-known that the proportion of the population endorsing a particular opinion will vary enormously according to the exact wording of the statement with which they are required to agree or disagree. Results of many opinion surveys have been seriously biased by the use of statements which are vague, ambiguous or loaded. Eysenck (1954) cites a striking example: 'Does small business need a government wet-nurse in all its daily activities?' Not surprisingly, 97% of people interviewed responded 'No'. Many attempts to assess attitudes by questionnaires have fallen into a similar trap.

Importance of item format
One of the problems with the directional statement form of item that is frequently used in both opinion polls and attitude questionnaires is the tendency for people to agree with almost any idea that is authoritatively and persuasively worded. This tendency has been called 'acquiescence response bias'. For example, referring to Table 14.2, there is no doubt that many people would happily agree with both the first (most strongly antiwar) and last (most pro-war) statement in the scale because the emotional conviction carried by the wording is sufficient to override any logical incompatibility between them. Apparently this can occur even if the items are not deliberately loaded as in the case quoted by Eysenck.

A solution to this problem that seems appropriate

Table 14.3   The Wilson–Patterson Attitude Inventory: instructions, items and format

WHICH OF THE FOLLOWING DO YOU FAVOUR OR BELIEVE IN?

(Circle 'Yes' or 'No'. If absolutely uncertain, circle '?'. There are no right or wrong answers; do not discuss; just give your first reaction. Answer all items)

1	death penalty	Yes	?	No	26	computer music	Yes	?	No
2	evolution theory	Yes	?	No	27	chastity	Yes	?	No
3	school uniforms	Yes	?	No	28	fluoridation	Yes	?	No
4	striptease shows	Yes	?	No	29	royalty	Yes	?	No
5	Sabbath observance	Yes	?	No	30	women judges	Yes	?	No
6	beatniks	Yes	?	No	31	conventional clothing	Yes	?	No
7	patriotism	Yes	?	No	32	teenage drivers	Yes	?	No
8	modern art	Yes	?	No	33	apartheid	Yes	?	No
9	self-denial	Yes	?	No	34	nudist camps	Yes	?	No
10	working mothers	Yes	?	No	35	church authority	Yes	?	No
11	horoscopes	Yes	?	No	36	disarmament	Yes	?	No
12	birth control	Yes	?	No	37	censorship	Yes	?	No
13	military drill	Yes	?	No	38	white lies	Yes	?	No
14	co-education	Yes	?	No	39	birching	Yes	?	No
15	Divine law	Yes	?	No	40	mixed marriage	Yes	?	No
16	socialism	Yes	?	No	41	strict rules	Yes	?	No
17	white superiority	Yes	?	No	42	jazz	Yes	?	No
18	cousin marriage	Yes	?	No	43	straitjackets	Yes	?	No
19	moral training	Yes	?	No	44	casual living	Yes	?	No
20	suicide	Yes	?	No	45	learning Latin	Yes	?	No
21	chaperones	Yes	?	No	46	divorce	Yes	?	No
22	legalised abortion	Yes	?	No	47	inborn conscience	Yes	?	No
23	empire-building	Yes	?	No	48	coloured immigration	Yes	?	No
24	student pranks	Yes	?	No	49	Bible truth	Yes	?	No
25	licensing laws	Yes	?	No	50	pyjama parties	Yes	?	No

for some purposes was proposed by Wilson and Patterson (1968). They suggested using brief catch-phrases to represent controversial issues without embodying them in any propositional context. The simplification involved here is that the evaluation of the issues occurs only in subjects' responses, not in the wording of the item itself. An example of such a questionnaire that has been widely used in attitude research is given in Table 14.3. Evidence suggests that the method is not only economical by comparison to statement-form questionnaires, it is at least equally reliable and valid, and relatively free of the effects of acquiescence and social desirability response biases (Wilson, 1973). Of course, this method is more appropriate to investigating broad attitude dimensions than scaling attitudes on specific issues such as war or fluoridation.

Indirect attitude measures

While questionnaires and inventories are far and away the most convenient and widely used of attitude assessment techniques, the transparency of their intent and their susceptibility to certain response biases has led some researchers to seek indirect and disguised methods. Physiological indices such as the G.S.R. and pupillary dilation/contraction have occasionally been employed in attitude research. These have the advantage of getting fairly directly at the central affective component of attitudes, but they are impractical for most experimental purposes and crude in the sense that it is always difficult to know precisely what internal or external event is responsible for a particular physiological response.

Some investigators study behaviour relating to the attitude object and infer the attitude from it. For example, the 'lost letter technique' involves the dispersal of letters addressed to a person or group which represents the attitude object (e.g. The John Birch Society; The Communist Party). The street address given will actually take all the letters to the investigator's headquarters. The favourability of attitude score is based simply on the number of letters that arrive at their destination, the assumption being that people are more likely to post a 'lost' letter to a person or organisation which they favour than one which they dislike. If people put their own stamp on such a letter, this is taken to indicate a higher level of favourability. Subject samples can be varied according to the locality in which the letters are dispersed (e.g. outside various clubs or churches). Behavioural methods such as this are of some theoretical interest and may be used to check results obtained by questionnaires, but of course, they are also too cumbersome to be used routinely.

Other indirect methods of attitude measurement are disguised as perceptual or judgmental tasks. A particularly neat example of such a technique is based on the previously mentioned discovery that the assignment of attitude statements to scale value categories in the Thurstone procedure is biased by the attitudes of the judges who are doing the assigning. It follows that it is possible to measure attitudes in people by having them rate a standard set of attitude statements in terms of their favourability/unfavourability with respect to the issue in question. Referring back to the scale of attitudes towards war, the individual who is strongly antiwar will tend to rate the statements as generally pro-war and *vice versa*. The reason seems to be that we tend to regard our own position on a controversial topic as fairly normal no matter how aberrant it actually is.

The indirect attitude measures have some specialised usefulness, but for general purposes they are unlikely to replace the questionnaire. Problems of falsification and social desirability response bias are actually not very pressing in attitude measurement because our own attitudes are usually by definition the 'good' and 'desirable' ones. Whether it is preferable to be described as liberal or conservative, for example, depends upon our own position on that continuum. For this reason it has been found less necessary to disguise the intent of attitude measures than techniques for assessing personality.

ATTITUDES AND BEHAVIOUR
The question has frequently been raised by laymen and experts alike, whether attitude measures are predictive of actual behaviour in relation to the attitude object. The general assumption pervading all of the early literature on attitudes and a great deal of contemporary research is that attitudes have causal priority in relation to overt behaviour. That is, holding a certain attitude is supposed to have a determining influence on one's behaviour toward the attitude object, e.g. a man is presumed to exercise discrimination against Jews because of his anti-Semitic attitude.

While this view of the attitude–behaviour relationship might appear self-evident to the layman, it is certainly not accepted by all psychologists. The strict behaviourist would argue that it is meaningless to attempt to explain behaviour as resulting from a mental event since we are never able to observe the mental event itself. According to the behavioural school of psychology, the attitude is inferred from the observation of behavioural consistencies and never represents more than a summary of all the responses observed (whether overt acts or answers to a questionnaire). The cognitive psychologist might reply that it is necessary to impute an attitude in order to explain why the behaviour shows any consistency in the first place. Once the locus of the attitude is established as

inside the organism, then the assumption that it has causal priority over behaviour appears far more reasonable.

There is, however, at least one sense in which attitudes are apparently a result of behaviour rather than a cause. The experiments of Leon Festinger and his colleagues on what they have called 'cognitive dissonance' phenomena show that if a person is compelled to behave in a particular way then his attitudes are likely to undergo a process of change which would tend to bring them into line (consonance or consistency) with that previously occurring behaviour. Apparently, attitudes may be adopted in order to justify or rationalise behaviour that has already occurred, e.g. the 'sour grapes' phenomenon. Thus there is no necessary or simple causal connection between attitudes on the one hand and overt behaviour on the other; they are mutually interdependent in a very complex way.

Let us consider the empirical evidence concerning the extent to which attitude measures are actually correlated with overt behaviour. Wicker (1969) summarised a large number of previous studies that he saw as bearing on the assumption that attitudes have consequences for behaviour outside of the testing situation. In general, the results showed that relationships between attitude measures and overt behaviour were significant but of a low order of magnitude. Correlation coefficients relating the two kinds of response were rarely greater than 0.3, and only seldom was as much as 10% of the variance in overt behaviour accounted for by the attitude measure. In studies in which data had been dichotomised into discrepant *v.* non-discrepant subject groups, substantial proportions of subjects showed an attitude–behaviour discrepancy. This finding apparently held true even when subjects scoring towards the polar extremes on the attitude measures were compared on the behavioural indices. Wicker concluded that there is 'little evidence to support the postulated existence of stable underlying attitudes within the individual which influence both his verbal expressions and his actions'.

Although the findings of this survey might appear discouraging to researchers who expect that their attitude measures will be predictive of overt behaviour, there are a number of reasons why they should be interpreted cautiously.

(1) We should not expect the correlation between attitudes and behaviour to be perfect anyway, because attitudes are not the only determinants of behaviour. There are many other classes of variables that need to be considered before it would be possible to even approximate a perfect prediction of behaviour. For example, whether or not a landlord manifests racial discrimination in selecting tenants might depend not only upon the extent to which he is prejudiced, but also on his knowledge of his liability to prosecution under the Race Relations Act, and his estimate of the

chances of an action being brought against him. Any given piece of behaviour is governed by a multiplex of personality and situational variables.

Wicker (1971) describes a study that was specifically conducted to investigate the possibility that measuring other variables in addition to attitudes would facilitate prediction of overt behaviour. Besides measuring attitudes toward the Church, he obtained verbal measures of (a) perceived consequences of taking part in various Church activities (e.g. Does church attendance set a good example to one's children?) (b) evaluation of participation in church activities (e.g. the degree of approval/disapproval attached to the idea of missing church twice a month), and (c) the judged influence of extraneous events (e.g. Would church attendance be affected by non-religious weekend guests?). All four variables were investigated as partial predictors of three behavioural criteria: Sunday service attendance, monetary contributions (both estimated from church records), and serving in responsible roles in church activities (self-report). Consistent with the 'other variables' explanation of attitude–behaviour discrepancies, addition of the verbal predictors to the attitude measures in a stepwise regression analysis did significantly improve predictions of the three behavioural criteria. The best single predictor of behaviour was judged influence of extraneous events (mean $r = .36$), followed by evaluation of behaviour (mean $r = .26$), attitude to the Church (mean $r = .22$), and perceived consequences of behaviour (mean $r = .15$). Clearly, attitudes are not the only predictors of behaviour; nor are they necessarily the best.

(2) It is not always possible to be certain what attitude will predict what behaviour. Kiesler *et al.* (1969) point out that 'our notions that a particular attitude correlates with a particular behaviour may be incorrect not because of a general failure of attitudes to have any relationship to behaviour, but because our intuitive notions about which attitudinal factors are correlated with which behavioural factors are incorrect'. In other words, we are in a better position to predict overt behaviour if we consider a variety of relevant attitudes, not just the one that is apparently the most directly related.

(3) As a general rule, measures of attitudes toward a specific kind of behaviour are better predictors of that behaviour than general attitudes toward relevant attitude objects. In Wicker's (1971) study, a measure of evaluation of church-related behaviour turned out to be more closely correlated with actual church participation than attitudes toward the church in general. This is in line with a frequently reported finding that the 'action tendency' (conative) component of attitudes is a better predictor of actual behaviour than beliefs or feelings in relation to the attitude object. In fact, close relationships between verbal and behavioural measures may turn out to be almost tautologi-

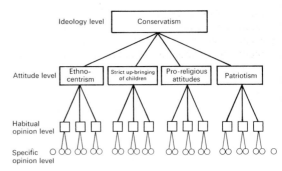

Figure 14.2 Hierarchical model of the relationship between opinions, attitudes, and ideology. (From Eysenck, 1954, by courtesy of Routledge and Kegan Paul)

cal, and trivial in the sense that the verbal measure lacks generalisability to other behaviours and situations because it fails to tap stable and broad personality characteristics or emotional orientations.

(4) The failure of an attitude measure to predict overt behaviour may simply reflect the inadequacy of the attitude measure, i.e. it may mean that the particular attitude measure is not valid, rather than attitude measurement in general. Since many of the studies reviewed by Wicker used tests such as the California F-Scale which are known to be suspect in validity (Wilson, 1973) we can be fairly certain that this explanation applies to at least some of the low correlations between attitude and behaviour that have been reported.

(5) Finally, it should not be forgotten that verbal report is itself a kind of behaviour that requires classification and explanation even if it does not correlate in any obvious and expected way with other forms of behaviour. In fact, one way of operationally defining an attitude that is implicitly adopted by many researchers is to regard an attitude as a cluster of opinions, i.e. as a factor underlying the correlations among several different opinion statements. A hierarchical model of the relationship between opinions, attitudes and ideology has been put forward by Eysenck (1954; Figure 14.2). Also, it is worth noting that questionnaire responses are not always entirely impotent and ineffectual forms of behaviour. For one thing, they determine who is to become President of the United States and Prime Minister of Britain.

MAJOR DIMENSIONS OF SOCIAL ATTITUDES

The classic work on the structure of social attitudes as revealed by factor analysis is that reported by Eysenck in *The Psychology of Politics* (1954). Eysenck identified two broad attitude dimensions which were fairly independent of each other. These he called radicalism–conservatism (R) and tough-mindedness–tender-mindedness (T). The position of various controversial attitudes in relation to these two factors is shown in Figure 14.3. The R factor accounts for somewhat more variation than the T factor. People at the conservative end display religious, nationalistic, ethnocentric and punitive attitudes, while people at the radical end favour redistribution of wealth, sexual permissiveness, pacifism, and world government. Recent research, however, has indicated a need to separate off socio-economic conservatism from general conservatism (conservatism with a small c). These two types of conservatism are fairly independent of each other; that is, issues which relate to capitalism *v*. socialism ('the class struggle') do not relate very closely to issues concerning religion, race, sex or punishments. This gives us three major factors in social attitudes which provide a fairly good summary of the way in which attitudes are organised. It is, of course, possible to break them up further into more specific components, in line with the hierarchical model shown in Figure 14.2; but from the psychological point of view it is the antecedents of the three major factors which are of primary interest.

These three factors have fairly clear demographic

correlates. General conservatism is quite strongly correlated with age (at least after the age of about 30); socio-economic conservatism relates to social class in a fairly predictable way (and, of course, political party affiliation and voting behaviour); tough-mindedness is associated with sex (males are on average more tough-minded than females). However, these demographic correlates do not entirely account for the three-factor attitude structure. Similar factors emerge even when the analysis is conducted on a sample of subjects that is fairly homogeneous with respect to age, sex and social class (e.g. male students). This suggests that other factors, such as personality, are also involved in the determination of social attitudes.

PERSONALITY AND ATTITUDES
Personality correlates of tough-mindedness have been recognised for some time and are well established. High T scores are associated with the P factor (psychoticism) in Eysenck's personality scheme, and possibly also extroversion. They also relate to many other similar traits such as aggressiveness, dominance,

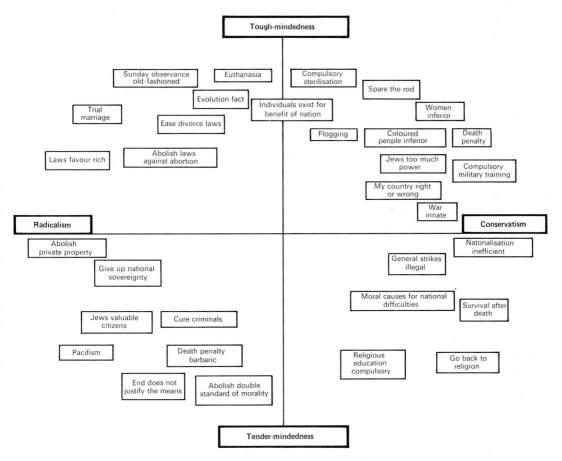

Figure 14.3   The position of various attitudes in relation to Eysenck's R and T factors

authoritarianism, dogmatism, rigidity and intolerance of ambiguity. It is noteworthy that these personality traits are more characteristic of men than women, which indicates a possible hormonal basis for tough-mindedness. Sex, however, is not the sole mediator of the correlations because they also emerge in analyses conducted separately within each sex. These relationships have been demonstrated not just by intercorrelating questionnaires but also with the use of perceptual tests such as the Dog–Cat Test of Intolerance of Ambiguity. This consists of a series of pictures of a dog changing into a cat through various transitional stages; more rigid subjects are inclined to cling to the percept of the dog long after it begins to look like a cat. Projective tests such as the T.A.T. and Rosenzweig Picture-Frustration Study have also supported the relationship between aggression and tough-mindedness. The T.A.T. is a series of vague pictures about which the subject has to write a story (see Chapter 9), while the Rosenzweig Test depicts a number of frustrating situations and the subject is invited to offer a verbal response by writing a comment into a cartoon-type speech-bubble. These two tests can be scored objectively for aggressive content. It has also been shown that Fascists and Communists (who are known to score high on tough-mindedness) likewise tend to be authoritarian, rigid, intolerant of ambiguity, and aggressive compared to controls (Eysenck and Coulter, 1972). All in all, the evidence linking tough-mindedness with traits of the aggressive/psychopathic/authoritarian/dogmatic type is very sound.

For a long time it was assumed that personality was not relevant to the radicalism–conservatism dimension; this was seen to reflect the interests of working-class people versus middle-class people. However, since the discovery that socio-economic conservatism needs to be separated from general conservatism, that view is recognised as an oversimplification. It now seems that socio-economic conservatism is based largely on class interests and is little affected by personality, while general conservatism is intimately bound up with personality.

Some recent research has been directed toward investigating the proposition that general conservatism reflects a characteristic response to situations of uncertainty. The various attitudes that go to make up the broad trait of conservatism can be identified with particular kinds of uncertainty all of which might present a degree of threat to the vulnerable individual. Some of these are located in the external environment, others (e.g. need conflict and freedom of choice) within the individual himself (Table 14.4). This idea began as an attempt to discover a common basis for the various attitudes that comprise the conservatism 'syndrome'. Since these attitude patterns could not be accounted for in terms of logical content overlap, a search was made for a motivational component common to each of the attitude areas which go together to make up the conservatism factor. The concept that seemed best able to account for this organisation of attitudes was that of 'uncertainty'. The suggestion is that some individuals seek to explore and manipulate their environment, and are prepared to accept a high degree of risk in order to satisfy their curiosity and need for variety; these people are prone to develop liberal or radical attitudes. Other people are more

Table 14.4   Fear of uncertainty as the hypothesised basis of conservative attitudes

	Source of threat	*Attitudinal manifestation*	
	Supernatural forces Death The unknown and unpredictable Ambiguity	Superstition Religious dogmatism	
	Anarchy Social disruption	Right-wing politics	
	Unfamiliar people Foreign influences Deviant behaviour	Ethnocentrism Militarism Intolerance of minorities	
FEAR OF UNCERTAINTY	Anomie Disorganisation Dissent	Authoritarianism Punitiveness	GENERAL CONSERVATISM
	Decisions Loss of control of own feelings and desires	Rigid morality Anti-hedonism Adherence to external authority	
	Complexity Novelty Innovation	Conventionality Conformity	
	Technological change Erosion of traditional ideas	Anti-science	

concerned about safety and security both in the physical and (probably more important) in the psychological sense, and these needs over-ride any need they might have for novelty and experience. Such people tend to develop a conservative pattern of attitudes. If we were to seek an evolutionary rationale for the significance of this variation, it could be argued that it is advantageous to a species to have some members engage in exploratory behaviour while others stay home to ensure the continuation of the species in case the more curious 'cats' get eliminated.

Support for this general proposition has come from studies of the personality and behavioural correlates of conservatism as measured by the Wilson–Patterson Inventory (Wilson, 1973). For example, high C scores are associated with a greater fear of death, a preference for safe and secure occupations, preference for types of humour that do not arouse sexual or aggressive feelings, a tendency to remain anonymous in filling out questionnaires, to avoid geographical displacement (e.g. migration) and to dislike paintings that involve a great deal of stimulus complexity. The results of the latter study are shown in Figure 14.4. In this study twenty paintings had been chosen by an art expert, five to represent each of four categories differing in degree of uncertainty: simple-representational, simple-abstract, complex-representational and complex-abstract. Conservative subjects liked the simple paintings but expressed a definite dislike of the complex works—their ratings were actually on the negative side of an indifference point in the rating scale. Studies such as this lend support to the idea that a generalised reaction against uncertainty is the psychological variable which accounts for the organisation of social attitudes along a general factor of

liberalism–conservatism. In this view, the tendency for the conservative person to subjugate his needs and feelings to the social order is seen as a means of reducing choice (response uncertainty).

GENETIC INFLUENCES ON SOCIAL ATTITUDES

The finding that major attitude factors are related to personality dispositions leads naturally to the question of whether genetic factors are involved in the development of attitude patterns. This possibility was recognised by the eminent American attitude researcher William J. McGuire (1969), though he admitted it with some trepidation 'because it seems to imply that "bad" attitudes like racial prejudice will be hard to change and that the genes for malevolent selfish attitudes will increase in frequency because they seem to offer survival value'. McGuire, however, is aware that unattractiveness of a hypothesis is not sufficient to invalidate it, and he goes on to describe some mechanisms by which attitudes might be affected by innate dispositions such as aggressiveness and intergroup hostility. For example, he cites a report that ants normally attack members of their own species who come from other colonies but tolerate with indifference visits to their nest from insects of other species. Thus he says, 'It would not be impossible' for xenophobia to be a partially innate attitude in the human'. McGuire also cites a variety of physiological conditions which are known to affect attitudes, including ageing, illnesses such as encephalitis, tuberculosis and epilepsy, certain drugs and brain surgery. On the basis of observations such as these, McGuire concludes that biological influences on attitudes are feasible, but he notes that in the absence of empirical research these ideas had to be quite conjectural.

The most important study of this question so far available is that of Eaves and Eysenck (1974). They studied the variation and covariation within and between pairs of monozygotic (identical) and dizygotic (fraternal) twins. Tests used were a new version of the Eysenck Personality Inventory, which measures psychoticism, extroversion and neuroticism, and a 60-item social attitude inventory measuring radicalism–conservatism, tough-mindedness, and tendency to give extreme opinions (emphasis). There were 706 pairs of like-sexed twins, 450 of them monozygotic and 256 dizygotic. The pairs had been separated for varying periods of time. Results showed clearly that a simple environmental hypothesis would not account for the co-variation of the six personality and attitude factors. On the other hand, an interactionist (genotype–environmental) hypothesis fitted the data reasonably well. Heritability estimates are given in Table 14.5.

These figures indicate that about half of the variance along these attitude dimensions is determined by heredity (perhaps a little more for the R dimension). Surprisingly, the heritability estimates for the attitude

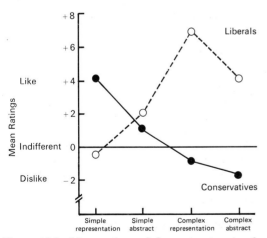

Figure 14.4 Mean ratings of four art categories for liberals and conservatives. (The four types of art are arranged on an *a priori* scale of stimulus uncertainty.) (From Wilson *et al.*, 1973, by courtesy of *J. Personal. Soc. Psychol.*)

Table 14.5 Heritability estimates for personality and social attitude variables based on a comparison of 450 MZ and 256 DZ twins (From Eaves and Eysenck, 1974, by courtesy of *Nature (London)*)

Trait	Heritability estimates
Radicalism–conservatism	0.65
Tough-mindedness	0.54
Emphasis	0.37
Psychoticism	0.35
Extroversion	0.48
Neuroticism	0.49

factors are actually higher than those for the personality dimensions, where a genetic basis has long been recognised (Chapter 10). Eaves and Eysenck were also able to establish from analysis of co-variation that the link between extroversion and tough-minded attitudes has a genetic basis rather than environmental, and that the relationship between psychoticism and tough-mindedness is at least partly genetic. Radicalism–conservatism, however, was not related to the particular personality variables measured by the Eysenck inventory.

Many people find it difficult to credit that attitudes can be so strongly affected by heredity. Many would ask: 'Doesn't this mean that children would have almost identical attitudes to their parents?' In fact, this is not so. Genetic models actually predict a certain degree of difference from one's parents. On the basis of the Eaves and Eysenck model, for example, we would predict parent–child correlations in attitudes to be about 0.2 to 0.3. Several studies of familial correlations in attitudes have produced correlations higher than this; too large in fact, to be consistent with a simple genetic model.

There is a sense in which attitudes are obviously determined by the environment. Whether or not a person favours legalisation of marijuana is going to be affected by the proportion of people in the population who hold different views on that issue. Since more people in the population favour legalisation of marijuana than legalisation of heroin, it follows that the chances of any individual person favouring marijuana will be higher than the chances of him favouring heroin. But this is not what the Eaves and Eysenck study was concerned with; they were investigating the heritability of co-variation in attitudes, i.e. the factors underlying characteristic attitude constellations. Attitudes on specific issues may be largely determined by situational factors and the prevailing social climate, but these sources of variation tend to be cancelled by co-variation analysis. In a similar way, our knowledge of the meaning of any particular word is affected by a great variety of 'chance' environmental factors, but the total size of our vocabulary is much more strongly influenced by our level of general intelligence. In other

words, the broader the factor, the more likely it is to show high heritability. The R and T factors studied by Eaves and Eysenck are quite broad in the sense that they span a wide variety of subject matter; this enables many of the environmental and situational influences to drop out, thus increasing the apparent influence of genetic, dispositional factors. Environmental influences on social attitudes are very real, however; some of the more important of them will be discussed below under the heading of attitude change.

ATTITUDES TO TREATMENT

Before going on to discuss the area of attitude change it might be useful for illustrative purposes to describe one extension of general attitude factor measurement into an applied/social field. One such area is that of attitudes to treatment. A number of recent studies have been concerned with the attitudes of psychiatric staff (doctors and nurses) to different types of treatment, and the way in which these tie in with social attitudes in general. Other studies in these series have investigated patients' attitudes to treatment and their expectations and preferences with respect to different types of treatment.

For purposes of this kind T. Caine and his colleagues at Claybury Hospital in Essex (e.g. Caine and Smail, 1969) have developed an Attitudes to Treatment Questionnaire (A.T.Q.) which patients and staff complete to reveal ward attitudes and liking for different kinds of treatment. In one study, conservative psychiatric nurses (according to scores on the Wilson–Patterson Inventory) were shown to have traditional views of hospital ward organisation, emphasising formal staff/patient relationships. Liberal nurses were more in favour of group psychotherapy and the therapeutic community approach.

A study by Pallis and Stoffelmayr (1972) revealed strong relationships between the attitudes to treatment of psychiatrists and their general social attitudes as measured by both the Wilson–Patterson and Eysenck Inventories. Conservatism was associated with a predilection for physical treatments (E.C.T., drugs, and psychosurgery), the need for hygiene, strict discipline and maintenance of the staff's image as omnipotent people. Tough-mindedness was also associated with these characteristics, though to a lesser degree. Another interesting finding was that the less conservative doctor chose his psychiatric specialisation earlier on in his medical career than the more conservative doctor. This might be interpreted as suggesting that the liberal psychiatrist has more of a humanitarian 'calling' to his specialisation. A group of psychiatrists who stated that they did not use psychotherapy in their practice were found to be significantly more conservative than those who did practise psychotherapy; they were also more physically oriented on the A.T.Q.

In another study, Pallis and Stoffelmayr (1973)

showed that psychiatrists who had received formal training in psychotherapy were more liberal and tender-minded than those who had not, and that they tended to favour psychological methods of treatment against physical treatments on the A.T.Q. Although these findings, like those above, do not establish causal relationships, the researchers argue that it is more likely that the psychiatrists choose their training because of the attitudes they hold rather than the other way about. In view of the broad base of the major attitude factors it does seem unlikely that they would be greatly modified by brief training in psychotherapy.

Caine and Leigh (1972) studied the attitudes of 85 neurotic out-patients. Those scoring high on conservatism tended to favour behaviour therapy while the liberals showed a preference for group therapy. This result suggests that behaviour therapy, being directive and authoritarian to a certain extent in its nature, and promising a simple, straight-forward cure, is more consistent with the expectations and personality needs of conservative patients. Verbal/insight therapies are presumably less acceptable because they are intraceptive, self-indulgent, and involve a great deal more psychological 'risk' and uncertainty.

Even more interesting was the discovery that patients assigned to behaviour therapy were more conservative than those assigned to group therapy. This implied to the authors that conservative patients must have presented their problems to the psychiatrist in a way that invited or 'demanded' a more authoritarian form of therapy. Caine and Leigh speculate that conservatives, in presenting their case, may have laid greater emphasis on symptomology than on interpersonal difficulties and so were more likely to be assigned to behaviour therapy for the removal of their symptoms. Whatever the precise mechanism, it is interesting to discover that the patient's general social attitudes are partial determinants of the doctor's decision as to what form of psychiatric treatment is appropriate.

Robertson and Kapur (1972) found that students who experience emotional distress are more likely to consult a doctor if they are high in conservatism. Apparently the more radical students are less likely to seek help from an 'establishment' doctor and are more inclined to see their problem as 'existential' and beyond the scope of traditional medical practice.

These studies taken together incline us towards several conclusions: (1) Behaviour therapy, with its emphasis on symptom removal rather than interpersonal relationships is perceived by both patients and psychiatric staff as more closely related to physical and traditional treatment procedures. (2) Behaviour therapy and physical treatments are favoured by conservative and tough-minded psychiatrists and patients alike. (3) The attitudes of both are involved in determining the kind of treatment that is prescribed

and received; together they may account for an appreciable amount of the variance in the assignment of different treatments. Future research might profitably consider the hypothesis that conservative and tough-minded patients would actually derive greater benefit from physical treatments and behaviour therapy compared with liberal and tender-minded patients who might be expected to do better with group therapy.

ATTITUDE CHANGE

We have seen that major attitude factors are strongly influenced by heredity. To this extent they are resistant to change. Nevertheless, nearly half of the variance in factors such as conservatism and tough-mindedness is contributed by environmental factors of various kinds. What is more, attitudes relating to specific issues such as marijuana, space travel, or women's liberation, are more open to the influence of experience—social effects, the 'media', vested interests, etc. Environmental influences such as these, and the factors which modify their effects, are usually discussed under the heading of attitude change.

Attitude change is one of the most central problems in social psychology, and its implications are most profound. Whenever we engage in debate or 'discussion' with other persons we are usually trying to effect some change in their attitudes, i.e. convert them to our own point of view. Advertisers, evangelists, political campaigners and propagandists are specifically engaged in changing people's attitudes, and much of the work of teachers and psychotherapists could be viewed in a similar way.

Like any technology, attitude change procedures can be used for purposes judged as good or bad; and how the change is evaluated depends upon one's point of view. If we are persuaded to smoke cigarettes the manufacturers will be pleased, but our life insurance company will not. For the individual, a knowledge of attitude change processes may be useful in helping us to convert others to our point of view and in resisting unwanted modification of our viewpoint.

Research on attitude change has dealt with four major components of the communication process: the source, the message, the medium (channel), and the audience. These will now be discussed in turn.

Studies that focus on the *source* of the communication are concerned with characteristics of the person or group from whom the message originates. One of the best studied characteristics of the source is its credibility. Attitude change is enhanced when the communicator is perceived as knowledgeable and trustworthy. This is the basis of the well-known advertising approach in which, for example, a man in a white coat seated at a desk and surrounded by various props such as a stethoscope, writing materials, and shelves of scientific volumes, is seen to recommend a particular toothpaste, shampoo or pain-killer. Specialised 'experts' are usually most persuasive, but prestige in any field will to some extent generalise to others. Thus people in high status occupations have been shown to pull greater weight on juries than people in low status occupations.

Also important in determining our readiness to accept a message is the motivation that we attribute to the agent who is addressing the message to us. Obviously we are more on our guard against persuasion by salesmen, political campaigners and religious proselytisers than we are against newscasters scientists, and teachers. Anybody with a strong personal investment in the message or anybody who seems to be working 'too hard' to change our attitudes is likely to evoke suspicion and resistance. There is some evidence that we are more open to persuasion if we are distracted during the presentation of the communication, or if we overhear it rather than have it addressed directly to us.

Altogether, the importance of source credibility seems to be well-established. However, it appears that its effect is sometimes short-lived. In a classic experiment by Hovland and Weiss (1951), statements attributed to highly credible sources gave rise to a significantly greater amount of attitude change than statements attributed to untrustworthy sources, but only when attitudes were assessed immediately after the communication. Four weeks later the difference between the two had completely disappeared; the amount of attitude change in the high-credibility group had dropped back, while the low-credibility group showed an increase in agreement with the communication (Figure 14.5). Apparently, the identity of

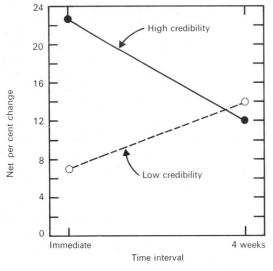

Figure 14.5 The effect of communicator credibility on attitude change as a function of time of assessment. (From Hovland and Weiss, 1951, by courtesy of *Publ. Opin. Quart.*)

the communicator becomes less salient over time compared to the content of the communication itself. This effect is presumably most marked when the communication is sufficiently well-reasoned to stand on its own merits.

Another important aspect of the source of a communication is its attractiveness. When a well-known actor or sportsman endorses a commercial product we are influenced not so much on the basis of his credibility but because we want to think of ourselves as similar to him. Attitude change is also enhanced if the audience see themselves as actually similar to the source. This identification process, as it is often called, may be strong enough to determine the very direction in which attitude change occurs. Several investigators have found that if the source is sufficiently unappealing to the audience a 'boomerang' effect may be observed, with attitudes hardening against the communicator.

There are many characteristics of the *message* which also affect the amount and direction of attitude change that may be expected to occur One of the most important is the extent to which the position advocated by the message differs from that originally held by the audience. Moderate levels of discrepancy produce a maximum amount of attitude change. Apparently the message needs to be close enough to the standing attitudes of the audience to allow assimilation to take place; if it is too alien to the audience it is likely to arouse antagonism and produce a contrast effect. The idea of shifting attitudes in one direction by having a fanatical stooge advocate the opposite point of view in a highly offensive manner has been consciously employed both in experimental and applied settings.

The concept of assimilation has further meaning. Attitude change is facilitated if the communicator begins by presenting material which is readily acceptable to the audience in order to gain their confidence. Once he is perceived by the audience as a moderate and reasonable person he can gradually shift his position along the scale in the desired direction, always being careful not to pull so far away from them that assimilation can no longer be sustained. A fine example of persuasion using this principle, among others, is found in Mark Antony's famous 'Friends, Romans, Countrymen' speech. The amount of discrepancy that is tolerable to the audience varies according to a number of other factors; for example, the extent to which they are committed or emotionally involved with the issue. If an audience is highly involved they will tolerate much less discrepancy before assimilation gives way to contrast.

A related question is whether the communicator or propagandist is best to acknowledge and refute the opposite point of view, or simply to ignore it. Research generally indicates that a two-sided presentation is superior when the audience initially holds a very discrepant point of view, and when they are highly intelligent. If the communication is fairly congruent with existing attitudes, or if the audience is fairly dull, a one-sided presentation may be superior. Two-sided presentations are generally at an advantage, though, in terms of building resistance to counter-propaganda; if the audience has already encountered the opposing point of view, perhaps in a weakened form (the 'inoculation' method), and given reasons for discounting it, they are better placed to resist attempts to reverse the previously established attitude change. Thus two-sided communications are not always more effective in changing attitudes but the effects, once achieved, tend to be more permanent.

Order of presentation is another variable that has been frequently studied. In accordance with the notion of assimilation it has been found better to deliver the more palatable material first and introduce less desirable arguments later on. Other research has suggested that an emotional appeal of some kind (e.g. arousal of fear, anger, or sympathy) followed by factual information is more effective in changing attitudes than factual information followed by an emotional appeal. This seems to be especially true if the factual information provides some degree of comfort in the form of cognitive understanding or a rational solution to the emotive problem that has been raised. If threat is used in a persuasive communication it is apparently best that it be in mild form; overly intense threats in a message once again seem to cause antagonism and thus rejection of the message.

To maximise the prospect of change the content of the communication should also take account of the motivational support of the original attitude. Ideally, the audience should be persuaded that the new position is consistent with the needs that were served by the original position, or the cardinal values expressed therein. For example, if a person is opposed to vivisection on the ground that it offends his humanitarian ideals, then propaganda emphasising the medical advances resulting from animal experiments and the consequent relief from suffering of sick people would be more effective than arguments based, say, on the dispensability of animals.

The effectiveness of propaganda also depends upon the *medium* (radio, television, newspaper, word-of-mouth etc.). This aspect of the communication process has received relatively little research attention; nevertheless some reasonably secure conclusions have been reached. For example, it has been shown that personal contact is nearly always more efficient than mass media in changing attitudes. Katz and Lazarsfeld (1955) studied the relative impact of personal influence and various kinds of mass media in determining changes in domestic produce preferences, hair styles, make-up, clothing, and choice of movies to attend. In each case, personal contact was found to have a stronger influence than any of the mass media. However, there was some evidence to suggest a 'two-step' process by which ideas are distilled from the media by certain influential persons, and passed on to the rest of the community by face to face contact with these 'opinion leaders'.

Individuals in the *audience* vary in the extent to which they are open to being persuaded. For example, women tend to be more suggestible (or less stubborn?) than men. Other studies have shown that people who are low in self-esteem are more susceptible to the effects of persuasive communications. Janis (1954), for example, found that students who displayed social inadequacy, inhibition of aggression, and depressive tendencies were most open to attitude change. On the other hand, students with other neurotic symptoms (e.g. obsessionality, anxiety and hysteria) were relatively impervious to persuasive communications. Intelligence is also a relevant factor, but its relationship to persuasibility is complex. Highly intelligent people are better able to comprehend, learn and draw appropriate conclusions from persuasive communications; they are also better able to assess the reliability of a source and are more critical of the conclusions drawn by the communicator.

If the audience can be made to participate actively in the communication process, this is likely to increase the extent to which attitude change occurs. Janis and King (1954) found that students who were induced to deliver a talk advocating a position different from their own changed their beliefs more than a group of passive listeners. A later experiment by the same researchers showed that the amount of opinion change produced through active participation was a function of the degree of improvisation. That is, beliefs are more markedly changed when the subject is required to reformulate the arguments, devise illustrations, and think of new ways in which to persuade others. However, there is a suggestion that in this area too, excessive pressure toward conformity may have a contrary effect on attitudes; some subjects appeared to resent the inducements to conform and displayed less opinion change than passive subjects who had not participated in presenting the message.

The studies of audience participation and attitude change provide an example of the general finding that changes in behaviour may be antecedent to changes in attitude. As noted previously, studies on forced compliance have indicated that if a subject is compelled to behave in a manner inconsistent with his attitudes, his attitudes may subsequently change so as to make them more consonant with the previous behaviour. This is related to the process of commitment, by which public statements of one's position lead to its further consolidation.

Interestingly, the less reason a person has for acting in a manner inconsistent with his attitudes, the greater is likely to be the amount of attitude change resulting from that action. The classic experiment showing this effect is that of Festinger and Carlsmith (1959). Subjects were paid either one dollar or twenty dollars to tell another person that a very boring experiment they had just participated in was really very interesting. When their attitudes to the experiment were subsequently measured, it was found that the heavily bribed subjects continued to regard the experiment as dull, but those paid only a nominal amount had come to believe it was in fact quite enjoyable. Festinger interprets this result in terms of his theory of 'cognitive dissonance'. He argues that mental discomfort is evoked when our behaviour is perceived as incompatible with our attitudes. Since it is too late to change our behaviour the only way to reduce this discomfort is to change the attitude. This however, is not necessary if another rationalisation of our unorthodox behaviour is available, and having received a large sum of money for it constitutes such an excuse. Presumably, the subjects who had been 'bought cheap' in the Festinger and Carlsmith experiment were unable to admit this to themselves, and so found it necessary to change their attitudes.

It is beyond the scope of this chapter to discuss Festinger's theory in detail. It is one of several theories that have been constructed in an attempt to make sense of the complexities of attitude change phenomena. The various 'consistency' theories that have been put forward have a great deal in common, but cognitive dissonance has probably stimulated the most research. The findings that are claimed in support of it are not always replicated; others are amenable to alternative interpretation. Nevertheless, it has proved valuable in suggesting many novel experiments in the field of attitude change and in making sense of certain phenomena that at first sight seem paradoxical in the framework of reinforcement theory (Chapter 4). These odd findings should not, however, blind us to the major principles operating in the field. In broad terms, attitudes develop and change as they serve important needs, motives and goals, i.e. they are instrumental in providing satisfaction, whether it be conceptualised at the mental or physiological level. Cognitive dissonance phenomena are at least consistent with this general statement.

References

Bogardus, E. S. (1925). Measuring social distance. *J. Appl. Sociol.*, 9, 299–308

Caine, T. M. and Smail, D. J. (1969). *The Treatment of Mental Illness: Science, Faith and the Therapeutic Personality* (London: University Press)

Caine, T. M. and Leigh, R. (1972). Conservatism in relation to psychiatric treatment. *Brit. J. Soc. Clin. Psychol.*, 11, 52–56

Coombs, C. H. (1964). *A Theory of Data* (New York: Wiley)

Eaves, L. J. and Eysenck, H. J. (1974). Genetics and the development of social attitudes. *Nature (London)*, 249, 288–289

Ehrlich, H. J. (1964). Instrument error and the study of prejudice. *Social Forces*, 43, 197–206

Eysenck, H. J. (1954). *The Psychology of Politics* (London: Routledge and Kegan Paul)

Eysenck, H. J. and Coulter, T. T. (1972). The personality and attitudes of working-class British Communists and Fascists. *J. Soc. Psychol.*, 87, 59–73

Festinger, L. and Carlsmith, J. M. (1959). Cognitive consequences of forced compliance. *J. Abn. Soc. Psychol.*, 58, 203–210

Guttman, L. (1950). The third component of scalable attitudes. *Int. J. Opin. Attitude Res.*, 4, 285–287

Hovland, C. I. and Weiss, W. (1951). The influence of source credibility on communication effectiveness. *Publ. Opin. Quart.*, 15, 635–650

Janis, I. L. (1954). Personality correlates of susceptibility to persuasion. *J. Personal.*, 22, 504–578

Janis, I. L. and King, B. T. (1954). The influence of role playing on opinion-change. *J. Abn. Soc. Psychol.*, 49, 211–218

Katz, E. and Lazarsfeld, P. F. (1955). *Personal Influence The Part Played by People in the Flow of Mass Communications* (Glencoe, Illinois: Free Press)

Kiesler, C. A., Collins, B. E. and Miller, N. (1969). *Attitude Change: A Critical Analysis of Theoretical Approaches* (New York: Wiley)

Krech, D. Crutchfield, R. S. and Ballachev, E. L. (1962). *Individuals in Society* (New York: McGraw-Hill)

Likert, R. A. (1932). A technique for the measurement of attitudes. *Arch. Psychol.*, No. 140

McGuire, W. J. (1969). The nature of attitudes and attitude research. In: *Handbook of Social Psychology* (2nd Ed.) (G. Lindzey and A. Aronson, editors) (London: Addison-Wesley)

Pallis, D. J. and Stoffelmayr, B. E. (1972). Training preferences, social attitudes, and treatment orientations among psychiatrists. *J. Clin. Psychol.*, 28, 216–217

Pallis, D. J. and Stoffelmayr, B. E. (1973). Social attitudes and treatment orientations among psychiatrists. *Brit. J. Med. Psychol.*, 46, 75–81

Peterson, R. C. and Thurstone, L. L. (1933). *Motion Pictures and the Social Attitudes of Children* (New York: Macmillan)

Robertson, A. and Kapur, R. L. (1972). Social change, emotional distress, and world view of students: An empirical study of the existentialist ethic and the spirit of suffering. *Brit. J. Sociol.*, 23, 462–477

Sherif, C. W., Sherif, M. and Nebergall, R. E. (1965). *Attitude and Attitude Change* (Philadelphia: Saunders)

Thurstone, L. L. (1931). The measurement of social attitudes. *J. Abn. Soc. Psychol.*, 26, 249–269

Wicker, A. W. (1969). Attitudes versus actions: The relationship of verbal and overt behavioural responses to attitude objects. *J. Soc. Issues*, 25, 41–78

Wicker, A. W. (1971). An examination of the 'other variables' explanation of attitude–behaviour inconsistency. *J. Personal. Soc. Psychol.*, 19, 18–30

Wilson, G. D. and Patterson, J. R. (1968). A new measure of conservatism. *Brit. J. Soc. Clin. Psychol.*, 7, 264–269

Wilson, G. D. (editor) (1973). *The Psychology of Conservatism* (London: Academic Press)

Wilson, G. D., Ausman, J. and Mathews, T. R. (1973). Conservatism and art preferences. *J. Personal. Soc. Psychol.*, 25, 286–288

ABNORMAL AND
APPLIED PSYCHOLOGY

Chapter 15

VARIETIES OF ABNORMAL BEHAVIOUR

D. K. B. Nias

INTRODUCTION

Mental disorders have been traditionally classified in terms of specific labels such as 'anxiety state' or 'paranoid schizophrenia', and in terms of general labels such as 'neurosis' or 'psychosis'. Official classifications have been provided by organisations such as the American Psychiatric Association (1968). Table 15.1 presents the framework of this system, which is based on the very detailed one set out by the World Health Organisation (1967) in the *International Classification of Diseases*.

One of the major distinctions in psychiatry is between organic disorders (i.e. those with an obvious physical cause) and functional disorders (i.e. those with no apparent physical cause). An example of the former would be mental retardation caused by brain damage, and of the latter a phobia due to faulty learning. Within the functional disorders another major distinction is between neurosis and psychosis. In neurosis, only a part of the personality is affected, the patient remains in contact with reality and he has insight into his disorder. The symptoms may involve sensory, sexual, motor or visceral disturbances and mental disturbances such as anxiety, phobias, trance-states, troublesome thoughts, difficulty in sleeping and lack of physical energy. A psychosis is more severe or disruptive, affecting all areas of a patient's life. The whole personality tends to be disturbed and reality has little meaning to the patient or is perceived in a distorted way. There is a failure to relate effectively to other people, there is sometimes a bizarre disturbance of language or thinking, and hallucinations or delusions may appear.

Personality disorders, which usually include psychopathy or sociopathy, are classified separately to neurosis and psychosis. Psychopathy is a disorder that is characterised by the patient causing distress to others rather than himself. This type of patient lacks the ability to experience normal emotions such as guilt, affection and genuine concern for the welfare of others. As a result he is unable to delay the gratification of his desires regardless of the consequences;

Table 15.1 Major categories of mental disorder. (From American Psychiatric Association, 1968)

I. Mental retardation	Phobic neurosis
II. Organic brain syndromes (disorders caused by or associated with impairment of brain tissue function, such as senile dementia and alcoholic psychosis)	Obsessive-compulsive neurosis
	Depressive neurosis
	Neurasthenic neurosis
	Depersonalisation neurosis
III. Psychoses not attributed to physical conditions listed previously	Hypochondriacal neurosis
Schizophrenia	Other
Simple type	V. Personality disorders and certain other non-psychotic mental disorders (such as paranoid personality, schizoid personality, and antisocial personality)
Hebephrenic type	
Catatonic type	
Paranoid type	
Acute schizophrenic episode	Sexual deviations (such as homosexuality, fetishism, and sadism)
Latent type	
Residual type	Alcoholism
Schizo-affective type	Drug dependence
Childhood type	VI. Psychophysiologic disorders (physical disorders, e.g., respiratory or gastrointestinal, of presumably psychogenic origin)
Chronic undifferentiated type	
Other	
Major affective disorders	VII. Special symptoms (such as speech disturbances, tics, disorders of sleep)
Involutional melancholia	
Manic-depressive illness (manic type, depressed type, or circular type)	VIII. Transient situational disturbances (during infancy, childhood, adolescence, adult life, or late life)
Paranoid states	IX. Behaviour disorders of childhood and adolescence (such as withdrawing reaction, overanxious reaction, and group delinquent reaction)
Other	
IV. Neuroses	
Anxiety neurosis	X. Conditions without manifest psychiatric disorder and non-specific conditions (such as marital maladjustment and occupational maladjustment)
Hysterical neurosis (conversion type or dissociative type)	

he is thus impulsive, hedonistic and irresponsible. The psychopath has insight into his condition and is often able to put on a convincing act by simulating normal emotions; nevertheless his social and sexual relationships remain superficial and demanding. Other disorders that tend to be classified separately to neurosis include those of children and those in the field of psychosomatic medicine.

Clinical observation rather than empirical study has given rise to descriptions such as the above. The classificatory system in Table 15.1 is similarly based on the majority vote of psychiatric committees rather than on explicit consideration of scientific evidence. Because of this limitation official classifications have often been subject to criticism, even to the point of questioning whether it is appropriate to apply the medical model of giving a specific diagnosis in the case of mental disorders. In general medicine it is meaningful to give a specific diagnosis, such as 'influenza' or 'tuberculosis', because such disorders tend to be discrete entities (i.e. mutually exclusive), to involve a specific cause or pathological agent (e.g. a virus), and to require treatment aimed at the eradication of this 'cause'. The classification of physical disorders, which began at a descriptive level, has thus come to be linked with a limited number of known causes, i.e. it has developed from a symptom- to an aetiological-classification. The position with mental disorders appears to be different. Many of the categories are overlapping rather than mutually exclusive, classification is still based largely at the descriptive level and these descriptions may, anyway, represent the extremes of normal variation rather than the effects of pathology. It may be noted in Table 15.1 that the principles of classification are not consistent; some of the categories are based on aetiology (e.g. organic brain syndromes) and others on similarity of displayed symptoms (e.g. the psychoses). While the traditional medical practice of arriving at a specific diagnosis is generally accepted for the former, its applicability to the latter has often been questioned.

The purpose of this chapter is to outline some of the scientific evidence relating to the fundamental issues that underlie the description of mental disorders. The emphasis will be on objective methods of approach and examples of new classifications, rather than on a comprehensive coverage of all areas of abnormal behaviour. First, methods for investigating the particular grouping of symptoms said to comprise the various diagnostic categories will be examined. Classifications resulting from studies employing these methods will be briefly described. Second, studies relevant to the question of whether or not mental disorders are different in kind from normal variation will be discussed. Third, a new approach to the classification of mental disorders, namely that based on dimensions, will be described. Finally, examples will be given of research that has followed the medical model in linking diagnosis with causative factors and with treatment.

TYPES OF ABNORMAL BEHAVIOUR

Analysis of symptom ratings

Abnormal behaviour can be described in terms of symptoms and at a more general level in terms of diagnostic categories. Clinical observation has provided a number of diagnostic categories but, being subjectively based, there has always been disagreement over the details of the system. For example, depression has been regarded by some authorities as one diagnosis ranging from neurotic (mild) to psychotic (severe), and by others as two separate diagnoses (neurotic and psychotic) each ranging in severity from mild to severe. Recently-developed statistical techniques offer an empirical means of settling such disputes, which hitherto have been argued on clinical grounds.

The present system of diagnosis was arrived at by assigning labels to groups of symptoms, or more generally 'signs', that were commonly found together. At a mathematical level the relationships between symptoms in a sample of patients can be expressed as correlation coefficients, and these coefficients can be summarised in terms of a number of factors by 'factor analysis' (Chapter 7). This method provides an objective means of checking the validity of subjectively determined traditional classifications, i.e. checking whether symptoms subsumed under each diagnostic label are indeed correlated more highly with each other than with symptoms belonging to other categories. In other words, factor analysis carries out objectively what the diagnostician does subjectively; it is therefore the method of choice in classification procedures. The approach is best illustrated by its application to the controversy over the classification of depression.

Types of depression

Factor analysis has been applied to the grouping of symptoms in patients diagnosed as suffering from depression in several studies. Eysenck (1970a) has described how the results from these studies generally support the idea of two separate factors of depression. The analyses have tended to give two factors, one with high loadings for 'neurotic depression' and the other with high loadings for 'psychotic depression'. There has been no general factor having positive correlations throughout, as would be required to support the concept of a single dimension.

The main items that comprised the two factors in a study by Kendell (1968) are listed in Table 15.2. This study involved analysing 42 items from the clinical records of 696 patients who had been given a primary diagnosis of some form of depression. Correlations were computed between the 42 items, and these correlations were summarised by the Promax method of factor analysis. Kendell first reduced the correlations to twelve factors labelled 'paranoid attitude', 'previous psychiatric symptoms', 'hypochondriacal attitude', etc. These factors were too specific to correspond to diagnoses but, because they were themselves inter-correlated, it was possible to summarise them further. This was done using a 'higher-order' analysis, which gave four factors that could be labelled 'neurotic depression', 'psychotic depression', 'suicidal feelings' and 'previous neurotic symptoms'. These factors in turn were reduced to the two given in Table 15.2; the items comprising 'previous neurotic symptoms' tended to fall into the neurotic depression rather than the psy-chotic depression dimension. At this level the two factors were independent, being correlated only −0.02. In other words, the symptoms of the two disorders are demonstrated to be unrelated.

Evidence for the need to revise official classifi-cations was provided by Kendell's study. His analysis did not, at any stage, reveal a factor of 'involutional

Table 15.2 Items comprising two factors of depres-sion. (From Kendell, 1968, by courtesy of Oxford University Press)

Neurotic depression	*Loading*
Previous anxiety symptoms	0.54
Previous subjective tension symptoms	0.53
Lengthy duration before admission	0.47
Previous hysterical symptoms	0.46
Childhood neurotic traits	0.45
Suicidal feelings	0.43
Previous obsessional symptoms	0.35
Previous mood variations	0.30
Important precipitating psychological cause	0.29
Rapid changes of mood	0.29
Previous preoccupation with bodily functions	0.28
Subjective sensory abnormalities	0.28
Irritable	0.27
Hypochondriacal attitude	0.27
Demonstrative suicidal attempt	0.26
Psychotic depression	
Gross disturbance of food intake	0.52
Gross disturbance of weight	0.48
Delusions of guilt, self reproach or unworthiness	0.47
Abnormal quality of speech	0.45
Ideas of reference	0.39
Retarded activity	0.39
Suspicious	0.36
Age (older)	0.36
Persecutory delusions	0.35
Severe insomnia	0.35
Social withdrawal	0.34
Abnormal rate of speech	0.31
Perplexed	0.28
Agitated	0.27
Apathetic	0.27
Delusions of bodily change or disorder	0.26
Sex (male)	0.26

melancholia', even though 55 of the patients had been diagnosed in this way and items supposedly relevant to such a diagnosis had been included. On the evi-dence of this study it appears that the nature of involutional melancholia is no different from that of psychotic depression; its inclusion in official classifi-cations is thus open to question.

Subdivisions of mood

An approach to the classification of a wide range of normal and abnormal mood states was undertaken by McNair and Lorr (1964); they were concerned with finding specific groupings of mood states rather than explicitly attempting to validate official classifications. Three samples of male psychotherapy patients rated themselves on a mood adjective check list. Intercorre-lations among the ratings were computed and the resulting matrix was factor analysed. Five factors emerged for all three samples and two other factors for two of the samples; these seven factors were taken to be reliable (i.e. not due to chance). Labels for the seven factors, together with high-loading items for each, are presented in Table 15.3. McNair and Lorr mention that these factors were intercorrelated but, unlike Kendell, they did not carry out a higher-order analysis; had they done so they would have arrived at more general factors that might have corresponded with traditional diagnostic categories.

Nowlis (1965) reported a similar analysis for a sample of 450 male students. The students completed a mood adjective rating scale before and after viewing films aimed at arousing different emotions; because students rather than patients were employed it was considered necessary to arouse various emotions in order to ensure that they would be represented in the analysis. From a total of 96 mood adjectives, five matrices were computed for the various 'arousing' and 'unarousing' conditions and the results factor ana-lysed. Four factors emerged from all five of the matrices and an additional four from four of the matrices; these eight were taken to be reliable. The eight factors, arranged in such an order as to facili-tate comparison with the McNair and Lorr factors, are included in Table 15.3. The close correspondence between the two sets of results provides a good check on their reliability, i.e. very similar factors have been found by different researchers using different subjects and rating scales. The close correspondence also suggests that the mood states of patients are similar in nature (but not degree) to those of normal students; further evidence on this question of whether neurotic states are extremes of normality rather than 'illnesses' will be discussed later.

Psychotic syndromes

Lorr *et al.* (1962) described the syndromes they obtained by factor analysing psychotic symptoms. Psychiatrists rated 296 psychotic patients on 42

Table 15.3   Items comprising factors of mood in patients and students. (From McNair and Lorr, 1964, by courtesy of *J. Abn. Soc. Psychol.* and Nowlis, 1965, by courtesy of Springer)

Patients' factor labels	*Items with highest loadings*
Tension or anxiety	tense, nervous, on edge, shaky
Anger or hostility	angry, furious, ready to fight
Depression or dejection	worthless, helpless, unhappy
Vigour or activity	lively, vigorous, full of pep, active
Fatigue or inertia	tired, fatigued
Friendliness	co-operation, good natured, understanding, cheerful
Confusion	forgetful, not able to concentrate or think clearly, inefficient
Students' factor labels	
Anxiety	clutched up, fearful, jittery
Aggression	defiant, rebellious, angry, grouchy, annoyed, fed-up
Sadness	regretful, sad, sorry
Surgency	carefree, playful, witty, lively, talkative
Fatigue	drowsy, dull, sluggish, tired
Social affection	affectionate, forgiving, kindly, warm-hearted
Concentration	attentive, earnest, serious, contemplative, concentrating, engaged in thought, intent, introspective
Scepticism	dubious, sceptical, suspicious

scales and assessed them for the presence or absence of 48 signs; 77 of these items were selected as statistically suitable for analysis. Nine factors were extracted and labelled and these, together with the items that loaded most highly on each factor, are presented in Table 15.4. Because these factors were intercorrelated it was possible to summarise them in terms of three main factors: excitement *v.* retarded withdrawal, hostile paranoia, and thinking disorganisation.

The factors emerging in the above study were similar to, but not identical with, traditional diagnostic categories. Before it can be concluded that these categories are in need of revision, it is necessary to evaluate the study in terms of certain criteria. First, it should be established that the sample is representative of psychotic patients. Lorr *et al.* mention that a postulated tenth factor (disorganisation) was not extracted because very few incoherent patients were included in the sample. Second, it should be established that the full range of psychotic signs are represented in the analysis. Although 77 items were analysed, many of these were very similar, and it is possible that diagnosticians make use of a wider range of signs. Finally, the factor analysis should ideally be performed several times, extracting a different number of factors each time. It may be considered that the optimum number of factors lies somewhere between the nine- and three-factor solutions reported by Lorr *et al.*

Other factor analytic studies have suffered from similar limitations to the above. Costello (1970) in reviewing these studies has constructed tables presenting the factors emerging from them. He points out that it is very difficult to compare the results from these studies because the investigators have tended to work from different sets of symptoms, and have extracted different numbers of factors. What is needed

is a more standardised approach in which investigators first decide on a fully comprehensive range of signs, and then explicitly set out to reproduce existing classifications. When this is done it will be possible to directly compare the factor analytic results with traditional classifications, and thus to see where revisions are needed.

Objective differences between patients

An empirical approach to the classification of abnormal behaviour has been provided by the factor analysis of symptom ratings. The main advantage of this method is that it allows the investigation of fundamental problems, such as whether there are one or two types of depression. In general, the syndromes emerging with this method have been similar to traditional diagnostic categories but, unfortunately, because factor analysis is usually based on subjective ratings the results may be influenced by personal opinions in the same way as clinical judgement. Raters observing a particular symptom in a patient may perceive other, supposedly related, symptoms merely because such symptoms are expected to be found together. The factors extracted in any one study may thus reflect the preconceived notions of the raters rather than the true state of affairs. A marked degree of such error, however, seems unlikely because similar factor analytic results have come from 'schools' holding different opinions. Nevertheless, alternative evidence is available that is based on objective differences between patients.

A major controversy in psychiatry has concerned the question of whether or not psychosis is functionally related to neurosis. Many psychoanalytic writers have postulated that schizophrenia, in particular, shares a common pathological basis with neurosis;

Table 15.4 Items comprising nine factors of psychosis. (From Lorr *et al.*, 1962, by courtesy of *J. Consult. Psychol.*)

	Loading
Excitement	
Speech hurried or pushed	0.51
Exhibits attitude of superiority	0.48
Overtalkative	0.47
Dramatises self and seeks attention	0.46
Body movements hurried	0.46
Paranoid projection	
Believes people are against him	0.54
Believes people talk about him	0.49
Suspicious of people and their motives	0.45
Hostile belligerence	
Manifests hostile or sullen attitude	0.53
Shows irritability or annoyance	0.47
Expresses feelings of bitterness and resentment	0.45
Agitated depression	
Apprehensive about vague future events	0.63
Blames and condemns self	0.59
Anxious about self, family or finances	0:58
Downcast or depressed in mood	0.57
Attitude of self-deprecation and inferiority	0.56
Withdrawal with retardation	
Speech slowed or deliberate	0.53
Voice flat and face is immobile	0.52
Apathetic and unresponsive in feeling	0.52
Body movements slowed or deliberate	0.48
Voice low or weak	0.48
Perceptual distortions	
Reports voices accuse or blame him	0.67
Reports hearing voices	0.63
Reports voices tell him to do things	0.53
Reports voices threaten him	0.52
Reports other hallucinations	0.40
Grandiose expansiveness	
Voices praise or extol him	0.60
Believes he has a distinct divine mission	0.55
Motor disturbances	
Exhibits peculiar repetitive movements	0.60
Makes unusual facial grimaces	0.58
Assumes bizarre postures	0.50
Conceptual disorganisation	
Speech is logically disconnected or incoherent	0.51
Rambles off the topic discussed	0.42

they have argued that a neurotic under stress may become schizophrenic. Wolpe (1970) in reviewing the evidence on this question concluded that the two disorders are quite independent. The types of objective evidence that were considered in coming to this conclusion will now be described.

Performance tests

Eysenck (1955) conducted a study designed to settle the controversy over whether psychosis represents an extreme form of neurosis or whether the two states are independent. The sample consisted of 20 normal people, 20 neurotics and 20 psychotics. A 'discriminant function analysis' was carried out to test whether one or more dimensions were needed for classifying the patients; this type of analysis is similar to factor analysis but has the advantage of allowing for tests of significance. Four objective performance tests, known from previous research to distinguish (on quantitative grounds) between the three groups, were chosen in preference to subjective symptom ratings. The tests were for visual acuity, object recognition, mental speed and visual accommodation. A score was derived for each person and the discriminant function analysis performed. The analysis gave two significant latent roots meaning that two dimensions, at least, were needed for distinguishing (qualitatively) the two groups of patients. Neurosis and psychosis were thus demonstrated to lie along different dimensions from normality; the scores for the three groups plotted against the two dimensions, labelled Y1 and Y2, are shown in Figure 15.1. This type of study has been repeated several times, with different tests and in different countries, and the same result has emerged each time.

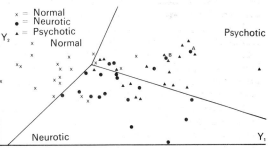

Figure 15.1 Distributions of scores for three groups of people on two dimensions. (From Eysenck, 1955, by courtesy of *Psychol. Rep.*)

The above study, apart from demonstrating that neurosis and psychosis are on independent dimensions, also demonstrates that objective performance tests are appropriate for diagnosing patients. With the three visually fitted lines in Figure 15.1, the test scores correspond to the original diagnosis in 45 of the 60 cases, i.e. 75% correct classification. Allowing for the known unreliability of psychiatric diagnosis (Zubin, 1967) this is about as close as could be expected. Moreover, the diagnosis of two of the misclassified 'neurotic' patients (labelled A and B) was later revised to psychosis in accordance with, but independent of, the test scores. This is consistent with the view that test scores provide a more reliable source of information than the interview upon which diagnoses are usually based.

Heredity

Genetic evidence relevant to the controversy over the classification of neurosis and psychosis has been provided by Cowie (1961). She predicted that if the two dimensions are truly independent, then on a genetic basis there should be no increased incidence of neurosis in the children of psychotics. The study involved comparing 330 offspring of at least one psychotic parent with 342 offspring of matched control parents. The mean age of the offspring was just under 20 years in each case. The psychotic parents were in-patients at a mental hospital and the control parents were out-patients at a general hospital reporting to an ante-natal or orthopaedic clinic, etc. A full psychiatric history of the offspring was taken from the parents and a teachers' report form was completed by the school and the parents. The Maudsley Personality Inventory (M.P.I.) was completed by those offspring who were of an appropriate age. As expected, the psychiatric histories indicated an increased incidence of psychosis in the offspring of psychotic parents, but only a very slightly increased incidence of neurosis and then only of a few symptoms. Moreover, the indices from the teachers' report form and the M.P.I. indicated that there was no significant difference in neuroticism between the two groups. This study thus provides strong evidence that neurosis and psychosis are independent.

With regard to the classification of depression, genetic studies support the factor analytic evidence that neurotic depression is distinct from psychotic depression. Shields (Chapter 10) reports that the two types tend to 'breed true', e.g. patients with psychotic depression are more likely to have relatives with this same disorder than to have relatives with neurotic depression. There is similar evidence that psychotic depression with mood swings is genetically distinct from psychotic depression without mood swings.

Physiological responses

Shagass and Jones (1958) reported being able to distinguish between several diagnostic groups by means of the 'sedation threshold test'. A patient's threshold was measured by injecting a barbiturate in stages until his voice began to slur and E.E.G. amplitude changes became apparent. The amount of drug per unit of body weight needed to produce this effect was different for various diagnostic groups. The largest difference was obtained between anxiety states, for whom a large amount of drug was needed, and hysterics (a category that includes patients with functional paralyses and loss of memory) for whom a small amount was sufficient. This finding is consistent with the clinical observation that it is particularly difficult to sedate an anxious patient. The two types of depression were also clearly distinguished; the sedation threshold of neurotic depressives was high and that of psychotic depressives was low. Considering the known unreliability of psychiatric diagnosis there was remarkably little overlap between the two groups as shown by the distribution of scores in Figure 15.2. We thus have

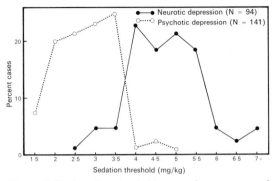

Figure 15.2   Sedation threshold scores for two types of depressed patients. (From Shagass and Jones, 1958, by courtesy of *Amer. J. Psychiatry*)

evidence that the two types of depression are distinct at the physiological level as well as at the genetic and behavioural (symptom) level.

Claridge (1967, 1970) describes subsequent work on the sedation threshold using a continuous injection of barbiturate and an arithmetic task as the means of determining a patient's threshold. The arithmetic task involves the patient doubling numbers until the effects of the drug are sufficient to cause repeated errors. Using this simple method instead of the E.E.G. recording it has been possible to confirm the main findings reported by Shagass and Jones. Other interesting findings have also emerged. In examining the responses of catatonic schizophrenics, Claridge reports the paradoxical finding that when in a stupor (these patients often assume a fixed posture for hours on end) they have a high sedation threshold along with anxiety patients. Moreover, the effect of the sedative drug is often to bring a catatonic out of his stupor making him more responsive behaviourally. These results are consistent with the theory that catatonics are highly aroused physiologically, their stupors serving the function of protecting the central nervous system from over-stimulation.

The 'Archimedes spiral' after-effect is another test that is related to diagnostic groups. This test involves measuring the strength of the visual illusion of after-movement following fixation of a rotating spiral. It is also related to the sedation threshold, e.g. anxiety patients who have high sedation thresholds tend to have long after-effects. With psychotics, however, there is a reversed relationship between the two tests. This inverse relationship in psychosis provides a useful means of distinguishing it from other disorders. The relationship between the two tests returns to normal when psychotics recover, as illustrated in Figure 15.3.

Results from the sedation threshold test and the Archimedes spiral are particularly useful in distinguishing between the schizophrenias. Simple schizophrenics who tend to be slow, socially withdrawn and emotionally flat have a low sedation threshold (like

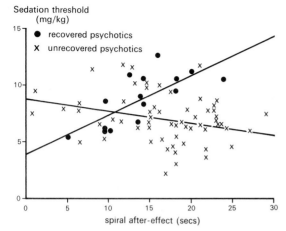

Sedation threshold
(mg/kg)

● recovered psychotics
X unrecovered psychotics

spiral after-effect (secs)

Figure 15.3 Sedation threshold and spiral after-effect scores for recovered and unrecovered psychotic patients. (From Claridge, 1967, by courtesy of Pergamon Press)

hysterics) and a long spiral after-effect (like anxiety patients). Schizophrenics who are behaviourally active, paranoid and thought disordered have a high sedation threshold (like anxiety patients) and a short spiral after-effect (like hysterics). These results were obtained during the early stages of schizophrenia. Different results were obtained during the late stages, indicating that physiological changes take place by the time the disorder has become chronic. A classificatory system should, ideally, reflect these physiological differences within the range of schizophrenic disorders; it would, at least, have implications for drug therapy.

RELATIONSHIP OF NORMAL TO ABNORMAL BEHAVIOUR

There have always been differences of opinion as to whether abnormal behaviour is qualitatively or quantitatively different from normal behaviour. A qualitative difference is seen to exist if the causes of the disorder are different from those that operate in the development of normal behaviour. The psychological effects of a brain tumour or lesion and the action of a rare gene causing mental abnormality are examples of a qualitatively different aetiology. A quantitative difference is seen to exist if the causes of the disorder are akin to normal processes. In this case symptoms are seen as graded traits that exist in normal people although, obviously, to a less extreme degree. This applies even to traits or predispositions that have to reach a certain level before manifesting themselves in overt behaviour; some forms of epilepsy and criminality are often given as examples in this connection.

In general medicine there is usually a qualitative difference between normal and abnormal in the sense that it is meaningful to make an 'either–or' judgment, i.e. a decision is taken as to whether a patient either

has or has not a given disease. The use of categories in diagnosis is clearly appropriate in these instances. In psychological medicine such a decision is often made difficult by the absence of any identifiable cause or pathology, and also because the symptoms may appear similar in nature to personality traits that exist in normal people. It is possible that many disorders simply represent the extremes of normal variation, including learning, rather than the effects of discrete pathological agents. Abnormally low intelligence provides an example of this dilemma. Low intelligence can be caused by the specific action of tumours, lesions and certain rare genes; it can also simply reflect the fact that the patient is towards the lower end of the scale of 'normal distribution'. The former cases would be referred to as constituting a qualitative difference and the latter as constituting a quantitative difference; a specific diagnosis would be required in the former cases whereas an I.Q. score would suffice in the latter.

There are two main sources of evidence relevant to the fundamental question of whether mental disorders differ in kind or just in degree from normal behaviour. The first are the statistical techniques of 'criterion analysis' and 'cluster analysis' and the second the investigation of genetic effects.

Criterion analysis

Eysenck (1950) developed the method of criterion analysis for deciding whether a quantitative or qualitative difference exists between two groups. The basic reasoning is that if the two groups differ quantitatively (i.e. are on a continuum) then tests or 'criteria' that discriminate between them will also discriminate within each of them. Criteria such as temperature discriminate various groups of physically ill people on the one hand, from well people on the other. Temperature also discriminates within the ill group (i.e. the ill from the more ill), but it does not discriminate within the well group. In this instance, criterion analysis would reveal a qualitative difference between illness and 'wellness'.

The mathematics of criterion analysis involves factor analysing the correlations among the tests for each group separately. A general factor from one group is obtained and then rotated into a position of maximum correlation with a 'criterion column' (the power of each test to discriminate between the two groups). The critical test is that there should be substantial correlations between the rotated factor and the criterion column if the two groups differ only in degree. The correlations should be at a chance level, however, if the two groups differ qualitatively.

Criterion analysis was first applied to neurosis. The two samples consisted of 105 hospital in-patients diagnosed as neurotic and 93 soldiers. Sixteen objective performance tests, known from previous research to discriminate between neurotics and normals, were chosen in preference to subjective ratings. The tests included the Maudsley Personality Inventory and measures of speed, fluency, flexibility, persistence, motor control and dark-adaptation. A general factor, neuroticism, was obtained from the correlations among the tests for the normal group; it was noted at this stage that the tests correlated positively meaning that they discriminated the normal from the very normal. The factor loadings were then rotated into a position of maximum correlation with the criterion column. The correlations between the two columns were predominantly positive averaging 0.57; this is evidence supporting the hypothesis that neurosis and normality are on a single continuum.

Eysenck (1952) carried out a similar analysis for testing the hypothesis that psychosis is continuous with normality. The two samples consisted of 100 hospital patients, diagnosed as suffering from some form of schizophrenia or manic-depression, and 100 soldiers. Twenty objective performance tests, known to discriminate psychotics from normals, were administered to both groups. The tests included verbal fluency (e.g. naming as many species of birds that you can think of), concentration (e.g. repeating the last six of a series of numbers read aloud to you), mirror drawing, and expressive movements (e.g. size of handwriting). The critical test again gave positive correlations thus supporting the hypothesis that psychosis is continuous with normality, i.e. the psychotics were not qualitatively different from the normals on the 20 measures used to discriminate between them.

Because the psychotic group in Eysenck's study was composed of both schizophrenics and manic-depressives, he was able to test Kretschmer's well-known hypothesis that there is a dimension running from schizothymia at one extreme to cyclothymia at the other. Criterion analysis did not support this hypothesis, the critical test giving correlations that were insignificant.

The above studies indicate that both neurosis and psychosis are continuous with normality. Many clinicians, however, still believe that these states, or at least psychotic states, are different in kind from normality. In spite of this disagreement the two studies have never been followed-up. This is surprising since an interesting extension to the research would be to employ symptom measures as the criteria, especially if the more bizarre psychotic symptoms were included. Symptoms such as paranoid beliefs and delusions certainly appear to exist in an attenuated form in normal people. For example, a paranoid patient may complain that enemy agents are spying on him or plotting to kill him, while a paranoid person may merely complain that strangers notice him in the street or try to provoke arguments with him. Symptoms such as thought-disorder and hallucinations, however, appear to be more of an 'all-or-nothing' phenomenon. These symptoms are usually so extreme and uninflu-

enced by external events that it is difficult to think of attenuated forms in normal people. By including tests for this sort of symptom in a criterion analysis, the hypothesis of a qualitative difference might then be supported. Until this research is carried out, however, it can only be stated that the statistical evidence indicates a difference in degree rather than kind between psychiatric patients and the general population.

Cluster analysis

It was mentioned above that an analysis involving tests of symptoms might reveal qualitative differences. Everitt *et al.* (1971) attempted to do this using subjective ratings of symptoms and cluster analysis, a statistical technique for sorting people into groups. This technique has the advantage, over factor analysis, of not assuming a continuous distribution in the variables being assessed. Thus cluster analysis might yield discrete groupings of, say, men and women, while factor analysis may need to be carried out separately for these two groups. Rather than comparing patients with normal people, the study attempted to find qualitative differences within a patient population. It was predicted that if diagnoses truly represent qualitatively distinct categories, then cluster analysis should produce groups composed largely of patients with the same diagnosis. The sample consisted of 480 patients classified into ten diagnostic groups and rated on 70 items. Cluster analysis produced one group composed largely of manic patients, another of paranoid schizophrenics, and a third of psychotic depressives. A fourth cluster was not so clear but did include a number of chronic schizophrenics. The results for these disorders are thus consistent with the hypothesis that they represent discrete 'illnesses'. The remaining clusters, however, were composed of mixed groups of patients; in particular, patients with neuroses and personality disorders showed no tendency to form distinct clusters.

Genetic evidence

Shields (Chapter 10) describes the genetic mechanisms responsible for disorders that differ in kind or just in degree from normal variation. A qualitative difference results from the action of a single or 'dominant' gene that has an all-or-nothing effect, cf. a virus in physical medicine. Quantitative variation results from the action of 'polygenes' interacting with environmental influences. While family studies indicate that the additive effects of polygenes are more common that the all-or-nothing effects of a single gene, there is in fact evidence for both mechanisms.

Slater's (1943) study on the effects of stress in World War II generally supported the polygenic hypothesis. Soldiers with many abnormalities of personality, even if only slight, were found to be more likely to break-down under stress than those with one major abnormality. In other words, the additive effect of tending towards the abnormal extreme on several factors is more likely to lead to mental disorder than the effect of being very high on just one factor. This finding led to the formulation of the theory that there is an inverse relationship between the number of abnormal personality 'markers' (i.e. polygenic predisposition) and the amount of stress needed to produce a break-down.

Examples of the specificity hypothesis are clearly provided by chromosome abnormalities and single genes resulting in disorders such as Down's syndrome (mongolism) and Huntington's chorea (a disease of the nervous system causing dementia, which starts in early middle age and is quickly fatal). With regard to the neuroses, there is also evidence for the operation of genes with a specific effect. Shields and Slater (1971) found that relative to fraternal twins, identical twins resemble each other more closely in specific symptomatology than in general diagnosis. The ratio of identical to fraternal concordance increased from 1.7 to 7.3 with the change from general diagnosis (presence or absence of psychiatric abnormality) to specific symptomatology (subdivisions of the World Health Organisation's classification).

Eysenck (1972) in reviewing the genetic evidence for schizophrenia describes how there is evidence for both specificity and generality. The prediction can be made that if a single gene is operating then the relatives of schizophrenics should tend to have the same disorder, whereas if many genes are operating then they may have other types of psychosis. Empirical studies indicate that while the relatives of schizophrenics are most likely to have this same disorder

(i.e. specificity model), there is also a tendency for them to have other psychoses such as manic-depression and, interestingly, psychopathy (i.e. generality model); as noted earlier (Cowie's study) they are not likely to have neurosis instead of psychosis. These findings have led to a two-part theory as follows. There is a general factor of psychoticism predisposing people to psychosis in varying degrees, which is inherited as a polygenic characteristic. There are also specific genes responsible for giving rise to sharply demarcated subtypes within the range of psychotic disorders. A parallel to this theory applies in the case of intelligence where specific factors such as verbal and numerical ability, although under different genetic control, are still related to the 'normally distributed' factor of general intelligence.

THE DIMENSIONAL APPROACH

The current practice in psychiatry is to give each patient a diagnosis that provides a summary of his most outstanding features. For the purposes of communication this works reasonably well for patients who present symptoms subsumed under only one diagnosis. For those who complain of other symptoms it is necessary to qualify the diagnosis by mentioning these or by giving a multiple diagnosis. In practice, it is found that most patients have symptoms belonging to several diagnostic categories, i.e. mixed disorders are more common than pure—unlike the position in general medicine. For example, a person suffering from anxiety is also likely to suffer from other symptoms such as depression. This presents a problem when attempting to arrive at a single diag-

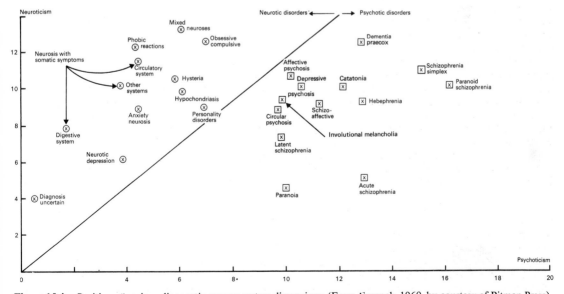

Figure 15.4   Position of various diagnostic groups on two dimensions. (From Eysenck, 1960, by courtesy of Pitman Press)

nosis, since to enquire whether a person is anxious or depressed is rather like asking whether he is tall or heavy. It would seem to be more logical to describe a patient in terms of his position on all relevant factors where he is towards the abnormal extreme. This is the rationale behind the 'dimensional' approach.

With the dimensional approach each patient would, ideally, be given a rating on all the dimensions of mental abnormality. For example, in describing a patient with neurotic features it would still be potentially useful to describe how he stands on the various psychotic factors, even if he is within the normal range. The disadvantage of this system is the practical one of complexity; it is much easier to describe a patient simply in terms of his most outstanding features. There is, however, a compromise solution.

Eysenck (1960, 1970b) has attempted to simplify the dimensional approach by describing patients in terms of their position on three important continua, namely psychoticism, neuroticism and introversion–extroversion. This method of classifying personality has been described by Wilson (Chapter 9). Factor analytic evidence indicates that many traits can be summarised in terms of these three dimensions; personality theorists although advocating the use of different subfactors seem to be in agreement on the existence of these major dimensions. In the same way that many personality traits can be defined in terms of these dimensions, it seems that many diagnostic categories can also be placed within this framework. Diagnosis is thus redefined as the point of intersection of a number of dimensions, i.e. a point in multifactor space. Patients would be classified together by virtue of a similar position on the relevant dimensions; a patient who differs on just one dimension would have a different diagnosis. This system is analogous to the way of defining colours; there are thousands of different colours but they can all be described by their position on just three dimensions, namely hue, saturation and brightness. Figure 15.4 presents the results of a study of symptom-ratings in which the factor scores of clinically diagnosed groups of patients were plotted along two dimensions. Apart from illustrating the position of different diagnoses, this figure also demonstrates the relevance of assessing patients on more than one dimension, e.g. patients with psychotic disorders also tend to have elevated neuroticism scores, which indicates that they require treatment for both types of disorder.

In order to incorporate the evidence discussed earlier of specific subtypes within a general diagnosis, the dimensional approach would need to be supplemented. As well as being assessed in terms of the three dimensions, a patient would also need to be given a specific diagnosis if his symptomatology warranted it. The analogy with intelligence, made earlier, will serve to illustrate this procedure. If a person has a specific cognitive defect, such as inability to spell, this assessment is best set against his general intelligence. This procedure may have implications for aetiology and treatment, e.g. a marked discrepancy between the two cognitive measures suggests the presence of a specific genetic abnormality or a brain lesion, while a smaller discrepancy might be accounted for in more 'normal' terms such as faulty learning techniques.

LINKS BETWEEN DIAGNOSIS, AETIOLOGY AND TREATMENT

One of the main aims of diagnosis is to arrive at a choice of treatment most likely to be effective for the individual patient. Bannister *et al.* (1964) conducted a survey on 1000 neurotic, psychotic and organic patients to determine the extent to which diagnosis is actually related to treatment. Their finding was that the most popular therapy for a given diagnosis was by no means always prescribed; two-thirds of the time a different therapy was given. Thus the conclusion was that there is very little in the way of a systematic link between diagnosis and choice of treatment. This may seem surprising in view of the many research studies presenting evidence that certain groups of patients respond better to certain forms of treatment. These studies, however, generally describe the patients in terms of many variables and, when prescribing treatment, it is these variables that a psychiatrist considers rather than the specific diagnosis that is entered in the case notes. The findings presented by Bannister *et al.* may thus be interpreted as reflecting the inadequacy of the traditional diagnostic approach rather than the psychiatrists' lack of awareness of the evidence linking patient characteristics with appropriate treatment. It would be interesting to see if a closer relationship exists when a dimensional system of diagnosis is adopted for such a survey.

Eysenck (1970b) has developed a theoretical model for explicitly linking diagnosis with aetiology in the expectation that this will lead to a more systematic approach to treatment. Predisposition is accounted for in terms of inherited differences in personality. Precipitation is accounted for in terms of environmental stress, conflict and learning effects generally. Three theories generated by this model are as follows. (a) Hysteria is hypothesised to result from strong stimulation (e.g. stress) of those parts of the central nervous system that mediate inhibition (which in turn causes paralysis, loss of memory, etc.). Predisposed people would thus include those who already have high levels of cortical inhibition. (b) Phobias are seen as being due to autonomic conditioning to neutral stimuli; the symptoms are regarded as conditioned responses that have become non-adaptive. Recovery from phobias is accounted for by simple extinction, whether occuring spontaneously or as a result of treatment. The finding that introverts are prone to phobias is attributed to the ease with which they condition as demonstrated in the laboratory. (c) Psychopathy is viewed as the absence of conditioned responses and, in particular, as a failure in the development of 'conscience'. Psychopaths tend to be extroverted and this is consistent with laboratory findings that it is difficult to condition extroverts without recourse to continuous and aversive reinforcement.

Eysenck's aetiological model, in directly linking diagnosis with appropriate treatment, is consistent with the behaviour therapy approach. With this approach, diagnosis consists of identifying the patient's symptoms and then applying various learning techniques in an attempt to eradicate them, i.e. diagnosis is directly linked to choice of treatment. There is also a basis for taking a patient's general personality into account when designing behaviour therapy, e.g. aversion therapy has been found to be more effective for patients low on neuroticism. Personality is also relevant when considering choice of drug treatment. At a very general level, stimulants are found to be more appropriate for extroverts and sedatives for introverts. Claridge (1970) quotes a study in which two groups differing in personality responded very differently to sedative and tranquillising drugs; the effect of the drugs was assessed using a nonsense syllable learning task. Figure 15.5 illustrates that relative to a placebo the drugs improved the learning performance for one group (introverts with high anxiety) but worsened it for the other group (extroverts with low anxiety).

Another example of the necessity to assess personality type before prescribing treatment is provided by Di Loreto (1971). He compared the outcome of three types of treatment on introverts and extroverts. The sample was 100 students who had high levels of general and social anxiety, and a desire for treatment.

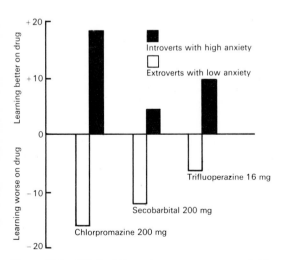

Figure 15.5 Effect of three drugs on nonsense syllable learning in two groups differing in personality. (From Claridge, 1970, by courtesy of Pergamon Press)

Systematic desensitisation, in which the patient is relaxed while visualising a graded series of anxiety provoking situations, was the most effective treatment overall working for both types of personality. Client-centred therapy, in which the patient is encouraged to disclose his feelings while the therapist merely clarifies what is said, was two and a half times more effective for extroverts than introverts. Rational–emotive therapy, in which the patient is confronted with his irrational and maladaptive life and encouraged to change, was three times more effective for introverts than extroverts.

CONCLUSIONS

An objective approach to diagnosis, namely factor analysis, has provided empirical support for many of the traditional diagnostic groups, i.e. symptoms subsumed under each label tend to be related when put to the statistical test. A problem arises, however, when efforts are made to assign patients to these groups; most patients have symptoms belonging not to one but to several diagnostic groups. In other words, while factor analysis reveals clearly defined clusters of symptoms, an individual's scores on these symptoms are almost as likely to place him between clusters as within a given cluster, i.e. 'person' space is not synonymous with 'factor' space. This is the essential difference between patterns of mental and physical symptomatology. The reason for this difference seems to be that a patient's mental symptomatology is to a large extent an exacerbation of 'normal' personality traits and the effects of learning experiences rather than the effects of specific pathology. Genetic evidence consistent with this explanation is provided by the finding that in mental disorders the operation of 'polygenes' is more common than that of specific 'dominant' genes. The conclusion that the nature of most psychiatric disorders is general rather than specific means that a categorical system of diagnosis, while appropriate for general medicine, is inappropriate for much of psychiatry.

Research studies concerned with reliability have demonstrated the limitations of the traditional system. Reasons for these limitations may now be offered. If patients do not fall into clearly defined categories then it is hardly surprising that measures of interjudge reliability based on this system are low. Added to this is the unreliability arising from a system that is not explicitly coded or standardised, e.g. it is left to the clinician's judgment as to how much weight to attach to different symptoms in arriving at a diagnosis. The findings of the U.S./U.K. diagnostic project (Cooper *et al.*, 1972) illustrate the repercussions of using this subjective system. One of the techniques employed in this project was to show videotape recordings of diagnostic interviews with selected patients to large audiences of American and British psychiatrists. The psychiatrists were asked to draw up a symptom profile of the patients and then diagnose according to the International Classification of Diseases. While the symptom profiles were similar, the American psychiatrists were much more likely to diagnose schizophrenia; the British psychiatrists tended to diagnose psychotic depression or personality disorder rather than schizophrenia.

The research evidence supports the logic of adopting a dimensional approach in psychiatric diagnosis. Being explicitly quantitative this approach would also meet the need for standardisation, e.g. factor loadings indicate the weights to attach to different symptoms in arriving at a diagnosis. There are, however, at least two ways in which the dimensional approach as first proposed by Kretschmer would need to be supplemented. First, it is necessary to take account of the evidence for specific sets of symptoms within a broader diagnosis, perhaps by incorporating certain categories within the dimensional approach. Second, as with the traditional system it will still be necessary to consider other variables, such as the patient's home environ-

ment, which may suggest suitable methods of treatment, e.g. changing the environment rather than the patient.

Because diagnosis on its own is not sufficient to lead to an optimum choice of treatment, it has often been suggested that attempts at diagnosis be abandoned and replaced by a direct concern with prescribing treatment. Arthur (1969) has reviewed various alternatives to diagnosis, such as Shapiro's experimental model of testing predictions made about the individual patient. The main feature of these alternative methods is to proceed according to an explicit set of rules, based on research evidence, designed to arrive at the most effective choice of treatment. Alternatives to diagnosis also have side-benefits such as not giving a person a potentially harmful label. Nevertheless, it is still necessary to meet the fundamental need in science for classification as an aid to theoretical understanding. This chapter has reviewed the objective methods that are appropriate for developing a modern classificatory system for abnormal behaviour.

References

American Psychiatric Association (1968). *Diagnostic and Statistical Manual of Mental Diseases* (2nd Ed.) (Washington: A.P.A.)

Arthur, A. Z. (1969). Diagnostic testing and the new alternatives. *Psychol. Bull.*, 72, 183–192

Bannister, D., Salmon, P. and Leiberman, D. M. (1964). Diagnosis–treatment relationships in psychiatry: a statistical analysis. *Brit. J. Psychiatry*, 110, 726–732

Claridge, G. S. (1967). *Personality and Arousal: A Psychophysiological Study of Psychiatric Disorder* (Oxford: Pergamon Press)

Claridge, G. S. (1970). *Drugs and Human Behaviour* (London: Allen Lane)

Cooper, J. E., Kendell, R. E., Gurland, B. J., Sharpe, L., Copeland, J. R. M. and Simon, R. (1972). *Psychiatric Diagnosis in New York and London* (London: Oxford University Press)

Costello, C. G. (1970). Classification and psychopathology. In: *Symptoms of Psychopathology: A Handbook* (C. G. Costello, editor) (New York: Wiley)

Cowie, V. (1961). The incidence of neurosis in the children of psychotics. *Acta Psychiatr. Scand.*, 37, 37–87

Di Loreto, A. O. (1971). *Comparative Psychotherapy: An Experimental Analysis* (Chicago: Aldine-Atherton)

Everitt, B. S., Gourlay, A. J. and Kendell, R. E. (1971). An attempt at validation of traditional psychiatric syndromes by cluster analysis. *Brit. J. Psychiatry*, 119, 399–412

Eysenck, H. J. (1950). Criterion analysis—an application of the hypothetico-deductive method to factor analysis. *Psychol. Rev.*, 57, 38–53

Eysenck, H. J. (1952). Schizothymia–cyclothymia as a dimension of personality: II. Experimental. *J. Personal.*, 20, 345–384

Eysenck, H. J. (1955). Psychiatric diagnosis as a psychological and statistical problem. *Psychol. Rep.*, 1, 3–17

Eysenck, H. J. (1960). Classification and the problem of diagnosis. In: *Handbook of Abnormal Psychology* (H. J.

Eysenck, editor) (London: Pitman Press)

Eysenck, H. J. (1970a). The classification of depressive illnesses. *Brit. J. Psychiatry*, 117, 241–250

Eysenck, H. J. (1970b). A dimensional system of psychodiagnostics. In: *New Approaches to Personality Classification* (A. R. Mahrer, editor) (New York: Columbia University Press)

Eysenck, H. J. (1972). An experimental and genetic model of schizophrenia. In: *Genetic Factors in 'Schizophrenia'* (A. R. Kaplan, editor) (Illinois: Thomas)

Kendell, R. E. (1968). *The Classification of Depressive Illnesses* (London: Oxford University Press)

Lorr, M., McNair, D. M., Klett, C. J. and Lasky, J. J. (1962). Evidence of ten psychotic syndromes. *J. Consult. Psychol.*, 26, 185–189

McNair, D. M. and Lorr, M. (1964). An analysis of mood in neurotics. *J. Abn. Soc. Psychol.*, 69, 620–627

Nowlis, V. (1965). Research with the Mood Adjective Check List. In: *Affect, Cognition and Personality* (S. S. Tomkins and C. E. Izard, editors) (New York: Springer)

Shagass, C. and Jones, A. L. (1958). A neurophysiological test for psychiatric diagnosis: results in 750 patients. *Amer. J. Psychiatry*, 114, 1002–1009

Shields, J. and Slater, E. (1971). Diagnostic similarity in twins with neuroses and personality disorders. In: *Man, Mind and Heredity* (J. Shields and I. I. Gottesman, editors) (Baltimore: Johns Hopkins Press)

Slater, E. (1943). The neurotic constitution: a statistical study of two thousand neurotic soldiers. *J. Neurol. Psychiatry*, 6, 1–16

Wolpe, J. (1970). The discontinuity of neurosis and schizophrenia. *Behav. Res. Ther.*, 8, 179–187

World Health Organisation (1967). *International Classification of Diseases* (Geneva: W.H.O.)

Zubin, J. (1967). Classification of the behaviour disorders. *Ann. Rev. Psychol.*, 18, 373–406

Chapter 16

CRIMINALITY AND DELINQUENCY

J. F. Allsopp

THE FIELD OF INVESTIGATION

There is an enormous range of behaviour that can be considered antisocial, delinquent, or criminal, ranging from that of the child in school whose disruptive behaviour prevents his classmates from working, to that of the violent robber, murderer, or rapist. Attempts to explain such varying types of behaviour abound in the sociological, psychological, and psychiatric literature. A vast number of sociological and psychological variables have been studied in an attempt to determine factors which distinguish delinquents and criminals from the remainder of the population. The time and effort expended on researches into various types of crime and criminals has been tremendous, yet criminologists are still not agreed whether or not it should be possible to propose a theoretical system capable of explaining a wide range of antisocial behaviour.

The usual method in criminological research has been to compare a group of convicted offenders with a control group drawn from the non-convicted general population. While this method has the advantage that groups of subjects are readily obtainable for testing, there are also a number of disadvantages. One is that criminality is clearly not an all-or-none criterion dependent on whether or not a person has been convicted of an offence. It is safe to assume that the majority of people convicted are criminals, but there are also, of course, many criminals who never get caught. And, on the other hand, we have the normal population, generally assumed to be comprised of non-criminals, and yet members of which vary widely in their degree of moral integrity. Another problem is that some measures of individual differences, such as personality tests, may be affected by the conditions under which they are obtained, so that apparent dissimilarities between prisoners and controls could be due, not to the former group being criminal, but to their being incarcerated.

It has been argued that more useful findings would be obtained if researchers concentrated their efforts on finely discriminated categories of offenders, rather than groups containing a mixture of people convicted of all types of offences. Some of the more recent studies have been conducted along these lines investigating, for example, groups of motoring offenders, sex offenders, and car thieves. There are similar problems here, however, to those encountered in trying to discriminate criminals as a whole. A man with many

prison sentences behind him may well have been convicted of all types of offences. Do we then classify him a thief, thug, or bank robber?

There is in fact considerable evidence for the generality of criminality. The person who commits one type of offence is likely to commit other offences. Dr T. Willett has provided some interesting data in this connection concerning motoring offences, which are often thought to have no relationship with other types of crime. He considered over 600 people who had been convicted for offences ranging from failure to be insured against third party risks to causing death by dangerous driving. About one-third of these people were found either to have criminal records for non-motoring offences, or to be known to the police as suspects for crimes in which it was not possible to prosecute. This proportion is far higher than would be obtained if these motoring offences were not related to other types of criminality.

There is also much evidence for the generality of antisocial behaviour over the individual's development. The boy who is very badly behaved in school is more likely to come to the attention of the courts for delinquent activity outside of school, and to later end up in prison for offences committed as an adult. There are, of course, many boys who behave very badly at school, and yet never get into trouble outside, and who grow up to lead blameless adult lives; and, on the other hand, many prisoners who were exceptionally well-behaved as youngsters. But, in general, childhood antisocial behaviour is predictive of adult antisocial behaviour. For example, Sir Cyril Burt reported that of a group of boys in a London area who had, many years previously, been picked out by their teachers as likely to develop into habitual offenders, 83% actually did drift into a life of regular and persistent crime.

In the criminological literature the term 'delinquent' is usually used, as in everyday speech, to refer to a younger category of offender than the term 'criminal', but there is considerable overlap in the age ranges of the offenders to which the terms have been applied. The terms used here generally follow those used by the investigators of the studies under discussion, and the original reports should be consulted if exact details of the subjects' ages are required. The studies to be discussed have been carried out on a wide range of subjects, and are divided into two sections according to whether the investigations have been concerned with the effect of social or individual factors on the development of antisocial behaviour. We conclude with a section in which possible theoretical explanations of antisocial behaviour are discussed.

SOCIAL FACTORS

In her book *Social Science and Social Pathology*, Barbara Wootton has examined the evidence relating to twelve well-known hypotheses about the causes or characteristic features of crime and delinquency. The studies reviewed were chosen on the basis of their methodological soundness, and had dealt with offenders of both sexes and varying ages and categories of offences. From a thorough examination of these studies, Wootton found it impossible to make more than vague generalisations in support of the hypotheses considered.

'On the whole, it seems that offenders come from relatively large families. Not infrequently (according to some investigators very frequently) other members of the delinquents' (variously defined) families have also been in trouble with the law. Offenders are unlikely to be regular churchgoers, but the evidence as to whether club membership discourages delinquency is "wildly contradictory". If they are of age to be employed, they are likely to be classified as "poor" rather than as "good" workers. Most of them come from the lower social classes, but again the evidence as to the extent to which they can be described as exceptionally poor is conflicting; nor is there any clear indication that their delinquency is associated with the employment of their mothers outside the home. Their health is probably no worse than that of other people, but many of them have earned poor reputations at school, though these may well be prejudiced by their teachers' knowledge of their delinquencies. In their schooldays they are quite likely to have truanted from school, and perhaps an unusually large proportion of them come from homes in which at some (frequently unspecified) time both parents were not, for whatever reason, living together; yet even on these points, the findings of some enquiries are negative. And beyond this we cannot go.'

The studies on which these conclusions were based were carried out from just prior to the First World War up to the mid-50s. Some of the hypotheses would no longer be considered important. For example, church attendance among the younger generation is now so low that its absence would not be seen as strongly related to the development of delinquent behaviour. Most of the conclusions, however, are likely to be of importance in attempting to understand the causes of such behaviour.

Wootton concluded that there is much evidence for a relationship between prison sentences and social class, but that this does not necessarily imply a prevalence of criminality among the lower classes. The relative absence of members of the upper social classes in prisons could be due to judges' prejudices in sentencing. The proportion of convicted persons who are imprisoned varies enormously from one category of offenders to another, and it can be argued that lower class offences such as petty thieving are dealt with more severely than upper class offences such as driving under the influence of drink.

A recent longitudinal survey, known as the Cambridge Study in Delinquent Development, designed to determine which factors, or combination of factors, would prove to be the clearest determinants of future delinquency is described by D. J. West in his book *Present Conduct and Future Delinquency*. Over 400 boys from a densely populated, working-class district are being followed-up from the age of eight to nine years to school leaving age or beyond. The results presented concerning the first stage of the investigation deal mainly with the boys' conduct at this early age, but, as would have been expected from previous studies, such behaviour was shown to be a strong indicator of later misconduct. The boys were classified into good, average, and bad categories on the basis of a combined assessment from teachers' ratings of behaviour in school, and ratings of conduct disorder made by psychiatric social workers. A follow-up at the age of 11 years showed that much the same group of boys were categorised as badly behaved at the two ages, and boys who had been so categorised were much more liable to juvenile court appearances at under 14 years of age. In contrast to what might have been expected from Wootton's conclusions, poor conduct was found to be related to virtually all factors which were considered in the study on the grounds that they had been frequently cited in the literature as having relevance to the development of juvenile delinquency.

By combining measures of inadequate family income, low socio-economic status, unsatisfactory housing, belonging to a large family, physical neglect of the child, neglect of the interior of the house, and whether the family was supported by social agencies, the boys were classified into three groups according to whether social handicap was absent, moderate, or severe. This combined measure of social handicap was strongly related to the conduct rating, 11% of the boys in whom social handicap was absent being categorised as badly behaved, whereas 48% of those with severe social handicap were so categorised.

In criminological research great importance has been attributed to the effects of permanently broken homes, or temporary separations of infants from their parents, in determining bad behaviour in later years. Boys were classified as having come from a broken home if either natural parent was no longer present, whether this was due to death, divorce, separation, or desertion. This classification did not necessarily mean that the boy was not looked after by two parental figures, as in some cases he had been placed in the care of step-parents or foster parents. Another group was identified who had been separated temporarily from their mother at an early age. A further group consisted of boys who did not fit into either of the above categories, and yet in whom there was evidence of physical neglect. Each of these three adverse categories, in comparison with the remainder of the sample, was associated with a more than doubly raised incidence of badly behaved boys. These findings are in line with the general trend shown by the studies of official offenders reviewed by Wootton. It seems that families where the parents are not consistently living together are likely to produce bad behaviour, and later delinquent and criminal conduct, in the children. The difficulty is to identify what it is about such families that causes the children to behave in this manner.

Another relationship showing similarity to the findings with official offenders, but which again involves considerable difficulty in interpretation, is that concerning criminality in the family. Having a father with a criminal conviction increased the probability of a poor conduct rating for the boy, and, as would have been expected from other research findings, families in which the father had been convicted showed increased rates of conviction for mothers and older brothers. But it is difficult to know how the family's criminality affects the boy. Does he, perhaps, follow their example, or is the relationship merely present because criminality is related to other adverse factors in the family which cause him to be badly behaved? It is even possible that the relationships between childhood delinquency and measures of parental inadequacy have little to do with any adverse environmental factors. The greater incidence of delinquent children in criminal families could be due mainly, not to the criminal influence of the parents, but to an inherited disposition towards criminality which would result in such behaviour even if the children were brought up in a completely different environment. We will see in the section on theoretical explanations that there is strong evidence for the inheritance of criminal behaviour, and the relationships with such adverse social factors as broken homes and parental criminality are likely to be partly explicable by this fact.

Factors to do with the method of upbringing and discipline adopted by the parents have a more obvious relationship to the development of the child's behaviour and the existence of this relationship in connection with official delinquency has been well-documented. In one of the most famous series of studies on criminality and delinquency, the American criminologists, Sheldon and Eleanor Glueck, constructed prediction tables by which prospective offenders might

be identified in advance. They carefully matched nearly 500 juvenile delinquents with a control sample for age, intelligence, race, and socio-economic status, and compared these two groups in respect to some 400 biological, psychological, psychiatric and socio-cultural factors. It took a considerable and highly-trained staff of social investigators eight years to compile and verify the 1000 necessary social case histories. They used the data to derive prediction tables by which prospective offenders might be identified in advance. Their Social Prediction Table, based on the five social factors which were found to best discriminate the delinquents from the non-delinquents, is presented as Table 16.1.

Table 16.1   Identification of potential juvenile delinquents based on five social factors

Predictive factors	Delinquency scores
Discipline of boy by father	
Firm but kindly	9.3
Lax	59.8
Overstrict or erratic	72.5
Supervision of boy by mother	
Suitable	9.9
Fair	57.5
Unsuitable	83.2
Affection of father for boy	
Warm (including overprotective)	33.8
Indifferent or hostile	75.9
Affection of mother for boy	
Warm (including overprotective)	43.1
Indifferent or hostile	86.2
Cohesiveness of family	
Marked	20.6
Some	61.3
None	96.9

The delinquency scores indicate the frequency of the occurrence of the factors amongst the delinquents. Thus 72.5% of the boys whose discipline was classifiable as overstrict or erratic were in the delinquent group compared to but 9.3% of the cases in which discipline was firm but kindly. A rating of unsuitable supervision was given where the mother left the child to his own devices without guidance, or in the care of an irresponsible person. The categorisation of indifferent affection was given where the parent was found to not pay much attention to the child, and of hostile affection where the parent rejected the child. The cohesiveness of the family was rated according to evidence of co-operativeness, group interests, pride in the home and affection for each other, as opposed to where self-interest of the members of the family exceeded group interest. It can be seen from Table

16.1 that such factors concerning family background were highly predictive of officially defined delinquency in the Gluecks' studies, and much the same relationships were found to hold with the ratings of the boys' conduct obtained in the Cambridge study.

Whereas the review by Wootton indicates that many of the social variables which are assumed to be linked with criminality may not in fact be so, West's report suggests that the conduct of primary school boys is related to virtually all variables which have been implicated in the study of delinquency. It is likely that many factors which affect the behaviour of the child in his home environment are not of importance in influencing the continuation of childhood misbehaviour into a later life of delinquent activity. Thus it can be expected that social factors will differ in their relative importance according to the type of antisocial behaviour under consideration. Not only may different social factors be related to the development of different categories of antisocial behaviour, but some factors relating to misconduct have been shown to operate selectively according to social circumstances. With such a complex set of relationships it is extremely difficult to tell which are important as possible causes of criminality.

Although many of the social factors which have been thought to relate to delinquency may not in fact do so, there is no doubt that some types of social and family background are far more likely than others to produce delinquents. The difficulty is to know how the background factors operate to cause the boy to become delinquent. And here the problem becomes even more complex for it has frequently been noted that some boys are so resistant to delinquent behaviour that they will conform to social requirements under extremely bad social conditions. Others are so susceptible that they become delinquent in environments where it appears that none of the adverse social factors usually associated with delinquency is present. It can be assumed that there are important individual factors which make some individuals vulnerable to social stress, and it is to a consideration of these that we now turn.

INDIVIDUAL FACTORS
Psychological variables have appeared as problematical as sociological ones for discovering consistent relationships with criminality. Metfessel and Lovell, in 1942, reviewing the literature on individual correlates of crime, found that age and sex were the only factors to hold up firmly, and also concluded that no reliable picture of a criminal personality could be drawn. In 1950, Schuessler and Cressey reported the evaluation of personality measurements obtained on criminals and non-criminals over the preceding 25 years. For 30 tests, used in all 113 times, no patterns of consistent results indicating reliable personality differences between the criminal and normal populations emerged.

More recent evidence suggests, however, that the use of more valid tests is capable of establishing reliable personality correlates of criminal behaviour.

The frequently noted relationship between poor academic performance and delinquency was for long accompanied by the assumption that criminality is closely related to low intelligence. However, with the development of more refined intelligence tests, which are less dependent on academic achievement, differences in intelligence quotients which early investigators found between groups of delinquents and non-delinquents tend no longer to be found.

It has for long been argued by psychiatrists that many persistent criminals possess some constitutional defect which prevents them from acquiring normal social values. The terms used to classify people showing such personality disorders have varied, but the term 'psychopath' is perhaps the best known. The psychopath is typically described as someone who, while not suffering from any structural disease of the brain, mental subnormality, or neurotic or psychotic disorder, is unable to make a satisfactory emotional adjustment or form lasting emotional relationships, is irresponsible, lacks self-control, and shows repeated acts of aggression. He shows no ordinary feelings of guilt, lacks insight into his own behaviour, and is clearly unable to profit from experience. Several studies have shown a marked lack of agreement between psychiatrists in the diagnostic labels they would apply to specific patients, and clearly psychopathy cannot be thought of in an all-or-none fashion. In order to get round this difficulty psychologists have devised dimensional systems of personality classification, and we look now at some studies which have shown reliable differences between delinquents or criminals and normals on various personality dimensions.

A series of studies by S. R. Hathaway and E. D. Monachesi has been carried out to investigate the relationships between juvenile delinquency and scores on various personality scales of an extensive questionnaire, known as the Minnesota Multiphasic Personality Inventory. There is an extensive literature on this instrument (commonly abbreviated and known as the M.M.P.I.) and a considerable body of objective and subjective information about the meaning of the wide variety of personality profiles that can be obtained from its use. It consists of a large number of items, varying combinations of which form scales to measure, for example, neurotic and psychotic factors as observed in adult maladjustment and indicators of the psychopathic deviate and paranoid behaviour disorders.

Some 4000 ninth grade schoolchildren (i.e. aged about 14 years) attending Minneapolis public schools during 1947–1948 were tested with the M.M.P.I., and a follow-up investigation made two years later. In this, each child was checked from official records for evidence of delinquent behaviour and was given a delinquency rating on the basis of these findings. The information was then related to earlier M.M.P.I. performance, and it was found that boys scoring high on certain combinations of the personality scales, namely psychopathic deviate, schizophrenia, and hypomania, tend to become delinquent with greater than average frequency. High scores on other combinations of the scales, namely social introversion, depression, and a scale indicative of general feminine interests as these appear in contrast to those of the average male, were shown to be predictive of low rates of later delinquency. Personality profiles in which the remainder of the clinical scales were dominant were predictive of approximately average delinquency rates. These three sets of M.M.P.I. scales were therefore termed, respectively, delinquency excitatory scales, delinquency inhibitory scales, and delinquency variable scales. Further follow-up studies were undertaken when the boys were 18 and 23 years of age, and it was found that in spite of the changes in delinquency patterns occurring over the longer periods of time the three sets of scales were still predictive of the later misconduct levels. The research was extended to include a further 11 000 ninth grade children who were given the M.M.P.I. during the 1953–1954 school year. The results closely replicated those of the earlier studies, and the girls provided very similar results to boys, although the delinquency rate with the girls was so low that it required this larger sample to properly develop the evidence. The authors

concluded that the method of their studies permits the objective identification of some boys and girls whose personality traits seem to presage delinquent behaviour. The results also clearly indicated that some boys and girls have measurable traits seemingly inimical to the occurrence of delinquency.

In another series of studies H. C. Peterson and D. R. Quay and their collaborators have attempted to determine the principal dimensions of personality associated with juvenile delinquency in samples of institutionalised adolescents. In order to do this they factor analysed responses to questionnaires whose items (some of which were taken from the M.M.P.I.) had in previous work been empirically shown to be related to delinquency. Consistently throughout the studies the majority of variance was found to be accounted for by three factors which were labelled psychopathic-unsocialised, neurotic-disturbed, and subcultural-socialised. The psychopathic factor was composed of items implying the presence of a tough, amoral, rebellious attitude, impulsiveness, and an open distrust of both social institutions and other people. Some items of the second factor also implied impulsive behaviour, but were accompanied by items suggesting the presence of remorse, tension, guilt and depression. The third factor contained items concerning a family and subcultural background of delinquent activity, and suggested the acceptance of delinquent mores without personality maladjustment. A fourth factor, labelled inadequacy-immaturity, also emerged on occasion in their analyses.

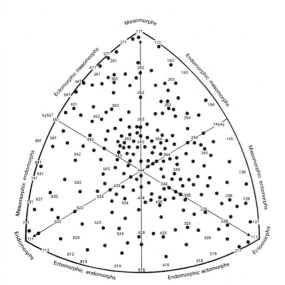

Figure 16.1 The distribution of somatotypes for a male college population of 4000. Each black dot represents 20 cases. (From W. H. Sheldon, E. M. Hartl and E. McDermott, 1949, *Varieties of Delinquent Youth*, by courtesy of Harper Brothers, New York)

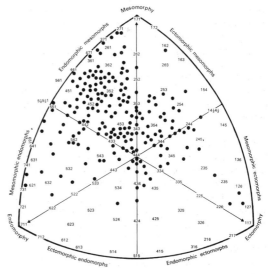

Figure 16.2 The distribution of somatotypes for 200 delinquent boys. (From W. H. Sheldon, E. M. Hartl and E. McDermott, 1949, *Varieties of Delinquent Youth*, by courtesy of Harper Brothers, New York)

In addition to work with personality questionnaires, this series of studies has attempted to determine personality dimensions associated with delinquency by analysing ratings of problem behaviour and case history data, and again the four factors described above have tended to emerge. A comparison of the results obtained from groups of institutionalised delinquents and of public school pupils showed a marked structure similarity across the varying samples, and Quay has argued that the degree of similarity between the results of the various studies indicates the presence of basic personality trait dimensions whose origin and maintenance are of considerable importance in the understanding of juvenile delinquency.

A different approach to the relationship between personality and delinquency was taken by W. H. Sheldon in his work on body build. This work renewed the long historical interest in the relationship between physical constitution and personality, and prompted a number of studies into the physical characteristics of criminals and delinquents. Sheldon postulated the existence of three main body types: the *endomorph* or thick-set type; the *mesomorph* or athletic type; and the *ectomorph* or lean, linear type. He did not adopt an all-or-none classification in the sense of categorising his subjects as belonging to one of three groups, but rather gave subjects three ratings, each on a seven point scale, to show the degree to which they tended towards each type. Thus while a person could be rated as tending predominantly towards one type of body build to the exclusion of the other two possible types, it was also possible to rate people showing a combination of the characteristics of all three. Links between physique and general personality traits are described in Chapter 9.

Sheldon provided a detailed biography including a number of criminological variables for each of a sample of 200 delinquent youths. He compared the somatotype distribution of this sample with that obtained from a sample of 4000 college students. These distributions are presented in Figures 16.1 and 16.2. A comparison of the two figures clearly shows a sharp departure of the delinquent population from the college distribution, with a distinct predominance of endomorphic mesomorphs. The delinquents tend more towards mesomorphy than endomorphy, but distinctly away from ectomorphy. There is, for example, a rarity of ectomorphic mesomorphs in comparison with the preponderance of endomorphic mesomorphs. The findings of Sheldon have been replicated by other workers. T. C. N. Gibbens, in a study of borstal boys, found similar physical differences between members of his sample and control subjects. Females have also been studied in this manner, P. Epps and R. W. Parnell having shown borstal girls, in comparison with university undergraduates of a similar age range, to be heavier in body build, and more muscular and fat.

In the above studies the use of undergraduates as control subjects leads to the possibility that the body build differences are due, not to delinquency, but to social class. However, as part of their extensive work on delinquency, which is not open to this criticism, the Gluecks compared anthropometric measurements and somatotype distribution, and also found that the delinquents were much more mesomorphic and less ectomorphic than the controls.

In general, then, various studies have pointed to a clear relationship between delinquency and body build along the lines suggested to exist by Sheldon. It is of further interest to note that of Sheldon's sample of 200, the group of 16 categorised as demonstrating 'primary criminality', who appeared to compose a small nucleus of really sincere, dedicated criminals, were all somatotyped as endomorphic mesomorphs. Generally such studies have also shown delinquents and non-delinquents to vary in their temperamental traits in a manner similar to that suggested by Sheldon. The studies are not strictly comparable, however, as different methods of personality assessment have been used.

The numerous studies which have been undertaken to determine personality differences between delinquents and controls are difficult to compare because of the different tests used. The clearest way to look for consistencies is probably via the system of personality classification adopted by H. J. Eysenck who, unlike proponents of other systems, lays emphasis on higher order factors (see Chapter 9). In addition to the well-known dimensions of extroversion and neuroticism, the presence of a third higher order factor of psychoticism has been implicit in Eysenck's writings for many years. He has hypothesised that there exists a set of correlated behaviour variables, indicative of predisposition to psychotic breakdown, demonstrable as a continuous variable in the normal population, and independent of extroversion and neuroticism. Eysenck describes the high psychoticism scorer as being characterised by the following traits: '(1) Solitary; not caring for other people. (2) Troublesome; not fitting in. (3) Cruel; inhumane. (4) Lack of feeling; insensitive. (5) Sensation-seeking; "arousal jag". (6) Hostile to others; aggressive. (7) Liking for odd, unusual things. (8) Disregard for danger; foolhardy. (9) Making fools of other people; upsetting them.'

Eysenck has proposed a theory of criminality based on his system of personality classification, which will be discussed in the next section. His theory leads to the predictions that criminals will score higher than control groups on all three of the major orthogonal dimensions of personality. Before seeing if it is possible to integrate the findings of the various studies concerning the personality of delinquents, we will look briefly at the results of several studies comparing criminals and controls on Eysenck's own dimensions. Table 16.2 summarises the published investigations

Table 16.2 **Summary of studies comparing criminals with control subjects on extroversion and neuroticism.** (From Eysenck, 1970, by courtesy of Paladin)

	ADOLESCENTS	E	N
1. Gibbens, T. C. N. (1963)	107 male delinquents	+	?
2. Glueck, S., Glueck, E. (1950)	500 male delinquents	+ +	?
3. Little, A. (1963)	290 male delinquents	=	+ +
4. Peterson, D. R. (1959; 1961)	116 male delinquents	+	+
5. Pierson, G. R., Kelly, R. F. (1963)	970 male delinquents	+ +	?
6. Price, J. R. (1968`	100 female delinquents	+ + +	+ + +
	ADULTS		
1. Bartholomew, A. A. (1957)	48 male and 24 female offenders (British)	=	+ +
2. Bartholomew, A. A. (1957)	100 male offenders (British)	=	+ +
3. Bartholomew, A. A. (1963)	150 male offenders, 159 female offenders (Australian)	+	+ +
4. Field, J. G. (1960)	369 male offenders (British)	+	+ +
5. Fitch, J. H. (1962)	700 male offenders (British)	=	+ +
6. Syed, I. (1964)	100 female offenders (British)	+	+ +
7. Warburton, F. W. (1965)	38 psychopathic criminals (American)	+ +	+ + +

which allow some reasonable assessment of the personality dimensions of extroversion and neuroticism. The signs given for extroversion (E) and neuroticism (N) 'signify whether the results are equivocal (=), support on the whole the hypothesis, but rather weakly (+), support the hypothesis significantly (++), or support the hypothesis very strongly (+++). Another sign is also used (?) to indicate that the data do not seem relevant to the personality trait in question.'

In general, results have supported the prediction concerning neuroticism more strongly than that concerning extroversion. This is possibly due to the effect of imprisonment on responses to items of the latter scale, especially these relating to the sociability aspect of extroversion. Prison life has such a curtailing effect on social intercourse that it is hardly surprising that prisoners should score low on sociability. Eysenck has distinguished between the sociability and impulsiveness components of extroversion, and it has been shown that when the scale is divided in this manner the impulsiveness items do successfully discriminate between prisoners and controls, even when the complete extroversion scale has failed to support the hypothesis.

Because of the only comparatively recent availability of psychoticism scales, little empirical work has been undertaken to test the prediction that criminals will be characterised by high psychoticism scores, but the studies which are available show that male prisoners are clearly higher, and female prisoners very much higher, than comparable groups of non-prisoners.

Nearly all the studies designed to test Eysenck's theory have been undertaken by comparing prisoners with control subjects. In an attempt to determine the applicability of Eysenck's theory to the misbehaviour of ordinary schoolchildren, M. P. Feldman and J. F. Allsopp have used a self-report questionnaire of anti-

social behaviour based on the work of H. B. Gibson. There is much evidence for the validity of such self-report measures, and both the antisocial behaviour score obtained with this questionnaire, and an objective measure of school misbehaviour based on school punishments received, have been shown to be positively related to extroversion, neuroticism and psychoticism in groups of boys and girls ranging from 11 to 16 years of age. Figure 16.3 shows antisocial behaviour and school misbehaviour scores for four groups of girls selected according to whether they had scored above average on all three, two, one, or none of the personality scales. It can be seen that the degree of misbehaviour varies markedly between these groups in the manner predicted by Eysenck's theory.

To what extent do the various approaches to the study of personality and delinquency link up? There would doubtless be many disagreements between the investigators we have considered here, but it does appear that there is a certain degree of consistency in the findings. Perhaps the hardest problem of interpretation is caused by the difference in the number of separate dimensions of personality which have been

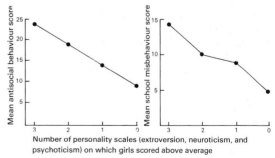

Number of personality scales (extroversion, neuroticism, and psychoticism) on which girls scored above average

Figure 16.3 Antisocial behaviour and school misbehaviour of groups of girls differing in personality. (See text for full explanation)

seen as important. Hathaway and Monachesi took the view that personality is so complex, and the number of different patterns of personality leading to delinquency so great, that it is unjustifiable to work with only a few personality variables. Yet their delinquency excitatory scales of Psychopathic deviate, Schizophrenia, and Hypomania bear a strong resemblance to the higher order factors of extroversion, neuroticism and psychoticism which Eysenck argues to be of importance in the development of delinquency. It is well-established that psychopaths score extremely high on both the extroversion and neuroticism scales of the Eysenck Inventories, and the psychopathic deviate scale of the M.M.P.I. has continually been shown to strongly discriminate delinquents from controls. There is a clear connection between Hathaway and Monachesi's delinquency excitatory scales and Eysenck's psychoticism dimension, but the delinquency inhibitory scales do not fit in so clearly with Eysenck's system. The finding that social introversion is an inhibitory scale does fit in, and that depression is an inhibitory scale may fit in, for a recent study has shown that whereas some neuroticism items discriminate strongly between prisoners and controls in line with Eysenck's theory, other items, if anything, discriminate in the opposite direction.

The work of Quay and Peterson, in which similar personality components associated with delinquency have been consistently obtained from studies using questionnaires, behaviour ratings, and case history data, points to the importance of psychopathy and neuroticism as continuous personality dimensions related to antisocial behaviour. Their studies have shown that these basic personality dimensions are not the exclusive property of institutionalised delinquents. It is merely that the scores on the personality dimensions are higher for the institutionalised delinquents than for non-institutionalised children showing problem behaviour. Their studies provide support for the notion of a continuum of antisocial behaviour related to basic personality trait dimensions, which again, if psychopathy is thought of as a combination of extroversion and neuroticism, show a marked similarity to Eysenck's higher order personality dimensions.

Sheldon distinguished two kinds of extroversion: viscerotonic and somatotonic. The former he called an extroversion of affect, the latter an extroversion of action. If we can go further and link his third component of temperament, cerebrotonia, with introversion, the studies on body build indicate, in Eysenck's terminology, that delinquents tend towards mesomorphy (impulsive extroversion?), somewhat less towards endomorphy (sociable extroversion?), and markedly away from ectomorphy (introversion?). It must be emphasised that this is in no way a conclusion about what the work on body build has shown,

but it does suggest a possible consistency between the results obtained from Sheldon's approach and those of other investigators who have used more standard measures of personality.

While the prospective studies of Hathaway and Monachesi strongly suggest that personality is predictive of later criminality, it could be argued that the findings of many of the investigations into the personality of criminals, especially those directly supporting Eysenck's theory, are due to the effects of incarceration. This explanation seems unlikely however. In the study by Sir Cyril Burt mentioned in the introductory section, the teachers rated the children for emotionality and for extroversion/introversion. A child was classified as highly emotional if the assessment placed him among the 25% most emotional children in the group. However, of those who became habitual offenders, 63% had been classified in this manner. The differences with respect to extroversion are even clearer, 54% of the offenders having been classified as 'extroverted' or 'unrepressed', and only 3% as 'introverted' or 'repressed'. If we can compare Burt's ratings of emotionality and extroversion/introversion with Eysenck's higher order factors of neuroticism and extroversion, we have strong evidence for the similarity of the findings obtained by two approaches to the study of the personality of criminals.

All these comparisons between different personality measures must be treated with caution, for it is easy to fall into the trap of considering two measures identical because the investigators who have used them have given them the same name. However, it can certainly be said that the findings of the various investigations into the personality of delinquency indicate that criminals and delinquents are characterised by personalities which differ, in a consistent manner, from the norm. In the following section we consider possible theoretical explanations for such differences.

THEORETICAL EXPLANATIONS

We have seen in the section on social factors the vast number of variables which have been implicated, through their empirically established relationship with criminality and delinquency, as possible causal factors in the development of antisocial behaviour. Even if it can be established which factors are actually important, and which relate to delinquency merely because of their association with an intervening variable, it is still necessary to attempt to explain how the adverse factors operate to help cause the delinquent conduct. It is clear that many of the factors which have been frequently implicated cannot, in the ordinary sense of the word, be regarded as causative.

One theory which makes much more intuitive sense than an explanation in terms of many social factors is that of 'differential association' proposed by Edwin H. Sutherland and Donald R. Cressey. According to this theory, criminal behaviour is learned in interaction with others, principally within intimate personal groups. The person who is not already trained in crime does not invent such behaviour. The necessary learning includes both techniques of committing crime, and the specific direction of motives and drives. The specific direction which is learned is dependent on the degree to which the person is surrounded by people who define the legal codes as rules either to be observed or to be violated. The principle of differential association refers to both criminal and anticriminal associations and concerns counteracting forces. When people become criminal, they do so because of contacts with criminal patterns and also because of isolation from anticriminal patterns.

Sutherland and Cressey are critical of the attempts of many scholars to explain criminal behaviour in terms of general drives and values such as the happiness principle, striving for social status, the money motive, or frustration because, they point out, these explain lawful behaviour as completely as they explain criminal behaviour. Their theory is useful in negating assertions that deviation from norms is simply the result of social adversity such as the family having insufficient income. Many social factors, such as the family's place of residence which is determined by income level, affect the kinds of associations a person has; but so too do individual factors such as the person's sociability. For example, an outgoing, active, sociable boy from a bad background will be more likely to develop criminal associations than a reserved, introverted boy. Thus the theory is able to indicate in a general way why it is that only some people with poor social backgrounds become delinquent. However, the theory is not precise enough to stimulate rigorous empirical test, and has been little explored by investigators.

It is commonly assumed that criminal behaviour is learned in a similar manner to other skills, and that if the results are unpleasant the conduct will be extinguished. However, the failure of long periods of forced isolation in depressing prison conditions to deter criminals from offending again suggests the need for some other explanation. In suggesting a possible explanation O. Hobart Mowrer argued that it is necessary to distinguish the process whereby the solutions to problems, or ordinary habits, are acquired, from the process whereby emotional learning, or conditioning, takes place. He differentiated these two processes by calling the first a teaching process and the second a training process. The first consists of learning which is individually helpful and the second of learning in which the primary object is social rather than individual. Mowrer argued that the normal socialised individual exhibits behaviour which is heavily influenced by the dictates of conscience. During infancy no demands are made on the individual, but there comes a time when socialisation

must begin, and an attempt is made to condition the child to acquire social attitudes and emotions which will act as his conscience and lay the basis for good character. At first this process will result in a good deal of resistance and resentment which is gradually overcome as the child moves towards adulthood. Sometimes, however, 'the opposition to authority and social sanctions which is aroused in the early attempts at socialisation is continued, relatively unmodified, on into later life. When this occurs we encounter a criminal, an individual . . . whose total energies are directed toward attacking, exploiting, and resisting the social order in which he finds himself'. This schematisation of the criminal personality type as representing the extreme in socialisation failure has proved extremely important in the development of theoretical explanations of criminality.

There is much in common between the manner in which children learn to inhibit unsuitable social behaviour and the phenomenon of passive avoidance conditioning which has been much investigated in animal laboratories. An example of this is where a hungry animal, which has learned to obtain food by pushing a bar, can be made to abandon this habit if a sufficiently strong electric shock is put on the bar. Mowrer's arguments concerning passive avoidance are theoretically quite complex but suggest basically that fear reactions become conditioned to stimuli produced during the first stages of the prohibited behaviour. In the example just given, once the bar has been connected up so as to provide shock, the animal will make several more attempts to obtain food by operating it and thus receive shock, but these attempts will eventually cease altogether. While they continue it is noticed that the animal's approach to the bar becomes increasingly jerky and hesitant, and Mowrer suggests this is due to internal (proprioceptive) stimuli, which are caused by the activity taking place and originate in the muscles, gradually becoming associated with the fear caused by the ultimate punishment. After a number of trials these conditioned stimuli evoke a state of anxiety sufficiently intense to prevent the behaviour occurring without the punishment being received. The advantage of this explanation is that it provides a rationale for the rat's behaviour involving a logical temporal sequence, for the animal makes the avoidance reaction following the occurrence of the conditioned state of anxiety.

Making extensive use of Mowrer's analysis, Gordon Trasler has attempted to develop a systematic theory of criminal action starting with the proposition that the criminal is someone for whom the process of social training has been defective. He proposes that the intensity of the anxiety reaction occurring in an individual who finds himself in a situation where he is tempted to commit a criminal act is a function of the severity of fear stimulated at the time of conditioning. Thus an effective deterrent against criminal activity will have been established in most individuals by the social training they have received during their childhood. This analysis would also help .to explain the apparent ineffectiveness of imprisonment as a deterrent against the continuation of criminal activity. It is popularly assumed that where fear acts as a deterrent the degree to which it will be effective is dependent on the likely severity of the sentence if the offender is caught. If Trasler's explanation is correct it may be that the threat of a long sentence will make little difference to the chance of a poorly socialised individual engaging in crime.

Trasler notes that the application of physical pain, as in the example given of passive avoidance conditioning in the rat, is not an essential element in passive avoidance training. As long as anxiety or fear can be stimulated by some means so that it immediately follows the conditioned stimulus on a number of successive occasions, passive avoidance conditioning will be established. Trasler suggests that there are, broadly, two ways in which parents can stimulate sufficiently intense anxiety when a child indulges in prohibited behaviour. There is, firstly, painful or unpleasant punishment in the form of a spanking or the withdrawal of a child's pleasures such as the use of his toys, which parallels the laboratory technique with animals discussed above. Here the anxiety aroused by the anticipation of the punishment must be sufficiently strong to counter the impulse to carry out the action, so the method will not be effective unless the parents are willing to apply a sanction which is severe enough to stimulate an adequate anxiety reaction. Secondly, there is the method of withdrawal of parental approval which is a powerful sanction in the early years of life when a child is highly dependent on his parents' affection. This will only work, however, when there is a constant relationship of emotional warmth between parent and child so that the threat of withdrawn approval will evoke an unpleasant anxiety reaction in marked contrast to the normal feeling of security. The method will prove ineffective on a child who is constantly fearful and insecure in his relationship with his parents. These two methods are used in combination by most parents and it is not possible to completely distinguish them. For example, a mild slap may serve more as a sign of parental disapproval than as a physical punishment in the laboratory sense.

Mowrer's explanation of the approach–avoidance type behaviour of the rat approaching the bar in terms of internal stimuli originating in the muscles and caused by the activity evoking a conditioned anxiety response is insufficient as an explanation of human avoidance behaviour as it is often impossible to identify any similar tentative movements towards the prohibited act. Trasler argues that this difficulty can be resolved by taking into account the human capacity for considering a course of action in advance. He suggests that the whole sequence of behaviour must

be thought of as comprising both the initial contemplation of, and the subsequent undertaking of, the observable physical actions. When training or conditioning has effectively taken place, the contemplation of the prohibited sequence of behaviour acts as a conditioned stimulus arousing the anxiety reaction which blocks the remainder of the behavioural sequence. Through stimulus-generalisation, this conditioned reaction will also be called out by situations which resemble the original one. Much depends on the ability the child develops at identifying the elements of the situation that are relevant, and this in turn is dependent on the adequacy with which the parents explain for what reason the child is being punished. If an effort is made to explain a general principle which underlies why a number of different isolated offences are wrong the child 'gradually acquires a set of moral values—anxiety reactions conditioned to generic notions or concepts—in the light of which he can determine the rightness or wrongness of a particular action, even in novel circumstances'.

If, as Trasler argues, socialisation consists mainly of passive avoidance training, it is necessary to account for individual differences in susceptibility to fear conditioning. An attempt to do so has been made by Eysenck who argues, on similar lines to Mowrer and Trasler, that a person's conduct during adulthood is determined very much by the quality of the conditioning received during childhood and by his degree of conditionability; that is the degree to which he is able to be conditioned by the stimuli which are presented to him. Eysenck suggests that what is normally termed our conscience is merely a set of autonomic responses conditioned according to ordinary Pavlovian conditioning. He argues that extroverted people will, because of physiological differences in conditionability, have weaker consciences than introverted people, and presents evidence that extroverts, both neurotic and stable, are in fact more difficult to condition than neurotic and stable introverts. There is also evidence available to show that psychopaths condition much more poorly than control subjects. But disconfirmatory results have also been obtained, some investigators having failed to obtain differences between psychopaths and others in the rate of conditioning. Conditioning is an extremely complex phenomenon and there are many different types of conditioning experiments which can be carried out. The studies in Eysenck's laboratories have mainly concerned eye-blink conditioning, but even when we restrict ourselves to the study of a specific type of response such as this there are still many parameters which when varied may alter the nature of the results obtained. Examples of such parameters are the nature and intensity of both the C.S. and U.C.S. and the interval of time between them. In the laboratory these parameters can be varied to optimise or reduce the degree of conditioning established. It is of interest that the largest differences in conditionability between introverts and extroverts have generally been obtained in experimentally controlled situations favouring a poor degree of conditioning, for these are clearly closer to the situation in which the child receives his training in real life. A vast amount of work still needs to be undertaken in order to determine to which categories of conditioning it is possible to apply Eysenck's postulate of individual differences in conditionability which are related to introversion.

From the proposition that it is the personality dimension of extroversion which is responsible for the differences between people in their degree of conditionability, Eysenck's theory predicts that extroverts are more likely than introverts to behave in an antisocial fashion. Further, he predicts, a high degree of neuroticism acts as a drive strongly reinforcing the extroverted or introverted tendencies towards or against antisocial behaviour. In his later work Eysenck has suggested that the addition of the psychoticism factor will make the relationship between personality and criminality more convincing. He gives two reasons for believing that psychoticism may be implicated in the causation of criminality. Firstly, he notes that the characteristics defining the high scorer on this personality dimension have much in common with the characteristics shown by many prisoners. The second reason lies in the consistent psychiatric observation that psychosis and criminality have a particularly close connection. Many studies have shown that a significantly high proportion of relatives of schizophrenics are classifiable as psychopaths or criminals. We discussed in the section on individual factors the evidence relating to these predictions, and

saw that criminals and delinquents have, indeed, been shown to be high on the extroversion, neuroticism, and psychoticism personality dimensions.

Can the theoretical explanations proposed by Mowrer, Trasler and Eysenck account for some of the social factors which are known to relate to delinquent and criminal behaviour? There is certainly evidence to suggest that they can. It is known that middle class parents place stronger emphasis on moral and socially approved behaviour, and on explaining the general principles behind why the child is being punished, than do working class parents. Table 16.3 shows that with increasing degrees of social handicap parental discipline rated as erratic or lax increased markedly while discipline rated as normal or strict showed a corresponding decrease. Both Trasler and Eysenck have argued that differences in the incidence of criminal behaviour between social groups may be caused by differences in the methods of socialisation applied. While there is a wide conceptual gap between conditioning schedules applied in the laboratory and ratings of parental discipline obtained in social research, the evidence available concerning differences in discipline at different social levels suggests that a theory based on conditioning is capable of accounting for many of the social variables which have been shown to be related to delinquency and criminality.

As we saw in the section on social factors, there is a mass of evidence on environmental factors which, with varying degrees of certainty, have been shown to relate to delinquent and criminal conduct. In contrast with the stress placed on environmental factors, however, most criminologists have neglected the possibility that the predisposition to criminality is inherited. Evidence for the inheritance of criminality

Table 16.3   **Maternal and paternal discipline related to three degrees of social handicap.** (From West, 1969, by courtesy of Heinemann)

	Boys with social handicap		
	Nil *(N=182)* *percentage*	*Moderate* *(N=174)* *percentage*	*Severe* *(N=55)* *percentage*
Maternal discipline			
Normal	550.6	40.8	25.5
Erratic or lax	19.8	33.9	61.8
Strict or very strict	20.8	16.1	7.2
Not rated or not applicable	8.8	9.2	5.5
	100	100	100
Paternal discipline			
Normal	47.8	42.5	29.1
Erratic or lax	15.4	25.9	43.6
Strict or very strict	26.4	17.2	18.2
Not rated or not applicable	10.4	14.4	9.1
	100	100	100

comes largely from twin studies, and has been discussed by J. Shields in Chapter 10. It has been established beyond doubt that monozygotic twins show higher concordance rates for officially defined criminality than dizygotic twins. From a review of the evidence concerning the genotypic determination of criminal conduct, Eysenck concluded that the facts support an interactionist theory. We need to consider the combination of both hereditary and environmental factors, and to specify the environmental conditions which predispose a person to crime, and some mechanism for the inheritance of criminality. It is clearly far more difficult to demonstrate any feasible mechanism for the inheritance of antisocial behaviour than it is to find environmental factors which relate to it, but the evidence for the importance of genetic factors makes it essential that they be considered in any adequate theoretical formulation.

Eysenck's theory is an attempt to explain how hereditary causes may work by linking the development of antisocial behaviour with inherited personality traits. There is considerable evidence that there is a strong hereditary basis for the personality dimensions of extroversion, neuroticism and psychoticism (see Chapter 10). We can assume that the personality differences which have been consistently obtained between delinquents or criminals and controls, using various measures such as the M.M.P.I. or the Eysenck Inventories, are in part due to genetic factors operating in an environment that permitted the development of antisocial behaviour.

The theoretical explanations based on differences in conditioning, such as those of Mowrer and Trasler, and the extended theory of Eysenck linking conditionability to inherited personality traits, do not claim to entirely explain the process whereby a person develops into a delinquent or criminal. Differences, caused by social factors of upbringing or individual factors of personality, in the degree to which people become conditioned to obey the rules of society are clearly important, but they are far from being all-important. Sociologists have shown that differing attitudes towards certain forms of criminal conduct are simply illustrations of differences in culture patterns. In some subcultures nothing is seen to be wrong in stealing from large stores or employers, whereas stealing from a friend will be seen to be strictly taboo. And, as Wootton has so clearly pointed out, in middle-class subcultures legally defined and clearly dangerous offences such as driving under the influence of alcohol are regarded as of no importance whereas petty thieving from a multimillion pound organisation is indeed seen to be criminal. Sheldon points out that our type of society has many individuals whose behaviour, while legally blameless in that it conforms to the official rules, is far more harmful to our wellbeing as a community than that of the average minor offender. He tells us that in the course of daily conversations for upwards of a decade with young men who had been labelled delinquent he became impressed that most of them also 'were playing according to rule and were fairly sure of *their* rules'.

In spite of the vast number of empirical relationships which have been found between social factors, individual factors, and various measures of antisocial behaviour, we are still unable to specify with any certainty which variables may be important, and which have merely been implicated because they are related to some other variable, perhaps never considered, which is important. Even when studies such as the Cambridge Study in Delinquent Development have hopefully managed to finally eliminate the need to consider many of the variables with which delinquency research has been concerned, there will still remain many important variables which will have to be taken into account in an attempt to develop more adequate theoretical explanations of criminality. These variables will doubtless include some which have thus far been barely considered. One obvious one is the sex difference in crime, which far outweighs any other factor that has been associated with delinquent or criminal behaviour. Wootton has pointed to the curious lack of research on this matter:

'Presumably, since the number of children of each sex is much the same, such experiences as the break-up of their homes, or the loss of parental affection, must fall with roughly equal frequency upon boys and girls. Yet no one asks why one sex should be nearly eight times more resistant to these shocks than the other. While there have been a few studies of women offenders, investigators have generally looked upon the difference between masculine and feminine criminality merely as a reason for eliminating female subjects from their researches on the ground that they provide insufficient material. Whether this insufficiency reflects a genuine difference in feminine propensity to crime, or merely the superior skill with which female lawbreakers elude detection, and how this difference is related to factors in the training and education of girls which they do not share with their brothers— these questions remain unanswered and indeed unasked.'

It is interesting in this connection that scores on Eysenck's psychoticism scales, which have been shown to be strongly related to criminality, are much higher for males than for females. Further, the M.M.P.I. scale measuring femininity of interests has been identified as a delinquency inhibitory scale. Environmental influences which are different for girls than for boys must be partly responsible for the relative lack of female criminality, but sex differences in inherited personality traits are also likely to be of importance.

In addition to the need for much more research to

facilitate the development of more adequate theoretical explanations for the complete range of antisocial behaviour encountered in our society, there is the important practical need for the development of methods to change the conduct of many delinquents and criminals on whom standard types of punishment have so little positive effect. There are grounds for optimism in this direction for in the same way as the development of learning theory has enabled the construction of theoretical explanations of criminality, it has also resulted in a rationale for the modification of such conduct through techniques of behaviour therapy (see Chapter 23). The theories and knowledge presently available are also suggestive of the possibility of preventing the onset of much antisocial behaviour. For example, the conduct problems encountered in many of our schools can be expected to be reduced by the adoption of methods of discipline based on the knowledge gained from psychological research. The practical and theoretical problems in criminology which remain to be investigated are vast, but the knowledge we possess is perhaps sufficient to justify optimism that the tremendous effort expended on criminological research may ultimately lead to the development of, firstly, adequate theories to explain the whole range of antisocial behaviour, and, secondly, methods to prevent the onset or continuation of criminal and delinquent activity, thus resulting in the reduction of many of the undesirable consequences of such behaviour.

Recommended reading

Detailed references to other studies can be obtained from the following list:

Eysenck, H. J. (1970). *Crime and Personality* (2nd Ed.) (London: Paladin)

Trasler, G. B. (1962). *The Explanation of Criminality* (London: Routledge and Kegan Paul)

Trasler, G. B. (1973). Criminal behaviour. In: *Handbook of Abnormal Psychology* (H. J. Eysenck, editor) (London: Pitman Press)

West, D. J. (1969). *Present Conduct and Future Delinquency* (London: Heinemann)

Wootton, B. (1959). *Social Science and Social Pathology* (London: George Allen and Unwin)

Chapter 17

PHYSICAL TREATMENTS

J. J. Wright

INTRODUCTION

Physical methods of treatment have played an important role in psychiatry ever since the neolithic period. In those days the first craniotomies were performed, probably with a view to releasing evil spirits. Since then there have been very considerable advances in technique, but it is uncertain whether the theory of the subject has changed much for the better.

Confronted with the mental anguish of a fellow man, and expected to do something dramatic to alleviate this suffering, today's psychiatrist must choose from a range of alternatives much like those of his prehistoric forebears. He can offer a potion selectively toxic to parts of the nervous system; he can render his patient temporarily unconscious in the hope that he will be better when he awakens; or if both he and his patient feel desperate he can recommend cranial surgery. Today's psychiatrist can do these things much better and with less untoward risk of ill-effects than ever before.

On the other hand, assessing the degree of effectiveness, and mode of action of these physical therapies has proved a difficult problem for science. All practising clinicians from the ancient shaman to the modern psychiatrist have held strong private views on the effectiveness of their preferred mode of treatment. Psychiatric patients likewise have strong expectations regarding the effects the physical therapies will have upon them, and thus very strong placebo effects can be generated. These placebo effects may influence the outcome of treatment in ways that are very difficult to predict. After treatment, if recovery ensues, it is usual for neither doctor nor patient to have any clear understanding of the degree to which spontaneous cure, physical therapy, or psychotherapy have contributed. Yet both may have strong opinions on the matter. It is in this emotionally difficult atmosphere that research on the psychological effects of physical treatment in psychiatry has to be conducted. Certain forms of physical therapy such as hydrotherapy, and insulin coma therapy stand as gruesome examples of the confusion of biological effects with accompanying psychotherapeutic and placebo effects.

The currently favoured method for the objective study of physical means of treatment is the double-blind controlled trial. In this method, treatment is administered to one group of patients while another group of patients receives some form of mock therapy. Neither the clinicians observing the patients, nor the patients themselves are supposed to know to which group any patient belongs. This is intended, ideally, to control for placebo, and general environmental effects. Regrettably, this type of study runs into numerous obstacles because of the complex side-effects produced by the physical treatments. These side-effects readily betray to clinician and patient whether or not the treatment is being given, in many cases. Replicating the side-effects in a control group may help in some circumstances, but this is often impossible or unethical. No complete solution to this difficulty is at present available.

There are still further barriers to clinical assessment of physical therapies. In many cases these therapies seem to exert effects which are different in kind, rather than degree, in mentally ill persons as compared to normal individuals or persons with illnesses of a different type. For example, antidepressant drugs appear to alleviate symptoms of depression in certain groups of patients. They do not affect other types of patient, nor do they induce feelings of euphoria in normal subjects. Since psychiatric diagnosis itself is often prone to cause disagreement among psychiatrists in any given case, then there are difficulties in making comparisons between the results of therapy with the same agent in different clinical groups, if these have been diagnosed in different clinics, or even by different psychiatrists in the same clinic.

In this review we will restrict attention to the major methods of treatment currently believed to have definite biological therapeutic effects, i.e. the tranquillisers, the antidepressant drugs, electroconvulsive therapy, some psychosurgical procedures, and treatment with lithium.

TRANQUILLISING DRUGS

The phenothiazines

These drugs are all chemically related to one parent compound; phenothiazine. Some of the best known members of the group are chlorpromazine, trifluoperazine and fluphenazine.

This group of compounds first found biological application as a treatment for infestations with worms. In 1950 chlorpromazine was first synthesised by Charpentier *et al.*, and was used to potentiate anaesthetics. It was soon noted that the drug did more than merely potentiate anaesthesia—it was itself calming to anxious patients. Its application in psychiatry soon followed and produced a deluge of enthusiastic, if poorly controlled, observations of its beneficial effects in the treatment of psychotics. Early studies made little allowance for the effects of therapeutic enthusiasm, and the wave of hopefulness which went through the back wards of mental hospitals when a phenothiazine treatment programme was introduced. Even so, it seemed clear that a definite therapeutic improvement had been produced.

The pharmacology of the phenothiazines is very complicated. If we take chlorpromazine as a representative example: within the nervous system, the drug becomes concentrated mainly in the stem of the brain, and is excreted very slowly, so that its action on the brain is very prolonged. The effects produced by the drug are partly dependent on the duration of treatment. At first, striking sedation is produced, but after a few days this wears off. Animal and human studies have shown that chlorpromazine reduces responsiveness to external stimulation and gross motor activity, without reducing motor power or co-ordination. Moderate doses severely affect performance in conditioned avoidance reactions, without comparable reduction in reflex time.

Psychological tests in man have mainly been conducted after single acute doses of the drug and in such tests the immediate sedative effect is such as to make the drug appear similar in effect to the barbiturates. It is the less understood chronic effects of the drug which are utilised clinically, especially in the treatment of schizophrenia. Controlled clinical trials of phenothiazine drugs in the treatment of schizophrenia have shown their striking superiority to inert placebo in controlling hallucinations and excitement, as well as reducing thought disorder and delusions. Inert placebo tablets are a very unsatisfactory placebo for such trials, because the numerous side-effects produced by phenothiazines make double-blind control virtually impossible. These side-effects include (as well as sedation in the early stages of treatment) dry mouth, blurred vision, low blood pressure (with subsequent tendency to attacks of fainting) and neuromuscular effects (due to an action on the basal ganglia) indistinguishable from Parkinson's disease.

Thus the use of barbiturates as placebo is also unsatisfactory, as any sophisticated patient, or psychiatric nurse can fairly easily distinguish which drug is being used. Because of this difficulty evidence of the specific therapeutic efficacy of phenothiazines sufficient to satisfy scientific purists is lacking. It has not been possible to separate the effects of the phenothiazines from the effects of enthusiasm for the drug, and changing social attitudes towards the schizophrenic patient. Since the introduction of phenothiazines the average duration of hospital stay for initial schizophrenic illnesses has been markedly reduced, and the subsequent rate of discharge as 'cured' or 'much improved' has also increased greatly. Readmission rates because of subsequent relapse have also increased, and the role of phenothiazines in altering the long-term prognosis of schizophrenia is still a matter of controversy. Although it is widely held that long-term phenothiazine treatment diminishes the chance of relapse of schizophrenia, Bleuler and others have advanced some figures on long-term follow-up which contradict this. These long-term follow-up statistics suggest that the long-term prognosis of schizophrenia is not as terrible as previously believed, and the phenothiazines may be receiving undue credit for the recovery of many patients.

Despite the absence of conclusive clinical studies, it is fair to say that present studies strongly suggest that phenothiazines exert a specific antipsychotic action in schizophrenia at least during the acute phases of the illness. Perhaps the best physiological explanation for this therapeutic action is that advanced by Bradley. He has demonstrated that while chlorpromazine does not diminish the transmission of nerve signals from the arousal controlling mechanisms of the brain stem to the cortex, it does diminish the effect of peripheral stimulation in activating the arousal controlling mechanisms. He concluded that chlorpromazine might therefore diminish the distracting and arousing effects of peripheral stimulation, without comparable disturbance of internal cortico–reticular interactions. This is in accord with contemporary theories which attribute schizophrenia to disturbances in the capacity to suppress irrelevant stimuli.

The butyrophenones

This group of drugs produce psychological effects not grossly different from the phenothiazines. Pharmacologically they produce much less effect on the peripheral nervous system, while producing the same central effects as phenothiazines, including sedation, and suppression of conditioned avoidance reactions and spontaneous activity. Controlled clinical trials have demonstrated no therapeutic advantage over phenothiazines in the treatment of psychosis.

The benzodiazepines

These compounds, and a few related drugs are known as minor tranquillisers, or anxiolytic sedatives. Their use is now wide spread among jittery people of all varieties—especially in the forms of chlordiazepoxide (Librium) and diazepam (Valium). These drugs are very different to the phenothiazines in action. Benzodiazepines produce a depression of neural activity especially in the limbic system (those parts of the brain especially involved in emotional behaviour), in the arousal mechanisms of the brain stem, and the neurones of the spinal cord. The result is a tranquillised, sedated and rather limp individual. In experimental animals, combativeness and conditioned avoidance reactions are depressed, without impairment of escape reactions, in a manner comparable to the phenothiazines. However, clinical trials have indicated that these drugs are quite ineffective in the treatment of psychosis. Their virtues as therapy for people suffering neurotic anxieties have been demonstrated in controlled trials, although they have never been shown to be convincingly superior to barbiturates. They are much safer than barbiturates in the event of a patient taking them as a means of attempting suicide, and this may partly account for their vastly extended use within the practice of general medicine.

ANTIDEPRESSANT DRUGS

A Swiss investigator (Kuhn) was investigating the hoped-for antipsychotic properties of the tricyclic drug imipramine in the late 1950s. This drug was expected to resemble the phenothiazines in action, but while it did not benefit schizophrenic patients, it seemed to benefit many patients who were depressed. Another drug, iproniazid, a monoamine oxidase inhibitor was undergoing investigations in patients suffering tuberculosis, because of its antibacterial properties. It was accidently found to produce euphoria in some of the patients.

Subsequent studies have largely confirmed that numerous members of these two groups of compounds have antidepressant properties. Both groups of drugs produce a relief of symptoms of depressive illness after an initial period of sedation lasting from four days to three weeks. Their efficacy has been theoretically linked closely to their effects on metabolism of monoamines in the brain. They have been shown to either block the reuptake of mono-

Table 17.1 Comparative evaluation of various forms of drugs tested for antidepressant action. (From Cole and Davis, 1967, *A Comprehensive Textbook of Psychiatry*, 1269 (Freedman and Kaplan, editors), by courtesy of The Williams and Wilkins Company, Baltimore)

Drug	Comparative studies in which	
	Drug more effective than placebo	Drug equal to or less effective than placebo
Imipramine	19	6
Amitriptylline	4	1
Iproniazid	2	1
Nialamide	1	2
Phenelzine	3	3
Isocarboxazid	3	2
Tranylcypromine	4	0
Nortriptyline	2	1
Desmethylimipramine	1	1
Amphetamine	0	3
Chlorpromazine	2	1

amine neurotransmitters to the nerve terminals (as is the case with tricyclic drugs) or to inhibit the enzyme degradation of monoamines (as is the case with the monoamine oxidase inhibitors). The causal connections from these observed phenomena, to the clinical action remain obscure at present, but monoamine neurotransmitters play a critical role in the regulation of those parts of the brain regulating subjective states of pleasure or aversion.

The tricyclic antidepressants

Imipramine, the first discovered tricyclic antidepressant, has been probably the most studied, and has often been subsequently used as a standard of comparison for other antidepressants.

Table 17.1 shows a representation of the results of double-blind trials of antidepressant drugs. It should be noted that these studies did not adequately allow for the possible placebo effect of the transient sedation experienced in early days of treatment, nor could a drug with numerous side-effects be very readily studied in a double-blind fashion, for reasons similar to those which made double-blind control of the phenothiazines difficult.

In the case of imipramine those studies which showed no significant therapeutic effect of imipramine can be criticised on the basis of having used too small a patient sample, too little drug, or too heterogeneous a sample of patients, including schizoaffective, elderly, and neurotic patients.

A good deal of work has been done to determine the characteristics of the group of patients who do respond to tricyclic antidepressants, since it seemed clear from the early days of their use, that not all depressed people could be expected to benefit from such treatment. Kiloh has performed a discriminant function analysis in patients treated with imipramine and shown that a good response was predominantly produced in patients showing the clinical features of 'endogenous' or 'psychotic' depression—i.e. depression of a different subjective quality to ordinary sadness, with associated feelings of guilt and unworthiness, retardation and agitation, early-morning insomnia and weight loss. Patients with hysterical or hypochondriacal features, and self-pity, with previous histories of long-standing neurotic difficulties did not respond well. Other studies have lent repeated support to this finding. Some clinical series have shown that there may be other groups of patients who also respond favourably, namely, obsessive–compulsive patients and patients with bizarre states of pain.

Monoamine oxidase inhibitors (M.A.O. Inhibitors)

Table 17.2 shows those studies in which M.A.O. inhibitors have been compared with imipramine.

They are in general less effective than the tricyclic antidepressants amitryptyline and desmethylinipra-

Table 17.2 Antidepressant effectiveness of M.A.O. inhibitors, compared to imipramine. (From Cole and Davis, 1967, *A Comprehensive Textbook of Psychiatry*, 1269 (Freedman and Kaplan, editors), by courtesy of The Williams and Wilkins Company, Baltimore)

M.A.O.I. Drug	Comparative studies in which		
	Treatment more effective than imipramine	Treatment equal to imipramine	Treatment less effective than imipramine
Phenelzine	0	3	2
Isocarboxazid	0	1	2
Tranylcypromine	0	2	0

mine, and better than phenothiazines (which also may have some antidepressant action).

M.A.O. inhibitors have proved dangerous in clinical practice, because by blocking monoamine oxidase they cause the body to accumulate quantities of amine chemicals found in food-stuffs such as red wine, cheese, broad beans and Marmite. These amines are known as pressor amines, because of their effect upon blood pressure. A patient taking a dose of these compounds in his diet, while receiving M.A.O. inhibitors may die of a cerebral haemorrhage.

This danger, plus the relative ineffectiveness of this group of drugs has led to their comparative disuse. Some clinicians, and in particular Sargent, have advanced the view that the M.A.O. inhibitors are most effective when given in combination with tricyclic antidepressants, and also that M.A.O. inhibitors influence a somewhat different type of depressed patient than the tricyclic drugs. These 'atypical depressives' said to respond better to M.A.O. inhibitors are similar in nature to the predominantly neurotic and hypochondriacal patients found by discriminant analysis to respond poorly to tricyclic drugs. This view has not been widely upheld by trial in other clinics.

ELECTROCONVULSIVE THERAPY (E.C.T.)

In 1935 von Meduna reported the induction of convulsions by intra-muscular injection of camphor in oil. These injections were given to schizophrenics in the belief that schizophrenia and epilepsy did not occur simultaneously in the same person. In 1935 and 1936 Cerletti *et al.* began the use of electroconvulsive therapy with the same rationale, but using electric current to induce a convulsion. It soon became fairly obvious that schizophrenia was improved. This success led to trial of the treatment in other conditions, and the most dramatic therapeutic responses were achieved in severe cases of depression.

E.C.T. produces the most rapid therapeutic responses seen in psychiatry, but no other form of therapy is less understood.

So far as is known, the neurological effects of electroconvulsive therapy are identical with those produced by a major epileptic seizure. The most striking immediate psychological effect is a con-

fusional state following each E.C.T. which leads to amnesia for the event, and later, to some degree of amnesia for the whole period of treatment. It has been shown by Neilsen and Fleming that this amnesia is not due to wiping of memory traces from the brain, but is an example of state-specific learning. That is, memory traces established during the period of recovery from treatment with E.C.T. are subject to recollection only in the period immediately following further E.C.T. Because of this effect, the patient subsequently has moderate to markedly impaired recollection of the period (usually of several weeks) during which he received E.C.T. regularly. In addition, during the course of treatment with E.C.T. the patient exhibits impairment of short-term and long-term memory (as measured by standard recall tests) as well as impaired recall of distant events (i.e. events preceding the beginning of E.C.T.). This confusional state during the course of treatment may become very gross—to the extent of complete disorientation for place and person. Such a degree of confusion is unlikely to occur if E.C.T. is given no more than three times weekly. The degree of confusion has been shown to be reduced if the electric shock intended to induce convulsion is delivered to the patient's non-dominant cerebral hemisphere. This finding may well reflect less impairment of verbal processing in the dominant hemisphere, but increased impairment of non-verbal processing in the 'minor' hemisphere could also be produced. This point has not been fully investigated. Follow-up investigations have established that complete recovery of memory for distant events occurs after weeks to months following discontinuation of treatment, but amnesia for the period of treatment, with variable amnesia for immediately preceding events persists in most cases.

It is important to note that there is no evidence that these changes in memory function have anything to do with the therapeutic effectiveness of E.C.T. There is no relationship between degree of amnesia produced and response to treatment. Many patients develop a considerable fear of E.C.T. for reasons which are not entirely clear, but again, fearfulness in treatment is not correlated with response to treatment, and folk-beliefs that E.C.T. is merely a variant of snake-pit therapy can be discounted.

Figure 17.1(a)   An early psychosurgeon at work.

Discriminant function analysis shows that a similar group of patients respond to E.C.T. as respond to antidepressant drugs—i.e. these patients best described as 'endogenous' or 'psychotic' depressives.

In addition to this large group of depressives who respond to E.C.T. there is a substantial group of patients with schizophrenic illnesses who also respond to E.C.T. Those schizophrenics with hallucinations and severe changes in affective state respond far better than patients with 'flattening' of affect. States of manic excitement are also well-controlled by E.C.T. It can thus be seen that E.C.T. is effective in the control of severely disordered emotional states of a psychotic nature. These disturbances are all also subject to control by pharmacological agents (tranquillisers, antidepressants) and E.C.T. is used clinically to control the severe forms of these disorders, when death might ensue from suicide or exhaustion unless rapid treatment is given.

Biochemical research presently links these psychotic disturbances with disturbances of cerebral amine metabolism, and also with disturbances in electrolyte metabolism. Depressives treated with E.C.T. show changes in amine and electrolyte metabolism consistent with reversion to normal, fairly early in a course of E.C.T. There is as. of yet, no evidence to show whether this is a direct consequence of E.C.T., or an indicator of beneficial changes produced by other mechanisms.

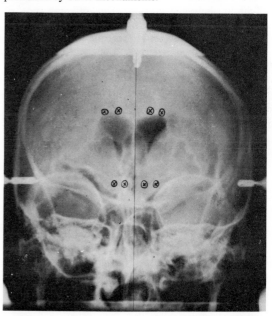

Figure   17.1(c)   Modern   stereotaxic   leucotomy—this antero-posterior air ventriculogram shows the intended sites (marked ⊗) at which localised removal of nervous tissue will be achieved by freezing. (Photograph by courtesy of Dr Desmond Kelly and Mr Alan Richardson, Atkinson Morley's Hospital, Wimbledon)

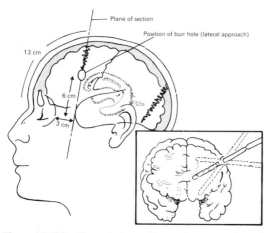

Figure 17.1(b)   The technique of leucotomy, as performed by Freeman and Watts. (From Eliott *et al.*, 1948, *A Text book of Physiological Psychology*, 547, by courtesy of John Wiley and Sons, New York)

PSYCHOSURGERY

Virtually all physical treatments in psychiatry were developed haphazardly. Psychosurgery was no exception (see Figure 17.1), but in this century animal experiments have been logically extended to human application. Fulton and Jacobson had reported in 1935 that frustration responses during training did not occur after ablation of the frontal lobes. Fulton reported, 'The most ferocious specimens have been reduced to a state of friendly docility'.

Moniz decided that this type of change might control the symptoms of patients suffering from irrational fears, obsessions and anxiety states, and so treated 20 patients. He was enthusiastic about the results. So were numerous others, and 20,000 people underwent frontal lobotomies in the next 15 years. These early procedures were very radical, and moderate to severe intellectual impairment was the rule, rather than the exception. The introduction of powerful psychoactive drugs, and the resurgence of psychiatric humanism was well on the way to making psychosurgery a thing of the past, until two recent developments resulted in a considerable rekindling of interest. Firstly, increased physiological analysis, plus examination of the most successful leucotomies at postmortem, had revealed that the most important beneficial effects were to be obtained by destruction of the fronto–limbic connections of the brain, rather than generalised destruction of the frontal lobes. Secondly, the technique of stereotaxic surgery has enabled much more precise and limited destruction of these connections in the brain.

Increasing application of these techniques has resulted in increasing controversy, and many critics act as though 1984 has arrived prematurely—sometimes with good reason.

Current psychosurgical procedures can be regarded as being of two main types:

1. Operations intended for the relief of intractable depression, anxiety states and obsessional neurosis. For these conditions the majority of operations are performed on the lower medial quadrant of the frontal lobe, the orbito-frontal region, and the cingulate region.
2. For severely abnormal aggressive behaviour various parts of a neural circuit interconnecting the amygdala and the hypothalamus have been operated on.

Operations of the first type have in common the relief of extreme subjective anxiety and sadness. On neurophysiological grounds it is believed that these operations produce clincial benefit by the interruption of pathways which normally enable neural systems involved in higher cognitive function to interact with neural systems involved in affective state. The patients undergoing such operations are usually fully able to give their rational consent to the procedures.

Modern techniques give good palliation of symptoms without intellectual impairment. A good example of this group of operations is that of limbic leucotomy, as performed at Atkinson Morley's Hospital. In this operation, small bilateral lesions are placed in both the cingulate gyrus and lower medial area of the frontal lobe. Patients typically have suffered for 10 years or more from chronic, intractable obsessional neurosis, depression or anxiety state. Average therapeutic response is fairly brisk, and improvement continues at later follow-up, as shown in Figure 17.2. Psychometric scores of anxiety, neuroticism and obsessions remain significantly reduced at 17 months postoperation. These results are superior to those reported for the old-style procedure of 'free-hand' lower medial quadrant operations, and in addition emotional blunting, disinhibition, postoperation epilepsy and excessive weight gain were not encountered in this series. Intelligence scores are slightly increased, if anything, following this operation. Workers at the Burden Neurological Institute have performed operations of a similar type, with the intent of 'tailoring' the operation to the specific patient, using chronic implantation of many hair-fine stimulating electrodes in the lower medial quadrant of the frontal lobe, and elsewhere. Over a period of months, these sites of electrode implantation are serially used to deliver a

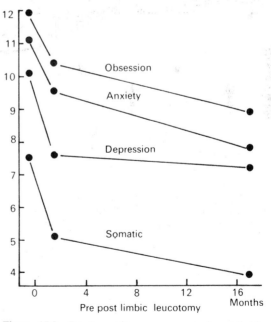

Figure 17.2 Psychometric scores pre- and post-limbic leucotomy. On Middlesex Hospital Questionnaire (phobic and hysterical scores not shown) N=29. (By courtesy of Dr Desmond Kelly, Atkinson Morley's Hospital, Wimbledon)

current which blocks transmission in the surrounding brain. Those sites in which blocking current produces a symptomatic improvement in the patient's mental state, are later subjected to electrocoagulation. Present clinical follow-up data suggests that results are similar to limbic leucotomy.

The second type of operation—procedures aimed more specifically at the control of pathological aggressive behaviour—has not found widespread acceptance on ethical grounds. Like leucotomy, these operations draw their inspiration from studies on animals. In this case the original studies were those performed by Kluver and Bucy, in which it was shown that damage to the amygdala, and related parts of the brain produced (among other effects) placidity and tractableness. Further animal studies have localised this 'taming' effect to lesions in amygdala and hypothalamic areas. Accordingly the operations of amygdalotomy and hypothalamotomy have been tried in humans. The patients have usually been highly aggressive and emotionally disturbed children, also suffering from epilepsy. These operations have produced 'marked calming effects' in 95% of cases, but have failed to entirely eliminate episodes of terror and outbursts of violence. There have also been attempts along similar lines to treat adult psychopathic prisoners. In view of the surgical dangers involved, and the meaninglessness of consent from prisoners or epileptic children, these operations have come to be regarded as ethically precarious.

Throughout the field of psychosurgery the role of non-operation factors in determining outcome is unknown. It is clear that the enormous potential placebo effect of undergoing intracranial surgery, and the role of postoperative rehabilitation programmes ought to be adequately allowed for. There has been uncertainty and debate about the provision of adequate control groups for such a study, as ideally this would require the performance of dummy operations on the control group. A working party of the Royal College of Psychiatrists has been set up to examine the question of a controlled prospective trial of psychosurgery, and will no doubt continue to examine the question for some time. In the meantime, these procedures are being limited in application to cases which have proved unresponsive to all other forms of therapy. Since this is the case, it can be reasonably inferred that the procedures are effective, as each patient acts as his own control.

LITHIUM THERAPY
Salts of the metallic ion lithium are specific treatment

for mania, as was discovered (accidentally) by Cade in 1949. It did not receive widespread application until claims by Schou in 1968 that lithium salts not only controlled mania, but were prophylactic against relapses of both the manic and depressive phases of manic depressive illness.

Lithium salts are unusual amongst psychiatric treatments, in that when given in controlled doses, with frequent tests of blood lithium content, they do not produce any discernible side-effects. Lithium is therefore reasonably easy to subject to double-blind controlled study. Several studies have shown its effectiveness as a prophylactic, including the multicentre trial undertaken by Copen *et al.* 86% of patients on lithium were rated as showing little or no affective symptoms, versus 8% of the placebo group. The duration of study was up to two years.

Given in excessive doses lithium produces drowsiness, ataxia, nausea, vomiting, diarrhoea, coma and death in a variety of ways. Its mode of action is unknown, but lithium is known to interfere with sodium, potassium and magnesium metabolism in various ways, and is also now known to interfere with cerebral amine metabolism in such a way as to increase turnover of noradrenaline.

CONCLUSIONS
It will be seen from this very brief résumé of physical psychiatric treatments that a number of very potent techniques exist. These techniques undoubtedly produce many complex changes in any person subjected to them. Which changes are therapeutically effective remains uncertain and the light has only just begun to permeate the mist. Well-controlled trials demonstrating the therapeutic benefit of these techniques are largely lacking, but it is probably fair to conclude that difficulties of providing adequate controls, rather than lack of therapeutic effects, are responsible for this deficiency. Another factor has been the very prolific introduction of different modes of treatment. Clinicians have been too busy exploring new treatment modes to conduct the painstaking work of determining which therapies work best. Investigators are only now beginning to seriously undertake this precise follow-up. Certainty of knowledge may duly emerge. We can reasonably expect that the introduction of further new therapies will severely interfere with the adequate assessment of our present modes of treatment. It is to be hoped that such a state of academic chaos truly reflects healthy growth.

Recommended reading

Ayd, F. J. and Blackwell, B. (editors) (1970). *Discoveries in Biological Psychiatry* (Philadelphia: J. B. Lippencott Company)

Ban, T. A. (1969). *Psychopharmacology* (Baltimore: Williams and Wilkins)

Bradley, P. B. (1968). Synaptic transmission in the central

nervous system and its relevance for drug action. *Int. Rev. Neurobiol.*, **II**, 1–56

Goodman, L. S. and Gilman, A. (1968). *The Pharmacological Basis of Therapeutics* (3rd Ed.) (London: Macmillan)

Kielholz, P. (editor) (1972). *Depressive Illness* (Bern: Hans Huber)

Laitinen, L. V. and Livingston, K. E. (editors) (1973). *Surgical Approaches in Psychiatry* (Lancaster: Medical and Technical Publishing Co.)

Mayer-Gross, W., Slater, E. and Roth, M. (1969). *Clinical Psychiatry* (3rd Ed.) (London: Bailliere, Tindall and Cassell)

Valzelli, L. (1973). *Psychopharmacology* (New York: Spectrum Publications)

Chapter 18

DYNAMIC THEORIES AND THERAPIES

G. D. Wilson

Psychodynamic theories have been a major influence on the thinking of Western psychologists and psychiatrists for close to 100 years. They remain dominant today as the basis of psychiatric practice and continue to exert a marked influence on academic psychology. Their appeal to the layman—artists, writers, dramatists, film directors etc.—has been so phenomenal that the man in the street often equates psychoanalysis and its off-shoots with the whole of psychology. There is clearly something very compelling and enduring about this approach, which makes it impossible to ignore in producing a text on human psychology.

Leading contemporary philosophers of science (e.g. Popper and Kuhn) have declared these theories unscientific on the grounds that their propositions are not falsifiable by any conceivable set of observations. While many psychoanalysts have shown an inclination to reinterpret negative research findings and clinical outcomes in their own favour, this viewpoint seems a little extreme and unfair. Some of the major propositions of psychoanalysis are testable, and have been tested. All that is necessary to bring these theories into the domain of science is to translate them into precise and unambiguous hypotheses, to provide operational (working) definitions of the concepts (i.e. state them in terms of the procedures used for observing and measuring them), and to accept the outcome of experimental studies without going back on the hypotheses after seeing the results. This chapter reviews the current state of scientific evidence for and against the claims of dynamic theorists, both as regards their statements about human personality and the efficacy of the therapeutic techniques that derive from them. The dynamic edifice is, of course, so gigantic that it will not be possible to tour it in detail; we must restrict ourselves to a few of its most central propositions. First, then, we will try to delineate more precisely what is meant by 'dynamic' theory and therapy.

CENTRAL PROPOSITIONS

Dynamic or 'depth' psychology is based largely on the ideas of Sigmund Freud and those following the school of 'psychoanalysis' that was founded by him around the turn of the century. Many other names come to mind as important in its history, mostly central Europeans (e.g. Charcot, Janet, Breuer, Jung, Adler), and more recently Americans of European descent (e.g. Horney, Fromm, Sullivan). Other notable

proponents have lived in England (e.g. Anna Freud, Melanie Klein, R. D. Laing), centred around the Tavistock Clinic of North London. In recent years, psychoanalytic ideas have merged with similar movements, especially 'Gestalt therapy', and to some extent 'humanistic psychology'; but the influence of Freud remains dominant, and it is mainly his theories with which this chapter is concerned.

Although the writings of these theorists are often vague, and there is likely to be disagreement as to how they should be interpreted, most would probably accept that the following statements summarise the most central ideas of dynamic psychology:

1. *Psychosexual development*—Adult personality and neuroses derive from experiences in early childhood, particularly those relating to the social control of basic instincts (e.g. weaning, toilet-training, punishment for masturbation).

2. *Psychic energy 'hydraulics'*—Instinctual energies whose outlets are blocked (frustrated) do not simply dissipate but are diverted elsewhere, manifesting themselves in behaviour or symptoms not directly related to their natural consummation (e.g. through displacement, sublimation, hysterical conversion reaction).

3. *Unconscious motivation and defence*—The individual is usually unaware of both the infantile origins and the hydraulic mechanisms determining his behaviour. They are prevented from reaching consciousness by certain 'ego-defence mechanisms' (e.g. repression, projection, reaction-formation and symbolism in dreams).

4. *Insight/cartharsis therapy*—Symptoms are removed by bringing them to consciousness. This is achieved by interpreting their meaning to the patient and having him relive the appropriate emotions. An important aid in this process is *transference*, in which the patient adopts a childlike dependency on the therapist (thus psychologically 'regressing') or identifies him with an important other person (e.g. parent or spouse) as a substitute target for emotional expression.

The scientific appraisal of these propositions has always been fraught with difficulties. Psychoanalysts (including Freud himself) have often claimed that no verification is necessary because their ideas are self-evidently true, at least to anyone with sufficient experience of the clinical phenomena from which they were derived. However clinical intuition unchecked by empirical studies is simply not trustworthy; for example, it was obvious to many psychiatrists in the last century that masturbation was a cause of insanity (Cade, 1973) —failure to adduce scientific evidence for this theory, added to a recent awareness of the widespread popularity of the practice, has led to deletion of the theory from the textbooks. Clinical observation may generate interesting hypotheses, but these need to be systematically tested before reliance can be placed on them. Appeal to authorities is frequently used by analysts in place of evidence. Hypotheses are transformed into facts simply by introducing them 'Freud has revealed to us . .', 'as Fenichel has told us . . .' etc. 'Outsiders' who question these authorities may be greeted with a condescending or hostile response.

Experimental psychologists who have been sufficiently interested in Freudian-type theories to attempt to put them on a scientific footing have found great difficulty in deriving clear, unambiguous hypotheses. They are often tempted to account for their findings after the fact in psychoanalytic terms; this is all too easily done, but open to the same criticism as that levelled at clinicians who always see their patients' problems in terms of their own theoretical orientation. It is not sufficient in science for a theory to explain everything—it must also be capable of a fair amount of prediction, otherwise it is completely useless. If, for example, a piece of behaviour is accounted for after its occurrence in terms of 'repressed Oedipal hostility', this may give satisfaction to the interpreter and others, but it is of no scientific value unless it leads to predictions of future behaviour which are verifiable (a) better than chance, and (b) better than alternative, especially more parsimonious (simple) theories, e.g. that the behaviour reflected a constitutional trait of aggressiveness. Let us now examine the evidence relating to each of the four major propositions in turn.

PSYCHOSEXUAL DEVELOPMENT
This is the area of dynamic psychology in which it has been found most easy to draw up clear hypotheses. Certain kinds of treatment in the first few years of life should have particular effects on adult life. For example, early weaning and bottle (v. breast) feeding should result in an 'oral incorporative personality'—a person who constantly seeks gratification through eating, drinking and smoking, and possibly also a general dependency on other people. Severe toilet-training should lead to an 'anal personality syndrome', consisting of obsessionality and meanness. Punishment for masturbation (fiddling with the genitals) around the ages of four or five should have marked effects on adult sex life—perhaps impotence, frigidity or homosexuality, though dynamic theorists are not clear on this point.

Some of these predictions seem straight-forward enough, so we might expect a clear answer to have emerged from the research carried out over the last 70

years. Unfortunately, though, the scientific evaluation of them has proved extremely difficult in practice. Observation of child-rearing practices must usually be retrospective, since longitudinal research would take at least 20 years and has seldom been attempted. Individuals are not able to report satisfactorily on the details of their own childhood experiences (especially since dynamic theory supposes that the critical experiences are unconscious or repressed); the memory of mothers and their motivation to report their infant rearing practices accurately must also be regarded as suspect. Even if access to the home is gained for the purpose of longitudinal studies, the behaviour of the parents may be modified by the awareness that they are being observed. One major difficulty, then, is in obtaining valid data concerning the way in which children were treated in the areas hypothesised to be critical.

Another problem is the difficulty of controlling for the effects of genetic and other constitutional factors in the development of personality. This is the major alternative theory of the origins of personality differences, for which there definitely is supportive evidence (see Chapter 10). For example, variations in child-rearing practices may reflect the personalities of the parents who choose them, which raises the possibility of genetically mediated connections between parental treatment and the personality of the child. Also, the constitutionally determined behaviour of the child may influence the way in which it is treated by the parents, giving rise to the same correlation that would be predicted on the basis of dynamic theory, but with a reversal of the direction of cause and effect. These issues may be clarified by reference to some particular classic studies in the field.

An exhaustive review of empirical studies of Freudian theories has been produced by Paul Kline in his book *Fact and Fantasy in Freudian Theory*, (1972). In his summary of the findings relating to psychosexual personality syndromes he is forced to state that, 'From the considerable number of studies attempting to relate infant rearing procedures to personality development only two studies give even slight support to the Freudian theory'. It would be most useful, then, to consider these two. The first is a study by Goldman-Eisler (1951) which attempted to verify the existence of the oral personality type described by psychoanalysts and its hypothesised connection with weaning events in infancy. First, she conducted a factor analysis of the set of traits (assessed by questionnaires) that were supposed, according to Freudian theory, to fall along a single dimension of 'oral optimism v. pessimism'—instead she discovered that they fell along two independent factors (Figure 18.1). Then she investigated the relationships between various weaning measures (based on the mothers' reports of what had happened at least 15 years previously) and these two personality factors. Only one statistically significant result was found: a tendency for individuals who had been weaned from the breast early to be withdrawn, negative and pessimistic in their outlook. Apparently, verification of the whole Freudian theory of orality rests on this one tenuous result, yet it is a prime example of an environmental explanation for a parent–child correlation being accepted when there is absolutely no evidence which would enable us to discount the genetic alternative. If unsociable, unhappy children turn out to have had 'rejecting' mothers who took them off the breast prematurely, could this not reflect a genetically transferred personality tendency such as neurotic–introversion? Again, perhaps the mother's weaning behaviour was partly influenced by the disposition of the child—the negative and withdrawn child showing less interest in the sociable act of breast-sucking and thus being taken off the breast earlier. A properly controlled experiment would require (a) that children be randomly assigned to parents, in order to control for genetic factors, and (b) that rearing practices be chosen randomly for the parents, and adhered to regardless of the behaviour of the infant. Such an experiment is, of course, impractical in a humane society, so we must sympathise with the researcher to some degree; however, she might have shown more awareness of these problems and made some attempt to control for them indirectly, e.g. by investigating reasons why the mothers adopted their respective weaning practices.

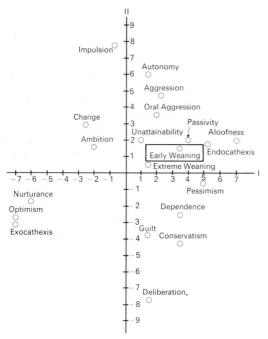

Figure 18.1 Factor loadings of 19 personality traits in relation to the variable of 'early weaning'. (From Goldman-Eisler, 1951, by courtesy of *J. Ment. Sci.*)

The only other study that Kline cites as providing any kind of support for Freudian psychosexual theory was, coincidentally, conducted by himself (1968). This study is held to confirm the hypothesis that obsessional adults are the victims of 'overenthusiastic' toilet-training. To a group of 46 students, Kline administered several questionnaires to measure obsessionality; then he solicited their reactions to a picture of a defaecating dog (the 'anal' item from the Blacky Pictures Test). Finding that his obsessional subjects expressed greater disturbance in response to the defaecating-dog picture, Kline concludes that Freudian theory concerning the aetiology of obsessional traits and syndromes is vindicated. This must be so, he says, because, 'there is no logical reason to link responses to a picture of a defaecating dog with obsessional traits'. Yet his own obsessionality measure contains many items relating to concern with cleanliness, e.g. 'When eating out do you wonder what the kitchens are like?' and (incredibly) 'Do you regard the keeping of household dogs as unhygienic?' Is it really unreasonable to expect answers to questions such as these to be linked with attitudes toward defaecating dogs? Concern with hygiene, cleanliness, tidiness and self-control (inevitably tapped by this particular Blacky picture) are central to the obsessional personality syndrome, and with this content overlap explanation in terms of toilet-training experience is not necessary to account for Kline's results.

If these two studies represent the best that can be offered by way of support for psychoanalytic notions about the relationship between child-rearing and subsequent adult personality, then we are forced to the conclusion that satisfactory evidence does not exist. This is not the same thing as saying that the hypotheses are false—the evidence is not good enough to enable us to say that either—but it is clear that they have become prematurely entrenched into our folklore. In the seventy years or so since these ideas were first promulgated, they have become widely accepted by child-care experts, educationalists and psychiatrists; the time has come to demand more adequate scientific support, despite the methodological difficulties in obtaining it, or we should consider abandoning them along with the masturbational madness theory mentioned previously.

The above is concerned only with specifically Freudian theories of child-rearing effects. What about the more general question of the influence of early experience on behaviour? Actually, this evidence is little better. Several independent reviews of the literature, e.g. Caldwell (1964), O'Connor (1968), Yarrow *et al.* (1968) and Berger (1973) suggest that there is generally little evidence to substantiate the influence of anything but the most extreme environmental intervention on the subsequent behaviour of children. For example, Yarrow *et al.* state that, 'the compelling legend of maternal influences on child behaviour that has evolved does not have its roots in solid data'. Reviewing all previous studies of maternal deprivation, O'Connor comments that, 'Despite the confidence of psychoanalysts and extensive research there would seem to be little satisfactory evidence which demonstrates a long-term effect of mother–child separation pure and simple'.

It is too soon to say for sure that infantile experiences are not important, but we should be aware of at least one faulty line of reasoning that would foster such a myth. This starts with the observation that individual differences in behaviour observed in the first year of life tend to persist into adulthood; many writers are so committed to an environmentalist position that they see this as evidence for the critical role of infantile learning. For example, Elizabeth Hurlock in her text on *Developmental Psychology* states:

'Because all experimental evidence to date indicates that personality traits established in babyhood are likely to remain relatively unchanged throughout life . . . it is apparent that babyhood is justly called a 'critical age' in the development of personality.'

Apparently she overlooks the fact that observation of personality traits that are stable from infancy is equally consonant with a theory stressing genetic and constitutional origins of personality. Furthermore the evidence for the constitutional alternative is, in fact, very good (Chapter 10).

One study that is particularly interesting in this connection was conducted by Thomas and coworkers (1968). They undertook a longitudinal study of 136 children in New York, following them through from infancy onwards by repeated interviews with the parents. Analysis of these records revealed a group of consistently 'difficult' children who as babies showed irregular biological functions, withdrawal reactions to novel stimuli, slowness in adapting to change, intense emotional reactions, and frequent displays of negative mood. The majority of this group (70%) developed marked behavioural disturbances in later childhood, despite the fact that their parents did not apparently differ from those of other children in their approach to child care. There were, however, later signs that some parents were beginning to react to the problems involved in handling the difficult children. There seems to be more evidence that the behaviour of children

has an effect upon their parents than *vice versa*! If non-genetic parental influences on the temperament of children and their proneness to psychiatric disorder are established in the future it is unlikely that they will turn out to be very marked.

PSYCHIC ENERGY HYDRAULICS

A second central assumption in dynamic psychology is that behaviour may be represented as the outcome of an energy system in which the 'libido' (sex) is the source of the energy, and the 'ego' (reason) and the 'superego' (conscience) operate the gates and dams which block the flow and divert it into alternative channels. This notion may be viewed as model or metaphor, but it is scientifically meaningless unless operational definitions are made available. In the general form stated above, this theory is certainly too vague to be tested; however, some more specific hypotheses concerning the connections between manifest symptoms and their underlying causes have been submitted to experimental test (e.g. Table 18.1). In order to present dynamic theory in the best possible light, we have selected for inclusion in this table only studies that have been cited by specialist critics such as Kline (1972) as good ones that have provided positive evidence in support of the chosen hypothesis. The two studies of neurotic conditions (Goldman-Eisler and Kline) were discussed above. We will now consider, as examples, two more studies from this list—one in the general area of psychosomatics (asthma) and one concerning a psychotic condition (paranoia).

The psychoanalytic hypothesis supposedly tested by Stein and Ottenberg (1958) was that asthmatic attacks represent 'a means of physiologically defending against the activation by odours of unresolved childhood conflicts'. In support of this they quote two findings: the first is that dirty, unpleasant smells are more likely to provoke attacks than pleasant perfumes and food smells (Table 18.2). This is adopted as support for Freudian theory simply by renaming the dirty smells 'anal'—from this it supposedly follows that toilet-training experiences in childhood must be involved. No evidence is presented to discount the hypersensitivity theory of asthma—i.e. that the symptoms involve a constriction of air passages to avoid taking in smells to which the individual is physiologically allergic (it seems quite probable that smells per-

Table 18.1 Some empirical studies of dynamic hypotheses concerning the origins of certain disorders

Symptom	Dynamic interpretation	Study
Antisocial behaviour	Early weaning	Goldman-Eisler (1951)
Obsessionality	Harsh toilet-training	Kline (1968)
Asthma	Unresolved anal conflicts	Stein and Ottenberg (1958)
Ulcers	Oral frustrations	Wolowitz and Wagonfeld (1968)
Appendicitis	Birth fantasies	Eylon (1967)
Paranoia	Repressed homosexuality	Zamansky (1958)

ceived as unpleasant by most people would produce severe aversion reactions in a few people). Note that the smell of actual faeces (the only one that could strictly be called 'anal') was implicated in only two out of the 61 cases. The second finding that the authors cite as support for Freudian theory was that asthmatic patients, compared to healthy controls, showed more emotional 'blocks' in giving word associations to a selection of odours (Figure 18.2); this also is supposed to implicate childhood conflicts concerning toilet-training. They do not appear to consider the possibility that the smells might be perceived as more threatening to asthma patients because they are liable to precipitate asthmatic attacks—perhaps the 'blocks' (about which we are told little) were themselves minor attacks. It is easy to suggest alternative explanations for the results of this experiment; but in any case, the authors have not adduced any real evidence for the Freudian hypothesis, they have merely interpreted their results in terms of this theory. Since there is no conceivable outcome that could not have been interpreted in dynamic terms, the theory is no stronger after this study than it was before.

The study by Zamansky (1958) is also a celebrated contribution to the literature on experimental psychoanalysis; it deals with the Freudian theory that paranoia is an outcome of 'powerful but unconscious homosexual strivings'. This theory arose from Freud's analysis of the case of a notorious German judge called Dr Schreber; actually he never met the patient but based his interpretation on a reading of Schreber's autobiography. Thereafter it became the orthodox psychoanalytic view that all cases of paranoia and

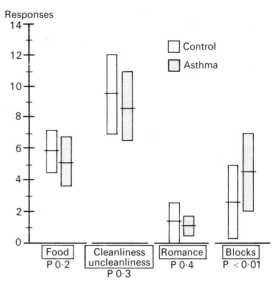

Figure 18.2   Content analysis of associative reactions to odours. The responses are expressed as the mean ± one standard deviation. (From Stein and Ottenberg, 1958, by courtesy of *Psychosom. Med.*)

Table 18.2   Classification of odorous substances that precipitated asthmatic attacks. (From Stein and Ottenberg, 1958, by courtesy of *Psychosom. Med.*)

Category	Odour	Number	Total
Food	Bacon	2	3 (5%)
	Onion, garlic	1	
	Urine	1	
	Sweat	2	
	Faeces	2	
	Disinfectant	7	
	Bleach	3	
Cleanliness	Camphor	2	
Uncleanliness	Dirty, musty	7	45 (74%)
	Smoke	6	
	Sulphur	5	
	Chemicals	2	
	Paint	5	
	Horses	2	
	Barn	1	
Romance	Perfume	10	
	Spring	2	13 (21%)
	Flowers	1	

paranoid schizophrenia involved repressed homosexual desires and the defence mechanism of projection. This tendency to arrive at a general theory following examination of a single case was quite characteristic of the thinking of Freud. For example, the psychoanalytic theory of appendicitis was derived from analysis of the case of Dora (1905); the theory of phobias and the notion of the castration complex arose out of the case of 'Little Hans' (1909), who was seen only once by Freud (the case material being provided by the boy's father, an ardent supporter of Freud's). The origins of the theory are unimportant, however, if it can be shown to have empirical support, so let us consider Zamansky's classic experiment.

Zamansky found two things: (1) Paranoid patients spent more time looking at pictures of men than a control group of non-paranoid schizophrenics, when given the options of looking at women or non-human objects in a double-viewing apparatus. (2) When asked which pictures they liked most, the paranoids expressed a greater preference for the women relative to controls. Doubtless Freudian theory could be invoked to 'explain' these findings; but is any theory really necessary? Paranoia is characterised by a tendency to be cagey, suspicious and sensitive to threat—given these traits the Zamansky findings follow logically. The paranoid patients would be more alert to men in the environment than either women or non-human objects simply because men offer more threat (after all, homosexual attraction to men is not the only possible reason for looking at them). On being asked which pictures they preferred, the paranoids would be more alert to the possibility of being labelled as homosexual by the treacherous 'shrinks', and would therefore be cautious about expressing any degree of liking for male pictures. Meanwhile, the regular schizophrenics, who are typically more thought-disordered than paranoids, would be responding to the task in their usual erratic and unsystematic way.

Zamansky had validated his picture-preference test by showing that it did discriminate overt homosexuals from normal men. This was a necessary but insufficient precaution. The fact that an experimental procedure can be a measure of homosexuality under some circumstances does not preclude the possibility that it measures something else as well. The vital control that is missing from Zamansky's study, and subsequent replications of it, is the use of other forms of threat not involving homosexuality, e.g. pictures of electrical apparatus such as might be used for aversion therapy. We would predict that paranoids would show greater sensitivity to these threats as well. In short, the paranoid's reaction to homosexual situations can be viewed as consistent with, and as part of his general suspiciousness and vigilance in relation to threatening stimuli. There is no need to invoke mysterious inner forces and complexes. In any event, it is doubtful that much would be gained by tracing the origin of paranoia to homosexual desires. We would still need to explain the homosexuality—pre-

sumably this would be ascribed to a repressed castration complex (or perhaps repressed paranoia?!)

These experiments have been discussed in some detail in order to point out their shortcomings as demonstrations of·dynamic principles. Space does not permit us here to repeat this procedure for all the many studies that purport to confirm Freudian theory; this has been done for the 20 or so most celebrated 'confirmations' of psychoanalytic theory by Eysenck and Wilson (1973). In every case, we found good reasons to discount the studies as proof of Freudian theories. Some were deficient in methodology or statistical analysis of data; others resorted to tricks such as reversing the dynamic hypothesis after seeing how the results turned out, e.g. by invoking the defence mechanism of 'reaction formation'. But far and away the most pervasive fault with these studies was their failure to take account of alternative hypotheses, which were generally much more simple and straightforward, involving fewer theoretical assumptions than psychoanalytic theory. The two examples described above are typical in this respect.

Before moving on, there is one other set of phenomena that should be mentioned, if only because it is so often cited as an example of a dynamic mechanism that is easily observed; this is the displacement (or 'scape-goating') theory of racial prejudice, still subscribed to by many social psychologists. According to the Freudian hypothesis, aggression that has arisen as a result of some kind of frustration has become redirected (displaced) onto the minority group, a vulnerable though innocent target. Numerous anecdotes (e.g. the clerk bawled out by the boss comes home and kicks the cat) and empirical studies (e.g. Campbell, 1947, see Figure 18.3) have been quoted as support for this general theory. But if aggression were actually displaced onto a new target such as a minority group in order to maintain a psychic energy balance, then it should no longer be possible to detect high levels of aggression in other aspects of the individual's behaviour. The alternative theory is that racial prejudice is simply one expression of a generalised aggressiveness or irritability which may arise either as a temperamental trait or a response to some environmental situation (e.g. stomach ulcers, unemployment, overcrowding). This generalisation hypothesis is clearly separable from the dynamic one, and is much simpler in that it involves no assumptions about 'energy hydraulics'. What is more, the available evidence clearly favours the generalisation theory. For example, Silverman and Kleinman (1967) repeated a classical study of the effects of frustration on racial prejudice, adding a number of attitude measures that were completely unrelated to prejudice (e.g. attitudes toward cheating on exams, the value of education, and democratic government). Frustration was induced in half of the subjects by arranging for them to fail dismally on a problem solving task. The results

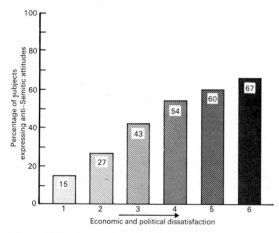

Figure 18.3 Economic and political dissatisfaction and attitudes toward Jews. The six bars represent the percentage of persons of varying degrees of economic and political dissatisfaction who express negative attitudes toward Jews. Bar 1 represents those *satisfied* in both economic and political matters; 2, those satisfied in one and intermediate in the other; 3, those intermediate in both; 4, those satisfied in one and dissatisfied in the other; 5, those dissatisfied in one and intermediate in the other; 6, those dissatisfied in both. It will be seen that the prevalence of anti-Semitic attitudes increases with degree of dissatisfaction. (From Krech, Crutchfield and Ballachey, 1962; based on the data of Campbell, 1947, by courtesy of McGraw-Hill)

(Figure 18.4) showed that the ·frustrated subjects expressed more prejudice than controls, but they also manifested more antisocial responses on the other three measures as well. The aggression induced by the frustrating situation did not ricochet cleanly onto the racial minority, it was scattered like shot to hit any target in the vicinity. The Freudian notion of the rechannelling of blocked energy is clearly too narrow to account for this finding.

Our conclusion, based on examination of these studies and others that are similar, is the same as that for the studies of child-rearing and psychosexual development. There is at present no acceptable confirmation of the psychoanalytic principle of psychic energy hydraulics. The theory in general is too vague to be scientifically useful; the specific hypotheses supposedly derived from it are either not proven or demonstrably wrong.

UNCONSCIOUS MOTIVATION AND DEFENCE

The third major aspect of dynamic theory is closely interconnected with the last. This is the idea that the major determinants of behaviour (particularly psycho-pathological symptoms) are unconscious desires and forgotten experiences—motivational forces which are kept out of awareness by repression and a variety of other defence mechanisms. One example has already been considered—the idea that paranoia is due to homosexual urges kept out of consciousness by re-action-formation and projection.

'. . . the proposition "I (a man) love him" is converted by reaction formation into "I hate him". As further insurance that the homosexual wish will not become conscious, this second proposition is transformed, by means of projection, into "He hates me"'.

(Zamansky, 1958)

We found that even if it is possible to translate this hypothesis into observables, there is as yet no evidence which can be held to support it.

In some senses it is obvious that unconscious events do influence our behaviour. We do not, for example, experience the genes which affect our personality and the quality of our thinking, nor are we aware of the electrochemical impulses that are whizzing around in our brain. The dynamic concept of the unconscious is more specific than this; it deals with internal states such as lust, anxiety and anger, that we are capable of experiencing at other times. Also, in dynamic theory, the unconscious state is assumed to influence behaviour in a way that is different from the usual effect of that state when it is conscious; otherwise the distinction would be irrelevant. Thus, in our previous example, the homosexual desires of the paranoid schizophrenic supposedly cause him to hate and fear men rather than seek them as sexual partners as would be the case if they were conscious. This idea of a battle between antagonistic conscious and unconscious minds for the control of the individual's behaviour is central in psychoanalytic theorising.

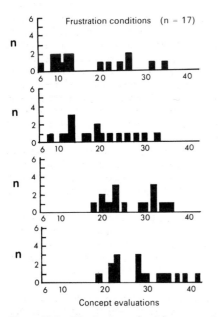
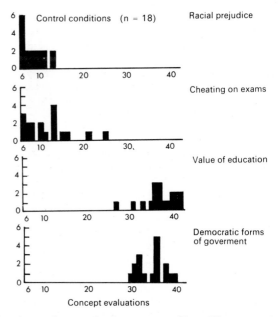

Figure 18.4   Distributions of opinion scores for frustrated and control groups for four concepts. (From Silverman and Kleinman, 1967, by courtesy of *J. Exp. Res. Personal.*)

After thus clarifying the definition of the unconscious as it is used in psychoanalytic theory, Brody (1972) proceeds to a ·critical review of the alleged empirical demonstrations of the phenomenon. His conclusion is uncompromising: 'Research conducted under controlled conditions does .not provide evidence for the kind of explanatory role assigned to the unconscious in traditional psychodynamic theories'. While it is not possible here to completely retrace the logic by which Brody arrives at this conclusion, we can briefly consider the objections to two laboratory phenomena that are perhaps most frequently cited as evidence for the unconscious—perceptual defence and posthypnotic suggestion.

Perceptual defence refers to the finding that under some circumstances people will show a physiological response (e.g. G.S.R.) to an emotional stimulus such as a four-letter word, whilst reporting verbally that they did not see it. This has been interpreted as meaning that our behaviour can be influenced by stimuli that are below the threshold of awareness. For a while there was great excitement in the psychological world; psychoanalysts embraced it as evidence for the unconscious and consumer psychologists claimed frightening powers for 'subliminal advertising'. More recently, however, researchers have found it more useful to think of perceptual defence phenomena in terms of discrepancies between different response modes and measures, which after all, is what they are. Many reasons have been discovered as to why the G.S.R. and verbal report should give slightly different indications as to whether or not a stimulus has been perceived. For example, the subject may perceive the stimulus but delay reporting it because he is too embarrassed to verbalise it. Alternatively, the G.S.R. may appear as a more sensitive indicator because it responds to uncertainty whereas the verbal report must wait upon a definite decision. This 're-sponse disparity' conceptualisation of perceptual defence obviates the need for assuming an unconscious mind and has led to much more precise and illuminating study of the phenomenon.

The other phenomenon that is frequently cited as evidence for the unconscious mind is *posthypnotic suggestion*. Subjects given a suggestion while under hypnosis to the effect that after being brought out of the trance they will perform a certain act in response to a given cue (e.g. scratch their left testicle every time the word 'coconut' is mentioned) are purported to comply without awareness of the reason. The problem here is that it has proved extremely difficult experimentally to distinguish the behaviour of hypnotised subjects from control subjects who have been asked to act as though they are hypnotised. So when subjects who have been hypnotised report amnesia regarding the suggestion that has been given to them, they may be simply conforming to the expectations of the role they are playing (Table 18.3). Certainly, the

experiments that have been reported have not succeeded in demonstrating otherwise; the odd differences that have been observed between hypnotised subjects and 'simulators' could well have arisen because the two groups are often playing slightly different roles, e.g. the simulator is in effect being asked to deceive the experimenter while the hypnotic subject believes he is co-operating. It might be revealing, following reports of amnesia for effective posthypnotic suggestions, to make a convincing offer of substantial payment for correctly recalling the suggestions; the subjects might then decide that the. new game is much more fun and display strikingly improved powers of recollection.

Table 18.3   Independent variables typically included in present-day 'hypnotic induction procedures'. (From Barber, 1965, by courtesy of *J. Abn. Psychol.*)

1. The situation is defined to the subject as 'hypnosis'.
2. Instructions are administered that are designed to motivate the subject to give a good performance.
3. Suggestions of eye-heaviness, eye-closure, relaxation, drowsiness, and sleep are administered.
4. It is suggested to the subject that he can now easily respond to test suggestions and can easily experience suggested effects.

So much for studies that attempt to establish directly the existence of the unconscious. What about studies that make an indirect approach to the question by investigating the so-called *ego-defence mechanisms*? We have already mentioned two of these—projection and reaction formation. *Projection* is the attribution of one's own unconscious undesirable characteristics to other people; ·two recent reviews of the empirical research on this hypothesised mechanism concur that there is no evidence to support it (Holmes, 1968; Kline, 1972). *Reaction-formation* refers to the display of attitudes or behaviour directly opposite to what is unconsciously intended. This notion has been found useful by psychoanalysts in 'explaining' outcomes which run counter to their predictions, but it is difficult to imagine what kind of observations could be used to verify it. There are numerous other hypothesised defence mechanisms, equally lacking in empirical support; it is necessary here to pass them by and concentrate on the central defence concept in dynamic theory—that of repression.

Repression was the first defence mechanism invented by Freud, and it is central in that it is implicated in the operation of all other defence mechanisms. It is the hypothesised process by which unacceptable desires, experiences and thoughts are kept from awareness. Analysts use it to account for their patients' resistances in free association, lateness, forgetting of appointments, failure to pay fees promptly, etc. It is also thought by many psychologists to have gained more experimental support than other defence mechanisms. Let us consider the state of the evidence by reference to its most classic alleged demonstrations.

Zeller (1950) introduced an experimental paradigm that is frequently cited as evidence for repression. In Zeller's experiment, subjects are required to learn a list of words; then half of them are 'ego threatened' by forcing them to fail on another task or giving them negative (insulting) personality feedback, while control subjects are not so threatened. A subsequent recall test reveals that the threatened group cannot remember the words as well as the controls. The dynamic interpretation of this finding is that anxiety induced by the threat procedure has resulted in repression of the word list. However, a study by Holmes (1972) tested the alternative hypothesis that the memory loss in this situation is due to *interference* rather than repression. He added to Zeller's paradigm a third group of subjects who were given 'ego-enhancing' personality feedback (an extremely flattering description of themselves supposedly based on the results of personality tests). This treatment, which can be presumed to be distracting without invoking anxiety, was found to be equally detrimental to verbal recall (Figure 18.5). Holmes notes that, 'This leaves the concept of repression in a precarious position with respect to the necessary experimental verification'.

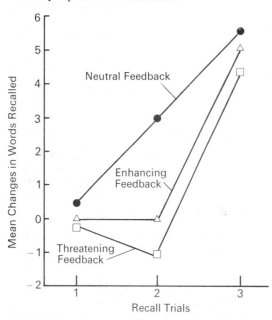

Figure 18.5 Mean changes in words recalled by subjects in ego-threatening, ego-enhancing, and neutral feedback conditions. Recall trial 1 was given before the distracting treatments; trial 3 was given after a debriefing designed to remove the distraction. The 'enhancing' and 'threatening' conditions do not differ significantly. (From Holmes, 1972, by courtesy of *J. Personal. Soc. Psychol.*)

Certainly Holmes' finding suggests that none of the studies using Zeller's paradigm can be used as evidence for repression. There are, however, other experimental studies of repression that are less open to interpretation in terms of interference. One such study, that has been widely acclaimed, is that of Levinger and Clark (1961); Kline goes as far as to claim that, 'This study provides irrefutable evidence for the Freudian concept of repression'. What did Levinger and Clark do? They recorded associations, reaction times, and G.S.R.s to 30 emotive and 30 neutral words balanced for frequency of usage in the English language. Subjects were then asked to repeat their original associations. It was found that forgotten associations were accompanied by higher G.S.R.s, that associations to emotive words were forgotten more than those to neutral words, and that associations to words which the subjects rated as highly emotional were forgotten more than those to words rated as unemotional. These results could be interpreted as evidence for repression (although the authors themselves largely resist this temptation); they are also perfectly in line with predictions from Walker's (1958) theory of memory, which is nowhere discounted as an alternative explanation.

Walker's theory suggests that long-term remembering is dependent on the transfer of learned material from short-term memory (consisting of reverberating circuits in the cerebral cortex) to long-term memory (chemical engrams in the cells). The process of transfer is called *consolidation*, and is facilitated by cortical arousal. During consolidation the relevant cells are occupied and less available for reproduction, hence memory for material giving rise to strong arousal (emotional, etc.) is less well-remembered immediately after learning. When consolidation is finished, however, e.g. after an hour to 24 hours, consolidation does not interfere any longer with reproduction, and emotional material is now better remembered. Numerous experimental studies (e.g. Kleinsmith and Kaplan, 1963) give evidence of this relationship between poor memory in the short run, and emotionality and G.S.R. production in certain words. In the long run, however, this relationship is reversed (Figure 18.6). Levinger and Clark (1961) gave their recall test immediately after the original word association test. So the results, as far as they go, are exactly as predicted by the Walker hypothesis. However, more recent results, such as these of Kleinsmith and Kaplan illustrated in Figure 18.6, could be regarded as deciding crucially between the two theories in question (Freud's and Walker's), and they have consistently tended to favour Walker by showing the cross-over effect predicted by him and not Freud. Certainly the Levinger–Clark study cannot be taken as 'irrefutable' evidence for repression.

Finally, before leaving the defence mechanisms, we shall consider *symbolism*, since in dynamic theory this

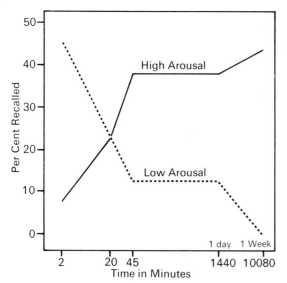

Figure 18.6 Differential recall of paired associates as a function of arousal level. (From Kleinsmith and Kaplan, 1963, by courtesy of *J. Exp. Psychol.*)

also serves the defensive function of keeping unacceptable thoughts out of consciousness. Note that the occurrence of symbolism itself is not a Freudian discovery; it has been recognised for thousands of years, at least since the time of the ancient Greeks. Nobody questions the fact that we sometimes think symbolically, or that we are particularly prone to do so when our rational powers are diminished by sleep or drugs. What is unique to dynamic psychology is a particular theory to explain why we adopt symbols in our thinking. According to Freudian theory we resort to symbols in dreams and elsewhere in order that we should not be confronted with the basic nature of our own thoughts and inclinations. These are supposedly so brutal and lustful that we translate them into symbols in order that nobody (except of course the analyst), but least of all ourselves, should recognise their significance. (Actually, symbolism is only the second line of defence in psychoanalytic theory; when the censor is operating more efficiently, as he normally does in the daytime, our libidinous thoughts do not even get that far.)

What are the alternative theories regarding the use of symbols in dreams? Interestingly enough, the ancient Greeks may have provided one:

'In their interpretation of dream symbolism, the Greeks seem to have inverted Freud (or perhaps we should rather say that Freud seems to have inverted the Greek view!). To judge from the few stories about famous dreams that we find in authors such as Herodotus, or in the records of miraculous cures at Epidaurus, they seem to have had overtly sexual dreams which were interpreted as having non-sexual significance. If a Greek dreamed that his mother enticed him into her bed, he would probably conclude that his motherland, i.e. his city-state, was going to bestow some exceptional honour upon him.'

(Eysenck and Wilson, 1973)

Here then is one alternative theory concerning the meaning of dreams, and it is extremely difficult to see how we could choose experimentally between this and the Freudian theory. Fortunately, there is a much simpler theory available which encompasses both sexual and non-sexual symbolism, and quite easily accounts for the available experimental evidence. This theory, which is stated most clearly by Eysenck (1957), holds that we adopt symbolism during sleep and other low arousal states because it is a more primitive form of thinking (in the evolutionary sense) than the highly abstract and verbal modes of thought that are typical of the waking state. Its function is not censorial but adjectival, i.e. it makes more precise the meaning of certain concepts. You may dream of your mother as a cow or a queen, depending upon whether her nutritive or disciplinary aspects are being emphasised.

A major way in which this theory of dreams differs from dynamic theories is that it assumes a continuity between our daytime and night-time thinking. In dreaming, our thoughts and desires are not disconnected from daytime concerns; characteristic motives and interests carry over into our dreams, even though they are likely to be in more pictorial and symbolic form. The vast amount of data on dreams accumulated by Calvin Hall and colleagues at the Institute of Dream Research may be readily explained on the basis of this theory. Thus, for example, the finding that men have more aggressive encounters with other men in their dreams than do women (Hall, 1963) does not require interpretation in terms of Oedipal hostility toward the father (supposedly symbolised by the male strangers); it can be attributed to the fact that men are generally more aggressive than women, and especially toward other men. This holds true for their night-time thinking as well as their day-time behaviour. Likewise, the 'discovery' that women dream more about babies and weddings than men is not necessarily a manifestation of 'displaced penis envy' (Hall and Van de Castle, 1963); it might simply reflect the fact that women are more interested in these things than men. There are, in fact, no empirical findings that would lead us to prefer the Freudian theory of symbolism in dreams over the simpler account based on the generalisation of conscious motives and interests.

INSIGHT/CARTHARSIS THERAPY

So far the evidence does not look good for dynamic approaches to personality, and consequently the prospects for a therapy ostensibly based upon them seem somewhat diminished. After all, if psychosexual experiences in childhood are not crucial, and if unconscious forces and defence mechanisms do not exist in any meaningful sense, then a therapy that is designed to manipulate these things is unlikely to have striking effects. However, it might affect patients' behaviour for reasons other than those postulated, and since psychoanalysis is widely believed to be helpful, it is certainly worthwhile evaluating its effectiveness as a question in its own right. What then, is the state of the evidence concerning the effects of psychotherapy?

In 1952 Eysenck published a now famous survey of the literature on the effects of psychotherapy. In this paper he emphasised the need to allow for the possibility that some patients may get better as a simple function of time alone, without any exposure to formal psychotherapy. For this purpose he produced an estimate of the 'spontaneous remission rate', derived from a variety of sources such as the percentage of neurotic patients discharged from state hospitals after receiving only custodial care, and the duration of claims against an insurance company for disability due to psychoneurosis. There is now fairly widespread agreement that about two-thirds of neurotic patients get better of their own accord after

Table 18.4 Percentages of patients cured or improved after about two years. (Based on data of Eysenck, 1952, by courtesy of *J. Consult. Psychol.*)

Psychoanalysis	44%
Eclectic psychotherapy	64%
No therapy	72%

two years (Figure 18.7). Eysenck then grouped all the published outcome studies into those that employed psychoanalysis and those using eclectic psychotherapy, totalled the number of patients reported as cured, much improved or improved, and arrived at figures of 44% and 64% respectively for the two types of treatment (Table 18.4). The figure of 44% for psychoanalysis could be raised to 66% by leaving out of the calculation the large number of patients who broke off treatment before their course was finished, but even so the improvement rate would be no better than spontaneous remission. Eysenck concluded, rather moderately, that psychotherapy's efficacy was not proven.

The appearance of this paper was hailed by angry protests from the psychotherapists. Most of them countered by pointing out that Eysenck had not proved that psychotherapy does not work, which raises the question of where lies the onus of proof. They did not, however, pretend that evidence for the effectiveness of psychotherapy was available, and more recent reviews (e.g. Rachman, 1971) show that this situation has not substantially altered in the two decades since Eysenck's revelation. There has been some interest in the possibility that improvements in some patients are offset by others getting worse, i.e. psychotherapy might work, but negatively just as

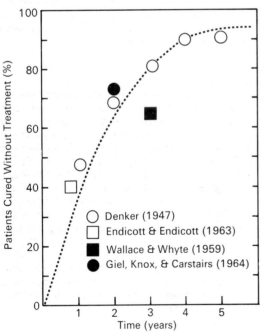

Figure 18.7 Spontaneous remission curve fitted to the data of four independent studies of patients cured without treatment. (From Eysenck, 1967, by courtesy of *Psychology Today*)

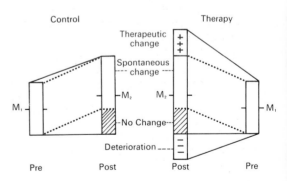

Figure 18.8 Schematic representation of pre- and post-test distributions of criterion scores in psychotherapy-outcome studies. (From Bergin, 1966, by courtesy of *J. Abn. Psychol.*)

often as positively, so that average results look no better than spontaneous remission (Figure 18.8). The latter view has led researchers to examine the effects of more specific variables such as the exact method of treatment, type of symptoms, personality of the patient and of the therapist (a healthy trend) but so far the results are not impressive. If anything, the case for psychotherapy is shifting from 'not proven' to 'rather unlikely'; such positive effects as have been reported are small and elusive.

In the face of this negative evidence there is an increasing tendency for psychotherapists to plead that even if their treatment does not work in the sense of directly contributing to improvement, it might offer a degree of comfort to the patient while his neurosis takes its natural course. In the same way, doctors admit that there is no cure for the common cold, but aspirins or whisky make it easier to live with. There might be some truth in this suggestion, but there is likewise no evidence to support it. Acceptance of this position would also necessitate abandoning claims to scientific respectability; psychoanalysis would then be on a level with animal magnetism, prayer, colour therapy, psychic acupuncture, and faith-healing, with the theory underlying it acknowledged as irrelevant. We also have to balance the value of such comfort against its potential harm, graphically illustrated by Joseph Wolpe in his foreword to R. B. Stuart's book on the subject, *Trick or Treatment* (1970):

'Physicians, when unable to establish a diagnosis of physical illness, often refer patients to psychiatrists for assessment and possible treatment. If a psychological attribution of the illness results, as it frequently does, one of its effects is to block further medical investigation of a condition that may have an organic basis after all. I think of a woman with persistent backache who turned out to have a spinal meningioma, of another whose attacks of dizziness were really due to Menière's disease, and a case of frigidity that I found to be due to a painful vaginal lesion, after the patient had wasted two years in psychoanalysis.'

While it is to be hoped that mistakes of this kind are infrequent, they do illustrate how the kind of thinking to which psychoanalytic theory and training is conducive may carry real dangers beyond the academic arguments about verification of hypotheses. If people's lives are being affected, it is not always in ways that they anticipate; here as elsewhere, it is important to establish the facts rather than hide behind dogmatic assertions.

THE VIRULENCE OF PSYCHOANALYSIS

If psychodynamic theories and therapies are so lacking in substantiation, how do we account for their popularity and persistence? Is this not in itself evidence for their validity? The answer is categorically no; especially since several other good reasons for their survival are apparent. Sex has always been very commerical; and Freud is full of it. Psychoanalysis as a treatment technique is self-indulgent fun for the patient, interesting and remunerative work for the therapist. Artists and writers find Freud's imagery colourful and evocative.

'Freud was a great novelist and dramatist himself; his theories are like a mediaeval morality play, with heroes, villains and monsters rushing about in all directions. Here the "ego", "id" and "superego" have their three-cornered fight; there the censor battles with the forces of the "unconscious"! Watch the celebrated "Oedipus complex" burrowing its way to the surface! See "sublimation" and "displacement" at work! Watch Eros battling against Thanatos! There is a tremendous cast, and their antics are astounding. The whole action of the play is centred on sex—what could be a greater draw than that?'

(Eysenck, 1971)

Perhaps even more important is the fact that dynamic theory can be easily used to 'explain' any behaviour or fantasy that people are capable of. It is especially well-equipped for doing so in deprecating terms—penis envy, Oedipal hostility, anal retentiveness, repressed homosexual urges, etc. What a way to get the best at a cocktail party! Moreover, there is usually no way by which you can be proved wrong. What more could anyone ask of a theory; except perhaps the power to predict?

CONCLUSION

The research effort to date seems to have failed to adduce any unequivocal evidence in support of the major assertions of psychoanalytic-type ('dynamic') theory. This does not rule out the possibility that such evidence might be unearthed in the future. Some of the hypotheses—especially those relating to the effects of different child-rearing practices and procedures of psychotherapy—would seem to be potentially testable, and while the tests so far conducted have not been favourable to them, it is fair to say that they have not all been decisively proved wrong. However, if a theory or approach shows no sign of being scientifically useful over an extended period of time, despite concerted research efforts to establish some predictive power, then we begin to wonder if our attention might be better directed toward other more promising theories.

References

Barber, T. X. (1965). Experimental analysis of 'hypnotic' behaviour. A review of empirical findings. *J. Abn. Psychol.*, 70, 132–154

Berger, M. (1973). Early experience and other environmental factors: An overview. In: *Handbook of Abnormal Psychology* (H. J. Eysenck, editor) (London: Pitman Press)

Bergin, A. E. (1966). Some implications of psychotherapy research for therapeutic practice. *J. Abn. Psychol.*, 71, 235–246

Brody, N. (1972). *Personality: Research and Theory* (New York: Academic Press)

Cade, J. F. J. (1973). Masturbational madness: an historical annotation. *Austral. N. Z. J. Psychiatry*, 7, 1–4

Caldwell, B. (1964). The effects of infant care. In: *Review of Child Development Research*, Vol. 1 (M. L. Hoffman and L. W. Hoffman, editors) (New York: Russell Sage Foundation)

Eylon, Y. (1967). Birth events, appendicitis and appendectomy. *Brit. J. Med. Psychol.*, 40, 317–332

Eysenck, H. J. (1952). The effects of psychotherapy: an evaluation. *J. Consult. Psychol.*, 16, 319–324

Eysenck, H. J. (1957). *Sense and Nonsense in Psychology* (Harmondsworth: Penguin)

Eysenck, H. J. (1967). New ways in psychotherapy. *Psychology Today*, (June), 39–47

Eysenck, H. J. (1971). The rise and fall of the Freudian empire. *Penthouse*, 6, No. 9

Eysenck, H. J. and Wilson, G. D. (1973). *The Experimental Study of Freudian Theories* (London: Methuen)

Goldman-Eisler, F. (1951). The problem of 'orality' and its origin in early childhood. *J. Ment. Sci.*, 97, 765–782

Hall, C. S. (1963). Strangers in dreams: an experimental confirmation of the Oedipus complex. *J. Personal.*, 31, 336–345

Hall, C. S. and Van de Castle, R. L. (1963). An empirical investigation of the castration complex in dreams. *J. Personal.*, 33, 20–29

Holmes, D. S. (1968). Dimensions of projection. *Psychol. Bull.*, 69, 248–268

Holmes, D. S. (1972). Repression or interference? A further investigation. *J. Personal. Soc. Psychol.*, 22, 163–170

Hurlock, E. B. (1968) *Developmental Psychology*, 170 (New York: McGraw-Hill)

Kleinsmith, L. J. and Kaplan, S. (1963). Paired associate learning as a function of arousal and interpolated interval. *J. Exp. Psychol.*, 65, 190–193

Kline, P. (1968). Obsessional traits, obsessional symptoms, and anal eroticism. *Brit. J. Med. Psychol.*, 41, 299–305

Kline, P. (1972). *Fact and Fantasy in Freudian Theory* (London: Methuen)

Krech, D., Crutchfield, R. S. and Ballachey, E. L. (1962). *Individual in Society* (New York: McGraw-Hill)

Levinger, G. and Clark, J. (1961). Emotional factors in the forgetting of word associations. *J. Abn. Soc. Psychol.*, 62, 99–105

O'Connor, N. (1968). Children in restricted environments. In: *Early Experience and Behaviour* (G. Newton and S. Levine, editors) (Springfield, Illinois: C. C. Thomas)

Rachman, S. J. (1971). *The Effects of Psychotherapy* (London: Pergamon Press)

Silverman, I. and Kleinman, D. (1967). A response deviance interpretation of the effects of experimentally induced frustration on prejudice. *J. Exp. Res. Personal.*, 2, 150–153

Stein, M. and Ottenberg, P. (1958). Role of odours in asthma. *Psychosom. Med.*, 20, 60–65

Stuart, R. B. (1970). *Trick or Treatment: How and When Psychotherapy Fails* (Champaign, Illinois: Research Press)

Thomas, A., Chess, S. and Birch, H. G. (1968). *Temperament and Behaviour Disorders in Children* (London: London University Press)

Walker, E. L. (1958). Action decrement and its relation to learning. *Psychol. Rev.*, 65, 129–142

Wolowitz, H. M. and Wagonfeld, S. (1968). Oral derivatives in the food preferences of peptic ulcer patients: an experimental test of Alexander's psychoanalytic hypothesis. *J. Nerv. Ment. Dis.*, 146, 18–23

Yarrow, M. R., Campbell, J. D. and Burton, R. V. (1968). *Childrearing* (San Francisco: Jossey-Bass)

Zamansky, H. S. (1958). An investigation of the psychoanalytic theory of paranoid delusions. *J. Personal.*, 26, 410–425

Zeller, A. F. (1950). An experimental analogue of repression II: The effects of individual failure and success on memory measured by relearning. *J. Exp. Psychol.*, 40, 411–422

Chapter 19

INTERVIEWING

J. S. Marzillier

INTRODUCTION

Interviewing is one of the most commonly used techniques for assessing and predicting human behaviour. It is in fact the only technique that is used by all the helping professions whatever their special interest or orientation. Interviews also enjoy widespread popularity and use outside of the clinical field, particularly in the areas of social research, market research and personnel selection. It would be difficult to imagine society functioning without interviews as the face-to-face conversational aspect of the interview seems to satisfy a need for personal involvement even if the interview is able to do little else. It is important, however, that an interview should do more than satisfy personal needs. Interviewers both in the clinical field and outside of it regard the interview as a vital technique by the use of which they are able to understand and predict human behaviour. This chapter consists of a critical examination of the claims of interviewing to serve this purpose, not in order to discredit or discard the technique. On the contrary it is hoped that by analysing its strengths and its weaknesses, interviewing may be put on a more scientific basis, thereby ensuring its better usage in clinical practice.

THE ASSESSMENT INTERVIEW IN SOCIAL RESEARCH

Interviews are most commonly used to collect information on the basis of which certain judgments are made. Such is, for example, the purpose of diagnostic interviewing by physicians and psychiatrists.

In contrast, interviewing is sometimes not used to collect information at all, but is conceived of as a means of producing change. The book, *The Psychiatric Interview* by Harry Stack Sullivan (1954), is a classic example of the therapeutic use of interviews. It is clear that 'interviewing', in this sense, is a form of treatment. Much of what is called psychotherapy is based on patient–therapist interviews. Similarly counselling, such as is found in welfare work, student help or probationary work consists in the main of interviews. It is beyond the scope of this chapter to review the vast and growing literature of the therapeutic effects of psychotherapeutic and counselling interviews. Readers are referred to other chapters in this book for an introduction to this field (Shapiro; Wilson). The term 'interviewing' in this chapter will thus exclusively refer to interviews used to collect information and to form judgments.

The field of social research has been one in which interviews have been most extensively studied. A number of useful general reviews exist and interested readers are referred to these for more detailed coverage than can be given here (Maccoby and Maccoby, 1954; Richardson *et al.,* 1965; Cannell and Kahn, 1968). It is true that while these studies are of interest in themselves, not all have a direct bearing on the clinical interview, for conditions that prevail in social research are often very different from those that exist in the clinic. For example, there is much discussion of the manner and status of the interviewer and the role he takes. In social research there is scope for considerable variability in these characteristics. Variability is much less, however, in clinical practice where the role of the interviewer, and of the respondent, is more clearly defined in terms of clinician and patient. Other differences, both minor and major, can be thought of. But one crucial difference is that social research interviewing takes place within a research setting; whereas clinical interviewing, although it can and has been used in research, is most frequently used as a part of everyday clinical practice. This distinction results in the interview being used with very different aims. Richardson *et al.* (1965) state quite clearly that for social research interviews their 'basic purpose is to collect information'. While this is true for a clinical interview, whether used by a psychiatrist, psychologist or other professional person, much more is demanded of the interviewer. He is continually forced to go beyond the data and form a judgment about the patient. This judgment could be a diagnosis, a decision to treat or some form of classification. Two processes are involved: one of gathering information; the other of clinical judgment. In social research, the interviewer is there fundamentally to collect data; inferences, predictions, judgments on the data are made separately at a later stage and usually by statistical techniques. The importance of this distinction should not be underestimated, as problems encountered in social research interviews may well be compounded in clinical interviews where immediate judgments are made by the interviewers at the time of interviewing.

In strict scientific terms, the interview should be evaluated on a par with other assessment devices such as psychological tests, questionnaires, or rating scales. Namely, high standards of reliability and validity such as are listed in 1966 American Psychological Association Manual are required. But the interview is notorious for its lack of reliability and its very poor validity. Social research reviews reveal that reliability studies are very often not carried out, despite the fact that the opportunities for error are enormous. Maccoby and Maccoby (1954) in their excellent review of the earlier research studies, list the possible sources of error in the interview. By 'error' they refer to any aspect of the interview that will tend to produce biassed or distorted information. One source of error is the way the questions are formulated.

Question formulation

There are many ways of looking at question formulation in interviews. One of the most commonly accepted distinctions is between open and closed questions. Closed questions are ones in which the answer is predicated by the question so that the respondent makes a choice out of two or more possible answers. The most common closed question is one which leads to a YES or a NO answer, e.g. 'Did you leave school at 14?' Another is where a multiple choice is indicated, e.g. 'Did you do X, Y or Z?' Error may arise in that a respondent makes a choice from alternatives which may not always be applicable and tends to give an answer where none may be indicated. Open questions are ones where no particular answer is predicated by the question, e.g. 'What was your life at school like?' Here error may arise in that relevant information may not be volunteered in response to the open question. Richardson *et al.* (1965) make the sensible point that all interviews must inevitably include both open and closed questions. Awareness of the error factor in both types of question is essential in designing an interview. Where the purpose of the interview is exploratory, such as an initial interview with a patient, open questions may well be an advantage, thereby not forcing the patient into a preconceived framework. These may then be followed-up by a series of closed questions covering specific subject areas such as symptomatology. Maccoby and Maccoby (1954) point out that closed questions have the advantage of leading to greater reliability in coding the responses. They are also more easily fitted into a structured interview and, as we shall see later, structured interviews tend to be both more reliable and more valid. Another type of question that may lead to error is the leading question, notorious from court-room dramas. 'When did you stop beating you wife?' is a leading question because it is based on an assumed premise which may be incorrect. It also may be based on a correct premise in which case, as Richardson *et al.* (1965) point out, it may in fact lead to more accurate information. Kinsey and his colleagues in their famous sex search claimed to obtain more information through such leading questions as, 'When did you first masturbate?' (Kinsey *et al.*, 1948). Sensitive clinicians may well use leading questions to prompt information that they realise is present but not volunteered by the patient. However, the danger in using leading questions is that a clinician will be obtaining answers that he is expecting to hear. This characterises the interpretive questions of some psychoanalytic interviewers where on the basis of very little evidence and a large number of assumed premises the patient's responses fall neatly into a predetermined psychoanalytic slot. Experimental work has shown that where information is difficult to recall, leading questions will produce more distorted information than where information is relatively more accessible (Marquis *et al.*, 1972b). Hence it would be wiser for interviewers to avoid leading questions unless they are certain that the assumed premises are correct ones and information they want readily accessible to the patient. The interrogative Kinsey-style interview where leading questions on a sensitive subject are shot off at a fast rate seems more appropriate to the police station than the psychiatric clinic.

Interviewer characteristics

A large number of studies in social research have been carried out on the characteristics of the interviewer and their effect on the interviewing process. There is overwhelming evidence indicating that a great many interviewer characteristics can result in biassed or inaccurate information being disclosed by the respondent. These characteristics range from demographic ones such as social class and race to individual ones such as the interviewer's manner, appearance, attitudes and expectations. Thus in a classic study Rice (1929) showed that in a survey of the causes of destitution among tramps and down-and-outs in the workhouse, one interviewer, a prohibitionist, consistently reported more cases of alcoholism, while another, a socialist, reported more social and industrial causes.

The influence the interviewer has on interview may well vary according to the type of interview, the information required and the motivation of the respondent. An unfamiliar interviewer attempting to prise information on political beliefs from a reluctant respondent is likely to obtain less accurate information than a doctor inquiring about illness from a willing patient. Nevertheless the documentation of 'interviewer error' in social research studies should be borne in mind in clinical interviewing especially where more obvious parallels can be drawn. Rapport is a good example. Contrary to popular belief the establishment of good rapport is not a *sine qua non* of good interviewing. Social research interviewers have long known that excessive friendliness on the part of interviewers may well lead to distorted reporting if only because respondents feel the need to please the interviewer and give him answers that they feel he expects. One way an interviewer achieves rapport is by reinforcing the respondent by social reinforcers.

That is, the interviewer will consistently look at the respondent, nod his head in response to the respondent's answers, smile, grunt and say 'Yes', 'Mmhm' and 'That's right' during the course of the interview. In other words he will pay the respondent a great deal of attention. The use of these reinforcers, however, is not always beneficial. Recent experimental evidence, for example, has shown that better educated subjects gave less accurate information when reporting chronic illness to an interviewer who used social reinforcers of this sort. For lesser educated subjects—in this study those who had not extended their education beyond high school—the interviewer's use of social reinforcement produced more accurate information (Marquis *et al.*, 1972a). A possible explanation of these findings is that the better educated subjects were put off by the interviewer's attempt to establish rapport. That is, the interviewer did not need to establish rapport because these subjects were already willing and able to provide the desired information. With the lesser educated subjects, on the other hand, rapport functioned in a useful way as it encouraged these subjects to provide more detailed information than they would otherwise have done. Good rapport has often been regarded as essential in clinical interviewing. But the findings of social research indicate that a good interviewer will be one who is able to relate rapport to the needs of the respondent and the demands of the interview. Thus with better educated patients a more professional approach may well be advisable, whereas lesser educated patients may respond better to a friendly, encouraging approach. This hypothesis could easily be tested by direct research into the clinical interview.

Recall of information

In both social research and clinical interviews a great demand is put on the respondent to recall items of information. Research has indicated that certain types of information are less reliably recalled than others. Recent events are generally more readily reported since older information will be subject to memory decay. Where events are associated with unpleasant emotional states, anxiety, for example, they may well be distorted. Attitudes and feelings are more often inaccurately reported than factual information. Social desirability and ego-enhancement can distort information. Mental illness and genito-urinary diseases are consistently under-reported, for example, charitable contributions consistently overestimated.

Certain methods of recording the data are subject to considerable error such as distortions, omissions, overcondensation of material and mechanical inaccuracies. Pure memory without the aid of tape-recordings, short-hand or long-hand transcriptions is most prone to error. Clinicians very often interview patients about serious illnesses, traumatic and unpleasant experiences, attitudes and feelings sometimes held and experienced many years previously, often in childhood, in an area where social desirability and ego-enhancement undoubtedly operate. Many interviewers will rely entirely on their memory in recording the information. On the basis of this flimsy, unreliable, poorly recorded information elaborate models of the patient's illness and personality are often constructed, given spurious validity by being inscribed into casenotes and 'substantiated' as more information is carefully fitted into the model. Clinicians should be more sensitive to the dangers of basing diagnostic or treatment formulations on interview data alone, particularly if no attempt is made to take account of the sources of error listed above. One safeguard would be to seek validation for their information by other means. Where possible, psychological, neurological tests and behavioural observations should be incorporated into the assessment procedure as a check on the data obtained by interview. Concurrently, attempt should be made to minimise error in interviews by more careful design and structure, ensuring that the information reported is systematically recorded.

THE PSYCHIATRIC ASSESSMENT INTERVIEW

Despite widespread usage of the interview in clinical practice, its evaluation as an assessment technique has been poor. As is well-known, the interview provides a major source of information for the psychiatrist in reaching a diagnosis, where it is used on patients and informants to uncover information about present state and aetiology. Research on diagnostic interviewing in the 1940s and 1950s appeared to show that the interview was fundamentally unreliable. Ash (1949) assessed the amount of agreement between three psychiatrists recording independent diagnoses following a joint interview, using five major and 60 specific diagnostic categories. He found very poor agreement on the 60 specific diagnoses and better agreement on the five major categories. However, total agreement across all three psychiatrists was obtained in less than half the cases seen, and 'pair' agreements—i.e. agreements between two out of three psychiatrists—for only 2/3 of the sample. In all there were more disagreements than agreements. Kreitman *et al.* (1961) studied the amount of agreement between two experienced clinicians working in a realistic clinical setting. No rating scales or schedules were used during the interviews but the psychiatrists filled in an Item sheet after each interview. While the clinicians reached a reasonable level of agreement on broad diagnostic categories (e.g. psychosis, organic disorder, neurosis, etc.) agreement dropped for the specific diagnoses and dropped further for specific symptomatology. In fact the two psychiatrists showed an average agreement of less than 50% on symptoms, with a range between 0 and 85%. Beck (1962), in an excellent review of a number of studies, showed that

Table 19.1   Level of diagnostic agreement by diagnostic category (patients). (From Kreitman *et al.* (1961), by courtesy of *J. Ment. Sci.*)

Level of diagnostic agreement	Organic	Functional psychoses	Neuroses	All
Specific*	75%	61%	28%	63%
Specific + generic*	85%	71%	52%	78%

*These terms refer to the type of diagnostic category used. 'Specific' refers to the level of agreement on a specific diagnostic category, e.g. schizophrenia. 'Generic' refers to cases where disagreement on the specific category is ignored, and agreement taken for the general diagnosis, e.g. functional psychosis.

in no study were psychiatrists able to obtain more than 30 to 40% agreement on specific diagnostic categories. As these categories are the ones most commonly used in clinical practice to predict response to treatment, the poor agreement between psychiatrists must cast serious doubts on the validity of their predictions.

There is also evidence that some diagnostic categories are less reliably arrived at than others. In all studies there is always better agreement on organic disorder and functional psychosis. Neurosis and personality disorder, on the other hand, are much more unreliably diagnosed at interview. This is clearly shown in the figures obtained by Kreitman *et al.* (1961) (Table 19.1).

The amount of agreement on specific neurotic categories should be noted, only 28%. Even when all the specific categories are collapsed into one broad category, 'neurosis', agreement is only 52%. In this study there were too few examples of 'personality disorder' to merit inclusion in the analysis. It is also the case that, when psychiatrists are asked to make a second choice diagnosis, the most common categories chosen are neurosis and personality disorder. It may well be the case that patients, whatever their disorder, show signs indicative of these two diagnostic categories. In other words, there is considerable overlap in the present classification system. This would make the psychiatrist's task at interview even more difficult.

In the studies reviewed so far the interview has been used in a relatively unstructured manner to form impressionistic judgments. In one sense this is fair as it represents what is common practice in many clinics. Admitting that such an approach is open to considerable error, it is perhaps most fruitful to look at ways and means in which this error can be reduced. There are a number of recent studies of psychiatric interviewing that are helpful in this respect.

Wing *et al.* (1967) developed a structured rating scale for assessing present state of psychiatric patients in a clinical interview. This rating scale is not standardised in the sense that a questionnaire is. Some of the questions are predetermined, and have to be read verbatim. These are screening questions that cover the main areas of symptomatology. A positive response to any one of these questions leads on to further questions, whose form and wording do not have to be strictly adhered to. The interviewer may pursue an interesting theme with further unspecified probes and questions if he so wishes. Two other aspects of this interview are worth noting. First, the enquiries are all restricted to the events and feelings of the past month, thereby reducing unreliability due to memory decay. Secondly, interpretative and overly obscure psychiatric terminology is excluded. As the interviewer proceeds from one symptom group to another he makes a rating of the presence and extent of the symptomatology, and at the end of the interview a categorisation (preliminary diagnosis) is made according to clearly defined criteria. Thus, the act of judging the patient—his assignment to a category—is separated from the recording process. The overall results are encouraging. High reliabilities are obtained for the categorisation, for two psychiatrists, either over two interviews or for the same interview. More importantly, reliabilities of 0.8 and 0.9 are achieved for most, though not all, the psychotic and neurotic symptomatology. This form of structured interview is standardised to a great extent, and yet flexible. The achievement of high reliabilities in the recording process has enabled these workers to carry out research on the diagnostic judgments made by different groups and in different countries. Striking differences have been found between American and British psychiatrists, particularly in the differential usage of the schizophrenic and manic depressive diagnoses. The fact that the structured interview is proved a reliable means of assessment enables the research workers to attribute those differences to a discrepancy in the judgmental process, and not to methodological faults or biasses in the recording process (Cooper *et al.*, 1969).

Further studies on the reliability of the interview have been carried out by Rutter and his co-workers (Rutter and Brown, 1966; Rutter and Graham, 1968). In these studies the major aim was to make the interview into a reliable and valid research instrument. In a sense the later study (Rutter and Graham, 1968) parallels the work carried out by Wing and his colleagues in the field of child psychiatry, and quite similar findings were obtained. This study consisted of an analysis of diagnostic interviewing with children to ascertain the presence and the severity of psycho-pathology. As with most other studies, the broad diagnostic categories were more reliably rated than the specific symptomatology. Reliabilities were interjudge, sometimes across two interviews, some-times in one interview. Behavioural observation constituted an important part of the diagnostic procedure, yet surprisingly proved to be less reliable than the more inferential decisions about symptoma-tology. Possible areas of psychopathology were covered systematically and the results coded, from which a categorisation was made. As in the interview used by Wing *et al.*, some questions were predeter-mined and some were at the interviewer's discretion. Although hard to assess accurately, the interview seemed to be less structured than in Wing's interviewing study and this may account for the somewhat lower reliabilities obtained for the individual symptoms.

The other study on the reliability of the inter-view (Rutter and Brown, 1966) differs in a number of respects. The interview was not used as a form of diagnostic assessment but to measure aspects of family life and relationships. Thirty families were involved, all of whom had at least one child under 15, and who came into contact with psychiatric services through the illness of one parent (psychoneurotic or depression). Interviews were conducted with the patient, the spouse, and jointly with both patient and spouse. The interviews were structured in an unusual way. Rutter and Brown made a preliminary distinc-tion between 'objective' and 'subjective' measures. Objective measures were measures of events and behaviours observed and reported by either husband or wife or both. The behaviours concerned were predetermined and ratings were quantitative. A short time period was covered, and specific rather than general questions asked. Examples of the type of events are frequency of sexual intercourse, partici-pation in household tasks, quarrelling. Subjective measures consisted of (1) self-reports of feelings in response to direct questions and (2) observed expres-sions of feelings spontaneously made at interview. Rutter and Brown stress that most reliance was put on the second measure. An assessment was also made of the quality of the marital relationship. The results of inter-rater reliabilities were encouragingly high. The 'objective' measures were as high as 0.9 to 0.95 for a single interview. Spontaneous expressions of feelings were only slightly less reliable (0.8 to 0.9).

The high reliabilities achieved in both types of study, but particularly in the Rutter and Brown study, are all the more encouraging because of the com-plexity of the subject matter covered. Marital relation-ships and interpersonal feelings would seem to be on face value, extremely difficult to assess reliably by interviews. Unfortunately, the design of all of these studies is such that no equivocal answer can be given as to what aspect of the interview procedure is of major importance in achieving high reliabilities, for in each case a variety of changes were made to the normal clinical interview. These changes, however, are worth summarising. In the first place, some form of interview schedule was used, thereby imposing much more structure on the interview and allowing data to be immediately recorded and coded for future judg-ment. The purpose of the interview was clearly defined; psychiatric jargon was avoided; and recent events were concentrated upon. Behavioural obser-vations of feelings were heavily relied on in the Rutter and Brown study, but proved less satisfactory in the study by Rutter and Graham. Finally all interviewers received some form of training. Although these interviews were originally designed as research instruments and in their present form would prove too cumbersome for everyday clinical use, some of the modifications may well be essential if the psychiatric interview is to survive as a viable assessment pro-cedure. There is no merit in continuing to use an error prone technique merely because it involves less time and less effort.

PREDICTION AND CLINICAL JUDGMENT

Thus far interviewing has been analysed and discus-sed mainly in terms of its ability to collect accurate and reliable information. As was mentioned earlier interviews are also used to form judgments and make predictions. In the clinical interview predictions can be couched in the form of diagnoses or in terms of the clinicians' judgments about the patient's likely re-sponse to various treatments. It is important to assess not only whether interviews are successful in making valid predictions but also whether the interview is the most efficient method for making such predictions. In the field of personnel selection, where the interview is one of a number of selection techniques, research has so far failed to give much support to the validity of the interview as a predictor of future behaviour.

PERSONNEL SELECTION

In the last ten years there have been three comprehen-sive reviews of the selection interview (Mayfield, 1964; Ulrich and Trumbo, 1965; Wright, 1969). A quite consistent pattern emerges from all the studies covered in these reviews. In the first place the inter-view is consistently shown to be a poor predictor of future performance, particularly if compared to other selection techniques such as biographical data, previous work history or psychometric assessment. In a five-year study on student selection, Kelly and Fiske (1951) looked at predictions made at various stages in the selection procedure using academic performance, objective tests of achievement and staff ratings as criteria against which the predictions were validated. The interview added so little to the success of the predictions that the time and expenditure involved could hardly be justified. Table 19.2 shows in quantitative terms how little a one-hour or two-hour interview added to the validity coefficients.

Table 19.2 Validity coefficients obtained in a sequential assessment of cumulative data. (From Kelly and Fiske, 1951, Validation Analyses, Part D, 170, by courtesy of The University of Michigan Press, Ann Arbor)

	Median values	
	Interviewer A	*Interviewer B*
Stage (1) Credential file only	0.24	0.22
(2) Objective tests	—	0.29
(3) Autobiography	—	0.28
(4) Projective tests	—	0.30
(5) Interviews	0.25	0.31

Interviewer A first assessed the candidate from his Credential file and then from an hour-long initial interview. Interviewer B assessed the candidates at five stages, the last of which was an intensive two-hour interview. Kelly and Fiske (1951) sum up the poor contribution of either interview: 'Neither of these interviews appears to have made an essential contribution to the assessment process. In each instance the median validity increases by only 0.01 over the previous value . . .'

A second consistent finding is that interviewers tend to make early decisions as to 'good' candidates, reflecting their particular bias or stereotype. The information gleaned later on in the interview is used merely to substantiate the decision made near the beginning. Thirdly, interviewers most commonly rely on negative or unfavourable information in reaching their decisions, using this information to support or disconfirm hypotheses held about the candidate. Thus the conception of the interviewer skilfully evaluating the candidate by careful and systematic interviewing seems to be a myth. No doubt such interviewers do exist, but research has shown that the majority of interviewers operate by using stereotypes arrived at early in the interview and as a result fail to make successful predictions about the candidates.

A further important finding that has consistently emerged from studies of the selection interview is that the more structured the interview becomes, the more agreement there is between interviewers and the more valid the predictions made. Yonge (1956) assessed the predictive validity of the interview in assessing successful job performance of employees in a pharmaceutical firm. By using an Item sheet, separated into six main sections and five subsections, coding and quantifying the responses, and a short 15–20 minute interview, substantially valid predictions were made. Ulrich and Trumbo (1965) conclude their review of the selection interview by suggesting that if the

interview is to have any validity it must be systematic, structured and made to answer specific rather than general questions. Similarly Wright (1969) is in no doubt that structure is an essential component of the selection interview. 'Virtually alone among techniques thus far, the structured (or patterned) interview has demonstrated consistent reliability and, although its validity as a selection tool has not been conclusively demonstrated, it serves to control some of the most distorting influences (e.g. interviewer bias) that impinge on the use of the interview as a selection device' (Wright, 1969).

CLINICAL JUDGMENT

Although the clinical interview is widely used to form judgments and predictions about patients, research into its validity as a source of prediction is virtually non-existent. There has been much more concern over the validity of the diagnostic classification system than over the interview itself. There is, however, one field where the validity of the interview has been specifically studied. Hunt and his colleagues in a series of studies have looked at the predictive validity of the psychiatric interview in military service, using discharge rate as their criterion (Hunt *et al.*, 1957). Although claiming that the brief psychiatric interview is a substantially valid predictor of future discharge rate, Hunt also acknowledges that the interview is 'a specific technique effective in some situations and not effective in others'. In fact his studies fail to show that the psychiatric interview can do more than differentiate 'normal' from 'abnormal' groups. In one study the interview failed miserably to differentiate between mild and moderate psychopathology, the results, in fact, almost reaching significance in the reverse direction! Moreover, a study by Plag (1961) showed that predictions from a psychiatric interview were no better than statistical predictions from biographical data alone, again with discharge rate as a criterion. The conclusion to be drawn from these predictive validity studies is that the brief psychiatric interview is not a successful predictor of discharge rate, except in the crudest manner where it is no better than less costly statistical prediction. In fairness to the interview, it should be pointed out that the five or ten-minute brief screening interview is not representative of most diagnostic interviews in a clinical setting which are generally considerably longer and more detailed. However, studies of the interview in personnel selection indicate that long interviews are not necessarily any better than short ones in making valid predictions. Moreover, as mentioned above, interviewers generally arrive at decisions early on in the interview. It is possible that similar processes occur in the longer diagnostic interviews.

Clinical judgments made at interviews involve somewhat different predictions than that of job performance or of discharge rate from the military service. The clinician is particularly concerned to predict the best course of treatment for the problems the patient presents. Despite the importance and prevalence of such clinical predictions, no systematic attempt has been made to assess how valid these predictions are. The evidence from the best researched field, personnel selection, suggests that interview-based predictions will not be valid, particularly if the interview is an unstructured one and its aims relatively unspecified. We have seen that the introduction of structure into a clinical interview as was done in the Wing and Rutter studies led to greater reliability and more accurate information. Further research is needed to assess the validity of the predictions made from such interviews. It seems important too that clinicians be aware of the potential dangers in interviewing. Considering how important clinical judgment is, it is surprising that little scientific research into it has been carried out.

ANALOGUE STUDIES OF INTERVIEWING

In the last decade there has been a substantial output of experimental work on the process of interviewing. That is, an attempt has been made to analyse, quantify and validate the events that take place during an interview. Unfortunately this research has been variable both in quality and in the areas covered, which may partly reflect the relative newness of the field and partly the difficulties in bringing the complex phenomena of the interview into experimental analysis.

One major obstacle in evaluating most process research is the doubtfulness that the findings are generalisable outside of the particular context. in which the research was carried out. The work of Joseph Matarazzo and his colleagues illustrates this problem very clearly (Matarazzo and Wiens, 1972). In a series of experimental studies on the interview, Matarazzo meticulously analysed speech patterns of interviewer and interviewee using an Interaction Chronograph, a device for measuring the amount of time each participant spoke. From these studies he concluded a certain synchrony existed in the amount spoken by both parties, the longer were the units of X's speech, the longer were the units of Y's replies. It is important to note that Matarazzo studied the duration of units of speech independent of content. He labelled this finding the inverted J curve of speech patterns. Although Matarazzo was able to replicate these findings in a series of experimental studies, it is significant to note that he was unable to find a similar effect in his analysis of seven ongoing psychotherapy sessions despite the fact that he and his colleagues were the counsellors (Matarazzo *et al.*, 1966). The failure to find similar synchrony in speech patterns in what must be the most analogous form of treatment to the experimental interview, counselling interviews, underlines the doubt about the generality and meaningfulness of this and other process research. It is worth

making the point that even if Matarazzo had found synchrony in his study on counselling interviews, this would not guarantee that synchrony would have been found in other forms of interviewing, not to mention other less 'verbal' forms of therapy.

The problem of generalisation is one major limitation of process research using analogue interviews. A second limitation is the fact that the majority of studies have concentrated on the operation of non-content variables. While Matarazzo has studied speech patterns others have studied eye contact, head-nods, grunts, hesitations, pauses, body movements and speech rate among many variables. It is understandable that research into this complex field has concentrated on the more obviously quantifiable aspect of the interview. Nevertheless until research is conducted into what people say, as well as how they say it, it is difficult to see what practical applications these findings will have.

Further, it is important that some research be directed to clinical interviewing of a more specific kind. Thus psychotherapeutic interviewing has been generally regarded as the clinical area where findings of experimental research can be applied. However, the considerable variability in the aims and methods of psychotherapeutic interviewing, as well as variations in the clients and their problems, suggests that experimental research might be more profitably concerned with assessment interviewing, where the aims and structure of the interview are more clear-cut. A start has been made in this direction in the work of Siegman and Pope (1972). They report a study assessing the effect of relatively ambiguous questions on the productivity of interviewee's responses in assessment interviews, finding that although ambiguous questions led to more productive responses in terms of amount spoken, it was not the case that ambiguity produced more 'meaningful' material as has been widely assumed by many clinicians. The proportion of 'meaningful' to 'neutral' material remained the same following specific or ambiguous questions. The findings of increased productivity following ambiguous questions have some practical application in assessment interviewing as clinicians may well cast their questions in a more ambiguous manner in order to collect more data. However, even in this context the variable of 'meaningfulness' of the data indicates that a simple generalisation cannot be made. Other variables remain uncontrolled, particularly the client variable. It is quite possible that categories of patients may respond very differently to ambiguous questions from the student nurses in Siegman and Pope's study.

Experimental work on process variables in interviewing is bedevilled by the uncertainty about generalisation, the limitations on the variables studied, the discrepancies in research quality and the doubtfulness about the practical relevance of the work. There is, however, a need for systematic research into what constitutes the process of interviewing in the clinical assessment interview, as this may throw light on how successful interviews can be conducted. It is hoped that as the body of process research grows, more studies will concentrate on this and other practically relevant areas.

CONCLUSIONS

In the introduction to this Chapter it was stated that its aim was not to discredit the interview as an assessment technique, but, by means of critical examination put the clinical interview on a more scientific basis. This examination indicates at least four important ways in which the clinical interview could usefully develop.

1. *Specification of objectives*

The consistent finding to emerge from research into the selection interview is the importance of specifying what objectives are aimed at in the interview. Global judgments on candidates' suitability for employment are not validly made at interview. However, it is possible that if interviewers are given specific aims then predictions can be made with better validity. Ulrich and Trumbo (1965), for example, suggest that the interviews may be most usefully employed to assess the motivation and sociability of candidates, although they fail to cite any evidence in support of this suggestion. The principle of greater specification would seem equally applicable to the clinical interview. In the first place it is necessary to separate assessment and treatment interviews. Further, the assessment interview can itself be broken down into various categories depending on the objectives in question. A speculative example of this would be the break-down of the psychiatric assessment interview into three types: an exploratory interview with the objective of getting to know the patient; a data-gathering interview whose aim is to collect factual information, as is done in obtaining educational or occupational histories; and, finally, a probing interview where sensitive problem areas are explored. By specifying the objectives of each interview, research can be conducted into the most effective style of interview and of interviewer for each objective. Hypotheses can be derived from work in other areas. In social research there is some evidence to indicate that open-ended questions would be most useful in an exploratory interview, whereas closed questions would predominate in a data-gathering interview. If this conclusion can be substantiated by clinical research, it would have important implications for interviewer training.

2. *Interviewer and patient variables*

Social research has shown that there are many different aspects of the interviewer and the respondent which influence the type of information obtained at interview. In general terms it has been documented that many interviewer characteristics tend to lead to biassed or inaccurate information. It is important that clinicians are at least aware of the potential sources of error in interviewing. Furthermore, there are methods by which error can be reduced. The use of scheduled interviews, avoidance of jargon, concentration on recent events, have all been proved useful in assuring that more reliable information is obtained. The studies of Rutter and Wing have shown the applicability of these methods to clinical interviews in a research setting. The extension to routine clinical practice should not prove too difficult.

A less general, but equally important finding, is the differential response of various subjects to different interviewing styles. Rapport has been shown to have a differential effect on better or lesser educated subjects in reporting chronic illness. It seems very likely that different categories of patients, at various stages in their illnesses, will be more responsive to certain types of interviewers. As yet there is no evidence to substantiate this assumption. However, if one diagnostic category is taken as an example, namely depression, it is apparent that a non-directive, open-ended style of interviewing is likely to be unprofitable in severely depressed patients where the overall level of responsiveness is very low. A structured interview with closed questions is likely to lead to more information. Research can be conducted to test this assumption, and, further, to assess the amount of accurate and meaningful material produced by the different interviewing styles. It would also be useful to test the generality of Siegman and Pope's finding that ambiguous questions lead to more information, though not necessarily more meaningful material. This finding may well vary according to the type of subjects interviewed. The general conclusion is that given a certain population of subjects, research should be conducted to assess what is the most effective style of interviewing for that population.

3. *Clinical judgment*

Clinical judgment is a feature of all clinical interviews. Yet, as we have seen from personnel selection, judgments based on interviews are notoriously subject to bias and error. A major step in reducing each error is to separate the data-gathering process from the judgmental one. When this is done, as it was in the Rutter and Wing studies, information is more reliably arrived at. It is then important to assess the validity of the clinical judgments made on the basis of this information. A similar procedure is required to that carried out by Plag (1961), when he compared predictions from other sources. In this study, clinical judgment proved no better than statistical prediction. Meehl (1954), in a controversial book, found that clinical judgment on the whole compares unfavourably with predictions arrived at by statistical techniques. Hence, it is important not only to validate clinical judgments made at interview, but also to compare such judgments with predictions made statistically. In other words, it is not only important to assess whether clinical judgments are correct, but also to assess whether they are the most useful way of arriving at predictions.

4. *Interviewing in relation to other techniques*

The interview is only one of many assessment techniques. In clinical practice, interviews are likely to be used in conjunction with other methods of assessment, such as psychological, neurological and medical tests, and behavioural observation and analysis. The specific contribution interviewing may make in an assessment needs to be established, not only in terms of clinical judgment, but also in terms of information gathering. Comparison of interviewing with other means of assessment will serve to delineate its particular value as well as its limitations. Behavioural analysis, for example, provides an objective and reliable means of assessing on-going behaviour (Kanfer and Saslow, 1969). Inferences can be made from interviews about the frequency and intensity of behaviour, but such inferences are less valid than measures obtained by observation and analysis. Therefore, where the objective of the assessment is to establish the prevalence of a particular behaviour, interviewing will not be the most valid or useful technique. However, interviewing may prove useful as part of an overall assessment. To take as an example aggressive behaviour in children, the methods of behavioural analysis have been well-established in assessing the frequency, duration, quality and variability of aggression in children. Interviewing, however, can play its part in, for example, assessing the attitudes of the parents towards their aggressive child. Thus, interviewing must be considered not simply as an individual technique, but as part of a general assessment procedure.

If further research can be conducted along these lines, interviewing will be sharpened into a more scientific, and hence more acceptable instrument. Its value as an assessment technique in the clinical field may then be increased to a level commensurate with its present popularity and usage.

References

Ash, P. (1949). The reliability of psychiatric diagnoses. *J. Abn. and Soc. Psychol.*, **44**, 272–276

Beck, A. T. (1962). Reliability of psychiatric diagnoses. I. Critique of systematic studies. *Amer. J. Psychiat.*, **119**, 210–216

Cannell, C. F. and Kahn, R. L. (1968). Interviewing. In: *Handbook of Social Psychology* (2nd Ed.) (G. Lindsey and E. Aronson, editors) (London: Addison-Wesley)

Cooper, J. E., Kendell, R. E., Gurland, B. J., Sartorius, N. and Farkas, T. (1969). Cross-national study of diagnosis of mental disorders: some results from the first comparative investigation. *Amer. J. Psychiatry*, Suppl. **125**, 21–29

Hunt, W. A., Herrmann, R. S. and Noble, H. (1957). The specificity of the psychiatric interview. *J. Clin. Psychol.*, **13**, 49–53

Kanfer, F. H. and Saslow, C. (1969). Behavioural diagnosis. In: *Behavior Therapy: Current Appraisal and Status* (C. Franks, editor) (New York: McGraw-Hill)

Kelly, E. L. and Fiske, D. (1951). *The Prediction of Performance in Clinical Psychology* (Ann Arbor: The University of Michigan Press)

Kinsey, A. C., Pomeroy, W. B. and Martin, C. E. (1948). *Sexual Behaviour in the Human Male* (Philadelphia: Saunders)

Kreitman, N., Sainsbury, P., Morissey, J., Towers, J. and Scrivener, J. (1961). The reliability of psychiatric assessment: an analysis. *J. Ment. Sci.*, **107**, 887–908

Maccoby, E. E. and Maccoby, N. (1954). The interview: a tool of social science. In: *Handbook of Social Psychology* (1st Ed.) (G. Lindsey, editor) (London: Addison-Wesley)

Marquis, K. H., Cannell, C. F. and Laurent, A. (1972a). Reporting of health events in interviews: effects of reinforcement, question length and interviews. *Vital and Health Statistics*, **Series 2, No. 45**

Marquis, K. H., Marshall, J. and Oskamp, S. (1972b). Testimony validity as a function of question form, atmosphere and item difficulty. *J. Appl. Soc. Psychol.*, **2**, 167–186

Matarazzo, J. D., Wiens, A. N., Matarazzo, R. G. and Saslow, G. (1968). Speech and silence behavior in clinical psychotherapy and its laboratory correlates. In: *Research in Psychotherapy*, Vol. 3, (J. M. Shlien, editor) (Washington: A.P.A.)

Matarazzo, J. D. and Wiens, A. N. (1972). *The Interview: research on its Anatomy and Structure* (Chicago: Aldine-Atherton)

Mayfield, E. C. (1964). The selection interview: a re-evaluation of published research. *Personnel Psychol.*, **17**, 239–260

Meehl, P. E. (1954). *Clinical vs Statistical Prediction* (University of Minnesota Press)

Plag, J. A. (1961). Some considerations of the value of the psychiatric screening interview. *J. Clin. Psychol*, **117**, 2–8

Rice, S. A. (1929). Contagious bias in the interview: A methodological note. *Amer. J. Sociol.*, **35**, 420–423

Richardson, S. A., Dohrenwend, N. S. and Klein, D. (1965). *Interviewing: Its Forms and Functions* (New York: Basic Books)

Rutter, M. and Brown, G. W. (1966). The reliability and validity of measures of family life and relationships in families containing one psychiatric patient. *Soc. Psychiatry*, **1**, 38–53

Rutter, M. and Graham, P. (1968). The reliability and validity of the psychiatric assessment of the child. I. Interview with the child. *Brit. J. Psychiatry*, **114**, 563–579

Siegman, A. W. and Pope, B. (1972). The effects of ambiguity and anxiety on interviewee behavior. In: *Studies in Dyadic Communication* (A. W. Siegman and B. Pope, editors) (Oxford: Pergamon Press)

Sullivan, H. S. (1954). *The Psychiatric Interview* (London: Tavistock Publication)

Ulrich, L. and Trumbo, D. (1965). The selection interview since 1949. *Psychol. Bull.*, 2, 100–116

Wing, J. K., Birley, J. L., Cooper, J. E., Graham, P. and Isaacs, A. D. (1967). Reliability of a procedure for measuring and classifying 'present psychiatric state'. *Brit. J. Psychiatry*, 113, 499–515

Wright, O. R. (1969). Summary of research on the selection interview since 1964. *Personnel Psychol.*, 22, 391–413

Yonge, K. A. (1956). The value of the interview: An orientation pilot study. *J. Appl. Psychol.*, 40, 25–31

Chapter 20

COUNSELLING

D. A. Shapiro

An ever-increasing number and variety of professional agencies offer 'personal' or 'psychological' help to those with problems in relationships, at work, or in 'life'. It is often felt that such essentially personal problems can only find resolution in a situation involving personal contact. This chapter is concerned with recent attempts to gain a scientific understanding and evaluation of these humanistically-oriented approaches to psychological treatment.

COUNSELLING AND PSYCHOTHERAPY

Although counselling and psychotherapy usually differ as to goals, professional background of their practitioners, settings, and methods, there is no single criterion by which they can be simply distinguished. However, several features which are more characteristic of counselling than of psychotherapy (Stefflre, 1965) have favoured the development of systematic research. Counselling was originated by psychologists, working in an academic setting; this contrasts with the medical orientation of psychotherapy. The recipients of counselling are called 'clients' rather than 'patients', and are less likely to be assigned a psychiatric diagnosis. Counselling tends to emphasise relatively modest goals, related to some relatively specific deficiency in the client's role functioning. As far as method is concerned, counselling tends to be completed in fewer sessions, with less emphasis on exploring the client's past experiences, and somewhat greater concern with cognitive clarification of the client's problems rather than exploration of its affective ambiguities. In all these matters of method, however, there is considerable overlap between the activites of practitioners calling themselves 'counsellors' and those calling themselves 'psychotherapists'.

THE CENTRAL ASSUMPTION OF COUNSELLING

Counselling is firmly rooted in a humanistic ethic, emphasising the inherent potential for growth and self-actualisation in every individual. This leads to the assumption, which is often uncritically accepted, that a certain type of counselling relationship is 'good' for any client. On this basis, a professional tradition of counselling has evolved, in advance of any scientific validation. Rogers (1957), however, attempted to articulate and formalise this assumption, for the purposes of subsequent empirical evaluation. He argued that there are certain 'necessary and sufficient conditions for constructive personality change' which are common to all forms of counselling and psychotherapy, and indeed to human relationships more generally. For one person to help another, Rogers suggested that the helper must be 'congruent' in the relationship, and must experience and communicate 'unconditional positive regard' for the person being helped, together with an 'empathic understanding of his internal frame of reference'.

As Rogers envisaged in his 1957 paper, a substantial body of research has developed, in which these conditions are rated from segments of sound recordings of interviews by trained raters, and the ratings correlated with therapeutic change in the clients. Much of this work is reviewed by Truax and Carkhuff (1967), who reproduce the manuals used in the training of the raters. These manuals define the attributes measured by each scale, giving descriptions and transcripted examples of therapists functioning at each level on each scale.

'Congruence' or 'genuineness' is rated on a five-point scale, defined as follows:

'This scale is an attempt to define five degrees of therapist genuineness, beginning at a very low level where the therapist presents a façade or defends and denies feelings; and continuing to a high level of self-congruence where the therapist is freely and deeply himself. A high level of self-congruence does not mean that the therapist must overtly express his feelings but only that he does not deny them. Thus, the therapist may be actively reflecting, interpreting, analysing, or in other ways functioning as a therapist; but this functioning must be self-congruent, so that he is being himself in the moment rather than presenting a professional facade. Thus the therapist's response must be sincere rather than phony; it must express his real feelings or being rather than defensiveness . . .'

Literal interpretation of this definition would require the rater to perform the impossible task of determining the extent to which the therapist is 'being himself' in the absence of any other information about the therapist. In practice, it is likely that much depends on the manner of the therapist's expression, voice tone, speech disturbances, and idiomatic features of content. A study by Shapiro (1973) suggests that some of these factors may not be equivalent for British and American raters.

'Unconditional positive regard' or non-possessive warmth' is also rated on a five-point scale. It is defined by Truax and Carkhuff (1967) as follows:

'. . . (it) ranges from a high level where the therapist warmly accepts the patient's experience as part of that person, without imposing conditions; to a low level where the therapist evaluates a patient or his feelings, expresses dislike or disapproval, or expresses warmth in a selective and evaluative way.

Thus a warm positive feeling toward the client may still rate quite low in this scale if it is given conditionally. Non-possessive warmth for the client means accepting him as a person with human potentialities. It involves a non-possessive caring for him as a separate person and, thus, a willingness to share equally his joys and aspirations or his depressions and failures. It involves valuing the patient as a person, separate from any evaluation of his behaviour or thoughts. Thus, a therapist can evaluate the patient's behaviour or his thoughts but still rate high on warmth if it is quite clear that his valuing of the individual as a person is uncontaminated and unconditional . . . at its highest level it involves . . . a prizing of the patient for himself regardless of his behaviour.

. . . the therapist's response to the patient's thoughts or behaviours is a search for their meaning or value within the patient rather than disapproval or approval.'

This scale appears to refer to two rather different aspects: one is the counsellor's warmth; the other is the degree to which his expression of warmth is conditional. Despite the emphasis on the apparent unconditionality of the therapist's warmth, the studies by Truax (1966a, 1968) suggest that it may be most effective when applied in a manner which is in fact conditional upon the patient's showing 'good' therapy behaviour.

The counsellor's 'empathic understanding' is rated on a nine-point scale of 'accurate empathy'. This is defined by Truax and Carkhuff (1967) in the following terms:

'Accurate empathy involves more than just the ability of the therapist to sense the client or patient's "private world" as if it were his own. It also involves more than just his ability to know what the patient means. Accurate empathy involves both the therapist's *sensitivity to current feelings* and his *verbal facility to communicate this understanding* in a language attuned to the client's current feelings.

It is not necessary—indeed it would seem undesirable—for the therapist to *share* the client's feelings in any sense that would require him to feel the same emotions. It is instead an appreciation and a sensitive awareness of those feelings. At deeper levels of empathy, it also involves enough understanding of patterns of human feelings and experience to sense feelings that the client only partially reveals. With such experience and knowledge, the therapist can communicate what the client knows as well as meanings in the client's experience of which he is scarcely aware . . .'

As with the genuineness scale, there are logical difficulties in the way of a literal interpretation of this definition. The rater would have to be himself sufficiently empathic to understand the client's communications, including the 'meanings in the client's experience of which he is scarcely aware', and then evaluate the counsellor's utterances by a matching procedure. However, a study by Truax (1966b) in which the patient's statements were edited out of tape recordings, with no apparent effect on the ratings given, indicates that no such matching is in fact necessary. Rather, it would seem that voice quality, vocabulary, and other correlates of empathic responding, together with the continuity of the interaction, are the main cues used by raters.

Another conceptual problem revealed by the above definitions is that of overlap between the characteristics assessed on the different scales. For example, a counsellor showing a total lack of empathy could scarcely be rated as showing the 'search for the meaning or value (of the patient's thoughts or behaviours) within the patient' characteristic of high 'non-possessive warmth'.

RELIABILITY AND VALIDITY OF THE SCALES

Any rating scale must be examined for reliability (to determine whether it measures consistently) and validity (to determine whether it measures what it purports to measure). In different studies, inter-rater reliabilities have ranged from 0·43 to 0·95 for empathy, from 0·50 to 0·95 for warmth, and from 0·25 to 0·95 for genuineness. This last scale has rather lower reliability than the others in most studies. These data indicate that although reliability is usually adequate, it can descend to an unacceptably low level. This may reflect the reliance of raters on becoming attuned to non-verbal cues and other attributes not made fully explicit in the rating scale manuals. The danger therefore arises that reliability may depend upon the non-standardised rater training procedure.

The chief source of evidence for the validity of the scales derives, of course, from studies relating them to patient change. However, there are other sources of relevant evidence which will be considered first. Several studies have been concerned with the kinds of information which can be tapped by the rater. Reliable ratings can be made on the basis of visual cues (J. G. Shapiro. 1968) and, in the case of warmth and of empathy, the therapist's utterances alone

(Truax, 1966c) and the words of the interaction alone, as recorded in transcripts (Gurman, 1971; Shapiro, 1970, 1973). These findings imply that several different aspects of the therapist's behaviour co-vary in a 'redundant' manner. An alarming possibility is raised by the finding of Caracena and Vicory (1969) that empathy ratings are correlated with the number of words spoken by the therapist, and with the proportion of the dialogue spoken by him. Empathy should mean more than mere verbosity! However, raters may be forced to depend upon the superficial, objective behaviours more readily accessible to them than is information about the more abstract and complex variable of empathic understanding.

Chinsky and Rappaport (1970; Rappaport and Chinsky, 1972) have criticised the analysis of the ratings of many recordings of each of a relatively small number of therapists as independent scores. Their argument is based partly on the statistical problem of correlated errors, and partly on the design problem of raters recognising the voices of the therapists heard repeatedly. Beutler *et al.* (1973) did not find the 'shrinkage' in inter-rate reliability predicted by Chinsky and Rappaport (1970) when accurate empathy ratings were summed for all the segments including each therapist. The voice recognition problem is not overcome by this finding, however, since the ratings were of transcripts rather than tapes.

An important aspect of the scales' validity is whether or not they measure functionally independent dimensions of behaviour, as Truax claims. Although experimental studies, in which therapists deliberately vary their levels of functioning, have shown that it is possible to vary one's empathy and warmth independently of genuineness, the three scales are usually positively intercorrelated in ordinary therapeutic practice (Truax and Carkhuff, 1967; Muehlberg *et al.*, 1969). Despite evidence that the three concepts are not interchangeable (Shapiro, 1973), it remains to be shown that these three dimensions, derived from an intuitive, clinical theory developed by Rogers, provide the most appropriate framework for the description of therapists' behaviour.

Studies of interpersonal behaviour more generally (Brown, 1965; Carson, 1970; Mehrabian, 1971) show partial agreement with the Truax framework. Although the major dimensions found in such research include friendliness, solidarity or evaluation (corresponding to warmth), the dimension of dominance, status or potency finds no counterpart in Truax's scheme. (This might, however, reflect the repudiation of both dominant and submissive behaviour envisioned by Rogerian theory. An empathic, warm and genuine therapist would lie somewhere at the centre of this dimension, being neither dependent upon the client nor demanding his obedience.) A third dimension found in the literature, that of activity or responsiveness, might relate to empathy. Independently of these factorial studies, Jourard (1971) has shown that self-disclosure or 'transparency' (corresponding to 'genuineness') has predictable and powerful effects on social behaviour. Notably, self-disclosure by one participant stimulated reciprocal self-disclosure by the other. This implies that acknowledgment of feelings by the counsellor may promote similar expression by the client.

THE 'THERAPEUTIC CONDITIONS' AND CLIENT CHANGE

Studies of the effects of the 'therapeutic conditions' have generally used a variety of measures of client change. These include various psychological tests, ratings by hospital staff, and relevant 'objective' data such as length of time spent outside the hospital or other institution, or academic grades. These 'objective' data are the most trustworthy source of evidence. The usual practice has been to use a battery of measures of different types, on the principle that no one measure can be taken on trust, but that diverse indices all pointing in the same direction are more credible than any one alone. This principle is reasonable enough, although many of the studies conducted by Truax and his colleagues have unjustifiably reported several scores from the same data as if they were independent from one another, and then concluded that (say) 14 of the 19 measures showed changes in the predicted direction.

Another criticism is that this 'broad spectrum' approach to the assessment of outcomes is far too vague and global to indicate the nature of the changes associated with a particular approach to treatment. A better strategy would be to specify a relatively objective outcome criterion for the type of client involved in the study, and to combine evaluation according to this criterion with measures with some specific relevance to it—test anxiety and study habits, for example, in the case of student under-achievers, for whom the target criterion would be improved grades (Mitchell and Ng, 1972).

Two types of design have been used in studies of the effects of the therapeutic conditions. The first involves comparison of clients receiving counselling characterised by a fairly high level of the conditions with untreated controls. Four studies have followed this design. These provide some evidence that 'high-conditions' counselling can help delinquents remain outside an institution (Truax *et al.*, 1966), and improve the academic performance of under-achievers (Dickenson and Truax, 1966). Disappointing results were obtained with hospitalised schizophrenics by Rogers *et al.* (1967). A three-month difference in hospitalisation over the year was not statistically significant. Carkhuff and Truax (1965), with a rather more mixed mental hospital population, obtained some evidence of the efficacy of their group counsellıng by lay personnel specifically trained to offer high levels of the 'therapeutic conditions', although there was some evidence of deterioration in the treated group. Another problem is that the ward staff completing the ratings knew which patients were involved in the groups, and the authors' assertion that 'the admitted and outspoken bias of the ward personnel involved in the behavioural ratings was against rather than for' the treatment does not altogether eliminate this difficulty.

The second type of study follows a correlational design, associating the levels of each of the conditions rated in the recordings of a given client's sessions to outcome measures obtained for that client. The usual procedure is as follows. Each of a number of therapists treats a number of clients, who are then split into two groups, according to the mean levels of the three conditions rated in three-minute segments of recordings of their sessions. A typical design might involve two segments from each of three of the 24 sessions of counselling. Psychological test changes, and more objective outcome data, are then compared for the two retrospectively assembled groups of clients receiving 'high' and 'low' therapeutic conditions. The analysis is repeated for each of the three scales in turn, and in some studies, for summed scores on all three scales.

Shapiro (1976) has reviewed eight studies of this type. They are difficult to evaluate. Each includes some 20 measures of outcome, with the repeated analysis for each of the three scales adding to the possibility of spuriously significant results. Whilst the majority of measures show differences in the expected direction in most studies, there are exceptions, and the differences do not often reach an acceptable level of statistical significance. Institutionalisation rate, the percentage of time spent outside the hospital in a year following counselling, failed to show significant results in any of the three studies in which it was obtained. An attempt by Truax (1970) to show differences in hospitalisation rate for the Rogers *et al.* (1967) patients is based on a dubious interpretation of differences in trend over a nine-year period between groups receiving high and low conditions.

In all, these results do not justify the optimistic assertions of Truax and Carkhuff (1967) and Truax and Mitchell (1971). The studies comparing supposedly 'high conditions' counselling with no-treatment controls showed quite promising results in terms of relevant, objective criteria (release from institution, academic grades). However, the evidence from the studies comparing high- and low-conditions counselling is no more than suggestive of an association between the three therapeutic conditions and favourable outcome of counselling. The number of significant results is not strikingly above what one would expect from chance variations, given the large number of outcome measures, and the repeated analysis of each set of data for the three scales in turn. The most objective data (institutionalisation) have failed to yield significant results. There are even examples of negative association between genuineness and warmth and outcome. Further caution in interpreting these results is made necessary by the conspicuous absence of experimental comparison between clients receiving different levels of the conditions. A stringent test of the hypothesis that the therapeutic conditions, considered as attributes of the therapist, produce beneficial changes in the client, would require that clients be randomly assigned to two groups of therapists, whose levels of conditions had been shown to differ with previous clients. Until this is done, any association between therapeutic conditions and outcome remains attributable to differences in the clients, or to interaction effects between therapist and client. Perhaps the client who is improving, or the client who is well-suited to the interpersonal style of his therapist, is easier for the therapist to empathise with than the client who is neither of these things. Client and interaction effects have emerged from studies in which each of several therapists sees each of several clients (Moos and MacIntosh, 1970). Furthermore, the experimental comparison of high- and low-conditions counselling is necessary in order to evaluate the studies using no-treatment control groups. It is an unfortunate fact in research such as this that we can never really know that a treatment works until we have some idea of why it works. Attention (the 'placebo effect') might be sufficient explanation of the difference between treated and untreated groups. In other words, the quality of the counselling might be irrelevant, unless we can show experimentally that clients assigned to 'good' counsellors do better than clients assigned to 'bad' counsellors.

INTERPERSONAL INFLUENCE IN COUNSELLING

Several researchers have studied the interactive process of counselling, in an attempt to understand the nature of the influence processes at work. The usual approach is to attempt to measure attributes of counsellor and client behaviour which are believed to be relevant to the helping process, and then to use these measures to find out how changes in the behaviour of one participant affect the behaviour of the other. Truax and his associates have developed a scale to rate the client's 'depth of self-exploration' following the Rogerian principle that it is by facilitating this self-exploration by the client that the 'therapeutic conditions' of empathy, warmth and genuineness have their effect. This scale is concerned with the extent to which the client is 'exploring his feelings, his values, his perception of others, his relationships, his fears, his turmoil, and his life-choices' (Truax and Carkhuff, 1967, page 206).

Ratings take into account the spontaneity and feeling with which the client talks about 'personally relevant material'.

Experimental studies by Truax and Carkhuff (1965), Holder *et al.* (1967), Piaget *et al.* (1967), Carkhuff and Alexik (1967) and Cannon and Pierce (1968) explored the effect of experimental manipulation of client or therapist behaviour within single interviews. Only when both participants function at a high level on their respective scales can the client's level of self-exploration be maintained in the face of a period of reduced empathy and warmth. Similarly, a co-operative, skilful client, by deliberately lowering her level of self-exploration, reduced the level of therapeutic conditions offered by therapists whose initial level was relatively low. 'Good' counsellors, however, were unaffected by the manipulation. They presumably attempted to empathise even with the seemingly trivial material produced by the client when reducing her self-exploration.

Contrary to the theoretical notion of unconditionality on the part of the counsellor, Truax (1966a) showed that Rogers' expressions of empathy and warmth varied in frequency according to the nature of the client's utterances. Truax suggests that this implies a mechanism of selective reinforcement, whose effectiveness can be seen in the increase over the series of interviews in the frequency of the client behaviours correlated with Rogers' expressions of empathy and warmth. These categories of behaviour have much in common with those described at the higher levels of the 'self-exploration' scale, with an interesting exception, 'similarity of patient style of expression to that of the therapist'. Imitation or modelling may be an important means of changing the client's style of relating. Truax (1968) found an association between 'reinforcement' for self-exploration and both levels of self-exploration and client outcome in group counselling.

The 'reinforcement' interpretation of these findings cannot be accepted without reservations, however. Truax analysed ratings of short segments of recorded sessions, each consisting of a counsellor statement, the following client statement, and finally the next counsellor statement. 'Reinforcement' was assessed in terms of the degree of correlation between ratings of the two counsellor statements taken together and ratings of the client statement separating them. It is not immediately obvious who is 'reinforcing' whom in the event of such a correlation being significant. Murray (1956), however, obtained similar results, classifying the client's statements solely on the basis of the 'approval' or 'disapproval' expressed by Rogers in the following utterance. 'Approved' statements occurred increasingly frequently over the course of interviews, whilst 'disapproved' statements diminished in frequency.

The studies following upon the work of Murray

Table 20.1 'Approach' and 'avoidance' behaviour by the counsellor. (From Bandura *et al.*, 1960, by courtesy of *J. Consult. Psychol.*)

Approach reactions

Approval

Client: I don't know but I got so mad when he came home.

Counsellor: Under the circumstances, how could you have felt otherwise?

Exploration

Client: For some reason I had a bad day, just couldn't fall asleep, I just felt aggravated.

Counsellor: Aggravated? Can you tell me a little about that?

Instigation

Client: I was pretty fatigued when I got home. I went to bed right off the bat but I just tossed and turned. When I woke up in the morning I had this pain in the leg. I went to the doctor and he gave me a shot.

Counsellor: Yes. Let's get back again to that evening, that irritated feeling you had.

Reflection

Client: And when the kids don't listen to me it rubs me the wrong way, I lose my temper.

Counsellor: You get mad.

Labelling

Client: I've picked up the tabs on that girl all my life. Always paying, always costing money. I think I resented her a good deal.

Counsellor: Maybe some of your resentment for Joyce is partly displaced from your mother in that your mother shipped her to you to take care of. You were mad at your mother as well as Joyce.

Avoidance reactions

Disapproval

Client: So I blew my top and hit her.

Counsellor: Just for that you hit her?

Topical transition

Client: My mother annoys me.

Counsellor: How old is your mother?

Silence (4 secs or more)

Client: I just dislike it at home so much at times.

Counsellor: (silence)

Client: So I just don't know what to do.

Ignoring

Client: I lose my temper over his tardiness.

Counsellor: What are the results of his being tardy?

Mislabelling

Client: When are you going to give me the results of those tests? I think I'm entitled to know.

Counsellor: You seem to be almost afraid to find out.

(1956), reviewed by Murray and Jacobson (1971), have indicated how complex are the influence processes between client and counsellor.

Bandura *et al.* (1960) developed a scheme for coding therapist responses as approach (encouraging the client to continue his current topic) and avoidance (discouraging such continuance by the client). Table 20.1 shows examples of responses which would be scored as 'approach' or 'avoidance' of the client's hostility. The immediate effects of these two types of response upon clients' continued expression of hostility were as predicted. Clients were more likely to continue expressing hostility to the same object following approach than following avoidance responses by the therapist. Similar findings were obtained in relation to clients' expressions of dependency by Winder *et al.* (1962), Caracena (1965) and Schuldt (1966). However, attempts to show that the approach and avoidance responses of the counsellor succeed in 'shaping' client behaviour over the duration of counselling have produced equivocal results (Caracena, 1965; Varble, 1968), attributed by Bandura (1968) to the unknown contingencies of reinforcement being applied by the therapist to competing responses not analysed in the studies. Bandura also points to the fact that categories such as 'hostile' are too broad, in that therapists are likely to distinguish between 'appropriate' and 'inappropriate' hostility expressions, and respond accordingly.

Another problem is the tendency in these studies to ignore the effect of client behaviour on the counsellor. In addition to the Carkhuff and Alexik (1967) study discussed above, the importance of this is indicated by the results obtained by Heller *et al.* (1963) and Gamsky and Farwell (1966). It might be more appropriate to consider the development of a counselling relationship in mutual, dyadic interactive terms, in which it is recognised that the determinants of a given utterance extend further back into the history of the interaction than the immediately preceding utterance alone. Vitalo (1970) found that ratings of 'therapeutic conditions' predict the efficacy of experimenters in a 'verbal conditioning' experiment. There is more to interpersonal influence than can be described in terms of simple reinforcement.

BEYOND COUNSELLING

There have been several developments 'beyond' counselling, extending the 'personal growth' philosophy of counselling to situations outside the conventional office setting. Various types of group experience designed to enhance interpersonal sensitivity and awareness of 'normal' people have sprung up, called 'T-groups' (Campbell and Dunette, 1968) or 'encounter groups' (Schutz, 1967; Rogers, 1970). Quite a number of research studies have been made of these groups (Cooper and Mangham, 1971), although methodological inadequacies and equivocal results leave us little the wiser as to their effects. Limitations of space prevent any further discussion of these techniques here. Another development has been into the 'social action' field, training unemployed, indigenous personnel to function in jobs such as 'casework aides' in welfare agencies (Carkhuff, 1971). The training of these personnel is based on an extension of the 'therapeutic conditions' methodology of Truax and Carkhuff (1967). Unfortunately, these fascinating developments into community action have been associated with an erosion of methodological standards, making it impossible to evaluate or understand the effects which are claimed.

TOWARDS SPECIFICITY IN COUNSELLING RESEARCH

Many of the difficulties encountered in the work reviewed so far are attributable to insufficient concern for the problem of specifying what types of counselling intervention produce what kinds of change in what types of client. Recently, several workers have responded to this need for greater specificity in counselling research. The first step in this is to specify a goal which is reliably measurable and clearly relevant to the type of client involved. From this, there usually follow some fairly clear implications for the technique or approach to be employed in counselling.

One example of this is in the field of delinquency, where the ability to keep out of further trouble is an appropriate goal. Persons (1966) conducted group therapy aimed at providing a sequence of:

  (i) establishment of supportive relationship,
 (ii) interpretation and differential reinforcement, including role-playing,
(iii) induction of stress concerning antisocial behaviour,
(iv) discussion of difficulties in returning to the community.

This sequence would seem to involve establishing a relationship in which the therapist acquires influence over the clients, and then systematically exercises this influence via modelling, shaping, persuasion and information, to direct the clients away from antisocial behaviour and toward acceptable behaviour. Disciplinary records during the period of institutionalisation favoured the treated group as compared with an untreated control group. The treated clients also had a lower recidivism rate over a one-year follow-up period. Massimo and Shore (1963) and Shore and Massimo (1966) report a vocationally-oriented programme, with involvement by the counsellor in all aspects of the adolescent delinquent clients' life. The principle here was of job-oriented, independence-fostering, broad involvement in the client's problems, focussing on practical and psychological assistance with problems which could prevent the establishment of a rewarding yet law-abiding life-style. Unfortunately, the numbers of clients involved were too small for proper statistical analysis. However, the information presented on the number and severity of offences committed over a two-year period indicated fewer and less serious misdemeanours by the treated than the control youths. Reading, vocabulary and arithmetic were better in the counselled group than the controls, this being attributed to the fact that more of them were successfully returned to school. A replication of this study with larger numbers would be of great interest. Finally, the Truax *et al.* (1966) study is relevant here. Group counselling by therapists offering high levels of empathy and warmth was associated with lower institutionalisation rates than those of untreated controls. Client-centred theory attributes delinquency to a felt insufficiency of 'good' relationships with authority figures.

Another example is in the facilitation of discharge from mental hospitals. Dreiblatt and Weatherley (1965) demonstrated the value to patients recently admitted to an organically-oriented psychiatric unit of brief contacts with counsellors. In particular, the second of their two studies compared different types of brief contact (all limited to twelve contacts of up to 10 minutes). They found that contacts not involving discussion of the patient's symptoms led to speedier discharge than control conditions of no contact and attention control (guessing task). The authors speculate that the contacts enhanced the patients' self-esteem, citing self-ideal correlations from *Q*-sorts in support of this. Whatever the precise mechanisms, it seems that brief contacts supplied something missing from the normal ward routine. This result stands in marked contrast to the failure of the Wisconsin Schizophrenia Project (Rogers *et al.*, 1967), suggesting that the more modest intervention by Dreiblatt and Weatherley (1965) was more appropriate to their patient population than the attempt to establish intensive counselling relationships with schizophrenic patients. This is not to say, however, that no counselling techniques are suitable for such patients. Mainord *et al.* (1965) found that 'confrontations' in group counselling increased the number of behavioural 'positive incidents' recorded by ward staff. A simplified, directive technique may be more appropriate to this group of patients.

A third example, which has been widely studied, is the counselling of under-achieving students. A review by Bednar and Weinberg (1970) suggests that about half (13 out of 23) of a series of studies yielded significant grade point average superiority in counselled as compared with non-counselled students. Furthermore, Bednar and Weinberg indicate that certain features of the counselling procedures of the various studies are associated with effectiveness in terms of this relatively objective criterion. These include:

(i) length of counselling (over 10 hours),
(ii) structuredness (i.e. directive, authoritarian, academic and prescriptive, rather than non-directive, client-centred, non-prescriptive or affectively oriented),
(iii) group procedures (rather than individual).

These findings are at variance with the traditional Rogerian theory of counselling. However, academic studies programmes alone tend to be ineffective, although effective in combination with counselling. Mitchell and Ng (1972) extend this principle to include behaviour therapy in conjunction with counselling, thus combining didactic and experiential approaches. They studied students who were highly anxious about examinations, and lacked study skills. Their experimental conditions included 'single-model' (such as desensitisation, or counselling) and 'multi-model' conditions in which elements of both types of procedure were combined. Desensitisation alone successfully reduced the test-anxiety towards which it was directed. However, only the 'multimodel' conditions brought about improvements in relation to both test-anxiety and study skills. Consequent changes in academic performance were consistent with this. Only the 'multimodel' groups showed improvement. The evidence on the duration of the effect of counselling on academic grades is discouraging. However, it seems to favour programmes combining directive, academic remedial help and counselling aimed at the social, motivational and emotional 'dynamics' of under-achievement (Bednar and Weinberg, 1970). The evidence on student counselling thus suggests that the relatively well-defined criterion of academic performance can be improved at an overall level better than chance. Although there is always the possibility of a bias towards the publication of positive as opposed to negative findings, the tentative identification of factors associated with success provides some basis for predicting successful outcomes of programmes combining the 'didactic' with the 'dynamic'.

The next step in the development of more adequate specificity in counselling research is to challenge the assumption that methods of counselling are universally applicable to all types of client. Two studies by Gilbreath (1967, 1968) have shown that 'structured' group counselling is effective in raising the grade point average of students showing evidence of high dependency needs, whereas 'unstructured' counselling is effective with students with low dependency needs. Given counselling 'inappropriate' to their personality, students do no better than untreated controls. These findings imply that the majority of students counselled in the studies reviewed by Bednar and Weinberg (1970) were relatively high in dependency, and thus were more likely to be helped by structured counselling. A similarly designed study by

Brown (1969) indicated that students admitting to high anxiety on a manifest anxiety scale were helped by unstructured counselling, as indicated by anxiety scale changes as well as grade point average, whereas those low in manifest anxiety scores were helped by structured counselling. Students who express anxiety in a self-report measure may be more inclined to express it verbally in the unstructured group situation than those who deny anxiety in the test. Students placed in groups inappropriate to their anxiety level showed increased anxiety over treatment, while those in appropriate groups showed a decrease. A fourth study comparing different approaches with students differing in personality was conducted by Di Loreto (1971). His subjects were students admitting to, and responding to an offer of treatment for, interpersonal anxiety. Di Loreto found that counselling based on rational–emotive theory (Ellis, 1962) was effective with introverts, client-centred counselling was effective with extroverts, and systematic desensitisation with both groups. His measures include self-reports, behaviour ratings and therapist ratings. With their respective 'appropriate' groups, the two counselling procedures were as effective as the behavioural method; with their 'inappropriate' groups, they were no more effective than a placebo control condition.

Interaction between client characteristics and the effectiveness of a treatment mode is not confined to personality variables. Love *et al.* (1972), investigating three types of clinical intervention with children referred for emotional and behaviour problems, found that socio-economic status moderated the effects of 'information feedback' to the family using videotapes and other informational aids as compared with more orthodox parental counselling. Information feedback resulted in improved school grades for children in upper socio-economic levels, whereas parent counselling led to improved grades for those from lower levels. There was some implication of fathers in this interaction, since there were more fatherless families in the low socio-economic group, and there was an association between success of the information feedback procedure and the presence of the father during the session. Perhaps the more concrete, 'factual' approach is more appropriate to men than to women.

CONCLUSIONS AND IMPLICATIONS

No attempt has been made in this chapter to be exhaustive in covering the very extensive literature on counselling. Rather, the emphasis has been on fairly detailed discussion of selected areas of research considered central to the problem of developing counselling techniques of proven efficacy. Unfortunately, the main conclusion must be that this has not yet been achieved. It is not possible to make firm recommendations for the practice of counselling on the basis of present knowledge. The 'central assumption' of counselling, with which we began, remains an assumption.

Indeed, the research literature undermines cherished beliefs in several areas. Unconditional acceptance of the client does not seem to occur, and the conditionality of the counsellor's responses may well be an important ingredient of his efficacy. We do not have to reduce the counsellor's behaviour to that of a reinforcement machine to appreciate that the implicit messages conveyed by the 'approach' and 'avoidance' responses of Table 20.1 are received and acted upon by the client. Counsellors and psychiatric interviewers alike should be aware of their subtle influence upon the responses of their clients or patients. Similarly, they should heed the evidence showing that their own behaviour is affected in turn by the client's demeanour.

The global nature of the 'central assumption' is also challenged by the research evidence. More didactic or structured approaches may be helpful for dependent, anxiety-denying, or introverted clients, whilst unstructured counselling following the Rogerian model may be helpful for independent, anxiety-admitting, or extroverted clients. The unstructured approach and the attempt to form an intensive counselling relationship with severely disturbed clients, such as schizophrenics, would appear to be inappropriate. Again, more directive techniques may be more useful.

The evidence in general favours relatively specific, modest goals, rather than the more ambitious attempts at far-reaching personality change. It may be more useful to establish brief contact counselling with each of a large number of psychiatric in-patients than to attempt the more intensive counselling or psychotherapy of a smaller number of clients which the practitioners so often prefer. There is greater assurance to be gained from the research literature to justify attempts to improve the academic performance of under-achievers than to resolve more general personality problems. It is desirable to tailor the technique of counselling to suit available knowledge of the client's personality, and presenting problems, together with such other factors (e.g. sex or social class) as may yet be shown relevant to counselling outcome.

This chapter may appear to be overloaded with methodological criticisms of research studies, and disappointingly lacking in constructive conclusions. This reflects the great difficulties inherent in studying the subject of counselling. It may also reflect an excessive reliance of researchers on clinically-derived theories. Rather than start with a conception of the 'good' counsellor as Rogers and Truax have done, it might be better to start by finding out how effective counsellors differ in their behaviour from ineffective counsellors. However, counselling research has now reached the point where we can expect increasingly precise answers to questions concerning the effects of specific types of counselling on specific types of client with specific problems.

References

Bandura, A., Lipsher, D. H. and Miller, P., E. (1960). Psychotherapists' approach–avoidance reactions to patients' expressions of hostility. *J. Consult. Psychol.*, 24, 1–8

Bandura, A. (1968). On empirical disconfirmations of equivocal deductions with insufficient data. *J. Consult. Clin. Psychol.*, 32, 247–249

Bednar, R. L. and Weinberg, S. L. (1970). Ingredients of successful treatment programs for underachievers. *J. Counsel. Psychol.*, 17, 1–7

Beutler, L. E., Johnson, D. T., Neville, C. W. and Workman, S. N. (1973). Some sources of variance in 'accurate empathy' ratings. *J. Consult. Clin. Psychol.*, 40, 167–169

Brown, R. (1965). *Social Psychology* (New York: Free Press)

Brown, R. D. (1969). Effects of structured and unstructured group counselling with high- and low-anxious college underachievers. *J. Counsel. Psychol.*, 16, 209–214

Campbell, J. P. and Dunnette, M. D. (1968) Effectiveness of T-group experiences in managerial training and development. *Psychol. Bull.*, 70, 73–104

Cannon, J. R. and Pierce, R. M. (1968). Order effects in the experimental manipulation of therapeutic conditions. *J. Clin. Psychol.*, 24, 242–244

Caracena, P. F. (1965). Elicitation of dependency expressions in the initial stage of psychotherapy. *J. Counsel. Psychol.*, 12, 268–274

Caracena, P. F. and Vicory, J. R. (1969). Correlates of phenomenological and judged empathy. *J. Counsel. Psychol.*, 16, 510–515

Carkhuff, R. R. and Truax, C. B. (1965). Lay mental health counselling: the effects of lay group counselling. *J. Consult. Psychol.*, 29, 426–431

Carkhuff, R. R. and Alexik, M. (1967). Effect of client depth of self-exploration upon high and low-functioning counsellors. *J. Counsel. Psychol.*, 14, 350–355

Carkhuff, R. R. (1971). Principles of social action in training for new careers in human services. *J. Counsel. Psychol.*, 18, 147–151

Carson, R. C. (1969). *Interaction Concepts of Personality* (London: George Allen and Unwin)

Chinsky, J. M. and Rappaport, J. (1970). Brief critique of the meaning and reliability of 'Accurate Empathy' ratings. *Psychol. Bull.*, 73, 379–380

Cooper, C. L. and Mangham, I. L. (editors) (1971). *T-Groups: A Survey of Research* (London: Wiley-Interscience)

Dickenson, W. A. and Truax, C. B. (1966). Group counselling with college underachievers: comparisons with a control group and relationship to empathy, warmth and genuineness. *Personnel Guid. J.*, 243–247

Di Loreto, A. O. (1971). *Comparative Psychotherapy: An Experimental Analysis* (Chicago: Aldine Atherton)

Dreiblatt, I. S. and Weatherley, D. (1965). An evaluation of the efficacy of brief-contact therapy with hospitalized psychiatric patients. *J. Consult. Psychol.*, 29, 513–519

Ellis, A. (1962). *Reason and Emotion in Psychotherapy* (New York: Lyle Stuart)

Gamsky, N. R. and Farwell, G. F. (1966). Counsellor verbal behaviour as a function of client hostility. *J. Counsel. Psychol.*, 13, 184–190

Gilbreath, S. H. (1967). Group counselling, dependence and college male under-achievement. *J. Counsel. Psychol.*, 14, 449–453

Gilbreath, S. H. (1968). Appropriate and inappropriate group counselling with academic underachievers. *J. Counsel. Psychol.*, 15, 506–511

Gurman, A. S. (1971). Rating of therapeutic warmth and genuineness by untrained judges. *Psychol. Rep.*, 28, 711–714

Heller, K., Myers, R. A. and Kline, L. V. (1963). Interviewer behavior as a function of standardized client roles. *J. Counsel. Psychol.*, 27, 117–122

Holder, T., Carkhuff, R. R. and Berenson, B. G. (1967). Differential effects of the manipulation of therapeutic conditions upon high- and low-functioning clients. *J. Counsel. Psychol.*, 14, 63–66

Jourard, S. M. (1971). *Self-Disclosure: an Experimental Analysis of the Transparent Self* (London and New York: Wiley-Interscience)

Love, L. R., Kaswan, J. and Bugental, D. E. (1972). Differential effectiveness of three clinical interventions for different socioeconomic groupings. *J. Consult. Clin. Psychol.*, 39, 347–360

Mainord, W. A., Burk, H. W. and Collins, L. G. (1965). Confrontation *v.* diversion in group therapy with chronic schizophrenics as measured by a 'positive incident' criterion. *J. Clin. Psychol.*, 21, 222–225

Massimo, J. L. and Shore, M. F. (1963). The effectiveness of a comprehensive, vocationally oriented psychotherapeutic program for adolescent delinquent boys. *Amer. J. Orthopsychiatry*, 33, 634–642

Mehrabian, A. (1971). Non-verbal communication. In: *Nebraska Symposium on Motivation* (J. K. Cole, editor) (Lincoln: University of Nebraska Press)

Mitchell, K. R. and Ng, K. T. (1972). Effects of group counselling and behaviour therapy on the academic achievement of test-anxious students. *J. Counsel. Psychol.*, 19, 491–497

Moos, R. H. and MacIntosh, S. (1970). Multivariate study of the patient–therapist system: a replication and extension. *J. Consult. Clin. Psychol.*, 35, 298–307

Muehlberg, N., Pierce, R. and Drasgow, J. (1969). A factor analysis of therapeutically facilitative conditions. *J. Clin. Psychol.*, 25, 93–95

Murray, E. J. (1956). A content-analysis method for studying psychotherapy. *Psychol. Mon.*, 70, (13, Whole No. 420)

Murray, E. J. and Jacobson, L. I. (1971). The nature of learning in traditional and behavioral psychotherapy. In: *Handbook of Psychotherapy and Behavior Change* (A. E. Bergin and S. L. Garfield, editors) (New York: Wiley)

Persons, R. W. (1966). Psychological and behavioral change in delinquents following psychotherapy. *J. Clin. Psychol.*, 22, 337–340

Piaget, G. W., Berenson, B. G. and Carkhuff, R. R. (1967). Differential effects of the manipulation of therapeutic conditions by high- and moderate-functioning therapists upon high- and low-functioning clients. *J. Consult. Psychol.*, 31, 481–486

Rappaport J. and Chinsky, J. M. (1972). Accurate empathy: confusion of a construct. *Psychol. Bull.*, 77, 400–404

Rogers, C. R. (1957). The necessary and sufficient conditions of therapeutic personality change. *J. Consult. Psychol.*, 21, 95–103

Rogers, C. R., Gendlin, G. T., Kiesler, D. V. and Truax, C. B. (1967). *The Therapeutic Relationship and its Impact: A Study of Psychotherapy with Schizophrenics* (Madison: University of Wisconsin Press)

Rogers, C. R. (1970). *Encounter Groups* (Harmondsworth: Allen Lane, The Penguin Press)

Schuldt, W. J. (1966). Psychotherapists' approach/avoidance responses and clients' expressions of dependency. *J. Counsel. Psychol.*, 13, 178–183

Schutz, W. C. (1967). *Joy: Expanding Human Awareness* (New York: Grove Press)

Shapiro, J. G. (1968). Relationships between visual and auditory cues of therapeutic effectiveness. *J. Clin. Psychol.*, 24, 236–239

Shapiro, D. A. (1970). The rating of psychotherapeutic empathy: a preliminary study. *Brit. J. Soc. Clin. Psychol.*, 9, 148–151

Shapiro, D. A. (1973). Naive British judgements of therapeutic conditions. *Brit. J. Soc. Clin. Psychol.*, 12, 289–294

Shapiro, D. A.' (1976). The effects of therapeutic conditions: positive results revisited. *Br. J. Med. Psychol.* In press

Shore, M. F. and Massimo, J. L. (1966). Comprehensive vocationally oriented psychotherapy for adolescent delinquent boys: a follow-up study. *Amer. J. Orthopsychiatry*, 36, 609–615

Stefflre, B. (1965). Function and present status of counselling theory. In: *Theories of Counseling* (B. Stefflre, editor) (New York: McGraw Hill)

Truax, C. B. and Carkhuff, R. R. (1965). The experimental manipulation of therapeutic conditions. *J. Consult. Psychol.*, 29, 119–124

Truax, C. B. (1966a). Reinforcement and non-reinforcement in Rogerian psychotherapy. *J. Abn. Soc. Psychol.*, 71, 1–9

Truax, C. B. (1966b). Influence of patient statements on judgments of therapist statements during psychotherapy. *J. Clin. Psychol.*, 22, 335–337

Truax, C. B. (1966c). Therapist empathy, warmth and genuineness and patient personality change in group psychotherapy: a comparison between interaction unit measures, time sample measures, patient perception measures. *J. Clin. Psychol.*, 22, 225–229

Truax, C. B., Wargo, D. G. and Silber, L. D. (1966). Effects of high accurate empathy and non-possessive warmth during group psychotherapy upon female institutionalized delinquents. *J. Abn. Psychol.*, 71, 267–274

Truax, C. B. and Carkhuff, R. R. (1967). *Toward Effective Counselling and Psychotherapy* (Chicago: Aldine)

Truax, C. B. (1968). Therapist interpersonal reinforcement of client self-exploration and therapeutic outcome in group psychotherapy. *J. Counsel. Psychol.*, 15, 225–231

Truax, C. B. (1970). Effects of client-centred psychotherapy with schizophrenic patients: nine years pre-therapy and nine years post-therapy hospitalization. *J. Consult. Clin. Psychol.*, 35, 417–422

Truax, C. B. and Mitchell, K. M. (1971). Research on certain therapist interpersonal skills in relation to process and outcome. In: *Handbook of Psychotherapy and Behavior Change* (A. E. Bergin and S. L. Garfield, editors) (New York: Wiley)

Varble, D. L. (1968). Relationship between the therapist's approach/avoidance reactions to hostility and client behavior in therapy. *J. Consult. Clin. Psychol.*, 32, 237–242

Vitalo, R. L. (1970). Effects of facilitative interpersonal functioning in a conditioning paradigm. *J. Counsel. Psychol.*, 17, 141–144

Winder, C. L., Ahmad, F. A., Bandura, A. and Rau, L. C. (1962). Dependence of patients, psychotherapists' responses, and aspects of psychotherapy. *J. Consult. Psychol.*, 26, 129–134

Chapter 21

SOCIAL TREATMENTS

F. N. Watts

It is a fundamental assumption of human psychology that people's behaviour is influenced by their social environment. This chapter will describe some practical applications of that principle in the field of abnormal behaviour. It would be misleading, however, to pretend that the methods of social treatment to be discussed here arose from a deliberate application of social psychology. They were developed in response to the realisation that institutions like mental hospitals seemed to be serving a custodial function and not a remedial one. Rather than improving their clients' social adaptation, they were adding 'institutionalisation' to their other handicaps (Wing and Brown, 1970).

The hope was that things could be organised differently, that a social environment could be created which would provide clients with an opportunity for improving their social adjustment. There were two basic assumptions underlying this. One was that unplanned round-the-clock social interaction exerts an influence on people's behaviour that is probably greater than that of official treatment sessions. The other was that where this influence is right, people's natural capacity for social learning will enable them to make a more normal adjustment.

One example of an attempt to create a 'normalising' social environment within a mental hospital has been the rehabilitation workshop (Black, 1970). Some of these have tried to replicate normal working conditions quite closely in terms of style of supervision, level and hours of work etc. Another example has been the 'therapeutic community' (Rapoport, 1960) in which patients have been given responsibility for the democratic running of their ward and for working towards the solution of each other's problems.

At first these methods were introduced without much interest either in evaluating their effectiveness or in understanding the processes at work in them. In 1955, Sir Aubrey Lewis commented that:

'. . . a great deal of rehabilitation is built up on faith, hope, and rule of thumb. We could do better than that. We could plan our programs so that they may disclose principles governing successful rehabilitation and the factors that restrict it. If one hitches one's wagon to a star, there can be a waste of energy that no community can really afford. Hence the need to define our aims in each patient, and judge the success of our method by whether we obtain that goal . . .'

In the years since those remarks were made there has been a considerable increase in scientific understanding of social treatment.

It has also emerged as a potentially important area of social psychology. Its interest lies in the fact that it is not open to the charge of triviality that has been levelled at much social psychological research. Too often social psychologists have confined themselves to studying brief interactions between anonymous strangers in which the participants are free to behave in quite artificial ways. At worst they have failed to study social behaviour at all and have tried, for example, to study interpersonal attraction by examining subjects' reactions to silhouette photographs. It is doubtful whether an exclusive reliance on such methods can lead to an adequate social psychology. The field of social treatment provides one opportunity of studying social behaviour in a less artificial way.

INDIRECT TREATMENT AIMS

The objectives of social treatment are complex and ambitious. The immediate aim is usually to achieve a higher level of social performance in some area or other. But there are often very important secondary aims such as the subject's psychological health, increasing his ability to maintain open employment and discharge his domestic obligations, and making him less likely to need hospital or other services in the future. One of the basic assumptions of the social treatment approach has thus been that a programme, designed to improve the social functioning of the client, can indirectly alleviate other problems.

There is some justification for this in the rather general inverse relationship that seems to exist between social adjustment and 'problem behaviour'. For example a relationship between premorbid social adjustment and recidivism has often been demonstrated for psychiatric patients. This relationship even holds where patients with good and poor premorbid adjustment do not differ in severity of illness (Phillips, 1968). A similar relationship between premorbid social adjustment and recidivism of criminals has been demonstrated (Blacker, 1968).

There are also some quite convincing examples of social treatments having more general effects. One is reported by Hunt and Azrin (1973) working with a group of alcoholics. Of a group of 16 patients admitted to hospital for alcoholism, half received only the standard programme of counselling and instruction on

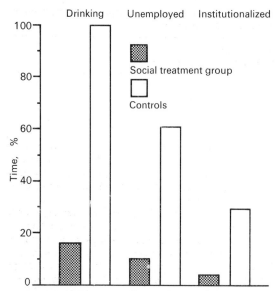

Figure 21.1 Comparison of social treatment and control groups: mean percentages of time spent drinking, unemployed, and institutionalised. (Adapted from Hunt and Azrin, 1973, by courtesy of *Behav. Res. Ther.*)

alcoholism. The other half also received a counselling programme for vocational, family and social problems. This latter group not only made a better social adjustment on discharge, as measured for example by the percentage of days in employment, they also spent fewer days drinking and in institutional care (Figure 21.1).

How is it that improved social adjustment had these more general results? The explanation suggested by Hunt and Azrin is that the alcoholics who had the social treatment programme led more satisfying lives on discharge (i.e. experienced greater reinforcement) and therefore had more to lose (as 'time out' from reinforcement) by drinking again. Though this explanation is quite plausible, others are possible. Perhaps better social adjustment exposed them to the influence of more people with non-alcoholic attitudes, or perhaps it enabled them to cope better with the stresses of life and thus removed the trigger for drinking. Unfortunately we have far too little evidence to assess the relative validity of these explanations.

Another example of social adjustment affecting abnormal behaviour comes from a study of schizophrenic patients in a mental hospital (Wing and Brown, 1970). In an initial survey of three mental hospitals it was found that the patients at the hospital where the most time was spent doing nothing were in the poorest clinical condition. Subsequent improvement in these patients was more closely related to a reduction in time spent doing nothing than to anything else. It thus seems likely that an active social

environment can minimise the severity of schizophrenic symptoms. However, it is again uncertain how this effect operates. It is doubtful whether it is possible to provide any single theory of the indirect effects of social treatments on problem behaviour. Though such effects seem to be very general, the exact mechanisms probably vary.

DIRECT TREATMENT AIMS
It is to cases in which social methods have been used to modify 'problem' behaviour that the term social treatment can be most strictly applied. However, in this chapter it is also being used in a more general way to refer to social measures that are aimed at improving social adjustment. It is admittedly unconventional to regard poor social adjustment as a category of abnormal behaviour requiring modification. But it is arguable that many clients of social treatment are handicapped more by this than by any other problem. It is therefore justifiable to regard the improvement of social adjustment as a treatment objective.

Unfortunately it has not been easy to develop a generally acceptable measure of social adjustment. Many workers seem to have made unjustified assumptions in doing so. For example it has sometimes been assumed that the number of social activities a person engages in is a reflection of his social adjustment. It is necessary to recognise that a good adjustment can be made in a great variety of equally satisfactory ways.

A commonly used outcome criterion of social treatment has been re-employment. This is at least objective and easily assessed, but it can be argued that it indicates the position subjects hold rather than their level of competence or adaptation. If the employer is tolerant, it can conceal a very low level of competence. On the other hand it is possible for subjects to improve their vocational competence without being able to get a job, especially if the general level of unemployment is high. There is also the problem that though re-employment is a widely shared aim, it is not held by everyone.

However the criterion of re-employment has been a very useful one in research, and makes vocational rehabilitation a good example of social treatment to consider in detail. It will serve to illustrate one of the emerging trends of social treatment research, that social adjustment is less affected by hospital-based training programmes than by the current social influences on the patient. Social treatment has therefore been moving from its initial institution-based phase to a new community-based phase in which family treatment is playing an important part.

A rather dramatic illustration of how little connection there can be between patients' adjustment in hospital and after discharge has been provided by Walker and McCourt (1965) (Table 21.1). They examined the association between patients who had

Table 21.1   **Relationship between numbers of patients with activity programmes in hospital and employment after discharge.** (From Walker and McCourt, 1965, by courtesy of *Amer. J. Psychiatry*)

		Some community employment	No employment
In-hospital	Active	57	55
	Inactive	42	57

activity programmes in hospital and those who were employed after discharge and found it to be negligible. It has indeed been suggested that there is a negative correlation between behaviour in hospital and after discharge. For example Ellsworth *et al.* (1968) have reported that the patients who were rated as most unpleasant and hostile in hospital were thought to have the best friendship skills after discharge.

REHABILITATION WORKSHOPS

A commonly used method for increasing patients' ability to return to employment is the rehabilitation workshop. These have varied widely in their principles of operation from those providing opportunities for low level work in somewhat casual conditions to those attempting to simulate a normal industrial environment. One relatively satisfactory evaluation of their effects is reported by Wing (1960). In this case the rehabilitation unit was one of the Industrial Rehabilitation Units operated by the Department of Employment. It was situated outside the hospital, and the patients travelled there each day for an eight-week rehabilitation programme. Psychiatric patients formed only a small proportion of the workshop population.

Thirty male schizophrenic patients were selected as being suitable for the study, of whom two-thirds were sent to the Unit, while a third were kept as controls. In each group half were rated as severely ill and half moderately ill. The results are shown in Table 21.2 below.

The Rehabilitation Unit made little impact on the severely ill group. However, among the moderately ill patients, those who were sent to the Rehabilitation Unit were more likely to be discharged and self-sup-

porting a year later. Equally encouraging results were obtained when a further series of 45 patients were sent to the Rehabilitation Unit, though on that occasion none of the subjects remained in hospital as controls (Wing *et al.*, 1964).

However, as often happens there remains some doubt as to exactly what it was about sending the patients to the Rehabilitation Unit that was responsible for their better outcome. There are at least two quite different interpretations of the results. Perhaps the most likely interpretation is that the occupational programme at the unit increased the patients' ability to work. Alternatively, going to the Rehabilitation Unit each day and mixing with the many non-psychiatric patients there might have increased the patients' interest in returning to the community and getting a job. Certainly attitudes to discharge improved during attendance at the unit and these changes were related to patients' follow-up status. Once the patients had returned to the community they might have sought employment because of financial and family pressures to do so. Discharge from hospital results in a fairly predictable proportion of patients becoming employed (Anthony *et al.*, 1972) and such pressures probably play an important part in this. It is thus uncertain how far the effects of the I.R.U. were due to its training function and how much due to its social influence function. (This distinction is similar to the classical one between learning and motivation in experimental psychology).

EMPLOYABILITY

Though rehabilitation workshops can play some part in facilitating patients' return to work, it has recently

Table 21.2   **Status of patients at one-year follow-up.** (From Wing, 1960, by courtesy of *Brit. J. Prev. Soc. Med.*)

	Discharged from hospital		Still resident in hospital	
	Self-supporting	Not employed	Self-supporting	Not employed
Moderately-ill patients				
Rehabilitation patients	6	1	1	2
Controls	—	1	—	4
Severely-ill patients				
Rehabilitation patients	—	1	—	9
Controls	—	—	—	5

emerged that the changes they produce are not in the most critical areas. The areas of functioning that best predict which patients will return to work seem not to be those that a rehabilitation course usually modifies.

The point is illustrated in a well-executed investigation reported by Hartmann (1972). From preliminary work on the structure of rehabilitation attitudes he was able to distinguish two separate attitudinal dimensions: insecurity and keenness to work. He then found that a course at a Rehabilitation Unit modified the clients' insecurity but not their keenness to work. On the other hand, while the subjects' keenness to work was related to their likelihood of obtaining employment, their insecurity was not. It thus seems that the effect of the rehabilitation unit, though perhaps valuable in other ways, did not increase their subjects' employability.

A similar conclusion about the importance of keenness arises from a study in which various aspects of patients' workshop behaviour were rated by supervisors (Cheadle and Morgan, 1972). They differed considerably in how well they predicted subsequent re-employment. The items have been shown to fall into four main groups (Griffiths, 1973). Most of the keenness items (e.g. works continuously, eager to work, looks for more work), the social items (e.g. gets on well with other people) and the response to supervision items (e.g. welcomes supervision) were significantly associated with employability. But none of the items assessing competence significantly differentiated the employable from the unemployable. Unfortunately Cheadle and Morgan did not report which aspects of workshop behaviour changed most during the period of rehabilitation, but the greatest gain seems more likely to have been in task performance (which probably improved with practice) than in keenness etc. So it seems that the areas most directly affected by rehabilitation programmes may be relatively unimportant in employability.

TREATMENT IN COMMUNITIES

This raises the interesting possibility of increasing employability by apparently more indirect social treatment procedures. Keenness, which seems to be of crucial importance, can perhaps be influenced as much by participation in a social group which places high value on work, as by a workshop training programme. There is some evidence that therapeutic communities can increase the number of patients who return to work.

Fairweather (1964) describes a programme in which patients met together each day in small 'task-groups' usually without any staff members present. A second group of patients had a treatment programme that was identical in other respects. The task groups had responsibility for dealing with problems relating to group members and for making recommendations about their progress through the programme. In addition the patients themselves formed a special 'employment committee' to facilitate resettlement in work. The task group patients showed a number of significant differences from the control group. They were more active in recreation time, more constructive in general ward meetings etc. But the crucial test of this kind of programme lies in its effect on patients after discharge. Here the results were less encouraging. On most of the follow-up variables examined, the two groups of patients did not differ. Another well-controlled evaluation of social treatment (Sanders *et al.*, 1962) also found that group therapy and patient government increased the number of patients returning to work.

But it is doubtful how long these effects lasted for. Fairweather followed-up his patients for only six months after discharge. Previous work (Fairweather and Simon, 1963) had shown that treatment in hospital affected employment six but not 18 months later. How long one would expect the results to last obviously depends on what model of the treatment process is adopted. As in rehabilitation it can be formulated either in terms of training or social influence. If a therapeutic community provides a training in personal relationships and responsibility, a permanent effect can be hoped for. If it influences patients' behaviour and values by group pressure, only a temporary effect can be expected.

The treatment processes of such therapeutic communities are not at all well-understood. The treatment rationale normally emphasises such elements as the democratic running of the unit, close cohesiveness of the whole community, and a combination of permissiveness of deviant behaviour with a high level of verbal confrontation. But it is an empirical question whether these elements are responsible for treatment results. For example Rapoport (1960) found that the patients who showed most improvement chose as their most admired person one of the core members of the staff (rather than one of the patients or junior staff). The senior staff may thus have played a more important role as models than the democratic philosophy of the unit would allow. Even more interestingly a number of variables which correlated with improvement in the unit, such as length of stay and adoption of the unit's values failed to correlate with long-term outcome. This suggests that the requirements for a satisfactory adjustment in the unit were rather different from those for adjustment to the outside world.

Both therapeutic communities and rehabilitation programmes constitute rather gross independent variables. Even where it is shown that they achieve better results than a conventional hospital regime, it is not clear exactly which aspects of the situation are responsible. It may well be that equivalent results could be obtained by less elaborate means. Some evidence suggesting this comes from a controlled evaluation of a social treatment programme reported by Ellsworth (1968). The social treatment regime was an unusually simple one and consisted of encouraging the non-professional aides employed by the hospital to have more contact with the patients, to treat them in a more normal and genuine way, and to take an interest in their progress. This not only improved the patients' behaviour in hospital, but also increased their chances of being discharged to the community for a year or more, and of making a better work and social adjustment there. The effects were especially impressive for the most chronic group of patients.

LONG-TERM SOCIAL INFLUENCE

There seem to be two main practical ways of ensuring that the effects of social treatment programmes are long-lasting. One is to set up a social treatment programme that can accommodate patients on a semipermanent basis. The other is to rely on the social influence processes of the natural environment, which is normally the family home. Fairweather *et al.* (1969) have reported an interesting project using the former approach. When some patients left hospital they were settled in small 'lodges' in the community, at first with supervision but later running autonomously. Other patients, forming a control group, were not allocated to lodges. Not surprisingly, many fewer of the lodge patients returned to hospital. In addition the employment rate of the lodge patients greatly exceeded that of the controls. It might be objected that such a system merely created 'ghettos' of mental hospital patients in the community and did not return them to a normal, independent life. But judged by the conventional, rather crude criteria of community tenure and re-employment, it seems that the method was highly successful.

The possibility of using the patient's domestic environment to affect employment is raised by some data reported by Freeman and Simmons (1963). Before patients were discharged their relatives were interviewed and asked whether they would expect patients to perform various normal social functions including full-time work. For most of these functions, there was a significant association between whether the relatives expected patients to do these things and whether the patients actually did them. The correlation for work was significant for the male but not the female patients. Of course such an association does not prove that the relatives' expectations influenced the patient's performance. However, there are some aspects of the results which suggest that this was the case. For example, there seems to have been an even closer relationship between what the relatives said they would insist on than what they would expect. The implication of this is that patients whose relatives are encouraged to set high standards for them should do better. However, so far there has been no systematic development and evaluation of such a programme.

This is an example of how the relatives of schizophrenics might be trained to exert a positive influence. It is also possible that relatives could be trained not to exert a negative influence. There is certainly reason to believe that the domestic environment can increase patients' level of disturbance and need for rehospitalisation. However, the factors that are relevant here are not the same as those influencing the level of social functioning. Freeman and Simmons found no connection between relatives' expectations of social performance and how long patients stayed out of hospital. The latter was associated with how ready the relatives had said they would be to contact the hospital if certain problems arose.

The possible contribution of relatives to the relapse and readmission to hospital of schizophrenics has been explored more fully by Brown *et al.* (1972) (Table 21.3). The relatives were classified as showing high or low expressed emotion. This was based on such things as the number of critical comments made about the patient during an interview with the relatives at the time of admission to hospital. A highly significant relationship was found between expressed emotion and subsequent relapse within nine months of being discharged back home. Indeed the expressed emotion of the relatives was a better predictor of relapse than was the patient's disturbed behaviour or work impairment (though the relatives' emotion was in turn strongly associated with the patient's disturbed behaviour).

Table 21.3 Relationship between relatives' expressed emotion and relapse. (From Brown *et al.*, 1972, by courtesy of *Brit. J. Psychiatry*)

	No relapse	Relapse
High emotional expression	19	26
Low emotional expression	47	9

$\gamma = 0.75, p < 0.001$

It may well prove more difficult to get relatives not to have such a negative effect on patients than to train them to have a positive one. However, there is one simple factor which determines the strength of the relatives' negative effects—the amount of time that the relatives and patients spend with each other. Among the patients whose relatives showed a high level of expressed emotion, the relapse rate was 79% for those who had more than 35 hours a week of face-to-face contact with them, but 29% for those with less contact.

It thus seems that it may be possible to have quite a big impact on the welfare of patients by giving training or advice to their relatives. Though this has not yet been demonstrated for the relatives of adult patients, there is good evidence that behaviour of disturbed children can be influenced by training their parents. When, using reinforcement principles, the mothers of disturbed children are trained to respond with attention only to normal behaviour and not to deviant behaviour the results can be quite impressive (Berkowitz and Graziano, 1972).

Family treatment has tended to proceed along rather different lines, however. Usually attention is given to the interaction of the family as a whole and not just to the way the patient is treated. Also treatment tends to be aimed primarily at reaching a general understanding of the family interaction, rather than at bringing about a few modest but precisely defined changes. This style of work makes it difficult to evaluate the effectiveness of the methods used, and is partly responsible for the poor scientific status of family therapy at present (Wells *et al.*, 1972).

However, there is one relatively satisfactory study showing that family therapy is one way of reducing hospitalisation (Langsley *et al.*, 1969). Of 150 referrals, half were admitted to hospital in the usual way and half were kept at home and given a short series of family treatment sessions. It proved unnecessary to hospitalise any of the patients referred for family therapy and they lost significantly fewer days of normal social functioning. Even more impressively, over the six months following treatment significantly fewer of the family treatment patients were re-referred to hospital. Presumably the family had either learned ways of reducing the level of disturbed behaviour or of tolerating it better.

THE FUTURE OF SOCIAL TREATMENT

Though the proponents of social treatment have not always been as careful to evaluate their methods as one could wish, it is clear that the approaches discussed here have shown considerable promise. It may be useful to suggest some principles to guide their future development. Perhaps the most important of these is the need to examine empirically how methods of social treatment work. This could lead to considerable increase in efficiency. It could ensure that treatment effort is directed at the modification of problems that are relevant to the objectives in hand. In particular it could avoid the wastage of resources that occurs when it is not known whether a method is having a short- or long-term effect.

Social treatment probably also needs to become less 'mass produced' than at present. It needs to specify with more care what its objectives are in each individual case. Also, if good results are to be obtained, these objectives need to be quite limited clearly and explicitly defined. (This applies particularly where it is hoped to bring about relatively permanent social learning.) In short, social treatment needs to move into a much more precise phase. Its future will depend on how successfully it can make the transition.

References

Anthony, W. A., Buell, G. J., Sharratt, S. and Althoff, M. E. (1972). Efficacy of psychiatric rehabilitation. *Psychol. Bull.*, **78**, 447–456

Berkowitz, B. P. and Graziano, A. M. (1972). Training parents as behaviour therapists: A review. *Behav. Res. Ther.*, **10**, 297–317

Black, B. J. (1970). *Principles of Industrial Therapy for the Mentally Ill* (New York: Grune and Stratton)

Blacker, C. (1968). Primary recidivism in adult men: Differences between men on first and second prison sentence. *Brit. J. Criminol.*, **8**, 130–169

Brown, G. W., Birley, J. L. T. and Wing, J. K. (1972). Influence of family life on the course of schizophrenic disorders: A replication. *Brit. J. Psychiatry*, **121**, 241–258

Cheadle, A. J. and Morgan, R. (1972). The measurement of work performance of psychiatric patients: A reappraisal. *Brit. J. Psychiatry*, **120**, 437–441

Ellsworth, R. B. (1968). *Nonprofessionals in Psychiatric Rehabilitation* (New York: Appleton-Century-Crofts)

Ellsworth, R. B., Foster, L., Childers, B., Arthur, G. and Kroeker, D. (1968). Hospital and community adjustment as perceived by psychiatric patients, their families and staff. *J. Consult. Clin. Psychol.*, **32**, Monograph Supplement, 1–41

Fairweather, G. and Simon, R. (1963). A further follow-up comparison of psychotherapeutic programs. *J. Consult. Psychol.*, **27**, 186

Fairweather, G. W. (editor) (1964). *Social Psychology in Treating Mental Illness: An Experimental Approach* (New York: Wiley)

Fairweather, G. W., Sanders, D. H., Cressler, D. L. and Maynard, H. M. (1969). *Community Life for the Mentally Ill* (Chicago: Aldine Publishing Company)

Freeman, H. E. and Simmons, O. G. (1963). *The Mental Patient Comes Home* (New York: Wiley)

Griffiths, R. D. P. (1973). A standardised assessment of the work behaviour of psychiatric patients. *Brit. J. Psychiatry*, **123**, 403–408

Hartmann, P. (1972). A study of attitudes in industrial rehabilitation. *Occupational Psychol.*, **46**, 87–97

Hunt, G. M. and Azrin, N. M. (1973). A community reinforcement approach to alcoholism. *Behav. Res. Ther.*, **11**, 91–104

Langsley, D. G., Flomenhaft, K. and Machotka, P. (1969). Follow-up evaluation of family crisis therapy. *Amer. J. Orthopsychiatry*, **39**, 753–760

Phillips L. (1968). *Human Adaptation and its Failures* (New York: Academic Press)

Rapoport, R. N. (1960). *Community as Doctor: New Perspectives on a Therapeutic Community* (London: Tavistock Publications)

Sanders, R., Weinman, B., Smith, R. S., Smith, A., Kenny, J. and Fitzgerald, B. J. (1962). Social treatment of the male chronic mental patient. *J. Nerv. Ment. Dis.*, **134**, 244–255

Walker, R. and McCourt, J. (1965). Employment experiences among 200 schizophrenic patients in hospital and after discharge. *Amer. J. Psychiatry*, **122**, 316–319

Wells, R. A., Dilkes, T. C. and Trivelli, N. (1972). The results of family therapy: A critical review of the literature. *Family Processes*, **11**, 189–207

Wing, J. K. (1960). Pilot experiment in the rehabilitation of long-hospitalised male schizophrenic patients. *Brit. J.*

Prev. Soc. Med., **14**, 173–180

Wing, J. K., Bennett, D. H. and Denham, J. (1964). *The Industrial Rehabilitation of Long-stay Schizophrenic Patients*, Medical Research Council Memo No. 42 (London: H.M.S.O.)

Wing, J. K. and Brown, G. W. (1970). *Institutionalism and Schizophrenia* (Cambridge; Cambridge University Press)

Chapter 22

SCHIZOPHRENIA AND ANTI-PSYCHIATRY

S. J. Rachman

INTRODUCTION

Schizophrenia is the most common of the psychotic disorders and also one of the most serious. It is usually distressing and all too often fails to remit, either spontaneously or in response to treatment. In the past decade it has also become the subject of a debate in which writers who oppose or disregard the accepted methods and theories of psychiatry, and also to some extent those of psychology, have used schizophrenia as a minor battleground. Schizophrenia is taken as the most characteristic form of madness and critics such as Laing have tried to show how the concept is abused—and why it is abused. The debate has also raised some fundamental methodological issues, sometimes inadvertently. Writers such as Laing and Cooper operate outside what have gradually emerged as the scientific guidelines of psychology. With rare exceptions they eschew experiments, hypothesis construction and testing, control strategies, statistical analyses and the like. In their place, they offer existential analyses. One purpose of this chapter is to show that existential approaches to psychological phenomena, whatever their general merits and faults, are still open to critical examination, or at least to the type of examination which aims to meet accepted academic standards. This chapter is intended to illustrate some of the consequences of carrying out an academic critique of an existentialist viewpoint, while at the same time evaluating the specific contributions of a Laingian approach to our understanding of schizophrenia.

TRUE MADNESS

The writings of Laing and his colleagues have achieved popularity with many students and lay people but few professional psychologists and psychiatrists appear to share this favourable view. Instead, their attitudes range from hostility to extreme hostility. It is plain, however, that Laing and his colleagues regard their work as being of exceptional importance: 'We believe that the shift of point of view that these descriptions both embody and demand has a historical significance no less radical than the shift from a demonological to a clinical viewpoint three hundred years ago' (Laing and Esterson, 1964, page 27). Cooper writes, 'We have sufficiently delineated the true nature of psychiatric madness . . . to take a step forward' (Cooper, 1967, page 104). Laing et al., (1964) argue that the results of their therapeutic trial,

'appear to us to establish at least a *prima facie* case for radical revision of the therapeutic strategy employed in most psychiatric units in relation to the schizophrenic and his family' (page 124).

Part of the hostility expressed by psychiatrists may be traced to the attacks made on them and their profession by Cooper and Laing. For example, Cooper (1967) asserts that it is the inferior doctors who turn to psychiatry—'In fact, many psychiatrists are second-rate doctors—-people who could not "make it" in general medicine' (page 124). However, the professional hostility to their writings rests on more serious grounds than personal slights; we will examine the basis of the disagreements and suggest some reasons for the gap which exists between professional and lay opinions. The examination covers their writings on psychological and psychiatric disturbances with special reference to schizophrenia and excludes their essays on literary and philosophical topics.

The approach

Laing's work can be divided into four categories. In the first place, he attempted an existential analysis of the schizoid personality, of schizophrenia and of the relations between these two concepts. Secondly, he tried to make psychiatric disorders 'intelligible' and in furtherance of this aim he and Esterson gave a detailed account of family interactions in a group of eleven female schizophrenic patients. Thirdly, Laing endorsed and elaborated the theory expounded by the American anthropologist Bateson that schizophrenia should be regarded as a valuable spiritual experience. Fourthly, Laing and his colleagues have criticised their psychiatric colleagues as being variously incompetent, insensitive and antihuman; they are particularly critical of current psychiatric techniques for the management of schizophrenia and in turn propose a 'radical revison' of therapeutic strategy.

In *The Divided Self*, Laing (1960) attempted his existentialist analysis of schizoid individuals, schizophrenia and the transition from the former to the latter. This speculative essay is illustrated by case material and deals largely with the concept of the self and the false self (sometimes referred to as 'persona') and the relation of these concepts to mental illness. The views expounded in this book are often interesting and ·occasionally revealing but are marred by a tendency to repetition and a weakness for paradoxes.

Scientifically, the material is best regarded as a fruitful source for the construction of hypotheses about the nature of what Laing calls 'schizoid' phenomena and the attributes of schizophrenics. As will be seen from the following selection of quotations he is not short of speculative proposals about the nature of the phenomena.

'The person whom we call "schizoid" feels both more exposed, more vulnerable to others than we do, and more isolated' (page 38). 'The schizoid individual fears a real live dialectical relationship with real live people. He can relate himself only to depersonalised persons, to phantoms of his own fantasies (Imagos), perhaps to things, perhaps to animals' (page 80). 'In schizoid individuals . . . the moods of futility, meaninglessness and purposelessness . . . are particularly insistent' (page 86). '. . . the schizoid individual abhors action . . .' (page 93). 'If there is anything the schizoid individual is likely to believe in, it is his own destructiveness . . . he regards his own love and that of others as being as destructive as hatred. To be loved threatens his self; but his love is equally dangerous to anyone else.' The schizoid individual, "begins by slavish conformity and compliance, and ends through the very medium of this conformity and compliance in expressing his own negative will and hatred' (page 109). 'The schizoid individual characteristically seeks to make his awareness of himself· as intensive and extensive as possible . . . and does not bask in the warmth of a loving self-regard. Self-scrutiny is quite improperly regarded as a form of narcissism. Neither the schizoid nor the schizophrenic is narcissistic in this sense' (page 120). 'The schizoid individual . . . is persecuted by his own insight and lucidity' (page 128).

Laing has a detailed and complex view of the people whom he defines as. schizoid. In theory it should be possible to take his descriptions, or at least some of them, and rephrase them in a way that would make them amenable to ordinary investigation (e.g. one could test the idea that they suffer from the mood disturbances described). At this point many professionals will wonder whether the effort required to elucidate Laing's multiple ideas about schizoid people is worthwhile. If there is a justification for recommending research of this type it is that some of the patients described in this and other books of Laing are clinically recognisable. Moreover, he is capable of conveying some part of their profound distress with skill and sympathy. The impatience and irritability of professional workers is more understandable when we come to examine Laing's account of the attributes of schizophrenics. For, despite his stated reservations about the value of the concept, Laing's retention of the term 'schizophrenic' has led to a confusion between the clinical condition and the existentialist interpretation of certain kinds of unusual behaviour Leaving aside these problems for the moment, here

are samples of Laing's account of schizophrenics (drawn from *The Divided Self*, Laing, 1960).

The schizophrenic 'is playing at being mad to avoid at all costs the possibility of being held *responsible* for a single coherent idea or intention' (page 179). 'In many schizophrenics, the self-body split remains the basic one' (page 177). Although Laing obviously feels that loving is of considerable importance· in schizophrenia, it is not always clear whether he feels that schizophrenics would do better to seek it out or to avoid it. 'To the schizophrenic, liking someone equals being like that person: being like a person is equated with being the same as that person, hence with losing identity. Hating and being hated may therefore be felt to threaten loss of identity less than do loving and being loved' (page 191). 'I have never known a schizophrenic who could say he was loved, as a man, by God the Father or by the Mother of God or by another man' (page 39). 'Despite his longing to be loved for his "real self" the schizophrenic is terrified of love. Any form of understanding *threatens* his whole defensive system' (page 178). 'The other's love, is therefore, feared more than his hatred, or rather all love is sensed as a version of hatred' (page 46). In *The Politics of Experience*, Laing (1971) states that, 'From the moment of birth . . . the baby is subjected to these forces of violence, called love . . . these forces are mainly concerned with destroying most of its potentialities' (page 50). On the other hand, we are told on the same page that, 'Love and violence, properly speaking, are polar opposites'. In *The Divided Self*, Laing (1960) states that the 'main agent in uniting the patient, in allowing the pieces to come together and cohere, is the physician's love, a love that recognises the patient's total being, and accepts it, with no strings attached' (page 180).

Evidence

Despite these contradictions and some obscurities, professional workers can take little exception to Laing's writings provided that they are understood to be entirely speculative. In *Sanity, Madness and the Family*, Laing and Esterson (1964) present excerpts from interviews carried out on eleven female schizophrenic patients and some members of their families. The interview material is preceded by a summary of the patient's clinical history, connected by some commentaries and summarised in tabular form at the end of each chapter. In the introduction, the authors claim that they are seeking to make the behaviour of the schizophrenic patient intelligible and they disclaim any intention to propose that the schizophrenia is caused by the behaviour of the patients' families. In the preface of the second edition they state, 'Such criticism would be justified if we had set out to test the hypothesis that the family is a pathogenic variable in the genesis of schizophrenia. But we did not set out to do this, and we have not claimed to have done so' (page 12). This specific disclaimer is often lost sight of in the discussion of Laing's views, particularly by some of his more enthusiastic followers, including those in the film world. It should be said however that there are grounds for concluding that Laing and his colleagues do claim a causal connection between family life and the development of schizophrenia in some of their writings. Even in *Sanity, Madness and the Family* (Laing and Esterson, 1964) there are two examples of this attribution. Their discussion of the Abbott case concludes with a statement that the patient's numerous and serious symptoms are 'more likely . . . the outcome of her interexperience and interaction with her parents' (page 49). Again, they come very close to a direct attribution of causality in their summing-up of. the Danzig case—'Once more, we have given, we hope, *enough* to establish the social intelligibility of the events in this family that have prompted the diagnosis of schizophrenia "in" one of its members' (page 130). Elsewhere Laing argues that the families of schizophrenic patients 'prevent' them from embarking on the long process of 'becoming well' (Laing, 1967, page 143). Cooper (1967) argues that the family finds the child's 'tentatively independent behaviour' unbearably anxiety-provoking and hence their attempts at 'autonomous self-assertion' are called illness, in fact schizophrenia (page 24).

Leaving aside the question of pathogenesis, how far are Laing and Esterson justified in claiming to make schizophrenia intelligible? At best they only partly succeed in making some aspects of the patients' behaviour intelligible. For example, however successful they sometimes are in making the patient's impoverished emotional responses meaningful to us, almost nowhere are they able to give an intelligible account of the development of hallucinations, or catatonic immobility, or prolonged apathy and so on. Most serious of all, in virtually all of the instances which they cite, there is a gaping disproportion between the apparently damaging behaviour of the relatives and the duration, extent and depth of the patient's handicaps. In many instances the family behaviour which is said to make the abnormal behaviour of the patient intelligible, seems to be trivial and can be matched with ease by examples of marital discord, occupational stress and the like, where no association with schizophrenia is claimed. It is hard to avoid the impression that they have set out to demonstrate that the exceedingly abnormal behaviour of the patients is a direct reflection of the equal or greater disturbance in the family members and to this end, they mix description with inference and inference with interpretation. Their evident sympathy for the patients does not extend to the relatives who are described and discussed with little sign of compassion. Sad to say, their tone is often that of the public prosecutor. In all it might have seemed more convincing if they had encountered at least some parents who were not completely devoid of insight or genuine affection.

The quality of the evidence is questionable. It is of course highly selected and what we read consists of selected fragments from selected interviews taken with selected patients and selected relatives. There are no external checks possible. Moreover, in a number of instances the material appears to contain contradictions. For example in the case of the Abbotts, we are told that the parents denied that the patient worried over school matters (Laing and Esterson, 1964, page 49) but on the other hand, we are told (page 31) that her parents were conscious of her school worries and had in the past dealt satisfactorily with them.

Why schizophrenia?

Presumably if we are to have an intelligible account of schizophrenia. it should include an explanation of the specific associations between the patient's experiences and her abnormal behaviour. This type of specificity is lacking in the work of Laing and Esterson. It is not at all clear why schizophrenia should develop in the cases they describe. Why not manic-depressive psychosis? Or for that matter why not neurotic behaviour or delinquency? Closely related to the problem of specificity, is the question of incidence. Their examples of family disturbance could be matched and surpassed by observations of families selected from the general population on a random basis and yet schizophrenia is statistically rare.

Having developed reliable means of studying and interpreting the family interactions, one would have to proceed to the construction and conduct of an acceptable study which would include those tedious but necessary control groups. Do the families described by Laing behave differently from those in which one member is a delinquent? Do they behave differently from those in which one member is brain-damaged or obsessional or asthmatic or plain normal? Even if we assume that differences can be demonstrated, further research would be needed before concluding that the observed differences are of special significance in relation to schizophrenic behaviour. Laing and Esterson claim that their main contribution is to make the apparently incomprehensible behaviour of the schizophrenic patient more meaningful. In my view the abnormal behaviour of the patients described in their book remains largely 'incomprehensible' in their terms. In the Danzig case for example, we appear to have a relatively mild family problem and yet the patient's behaviour was abnormal and bizarre for a prolonged period. The writers suggest that the girl's apparently unintelligible behaviour, called schizophrenia by her doctors, was caused or at least precipitated by her bewilderment on discovering that the family operated double standards. These double standards included such common examples as minor evasions of income tax and a gap between their religious pretensions and their ritual practices. Contrary to the claims of Laing and Esterson, they have not done 'enough to establish the social 'intelligibility of the events in this family that have prompted the diagnosis of schizophrenia in one of its members' (Laing and Esterson, 1964, page 130). There is nothing in their accounts of the behaviour of her family to explain why the patient had 'bizarre ideas' such as her false report that she had been sexually assaulted, that people on television were talking about her, that people were plotting against her and so forth. It is not made plain why she lay in bed all day, nor why she was mute for some time. It is not clear why, if the family's double standards were so damaging, the patient's older and younger siblings were apparently quite normal. It might be objected that the Danzig family is one of the weakest examples provided by Laing and Esterson and therefore should not be chosen for close analysis. Here one can only rely on comparative judgments of all eleven families and for what it is worth, my view is that the Danzig family *is* a weak example but many of the other cases are equally thin.

Four interpretations

This is not to deny that the transcripts presented by Laing provide evidence of disturbed behaviour and attitudes in most of the eleven families. It has been shown by many research groups that the families of schizophrenic patients do in fact demonstrate disturbed behaviour and attitudes. This may be interpreted as evidence in support of a hypothesis that schizophrenia is caused by the patient's family. Four other possible interpretations are: (i) the family disturbance is a consequence of the patient's serious disorder (ii) the patient's disorder is caused by extra-familial factors, but is exacerbated by the occurrence of disturbance in the family (iii) the family disturbance is initially caused by coping with the patient's disorder, but then becomes a factor in exacerbating the disorder (iv) the family disturbance is a manifestation of genetically determined disorders of behaviour in the relatives of a person known to be genetically vulnerable (by virtue of his schizophrenic disorder).

It is not possible to examine each of these alternatives in detail but a few observations are in place. On the face of it, the occurrence of one of the most serious psychological disorders is likely to cause considerable distress in the entire family as well as in the patient himself. In a well-known study, Klebanoff found that the parental attitudes of mothers of schizophrenic children were indeed pathological; but only slightly less pathological than the parental attitudes of mothers of children with brain injuries. 'The finding that mothers of schizophrenic children showed less rather than more pathological attitudes than the mothers of brain damaged and retarded children tends

to cast doubt on the hypothesis that maternal attitudes cause schizophrenia' (Klebanoff, 1959, page 44). It is also known that parents of children with other types of chronic or severe illness such as cerebral palsy, behave in seemingly unfortunate ways. Their parental attitudes and behaviour are frequently marked by inconsistency and by swings between over-indulgence and over-restriction. The apparently pathogenic behaviour of parents of schizophrenic patients may be the outcome of the uncertainty and stress involved in caring for a child with this serious disorder and may arise in a similar manner to that noted in the parents of other severely ill offspring. Although the parents of the people affected may display pathogenic attitudes, no one would claim that cerebral palsy, brain injury or mental retardation are caused by abnormal attitudes. Moreover, one may pose the question of how the biological or foster parents of chronically ill or disordered children should behave? In caring for the severely disabled, what is 'normal' behaviour and what are 'normal' attitudes? With the possible exception of behavioural psychologists, it must be admitted that we have been more successful in identifying abnormal parental behaviour than in providing practical alternatives or assistance.

A second interpretation of the disturbances observed in families of schizophrenics is that family tension exacerbates an existing disorder. Brown *et al.* (1966) found, for example, that 76% of a sample of schizophrenics who returned from hospitals to families in which a good deal of emotion was expressed, deteriorated after discharge. They suggested that the patients fared better in families which were concerned and caring but did not have what the writers describe as 'high emotional involvement'. Other research has revealed that the admission or readmission to hospital of schizophrenic patients is frequently precipitated by disturbing events (not only within the family of course) and/or a failure to take the prescribed amount of phenothiazine medication. Family discord then is one of several precipitating factors. It should be remembered however that many of the factors that appear to precipitate schizophrenia (such as discord, bereavements, illness, work failure and so on) are also capable of precipitating neurotic and other types of psychological upset. Also, Birley and Brown (1970) have noted that the 'symptomatology of acute schizophrenia is largely unrelated to its precipitants'. On the main question however it seems reasonable to accept that family discord or pressures can precipitate schizophrenic disorders. This is at best a partial explanation because we know that other types of stress can act as precipitants, that there is a genetic component in schizophrenia, that the symptoms are often unrelated to the precipitants and finally that the same family pressures are able to precipitate disorders quite other than schizophrenia.

The third interpretation of observed disturbances in

the families of schizophrenics, that the patient's disorder disrupts the family and this discord in turn comes to act as a contributor to the patient's problems, combines the first two interpretations and hence will not be expanded here.

A fourth interpretation of the observed disturbances in the families of schizophrenics might be offered by proponents of a genetic model: the family disturbance reflects the increased risk of mental illnesses in relatives of a schizophrenic. According to Slater and Cowie (1971), 'It is undoubtedly the case that near relatives of schizophrenic patients who may be supposed to carry some enhanced predisposition to schizophrenia, not only show an incidence of schizophrenic psychoses higher than in the general population, but also increased risks of other forms of mental illness, of suicide, of abnormalities of personality, and possibly also of alcoholism, criminality and other abnormalities of behaviour' (page 23). Once again, however, we are confronted by the problem of determining whether the increased incidence of these disorders is best accounted for mainly on environmental or mainly of genetic grounds. The growing evidence from studies of schizophrenics (or their offspring) who are reared in foster homes seems to indicate a strong genetic contribution. For example, in a group of forty-seven children born to schizophrenic mothers but reared in foster homes, no less than five were found to be schizophrenic, nine were sociopaths, seven were criminals, four were retarded and thirteen were neurotic. In the control group of fifty foster children born of non-schizophrenic parents, there were no cases of schizophrenia, no cases of retardation and far fewer sociopaths, criminals or neurotics. It will be some time before we are in possession of sufficient evidence to reach firm conclusions on the worrying possibility that schizophrenia is a sign of a general mental vulnerability with ramifications for the entire family, but it cannot be ruled out at this stage.

Returning to the observation of disturbances in the families of schizophrenics, it is plain that the fact is open to at least four plausible interpretations over and above that of direct causation of schizophrenia by the family. These alternative interpretations need to be excluded by any theory which rests on the claim that schizophrenia has its genesis within the family.

GENETIC CONTRIBUTION

As no discussion of schizophrenia is complete without reference to the possibility of a significant genetic contribution, it is necessary to review some of the current evidence on this subject. While most professionals agree that there is a significant genetic contribution in the aetiology of schizophrenia, no one asserts that it is a purely genetic disorder (see Chapter 10). The major types of evidence which suggest a genetic component are worth summarising (see Rosenthal and Kety, 1968; Slater and Cowie, 1971).

There is a correlation between degree of blood relationship and the incidence of schizophrenia in relatives. Although the figures drawn from the eleven main investigations show a wide range, the study of monozygotic twins reveal that in more than 30% of cases, both twins have schizophrenia. In those rare instances (only sixteen recorded pairs) where a monozygous pair were separated early in life and schizophrenia was diagnosed at some stage, no less than ten of the sixteen separated pairs were similarly affected. Comparisons between 'identical' and fraternal twins reared in the same home enable one to obtain a rough measure of the relative contributions of heredity and environment and in the case of schizophrenia, the evidence suggests an important genetic component. The likelihood of 'identical' twins both having schizophrenia is from three to six times greater than the likelihood of fraternal twins being similarly affected. In fact, the incidence of schizophrenia among fraternal twins is close to the incidence of schizophrenia among siblings. There is an association between the severity of schizophrenic illness in the index twin and the likelihood of his co-twin being affected; the more severe the illness, the greater the likelihood. Moreover, comparatively few monozygous co-twins of cases of typical schizophrenia are found to be normal. Children fostered by schizophrenic parents do not show an increased incidence of schizophrenia. Lastly, studies on children of a schizophrenic parent who were adopted at an early age show that the incidence of the illness observed in the adoptees resembles that of the biological and not the adopted family. Along similar lines, an Icelandic study was carried out on the biological and foster siblings of schizophrenics who had been adopted before the age of one year. Six of the twenty-nine biological siblings were schizophrenic and none of the foster siblings.

The quality of much of the evidence on genetic factors is satisfactory and recent advances in research strategy have led to a reduction of those distorting influences (e.g. bias in samples, rater contaminations etc.) which impaired research ten and more years ago. In view of the extent of the interlocking evidence, it now seems inescapable that genetic factors play a significant part in the genesis of schizophrenia. Shields discusses current evidence and interpretations in Chapter 10. Recognition of these genetic factors by no means rules out different and supplementary approaches to schizophrenia and in particular, does not preclude an existentialist analysis of the experiences of people affected.

SCHIZOPHRENIA AS A HEALING VOYAGE

Turning to *The Politics of Experience*, Laing (1971) argues that schizophrenia, far from being a pathological disorder, may instead be regarded as an especially valuable experience. Central to an understanding of this view is Laing's endorsement of

Bateson's theory that there is an analogy between schizophrenia and primitive initiation processes. According to Bateson, the patient embarks on a voyage of discovery (a death) and returns (rebirth) to the normal world with new insights. This voyage may be 'precipitated by his family life' or by chance circumstances. The normal outcome is a return to the 'real world' but some people fail to return and Bateson suggests that attempts at therapy are sometimes the reason for this failure (Laing, 1971, page 97). Taking up the thread Laing argues that schizophrenia might be regarded as a voyage 'into inner space' and may constitute 'a natural *healing* process' (page 105). He postulates that, 'The journey is experienced as going further in, as going back through one's personal life, in and back and through and beyond into the experience of all mankind, of the primal man, of Adam and perhaps even further into the being of animals, vegetables and minerals' (page 104). I regret being unable to grasp the meaning of 'cosmic foetalisation' or what it means to return to the experiences of the garden pea but until better arguments are available, there seems little reason to pursue the curious analogy between initiation rites and schizophrenia.

Laing complains that the 'natural sequence' of schizophrenia is 'seldom allowed to occur because we are so busy "treating" the patient, whether by chemotherapy, shock therapy, milieu therapy, group therapy, psychotherapy, family therapy—sometimes now in the very best, most advanced places. by the lot' (page 102).

In the appendix of *Psychiatry and Anti-psychiatry*, Cooper. Laing and Esterson describe their therapeutic experiment carried out on forty-two schizophrenic patients. The 'twenty male and twenty-two female schizophrenics were treated by conjoint family and by milieu therapy, with reduced use of tranquillisers' (page 124). As a pilot study, their report could pass muster but the absence of elementary controls, combined with an inadequate and contaminated outcome criterion. a mixture of treatments and an absence of essential detail, make it unnecessary to subject their meagre results to detailed analysis. One cannot be sure that their therapeutic results, which were in the average range for this type of report, can be attributed solely to the use of chlorpromazine. Certainly there are grounds for believing that in our present state of limited knowledge, the greatest benefits to be derived in the treatment of schizophrenia are attributable to drug effects (e.g. the thorough, large-scale study reported from the Neuropsychiatric Institute in California—May, 1968).

Three contradictions are worth mentioning, although only one of them is of major dimension. Having criticised the concept of psychiatric cure, 'Curing patients . . . curing is so ambiguous a term; one may cure bacon, hides, rubber or patients' (page 107), Cooper (1967) talks about their recovery rate in terms of cures (page 110). The second, minor, contradiction occurs in their use of statistics to ascertain the significance of their outcome figures. On more than one occasion Cooper expresses his disdain for 'massified abstraction' (page 112) and castigates statistical analyses of this type as perpetuating a form of pseudoscience. None of this prevents them from carrying out two of their main statistical analyses on samples of five and six patients respectively.

A third contradiction appears in Cooper's attitude to psychiatric hospitals which he likens to Nazi extermination camps (page 97) and then argues for the desirability of allowing patients to stay in hospital for prolonged periods (page 110). He argues that, 'To my mind (it is) indefensible to resort to economic arguments in terms of reducing hospital beds to justify this form of therapeutic ruthlessness' (page 108). The major contradiction however will not have escaped the reader; having argued that schizophrenia is a valuable experience and even, in Cooper's words 'a more advanced human state' (page 79). they appear to follow conventional psychiatric practice in their treatment of the forty-two patients described in their study—family therapy, tranquillisers and all.

In most of Laing's writings there seems to be an unresolved conflict between regarding schizophrenia as a form of violence inflicted by parents and society on people who seek autonomy and independence, with the contrasting view that it is a special and valuable spiritual experience that should be encouraged rather than discouraged. This latter view is clearly expressed in *The Politics of Experience* (Laing, 1971) where he states that, 'We need . . . an initiation ceremonial through which the person will be guided with full social encouragement and sanction into inner space and time by people who have been there and back again. Psychiatrically, this would appear as ex-patients helping future patients to go mad' (page 106).

When he is attempting to provide an existentialist view of schizophrenic experiences, Laing has interesting observations to make. Moreover some of these views are potentially capable of being investigated in a conventional manner. Unfortunately, his family studies add little to the model provided in *The Divided Self* (Laing, 1960) and the analogy of schizophrenia and initiation ceremonies seems to constitute a break with the earlier analysis, if not a direct contradiction. His venture into a therapeutic experiment would appear to have been ill-advised on several grounds but perhaps the most important is that it is in contradiction to almost all of the views which he has expressed on the nature of schizophrenia and the way in which the parents, doctors and society 'manage' people who display this kind of behaviour. The veiled suggestion that families induce schizophrenia in one of their members, despite the disclaimer by Laing and Esterson (1964), appears to have been misunderstood and misused. If taken seriously, this opinion when stated as an established, accepted piece of knowledge may well add to the already considerable distress of the schizophrenic and his relatives and friends.

THE APPEAL OF LAING'S VIEWS

Finally, we return to the question of why it is that Laing's views appear to appeal to so many non-professional people. It may well appeal to people who hold radical attitudes as Laing's work on madness and the family repeatedly suggests that the attribution of schizophrenia is an attempt on the part of the parents to suppress the youngster's striving for independence and personal freedom. The attacks on psychiatry and psychiatric hospitals fall on fertile ground because current psychiatric practice is often rudimentary and too often a matter of incompetence. The abuse of some patients in long-stay institutions is now a matter of public knowledge and we also have evidence of the unfortunate effects which prolonged residence in a psychiatric institution may have on a person's initiative, sense of responsibility and dignity. On the positive side, Laing shows in *The Divided Self* an appealing humanitarianism in his attempts to sympathise and empathise with those unfortunate people who suffer from distressing·and bizarre experiences (Laing, 1960).

The political overtones of 'antipsychiatry', hinting at conspiracy, also have some appeal. Laing has asserted that, 'Only under certain socio-economic circumstances will people suffer from schizophrenia' (Laing, 1967, page 145). In fact schizophrenic disorders are observed in all countries. They are seen in Leeds and Chungking, in Beverly Hills and Zululand. The content of the disorder is culturally coloured of course but the main pathological features and incidence figures are similar in societies as different as capitalist America and communist China. Laing's assertion that the diagnosis of schizo-phrenia is a political event is not absolutely misleading but it would have been more accurate to state that the diagnosis may have legal consequences. His account of hospital admissions is a caricature as far as this country is concerned. 'After being subjected to a degradation ceremonial known as psychiatric examination he is bereft of his civil liberties in being imprisoned in a total institution known as a "mental" hospital. More completely, more radically than anywhere else in our society, he is invalidated as a human being' (Laing, 1971, page 101). To take one aspect of Laing's account, according to the 1970 Annual Report of the Department of Health, 93% of psychiatric in-patients were voluntary patients. The great majority of admissions to psychiatric hospitals are of short duration and voluntary in nature. Melodramatic accounts of psychiatric procedures may cause undue alarm and also distract people from attending to the numerous and serious deficiencies in our prevailing arrangements for assisting, advising and comforting people suffering from the various forms of psychological distress. Accusations of malicious imprisonment and degradation will always find a ready response but are unlikely to give rise to realistic improvements.

In conclusion, the interesting part of Laing's work is to be found in his inventive and original existential analysis of certain bizarre experiences. His views on the role of the family in schizophrenia rest on poor foundations and omit a good deal of contrary information. The analogy between schizophrenia and primitive initiation ceremonies is far-fetched and leads to unrestrained speculations of an unhelpful character. Lastly, the melodramatic quality of many of his criticisms of current psychiatric practice permits people to continue ignoring the serious deficiencies in our present services for assisting those in psychological distress.

References

Birley, J. and Brown, G. (1970). Crises and life changes preceding the onset or relapse of acute schizophrenia: clinical aspects. *Brit. J. Psychiatry*, 116, 327–33

Brown, G., Wing, J. et al. (1966). *Schizophrenia and Social Care* (Oxford: Oxford University Press)

Cooper, D. (1967). *Psychiatry and Anti-psychiatry* (London: Tavistock Publications)

Department of Health and Social Security (1970). *Annual Report* (London: H.M.S.O.)

Klebanoff, L. (1959). Parental attitudes of mothers of schizophrenic, brain-injured and retarded and normal children. *Amer. J. Orthopsychiatry*, 29, 445–454

Laing, R. D. (1960). *The Divided Self* (Chicago: Quadrangle Books)

Laing, R. D. (1967). The study of family and social contexts in relation to the origin of schizophrenia. In: *The Origins of Schizophrenia* (J. Romano, editor) (Amsterdam: Excerpta Medica)

Laing, R. D. (1969). *Self and Others* (Revised Ed.) (London: Tavistock Publications)

Laing, R. D. (1971). *The Politics of Experience* (London: Penguin Books)

Laing, R. D., Cooper, D. G. and Esterson, A. (1964). *Reason and Violence* (London: Tavistock Publications)

Laing, R. D. and Esterson, A. (1964). *Sanity, Madness and the Family* (London: Penguin Books)

May, P. (1968). *Treatment of Schizophrenics* (New York: Science House)

Rosenthal, D. and Kety, S. (editors) (1968). *The Transmission of Schizophrenia* (Oxford: Pergamon Press)

Slater, E. and Cowie, V. (1971). *The Genetics of Mental Disorder* (Oxford University Press)

Chapter 23

BEHAVIOUR MODIFICATION

H. R. Beech

An interest in the modification of behaviour is certainly not confined to clinicians involved in the treatment of psychological disorders. Such an objective is shared by many, including educationalists, advertising agencies, politicians, and so on. In pursuing this aim numerous different methods have been utilised but all have involved, in one way or another, the use of rewards and punishments.

The psychologist's interest in this area, however, has diverged from that of others in that stress has been placed upon achieving an understanding of the processes by which the behaviour of organisms is changed or modified and, also, in that emphasis is given to the need for systematic and careful experimentation in accomplishing this end.

Often such investigations have contributed to the elaboration of theories, such as that of Clark Hull (1943), but not infrequently the results have presented problems which cannot yet be integrated into a cogent conceptual system. Such work has made important contributions to understanding, although it is abundantly clear that many years of patient endeavour will be needed before our accounts and practice of behaviour modification are sufficiently refined, sophisticated, and usefully predictive, to meet existing needs.

Nevertheless, it is possible, even at this early stage of the development of behavioural theories and techniques, to offer a plausible (albeit partial) account of human behaviour and to translate such an account into viable practical modification procedures.

Behaviour modification practices can, of course, emanate from any theoretical formulation which deals with this subject matter. However, the term has been largely restricted to theories and procedures which derive from the principles of learning and conditioning, many of which were first elucidated by Pavlov and Bechterev (Pavlov, 1927).

Early experimental studies in the area, almost exclusively employing animals, had been largely attempts to understand normal processes. True, Pavlov's redoubtable work, summarised in the Anrep translation of *Conditioned Reflexes* (1927), contained reference to abnormalities of functioning which might arise under certain environmental arrangements and, indeed, the circle-and-ellipse experiment was an important landmark in this respect, being an early example of the way in which 'neurotic' behaviour can be contrived in the laboratory.

Briefly, the experimental animal was taught to discriminate between a circle and an ellipse, allowing food to follow presentation of the former, but not the latter. In the next stage the procedure was adopted of gradually changing the shape of the ellipse so that it became more and more circular in appearance, until the animal could no longer determine whether the shape was one to which it should respond (as a cue preceding food) or should not do so. Its reactions became strongly emotional, with howling, biting, struggling to be free of the harness, and so on, and such behaviour was readily apparent on subsequent occasions when the animal was returned to the laboratory situation.

In short, some experimental condition had been established which allowed for the development of an emotional reaction which persisted over time.

Numerous other studies of what have been called 'experimental neuroses' have confirmed the main findings of Pavlov's experiment. Liddell (1944) for example, using sheep, forced these animals to make difficult discriminations between signals, some of which were followed by strong electric shock and others which were not. The result again was an emotional instability which showed considerable persistence over several months of observation.

Such experimental studies succeeded in demonstrating in an unequivocal way that aberrant behaviour might be established in animals as the direct outcome of certain conditioning procedures. Thus the possibility existed that all 'neurotic' behaviour could be attributed to this kind of mechanism, and that all modifications of behaviour, with beneficial or adverse outcomes, could be explained in terms of conditioning.

However, this kind of model had seldom been applied to the modification of human behaviour and there was no strong interest in reversing the ill-effects of any learning/conditioning. To meet the second of these points would require the establishment of abnormal reactions by conditioning procedures, followed by some attempt at removing or extinguishing the abnormal behaviours (deconditioning).

Masserman's (1943) experiment achieved this important step. Using cats as his subjects he first set about creating experimental neuroses in these animals by presenting food in the context of noxious stimulation. The cats were kept in special cages and, as a preliminary step, were trained to press a lever to obtain food. When they had successfully acquired this skill the procedure was changed so that any attempt to take food from the dish was greeted by a strong blast of air or an electric shock. Under this regime there was often a refusal to approach the food tray and eat, even though the animals might be very hungry.

Masserman then compared several methods of treatment which might restore the animal to normal feeding and remove the 'anxiety' which was occasioned by placing it in the experimental cage.

Two of these are deserving of special mention. One was that of physically forcing the cat to approach the food dish, and which was largely unsuccessful. The other was that of creating some condition which counteracted the 'anxiety' experienced by the animal, so that it could once again come to 'know' that food-approach did not lead to unpleasant consequences.

This latter method involved stroking and patting the animals, feeding them by hand, first outside, and then in the cage, and only gradually approaching the original experimental feeding situation. Indeed the importance of a careful and unhurried retraining programme was underlined in Masserman's findings, for failure to observe this little-by-little approach could result in renewed instability and fearfulness in the animal. In essence, then, this method had two main elements, the employment of some means of counteracting the negative emotionality, and the use of a graduated approach to the feared situation.

The further study and elaboration of these important therapeutic possibilities was undertaken by Wolpe (1952). In doing so he pointed out that whereas most other experimental neurosis studies had assumed conflict to be a necessary condition for emotional instability (e.g. the strong approach-to-food tendency of the hungry cat being present at the same time as a strong avoidance of electric shock), equally dramatic results could be obtained simply as the outcome of repeatedly applying some inescapable noxious stimulation (e.g. a strong electric shock).

The 'neurotic' reactions of trembling, howling. spitting, crouching, and violent motor activity of the cats soon became fixed and would appear whenever the animal was placed in the experimental cage. Furthermore, such reactions showed little or no reduction over a period of time, even though there was no further exposure to shock, and the learned fear appeared to have acquired some degree of permanence.

Using Masserman's procedure Wolpe was able to confirm that a gradual approach combined with feeding by hand could be successful in eliminating such 'neurotic' reactions.

The importance of Wolpe's contribution is clear. First, he was able to provide a more cogent explanation for the 'treatment' than any which had previously been offered and, secondly, he went on to elaborate the programme of retraining necessary for

stabilising the emotional responsivity of the animal. Both these points will be dealt with in the appropriate later section of this chapter.

Perhaps the most important issues to raise here are two-fold. In the first place it is important to question the mechanisms of conditioning/learning as a satisfactory explanation of human psychological abnormalities.

Secondly, although one may subscribe to the view that learning/conditioning principles have much to offer, both in terms of explanation as well as treatment, would the account be full and satisfactory if the role of temperament is excluded?

Clearly there are many important objections to be raised to any view which holds that comparatively simple laboratory studies of animals low in the phylogenetic scale have provided the key to the relatively complex phenomena of the human neurotic state. Nevertheless, certain studies have provided evidence which is at least consistent with the view that psychological abnormalities could have their origin in either unwanted (superfluous) conditioning, or in a deficiency in conditioning, and that such abnormalities can be rectified by making use of principles deriving from the conditioning laboratory.

One of the earliest studies which pointed to the relevance of conditioning to the acquisition of a phobia is the celebrated case of Little Albert (Watson, 1920). This stolid and relatively placid child of nine months was first exposed to a regular routine in which his reactions were noted to the sudden presentation of a white rat, a rabbit, a dog, and various other stimuli. While Albert would frequently reach out for them, not once did he show any sign of fear. On the other hand, not unexpectedly, a loud and unpleasant noise could produce signs of distress in the child.

The next step in Watson's study was to attempt to transfer the fear occasioned by the noise to the white rat, which was accomplished by the simple process of making the noise whenever Albert reached out for the animal. Only seven such associations were necessary to effect this piece of conditioning which not only involved the reaction of fear whenever the rat was shown to the child, but included a spreading or generalisation of the fear reaction to stimuli in some way similar to the rat, such as a fur coat.

In short, Watson's study demonstrated that a simple conditioning procedure could bring about an unadaptive fear response of a lasting kind.

The plausibility of the conditioning model is also revealed in quite a different kind of study by Goldiamond and his colleagues (1965). In an initial experiment a group of stutterers were required to read aloud for 90 minutes, during the first 30 of which their stuttering frequency was noted. In the next 30-minute period an aversive stimulus (a loud and unpleasant noise) was presented following each disfluent utterance, while in the final 30 minutes there was, once again, simple observation of the number of stuttered words. The results showed clearly that the frequency of stuttering dropped during the second (punishment) period, and that this benefit persisted into the final period of measurement.

In a second study by the same experimenters the punishment (negative reinforcement) was used in an escape context for here it was arranged that any stuttered words would *switch off* the noxious noise. In this situation the rate of stuttering increased markedly.

This study provides a useful illustration of the dual role of the negative reinforcer; used in one way the outcome can be beneficial, while used in another the opposite result may be obtained. But it also provides an interesting example of the way in which a simple arrangement of contingencies can have important behavioural consequences.

As a further example of the way in which a simple conditioning paradigm can produce modifications of behaviour one might quote Rachman's (1966a) study of conditioned sexual responses. The question which Rachman posed was that of whether a conditioning procedure can account for the development of sexual fetishes. It is, admittedly, an analogue study and, as Rachman points out, positive results cannot be taken to indicate that any or all fetishes are attributable to this mechanism; all one can say is that deviant behaviour *could* arise out of a conditioning process.

His study first involved showing that while slides of pretty and naked women could produce reliable erectile responses in three young male subjects, pictures of various kinds of boots did not do so. The attempt to transfer sexual arousal to the 'neutral' object was made by first showing a slide of the boots closely followed by one of the 'pin-up' girl. By this means a reliable increase in penis volume to 'boots' alone was achieved in from 24 to 65 trials.

Such demonstrations as these tend to increase our confidence in the relevance of conditioning principles to behavioural changes, and the application of these techniques to the treatment of psychological problems seems less remote.

Certainly the importance of the inherent characteristics of the organism in determining the reaction to conditioning has been repeatedly demonstrated in animal work. Petrova, for example, a colleague of Pavlov, reported upon the marked differences between two dogs when exposed to delayed reinforcement (reward) following presentation of a signal, or to strong electric shock. Such demonstrations led Pavlov to postulate two processes of nervous activity, excitation and inhibition, having the properties of strength, mobility, and equilibrium, which allow for numerous different *types* of organisms that can be differentiated by several aspects of conditioning responsivity.

Indeed, differences in conditionability attributable to existing characteristics of the organism have been frequently observed and are recorded in the literature.

Certain theorists (e.g. Eysenck, 1967) have in fact devoted very considerable time to investigating these individual differences.

In the study previously mentioned, for example, Masserman noted that not all cats became disturbed, and that some learned to overcome their fear and readily ate from the food dish even when given shocks or blasts of air. Similarly, Gantt (1944) has reported upon the differences in behaviour of dogs in experimental conditions, as have Liddell (1944) and others. In the human sphere, too, there is much evidence that temperament can produce differences in learning and conditioning (see Eysenck, 1967).

In practice the utilisation of conditioning principles in therapeutic work has resulted in a proliferation of relatively standard techniques, not all of which have proved useful, or are supported by strong evidence of their value. Accordingly, it is appropriate in this chapter to confine the discussion and evaluation of the available techniques to those which have not only found popularity with therapists, but for which a certain amount of positive evidence has been forthcoming.

DESENSITISATION

This technique has a comparatively long history, probably being first employed in a systematic way by Jones (1924). The elaboration of this method into a routine form of behaviour modification, however, is largely due to Wolpe's (1952) important contribution.

It is a technique which sets out very specifically to deal with psychological problems in which anxiety is the main feature and, hence, has been used extensively in the treatment of phobias. It utilises, as the earlier section of this chapter indicated, two important elements, the gradual and progressive exposure of the individual to the object of his fear, and the induction of a state incompatible with the presence of anxiety.

In practice the therapist prepares, with the afflicted individual's help, a list of situations, called a hierarchy, graded according to the degree of fear which such situations would cause to the patient. These are presented to him, starting with the least evocative items and proceeding to those which would ordinarily produce strong, negative emotions, while the patient is in a state of deep relaxation. It is argued that to make such presentations while the subject is in a state of profound muscular relaxation is necessary for building up the tolerance of the patient—the relaxed state being to some extent antagonistic to the presence of anxiety.

Each scene or item is presented repeatedly until such time as the patient can tolerate it without experiencing any discomfort. Typically, the therapist will ensure reaching this criterion for each step in the hierarchy before passing to the next one in the list.

Thus, scenes which are presented to the spider phobic person might begin with asking the patient to imagine that he is at some distance from a small dead spider, through those which depict a more active but small specimen, to the close proximity of a large, hairy, scuttling spider having all the frightening characteristics specified by the patient as causing panic. It is generally found that the afflicted individual not only comes to tolerate the imagined scenes without anxiety, but that this benefit transfers to the real life situation.

The earliest reports on the use of this method lacked the kind of experimental controls necessary to adequate evaluation. Wolpe's (1958) data, obtained from 210 patients, suffered this defect, and it is difficult to attach significance to his report that about 90% of neurotic patients respond favourably to desensitisation. The same may be said of data published by Lazarus (1963) concerning the treatment of 408 neurotic patients. However, what is interesting in this latter study is the differential results obtained with patients suffering from more severe forms of disturbance. Overall, the figure for 'cure' or 'much improved' was 78%, but the same statistic for the severely disturbed group was only 62%; in other words it appears that desensitisation works better with milder forms of neurotic disorder than the more severe kinds.

Far more satisfactory studies have been conducted by several authors, although these were concerned with phobias in otherwise normal rather than psychiatrically disturbed subjects, and do not serve to inform us about the value of desensitisation in the abnormally disturbed.

Lang and Lazovik's (1963) study, for example, concerned the treatment of snake phobia in 24 normal students, in which systematic desensitisation was compared with simple repeated exposure to phobic stimuli. Lang *et al.* (1966), in another study, also employed a non-psychiatric sample suffering from snake phobia, dividing the subjects into a non-treatment group, a pseudotherapy group, and a group receiving orthodox systematic desensitisation.

Both studies produced results strikingly favourable to desensitisation therapy, as did other experiments in which normal individuals having minor phobic reactions were used. (Rachman, 1965; Cooke, 1966; Paul, 1966; Paul and Shannon, 1966; Davison, 1968.)

Less satisfactory results have been obtained in studies of psychiatrically disturbed patients, as opposed to 'normals'. However, even here the value of desensitisation has been repeatedly confirmed as a technique for ridding the patient of maladaptive anxiety.

Two early attempts to provide this kind of evidence involved retrospective studies, i.e. an examination of the results obtained in treatment of individual cases which, when compiled, will satisfy some of the requirements of a controlled experiment.

In the first of these Cooper (1963) was able to compare 30 patients given a variety of behaviour

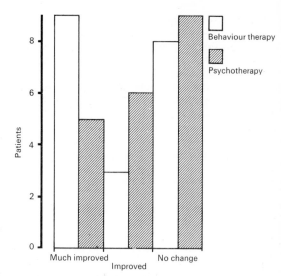

Figure 23.1 Comparison of results achieved from psychotherapy and behaviour therapy. (From Marks and Gelder, 1965, by courtesy of *Brit. J. Psychiatry*)

modification procedures with a matched group who had received psychotherapy. However, this study, while showing an overall result favourable to the behaviour modification procedures, did not allow a separate assessment of desensitisation to be made.

In a later study (Cooper *et al.*, 1965) the numbers involved in Cooper's original (1963) study were augmented, and it was possible to examine the independent contribution made by desensitisation therapy. At the end of such treatment all patients had shown benefit, although some of this improvement had been lost on later follow-up.

Marks and Gelder (1965) also conducted a retrospective study which enabled a useful comparison to be made between desensitisation therapy and psychotherapy, and the respective contributions which these treatments made to different types of phobic patients (Figure 23.1). The outcome in general was decidedly favourable to desensitisation where phobias other than agoraphobia were concerned, particularly in the period immediately following treatment. For agoraphobias there was little difference between the two treatments given, neither of which appeared to be specially beneficial.

A prospective* study by Gelder and Marks (1966) focussed particularly upon agoraphobic patients, and they reported that while some patients showed improvements with both psychotherapy and desensitisation, neither treatment produced impressive results. Furthermore, any useful outcome tended to be lost over a period of time.

*A study in which samples are gathered for the specific purpose which the experimenter has in mind.

Gelder *et al.* (1967) then embarked upon an experiment to compare the effects of desensitisation with both individual and group psychotherapy, and employing different types of phobic patients. Desensitisation was clearly the most effective of the three treatments, both in terms of the numbers of patients who responded favourably and the speed at which the relief was achieved.

Not only does this kind of evidence indicate the usefulness of desensitisation but also strongly suggests the superiority of desensitisation over the more traditional types of therapy. On the other hand, desensitisation does not produce unequivocally good results, and it is important to note that for some patients the benefits may not be enduring.

FLOODING

For a considerable period of time, certainly since the early reports from Jones (1924) and Jersild and Holmes (1935), the exposure of organisms to massive 'doses' of the feared stimuli has looked unpromising. While this procedure received some cursory attention from Wolpe (1952) and was applied to students suffering from examination anxiety by Malleson (1961), serious interest in the method as a treatment was first kindled by Stampfl (1967) who used the term 'implosive therapy'.

One of the early views of neurotic symptoms was that they simply represent avoidance behaviours which, as they lead to escape from anxiety, are in a sense reinforcing (rewarding). Stampfl and Levis (1968) argue that when anxiety is evoked by certain cues, their repeated presentation in the absence of a primary reinforcement should lead to extinction and, in turn, to the elimination of avoidance behaviour. This is, therefore, much the same process as the extinction of a salivary response in a Pavlovian experiment where, following establishment of the conditioned response of salivation to a bell, the bell is presented many times without food (primary reinforcement), leading to the eventual disappearance of any salivation to the bell alone.

However, Stampfl and Levis (1967) appear to think that things other than straight-forward conditioning are involved, and attach importance to what might be seen as 'unconscious' processes, i.e. those of which the patient is unaware but which serve to activate his feelings and behaviour. Accordingly, some therapists who make use of implosion attempt to recreate the original trauma assumed to be responsible for the patient's intense emotional reactions.

The method is, of course, quite opposite from that employed in systematic desensitisation. Instead of proceeding cautiously from step to step in the hierarchy of fear-inducing situations, the implosive therapy requires that, either in imagination or in the real-life context, the patient is exposed to continuous presentation of the most anxiety-evoking stimuli.

Keeping him in this situation, and preventing him from engaging in his usual escape reactions, allows him to 'discover' that the anticipated traumatic event does not occur, and the anxiety will then extinguish.

One or two early studies by Lang and Lazovik (1963), and Rachman (1966b), suggested that this may not be a useful therapy, although Wolpin and Raines (1966) had found the method effective.

However, there were some differences in technique which might well have accounted for the discrepancies. For example, Rachman had asked his subjects to rehearse their *anxiety responses* to the presence of the feared stimulus, while Wolpin and Raines had required theirs to rehearse *adaptive* responses. Furthermore, Staub (1968) reasons that Rachman used periods of exposure to the feared situation which were too brief to allow extinction to take place.

The technique itself can appear rather startling, since its deliberately conceived purpose is to *maximise* anxiety associated with the cues to fear. Hogan and Kirchner (1967), for example, treated a group of students for their fear of rats who were asked to imagine the most horrifying scene involving these animals. They were told to imagine that rats were running all over their bodies, getting inside their bodies, gnawing at their organs, and so on. In another context Wolpe (1969) has reported the use of implosive (flooding) treatment in a dentist who could not give injections to his patients in case they died in his surgery. Therapy involved the vivid portrayal of the dentist giving an injection, withdrawing the syringe, and then observing the patient slump forward, dead. The earliest reponse of patients to implosion is, not surprisingly, acute distress, but this tends to give place to a calmer state as the 'scene' continues, until all anxiety may disappear.

However, Wolpe (1969) has pointed out that while some patients benefit greatly from flooding, others fare badly and can become worse. He quotes a case from his own experience of a doctor, greatly afraid of insane persons, taking a post in a psychiatric hospital where, presumably, he was exposed in a very intensive way to 'insanity', but who became increasingly disturbed by the experience. Furthermore, he points out that there is little evidence favourable to a 'repeated exposure' technique in the studies of experimental neurosis; animals tend to remain fearful after very many occasions of placing them in the experimental environment and it is unclear as to why humans should sometimes react differently.

Relatively few experimental studies are available as yet. In one, Hogan and Kirchner (1967) demonstrated that, certainly with the students who took part, a fear of rats can be successfully dealt with by implosion. Following only one treatment session 14 of the 21 individuals having implosion could pick up a laboratory rat, while only two of those who did not receive treatment could do so.

A further study by the same authors (Hogan and Kirchner, 1968), again using non-psychiatric patients, found a striking reduction in fear of snakes in subjects given implosive treatment.

More recently there has been some suggestion, from experimental studies as well as from clinical practice, that the more severely disturbed patient may be most responsive to implosion. Furthermore, it is thought possible that desensitisation and implosion may be useful complementary treatments, dealing with patients of varying degree of disturbance. However, Gelder *et al.* (1973), in a careful and systematic inquiry, have been unable to confirm an earlier report that agoraphobic patients respond better to implosive than to desensitisation treatment.

Meyer *et al.* (1974) have found that massive exposure to the object of a patient's fear, when combined with other training, can produce excellent results in the severely handicapped obsessional patient (Figure 23.2). Briefly, they have found that the anxiety such patients experience when brought into contact with some source of imagined 'contamination', can be brought under control if the individual is exposed to contamination and is prevented from either running away or engaging in some ritualistic activity.

However, there are still too few adequately controlled experimental studies of implosive therapy, particularly where psychiatric patients are concerned. Until such studies have been conducted it is difficult to arrive at a sound and balanced view of the contribution which this method makes. In addition, it will be necessary to know far more about the theoretical basis of implosion than is presently the case.

MODELLING

Several types of treatment, deriving from social-learning principles, have been developed by Bandura (1969). These are based upon the idea that learning can take place not only as a result of direct experience, but can be vicarious, i.e. as a function of *witnessing* the behaviour and the outcome of that behaviour for other people.

Bandura argues that effective observational learning requires the operation of four subsystems. In the first place it is obvious that simple exposure to a model is not enough, and it is necessary that the model is attended to. Secondly, there must be adequate retention of the desirable behaviour in the absence of the cues which have served as the model to be copied. Thirdly, there must be little or no limitation in the ability to reproduce the behaviour demonstrated and, finally, the continued appearance of newly acquired behaviours requires that appropriate incentives are available.

Given that the above conditions are satisfied then, as Bandura has shown, learning can take place in the absence of any opportunity to perform the responses, but in the presence of a model who *does* emit the desirable behaviour.

One of the first studies employing modelling (Jones, 1924) found this technique (which she labelled 'social imitation') useful in dealing with children's fears. Here, the fearlessness of the model in the presence of the phobic object (an insect, etc.) would encourage a like performance in the fearful child. Interestingly, Jones also noted that the same mechanism (social imitation) was probably an important means by which fears are *acquired*.

Later experimental studies were concerned with the transfer of aggressive behaviour through vicarious learning. Bandura *et al.* (1961), for example, were able to demonstrate that children exposed to an aggressive model showed a significant tendency to imitate such behaviour, both verbally and non-verbally. In another study (Bandura and Rosenthal, 1966) it was shown that an anxious state could be acquired by the modelling process. Here the model feigned a reaction to an electric shock, with a buzzer as the C.S. and G.S.R.* deflection as the C.R., and concomitant measurement of the G.S.R. responses of those watching the model showed that affective reactions were induced in these observers.

Some research in this field has been concerned with experiments employing subjects with minor fears. The outcome has tended to be favourable to modelling

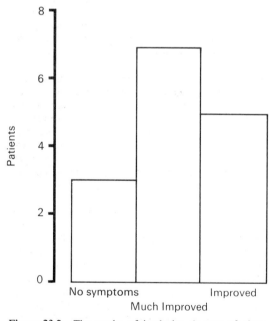

Figure 23.2 The results of implosive therapy of obsessional patients. (From Meyer *et al.*, 1974, *Obsessional States*, H. R. Beech, (ed.) by courtesy of Methuen and Co. Ltd.)

*A measure of change in an individual's skin resistance to a small electrical current. The amount of skin resistance is associated with emotional state

procedures in the sense that fears have shown greater reduction than has been the case using control 'treatments' and the benefit has shown generalisation to situations and stimuli outside the context in which the experiment has been performed. It has also been found that when symbolic modelling (e.g. seeing a *recorded* example of an undisturbed person dealing with the phobic object) is supported by participant modelling (where model and subject take part in a *live* exercise) the improvement is further increased.

A further important possibility arises from the study of Bandura *et al.* (1969), who found that modelling proved superior to desensitisation as a means of dealing with snake phobias. However, too little is known about this method and its value with psychiatric patients to be certain about its potential, particularly in pathological states. Certainly there is not sufficient evidence to form any clear idea of the comparative efficiency of modelling and other behavioural procedures.

Nevertheless, a study by Rachman *et al.* (1971) offers some hope that the technique might be useful in treating obsessional compulsive neurosis. In their experiment 10 such patients were given a control treatment (relaxation) following which they were allocated either to 15 sessions of flooding or modelling therapy.

Relaxation training involved asking the patient to think about one of his obsessional worries while relaxing during the final 10 minutes of each of the 15 sessions.

Flooding (*in vivo*) involved persuading the patient to 'enter' the situation which disturbed him most, during which time the therapist was 'calming and reassuring'. The patient, for example, would be asked to 'contaminate'* himself but refrain from engaging in any ritualistic behaviour.

Modelling *in vivo* was carried out by having the patient deal with a hierarchy of disturbing situations (similar to desensitisation), each one of which was first demonstrated (modelled) by a calm, reassuring therapist.

Both flooding and modelling produced significantly better results than did the 'control' treatment (relaxation), but there was no observable difference in the success attending the first two methods. While the experiment itself has numerous shortcomings, it suggests the possibility that the technique of modelling might compare with flooding in the treatment of certain disturbances, such as obsessional states, which tend to be resistant to other behavioural strategies, including desensitisation.

Finally, one might point out that a social learning/imitation model has a ready appeal in terms of explaining the *acquisition* of abnormalities in terms of

*To touch some object or substance which the patient may think of as dirty or dangerous

conditioned trauma, e.g. that someone has learned to avoid a certain situation because of an unpleasant and aversive event which took place there. No such personal traumatic event, or series of smaller events in combination, is evident in many cases. The social-learning/imitation model does not need to assume that such events *are* part of the individual's history. Of course the account does require that exposure to vicarious learning has taken place, and it is notable that a patient with a phobia sometimes has a parent who had the same fear. Unhappily, of course, opportunities for vicarious learning in the individual's history cannot be easily traced and identified.

Indeed, the modelling explanation of fear acquisition presents a difficult problem: so many fear models—in films, T.V. and elsewhere—bear in upon the individual that perhaps phobias should be a good deal more common than they are. No doubt the salience of the fear model experience for the individual, the degree to which he can detach himself from that experience, and the temperament he brings to the situation, are all relevant considerations here.

AVERSION THERAPY

This strategy for dealing with problems of behaviour modification has been primarily used in the treatment of socially undesirable characteristics. Alcoholism, sexual deviations, drug addiction, and criminal behaviours fall into this category and all, to some degree, might be said to provide gratification to the individual concerned, i.e. they carry positively re-inforcing qualities. However, not all problems to which aversion therapy has been applied can be so described. The muscular spasms of writer's cramp, for example, are probably distressing to the afflicted individual, yet have been successfully dealt with by this kind of treatment.

Basically aversion therapy involves the evocation of the 'undesirable' behaviour—the muscular spasm, the drug injections, and so on—and following this with a strong aversive stimulus, such as an electric shock. By this means it is hoped that the response which previously afforded pleasure (maybe even the muscle spasm could be said to provide a source of relief to the writer's cramp sufferer) comes to be associated with pain and anxiety and will, in time, be avoided by the individual concerned.

Clearly this approach to helping people with problems is fraught by difficulties which go beyond technical and theoretical considerations. The ethical arguments often advanced against using aversion therapy certainly carry some weight, and these must be set against the reasoning that, often, no alternative treatments may be available, that the patient's strong desire to change must be considered, and that one must presume the integrity of the therapist as is the case in any other treatment endeavour.

It may be that the relatively poor success rates of

using aversion therapy to effect behaviour modification stem from some of these problems. There is a tendency, for example, to use only weak aversive stimuli and to make the training situation as brief as possible, so as to avoid too great a commitment to 'punishment'. Neither tendency is conducive to effective learning.

However, perhaps one of the most pressing problems is that while desensitisation training often liberates the individual to enjoy much more of life than before, aversion therapy can create new difficulties for the patient to face. Blocking some behaviour which has afforded satisfaction may leave the individual without any readily available alternatives; the homosexual, deprived of his deviant impulse, does not 'naturally' become a well-adjusted heterosexually-orientated individual, and the alcoholic who has become a non-drinker has lost many friends and is left with an 'occupational' void.

Obviously, aversion therapy would be more successful if it were accompanied by some other type of training which helps the individual to realise other forms of satisfaction which could be available. To some extent recent endeavours in the field have attempted to do just this. In a study by Feldman and McCulloch (1965), for example, not only is the homosexual patient given electric shocks when homosexual scenes are depicted, but he is exposed to training in which the shock is *switched off* when heterosexual scenes are shown. Taken at face value this could result in the avoidance of homosexual stimuli, but makes the heterosexual stimuli attractive since they are associated with relief from pain and anxiety.

Whether such measures are adequate remains open to doubt, but at least there is an awareness of the problem and there are many possibilities to explore in attempting to overcome it.

Three main types of aversive stimuli have been used: chemicals which produce unpleasant effects, electrical shocks, and images which the patient finds distressing in some way. The use of chemical agents is attended by certain difficulties, notably the lack of control over the timing of the effects which are produced and the intensity with which they are experienced, the reduced possibility of giving numerous aversive 'trials', and the possibility of side effects which may impair the patient in some way.

Emetine and apomorphine have been frequently employed chemical agents to produce aversive reactions. Typically the patient is taken to a room where various types of alcohol are available and where the drug is injected. When the patient begins to feel slightly nauseated as a reaction to the drug, he is induced to smell and taste a selection of his favourite drinks, during which time his feelings of nausea are increasing until, quite frequently, vomiting occurs. This association is repeated as many times as possible, usually over a period of one or two weeks.

Not entirely typical of chemically induced aversion, yet of considerable interest, is the employment of the drug scoline which produces muscle and respiratory paralysis. Sanderson *et al.* (1963) 1964) have reported on the use of this drug in the treatment of alcoholism, which is injected immediately after the patient has looked at, and sniffed, his chosen drink, and he is allowed to sip a little just before the expected onset of paralysis. The patient remains completely conscious while the drug is acting, but cannot speak, move or breathe for a minute or so, and the experience is very traumatic.

The use of electric shock is well-illustrated in the study by Sylvester and Liversedge (1960) who treated a selection of patients suffering from occupational cramps. Analysis of the difficulties of writer's cramp sufferers revealed the presence of two distinct abnormalities, tremor and muscle spasm, each of which required separate attention.

To deal with the tremor a metal plate was drilled with holes of graduated size and the patient was required to insert a metal stylus into these, starting with the largest. Any marked tremor would lead to contact between stylus and metal plate, which would complete an electrical circuit resulting in a strong shock being given. This aversive stimulus would lead to avoidance of the aberrant activity (tremor), and the patient could then proceed to increase his control using one of the smaller holes.

The use of disturbing images has not yet received the degree of attention which has been given to electric shock or drugs as aversive stimuli. The practice depends upon the patient's capacity to experience discomfort when the therapist describes disagreeable feelings and sensations accompanying some undesirable activity. Cautela (1966), who calls this procedure 'covert sensitisation', described its application to the control of overeating in a middle-aged lady.

First the patient was relaxed by the therapist and while she was in this state, was required to imagine that she was in process of preparing a meal. While she was busily occupied in this work it was suggested that she reached for some food but, at once, began to feel a little sick. The therapist then goes on to describe how these feelings increase, how vomit comes into her mouth spilling over the meal she is preparing, and how a sense of revulsion is experienced. Such scenes, associating some 'undesirable' behaviour in connection with noxious ideas, are repeated as many times as necessary.

Many reports of aversion therapy have tended to focus upon the treatment of individuals, typical of which is that by Blakemore *et al.* (1963). This patient was a transvestite who had, since the age of four, derived pleasure from dressing in female clothing. In his twenties he frequently cross-dressed and appeared publicly, as he described it, as a 'complete woman'.

Although he married, his aberration persisted, and he began to find that sexual relationships with his wife were unsatisfactory unless he cross-dressed.

Aversion therapy involved having the patient 'dress up' while standing on an electrified grid so that, at any time the therapist chose, a shock could be delivered while the patient was engaged in the pleasurable activity. The shock would be given repeatedly until the patient had divested himself of female clothing.

Treatment was intensive, five 'trials' of the kind described above being given at half-hourly intervals for about eight hours each day, over a six-day period.

The outcome was successful in this case, and remained so over the six months of follow-up. Not only was the patient able to resist any temptation to cross-dress, but his relationship with his wife also showed an understandable improvement.

Voegtlin and his colleagues (Voegtlin and Lemere, 1942; Lemere and Voegtlin, 1950) have reported upon the treatment of over 4000 alcoholics, using aversion therapy (Figure 23.3). Their studies indicate an overall abstinence rate, following treatment, of 51%. However, this, like most other studies in aversion therapy, lacks the kind of refinements and experimental controls which allow us to form an accurate impression of the value of aversion therapy.

Roughly similar success rates to the above were obtained by Feldman and McCulloch (1965) in their treatment of homosexuals. Basically their procedure involved shock which accompanied the presentation of a 'homosexual' picture, which could be avoided if the patient rejected the picture quickly enough.

Rejection of the male picture was arranged to coincide with the presentation of the picture of an attractive female, in an attempt to form an association between relief from anxiety and the presence of a heterosexual stimulus.

Finally, mention may be made of a study by Marks and Gelder (1965), in which a careful assessment was made of five patients with fetishes and/or transvestism. Aversion therapy was given for two hours each day for two weeks and, since it is widely held that 'booster' courses are a helpful way of preventing relapse, further treatment was given, first weekly, then monthly, for a period of time.

The electric shocks used in this treatment were given both when the patient deliberately engaged in fantasies about his deviant behaviour, and also when he carried out such behaviour in reality. In this way both imaginal and actual involvement in the aberration were being dealt with. Furthermore, shock was given only intermittently, since evidence has accumulated indicating that this procedure leads to better preservation of some newly acquired learning than when a reinforcement is given on every learning trial.

It was observed that one of the earliest reactions to treatment was a difficulty in conjuring up the required fantasy, which increased until the fantasy became very delayed or could not be obtained at all. This effect was paralleled by an increasing difficulty, throughout treatment, in obtaining penile erections to 'stimuli' such as a blouse, a skirt, and so on. In 'behavioural' terms, therefore, progress was in the direction predicted.

Rather curiously the attitudes which patients entertained concerning the items which, prior to treatment, had been sexually exciting (panties, skirt etc.) simply became 'neutralised' rather than assuming aversive properties. Perhaps this outcome was for the best since ordinary items of female apparel would be difficult to avoid without retiring to a monastery.

As Rachman and Teasdale (1969) have argued, there is now sufficient evidence from experimental studies to justify a certain guarded optimism about aversion therapy. However, there is still a serious lack of well-controlled investigations, which leaves us in doubt about the precise contribution which this treatment can make.

OPERANT CONDITIONING

It is not at all easy in practice to distinguish aversion therapy from operant approaches to treatment. Ordinarily, at least in theory, the two are different in that in aversion therapy (classical conditioning) some stimulus is employed which precedes and elicits the response, while in operant conditioning the individual emits a response which leads to some environmental event. Furthermore, it is usual for those employing operant training to see the individual as an active organism, doing things to and in his environment which produces certain consequences. The focus of

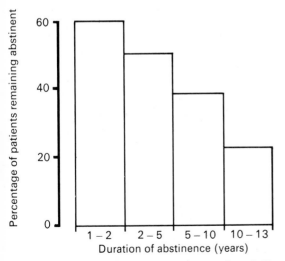

Figure 23.3 Outcome of aversion therapy of alcoholic patients. Data compiled from Voegtlin and Lemere's studies.

the approach is upon manipulating these consequences which are held to determine the future occurrence of particular behaviours.

Briefly, if a behaviour is followed by 'rewards' (positive reinforcements), then it will tend to occur more frequently; but if punishment is the consequence (negative reinforcement), then that behaviour will be weakened and may disappear completely from the individual's repertoire.

This somewhat oversimplified description does not do justice to the complex and detailed work which has often emanated from those concerned with this approach. The emphasis upon careful and meticulous analysis of behaviour, the care and concern with experimental procedure, and the substantial body of facts and principles from laboratory studies, are all part and parcel of an approach which has gained widespread acceptance in clinical settings.

Apart from the techniques and practices, however, the operant approach has become associated with a particular philosophy concerning aberrant behaviour. This involves a rejection of the 'medical' or 'disease' model of human behavioural dysfunction in favour of a view which holds that changing the individual's behaviour produces real and possibly enduring changes in *him*. Put in another way, the medical model tends to assume some underlying causes of unacceptable behaviour which themselves must be eradicated before that behaviour can change: the operant viewpoint argues that a direct attack upon the behaviour itself can produce all the alterations in external behaviour and internal state which are needed.

The contrast between the two viewpoints may be illustrated, with advantage to the operant approach, by the example of the disordered speech of schizophrenic patients. Where this abnormality is found it is often regarded as part of a disease process and therefore not amenable to modification until the illness has been cured or has remitted. Ullman *et al.* (1964), however, were able to demonstrate that the bizarre verbalisations of schizophrenic patients can be made more normal using reinforcements contingent upon speech. The method involved providing social reward (a nod, a smile, or an encouraging 'mmhm-hmm') when acceptable talk was emitted, but witholding such 'rewards' when peculiar utterances were heard.

Similarly, an investigation by Bachrach *et al* (1965) showed gratifying confirmation of the way in which the manipulation of reinforcement can produce remarkable changes in behaviour that could not be predicted from the 'disease' model. Their single case was that of a 37-year-old woman suffering from the condition known as anorexia nervosa, in which an ordinary diet is refused. Before training began she was described as being 'so cachectic and shrunken about her skeleton as to give the appearance of a poorly preserved mummy suddenly struck with the breath of life'. Indeed, weighing a mere 47 pounds, she was quite unable to stand without support, and serious concern for her survival was expressed.

The patient was placed in a 'barren experimental box' and was told that three people concerned with her treatment would each come and eat one meal with her every day. Any movement associated with eating, from spearing a piece of food with her fork, to swallowing some morsel, were positively reinforced. Initially these reinforcers consisted of talking to her about something which she found interesting, but later, access to radio, T.V., and so on were used as incentives. Should she fail to make any suitable responses, nothing would be done and she would be simply left in her 'box' until the next meal time.

As this treatment progressed more was required from the patient before a reward would be given, and new types of reinforcement were introduced, such as receiving visitors and going out for walks.

By the end of her training her weight had doubled, she was much more active socially, and took a greater interest in her appearance. Later she found a job and, while still remaining very thin, was able to lead a reasonably normal existence.

Not all problems which have received attention by operant procedures have been characterised by this degree of seriousness. Indeed, what has been remarkable is the range of very different disturbances, both in type and severity, which have remitted to this type of therapy.

A study by Hart *et al.* (1964), for example, illustrates the application of operant training to a very minor problem. Bill and Alan were both four-year-old kindergarten children with an exaggerated tendency to burst into tears. This, quite frequently, was associated with catching the teacher's eye, and the crying would then begin and continue until lots of attention had been given. Thus the undesirable behaviour appeared to be 'operant' in the sense of being dependent upon, and maintained by, the environmental consequences of crying, rather than as a result of painful accidents.

To discourage the tearful outbursts it was decided to withdraw the social reinforcement of attention-giving, and ignore operant crying completely. On the other hand, attention was given for behaviour deemed to be appropriate. The outcome of putting this programme into practice was that, within one week, the unwanted behaviour was eliminated.

However, much of the work in this area has been concerned with severely handicapped patients, primarily those classified as chronic patients in large psychiatric institutions. While restoration of normal functioning has frequently been the concern of the therapists involved, there are many problem behaviours that such patients exhibit which make their daily lives impoverished and render them difficult to care for. In this context, and because of the very large scale of the problems involved, token economy programmes have been devised. These are special cases of the application of operant training principles and have become important since their development in the 1960s.

Briefly, such programmes involve the designation of certain behaviours as 'desirable' and, therefore, to be positively reinforced. Arrangements are made to provide tokens (cards, plastic discs, etc.) as reinforcements which can be exchanged, at some stage, for a more tangible reward (such as sweets, cigarettes, special outings, and so on). Ayllon and Azrin (1965, 1968) were first to report on such treatment programmes in the context of the psychiatric institution.

The kind of behaviours which they wished to encourage included self-care and various ways of helping in the daily hospital routine (e.g. cleaning, washing dishes, sorting laundry). The reinforcements chosen were varied, and included sweets, cigarettes, access to T.V. and a chance to talk with hospital staff.

The outcome clearly demonstrated the way in which tokens became an established currency that patients would value and work for. The new behaviours, which came to replace the old apathetic state of patients, were maintained as long as the reinforcement continued.

Naturally, the large scale management of patients which is implied in token economy programmes requires meticulous attention to the training of staff, to the behavioural analysis of the patient difficulties involved, and so on. Much of the success of this type of training depends upon the systematic and precise application of reinforcements, and misuse of these procedures can arise out of the apparent simplicity of the method. Indeed, it has been said that there are so many examples of poor application and consequent failure that the whole field is 'in danger of being ruined by amateurs'.

Mention must also be made of a relatively new application of operant principles which is currently achieving prominence and appears to have considerable potential, namely, bio-feedback.

It has been reasonably well-established in experimental settings that the physiological response to emotional situations can be reduced if the individual exercises his 'mind' to deny its significance or diminish it in some way. Similarly, if an individual is mentally prepared to be afraid the physiological reaction to the emotion-evoking event will be more intense.

It has also been shown that there can be a reciprocal relationship between the mental state of the individual and his physiological state so that, for example, an expectation of something fearful may lead to increased heart rate which, in turn, makes the individual more anxious since there is a 'real' cue to inform him of his anxious state. But such interactions may offer interesting therapeutic possibilities. Shearn (1962) first showed that changes in heart rate could

come under the control of environmental manipulations, and there have been other demonstrations which suggest that blood pressure, muscle activity, sweat gland activity, and E.E.G. (electrical activity of the brain) are amenable to modification.

In the operant control of E.E.G., for example, Kamiya (1968) has reported that individuals can very significantly increase the period of time during which they manifest alpha waves (associated with lessened tension and anxiety), if rewarded for keeping 'on target'. Such demonstrations have suggested the possibility of control over the disorganised electrical activity of the brain found in epileptic seizures.

Similarly, Stoyva (see Lang, 1971) has reported upon the successful use of feedback from striate muscles in obtaining psychological and physiological relaxation.

However, while reports of striking achievements in altering behavioural and other abnormalities, using feedback in conjunction with reinforcements have been published, the potential of this application of operant conditioning has not yet been properly established.

PROBLEMS OF BEHAVIOUR MODIFICATION

There is little doubt that behaviour modification procedures have proved to be useful in dealing with many types of psychological disorder. Their importance concerns not only the actual success rate which attends the application of these methods, but the degree to which a change in emphasis in approach has altered the climate of opinion in therapy. In making the latter point it may be useful to contrast psychoanalytic procedures, and related theories and treatments, with the behaviour modification approach. Basically this is bound up with the relevance which we attach to scientific method and experimental procedure as a means of making discoveries.

Behaviour modification, unlike traditional psychological approaches to remedial work, has stressed the importance of experimentation as a means of gathering data and testing propositions, hoping in this way to establish a body of fact and theory which will be valid and enduring. At least such an approach might be expected to inform us as to the incorrectness of some idea or model about human functioning, even if we fail to produce any startling revelation which confers a greater understanding of behaviour. It has been pointed out on many occasions that numerous practices and techniques in treatment or education survive simply because they have not been subjected to an adequate, if indeed any, evaluative scrutiny (Beech, 1969).

By and large behaviour modification techniques, then, have developed within the framework of experimental science, and this has been a refreshing and valuable contribution. Nevertheless, problems have arisen, and continue to arise, in connection with such approaches, and it is useful to briefly review some of them.

Not infrequently questions have been asked concerning the ethical considerations involved. Such doubts have been discussed (Eysenck and Beech, 1971), particularly in the context of aversion therapy. Thus the fear has been expressed that aversion therapy may be employed solely to secure conformity to the laws of society and is, in this sense, better suited to the function of the policeman than the therapist. Certainly, it is of paramount importance to establish that such treatments are in the interests of the individual who is actively seeking change, but this is not always an easy problem for the therapist to decide.

Whether one can have an acceptable treatment which apparently involves the infliction of punishment is yet another issue. Of course the issue is not confined to aversion therapy, for surgery, dentistry, and other therapies frequently involve inflicting considerable amounts of pain. Most likely it is the deliberate and calculated use of pain as a means of obtaining change which some may find unacceptable, and they will point out that the pain of the dentist's drill is a by-product which the dentist does his best to minimise.

The dilemma in which the therapist· may find himself is well-illustrated in Tate and Baroff's (1966) report on Sam. This little psychotic boy of nine years had engaged for some time in numerous acts of self injury, banging his head against walls and floors, kicking and punching himself, and so on. At the time the therapists undertook his treatment Sam had only a little residual vision in one eye, and it was clear that further self-injurious behaviour would probably render him completely blind.

Accordingly, treatment was given which involved placing him on a bed, with his feet restrained, and being spoken to in a pleasant and affable way. He was told (although it is unclear how much understanding he had of this) that any attempt to hit himself would result in an electric shock to his leg. At the same time any non-self-injurious behaviour was lavishly praised.

At first sight such treatment appears to be utterly barbaric, involving the deliberate application of shock to a young child of deficient intelligence and understanding, under conditions of restraint. Yet the outcome was successful (Sam began to enjoy life more, to play more happily, and did not engage in further self-destructive behaviour), and there was no obvious alternative means of preserving the child's sight.

In quite another context Krasner (1971) has described what he believes to be a programme of coercion, rather than operant training in a therapeutic sense. The example he quotes is Cotter's attempt to induce Vietnamese psychiatric patients to work rather than to remain in hospital. The means adopted was to have the patients choose between receiving E.C.T.

(electroconvulsive therapy) three times each week while living in hospital, or working for their living. Having failed to induce a good part of his sample to work under these conditions of 'negative reinforcement', Cotter then introduced an alternative condition, either to work or to receive no food. This choice was more successful in that more patients chose the 'work' alternative.

Finally Krasner refers to Cotter's 'major achievement' which involved having patients work under Viet Cong gunfire as a way of helping the war effort in Vietnam.

While this is undoubtedly a parody of how learning principles should be applied, there is an important conclusion for therapists to draw. The aim should be to encourage new adaptive behaviours to emerge, which the patient will adopt and which will be in his interests; the attempt to change behaviour by coercion is not only morally unacceptable but is unlikely to do more than secure 'good' behaviour just so long as the goad is present.

Other and quite different problems of behaviour modification arise in connection with theoretical considerations. It has been pointed out, for example (Eysenck and Beech, 1971), that theoretical formulations in respect of aversion therapy are far less well-developed than is the case for desensitisation treatment. Even so, there are several available accounts of how desensitisation works which, as yet, we cannot decide between. Certainly some of the conditions formerly held to be essential to successful desensitisation no longer seem to be so necessary (see Eysenck and Beech, 1971; Murray and Jacobson, 1971) and suggest that Wolpe's original formulation requires either amendment or rejection.

At a more general level it has been argued that learning and conditioning theories themselves are so unsatisfactory as to be quite inadequate as a foundation for treatment strategies. Certainly it is the case that there are different theories within the area of learning and conditioning, and that these are to some extent in conflict with each other. Furthermore, these formulations quite often have difficulty in providing a satisfactory account of even the comparatively simple phenomena of the laboratory experiment, let alone the complexity of the real life situation.

It is important, however, to relate these criticisms to the development of psychology as a science. It is not unusual, but rather typical, that the forefront of scientific development is marked by the existence of several alternative 'weak' theories. These serve a most valuable purpose in stimulating research work and cannot be discarded simply because none is completely satisfactory. We must, as Thomson argues, regard theory in science as a policy, rather than a creed. In short, rather than reject all models and the strategies which derive from them, we must make full use of them, ever watchful to make crucial comparisons where we can, and always prepared to reject those theories which constantly fail to be substantiated. Some may feel that we have already reached this stage in behaviour modification. Murray and Jacobson (1971), for example, in their review of the shortcomings of current theories in this 'topic area', feel that existing models fall so far short of adequate that it may be necessary to devise a 'framework radically different from any now known'. However, while it may be agreed that there are many difficulties, it would seem unwise to reject the existing frameworks before each has been thoroughly explored, tested, and its value properly determined.

It is often said by the critics of behaviour modification theories that there is a serious neglect of 'internal' processes. It must be agreed that there is, partly as a result of the historical. origins of these methods, an emphasis upon observable behaviour, and sometimes a relative neglect of the inner world of attitudes, thoughts and emotions. It is also true that many applications of behaviour modification techniques involve a dependence upon little-understood internal processes, such as asking the patient to imagine a scene in desensitisation or to conjure up a fantasy of sexual activity in the course of aversion therapy. In these circumstances there is a paucity of information concerning what is actually going on in the patient's 'mind', and this must be regarded as a serious problem and hazard for current theoretical formulations.

However, techniques are available which, albeit rudimentary, do enable us to anchor these intervening variables on both the stimulus and response side. We can, for example, present some stimulus (such as a pornographic slide) and draw reasonable inference about the intervening processes when noting that penile erections occur as the response. We can present a harrowing scene as the stimulus and note signs of distress in the patient as a response, with acceptable deductions as to what the state of the organism is between these two events. Again, direct physiological recording, for example of the changes in the resistance of the skin to an electrical current, can be related to statements about the way a patient feels when he reports upon his state.

However, perhaps the problem becomes rather more difficult when we come to consider the power which cognitive (thinking) events can assume in the learning process. One of the clearest examples of this comes from Wilson (1968) who began by training his experimental subjects to expect shock to a blue stimulus, but not to a yellow one, and showing that they rapidly achieved conditioned skin (G.S.R.) responses to the colour blue, i.e. they would react strongly even if no shock was given.

At this stage Wilson gave a further instruction, to the effect that shock would henceforth be given for the yellow stimulus rather than the blue. In fact no further shocks were given at all, yet individuals showed an immediate transfer of skin reaction to yellow and instantly lost their well-conditioned reaction to blue. Clearly, therefore, a change in 'mental set' can produce both the elimination of existing conditioned responses and the establishment of new reactions which have not resulted directly from training. This is not a remarkable finding in the sense that it amply confirms our everyday experience of life and our reactions to it, yet it presents intriguing problems for learning/conditioning theories and therapies. How far can we and do we use cognitions to enhance our treatment strategies, and how far are these treatments affected adversely by 'mental' events?

Apart from the above, behaviour modification procedures are attended by numerous technical problems. Not least of these is that of quantifying the parameters with which we are dealing. The assessment of anxiety, for example, still rests pretty substantially upon the verbal report of the individual concerned, so that in building the anxiety-hierarchy for desensitisation therapy the precise arrangement of items according to their fear-evoking potential is not possible. Psychophysiological methods of assessment may sometimes be a useful adjunct to self-report, and they may add a certain precision to data gathering, but these procedures themselves have numerous disadvantages.

Imagery, too, presents a problem in measurement since it is entirely dependent upon the patient's volition and desire to co-operate. Clearly, there must be certain reservations about what is happening when we treat a patient by giving electric shocks whenever he reports having a particular fantasy; is his tendency to report fewer fantasies an index of improvement, is it the result of a calculated unwillingness to think about this scene, or is the patient having the fantasy, but refusing to report it?

The part which motivation plays in treatment and how this may be assessed constitutes a further difficulty. It seems very probable, from published evidence, that patients who are pressed to seek treatment by the courts, by marriage partners, and the like, do less well than those who seek help of their own volition. These and numerous other technical issues remain serious problems.

Practical problems are a further area of difficulty in behaviour modification, just as they are in other treatment procedures. One which the therapist encounters, not infrequently, is that of arranging that changes in behaviours which are effected in the clinical setting will show transfer to the actual life situation of the individual concerned. Relatively few published accounts make any serious reference to the differentiations which an individual may make between behaviour produced under the therapist's gaze and that which may be emitted in the naturalistic setting, yet such problems are not uncommon.

Consider the example of the small boy treated by operant procedures for persistent thumb-sucking. It was discovered that this habit could be brought under control if a cartoon film which he was watching was shown only when his thumb was out of his mouth. The outcome indicated that, while the child learned very well not to suck his thumb during the film show, this had no effect upon his behaviour outside the 'laboratory'. Perhaps it is salutary and surprising that such differentiations are not observed more frequently in the context of aversion therapy. We might expect, for example, that the patient can very well differentiate the conditions under which he receives strong electric shocks for certain behaviours (in the clinic), from those in which no such noxious events are likely.

Related to this problem is that of the relatively uncontrollable factors in the real life situation. For example, an individual undergoing imaginal desensitisation therapy may cope perfectly well with the limited scenes portrayed, yet the 'same' situation re-enacted in the natural setting may contain frightening elements over which he has no control and which could reverse the treatment process. The clerk may be curt, rather than courteous, the dog may bite rather than lick, the train may make an unscheduled stop, and so on. Securing the transfer to the real world, and testing out one's capacity to 'cope' in that setting, remain problems.

Practical problems often arise within the hospital or clinic settings which abort or disrupt attempts at behaviour modification. It is not uncommon to find that the manipulation of reinforcements in operant conditioning programmes is made difficult by patients who receive unscheduled rewards from friends, relatives, or other patients. It is not uncommon to find the alcoholic patient, before coming to hospital for treatment, has thoughtfully arranged a secret supply of his favourite beverage. It is not untypical that drug-addicted patients should continue to receive supplies from a kindly visiting friend.

Problems, whether ethical, theoretical, technical, or practical, attend most human endeavours. The fact that they are commonplace and not peculiar to behaviour modification procedures does not diminish the responsibility to deal with them energetically and promptly. However, it is important to note that the various shortcomings of these techniques have, from no quarter, received greater attention than from those involved in their administration. Indeed, the field is remarkable for the degree of concern shown for the problems involved, and it is doubtful whether any alternative approach has been characterised by a greater degree of self-criticism and appraisal. Such a situation is not only satisfactory in that necessary safeguards are examined closely, but it ensures the important monitoring of work which provides a much-needed impetus to improve theory and technique. The research into desensitisation is an excellent example of the way in which a successful technique, backed by a plausible theory, has been subjected to careful scrutiny. The fact that we can now express doubts about what the important ingredients of desensitisation are, and about the theoretical underpinnings of the procedure, is a cause for congratulation rather than alarm. Fortunately, at least at this point in time, behaviour modification has not become an ossified, static, doctrinaire body of practices and theory, and itself continues to be modified.

References

Ayllon, T. and Azrin, N. H. (1965). The measurement and reinforcement of behaviour of psychotics. *Exp. Anal. Behav.*, **8**, 357–383

Ayllon, T. and Azrin, N. H. (1968). *The Token Economy: A Motivational System for Therapy and Rehabilitation* (New York: Appleton-Century-Crofts)

Bachrach, A. J., Erwin, W. J. and Mohr, J. P. (1965). *Case Studies in Behaviour Modification* (Ullman and Krasner, editors) (London: Holt, Rinehart and Winston)

Bandura, A., Ross, D. and Ross, S. A. (1961). Transmission of aggression through imitation of aggressive models. *J. Abn. Soc. Psychol.*, **63**, 575–582

Bandura, A. and Rosenthal, T. L. (1966). Vicarious classical conditioning as a function of arousal level. *J. Personal. Soc. Psychol.*, **3**, 54–62

Bandura, A. (1969). *Principles of Behaviour Modification* (New York: Holt, Rinehart and Winston)

Bandura, A., Blanchard, E. B. and Ritter, B. (1969). The relative efficacy of desensitisation and modelling approaches for inducing behavioural, affective, and attitudinal changes. *J. Personal. Soc. Psychol.*, **13**, 173–199

Beech, H. R. (1969). *Changing Man's Behaviour* (Pelican Original) (Harmondsworth: Penguin Books)

Blakemore, C. B., Thorpe, J. G., Barker, J. C., Conway, C. G. and Levin, N. I. (1963). The application of faradic aversion conditioning in a case of transvestism. *Behav. Res. Ther.*, **1**, 29–34

Cautela, J. B. (1966). Treatment of compulsive behaviour by covert sensitisation. *Psychol. Rec.*, **16**, 33–41

Cooke, G. (1966). The efficacy of two desensitisation procedures: An analogue study. *Behav. Res. Ther.*, **4**, 17–24

Cooper, J. E. (1963). A study of behaviour therapy in 30 psychiatric patients. *Lancet*, **1**, 411–415

Cooper, J. E., Gelder, M. G. and Marks, T. M. (1965). Results of behaviour therapy in 77 psychiatric patients. *Brit. Med. J.*, **1**, 1222–5

Davison, G. (1968). The influence of systematic desensitisation, relaxation and graded exposure to imaginal stimuli in the modification of phobic behaviour. *J. Abn. Psychol.*

Eysenck, H. J. (1967). *The Biological Basis of Personality* (Springfield: C. C. Thomas)

Eysenck, H. J. and Beech, H. R. (1971). Counterconditioning and related methods in behaviour therapy. In: *Handbook of Psychotherapy and Behaviour Change*, (Bergin and Garfield, editors) (London: John Wiley)

Feldman, M. P. and McCulloch, M. J. (1965). The application of anticipatory avoidance learning in the treatment of homosexuality. *Behav. Res. Ther.*, 2, 165–183

Gantt, W. H. (1944). *Experimental Basis for Neurotic Behaviour* (New York: Hoeber)

Gelder, M. G. and Marks, I. M. (1966). Severe agoraphobia: A controlled prospective trial of behaviour therapy. *Brit. J. Psychiatry*, 112, 309–319

Gelder, M. G., Marks, I. M. and Wolff, H. H. (1967). Desensitisation and psychotherapy in the treatment of phobic states: A controlled inquiry. *Brit. J. Psychiatry*, 113, 54–73

Gelder, M. G., Bancroft, J. H. J., Gath, D. H., Johnston, D. W., Mathews, A. M., and Shaw, P. M. (1973). Specific and non-specific factors in behaviour therapy. *Brit. J. Psychiatry*, 123, 445–462

Goldiamond, I. (1965). Stuttering and fluency as manipulable response classes. In: *Research in Behaviour Modification* (Krasner and Ullman, editors) (London: Holt, Rinehart and Winston)

Hart, B. M., Allen, K. E., Buell, J. S., Harris, F. R. and Wolf, M. M. (1964). Effects of social reinforcement on operant crying. *J. Exp. Child. Psychol.*, 1, 145–153

Hogan, R. A. and Kirchner, J. H. (1967). Preliminary report of the extinction of learned fears via short-term implosive therapy. *J. Abn. Psychol.*, 72, 106–109

Hogan, R. A. and Kirchner, J. H. (1968). Implosive, eclectic, verbal, and bibliotherapy in the treatment of fears of snakes. *Behav. Res. Ther.*, 6, 167–171

Hull, C. L. (1943). *Principles of Behaviour* (New York: Appleton-Century)

Jersild, A. T. and Holmes, F. B. (1935). Methods of overcoming children's fears. *J. Psychol.*, 1, 25–83

Jones, M. C. (1924). The elimination of children's fears. *J. Exp. Psychol.*, 7, 383–390

Kamiya, J. (1968). Conscious control of brain waves. *Psychology Today*, 1, 57–60

Krasner, L. (1971). The operant approach in behaviour therapy. In: *Handbook of Psychotherapy and Behaviour Change* (Bergin and Garfield, editors) (London: John Wiley)

Lang, P. J. and Lazovik, A. D. (1963). Experimental desensitisation of a phobia. *J. Abn. Soc. Psychol.*, 66, 519–525

Lang, P. J., Lazovik, A. D. and Reynolds, D. J. (1965). Desensitisation, suggestibility and pseudo-therapy. *J. Abn. Psychol.*, 70, 395–402

Lang, P. J. (1971). The application of psychophysiological methods to the study of psychotherapy and behaviour modification. In: *Handbook of Psychotherapy and Behaviour Change* (Bergin and Garfield, editors) (London: John Wiley)

Lazarus, A. A. (1963). The results of behaviour therapy in 126 cases of severe neurosis. *Behav. Res. Ther.*, 1, 65–78

Lemere, F. and Voegtlin, W. L. (1950). An evaluation of the aversion treatment of alcoholism. *Quart. J. Stud. Alcohol.*, 11, 199–204

Liddell, H. (1944). Conditioned reflex method and experimental neurosis. In: *Personality and the Behaviour Disorders* (J. McV. Hunt, editor) (New York: Ronald Press)

Malleson, N. (1961). Panic and phobia. *Lancet*, 1, 225–227

Marks, I. M. and Gelder, M. G. (1965). A controlled retrospective study of behaviour therapy in phobic patients. *Brit. J. Psychiatry*, 111, 561–573

Masserman, J. H. (1943). *Behaviour and Neurosis* (Chicago: University of Chicago Press)

Meyer, V., Levy, R. and Schnurer, A. (1974). The behavioural treatment of obsessive-compulsive disorders. In: *Obsessional States* (Beech, editor) (London: Methuen)

Murray, E. J. and Jacobson, L. I. (1971). The nature of learning in traditional and behavioural psychotherapy. In: *Handbook of Psychotherapy and Behaviour Change* (Bergin and Garfield, editors) (London: John Wiley)

Paul, G. L. (1966). *Insight vs. Desensitisation in Psychotherapy* (Stanford: Stanford University Press)

Paul, G. L. and Shannon, D. T. (1966). Treatment of anxiety through systematic desensitisation in therapy groups. *J. Abn. Psychol.*, 71, 124–135

Pavlov, I. P. (1927). *Conditioned Reflexes* (Oxford: Oxford University Press)

Rachman, S. (1965). Studies in desensitisation. *Behav. Res. Ther.*, 3, 245–251

Rachman, S. (1966a). Studies in desensitisation. *Behav. Res. Ther.*, 4, 1–6

Rachman, S. (1966b). Studies in desensitisation. *Behav. Res. Ther.*, 4, 7–15

Rachman, S. and Teasdale, J. D. (1969). *Aversion Therapy* (London: Routledge and Kegan Paul)

Rachman, S., Hodgson, R. and Marks, I. M. (1971). The treatment of chronic obsessive-compulsive neurosis. *Behav. Res. Ther.*, 9, 237–247

Rachman, S. (1972). Clinical applications of observational learning, imitation, and modelling. *Behav. Ther.*, 3, 379–397

Sanderson, R. E., Campbell, D. and Laverty, S. (1963). Traumatically conditioned responses acquired during respiratory paralysis. *Nature (London)*, 196, 1235–6

Sanderson, R. E., Campbell, D. and Laverty, S. (1964). An investigation of a new aversive conditioning technique for alcoholism. In: *Conditioning Techniques in Clinical Practice and Research* (C. M. Franks, editor) (Springer)

Shearn, D. W. (1962). Operant conditioning of heart rate. *Science*, 137, 530–531

Stampfl, T. (1967). Implosive therapy. In: *Behaviour Modification Techniques in the Treatment of Emotional Disorders* (Armitage, editor) (Michigan: V. A. Publication)

Stampfl, T. and Levis, D. (1967). Essentials of implosive therapy. *J. Abn. Psychol.*, 72, 496–503

Stampfl, T. and Levis, D. (1968). Implosive therapy—a behavioural therapy? *Behav. Res. Ther.*, 6, 31–36

Staub, E. (1968). Duration of stimulus-exposure as determinant of the efficacy of flooding procedures in the elimination of fear. *Behav. Res. Ther.*, 6, 131–132

Sylvester, J. D. and Liversedge, L. A. (1960). Conditioning and the occupational cramps. In: *Behaviour Therapy and the Neuroses* (H. J. Eysenck, editor) (Oxford: Pergamon Press)

Tate, B. G. and Baroff, G. S. (1966). Aversive control of self-injurious behaviour in a psychotic boy. *Behav. Res. Ther.*, 4, 281–287

Ullman, L. P., Krasner, L. and Edinger, R. L. (1964). Verbal conditioning of common associations in long-term schizophrenic patients. *Behav. Res. Ther.*, 2, 15–18

Voegtlin, W. L. and Lemere, F. (1942). The treatment of alcohol addiction. *Quart. J. Stud. Alcohol.*, 2, 717–803

Watson, J. B. and Rayner, R. (1920). Conditioned emotional reactions. *J. Exp. Psychol.*, 3, 1–14

Wilson, G. D. (1968). Reversal of differential GSR conditioning by instructions. *J. Exp. Psychol.*, **76**, 491–493

Wolpe, J. (1952). Experimental neuroses as learned behaviour. *Brit. J. Psychol.*, **43**, 243–268

Wolpe, J. (1969). *The Practice of Behaviour Therapy* (Oxford: Pergamon Press)

Wolpin, M. and Raines, J. (1966). Visual imagery, expected roles and extinction as possible factors in reducing fear and avoidance behaviour. *Behav. Res. Ther.*, **4**, 25–38

INDEX

INDEX OF AUTHORS